Universal's
Concise Commentary
on

The Motor Vehicles Act, 1988

(59 of 1988)

with

Exhaustive Case Law

First Edition 2015

Universal's Concise Commentary on

The Motor Vehicles Act, 1988

(59 of 1988)

with

Exhaustive Case Law

Universal
Law Publishing
an imprint of LexisNexis

LexisNexis®

This book is a publication of **LexisNexis®**
(A Division of Reed Elsevier India (Pvt) Ltd)
14th floor, Building No 10, Tower–B, DLF Cyber City, Phase-II,
Gurgaon–122002, Haryana, India.
Tel : + 91 124 4774444 Fax: + 91 124 4774100
Website : www.lexisnexis.co.in / E-mail : help.in@lexisnexis.com

---

Universal's Concise Commentary - *The Motor Vehicles Act, 1988,* First Edition 2015

ISBN: 978-93-5035-592-3

Printed by: Sita Fine Arts Pvt. Ltd., New Delhi

Printed and bound in India.

THE MOTOR VEHICLES ACT, 1988

CONTENTS

CHAPTER III

LICENSING OF CONDUCTORS OF STAGE CARRIAGES

CHAPTER V

CONTROL OF TRANSPORT VEHICLES

CHAPTER VII

CONSTRUCTION, EQUIPMENT AND MAINTENANCE OF MOTOR VEHICLES

CHAPTER VIII

CONTROL OF TRAFFIC

CHAPTER IX

MOTOR VEHICLES TEMPORARILY LEAVING OR VISITING INDIA

CHAPTER X

LIABILITY WITHOUT FAULT IN CERTAIN CASES

CHAPTER XI

INSURANCE OF MOTOR VEHICLES AGAINST THIRD PARTY RISKS

CHAPTER XII

CLAIMS TRIBUNALS

TABLE OF CASES

THE MOTOR VEHICLES ACT, 1988

INTRODUCTION

The first enactment relating to motor vehicles in India was the Indian Motor Vehicles Act, 1914, which was subsequently replaced by the Motor Vehicles Act, 1939. The Act of 1939 had been amended several times. Inspite of several amendments it was felt necessary to bring out a comprehensive legislation keeping in view the changes in the transport technology, pattern of passenger and freight movements, development of the road network in the country and particularly the improved techniques in the motor vehicles management. Various Committees as well as the Law Commission had gone into different aspects of road transport. Several Members of Parliament had also urged for comprehensive review of the Motor Vehicles Act, 1939. A Working Group was, therefore, constituted in January, 1984 to review all the provisions of the Act of 1939. This Working Group took into account the suggestions and recommendations earlier made by various bodies and institutions and made certain recommendations. On the recommendations of the Working Group State Governments were asked to submit their comments. The recommendations made by the Working Group and comments received from the State Governments were discussed at a special meeting of Transport Ministers of all States and Union Territories. Based on the conclusions reached in the meeting of Transport Ministers and suggestions made by the Supreme Court in a case the Motor Vehicles Bill was introduced in the Parliament.

STATEMENT OF OBJECTS AND REASONS

The Motor Vehicles Act, 1939 (4 of 1939), consolidates and amends the law relating to motor vehicles. This has been amended several times to keep it up-to-date. The need was, however, felt that this Act should, now *inter alia,* takes into account also changes in the road transport technology, pattern of passenger and freight movements, development of the road network in the country and particularly the improved techniques in the motor vehicles management.

Various Committees like National Transport Policy Committee, National Police Commission, Road Safety Committee, Low Powered Two-wheelers Committee, as also the Law Commission have gone into different aspects of road transport. They have recommended updating, simplification and rationalization of this law. Several Members of Parliament have also urged for comprehensive review of the Motor Vehicles Act, 1939, to make it relevant to the modern-day requirements.

A Working Group was, therefore, constituted in January, 1984 to review all the provisions of the Motor Vehicles Act, 1939, and to submit draft proposals for a comprehensive legislation to replace the existing Act. This Working Group took into account the suggestions and recommendations earlier made by various bodies and institutions like Central Institute of Road Transport, Automotive Research Association of India, and other transport organisations including the manufacturers and the general public. Besides, obtaining comments of State Governments on the recommendations of the Working Group, these were discussed in a specially convened meeting of Transport Ministers of all States and Union Territories. Some of the more important modifications so suggested related for taking care of—

(a) the fast increasing number of both commercial vehicles and personal vehicles in the country;

(b) the need for encouraging adoption of higher technology in automotive sector;

(c) the greater flow of passenger and freight with the least impediments so that islands of isolations are not created leading to regional or local imbalances;

(d) concern for road safety standards, and pollution-control measures, standards for transportation of hazardous and explosive materials;

(e) simplification of procedure and policy liberalizations for private sector operations in the road transport field; and

(f) need for effective ways of tracking down traffic offenders.

The Supreme Court in *M.K. Kunhimohammed* v. *P.A. Ahmedkutty,* (1987) 4 SCC 284: AIR 1987 SC 2158: JT 1987 (4) SC 465, has made certain suggestions to raise the limit of compensation payable as a result of motor accidents in respect of death and permanent disablement in the event of there being no proof of fault on the part of the person involved in the accident and also in hit and run motor accidents and to remove certain disparities in the liability of the insurer to pay compensation depending upon the class or type of vehicles involved in the accident. The above suggestions made by the Supreme Court have been incorporated in the Bill.

The proposed legislation has been prepared in the light of the above background. Some of the more important provisions of the Bill provide for the following matters, namely:—

(a) rationalization of certain definitions with additions of certain new definitions of new types of vehicles;

(b) stricter procedures relating to grant of driving licences and the period of validity thereof;

(c) laying down of standards for the components and parts of motor vehicles;

(d) standards for anti-pollution control devices;

(e) provision for issuing fitness certificates of vehicles also by the authorised testing stations;

(f) enabling provision for updating the system of registration marks;

(g) liberalised schemes for grant of stage carriage permits on non-nationalised routes, All India Tourist Permits and also national permits for goods carriages;

(h) administration of the Solatium Scheme by the General Insurance Corporation;

(i) provision for enhanced compensation in cases of "no fault liability" and in "hit and run" motor accidents;

(j) provision for payment of compensation by the insurer to the extent of actual liability to the victims of motor accidents irrespective of the class of vehicles;

(k) maintenance of State registers for driving licences and vehicle registration;

(l) constitution of Road Safety Councils.

The Bill also seeks to provide for more deterrent punishment in the cases of certain offences.

The Notes on clauses explain the provisions of the Bill.

The Bill seeks to achieve the above objectives.

ACT 59 OF 1988

The Motor Vehicles Bill having been passed by both the Houses of Parliament, received the assent of the President on 14th October, 1988. It came on the Statute Book as THE MOTOR VEHICLES ACT, 1988 (59 of 1988).

AMENDING ACTS

1. The Motor Vehicles (Amendment) Act, 1994 (54 of 1994) (w.e.f. 14-11-1994).
2. The Motor Vehicles (Amendment) Act, 2000 (27 of 2000) (w.e.f. 11-8-2000).
3. The Motor Vehicles (Amendment) Act, 2001 (39 of 2001) (w.e.f. 27-9-2001).

THE MOTOR VEHICLES ACT, 1988

(59 of 1988)

[*14th October, 1988*]

An Act to consolidate and amend the law relating to motor vehicles.

Be it enacted by Parliament in the Thirty-ninth Year of the Republic of India as follows:—

CHAPTER I

PRELIMINARY

1. Short title, extent and commencement.—(1) This Act may be called the Motor Vehicles Act, 1988.

(2) It extends to the whole of India.

(3) It shall come into force on such date[1] as the Central Government may, by notification in the Official Gazette, appoint; and different dates may be appointed for different States and any reference in this Act to the commencement of this Act shall, in relation to a State, be construed as a reference to the coming into force of this Act in that State.

2. Definitions.—In this Act, unless the context otherwise requires,—

(1) "area", in relation to any provision of this Act, means such area as the State Government may, having regard to the requirements of that provision, specify by notification in the Official Gazette;

(2) "articulated vehicle" means a motor vehicle to which a semi-trailer is attached;

(3) "axle weight" means in relation to an axle of a vehicle the total weight transmitted by the several wheels attached to that axle to the surface on which the vehicle rests;

(4) "certificate of registration" means the certificate issued by a competent authority to the effect that a motor vehicle has been duly registered in accordance with the provisions of Chapter IV;

(5) "conductor" in relation to a stage carriage, means a person engaged in collecting fares from passengers, regulating their entrance into, or exit from, the stage carriage and performing such other functions as may be prescribed;

(6) "conductor's licence" means the licence issued by a competent authority under Chapter III authorising the person specified therein to act as a conductor;

(7) "contract carriage" means a motor vehicle which carries a passenger or passengers for hire or reward and is engaged under a contract, whether expressed or implied, for the use of such vehicle as a whole for the carriage of passengers mentioned therein and entered into by a person with a holder of a permit in relation to such vehicle or

---

1. Came into force on 1-7-1989. *Vide* S.O. 368 (E), dated 22nd May, 1989, published in the Gazette of India, Extra., Pt. II, Sec. 3 (ii), dated 22nd May, 1989.

any person authorised by him in this behalf on a fixed or an agreed rate or sum—

(a) on a time basis, whether or not with reference to any route or distance; or

(b) from one point to another,

and in either case, without stopping to pick up or set down passengers not included in the contract anywhere during the journey, and includes—

(i) a maxicab; and

(ii) a motor cab notwithstanding that separate fares are charged for its passengers;

(8) "dealer" includes a person who is engaged—

[1][***]

(b) in building bodies for attachment to chassis; or

(c) in the repair of motor vehicles; or

(d) in the business of hypothecation, leasing or hire-purchase of motor vehicle;

(9) "driver" includes, in relation to a motor vehicle which is drawn by another motor vehicle, the person who acts as a steersman of the drawn vehicle;

(10) "driving licence" means the licence issued by a competent authority under Chapter II authorising the person specified therein to drive, otherwise than as a learner, a motor vehicle or a motor vehicle of any specified class or description;

(11) "educational institution bus" means an omnibus, which is owned by a college, school or other educational institution and used solely for the purpose of transporting students or staff of the educational institution in connection with any of its activities;

(12) "fares" includes sums payable for a season ticket or in respect of the hire of a contract carriage;

(13) "goods" includes livestock, and anything (other than equipment ordinarily used with the vehicle) carried by a vehicle except living persons, but does not include luggage or personal effects carried in a motor car or in a trailer attached to a motor car or the personal luggage of passengers travelling in the vehicle;

(14) "goods carriage" means any motor vehicle constructed or adapted for use solely for the carriage of goods, or any motor vehicle not so constructed or adapted when used for the carriage of goods;

(15) "gross vehicle weight" means in respect of any vehicle the total weight of the vehicle and load certified and registered by the registering authority as permissible for that vehicle;

(16) "heavy goods vehicle" means any goods carriage the gross vehicle weight of which, or a tractor or a road-roller the unladen weight of either of which, exceeds 12,000 kilograms;

1. Sub-clause (a) omitted by Act 54 of 1994, sec. 2 (w.e.f. 14-11-1994).

(17) "heavy passenger motor vehicle" means any public service vehicle or private service vehicle or educational institution bus or omnibus the gross vehicle weight of any of which, or a motor car the unladen weight of which, exceeds 12,000 kilograms;

(18) "invalid carriage" means a motor vehicle specially designed and constructed, and not merely, adapted, for the use of a person suffering from some physical defect or disability, and used solely by or for such a person;

(19) "learner's licence" means the licence issued by a competent authority under Chapter II authorising the person specified therein to drive as a learner, a motor vehicle or a motor vehicle of any specified class or description;

(20) "licensing authority" means an authority empowered to issue licences under Chapter II or, as the case may be, Chapter III;

(21) "light motor vehicle" means a transport vehicle or omnibus the gross vehicle weight of either of which or a motor car or tractor or road-roller the unladen weight of any of which, does not exceed [1][7,500] kilograms;

[2][(21A) "manufacturer" means a person who is engaged in the manufacture of motor vehicles;]

(22) "maxicab" means any motor vehicle constructed or adapted to carry more than six passengers, but not more than twelve passengers, excluding the driver, for hire or reward;

(23) "medium goods vehicle" means any goods carriage other than a light motor vehicle or a heavy goods vehicle;

(24) "medium passenger motor vehicle" means any public service vehicle or private service vehicle, or educational institution bus other than a motor cycle, invalid carriage, light motor vehicle or heavy passenger motor vehicle;

(25) "motorcab" means any motor vehicle constructed or adapted to carry not more than six passengers excluding the driver for hire or reward;

(26) "motor car" means any motor vehicle other than a transport vehicle, omnibus, road-roller, tractor, motor cycle or invalid carriage;

(27) "motor cycle" means a two-wheeled motor vehicle, inclusive of any detachable side-car having an extra wheel, attached to the motor vehicle;

(28) "motor vehicle" or "vehicle" means any mechanically propelled vehicle adapted for use upon roads whether the power of propulsion is transmitted thereto from an external or internal source and includes a chassis to which a body has not been attached and a trailer; but does not include a vehicle running upon fixed rails or a vehicle of a special type adapted for use only in a factory or

1. Subs. by Act 54 of 1994, sec. 2, for "6000" (w.e.f. 14-11-1994).
2. Ins. by Act 54 of 1994, sec. 2 (w.e.f. 14-11-1994).

in any other enclosed premises or a vehicle having less than four wheels fitted with engine capacity of not exceeding [1][twenty-five cubic centimetres];

(29) "omnibus" means any motor vehicle constructed or adapted to carry more than six persons excluding the driver;

(30) "owner" means a person in whose name a motor vehicle stands registered, and where such person is a minor, the guardian of such minor, and in relation to a motor vehicle which is the subject of a hire-purchase agreement*, or an agreement of lease or an agreement of hypothecation, the person in possession of the vehicle under that agreement;

(31) "permit" means a permit issued by a State or Regional Transport Authority or an authority prescribed in this behalf under this Act authorising the use of a motor vehicle as a transport vehicle;

(32) "prescribed" means prescribed by rules made under this Act;

(33) "private service vehicle" means a motor vehicle constructed or adapted to carry more than six persons excluding the driver and ordinarily used by or on behalf of the owner of such vehicle for the purpose of carrying persons for, or in connection with, his trade or business otherwise than for hire or reward but does not include a motor vehicle used for public purposes;

(34) "public place" means a road, street, way or other place, whether a thoroughfare or not, to which the public have a right of access, and includes any place or stand at which passengers are picked up or set down by a stage carriage;

(35) "public service vehicle" means any motor vehicle used or adapted to be used for the carriage of passengers for hire or reward, and includes a maxicab, a motorcab, contract carriage, and stage carriage;

(36) "registered axle weight" means in respect of the axle of any vehicle, the axle weight certified and registered by the registering authority as permissible for that axle;

(37) "registering authority" means an authority empowered to register motor vehicles under Chapter IV;

(38) "route" means a line of travel which specifies the highway which may be traversed by a motor vehicle between one terminus and another;

[2][(39) "semi-trailer" means a vehicle not mechanically propelled (other than a trailer), which is intended to be connected to a motor vehicle

---

1. Subs. by Act 54 of 1994, sec. 2, for "thirty-five cubic centimetres" (w.e.f. 14-11-1994).

* **Ed.**—In clause (30) (relating to "owner") after the words "hire-purchase" and before the word "agreement" there is a comma as printed in the Government publication (Acts of Parliament, 1988), whereas there should be no comma after the words "hire-purchase" and before the word "agreement" hence comma has been deleted. In this respect, see *Dhulchand* v. *Kanti Lal*, AIR 2004 Raj 267: 2005 (2) CCC 25: 2006 (1) ACJ 276.

2. Subs. by Act 54 of 1994, sec. 2, for clause (39) (w.e.f . 14-11-1994).

and which is so constructed that a portion of it is super-imposed on, and a part of whose weight is borne by, that motor vehicle;]

(40) "stage carriage" means a motor vehicle constructed or adapted to carry more than six passengers excluding the driver for hire or reward at separate fares paid by or for individual passengers, either for the whole journey or for stages of the journey;

(41) "State Government" in relation to a Union territory means the Administrator thereof appointed under article 239 of the Constitution;

(42) "State transport undertaking" means any undertaking providing road transport service, where such undertaking is carried on by,—

(i) the Central Government or a State Government;

(ii) any Road Transport Corporation established under section 3 of the Road Transport Corporations Act, 1950 (64 of 1950);

(iii) any municipality or any corporation or company owned or controlled by the Central Government or one or more State Governments, or by the Central Government and one or more State Governments.

[1][(iv) Zila Parishad or any other similar local authority.]

Explanation.—For the purposes of this clause, "road transport service" means a service of motor vehicles carrying passengers or goods or both by road for hire or reward;

(43) "tourist vehicle" means a contract carriage, constructed or adapted and equipped and maintained in accordance with such specifications as may be prescribed in this behalf;

(44) "tractor" means a motor vehicle which is not itself constructed to carry any load (other than equipment used for the purpose of propulsion); but excludes a road-roller;

(45) "traffic signs" includes all signals, warning sign posts, direction posts, markings on the road or other devices for the information, guidance or direction of drivers of motor vehicles;

(46) "trailer" means any vehicle, other than a semi-trailer and a side-car, drawn or intended to be drawn by a motor vehicle;

(47) "transport vehicle" means a public service vehicle, a goods carriage, an educational institution bus or a private service vehicle;

(48) "unladen weight" means the weight of a vehicle or trailer including all equipment ordinarily used with the vehicle or trailer when working, but excluding the weight of a driver or attendant; and where alternative parts or bodies are used the unladen weight of the vehicle means the weight of the vehicle with the heaviest such alternative part or body;

(49) "weight" means the total weight transmitted for the time being by the wheels of a vehicle to the surface on which the vehicle rests.

1. Ins. by Act 54 of 1994, sec. 2 (w.e.f. 14-11-1994).

SYNOPSIS

1. Autorickshaws are not Trailors
2. Manufacturer includes Assemblers
3. Educational Institution Bus Transporting Students and Staff is not Public Service Vehicle
4. Vehicle Used for Carrying Employees is Private Service Vehicle
5. Private Service Vehicle
6. Distinct Licence
7. Tractor Trailer a Goods Carriage
8. Tractor not Goods Carriage
9. When Contract *De Hors*
10. Motor Car is not Tractor
11. Road Roller
12. Omnibus or Motor Car
13. Public Place
14. Private Service Vehicle
15. Mechanically Propelled Vehicles
16. Ownership not Dependent upon Entries in Registration Certificate
17. Stage Carriage Permit
18. Liability Owner of School Buses to Pay Additional Tax
19. Lease Executed in Favour of Person
20. Driving License – Valid License to Drive Light Motor Vehicle
21. Person in Possession of Vehicle under Hypothecation Agreement

COMMENTS

1. Autorickshaws are not Trailors – Definition of motor vehicle in the Act clearly goes to show that it means any mechanically propelled vehicle adapted for use on roads. Autorickshaws are mechanically propelled vehicles. They are not being driven by drawn vehicles. Therefore, the submission that provision of rule 126 would not apply to autorickshaws assembled by them on the ground that they are trailers is not only illogical but illegal and unsustainable. This provision is applicable to the autorickshaws as this provision of rule 126 makes it very clear that it applies to all motor vehicles except trailors and semi-trailers. Therefore, in case of manufacturing of any motor vehicle, other than trailers and semi-trailers, the test and the requirement provided in rule 126 will have to be undergone; *Shakti Auto Garage* v. *Assistant Regional Transport Officer*, AIR 1996 Guj 54: 1995 (3) Civ LJ 856: 1996 (1) Cur CC 522.

2. Manufacturer includes Assemblers – Assemblers are included in the expression 'manufacturer'. Therefore, the provisions of rule 126 are attracted to autorickshaws. Autorickshaws assembled by the petitioners are held to be motor vehicle manufactured under the Act. The fact that the parts of assembled autorickshaws are not originally manufactured by the petitioners does not make any difference insofar as applicability of provisions of rule 125 is concerned. The underlying object of rule 126 read with section 52 of the New Act undoubtedly goes to show that all the manufacturers of motor vehicles are statutorily obliged to first get the prototype of vehicles approved and even in case of any alteration, approval of the registering authority is required. It cannot be said that the provision would not apply in case of manufacturing or assembling different parts. What is required to be approved is a motor vehicle made by genuine parts, original parts or assembled cannot be used on road without prototype of design being approved by the statutory authority. Section 52 of the new Act clearly provides for making alteration in motor vehicle and empowers the registering authority to make necessary alteration in the certificate of registration. In short, provision of New rule 126 cannot be avoided on the ground that motor vehicles are assembled by purchasing parts. Assembling as such is process of manufacturing and, therefore, manufacturers are required to observe and satisfy the conditions incorporated in rule 126; *Shakti Auto Garage* v. *Assistant Regional Transport Officer*, AIR 1996 Guj 54.

3. Educational Institution Bus Transporting Students and Staff is not Public Service Vehicle – Transportation of passengers undertaken as a business activity for hire or reward by the owner of any motor vehicles is an essential ingredient of the expression "public service vehicle". "Private Service Vehicle" on the other hand is meant to be used by the owner or any other person for or in connection with owner's trade or business otherwise than for hire or reward. Transportation of students in an "educational institution bus" owned by a college, school or other educational institutions is undertaken in furtherance of and in connection with the activities of the institution otherwise than for "hire or reward" and not as a business activity "for hire or reward". The educational institution bus would thus not qualify itself to be called "public service vehicle" which includes a maxi-cab, a motor-cab, contract carriage, and stage carriage. If, therefore, a motor vehicle is registered as an "educational institution bus" and used for transporting the students to and from the institutions otherwise than on "hire or reward" additional tax under section 6 of the Act would not be leviable/payable in respect of such vehicle. On the other hand if a motor vehicle is registered as "stage carriage" or other "public service vehicle" it would be liable to tax as well as additional tax unless it is exempted wholly or partially from such liability; *A.I.P. School's Welfare Society, Ghaziabad* v. *State of Uttar Pradesh,* AIR 2000 All 85: 2000 AIHC 2252: 2000 All LJ 606.

4. Vehicle Used for Carrying Employees is Private Service Vehicle – Vehicle used only for the purpose of carrying on its employees and their children under a welfare scheme for the employees is a private service vehicle and not a public service vehicle which includes contract carriage and stage carriage. Therefore, no charge of passenger tax can be levied on such vehicles. When only employees and the school going children are permitted to use the said vehicles on the basis of the terms and conditions of their service and the amount collected do not represent hire or reward, it would neither be a stage carriage nor a contract carriage nor the passengers carried would be passengers within the meaning of the Act; *I.T.I. Ltd., Allahabad* v. *Passenger Tax Officer,* AIR 1996 All 79: 1996 All LJ 342.

5. Private Service Vehicle – The subject vehicle was leased in favour of the company under the agreement dated 1-4-1999. It is also admitted position and the possession of the subject vehicle was handed over to the company in terms of the agreement. Therefore, the company satisfies the definition of the term 'owner' as defined under section 2(30) of the Act. If that is so, it is satisfactorily shown that the subject vehicle is ordinarily used by or on behalf of the respondent-company, which is the owner of the subject vehicle, for the purpose of carrying its employees. It is nobody's case that any passenger is carried in the subject vehicle for hire or reward. It is a fact that only the employees of the respondent-company are transported to and from the factory in connection with the trade or business of the respondent-company. The subject vehicle also stands registered in the name of the company and, therefore, the company will be deemed to be the owner thereof. Since the subject vehicle answers the description of a 'private service vehicle' the company is justified in insisting that the subject vehicle should be shown and recorded as 'private service vehicle' in the RC book; *R.T.O. Bangalore Central* v. *Tata Infotech Ltd.,* AIR 2005 Kant 409: 2005 (4) ACC 444: 2005 (5) Kant LJ 590.

6. Distinct Licence – Although the definition of the 'light motor vehicle' brings within its umbrage both 'transport vehicle' or 'omnibus', indisputably, a distinction between an effective licence granted for transport vehicle and passenger motor vehicle exists. A transport vehicle may be a light motor vehicle but for the purpose of driving the same, a distinct licence is required to be obtained. The distinction between a 'transport vehicle' and a 'passenger vehicle' can also be noticed from section 14 of the Act; *Oriental Insurance Co. Ltd.* v. *Angad Kol,* AIR 2009 SC 2151: 2009 AIR SCW 2747: 2009 (3) SCALE 749.

7. Tractor Trailer a Goods Carriage – A combined reading of the definitions under sections 2(14) and 2(47), shows that the definition of "motor vehicle" includes any mechanically propelled vehicle apt for use upon roads irrespective of the source of power and it includes a trailer. Therefore, even though a trailer is drawn by a motor vehicle, it by itself being a motor vehicle, the tractor-trailer would constitute a "goods carriage" under section 2(14) and consequently, a "transport vehicle" under section 2(47).; *Natwar Parikh and Co. Ltd.* v. *State of Karnataka,* AIR 2005 SC 3428: 2005 AIR SCW 4361: (2005) 7 SCC 364.

8. Tractor not Goods Carriage – A tractor is not a goods carriage. A tractor fitted with a trailer may or may not answer the definition of goods carriage contained in section 2(14) of the Motor Vehicles Act; *National Insurance Co. Ltd.* v. *V. Chinnamma,* 2004 AIR SCW 5116: AIR 2004 SC 4338: JT 2004 (7) SC 167: 2004 (8) SCC 697: 2004 (6) Supreme 379.

9. When Contract *De Hors* – The very permit for which the contract for carriage of the passengers granted should contain the names of the passengers to carry from one destination to another destination without picking up or setting down *en route* for hire or reward but when the holder of a permit is another and permits them to carry the passengers and makes the contract *de hors* those mentioned in the list of passengers enclosed to the permit as contract carriage and takes the passengers from one destination to another, even without picking up or getting down *en route,* the necessary consequence would be that the vehicle has been or is being used as a stage carriage but not a contract carriage; *Nirmala Jagdishchandra Kabra* v. *Transport Commissioner,* AIR 1997 SC 1405: 1997 AIR SCW 1530: (1997) 2 SCC 227.

10. Motor Car is not Tractor – In the definition of motor car, as contained in sub-section (26) of section 2, tractor "is not included. It may be a light vehicle for purposes of sub-section (24) of section 2. These findings get support from the fact that expression "tractor" has specifically been defined under sub-section (44) of section 2. It is clear beyond any pale of controversy that a motor car, is not a tractor; *National Insurance Co. Ltd.* v. *Shinder Kumar,* AIR 1998 P&H 184: 1998 (2) ACJ 880: 1998 (1) Rec Civ R 302.

11. Road Roller – Road roller comes within the definition of the "motor vehicle" as contained in sub-section (28) of, section 2 of the Act; *State of Uttar Pradesh* v. *Suresh Chandra,* AIR 1995 All 253: 1995 (1) ACC 177: 1995 (1) ACJ 245.

12. Omnibus or Motor Car – As per sub-section (29) of section 2 any motor vehicle constructed or adapted to carry more than six persons excluding the driver irrespective of the use will be an omnibus. In that view Tata-mobile 207 cannot be a motor car since the vehicle had been constructed or adapted to carry more than six persons; *Saramma Philipose* v. *Regional Transport Officer, Ernakulam,* AIR 1966 Ker 44: 1995 (2) Ker LJ 472: 1995 (2) Ker LT 450.

13. Public Place – Inside the mines area there are roads though on these roads entry is restricted but the members of the public have also access on these roads by permission. That would not mean that it would cease to be a public place as defined in sub-section (34) of section 2; *National Insurance Co. Ltd.* v. *Sahiba Khatun,* AIR 1998 MP 238: 2000 (1) ACJ 168: 1998 (3) Civ LJ 396.

The definition of 'public place' under the Act is, wide enough to include any place which members of public use and to which they have a right of access. The rights of access may be permissive, limited, restricted or regulated by oral or written permission, by tickets, passes or badges or on payment of fee. The use may be restricted generally or to particular purpose or purposes. What is necessary is that place must be accessible to members of public and be available for their use, enjoyment, avocation or other purpose. Hence all places where members of public and/or their property are likely to come in contact with vehicle can legitimately be said to be in its view when legislature made relevant provisions for compulsory insurance. Therefore, all places where members of public have an access, for whatever reasons, whether as of right or controlled in any manner whatsoever, would be covered by definition of 'public place' in section 2(34) of the Act. In instant case evidence on record shows that land in question was recorded as 'Nayanjori', abutting public road, to which public had free and easy access same does not cease to be a public place, merely because land stood recorded in name of a private individual. Thus, conclusion is irresistible that land in question, on which accident took place, was a 'public place' and therefore, insurer is liable to pay compensation; *M.K. Bhaumik* v. *Sukura Singh,* AIR 2011 Ori 144.

14. Private Service Vehicle – As per notification private service vehicle as defined in section 2(33) of the Motor Vehicles Act registered in the name of an individual can be used for private purpose unconnected with the business or trade of the owner of such vehicle. Therefore, a businessman who purchases a motor vehicle which answers the definition of the term "private service vehicle" can have the vehicle specified as a private service vehicle for personal use, if it is registered in his name and he gives a declaration to the effect that the vehicle is intended to be used by him solely for personal use; *Jagan Thomas* v. *State of Kerala,* AIR 2012 Ker 154: 2012 (2) Ker LJ 363: 2012 (2) Ker LT 365.

15. Mechanically Propelled Vehicles – The tractors, trucks with six wheels or ten wheels or bigger trucks/turbos are motor vehicles within the definition of section 2(28) of the Act. They are all also mechanically propelled vehicles. The authority to levy tax on such vehicle vests in the State Government alone. In any case, the tax which has been sought to be realised by the Gram Panchayat in the name of vehicle development tax is analogous to road tax, which is; leviable only by the State Government. There cannot be any duplicity of such tax. Even otherwise, though as it is, the Gram Panchayats have not been able to show authority to levy such tax, the tax can be levied and realised only under the authority of law. In the absence of expressed authority conferring the power upon the Gram Panchayat, such tax could not be levied. In the present case, the Gram Panchayats have though not directly levied the tax on excavation of minerals, but indirectly it leads to this only because they have levied the tax on passage of only such vehicles through their territory, which are found to carry the minerals excavated. No such power is conferred upon the Gram Panchayats to levy this type of tax either under section 65 or elsewhere under any other statute or the Rules framed thereunder. Thus the imposition of vehicle tax by the Gram Panchayat is not proper; *Arjun Singh* v. *State,* AIR 2013 Raj 136: 2013 (4) WLC 142.

16. Ownership not Dependent upon Entries in Registration Certificate – The ownership of a movable property is not dependent upon the entries in the registration certificate. The act of transfer of owner in the registration certificate is required to be performed by the transferee. If the transferee does not effect the ownership transferred in the registration certificate in his name, he will be liable for punishment but the property in the vehicle will stand transferred in terms of section 19 of the Sale of Goods Act, when it was intended, it being movable property; *Munni Ram* v. *Fakir Chand,* AIR 2010 P&H 50: 2011 (1) ACC 302: 2011 (2) ACJ 747.

17. Stage Carriage Permit – Even after the Motor Vehicles Act, 1988 was enacted and brought into force, a person other than the registered owner of a vehicle can apply for a regular permit or a temporary permit. Stage carriage permit can be issued to person other than registered owner of vehicle. Thus person in lawful possession of vehicle under lease agreement with registered owner is entitled to stage carriage permit; *Anil Kumar S. Anupam* v. *Secretary, Regional Transport Authority, Kollam,* AIR 2010 Ker 94: 2010 (2) ACC 497: 2010 (1) Ker LT 758.

18. Liability Owner of School Buses to Pay Additional Tax – The petitioner is paying the road tax on the school buses at par with the tax which is leviable upon the other type of the vehicles named in the definition of the transport vehicle given in section 2(47) of the Act of 1988. Therefore, the petitioner who did not challenge the definition of the transport vehicle which included the educational institution buses in the definition and category of transport vehicle and are paying the road tax as such, yet they have only objection with respect to the levy of additional tax by projecting the difference in use of vehicle only for the purpose of levy of additional tax. Meaning thereby, the root of the additional tax is leviable according to the writ petitioner himself and his contention is that even then he is not liable to pay the additional tax. If the contention of the writ petitioner is accepted, then that will make one vehicle covered by one definition in two categories of vehicle–one for the purpose of levying of tax and another for the purpose of levy of additional tax. One, at par with other vehicles, which are included in the definition of transport vehicle for the purpose of levy of road tax whereas for the purpose of levy of additional tax, that particular vehicle shall stand excluded. Further more, according to writ petitioner itself the tax in either case is levied according to vehicles use on the road and it's sitting capacity. The petitioner failed to justify how their case be given different treatment to the vehicle for taxing in that fact situation? Also apart from the fact that there is no reason to treat these vehicles different when they are treated at par in section 2(47) of the Act of 1988. Thus once the educational institution bus has been included in the category of transport vehicle and validity of that provision is not under challenge and the petitioner himself has accepted, this position and paying the road tax levied because of that categorization has no right to challenge the additional tax on the ground that the motor vehicles plied by the educational institutions have limited role and meant for only limited purpose; *Rajkamal Saraswati Vidya Mandir, Dhanbad* v. *State of Jharkhand*, AIR 2012 Jhar 35: 2012 (1) AIR Jhar R 437: 2012 (2) Civ LJ 455.

19. Lease Executed in Favour of Person – Can be deemed to be owner of vehicle; *Rishikesh Singh* v. *Seema Arora*, AIR 2015 MP 10.

20. Driving License – Valid License to Drive Light Motor Vehicle – Driver authorised to drive light goods vehicle; *Ashvinbhai Jayantilal Modi* v. *Ramkaran Ramchandra Sharma*, (2015) 2 SCC 180.

21. Person in Possession of Vehicle under Hypothecation Agreement – Treated as owner; *HDFC Bank Limited* v. *Reshma*, (2015) 3 SCC 679.

CHAPTER II

LICENSING OF DRIVERS OF MOTOR VEHICLES

3. Necessity for driving licence.—(1) No person shall drive a motor vehicle in any public place unless he holds an effective driving licence issued to him authorising him to drive the vehicle; and no person shall so drive a transport vehicle [other than [1][a motor cab or motor cycle] hired for his own use or rented under any scheme made under sub-section (2) of section 75] unless his driving licence specifically entitles him so to do.

(2) The conditions subject to which sub-section (1) shall not apply to a person receiving instructions in driving a motor vehicle shall be such as may be prescribed by the Central Government.

SYNOPSIS

1. Effecting Driving Licence
2. Valid Driving Licence
3. Driver Holding American Driving Licence
4. Driving without Licence
5. Effective and Valid Licence
6. Driving License – Automated Driving Test – Grant on Basis not Improper

COMMENTS

1. Effecting Driving Licence – A learner's licence indisputably is a licence within the meaning of provisions thereof. A person holding a learner's licence is also entitled to drive a vehicle but it is granted for a specific period. Holding of a learner's licence is imperative for filing an application for grant of licence. Converse however is not true. Only because the appellant held a learner's licence which had expired and was not valid on the date of accident, he cannot be said to be duly licensed; *Bhuwan Singh* v. *M/s. Oriental Insurance Co. Ltd.*, AIR 2009 SC 2177: 2009 AIR SCW 2865: 2009 (5) SCC 136: 2009 (3) SCALE 798.

---

1. Subs. by Act 54 of 1994, sec. 3, for "a motor cab" (w.e.f. 14-11-1994).

2. Valid Driving Licence – A licence to drive a transport vehicle will be effective for a period of three years whereas in the case of any other vehicle it can be issued or renewed for a period of 20 years from the date of issuance or renewal. The fact that the licence was granted for a period of 20 years, thus, clearly shows that the, driver of the vehicle, was not granted a valid driving licence for driving a transport vehicle. The driver of the vehicle was not holding an effective licence. Possession of an effective licence is necessary in terms of section 10 of the Motor Vehicles Act; *New India Assurance Co. Ltd.* v. *Roshanben Rahemansha Fakir*, AIR 2008 SC 2266: 2008 AIR SCW 4048: 2008 (8) SCC 253: 2008 (8) SCALE 572.

3. Driver Holding American Driving Licence – In India, the driver is always on the defensive due to various reasons. Pedestrians in India seldom use footpaths nor respect Zebra lines or traffic lights, two wheelers, auto rickshaws, cyclists and street vendors are common sights on Indian roads. A driver on Indian roads should expect the unexpected always, therefore, the plea that the accused has an American driving licence is not an answer for driving in Indian roads unless it is recognized in India or that person is having a driving licence issued by the Licensing Authority in India; *State Tr. P.S. Lodhi Colony, New Delhi* v. *Sanjeev Nanda*, AIR 2012 SC 3104: 2012 Cr LJ 4174: 2012 AIR SCW 4506.

4. Driving without Licence – The minor person came from behind on the motorcycle and hit the scooter of the deceased from behind. The responsibility in causing the accident was, therefore, found to be solely that of the minor. However, since he was a minor and it was the responsibility of the petitioner to ensure that his motorcycle was not misused and that too by a minor who had no licence to drive the same, the Motor Accident Claims Tribunal quite rightly saddled the liability for payment of compensation on the Petitioner and, accordingly, directed the Insurance Company to pay the awarded amount to the awardees and, thereafter, to recover the same from the Petitioner. The story that the minor came into the house of the petitioner and took the keys of the motorcycle without any intimation to the petitioner, appears to be highly improbable and far-fetched. It is difficult to accept the defence of the petitioner that the keys of the motorcycle were taken by the minor without his knowledge; *Jawahar Singh* v. *Bala Jain*, AIR 2011 SC 2436: 2011 AIR SCW 3625: (2011) 6 SCC 425.

5. Effective and Valid Licence – The driver and the owner of the vehicle did not examine themselves. The driving licence was not produced. The application form praying for grant of driving licence was also not produced. The witness of the Opposite Party of the Regional Transport Authority has stated that the driver had licence to drive Light Motor Vehicle but the vehicle involved is a Light Goods Vehicle. The holder of the licence had to obtain an endorsement to drive goods vehicles but it has not been established whether the vehicle involved in the accident is a goods vehicle and whether the holder of the licence was entitled to drive a goods carriage vehicle. It has also not been established that the vehicle involved was a goods carriage vehicle. The Opposite Party could not establish that the vehicle was driven contrary to the terms and conditions of the insurance. As a result the Opposite Party has not been able to establish that the driver of the vehicle which caused the accident did not have an effective and valid licence. Hence the vehicle was not driven contrary to the conditions of the insurance contract. *Oriental Insurance Co. Ltd.* v. *Angad Kol*, 2009 AIR SCW 2747: AIR 2009 SC 2151: (2009) 3 SCALE 749.

The stand of the claimant before was that since the deceased driver was holding a valid licence and had not been disqualified from holding an effective licence, the stipulation in the afore-extracted condition was not infringed. But the argument is stated to be rejected. The licence could not be renewed with effect from the date of its expiry as having failed to apply for renewal of the driving licence within 30 days from the date of its expiry in terms of section 15 of the Act, and therefore, between the deceased driver had no valid and effective driving licence as contemplated under section 3 of the Act. The driver did not hold at all an effective driving licence, as required in the terms and conditions governing the policy on the date of accident. As a matter of fact, in view of the clear mandate of section 3 of the Act, the deceased driver was not even permitted to drive the insured vehicle in a public place. Furthermore, the claimant not only committed breach of the terms of the policy, he also violated the provisions of section 5 of the Act by entrusting the vehicle to a person who did not hold a valid licence on the date of the accident. The licence was not and could not be renewed after the death of the licence-holder. Therefore, the appellant was not liable to indemnify the claimant for the loss suffered by him in the accident of the insured vehicle; *New India Assurance Co. Ltd.* v. *Suresh Chandra Aggarwal*, 2009 AIR SCW 4801: AIR 2009 SC 2987: (2009) 9 SCALE 449.

Section 3(1) of the Act requires holding of driving licence which is material. If a vehicle is 'Light Motor Vehicle', but falls under the category of Transport Vehicle, the driving licence has to be duly endorsed under section 3 of the Act. Section 3, therefore, required the driver to have an endorsement which would entitle him to ply such vehicle. If it is not done, a person holding driving licence to ply Light Motor Vehicle cannot ply transport vehicle. In the instant case, the driver was having licence to drive Light Motor Vehicle. The licence was not endorsed as required and hence, he could not have driven the vehicle in absence of requisite endorsement and Insurance Company could not be held liable; *New India Assurance Co. Ltd.* v. *Prabhu Lal*, 2007 AIR SCW 7677: AIR 2008 SC 614: (2008) 1 SCC 696.

6. Driving License – Automated Driving Test – Grant on Basis not Improper – Automated Driving Test is in the interest of general public and not contrary to public interest; *Bhupendra Mangaldas Patel* v. *State of Gujarat*, AIR 2015 Guj 65.

4. Age limit in connection with driving of motor vehicles.—(1) No person under the age of eighteen years shall drive a motor vehicle in any public place:

Provided that [1][a motor cycle with engine capacity not exceeding 50cc] may be driven in a public place by a person after attaining the age of sixteen years.

(2) Subject to the provisions of section 18, no person under the age of twenty years shall drive a transport vehicle in any public place.

(3) No learner's licence or driving licence shall be issued to any person to drive a vehicle of the class to which he has made an application unless he is eligible to drive that class of vehicle under this section.

SYNOPSIS

COMMENTS

1. Minor Driving Motorcycle – The minor person came from behind on the motorcycle and hit the scooter of the deceased from behind. The responsibility in causing the accident was, therefore, found to be solely that of the minor. However, since he was a minor and it was the responsibility of the petitioner to ensure that his motorcycle was not misused and that too by a minor who had no licence to drive the same, the Motor Accident Claims Tribunal quite rightly saddled the liability for payment of compensation on the Petitioner and, accordingly, directed the Insurance Company to pay the awarded amount to the awardees and, thereafter, to recover the same from the Petitioner. The story that the minor came into the house of the petitioner and took the keys of the motorcycle without any intimation to the petitioner, appears to be highly improbable and far-fetched. It is difficult to accept the defence of the petitioner that the keys of the motorcycle were

1. Subs. by Act 54 of 1994, sec. 4, for "a motor cycle without gear" (w.e.f. 14-11-1994).

taken by the minor without his knowledge; *Jawahar Singh* v. *Bala Jain,* AIR 2011 SC 2436: 2011 AIR SCW 3625: (2011) 6 SCC 425.

2. Adjustment of Higher Tax Amount cannot be Found Fault with – When there is a conversion in the use of the vehicle, the owner or person who is in possession of the vehicle has to pay the differential rate of tax, if the rate of tax applicable to such class of vehicle is higher. Section 4 of the Motor Vehicles Act, 1988, envisages that the tax levied under the Act shall subject to the provisions of sub-section (1-A), be paid in the manner prescribed by the registered owner or by any other person having possession or control of the motor vehicle, at his choice, either quarterly, half yearly or annually, on a licence to be taken out by him for that quarter, half-year or year, as the case may be. As per section 3(2) of the Act, the Government is empowered to increase the rate of tax specified in the schedule by notification from time to time. In the case on hand, the user of the vehicle is now changed non-transport vehicle to private service vehicle and therefore, the respondent is empowered to levy appropriate tax for that class of vehicle as per section 3 of the Act, and can levy or demand tax not more than the amount specified in the II Schedule to the above said Act. Therefore, if a higher rate of tax has to be paid by the registered owner or any other person having possession or control of the vehicle, the adjustment of the amount cannot be found fault with. However, taking into consideration, the averments made in the counter-affidavit that the matter has already been referred to the first respondent for appropriate orders and the same is still pending consideration, the respondents are directed to pass appropriate orders on the application of the petitioner, on merits and in accordance with law; *V.I. Micro System Pvt. Ltd.* v. *State of Tamil Nadu,* AIR 2008 Mad 232: 2008 AIHC 961 NOC: 2008 (6) AKAR (NOC) 1053: 2008 (5) Mad LJ 1333.

5. Responsibility of owners of motor vehicles for contravention of sections 3 and 4.—No owner or person in charge of a motor vehicle shall cause or permit any person who does not satisfy the provisions of section 3 or section 4 to drive the vehicle.

6. Restrictions on the holding of driving licences.—(1) No person shall, while he holds any driving licence for the time being in force, hold any other driving licence except a learner's licence or a driving licence issued in accordance with the provisions of section 18 or a document authorising, in accordance with the rules made under section 139, the person specified therein to drive a motor vehicle.

(2) No holder of a driving licence or a learner's licence shall permit it to be used by any other person.

(3) Nothing in this section shall prevent a licensing authority having the jurisdiction referred to in sub-section (1) of section 9 from adding to the classes of vehicles which the driving licence authorises the holder to drive.

COMMENTS

Policy Decision – Validity – Section 6 of the Act provides for restrictions on holding the driving licence as it deals with other eligibility conditions for having a permit and also prohibits its use by any other person *i.e.,* licence not been transferable. The Legislature in its wisdom has given a very comprehensive scheme providing for a driving licence explaining its necessity and responsibility of the owner in case he hands over the vehicle to a person, who is not having a valid driving licence. There is no bar under the statute to apply for grant of permit by a handicapped person, however under the impugned condition that such a person has to drive its own vehicle would be depriving him of his source of livelihood. Likewise, a woman would not be able to drive in odd hours in night or beyond particular distances. Further, if a person having the permit of autorikshaw dies and the widow of the permit holder succeeds the possession of the vehicle and ask for transfer of the permit under the statutory provisions, her application would automatically be rejected, if she is not in a position to drive or does not have a valid driving licence, under the impugned condition. Such a condition deprives a person to have permits of more than one Auto-Richshaw which has not been the intention of the Legislature. Moreso, it is discriminatory as no such treatment has been given to the permit-holders of other vehicles like buses and goods vehicles. In case of death of the permit-holder, person in possession of the vehicle may not be able to get the permit transferred in his name for want of driving licence which is also not in consonance with the statutory requirement. In view of the fact that the policy decision taken by the RTA providing permit-holders for plying of auto-rickshaw within municipal limits only is unreasonable and unworkable and also discriminatory *qua* higher income group who can afford to have any number of vehicles on many routes or having buses, the policy decision does not stand on the judicial scrutiny and is liable to be struck down; *Rajasthan Auto Chalak Union (Intack)* v. *State of Rajasthan*, AIR 2003 Raj 194: 2003 (3) Raj LR 683: 2003 (3) Raj LW 1543.

7. Restrictions on the granting of learner's licences for certain vehicles.—[1][(1) No person shall be granted a learner's licence to drive a transport vehicle unless he has held a driving licence to drive a light motor vehicle for at least one year.]

(2) No person under the age of eighteen years shall be granted a learner's licence to drive a motor cycle without gear except with the consent in writing of the person having the care of the person desiring the learner's licence.

8. Grant of learner's licence.—(1) Any person who is not disqualified under section 4 for driving a motor vehicle and who is not for the time being disqualified for holding or obtaining a driving licence may, subject to the provisions of section 7, apply to the licensing authority having jurisdiction in the area—

(i) in which he ordinarily resides or carries on business, or

(ii) in which the school or establishment referred to in section 12 from where he intends to receive instruction in driving a motor vehicle is situate,

for the issue to him of a learner's licence.

(2) Every application under sub-section (1) shall be in such form and shall be accompanied by such documents and with such fee as may be prescribed by the Central Government.

(3) Every application under sub-section (1) shall be accompanied by a medical certificate in such form as may be prescribed by the Central Government and signed by such registered medical practitioner, as the State Government or any person authorised in this behalf by the State Government may, by notification in the Official Gazette, appoint for this purpose:

[2][Provided that no such medical certificate is required for licence to drive a vehicle other than a transport vehicle.]

(4) If, from the application or from the medical certificate referred to in sub-section (3), it appears that the applicant is suffering from any disease or disability which is likely to cause the driving by him of a motor vehicle of

1. Subs. by Act 54 of 1994, sec. 5, for sub-section (1) (w.e.f. 14-11-1994).
2. Added by Act 54 of 1994, sec. 6 (w.e.f. 14-11-1994).

the class which he would be authorised by the learner's licence applied for to drive to be a source of danger to the public or to the passengers, the licensing authority shall refuse to issue the learner's licence:

Provided that a learner's licence limited to driving an invalid carriage may be issued to the applicant, if the licensing authority is satisfied that he is fit to drive such a carriage.

(5) No learner's licence shall be issued to any applicant unless he passes to the satisfaction of the licensing authority such test as may be prescribed by the Central Government.

(6) When an application has been duly made to the appropriate licensing authority and the applicant has satisfied such authority of his physical fitness under sub-section (3) and has passed to the satisfaction of the licensing authority the test referred to in sub-section (5), the licensing authority shall, subject to the provisions of section 7, issue the applicant a learner's licence unless the applicant is disqualified under section 4 for driving a motor vehicle or is for the time being disqualified for holding or obtaining a licence to drive a motor vehicle:

Provided that a licensing authority may issue a learner's licence to drive a motor cycle or a light motor vehicle notwithstanding that it is not the appropriate licensing authority, if such authority is satisfied that there is good reason for the applicant's inability to apply to the appropriate licensing authority.

(7) Where the Central Government is satisfied that it is necessary or expedient so to do, it may, by rules made in this behalf, exempt generally, either absolutely or subject to such conditions as may be specified in the rules, any class of persons from the provisions of sub-section (3), or sub-section (5), or both.

(8) Any learner's licence for driving a motor cycle in force immediately before the commencement of this Act shall, after such commencement, be deemed to be effective for driving a motor cycle with or without gear.

COMMENTS

Issuance of Learner's Licence – The Transport Authorities are not empowered to accept the medical Certificates issued by the Registered Medical Practitioners without having the minimum qualification of MBBS Degree in Allopathy or equalivalent degree granted by any University established as per the notification in GO. Ms. No. 25, Transport, Roads and Buildings (Tr. II) Department; *B.S.S. Sanadha Raj* v. *Commr. of Transport, Hyderabad,* AIR 2001 AP 162: 2001 (2) Andh LD 85: 2001 (1) Andh LT 705.

9. Grant of driving licence.—(1) Any person who is not for the time being disqualified for holding or obtaining a driving licence may apply to the licensing authority having jurisdiction in the area—

(i) in which he ordinarily resides or carries on business, or

(ii) in which the school or establishment referred to in section 12 from where he is receiving or has received instruction in driving a motor vehicle is situated.

for the issue to him of a driving licence.

(2) Every application under sub-section (1) shall be in such form and shall be accompanied by such fee and such documents as may be prescribed by the Central Government.

[1][(3) If the applicant passes such test as may be prescribed by the Central Government, he shall be issued the driving licence:

Provided that no such test shall be necessary where the applicant produces proof to show that—

(a) (i) the applicant has previously held a driving licence to drive such class of vehicle and that the period between the date of expiry of that licence and the date of the application does not exceed five years, or

(ii) the applicant holds or has previously held a driving licence to drive such class of vehicle issued under section 18, or

(iii) the applicant holds a driving licence to drive such class of vehicle issued by a competent authority of any country outside India, subject to the condition that the applicant complies with the provisions of sub-section (3) of section 8,

(b) the applicant is not suffering from any disability which is likely to cause the driving by him to be a source of danger to the public; and the licensing authority may, for that purpose, require the applicant to produce a medical certificate in the same form and in the same manner as is referred to in sub-section (3) of section 8:

Provided further that where the application is for a driving licence to drive a motor vehicle (not being a transport vehicle), the licensing authority may exempt the applicant from the test of competence to drive a vehicle prescribed under this sub-section, if the applicant possesses a driving certificate issued by any institution recognised in this behalf by the State Government.]

(4) Where the application is for a licence to drive a transport vehicle, no such authorisation shall be granted to any applicant unless he possesses such minimum educational qualification as may be prescribed by the Central Government and a driving certificate issued by a school or establishment referred to in section 12.

[2][(5) Where the applicant does not pass the test, he may be permitted to re-appear for the test after a period of seven days:

Provided that where the applicant does not pass the test even after three appearances, he shall not be qualified to re-appear for such test before the expiry of a period of sixty days from the date of last such test.]

(6) The test of competence to drive shall be carried out in a vehicle of the type to which the application refers:

Provided that a person who passed a test in driving a motor cycle with gear shall be deemed also to have passed a test in driving a motor cycle without gear.

(7) When any application has been duly made to the appropriate licensing authority and the applicant has satisfied such authority of his competence to drive, the licensing authority shall issue the applicant a driving licence unless the applicant is for the time being disqualified for holding or obtaining a driving licence:

1. Subs. by Act 54 of 1994, sec. 7, for sub-section (3) (w.e.f. 14-11-1994).
2. Subs. by Act 54 of 1994, sec. 7, for sub-section (5) (w.e.f. 14-11-1994).

Provided that a licensing authority may issue a driving licence to drive a motor cycle or a light motor vehicle notwithstanding that it is not the appropriate licensing authority, if the licensing authority is satisfied that there is good and sufficient reason for the applicant's inability to apply to the appropriate licensing authority:

Provided further that the licensing authority shall not issue a new driving licence to the applicant, if he had previously held a driving licence, unless it is satisfied that there is good and sufficient reason for his inability to obtain a duplicate copy of his former licence.

(8) If the licensing authority is satisfied, after giving the applicant an opportunity of being heard, that he—

(a) is a habitual criminal or a habitual drunkard; or

(b) is a habitual addict to any narcotic drug or psychotropic substance within the meaning of the Narcotic Drugs and Psychotropic Substances Act, 1985 (61 of 1985); or

(c) is a person whose licence to drive any motor vehicle has, at any time earlier, been revoked,

it may, for reasons to be recorded in writing, make an order refusing to issue a driving licence to such person and any person aggrieved by an order made by a licensing authority under this sub-section may, within thirty days of the receipt of the order, appeal to the prescribed authority.

(9) Any driving licence for driving a motor cycle in force immediately before the commencement of this Act shall, after such commencement, be deemed to be effective for driving a motor cycle with or without gear.

SYNOPSIS

1. Grant of Licence
2. Submission of Fresh Application and Fees for Re-appearance is not Improper
3. Ceiling of Three Tests for Driving Licence
4. Using School's Address as Temporary Address

COMMENTS

1. Grant of Licence – The licensing authority having jurisdiction in a particular area can grant driving licence to any person who resides or carries on business in his area or in which the school or establishment referred to in section 12, from which he was receiving instructions in driving, is situated; *Jain Motor Driving Training College* v. *Deputy Transport Commissioner, Meerut Zone,* AIR 1993 All 65: 1992 All WC 1640: 1994 All LJ 293.

2. Submission of Fresh Application and Fees for Re-appearance is not Improper – The object of section 9(5) is only to provide an opportunity for a repeater in the event of a failure and a time schedule is fixed in the Act. That would not mean that there should be no application and no fees. Any such understanding would be ruinous to the very understanding of the Act. The section is very clear with regard to payment. It is not possible to read something more into the section for the purpose of interpretation of the section read with rules. Therefore, the argument of no fresh application and no fresh fee for three tests is liable to be rejected. What is provided under section 9(5) is only an opportunity with time schedule and nothing else; *Prabhakar Y.D.* v. *State of Karnataka,* AIR 2003 Kant 466: 2003 (5) Kant LJ 514: 2003 (12) All Ind Cas 707.

3. Ceiling of Three Tests for Driving Licence – Most of the accidents are attributable to reckless driving of the vehicle without caring for human life and human misery. In these circumstances, the authorities are to ponder over to arrest these unfortunate accidents resulting in loss of life in addition to misery. One method that can be adopted is to put a ceiling of only three purposeful tests for the purpose of driving licence. If a person is unable to pass the driving test in three attempts, any further concession can not be shown to him. It is not unknown that ceiling, is fixed in the matter of examinations. Hence, the court deem it proper to observe that the Government may take note of this judgment and effect necessary amendment thereby creating a ceiling of only three attempts for obtaining licence in the larger interest of saving human life and in the larger interest of avoiding accidents as a whole in the State. This three tests ceiling is to be fixed after providing sufficient safe guards for a sincere applicant in the matter of test by the officials, and see that an honest and sincere aspirant is not deprived of his/her driving licence; *Prabhakar Y.D.* v. *State of Karnataka*, AIR 2003 Kant 466: 2003 (5) Kant LJ 514.

4. Using School's Address as Temporary Address – For applying for licence, it is necessary to give a certificate that the applicant has undergone the training in the school and to prevent the applicant from using the school's address as temporary address is without any basis. The Act itself gives the applicant to apply for licences within the jurisdiction of the driving school. It may be that a person may not have any temporary address in a city. He may be permanently employed in a place outside the city. But when he comes to city for learning driving, he cannot give his permanent address as temporary address. The school imparts training and education. It will be the temporary home of the applicant. If the owners of the schools commit any manipulations, it is for the authorities to take action. But, that should not prevent the students who study in the School to give the address of the School as temporary address; *All Kerala M.D.S. Workers Welfare Assocn.* v. *State of Kerala*, AIR 1999 Ker 337: 1999 (1) Ker LJ 782: 1999 (2) Ker LT 217.

10. Form and contents of licences to drive.—(1) Every learner's licence and driving licence, except a driving licence issued under section 18, shall be in such form and shall contain such information as may be prescribed by the Central Government.

(2) A learner's licence or, as the case may be, driving licence shall also be expressed as entitling the holder to drive a motor vehicle of one or more of the following classes, namely:—

(a) motor cycle without gear;

(b) motor cycle with gear;

(c) invalid carriage;

(d) light motor vehicle;

[1][(e) transport vehicle;]

(i) road-roller;

(j) motor vehicle of a specified description.

SYNOPSIS

1. Driving Different Class of Vehicle
2. Driving Licence is not Required for Operation of Power Tiller
3. Offending Vehicle Type Different From Vehicle Authorised

COMMENTS

1. Driving Different Class of Vehicle – The cause of death of the deceased in road accident had occurred due to rash and negligent driving of scooter. The driver admittedly had no valid and effective licence to drive the vehicle on the day of accident. The scooterist was possessing driving licence of driving Heavy Motor Vehicle and he was driving totally different class of vehicle which act is in violation of section 10(2)

1. Subs. by Act 54 of 1994, sec. 8, for clauses (e) to (h) (w.e.f. 14-11-1994).

of the MV Act. Insurance Company cannot be held liable; *Oriental Insurance Co. Ltd.* v. *Zaharulnisha,* AIR 2008 SC 2218: 2008 AIR SCW 3251: 2008 (7) SCALE 310.

2. Driving Licence is not Required for Operation of Power Tiller – Section 10 of the M.V. Act deals with the form and contents of a licence to drive. Sub-section (1) says that the learners licence and driving licence shall be in such form as may be prescribed. Sub-section (2) says that the learners licence and the driving licence shall express the class of vehicle or vehicles which the holder of the licence was entitled to drive. It mentions of the following classes of vehicles (a) motor cycle without gear (b) Motor cycle with gear (c) invalid carriage, (d) light motor cycle, (e) transport vehicle (f) road roller and (g) motor vehicle of the specified description. The above classes do not include a Power Tiller and it was not specified too and as such a driving licence is necessary for the operation of a Power Tiller which is not ordinarily used for transport purpose. The main purpose of the Power Tiller is for the agricultural work and for that purpose it requires movement. Yet Power Tiller would come in category of a motor vehicle and there by registration under the Motor Vehicles Act was necessary. But for operating the above, the law does not contemplate the requirement of a driving licence as the vehicle itself does not provide any seat for accommodating a driver. Hence, the argument that a driving licence under the M.V. Act is not required for the operation of a Power Tiller has only to be accepted. There is no provision of law or any circumstances so as to hold that a driving licence was required for the operation of the Power Tiller. But in respect of other vehicles law specifically mentions of the requirements of a driving licence; *Secretary, P.P.S.C. Co-op. Socy. Ltd.* v. *Ponnappan,* AIR 2004 Ker 46: 2004 (1) Ker LJ 156: 2003 (3) Ker LT 997.

3. Offending Vehicle Type Different from Vehicle Authorised – The insurance company has felt contended with mere pleading that the driver of offending vehicle did not have effective driving license without any proof to establish such pleadings before the Tribunal. While there can be no dispute with the legal prepositions that the insurance company to be saddled with the liability to indemnify the insured, the driver of the offending vehicle must have a valid and effective driving license, yet in absence of reliable and credit-worthy evidence that the offending vehicle was of a type different from the vehicle, the respondent was competent to drive, the insurance company cannot wriggle out of its responsibility to indemnify the insured and pay compensation assessed by the Tribunal to the respondents; *National Insurance Co. Ltd.* v. *Fatima,* AIR 2011 J&K 125.

11. Additions to driving licence.—(1) Any person holding a driving licence to drive any class or description of motor vehicles, who is not for the time being disqualified for holding or obtaining a driving licence to drive any other class or description of motor vehicles, may apply to the licensing authority having jurisdiction in the area in which he resides or carries on his business in such form and accompanied by such, documents and with such fees as may be prescribed by the Central Government for the addition of such other class or description of motor vehicles to the licence.

(2) Subject to such rules as may be prescribed by the Central Government, the provisions of section 9 shall apply to an application under this section as if the said application were for the grant of a licence under that section to drive the class or description of motor vehicles which the applicant desires to be added to his licence.

12. Licensing and regulation of schools or establishments for imparting instruction in driving of motor vehicles.—(1) The Central Government may make rules for the purpose of licensing and regulating, by the State Governments, schools or establishments (by whatever name called) for imparting instruction in driving of motor vehicles and matters connected therewith.

(2) In particular, and without prejudice to the generality of the foregoing power, such rules may provide for all or any of the following matters, namely:—

(a) licensing of such schools or establishments including grant, renewal and revocation of such licences;

(b) supervision of such schools or establishments;

(c) the form of application and the form of licence and the particulars to be contained therein;

(d) fee to be paid with the application for such licences;

(e) conditions subject to which such licences may be granted;

(f) appeals against the orders of refusal to grant or renew such licences and appeals against the orders revoking such licences;

(g) conditions subject to which a person may establish and maintain any such school or establishment for imparting instruction in driving of motor vehicles;

(h) nature, syllabus and duration of course or courses for efficient instruction in driving any motor vehicle;

(i) apparatus and equipments (including motor vehicles fitted with dual control) required for the purpose of imparting such instruction;

(j) suitability of the premises at which such schools or establishments may be established or maintained and facilities to be provided therein;

(k) qualifications, both educational and professional (including experience), which a person imparting instruction in driving a motor vehicle shall possess;

(l) inspection of such schools and establishments (including the services rendered by them and the apparatus, equipments and motor vehicles maintained by them for imparting such instruction);

(m) maintenance of records by such schools or establishments;

(n) financial stability of such schools or establishments;

(o) the driving certificates, if any, to be issued by such schools or establishments and the form in which such driving certificates shall be issued and the requirements to be complied with for the purposes of issuing such certificates;

(p) such other matters as may be necessary to carry out the purposes of this section.

(3) Where the Central Government is satisfied that it is necessary or expedient so to do, it may, by rules made in this behalf, exempt generally, either absolutely or subject to such conditions as may be specified in the rules, any class of schools or establishments imparting instruction in driving of motor vehicles or matters connected therewith from the provisions of this section.

(4) A school or establishment imparting instruction in driving of motor vehicles or matters connected therewith immediately before the commencement of this Act, whether under a licence or not, may continue to impart such instruction without a licence issued under this Act for a period of one month

from such commencement, and if it has made an application for such licence under this Act within the said period of one month and such application is in the prescribed form, contains the prescribed particulars and is accompanied by the prescribed fee, till the disposal of such application by the licensing authority.

13. Extent of effectiveness of licences, to drive motor vehicles.—A learner's licence or a driving licence issued under this Act shall be effective throughout India.

14. Currency of licences to drive motor vehicles.—(1) A learner's licence issued under this Act shall, subject to the other provisions of this Act, be effective for a period of six months from the date of issue of the licence.

(2) A driving licence issued or renewed under this Act shall,—

(a) in the case of a licence to drive a transport vehicle, be effective for a period of three years: [1][***]

[2][Provided that in the case of licence to drive a transport vehicle carrying goods of dangerous or hazardous nature be effective for a period of one year and renewal thereof shall be subject to the condition that the driver undergoes one day refresher course of the prescribed syllabus; and]

(b) in the case of any other licence,—

(i) if the person obtaining the licence, either originally or on renewal thereof, has not attained the age of [3][fifty years] on the date of issue or, as the case may be, renewal thereof,—

(A) be effective for a period of twenty years from the date of such issue or renewal; or

(B) until the date on which such person attains the age of [3][fifty years],

whichever is earlier;

[4][(ii) if the person referred to in sub-clause (i), has attained the age of fifty years on the date of issue or as the case may be, renewal thereof, be effective, on payment of such fee as may be prescribed, for a period of five years from the date of such issue or renewal:]

Provided that every driving licence shall, notwithstanding its expiry under this sub-section continue to be effective for a period of thirty days from such expiry.

COMMENTS

No Provision should be Considered as Surplusage – Motor Vehicles Act, 1988 provides for grant of learner's licence. A learner's licence is, thus, also a licence within the meaning of the provisions of the said Act. It cannot, therefore, be said that a vehicle when being driven by a learner subject to the conditions mentioned in the licence, he would not be a person who is not duly licensed resulting in conferring a right on the insurer to avoid the claim of the third party. It cannot be said that a person holding a

1. The word "and" omitted by Act 54 of 1994, sec. 9 (w.e.f. 14-11-1994).
2. Ins. by Act 54 of 1994, sec. 9 (w.e.f. 14-11-1994).
3. Subs. by Act 54 of 1994. sec. 9, for "forty years" (w.e.f. 14-11-1994).
4. Subs. by Act 54 of 1994. sec. 9, for sub-clause (ii) (w.e.f. 14-11-1994).

learner's licence is not entitled to drive the vehicle. Even if there exists a condition in the contract of insurance that the vehicle cannot be driven by a person holding a learner's licence, the same would run counter to the provisions of section 149(2) of the said Act. Learner's licences are granted under the rules framed by the Central Government or the State Governments in exercise of their rule-making power. Conditions are attached to the learner's licences granted in terms of the statute. A person holding learner's licence would, thus, also come within the purview of "duly licensed" as such a licence is also granted in terms of the provisions of the Act and the rules framed thereunder. Thus Rules validly framed become part of the statute. Such Rules are, therefore, required to be read as a part of main enactment. Further for the interpretation of statute an attempt must be made to give effect to all provisions under the rule. No provision should be considered as surplusage; *National Insurance Co. Ltd.* v. *Swaran Singh,* AIR 2004 SC 1531: 2004 AIR SCW 663: (2004) 3 SCC 297.

15. Renewal of driving licences.—(1) Any licensing authority may, on application made to it, renew a driving licence issued under the provisions of this Act with effect from the date of its expiry:

Provided that in any case where the application for the renewal of a licence is made more than thirty days after the date of its expiry, the driving licence shall be renewed with effect from the date of its renewal:

Provided further that where the application is for the renewal of a licence to drive a transport vehicle or where in any other case the applicant has attained the age of forty years, the same shall be accompanied by a medical certificate in the same form and in the same manner as is referred to in sub-section (3) of section 8, and the provisions of sub-section (4) of section 8 shall, so far as may be, apply in relation to every such case as they apply in relation to a learner's licence.

(2) An application for the renewal of a driving licence shall be made in such form and accompanied by such documents as may be prescribed by the Central Government.

(3) Where an application for the renewal of a driving licence is made previous to, or not more than thirty days after the date of its expiry, the fee payable for such renewal shall be such as may be prescribed by the Central Government in this behalf.

(4) Where an application for the renewal of a driving licence is made more than thirty days after the date of its expiry, the fee payable for such renewal shall be such amount as may be prescribed by the Central Government:

Provided that the fee referred to in sub-section (3) may be accepted by the licensing authority in respect of an application for the renewal of a driving licence made under this sub-section if it is satisfied that the applicant was prevented by good and sufficient cause from applying within the time specified in such-section (3):

Provided further that if the application is made more than five years after the driving licence has ceased to be effective, the licensing authority may refuse to renew the driving licence, unless the applicant undergoes and passes to its satisfaction the test of competence to drive referred to in sub-section (3) of section 9.

(5) Where the application for renewal has been rejected, the fee paid shall be refunded to such extent and in such manner as may be prescribed by the Central Government.

(6) Where the authority renewing the driving licence is not the authority which issued the driving licence it shall intimate the fact of renewal to the authority which issued the driving licence.

SYNOPSIS

COMMENTS

1. Renewal cannot Cure Inherent Fatality – Where originally the license was a fake one, renewal cannot cure the inherent fatality in fake licence; *National Insurance Co. Ltd.* v. *Laxmi Narain Dhut*, AIR 2007 SC 1563: 2007 AIR SCW 2279: 2007 (3) SCC 700: 2007 (4) SCALE 36: 2007 (2) Supreme 721.

If a fake driving licence happened to be renewed by the statutory authorities, the fakeness of the original document does not get legally sanctified. The Insurance Company shall not be liable to pay compensation in respect of a motor accident occurred while the vehicle was driven by a person holding such a sham licence. No licensing authority has the power to renew a fake licence and, therefore, a renewal if at all made cannot transform a fake licence as genuine; *New India Assurance Co., Shimla* v. *Kamla*, AIR 2001 SC 1419: 2001 AIR SCW 1340: JT 2001 (4) SC 235: 2001 (4) SCC 342: 2001 (3) SCALE 18: 2001 (3) Supreme 84.

If the licence is fake, renewal cannot take away the effect of fake licence; *Oriental Insurance Co. Limited* v. *Prithvi Raj*, (2008) 2 SCC 338: (2008) 1 SCR 1180: AIR 2008 SC 1408.

2. Application for Renewal of Driving Licence must be Filed within 30 Days from Date of its Expiry – The driving licence of the deceased driver had expired four months prior to the date of accident and it was renewed. It is not the case of the claimant that the driver had applied for renewal of the licence within 30 days of the date of its expiry. From a plain reading of section 15 of the Act, it is clear that if an application for renewal of licence is made within 30 days of the date of its expiry, the licence continues to be effective and valid without a break as the renewal dates back to the date of its expiry. Whereas, when an application for renewal is filed after more than 30 days after the date of its expiry, proviso to sub-section (1) of section 15 of the Act, gets attracted and the licence is renewed only with effect from the date of its renewal, meaning thereby that in the interregnum between the date of expiry of the licence and the date of its renewal, there is no effective licence in existence. The provision is clear and admits of no ambiguity. However, the stand of the claimant was that since the deceased driver was holding a valid licence and had not been disqualified from holding an effective licence, the stipulation in the afore-extracted condition was not infringed. Thus the argument is stated to be rejected. Admittedly, having failed to apply for renewal of the driving licence within 30 days from the date of its expiry in terms of section 15 of the Act, the licence could not be renewed with effect from the date of its expiry and therefore, the deceased driver had no valid and effective driving licence as contemplated under section 3 of the Act. Thus he did not hold at all an effective driving licence, as required in the terms and conditions governing the policy on the date of accident. In view of the clear mandate of section 3 of the Act, the deceased driver was not even permitted to drive the insured vehicle in a public place. Furthermore, the claimant not only committed breach of the terms of the policy, he also violated the provisions of section 5 of the Act by entrusting the vehicle to a person who did not hold a valid licence on the date of the accident. Therefore, the appellant was not liable to indemnify the claimant for the loss suffered by him in the accident of the insured vehicle; *New India Assurance Co. Ltd.* v. *Suresh Chandra Aggarwal,* 2009 AIR SCW 4801: AIR 2009 SC 2987: (2009) 9 SCALE 449.

A bare perusal of the provisions of section 15 appear that the licence is renewed in terms of the said Act and the rules framed thereunder. The proviso appended to section 15(1) of the Act in no uncertain terms states that whereas the original licence granted despite expiry remains valid for a period of 30 days from the date of expiry, if any application for renewal thereof is filed thereafter, the same would be renewed from the date of its renewal. As on the date the accident, the renewal application had not been filed, the driver, did not have a valid licence on the date when the vehicle met with the accident; *Ishwar Chandra* v. *Oriental Insurance Co. Ltd.,* AIR 2007 SC 1445: 2007 AIR SCW 1889: (2007) 4 SCALE 292.

3. Authorities have No Power to Reject Application for Renewal on Lapse of Tenure – A person whose licence is ordinarily renewed in terms of the Motor Vehicles Act and the Rules framed thereunder, despite the fact that during the interregnum period, namely, when the accident took place and the date of expiry of the licence, he did not have a valid licence, he could during the prescribed period apply for renewal thereof and could obtain the same automatically without undergoing any further test or without having been declared unqualified therefor. Proviso appended to section 14 in unequivocal terms states that the licence remains valid for a period of thirty days from the day of its expiry. Section 15 of the Act does not empower the authorities to reject an application for renewal only on the ground that there is a break in validity or tenure of the driving licence has lapsed, as in the meantime the provisions for disqualification of the driver contained in sections 19, 20, 21, 22, 23 and 24 will not be attracted, would indisputably confer a right upon the person to get his driving licence renewed. Thus he cannot be said to be delicensed and the same shall remain valid for a period of thirty days after its expiry; *National Insurance Co. Ltd.* v. *Swaran Singh,* AIR 2004 SC 1531: 2004 AIR SCW 663: (2004) 3 SCC 297.

4. Once License is Fake One Renewal cannot take Away Effect of Fake License – Once the license is a fake one the renewal cannot take away the effect of fake license. A fake licence cannot get its forgery outfit stripped off merely on account of some officer renewing the same with or without knowing it to be forged. Section 15 of the Act only empowers any Licensing Authority to "renew a driving licence issued under the provisions of this Act with effect from the date of its expiry". No Licensing Authority has the power to renew a fake licence and, therefore, a renewal if at all made cannot transform a fake licence as genuine. Any counterfeit document showing that it contains a purported order of a statutory authority would ever remain counterfeit albeit the fact that other persons including some statutory authorities would have acted on the document unwittingly on the assumption that it is genuine; *New India Assurance Co., Shimla* v. *Kamla,* AIR 2001 SC 1419: 2001 AIR SCW 1340: (2001) 4 SCC 342.

5. No Licensing Authority has Power to Renew Fake Licence – No Licensing Authority has the power to renew a fake licence and, therefore, a renewal if at all made cannot transform a fake licence as genuine. Any counterfeit document showing that it contains a purported order of a statutory authority would ever remain counterfeit albeit the fact that other persons including some statutory authorities would have acted on the document unwittingly on the assumption that it is genuine; *New India Assurance Co., Shimla* v. *Kamla,* AIR 2001 SC 1419: 2001 AIR SCW 1340: (2001) 4 SCC 342.

6. Whether Forged or Fake Licence, if Renewed would Get Validated or not – There was a motor accident which gave rise to a claim for compensation, duly set up by the claimants/respondents. One of the questions which was brought to the fore was whether the offending motor vehicle was being driven by a driver holding a valid driving licence. The matter was put to issue and the conclusion arrived at by the Tribunal was that the driver held a valid licence which had validly been renewed. This finding stood affirmed in appeal before the High Court. Yet it was taken by the High Court that a question of law arose as to whether a forged or a fake licence, if renewed would get validated or not so as to work out the liabilities under the Motor Vehicles Act. The question gathered momentum inasmuch as when the cause was before a Division Bench of the High Court, it referred the matter so a Full Bench of three Hon'ble Judges which in turn pronounced as: "(1) A forged driving licence though may be validly renewed, would not become a valid driving licence or a duly issued driving licence in accordance with the Motor Vehicles Act. (2) The insured *bonafidely* believing in the validity of a forged driving licence employing the holder of a fake driving licence renewed by a competent authority, would not amount to violation of the conditions of contract or of the insurance policy. It would not be violating either conditions of indemnity or the insurance policy or the contract or violation of any statutory provisions. Under these circumstances, merely employing a driver with a forged driving licence would not absolve the insurer of its liability. (3) In the absence of *mens rea* or knowledge or intention to violate the terms of policy or the provisions of the Act by the insured, the insurance company would not be discharged of its liability from indemnifying the insurer or of its statutory liability to third party. (4) The insurance company cannot refuse to meet its liability quo third party for any act or omission *bonafidely* or otherwise committed by the insured or its liability inasmuch as third party for whose benefit the insurance has been provided, is not a privity to any breach as being not in control of the act or conduct of the insured or its employee or insurer. Thus, the insurance company cannot refuse to meet its liability quo third party. (5) The insurer is duty bound and liable, statutorily as well as contractually to reimburse third party claim, for the tortuous act committed by the insured or his employee as well as the liability incurred by insured or his employee under the Motor Vehicles Act. (6) The insurance company can neither refuse to indemnify nor is discharged from its liability to the insured or the claimants for an act of fraud committed by the third party quo the insured though it has a right to recover any loss suffered by it from the person, who committed the fraud or from any other authority, as permissible either under tort or any other statute; and (7) The insurance company would be entitled to recover the amount, which it has paid to the claimant from the insured or his driver or employee who has perpetuated fraud and the insurance company was made to reimburse third party who suffered loss because of the tortuous act of the insured or his employee. The insurer would not be left without remedy to reimburse itself. It would be at liberty to approach under tort in accordance with law for the failure of the State to discharge common duty care as well as the insured for not observing due care of an ordinary prudent person, expected from the insured, as a duty towards the insurer as well as the person who has committed the fraud. Remedy as available to the insurer is not a decision by this Court while dealing with the question, rather it is left open to be determined as and when a question arises in the facts and circumstances of a particular case." But this court do not approve of the High Court having gone on the endeavour streamlining the law when its ratio on the fact situation was likely to be rendered totally obiter. There was a concurrent finding recorded by the Tribunal as well by the High Court that the offending vehicle was driven by a driver who had held a valid licence and it stood renewed on the date of the accident. There was thus no occasion for the High Court to have ruled on suppositions to the contrary in order to interpret the law and that too on a fact situation not available to it. Thus the entire exercise of the High Court in that direction was obiter, not at all a binding precedent. In that sense, the court strike off from the impugned order observations and findings pertaining thereto. Yet at the same time, the court has affirmed the substantive part of the order, in holding that the claimants/respondents had rightly been granted compensation on account of the motor accident, on the basis of the recorded finding of fact; *National Insurance Co. Ltd.* v. *Santro Devi*, 1998 AIR SCW 346: AIR 1998 SC 1485: (1998) 1 SCC 219.

7. Driving License – Renewal – Driver of Vehicle not holding valid driving license from date of expiry till renewal; *Oriental Insurance Company Limited, Chalakudy, Kochi* v. *Poulose*, AIR 2015 Ker 148.

8. 'Duly Licensed' – Driving license expired on the date of road accident and not renewed subsequently within statutory period- Requirement of 'duly licensed' not fulfilled; *Oriental Insurance Company Limited, Chalakudy, Kochi* v. *Poulose*, AIR 2015 Ker 148.

16. Revocation of driving licence on grounds of disease or disability.— Notwithstanding anything contained in the foregoing sections, any licensing authority may at any time revoke a driving licence or may require, as a condition of continuing to hold such driving licence, the holder thereof to produce a medical certificate in the same form and in the same manner as is referred to in sub-section (3) of section 8, if the licensing authority has reasonable grounds to believe that the holder of the driving licence is, by virtue of any disease or disability, unfit to drive a motor vehicle and where the authority revoking a driving licence is not the authority which issued the same, it shall intimate the fact of revocation to the authority which issued that licence.

SYNOPSIS

1. Right of Appeal
2. Power Vested in Taxing Officer to Decide whether Tax in Respect of Vehicle Paid or Not

COMMENTS

1. Right of Appeal – As per the endorsement the petitioner had received a copy of order of suspension on 20-3-2012. Section 16(3) of the Act confers a right of appeal on the petitioner. The right of appeal was to be exercised within a period of 30 days of receipt of the order. Though the petitioner had received a copy of the order on 20-3-2012, he had not chosen to file a statutory appeal within the time stipulated in section 16. If the petitioner's case that he had not been heard before the issue of order of suspension were *bona fide*, he would certainly have challenged the order of suspension in appeal within the statutory period of 30 days prescribed by section 16(3). This Writ Petition is filed long after the said period had expired, on 5-6-2012. The above conduct of the petitioner also does not inspire confidence; *Peethambaran T.R.* v. *Additional Licensing Authority*, AIR 2013 Ker 46: 2012 (3) Ker LJ 547: 2012 (3) Ker LT 622.

2. Power Vested in Taxing Officer to Decide whether Tax in Respect of Vehicle Paid or Not – Power is vested in the Taxing Officer to decide whether tax in respect of the vehicle has been paid and if the same has not been paid, to recover the same from sale of the vehicle, if necessary. Thus, the High Court should not have straightway come to the conclusion in the writ petition that the tax in respect of the vehicle has been paid; *State of West Bengal* v. *Mani Bhushan Kumar*, AIR 2012 SC 184: 2011 AIR SCW 6366: (2011) 10 SCC 147.

17. Orders refusing or revoking driving licences and appeals therefrom.— (1) Where a licensing authority refuses to issue any learner's licence or to issue or renew, or revokes any driving licence, or refuses to add a class or description of motor vehicle to any driving licence, it shall do so by an order communicated to the applicant or the holder, as the case may be, giving the reasons in writing for such refusal or revocation.

(2) Any person aggrieved by an order made under sub-section (1) may, within thirty days of the service on him of the order, appeal to the prescribed authority

which shall decide the appeal after giving such person and the authority which made the order an opportunity of being heard and the decision of the appellate authority shall be binding on the authority which made the order.

18. Driving licences to drive motor vehicles, belonging to the Central Government.—(1) Such authority as may be prescribed by the Central Government may issue driving licence valid throughout India to persons who have completed their eighteenth year to drive motor vehicles which are the property or for the time being under the exclusive control of the Central Government and are used for Government purposes relating to the defence of the country and unconnected with any commercial enterprise.

(2) A driving licence issued under this section shall specify the class or description of vehicle which the holder is entitled to drive and the period for which he is so entitled.

(3) A driving licence issued under this section shall not entitle the holder to drive any motor vehicle except a motor vehicle referred to in sub-section (1).

(4) The authority issuing any driving licence under this section shall, at the request of any State Government, furnish such information respecting any person to whom a driving licence is issued as that Government may at any time require.

19. Power of licensing authority to disqualify from holding a driving licence or revoke such licence.—(1) If a licensing authority is satisfied, after giving the holder of a driving licence an opportunity of being heard, that he—

(a) is a habitual criminal or a habitual drunkard; or

(b) is a habitual addict to any narcotic drug or psychotropic substance within the meaning of the Narcotic Drugs and Psychotropic Substances Act, 1985 (61 of 1985); or

(c) is using or has used a motor vehicle in the commission of a cognizable offence; or

(d) has by his previous conduct as driver of a motor vehicle shown that his driving is likely to be attended with danger to the public; or

(e) has obtained any driving licence or a licence to drive a particular class or description of motor vehicle by fraud or misrepresentation; or

(f) has committed any such act which is likely to cause nuisance or danger to the public, as may be prescribed by the Central Government, having regard to the objects of this Act; or

(g) has failed to submit to, or has not passed, the tests referred to in the proviso to sub-section (3) of section 22; or

(h) being a person under the age of eighteen years who has been granted a learner's licence or a driving licence with the consent in writing of the person having the care of the holder of the licence and has ceased to be in such care,

it may, for reasons to be recorded in writing, make an order—

(i) disqualifying that person for a specified period for holding or obtaining any driving licence to drive all or any classes or descriptions of vehicles specified in the licence; or

(ii) revoke any such licence.

(2) Where an order under sub-section (1) is made, the holder of a driving licence shall forthwith surrender his driving licence to the licensing authority making the order, if the driving licence has not already been surrendered, and the licensing authority shall,—

(a) if the driving licence is a driving licence issued under this Act, keep it until the disqualification has expired or has been removed; or

(b) if it is not a driving licence issued under this Act, endorse the disqualification upon it and send it to the licensing authority by which it was issued; or

(c) in the case of revocation of any licence, endorse the revocation upon it and if it is not the authority which issued the same, intimate the fact of revocation to the authority which issued that licence:

Provided that where the driving licence of a person authorises him to drive more than one class or description of motor vehicles and the order, made under sub-section (1), disqualifies him from driving any specified class or description of motor vehicles, the licensing authority shall endorse the disqualification upon the driving licence and return the same to the holder.

(3) Any person aggrieved by an order made by a licensing authority under sub-section (1) may, within thirty days of the receipt of the order, appeal to the prescribed authority, and such appellate authority shall give notice to the licensing authority and hear either party if so required by that party and may pass such order as it thinks fit and an order passed by any such appellate authority shall be final.

SYNOPSIS

1. Authorises Authority to Disqualify Any Person from Holding Driving Licence
2. Suspension of Licence would not be Deprivation of means to Earn Livelihood
3. Validity of Suspension of Driving License for One Year
4. Suspension of Licence not Dependent upon Conviction of Offender

COMMENTS

1. Authorises Authority to Disqualify Any Person from Holding Driving Licence – Section 19 authorises the licensing authority to disqualify any person from holding a driving licence or revoke such a licence if the licensing authority is satisfied that the holder of the driving licence is indulging in any of the acts, detailed in section 19(1) of the Act. Indubitably, no such order had been passed against the driver of the vehicle involved in the accident. The stand of the appellant is that the claim preferred by the claimant could not be processed and had to be repudiated because special condition No. 5 of the insurance policy had been violated inasmuch as the driver of the insured vehicle did not have an effective driving licence at the time of the accident. Special condition contemplates that apart from the insured, any other person, authorised by the insured, could also drive the vehicle provided the person driving the vehicle "holds or had held and has not been disqualified" from holding an effective driving licence. In the instant case, as per the certificate issued by the licensing authority, the driving licence of the deceased driver had expired four months prior to the date of accident and it was renewed. Having failed to apply for renewal of the driving licence within 30 days from the date of its expiry in terms of section 15 of the Act, the licence could not be renewed with effect from the date of its expiry and therefore, the deceased driver had no valid and effective driving licence; *New India Assurance Co. Ltd.* v. *Suresh Chandra Aggarwal*, 2009 AIR SCW 4801: AIR 2009 SC 2987: (2009) 9 SCALE 449.

2. Suspension of Licence would not be Deprivation of means to Earn Livelihood – It is contended that the action of suspension of licence for a period of one year has deprived the petitioner of his means to earn his livelihood as he is not able to work as a driver for the purpose of earning a livelihood. The right to earn a livelihood by working as the driver of a transport vehicle is regulated by the provisions of the Motor Vehicles Act and the Rules therein. The licence granted to the petitioner does not confer on him a right to drive his vehicle dangerously or carelessly or in such a way as to cause injury, damage or loss of life to another. Any such conduct on his part amounts to violation of the terms and conditions subject to which he has been licenced to drive a motor vehicle. Therefore, for violation of the terms of the licence, the licensing authority is within its powers to suspend and if necessary, revoke the licence that has been granted. When such action is initiated, it is not open to the licencee to contend that such action has deprived him of his means of livelihood. The device of licensing itself operates by prohibiting a particular act and then permitting the said act subject to the terms of a licence that is issued only to persons who are considered to be competent to be granted such licence. Therefore, in the case of driving also, there is a general prohibition in force, which is relaxed in the case of persons who are granted a licence, by permitting them to drive provided they abide by the conditions of the licence. Since the licensing authority is satisfied that the petitioner has violated the terms of the licence, it is certainly within the powers of the said authority to suspend the licence. The suspension is only for a period of one year. Such suspension is only reasonable. It is open to the petitioner to engage himself in any other avocation to earn a livelihood; *Peethambaran T.R.* v. *Additional Licensing Authority*, AIR 2013 Ker 46: 2012 (3) Ker LJ 547: 2012 (3) Ker LT 622.

3. Validity of Suspension of Driving License for One Year – It is contended that since the licensee was not habitual criminal or offender, the provision of section 19 could not be invoked. The license was suspended because the licensee was involved in motor accident causing the death of a person. Section 19 could be invoked when licensee uses his vehicle in commission of a cognizable offence like causing death of a human being. The license has been granted to the licensee but that would not confer on him right to drive dangerously thus when he drives dangerously he violates the terms of license, Therefore, the provision of section 19 is squarely applicable and suspension of the driving licence is not invalid; *Peethambaran T.R.* v. *Additional Licensing Authority*, AIR 2013 Ker 46: 2012 (3) Ker LJ 547: 2012 (3) Ker LT 622.

4. Suspension of Licence not Dependent upon Conviction of Offender – The power of suspension is to be exercised in appropriate cases by the Court, upon conviction of a person. Therefore, the power of the licensing authority and that of the Court, operates in different spheres. The suspension of a licence under section 19 is not dependent upon a conviction of the offender. The same can be invoked immediately upon commission of the offence where the licensing authority is satisfied of the existence of the other conditions stipulated by the provision. For the above reasons, the impugned action would not constitute double jeopardy as contended; *Peethambaran T.R.* v. *Additional Licensing Authority*, AIR 2013 Ker 46: 2012 (3) Ker LJ 547: 2012 (3) Ker LT 622.

20. Power of Court to disqualify.—(1) Where a person is convicted of an offence under this Act or of an offence in the commission of which a motor vehicle was used, the court by which such person is convicted may, subject to the provisions of this Act, in addition to imposing any other punishment authorised by law, declare the persons so convicted to be disqualified, for such period as the Court may specify, from holding any driving licence to drive all classes to description of vehicles, or any particular class or description of such vehicles, as are specified in such licence:

Provided that in respect of an offence punishable under section 183 no such order shall be made for the first or second offence.

(2) Where a person is convicted of an offence under clause (c) of sub-section (1) of section 132, section 134 or section 185, the Court convicting any person of any such offence shall order the disqualification under sub-section (1), and if the offence is relatable to clause (c) of sub-section (1) of section 132 or section 134, such disqualification shall be for a period of not less than one month, and if the offence is relatable to section 185, such disqualification shall be for a period of not less than six months.

(3) A Court shall, unless for special reasons to be recorded in writing it thinks fit to order otherwise, order the disqualification of a person—

(a) who having been convicted of an offence punishable under section 184 is again convicted of an offence punishable under that section,

(b) who is convicted of an offence punishable under section 189, or

(c) who is convicted of an offence punishable under section 192:

Provided that the period of disqualification shall not exceed, in the case referred to in clause (a), five years, or, in the case referred to in clause (b), two years or, in the case referred to in clause (c), one year.

(4) A Court ordering the disqualification of a person convicted of an offence punishable under section 184 may direct that such person shall, whether he has previously passed the test of competence to drive as referred to in sub-section (3) of section 9 or not, remain disqualified until he has subsequent to the making of the order of disqualification passed that test to the satisfaction of the licensing authority.

(5) The court to which an appeal would ordinarily lie from any conviction of an offence of the nature specified in sub-section (1) may set aside or vary any order of disqualification made under that sub-section notwithstanding that no appeal would lie against the conviction as a result of which such order of disqualification was made.

21. Suspension of driving licence in certain cases.—(1) Where, in relation to a person who had been previously convicted of an offence punishable under section 184, a case is registered by a police officer on the allegation that such person has, by such dangerous driving as is referred to in the said section 184, of any class or description of motor vehicle caused the death of, or grievous hurt to, one or more persons, the driving licence held by such person shall in relation to such class or description of motor vehicle become suspended—

(a) for a period of six months from the date on which the case is registered, or

(b) if such person is discharged or acquitted before the expiry of the period aforesaid, until such discharge or acquittal, as the case may be.

(2) Where by virtue of the provisions of sub-section (1), the driving licence held by a person becomes suspended, the police officer, by whom the case referred to in sub-section (1) is registered, shall bring such suspension to the notice of the Court competent to take cognizance of such offence, and thereupon, such Court shall take possession of the driving licence, endorse the suspension thereon and intimate the fact of such endorsement to the licensing authority by which the licence was granted or last renewed.

(3) Where the person referred to in sub-section (1) is acquitted or discharged, the Court shall cancel the endorsement on such driving licence with regard to the suspension thereof.

(4) If a driving licence in relation to a particular class or description of motor vehicles is suspended under sub-section (1), the person holding such licence shall be debarred from holding or obtaining any licence to drive such particular class or description of motor vehicles so long as the suspension of the driving licence remains in force.

COMMENTS

Suspension of Licence would not Constitute Double Jeopardy – It is contended that the action of suspension of licence would constitute double jeopardy as the petitioner is already facing a criminal prosecution for the various offences alleged against him by the Police and the criminal Court is also empowered to suspend or cancel the petitioner's driving licence under sections 21 and 22 of the Act. The power of suspension is to be exercised in appropriate cases by the Court, upon conviction of a person. Therefore, the power of the licensing authority and that of the Court, operates in different spheres. The suspension of a licence under section 19 is not dependent upon a conviction of the offender. The same can be invoked immediately upon commission of the offence where the licensing authority is satisfied of the existence of the other conditions stipulated by the provision. For the above reasons, the impugned action would not constitute double jeopardy as contended; *Peethambaran T.R.* v. *Additional Licensing Authority*, AIR 2013 Ker 46: 2012 (3) Ker LJ 547: 2012 (3) Ker LT 622.

22. Suspension or cancellation of driving licence on conviction.—(1) Without prejudice to the provisions of sub-section (3) of section 20 where a person, referred to in sub-section (1) of section 21 is convicted of an offence of causing, by such dangerous driving as is referred to in section 184 of any class or description of motor vehicle the death of, or grievous hurt to, one or more persons, the Court by which such person is convicted may cancel, or suspend for such period as it may think fit, the driving licence held by such person in so far as it relates to that class or description of motor vehicle.

(2) Without prejudice to the provisions of sub-section (2) of section 20, if a person, having been previously convicted of an offence punishable under section 185 is again convicted of an offence punishable under that section, the Court, making such subsequent conviction, shall, by order, cancel the driving licence held by such person.

(3) If a driving licence is cancelled or suspended under this section, the court shall take the driving licence in its custody, endorse the cancellation or, as the case may be, suspension, thereon and send the driving licence so endorsed to the authority by which the licence was issued or last renewed and such authority shall, on receipt of the licence, keep the licence in its safe custody, and in the case

of a suspended licence, return the licence to the holder thereof after the expiry of the period of suspension on an application made by him for such return:

Provided that no such licence shall be returned unless the holder thereof has, after the expiry of the period of suspension, undergone and passed, to the satisfaction of the licensing authority by which the licence was issued or last renewed, a fresh test of competence to drive referred to in sub-section (3) of section 9 and produced a medical certificate in the same form and in the same manner as is referred to in sub-section (3) of section 8.

(4) If a licence to drive a particular class or description of motor vehicles is cancelled or suspended under this section, the person holding such a licence shall be debarred from holding, or obtaining, any licence to drive such particular class or description of motor vehicles so long as the cancellation or suspension of the driving licence remains in force.

COMMENTS

Suspension of Licence would not Constitute Double Jeopardy – It is contended that the action of suspension of licence would constitute double jeopardy as the petitioner is already facing a criminal prosecution for the various offences alleged against him by the Police and the criminal Court is also empowered to suspend or cancel the petitioner's driving licence under sections 21 and 22 of the Act. The power of suspension is to be exercised in appropriate cases by the Court, upon conviction of a person. Therefore, the power of the licensing authority and that of the Court, operates in different spheres. The suspension of a licence under section 19 is not dependent upon a conviction of the offender. The same can be invoked immediately upon commission of the offence where the licensing authority is satisfied of the existence of the other conditions stipulated by the provision. For the above reasons, the impugned action would not constitute double jeopardy as contended; *Peethambaran T.R.* v. *Additional Licensing Authority*, AIR 2013 Ker 46: 2012 (3) Ker LJ 547: 2012 (3) Ker LT 622.

23. Effect of disqualification order.—(1) A person in respect of whom any disqualification order is made under section 19 or section 20 shall be debarred to the extent and for the period specified in such order from holding or obtaining a driving licence and the driving licence, if any, held by such person at the date of the order shall cease to be effective to such extent and during such period.

(2) The operation of a disqualification order made under section 20 shall not be suspended or postponed while an appeal is pending against such order or against the conviction as a result of which such order is made, unless the appellate Court so directs.

(3) Any person in respect of whom any disqualification order has been made may at any time after the expiry of six months from the date of the order apply to the Court or other authority by which the order was made, to remove the disqualification; and the Court or authority, as the case may be, may, having regard to all the circumstances, either cancel or vary the disqualification order:

Provided that where the Court or other authority refuses to cancel or vary any disqualification order under this section, a second application thereunder shall not be entertained before the expiry of a period of three months from the date of such refusal.

24. Endorsement.—(1) The Court or authority making an order of disqualification shall endorse or cause to be endorsed upon the driving licence if any, held by the person disqualified, particulars of the order of disqualification and of any conviction of an offence in respect of which an order of disqualification is made; and particulars of any cancellation or variation of an order of disqualification made under sub-section (3) of section 23 shall be similarly so endorsed.

(2) A Court by which any person is convicted of an offence under this Act as may be prescribed by the Central Government, having regard to the objects of this Act, shall, whether or not a disqualification order is made in respect of such conviction, endorse or cause to be endorsed particulars of such conviction on any driving licence held by the person convicted.

(3) Any person accused of an offence prescribed under sub-section (2) shall when attending the Court bring with him his driving licence if it is in his possession.

(4) Where any person is convicted of any offence under this Act and sentenced to imprisonment for a period exceeding three months the Court awarding the sentence shall endorse the fact of such sentence upon the driving licence of the person concerned and the prosecuting authority shall intimate the fact of such endorsement to the authority by which the driving licence was granted or last renewed.

(5) When the driving licence is endorsed or caused to be endorsed by any Court, such Court shall send the particulars of the endorsement to the licensing authority by which the driving licence was granted or last renewed.

(6) Where on an appeal against any conviction or order of a Court, which has been endorsed on a driving licence, the appellate court varies or sets aside the conviction or order, the appellate court shall inform the licensing authority by which the driving licence was granted or last renewed and such authority shall amend or cause to be amended the endorsement.

25. Transfer of endorsement and issue of driving licence free from endorsement.—(1) An endorsement on any driving licence shall be transferred to any new or duplicate driving licence obtained by the holder thereof until the holder becomes entitled under the provisions of this section to have a driving licence issued to him free from endorsement.

(2) Where a driving licence is required to be endorsed and the driving licence is not in the possession of the Court or authority by which the endorsement is to be made, then—

(a) if the person in respect of whom the endorsement is to be made is at the time the holder of a driving licence, he shall produce the driving licence to the Court or authority within five days, or such longer time as the court or authority may fix; or

(b) if, not being then the holder of a driving licence, he subsequently obtains a driving licence, he shall within five days after obtaining the driving licence produce it to the Court or authority,

and if the driving licence is not produced within the time specified, it shall, on the expiration of such time, be of no effect until it is produced for the purpose of endorsement.

(3) A person whose driving licence has been endorsed shall, if during a continuous period of three years after such endorsement no further endorsement has been made against him, be entitled on surrendering his driving licence and on payment of a fee of five rupees, to receive a new driving licence free from all endorsements:

Provided that if the endorsement is only in respect of an offence contravening the speed limits referred to in section 112, such person shall be entitled to receive a new driving licence free from such endorsements on the expiration of one year of the date of the endorsement:

Provided further that in reckoning the said period of three years and one year, respectively, and period during which the said person was disqualified for holding or obtaining a driving licence shall be excluded.

26. Maintenance of State Registers of Driving Licences.—(1) Each State Government shall maintain, in such form as may be prescribed by the Central Government, a register to be known as the State Register of Driving Licences, in respect of driving licences issued and renewed by the licensing authorities of the State Government, containing the following particulars, namely:—

(a) names and addresses of holders of driving licences;

(b) licence numbers;

(c) dates of issue or renewal of licences;

(d) dates of expiry of licences;

(e) classes and types of vehicles authorised to be driven; and

(f) such other particulars as the Central Government may prescribe.

(2) Each State Government shall supply to the Central Government a [1][printed copy or copy in such other form as the Central Government may require], of the State Register of Driving Licences and shall inform the Central Government without delay of all additions to and other amendments in such register made from time to time.

(3) The State Register of Driving Licences shall be maintained in such manner as may be prescribed by the State Government.

27. Power of Central Government to make rules.—The Central Government may make rules—

(a) regarding conditions referred to in sub-section (2) of section 3;

(b) providing for the form in which the application for learner's licence may be made, the information it shall contain and the documents to be submitted with the application referred to in sub-section (2) of section 8;

(c) providing for the form of medical certificate referred to in sub-section (3) of section 8;

(d) providing for the particulars for the test referred to in sub-section (5) of section 8;

(e) providing for the form in which the application for driving licence

1. Subs. by Act 54 of 1994, sec. 10, for "printed copy" (w.e.f. 14-11-1994).

may be made, the information it shall contain and the documents to be submitted with the application referred to in sub-section (2) of section 9;

(f) providing for the particulars regarding test of competence to drive, referred to in sub-section (3) of section 9;

(g) specifying the minimum educational qualifications of persons to whom licences to drive transport vehicles may be issued under this Act and the time within which such qualifications are to be acquired by such persons;

(h) providing for the form and contents of the licences referred to in sub-section (1) of section 10;

(i) providing for the form and contents of the application referred to in sub-section (1) of section 11 and documents to be submitted with the application and the fee to be charged;

(j) providing for the conditions subject to which section 9 shall apply to an application made under section 11;

(k) providing for the form and contents of the application referred to in sub-section (1) of section 15 and the documents to accompany such application under sub-section (2) of section 15;

(l) providing for the authority to grant licences under sub-section (1) of section 18;

(m) specifying the fees payable under sub-section (2) of section 8, sub-section (2) of section 9 and sub-sections (3) and (4) of section 15 for the grant of learner's licences, and for the grant and renewal of driving licences and licences for the purpose of regulating the schools or establishments for imparting instructions in driving motor vehicles;

(n) specifying the acts for the purposes of clause (f) of sub-section (1) of section 19;

(o) specifying the offences under this Act for the purposes of sub-section (2) of section 24;

(p) to provide for all or any of the matters referred to in sub-section (1) of section 26;

(q) any other matter which is, or has to be, prescribed by the Central Government.

SYNOPSIS

1. Device as an In-built Mechanism to Reduce Pollution
2. Driving Test – Restriction of Sub-centres not Correct
3. Driving Training School Licence – Cancellation of
4. Central Government has No Power Providing Exception from Wearing of Protective Headgear
5. Grant of Badge to Drive Transport Vehicle – Eligibility

COMMENTS

1. Device as an In-built Mechanism to Reduce Pollution – The heavy vehicles operating in the city being the buses, trucks and defence vehicle constitute the main contributing factor to pollution. It is necessary, therefore, that more of attention is directed against these vehicles. Particulars of the prosecution said to have been undertaken should be made available to the Court so that the Court would be in a position to appreciate the steps taken and to what extent this measure is effective. Therefore, direction is given to the Delhi Administration to place before the Court a complete list of the prosecution launched against the vehicles for causing pollution by infringement of the various requirements of the law with particular reference to the vehicles, nature of the vehicles dates of prosecution, the nature of offences for which prosecutions have been launched and the result, if any, of such prosecutions. Similarly, particulars of the vehicles registration of which is said to have been suspended must be provided with specific mention of the nature of the vehicle and a brief indication as to why suspension has been directed. Follow up action after suspension must also be indicated, if anything has been done. In supplying the particulars of the two categories, namely, prosecutions and suspension, the classification as to whether the vehicles belong to the Delhi Administration or the Central Government or the public sector undertakings and/ or the public transport system should be specified. Rules 115(6) and 126 and 127 of the Rules should be made operative. The National Environment Engineering Research Institute, Nagpur has brought out a device which would reduce the pollution content and the Ministry of Environment is aware of this fact. Thus the Environment Ministry should carry out appropriate experiments with the aid of the same device to find out its effectiveness within two months from today and in case it is found to be effective steps should be taken to ensure that every vehicle to be manufactured to have that device as an in-built mechanism to reduce pollution. Whether vehicles which have already been operating can also adopt the said device should also be examined and in case that also is found feasible, the Environment Ministry should place the material for consideration of the Court; *M.C. Mehta* v. *Union of India,* AIR 1991 SC 1132: 1992 (1) BLJ 261: (1991) 2 SCC 137.

2. Driving Test – Restriction of Sub-centres not Correct – The main contention of the petitioners was that without any basis the training schools are being ignored and they have not been treated properly. The Act itself gives power to an applicant to file an application for licence before the Regional Transport Officer, who is within the jurisdiction of the driving school. The grievance of the petitioner is that in spite of the fact that both the Act and the Central Rules allows to give both permanent and temporary addresses, the circulars in question the address of a driving school will not be treated as a temporary address. In fact, in the Circulars issued by the Transport Commissioner it is stated that candidate should be advised to furnish his own temporary address in column 4 of the application. The address of the driving school will not be accepted as temporary address. There was no basis for such restriction. For applying for licence, it is necessary to give a certificate that the applicant has undergone the training in the school and to prevent the applicant from using the school's address as temporary address is without any basis. The Act itself gives the applicant to apply for licence within the jurisdiction of the driving school. It may be that a person may not have any temporary address in a city. He may be permanently employed in a place outside the city. But when he comes to city for learning driving, he cannot give his permanent address as temporary address. The school imparts training and education. It will be the temporary home of the applicant. If the owners of the schools commit any manipulations, it is for the authorities to take action. But, that should not prevent the student who study in the school to give the address of the school as temporary address. Therefore, the Circulars issued by the Transport Commissioner state that the school's address cannot be taken as a temporary address, is struck down. If an application contains the temporary address as that of the school, that application should not be rejected. Similarly all the licensing authorities should see that testing centres are opened in sub-regions as expeditiously as possible; *All Kerala M.D.S. Workers Welfare Assocn.* v. *State of Kerala,* AIR 1999 Ker 337: 1999 (1) Ker LJ 782: 1999 (2) Ker LT 217.

3. Driving Training School Licence – Cancellation of – After issuing a show cause notice and personal hearing, the District Transport Officer has recorded a categorical finding that the petitioner is involved in issuance of fake driving licence to four persons. It has further been found that such an act on the part of the petitioner is against the terms and conditions on the basis of which the petitioner was Issued driving school licence. One of the conditions in the licence was that the petitioner would comply with all the conditions contemplated by rule 27 of the Central Motor Vehicles Rules, 1989. According to sub-rule (k) of rule 27, petitioner was not to act in a manner calculated which may mislead any person making an application for procuring a licence for such person other than in accordance with these rules or to connive with any person in acts of commission or omission with a view to circumvent the provision of chapter and the rules. A copy of the licence issued to the petitioner's school is taken on record. Rule 27(k) makes it amply clear that the petitioner has connived with other person in the issuance of driving licence which was prohibited by the terms and conditions laid down when the licence for establishment of driving school was issued to the petitioner. Thus cancellation of the Driving Training School licence is proper; *Bahadur Singh Bhogal* v. *State of Punjab*, AIR 2008 P&H 157.

4. Central Government has No Power Providing Exception from Wearing of Protective Headgear – The contention of the counsel that under section 27(q), the Central Government is competent to make rules providing for exception to the provisions of section 129 is wrong and unacceptable. Clauses (a) to (p) of section 27 confer power on the Central Government to make rules regarding the specific matters mentioned therein. The matter dealt with in section 129 is not covered by clauses (a) to (p) of section 27. Even under clause (q) Central Government can exercise the power to make rules only regarding a "matter which is, or has to be, prescribed by the Central Government." Any exception to the provisions of section 129 is not a matter which is, or has to be, prescribed by the Central Government. It is a matter which is, or has to be, prescribed by the State Government. In fact, the State Government has already made the rules regarding that matter by issuing the U.P. Motor Vehicles Rules, 1998. Hence the Motor Vehicles (Protective Headgears) Rules, 1980 cannot be deemed to have been issued under the provisions of the Motor Vehicles Act, 1988 and the said Rules are no more in force. Merely because there is a provision under section 12 of the Motor Vehicles Act, 1988 empowering the State Government to make rules providing for exception to the provision of section 129, it does not mean that rule 3 of the Motor Vehicles (Protective Headgears) Rules, 1980 issued under section 85A of the Motor Vehicles Act, 1939 providing for exception to the provisions of the said section 85A, can be deemed to be valid and operative even now. Any provision contained in the Motor Vehicles (Protective Headgears) Rules, 1980, which is inconsistent with the provisions contained in section 129 of the Motor Vehicles Act, 1988 cannot be operative or applicable after the commencement of Motor Vehicles Act, 1988. No person can be given exemption from the application of section 129 of the Motor Vehicles Act, 1988 otherwise than by the Rules made by the State Government under the second proviso to section 129. In fact the U.P. Motor Vehicles Rules, 1998 have been issued by the Government of U.P. in exercise of the powers conferred by the Motor Vehicles, Act, 1988; *Uttaranchal Sikh Federation* v. *State of Uttaranchal*, AIR 2006 Uttaranchal 67.

5. Grant of Badge to Drive Transport Vehicle – Eligibility – The minimum educational qualification required for obtaining driving licence to drive transport vehicle is pass of 8th standard but the Kerala Motor Vehicle Rules has authorized a person who has studied upto 4th standard to drive a transport vehicle. The power to make rules specifying the minimum educational qualifications of persons to whom licences to drive transport vehicles may be issued under the Act is vested in the Central Government. The rule making power of the State Government is contained in section 28 of the Act. It is in exercise of the power under section 27(g) of the Act that rule 8 of the Central

Motor Vehicles Rules has been enacted. The said Rule does not venture to prescribe any qualifications for the grant of permission to drive transport vehicles. However, the proviso enacts a prohibition that the licencing authority concerned shall not authorize a person to drive a transport vehicle unless he has passed standard IV as his minimum educational qualification. The said provision can have no application after the introduction of the present rule 8 of the Central Rules. At any rate, it cannot supersede or set at naught, the mandate of rule 8 of the Central Rules. The provision ought to have been suitably amended so as to conform to the Central Rules. The petitioner is not entitled to claim any benefit on the basis of the said proviso, which has become redundant, with the coming into force of rule 8 of Central Rules; *Ousephkutty V.T.* v. *Regional Transport Officer, Alappuzha*, AIR 2012 Ker 172: 2012 (3) Ker LJ 6: 2012 (3) Ker LT 29.

28. Power of State Government to make rules.—(1) A State Government may make rules for the purpose of carrying into effect the provisions of this Chapter other than the matters specified in section 27.

(2) Without prejudice to the generality of the foregoing power, such rules may provide for—

(a) the appointment, jurisdiction, control and functions of licensing authorities and other prescribed authorities;

(b) the conduct and hearing of appeals that may be preferred under this Chapter, the fees to be paid in respect of such appeals and the refund of such fees:

Provided that no fee so fixed shall exceed twenty-five rupees;

(c) the issue of duplicate licences to replace licences lost, destroyed or mutilated, the replacement of photographs which have become obsolete and the fees to be charged therefor;

(d) the badges and uniform to be worn by drivers of transport vehicles and the fees to be paid in respect of badges;

(e) the fee payable for the issue of a medical certificate under sub-section (3) of section 8;

(f) the exemption of prescribed persons, or prescribed classes of persons, from payment of all or any portion of the fees payable under this Chapter;

(g) the communication of particulars of licences granted by one licensing authority to other licensing authorities;

(h) the duties, functions and conduct of such persons to whom licences to drive transport vehicles are issued;

(i) the exemption of drivers of road-rollers from all or any of the provisions of this Chapter or of the rules made thereunder;

(j) the manner in which the State Register of Driving Licences shall be maintained under section 26;

(k) any other matter which is to be, or may be, prescribed.

SYNOPSIS

1. Prohibition of Exhibition of Advertisements on Transport Vehicles
2. Licensing Authorities can make Regulations Subject to Instructions of Commissioner
3. Rules for Badges and Uniform taken to be Regulatory Measures for Administrative Convenience

COMMENTS

1. Prohibition of Exhibition of Advertisements on Transport Vehicles – The question that arises for consideration is whether the impugned action of the respondent in prohibiting the exhibition of advertisements and writings on the transport vehicles is illegal being arbitrary or without jurisdiction? The rule 127(1) of the Karnataka Motor Vehicles Rules (KMV), 1989 makes it clear that there is a prohibition for a transport vehicle to exhibit any advertising device, figure or writing. However, the authorities are empowered to grant permission either by issuing general or special orders. In fact, pursuant to the said power conferred on the authority, the authority permitted the exhibition of such advertisements on the transport vehicles with prior permission after paying the prescribed fees. But by the impugned resolution the authority has resolved that no such permission will be given in the interest of road safety and in public interest. The authorities have kept in mind the fact that such advertisements carried on the transport vehicles tend to divert or distract the attention of the drivers of the other vehicles which may endanger the safety on the road. It cannot be said that this reason assigned for taking such an action is unreasonable or arbitrary. In the present circumstances, road safety has become a prime concern of the authorities. The initiation of such action, that too, pursuant to the provisions contained under rule 127 of the KMV Rules cannot be characterized as arbitrary or unreasonable. Petitioner cannot claim any vested right to exhibit such advertisements on the transport vehicles. Therefore, the contention that the action is without jurisdiction and is arbitrary and unreasonable cannot be accepted. The power and the jurisdiction to take such action is traceable to rule 127(1) of KMV Rules. In fact, there is no right in the owners of the transport vehicle to exhibit such advertisements as there is a prohibition under rule 127(1) of the KMV Rules. It is only by the permission of the authorities that any such exhibition can be allowed. When the authorities decided that such permission cannot be given in the interest of the road safety of the public, the same cannot be found fault with; *T. Rajagopal* v. *Regional Transport Authority, Bangalore,* AIR 2007 Kant 103: 2007 AIHC 1059: 2007 (2) Kant LJ 137.

2. Licensing Authorities can make Regulations Subject to Instructions of Commissioner – Under section 28 of the Act, the State Government is empowered to make necessary rules for the appointment, jurisdiction, control and functions of the licensing authorities and other prescribed authorities. Similarly under rule 405 of the Kerala Rules, all the officers including the Regional Transport Officers and the Joint Regional Transport Officers are to be regarded as officers of the Motor Vehicles Department and shall exercise powers and perform duties as per the Act and the Rules. It is further stated that they shall carry out the instructions and orders issued by the Transport Commissioner from time to time. Thus, with regard to the powers of the licensing authorities, the Commissioner is entitled to issue orders in the form of Circulars or notifications in order to guide the licensing authorities. It cannot be said that only the licensing authority can make regulations. The licensing authorities can make regulations subject to the instructions of the Commissioner. Hence, the Circulars issued by the Commissioner are valid in law; *All Kerala M.D.S. Workers Welfare Assocn.* v. *State of Kerala,* AIR 1999 Ker 337: 1999 (1) Ker LJ 782: 1999 (2) Ker LT 217.

3. Rules for Badges and Uniform taken to be Regulatory Measures for Administrative Convenience – Under section 28 of the Act the State Governments are authorised to make rules for the purpose of carrying into effect the provisions of Chapter 2 of the Act other than the matters specified in section 27 of the Act. In other words, the rule making power of the State is expressly made subject to the rule making power of the Central Government. Section 28(2)(d) of the Act envisages the rule making power of the State in relation to "badges and uniform" to be worn by the driver of a transport vehicle and fees to be paid in respect of the badges. A particular State Government may frame rules prescribing the "badges and uniform" for a driver of a transport vehicle which may not be contemplated in the rule of another State. Since under section 13 of the Act, a licence issued in any State is valid throughout India, it may so happen that the person authorised to drive a transport vehicle in a particular State may not be required to wear badges and uniforms whereas such provisions may be there in another State. A combined reading of the provisions contained in Chapter 2, particularly, the provisions contained in sections 3, 8, 9, 10, 13 and 27 of the Act, leaves no room for doubt that the licence is to be issued in accordance with rules prescribed by the Central Government. Though rule 71 of the Orissa Motor Vehicle Rules, 1993, framed under section 28 of the Act, contemplates that driver of a public service vehicle should wear a badge and in fact a particular dress, there is nothing in the Act or Rules framed by the Central Government that issuance of a badge to a driver is a condition precedent authorising such driver to drive a transport vehicle. The provisions in the rules prescribing for badges and uniform must be taken to be regulatory measures for identity and administrative convenience and as a *sine qua non* for a valid driving licence authorising a person to drive a transport vehicle; *National Insurance Co. Ltd.* v. *Raisa Bibi,* AIR 1999 Ori 78: 2000 (1) ACJ 600: 1999 (2) TAC 298.

CHAPTER III

LICENSING OF CONDUCTORS OF STAGE CARRIAGES

29. Necessity for conductor's licence.—(1) No person shall act as a conductor of a stage carriage unless he holds an effective conductor's licence issued to him authorising him to act as such conductor; and no person shall employ or permit any person who is not so licensed to act as a conductor of a stage carriage.

(2) A State Government may prescribe the conditions subject to which sub-section (1) shall not apply to a driver of a stage carriage performing the functions of a conductor or to a person employed to act as a conductor for a period not exceeding one month.

30. Grant of conductor's licence.—(1) Any person who possesses such minimum educational qualification as may be prescribed by the State Government and is not disqualified under sub-section (1) of section 31 and who is not for the time being disqualified for holding or obtaining a conductor's licence may apply to the licensing authority having jurisdiction in the area in which he ordinarily resides or carries on business for the issue to him of a conductor's licence.

(2) Every application under sub-section (1) shall be in such form and shall contain such information as may be prescribed.

(3) Every application for a conductor's licence shall be accompanied by a medical certificate in such form as may be prescribed, signed by a registered medical practitioner and shall also be accompanied by two clear copies of a recent photograph of the applicant.

(4) A conductor's licence issued under this Chapter shall be in such form and contain such particulars as may be prescribed and shall be effective throughout the State in which it is issued.

(5) The fee for a conductor's licence and for each renewal thereof shall be one-half of that for a driving licence.

COMMENTS

Authorities have No Power to Accept Medical Certificates Issued by Registered Medical Practitioners – A notification has been issued in exercise of the powers conferred by sections 8(3) and 30(3) of the Motor Vehicles Act, 1988 read with rules 43 and 77 of the Andhra Pradesh Motor Vehicles Rules, 1989 declaring that the Registered Medical

Practitioners possessing the Degree of MBBS in Allopathy or any equivalent qualification of any University in India established or incorporated by or under Central Act or a State Act or an institution recognised by the University Grants Commission shall be the authorities competent to issue a Medical Certificate for the purpose of obtaining a Learner's Licence and Conductor's Licence. Further the Medical Certificates issued by the Registered Medical Practitioners possessing the Degree qualification of MBBS in Allopathy or equalivalent qualification alone shall be accepted for the purpose of giving learner's Licence, Conductor's Licence, etc., and the declaration as to the physical fitness to be given by the applicant in Form (a) to (g) of Part I and (a) to (c) under Part II of Form I shall be certified by the Registered Medical Practitioners of Allopathy with a minimum qualification of MBBS alone. Thus the Transport Authorities are not empowered to accept the medical Certificates issued by the Registered Medical Practitioners without having the minimum qualification of MBBS Degree in Allopathy or equalivalent degree granted by any University established as per the notification in GO. Ms. No. 25, Transport, Roads and Buildings (Tr. II) Department, dated 6-2-1992; *B.S.S. Sanadha Raj* v. *Commr. of Transport, Hyderabad,* AIR 2001 AP 162: 2001 (2) Andh LD 85: 2001 (1) Andh LT 705.

31. Disqualifications for the grant of conductor's licence.—(1) No person under the age of eighteen years shall hold, or be granted, a conductor's licence.

(2) The licensing authority may refuse to issue a conductor's licence—

(a) if the applicant does not possess the minimum educational qualification;

(b) if the medical certificate produced by the applicant discloses that he is physically unfit to act as a conductor; and

(c) if any previous conductor's licence held by the applicant was revoked.

32. Revocation of a conductor's licence on grounds of disease or disability.—A conductor's licence may at any time be revoked by any licensing authority if that authority has reasonable grounds to believe that the holder of the licence is suffering from any disease or disability which is likely to render him permanently unfit to hold such a licence and where the authority revoking a conductor's licence is not the authority which issued the same, it shall intimate the fact of such revocation to the authority which issued that licence:

Provided that before revoking any licence, the licensing authority shall give the person holding such licence a reasonable opportunity of being heard.

33. Orders refusing, etc., conductor's licences and appeals therefrom.—(1) Where a licensing authority refuses to issue or renew, or revokes any conductor's licence, it shall do so by an order communicated to the applicant or the holder, as the case may be, giving the reasons in writing for such refusal or revocation.

(2) Any person aggrieved by an order made under sub-section (1) may, within thirty days of the service on him of the order, appeal to the prescribed authority which shall decide the appeal after giving such person and the authority which made the order an opportunity of being heard and the decision of the appellate authority shall be binding on the authority which made the order.

34. Power of licensing authority to disqualify.—(1) If any licensing authority is of opinion that it is necessary to disqualify the holder of a conductor's licence for holding or obtaining such a licence on account of his previous conduct as a conductor, it may, for reasons to be recorded, make an order disqualifying that person for a specified period, not exceeding one year, for holding or obtaining a conductor's licence:

Provided that before disqualifying the holder of a licence, the licensing authority shall give the person holding such licence a reasonable opportunity of being heard.

(2) Upon the issue of any such order, the holder of the conductor's licence shall forthwith surrender the licence to the authority making the order, if the licence has not already been surrendered, and the authority shall keep the licence until the disqualification has expired or has been removed.

(3) Where the authority disqualifying the holder of a conductor's licence under this section is not the authority which issued the licence, it shall intimate the fact of such disqualification to the authority which issued the same.

(4) Any person aggrieved by an order made under sub-section (1) may, within thirty days of the service on him of the order, appeal to the prescribed authority which shall decide the appeal after giving such person and the authority which made the order an opportunity of being heard and the decision of the appellate authority shall be binding on the authority which made the order.

35. Power of Court to disqualify.—(1) Where any person holding a conductor's licence is convicted of an offence under this Act, the court by which such person is convicted may, in addition to imposing any other punishment authorised by law, declare the person so convicted to be disqualified for such period as the Court may specify for holding a conductor's licence.

(2) The Court to which an appeal lies from any conviction of an offence under this Act may set aside or vary any order of disqualification made by the court below, and the court to which appeals ordinarily lie from such Court, may set aside or vary any order of disqualification made by that Court, notwithstanding that no appeal lies against the conviction in connection with which such order was made.

36. Certain provisions of Chapter II to apply to conductor's licence.—The provisions of sub-section (2) of section 6, sections 14, 15 and 23, sub-section (1) of section 24 and section 25 shall, so far as may be, apply in relation to a conductor's licence, as they apply in relation to a driving licence.

37. Savings.—If any licence to act as a conductor of a stage carriage (by whatever name called) has been issued in any State and is effective immediately before the commencement of this Act, it shall continue to be effective, notwithstanding such commencement, for the period for which it would have been effective, if this Act had not been passed, and every such licence shall be deemed to be a licence issued under this Chapter as if this Chapter has been in force on the date on which that licence was granted.

38. Power of State Government to make rules.—(1) A State Government may make rules for the purpose of carrying into effect the provisions of this Chapter.

(2) Without prejudice to the generality of the foregoing power, such rules may provide for—

(a) the appointment, jurisdiction, control and functions of licensing authorities and other prescribed authorities under this Chapter;

(b) the conditions subject to which drivers of stage carriages performing the functions of a conductor and persons temporarily employed to act as conductors may be exempted from the provisions of sub-section (1) of section 29;

(c) the minimum educational qualifications of conductors; their duties and functions and the conduct of persons to whom conductor's licences are issued;

(d) the form of application for conductor's licences or for renewal of such licences and the particulars it may contain;

(e) the form in which conductor's licences may be issued or renewed and the particulars it may contain;

(f) the issue of duplicate licences to replace licences lost, destroyed or mutilated, the replacement of photographs which have become obsolete and the fees to be charged therefor;

(g) the conduct and hearing of appeals that may be preferred under this Chapter, the fees to be paid in respect of such appeals and the refund of such fees:

Provided that no fee so fixed shall exceed twenty-five rupees;

(h) the badges and uniform to be worn by conductors of stage carriages and the fees to be paid in respect of such badges;

(i) the grant of the certificates referred to in sub-section (3) of section 30 by registered medical practitioners and the form of such certificates;

(j) the conditions subject to which, and the extent to which, a conductor's licence issued in another State shall be effective in the State;

(k) the communication of particulars of conductor's licences from one authority to other authorities; and

(l) any other matter which is to be, or may be, prescribed.

CHAPTER IV

REGISTRATION OF MOTOR VEHICLES

39. Necessity for registration.—No person shall drive any motor vehicle and no owner of a motor vehicle shall cause or permit the vehicle to be driven in any public place or in any other place unless the vehicle is registered in accordance with this Chapter and the certificate of registration of the vehicle has not been suspended or cancelled and the vehicle carries a registration mark displayed in the prescribed manner:

Provided that nothing in this section shall apply to a motor vehicle in possession of a dealer subject to such conditions as may be prescribed by the Central Government.

SYNOPSIS

1. Prohibits Anybody to Drive Motor Vehicles unless Vehicle is Registered
2. Tax has Reasonable Nexus with Vehicles Does not Violate Article 302 or Article 304
3. Allotment of Fancy Registration Mark – Validity
4. Fresh Auction-cum-Tender

COMMENTS

1. Prohibits Anybody to Drive Motor Vehicles unless Vehicle is Registered – Section 39 of the Motor Vehicles Act deals with necessity of registration and prohibits anybody to drive motor vehicles unless the vehicle is registered. Section 56 of the Act requires certificate of fitness of transport vehicles. Once these documents are surrendered, it cannot be presumed that the vehicle is used or kept for use and, therefore, the advance tax is leviable. Therefore, it cannot be said that it is competent for the State to levy vehicle tax if the vehicles are kept for use within State and liability to pay tax is attracted on omnibuses getting registration within State as it is kept for use by the owner. *A.G.P.V.S. Mahamandal* v. *State of Gujarat*, AIR 2002 Guj 121: 2002 (1) Guj LH 21: 2002 (1) Guj LR 58.

2. Tax has Reasonable Nexus with Vehicles Does not Violate Article 302 or Article 304 – The submission that section 6 of the impugned Taxation Act is repugnant and is in conflict with section 39 of the Central Act, 1988 and some of the rules framed thereunder has been rejected. So far as the challenge to section 6 of the impugned Taxation Act on the ground of violation of Articles 302 and 304 of the Constitution of India is concerned, since the tax has a reasonable nexus with the vehicles being suitable for use upon roads, it is compensatory in nature as the tax is levied upon vehicles which are suitable for use on roads. It does not violate either Article 302 or Article 304 of the Constitution of India. Moreover, it is not even agreed before us that the levy under the impugned Taxation Act impedes the free flow of inter State trade and commerce. Such being the fact situation, even if the levy be held not to be compensatory in nature, it will not affect the validity of the law which clearly falls within the legislative jurisdiction of the State legislature. No authority has been cited before us for the proposition that in the exercise of its legislative power under Entry 57 of List II, the State can only levy a tax which is compensatory in nature, even if there is no challenge to the levy on the ground of breach of Article 301 of the Constitution of India; *Tata Engineering and Locomotive Company Ltd.* v. *State of Bihar*, AIR 1999 Pat 62: 1998 (3) Pat LJR 457.

3. Allotment of Fancy Registration Mark – Validity – The procedure for allotment of the fancy registration mark is not only governed by rule 95 of the Rules but also by the Circular issued by the Transport Commissionerate. The clause of the said Circular states that the tender process and the auction process should proceed parallely and the applicant who had quoted in the tender or bid in the auction for the highest amount is to be adjudged successful. The application put in by the petitioner- allottee was accompanied by a sealed cover containing an offer letter quoting an amount of Rs.10,600 accompanied by a demand draft for half of the amount quoted. The respondent-objector did not submit any sealed cover for participating in the tender and was rest contended with participating in the auction that followed. The petitioner-allottee bid for an amount of Rs.1000 whereas the respondent-objector bid for an amount of Rs.2000 in the auction conducted by the Regional Transport Officer and none bid for a higher amount. The tender register and the auction register shows no irregularity or impropriety in the conduct of tender and auction. Thus the allotment in favour of highest bidder-allottee is not invalid; *Thambi T.G.* v. *State of Kerala*, AIR 2013 Ker 129: 2013 (1) Ker LJ 779: 2013 (1) Ker LT 730.

4. Fresh Auction-cum-Tender – The decision making process can be annulled only if the same is found to be vitiated by *mala fides*, arbitrariness or total unreasonableness. Attempts by unsuccessful tenderers with imaginary grievances, wounded pride and business rivalry to make mountains out of molehills and persuade courts to interfere by judicial review should be resisted. The Regional Transport Officer has to be directed to proceed further for allotment of the fancy registration mark to the petitioner; *Thambi T.G.* v. *State of Kerala*, AIR 2013 Ker 129: 2013 (1) Ker LJ 779: 2013 (1) Ker LT 730.

40. Registration, where to be made.—Subject to the provisions of section 42, section 43 and section 60, every owner of a motor vehicle shall cause the vehicle to be registered by a registering authority in whose jurisdiction he has the residence or place of business where the vehicle is normally kept.

SYNOPSIS

1. Imposition of Condition Regarding Registration
2. Payment of Tax in Advance before Regular Registration does not Affect Liability for Tax
3. Levy of Tax can only be During Period of Permanent Registration

COMMENTS

1. Imposition of Condition Regarding Registration – Provisions in section 40 of the Act, 1988 have not created any right of the owner of a motor vehicle; they have rather created an obligation to be discharged by him, if he wants to use the motor vehicle. They require him to register it. They only give him a choice to register it either with the registering authority in whose jurisdiction he is a resident, or with the registering authority in whose jurisdiction he has place of business where the vehicle is normally kept. Hence it cannot be said that by imposing the condition regarding registration the authority has acted illegally or arbitrarily or unfairly or unreasonably; *Jugal Mondal* v. *State of West Bengal,* AIR 2006 Cal 189: 2006 AIHC 2732: 2006 (4) ACC 663.

2. Payment of Tax in Advance before Regular Registration does not Affect Liability for Tax – Tax endorsement under Taxation Act is made only after regular registration which is done only on producing certificate of insurance for the vehicle, proof of residence, identity etc., of the purchaser as required under the Act and the Rules. The 2nd proviso to section 3(1) of Taxation Act, which provides for levy of tax on new vehicles, clearly states that levy of tax on new vehicles is to be made at the time of "first registration" of the vehicle. Even though it is stated that for new vehicles one-time tax at the rate as specified is payable from the date of purchase of the vehicle, the rate of tax applicable is as on the date of first registration of the vehicle. Thus, there is no provision in the Taxation Act to levy tax during the period a new vehicle is granted temporary registration; *Hilal B.* v. *State of Kerala,* AIR 2013 Ker 19: 2012 (3) Ker LJ 503: 2012 (3) Ker LT 438.

3. Levy of Tax can only be During Period of Permanent Registration – There is no provision in the Taxation Act to levy tax during the period a new vehicle is granted temporary registration. So much so, the first registration cannot be temporary registration granted under section 43 of the Act of 1988 read with rule 94 of the Kerala Motor Vehicles Rules, but can only be the permanent registration granted under section 40 of Act. Where date of increase of tax was known to purchasers and therefore they remitted tax in advance at time of granting temporary registration, which they were not required to pay at that time, payment of tax in advance before regular registration is granted does not affect liability for tax which has to be considered with reference to charging provision of Taxation Act and rate of tax applicable is rate in force as on date of granting regular registration; *Hilal B.* v. *State of Kerala,* AIR 2013 Ker 19: 2012 (3) Ker LJ 503: 2012 (3) Ker LT 438.

41. Registration, how to be made.—(1) An application by or on behalf of the owner of a motor vehicle for registration shall be in such form and shall be accompanied by such documents, particulars and information and shall be made within such period as may be prescribed by the Central Government:

Provided that where a motor vehicle is jointly owned by more persons than one, the application shall be made by one of them on behalf of all the owners and such applicant shall be deemed to be the owner of the motor vehicle for the purposes of this Act.

(2) An application referred to in sub-section (1) shall be accompanied by such fee as may be prescribed by the Central Government.

(3) The registering authority shall issue to the owner of a motor vehicle registered by it a certificate of registration in such form and containing such particulars and information and in such manner as may be prescribed by the Central Government.

(4) In addition to the other particulars required to be included in the certificate of registration, it shall also specify the type of the motor vehicle, being a type as the Central Government may, having regard to the design construction and use of the motor vehicle, by notification in the Official Gazette, specify.

(5) The registering authority shall enter the particulars of the certificate referred to in sub-section (3) in a register to be maintained in such form and manner as may be prescribed by the Central Government.

(6) The registering authority shall assign to the vehicle, for display thereon, a distinguishing mark (in this Act referred to as the registration mark) consisting of one of the groups of such of those letters and followed by such letters and figures as are allotted to the State by the Central Government from time to time by notification in the Official Gazette, and displayed and shown on the motor vehicle in such form and in such manner as may be prescribed by the Central Government.

(7) A certificate of registration issued under sub-section (3), whether before or after the commencement of this Act, in respect of a motor vehicle, other than a transport vehicle, shall, subject to the provisions contained in this Act, be valid only for a period of fifteen years from the date of issue of such certificate and shall be renewable.

(8) An application by or on behalf of the owner of a motor vehicle, other than a transport vehicle, for the renewal of a certificate of registration shall be made within such period and in such form, containing such particulars and information as may be prescribed by the Central Government.

(9) An application referred to in sub-section (8) shall be accompanied by such fee as may be prescribed by the Central Government.

(10) Subject to the provisions of section 56, the registering authority may, on receipt of an application under sub-section (8), renew the certificate of registration for a period of five years and intimate the fact to the original registering authority, if it is not the original registering authority.

(11) If the owner fails to make an application under sub-section (1), or, as the ease may be, under sub-section (8) within the period prescribed, the registering authority may, having regard to the circumstances of the case, require the owner to pay, in lieu of any action that may be taken against him under section 177, such amount not exceeding one hundred rupees as may be prescribed under sub-section (13):

Provided that action under section 177 shall be taken against the owner where the owner fails to pay the said amount.

(12) Where the owner has paid the amount under sub-section (11), no action shall be taken against him under section 177.

(13) For the purposes of sub-section (11), the State Government may prescribe different amounts having regard to the period of delay on the part of the owner in making an application under sub-section (1) or sub-section (8).

(14) An application for the issue of a duplicate certificate of registration shall be made to the [1][last registering authority] in such form, containing such particulars and information along with such fee as may be prescribed by the Central Government.

STATE AMENDMENT

Rajasthan.—In section 41,—

(a) in sub-sections (7) and (8), the expression, "other than a transport vehicle," shall be omitted;

(b) after sub-section (7) so amended, insert the following proviso, namely:—

"Provided that in the case of transport vehicles, State Government may require the transport vehicles to be re-registered in the manner prescribed, subject to the age limit, if any, prescribed under section 59 of the Act."; and

(c) in sub-section (10), after the words "for a period of five years" and before the words "and intimate", insert the expression "on payment of all taxes, penalties and interest, if any, levied by the State Government".

[Rajasthan Act 1 of 2002, sec. 2 (w.e.f. 13-3-2002).]

NOTIFICATION

In exercise of the powers conferred by sub-section (4) of section 41 of the Act the Central Government has specified the type of motor vehicles as mentioned in columns 1 and 2 of the Table below:—Vide S.O. 1248(E), dated 5th November, 2004.

TABLE

Transport Vehicle	Non-Transport Vehicle
(i) Motor cycle with side car for carrying goods	(i) Motor cycle with or without side car for personal use
(ii) Motor cycle with trailer to carry goods	(ii) Mopeds and motorized cycle (Engine capacity exceeding 25 cc)
(iii) Motor cycle used for hire to carry one passenger on pillion and motorized cycle rickshaw for goods or passengers on hire	(iii) Invalid carriage
(iv) Luxury Cab	(iv) Three wheeled vehicles for personal use.
(v) Three wheeled vehicles for transport of passenger/goods	(v) Motor car
(vi) Goods carrier trucks or tankers or mail carriers (N_1—N_3 category)	(vi) Fork lift
(vii) Power tiller and Tractors using public roads	(vii) Vehicles or trailers fitted with equipments like rig, generator, compressor

1. Subs. by Act 54 of 1994, sec. 11, for "original registering authority" (w.e.f. 14-11-1994).

Transport Vehicle	Non-Transport Vehicle
(viii) Mobile clinic or X-Ray van or library vans	(viii) Crane mounted vehicle
(ix) Mobile Workshops	(ix) Agricultural Tractor and Power Tiller
(x) Mobile canteens	(x) Private service vehicle, registered in the name of an individual and if declared to be used by him solely for personal
(xi) Private Service Vehicle	(xi) Camper van or trailer for private use
(xii) Public Service Vehicle such as maxi cab, motor cab, stage carriages and contract carriages including tourist vehicles	(xii) Tow trucks, Breakdown Van and Recovery Vehicles
(xiii) Educational Institution buses	(xiii) Tower Wagons and tree trimming vehicles owned by Central, State and local authorities
(xiv) Ambulances#	(xiv) Construction Eqı ρment Vehicles as defined in rule 2(ca)*
(xv) Animal ambulances##	
(xvi) Camper† vans or trailers	
(xvii) Cash vans	
(xviii) Fire tenders, snorked ladders, auxiliary trailers and fire fighting vehicles	
(xix) Articulated vehicles	
(xx) Hearses	
(xxi) Omnibus††	

\# (a) "Ambulance" means vehicle specially designed constructed or modified and equipped and intended to be used for emergency transportation of persons who are sick, injured, wounded or otherwise incapacitated.

\## (b) "Animal ambulance" means a motor vehicle intended to be used for the emergency transportation of sick, injured, wounded or otherwise incapacitated animals.

† (c) "Camper van" means a special purpose M1 category vehicle constructed to include living accommodation which contains at least the following equipment:—

— Seats and table
— Sleeping accommodation which may be converted from the seats
— Cooking facilities, and

— Storage facilities.

This equipment shall be rigidly fixed to the living compartment; however, the table may be designed to be easily removable.

††(d) The "Omnibus" has been kept in the category of transport vehicle with a view to bringing it under the purview of fitness regime as it is exhaustively used on road. However, the taxes to be levied on such vehicle would fall within the jurisdiction of State Governments.

*(e) Under rule 2(ca), use of public road by Construction Equipment Vehicles is incidental to the main off-road function. However, when the public road is being used regularly for carrying on commercial activities, then Construction Equipment Vehicles such as dumpers and excavators being used for such activities, shall be deemed as transport vehicles.

NOTIFICATION

In exercise of the powers conferred by sub-section (6) of section 41 of the Act the Central Government has allotted to the States and Union Territories the groups of letters for the use as registration mark as given in the table below—vide S.O. 444(E), dated 12th June, 1989 and as amended by S.O. 827(E), dated 11th November, 1992, by S.O. 1080(E), dated 30th November, 2000, by S.O. 14(E), dated 5th January, 2001 and S.O. 606(E), dated 19th April, 2007.

TABLE

State/Union Territories	Group of letters	State/Union Territories	Group of letters
1. Andaman and Nicobar	AN	17. Lakshadweep	LD
2. Andhra Pradesh	AP	18. Madhya Pradesh	MP
3. Arunachal Pradesh	AR	19. Maharashtra	MH
4. Assam	AS	20. Manipur	MN
5. Bihar	BR	21. Meghalaya	ML
6. Chandigarh	CH	22. Mizoram	MZ
6A. Chhatisgarh	CG	23. Nagaland	NL
7. Dadra and Nagar Haveli	DN	24. Orissa	OR
8. Daman and Diu	DD	25. Pondicherry	PY
9. Delhi	DL	26. Punjab	PN
10. Goa	GA	27. Rajasthan	RJ
11. Gujarat	GJ	28. Sikkim	SK
12. Haryana	HR	29. Tamil Nadu	TN
13. Himachal Pradesh	HP	30. Tripura	TR
14. Jammu and Kashmir	JK	31. Uttar Pradesh	UP
14A. Jharkhand	JH	31A. Uttarakhand	UK
15. Karnataka	KA	32. West Bengal	WB
16. Kerala	KL		

SYNOPSIS

COMMENTS

1. Manner and Contents of Information of Registration Certificate – Where the condition in the tender inviting bids for preparation of smart cards for registration of motor vehicle provided that the Smart Card for registration of motor vehicle was to be given for Rs. 440, it would be against the proviso to rule 81 which prescribes additional fee of Rs. 200 only no State Government can prescribe a format for tender or smart card and charge a fee which is contrary to the rules. The State Government does not have any power to prescribe the form, manner and contents of information of the registration certificate or the fee to be charged for issuing registration certification of a motor vehicle, since the Central Government has already done so in the Motor Vehicles Rules. The State Government by issuing a tender cannot prescribe the form contents of information, and fee contrary to the Rules; *Smart Chip Ltd* v. *State of Uttar Pradesh,* AIR 2003 All 80.

2. Entry in Registration Certificate not Condition Precedent for Ownership of Movable Property – The ownership of a movable property is not dependent upon the entries in the registration certificate. For the delay in seeking mutation of change in the registration certificate, the transferor or the transferee, as the case may be, can be penalized and proceeded against in terms of section 177 of the M.V. Act, 1988. Such default is again compoundable on payment of prescribed fee under sub-section (5) of section 50 of the M.V. Act, but the ownership of the movable property is not dependent upon the registration certificate. The act of transfer of owner in the registration certificate in terms of section 31 of the M.V. Act, 1939 or in terms of section 50 of the M.V. Act, 1988 is required to be performed by the transferee. If the transferee does not effect the ownership transferred in the registration certificate in his name, it may liable him for punishment in terms of section 112 of the M.V. Act, 1939 and 177 of the M. V. Act, 1988 but the property in the vehicle will stand transferred in terms of section 19 of the Sale of Goods Act, when it was intended, it being movable property. Thus, where appellant has admitted that both the parties have purchased the vehicle by contributing equal amount and are owner of the truck in equal shares, therefore, though the registration of the vehicle is in the name of the appellant alone but the title of the movable property would vest with the plaintiff as well and entry in the registration certificate would not be a condition precedent for ownership of the movable property; *Munni Ram* v. *Fakir Chand,* AIR 2010 P&H 50: 2011 (1) ACC 302: 2011 (2) ACJ 747.

3. Application for Registration of Vehicle – As per notification private service vehicle as defined in section 2(33) of the Motor Vehicles Act registered in the name of an individual can be used for private purpose unconnected with the business or trade of the owner of such vehicle. Therefore, a businessman who purchases a motor vehicle which answers the definition of the term "private service vehicle" can have the vehicle specified as a private service vehicle for personal use, if it is registered in his name and he gives a declaration to the effect that the vehicle is intended to be used by him solely for personal use. In the present case, the petitioner-proprietor of bakery had given such a declaration by filing application along with the application for registration. Also in the sale certificate the business address of the petitioner was given by itself would not make the business concern the owner of the vehicle. That apart, a proprietary concern is not a natural person or a juristic person and it cannot be the owner of a motor vehicle. The apprehension if any entertained by the transport authorities that the petitioner who was running a bakery was likely to use vehicle either for his business purposes or as contract carriage after registering it as private service vehicle of personal use and paying tax at rate applicable to non-transport vehicle, cannot be reason to deny registration of the vehicle as private service vehicle for personal use. If later, after registration and classification as a private service vehicle for personal use, the petitioner was found to use the vehicle for the purpose of his trade or business and not for personal use or is found to use it as a contract carriage, transport authorities would be entitled to seize the vehicle and reclassify it as a private service vehicles with liability to pay tax at the rate applicable to transport vehicle with effect from the date of its original registration. Thus, application of petitioner-proprietor of bakery for registration of vehicle as private service vehicle for personal use liable to be allowed; *Jagan Thomas* v. *State of Kerala,* AIR 2012 Ker 154: 2012 (2) Ker LJ 363: 2012 (2) Ker LT 365.

42. Special provision for registration of motor vehicles of diplomatic officers, etc.—(1) Where an application for registration of a motor vehicle is made under sub-section (1) of section 41 by or on behalf of any diplomatic officer or consular officer, then, notwithstanding anything contained in sub-section (3) or sub-section (6) of that section, the registering authority shall register the vehicle in such manner and in accordance with such procedure as may be provided by rules made in this behalf by the Central Government under sub-section (3) and shall assign to the vehicle for display thereon a special registration mark in accordance with the provisions contained in those rules and shall issue a certificate (hereafter in this section referred to as the certificate of registration) that the vehicle has been registered under this section; and any vehicle so registered shall not, so long as it remains the property of any diplomatic officer or consular officer, require to be registered otherwise under this Act.

(2) If any vehicle registered under this section ceases to be the property of any diplomatic officer or consular officer, the certificate of registration issued under this section shall also cease to be effective, and the provisions of sections 39 and 40 shall thereupon apply.

(3) The Central Government may make rules for the registration of motor vehicles belonging to diplomatic officers and consular officers regarding the procedure to be followed by the registering authority for registering such vehicles, the form in which the certificates of registration of such vehicles are to be issued, the manner in which such certificates of registration are to be sent to the owners of the vehicles and the special registration marks to be assigned to such vehicles.

(4) For the purposes of this section, "diplomatic officer" or "consular officer" means any person who is recognised as such by the Central Government and if any question arises as to whether a person is or is not such an officer, the decision of the Central Government thereon shall be final.

43. Temporary registration.—(1) Notwithstanding anything contained in section 40 the owner of a motor vehicle may apply to any registering authority or other prescribed authority to have the vehicle temporarily registered in the prescribed manner and for the issue in the prescribed manner of a temporary certificate of registration and a temporary registration mark.

(2) A registration made under this section shall be valid only for a period not exceeding one month, and shall not be renewable:

Provided that where a motor vehicle so registered is a chassis to which a body has not been attached and the same is detained in a workshop beyond the said period of one month for being fitted [1][with a body or any unforeseen circumstances beyond the control of the owner], the period may, on payment of such fees, if any, as may be prescribed, be extended by such further period or periods as the registering authority or other prescribed authority, as the case may be, may allow.

[2][(3) In a case where the motor vehicle is held under hire-purchase agreement, lease or hypothecation, the registering authority or other prescribed authority

1. Subs. by Act 54 of 1994, sec. 12, for "with a body" (w.e.f. 14-11-1994).
2. Ins. by Act 54 of 1994, sec. 12 (w.e.f. 14-11-1994).

shall issue a temporary certificate of registration of such vehicle, which shall incorporate legibly and prominently the full name and address of the person with whom such agreement has been entered into by the owner.]

SYNOPSIS

1. Levy of Tax can Only be During Period of Permanent Registration
2. Payment of Tax in Advance before Regular Registration does not Affect Liability for Tax

COMMENTS

1. Levy of Tax can Only be During Period of Permanent Registration – There is no provision in the Taxation Act to levy tax during the period a new vehicle is granted temporary registration. So much so, the first registration cannot be temporary registration granted under section 43 of the Act of 1988 read with rule 94 of the Kerala Motor Vehicles Rules, but can only be the permanent registration granted under section 40 of Act. Where date of increase of tax was known to purchasers and therefore they remitted tax in advance at time of granting temporary registration, which they were not required to pay at that time, payment of tax in advance before regular registration is granted does not affect liability for tax which has to be considered with reference to charging provision of Taxation Act and rate of tax applicable is rate in force as on date of granting regular registration; *Hilal B.* v. *State of Kerala*, AIR 2013 Ker 19: 2012 (3) Ker LJ 503: 2012 (3) Ker LT 438.

2. Payment of Tax in Advance before Regular Registration does not Affect Liability for Tax – Tax endorsement under Taxation Act is made only after regular registration which is done only on producing certificate of insurance for the vehicle, proof of residence, identity etc., of the purchaser as required under the Act and the Rules. The 2nd proviso to section 3(1) of Taxation Act, which provides for levy of tax on new vehicles, clearly states that levy of tax on new vehicles is to be made at the time of "first registration" of the vehicle. Even though it is stated that for new vehicles one-time tax at the rate as specified is payable from the date of purchase of the vehicle, the rate of tax applicable is as on the date of first registration of the vehicle. Thus, there is no provision in the Taxation Act to levy tax during the period a new vehicle is granted temporary registration. So much so, the first registration referred to in the 2nd proviso to section 3(1) cannot be temporary registration granted under section 43 of the Act of 1988 read with rule 94 of the Kerala Motor Vehicles Rules, but can only be the permanent registration granted under section 40 of Act. Where date of increase of tax was known to purchasers and therefore they remitted tax in advance at time of granting temporary registration, which they were not required to pay at that time, the payment of tax in advance before regular registration is granted does not affect liability for tax which has to be considered with reference to charging provision of Taxation Act and rate of tax applicable is rate in force as on date of granting regular registration; *Hilal B.* v. *State of Kerala*, AIR 2013 Ker 19: 2012 (3) Ker LJ 503: 2012 (3) Ker LT 438.

44. Production of vehicle at the time of registration.—The registering authority shall before proceeding to register a motor vehicle or renew the certificate of registration in respect of a motor vehicle, other than a transport vehicle, require the person applying for registration of the vehicle or, as the case may be, for renewing the certificate of registration to produce the vehicle either before itself or such authority as the State Government may by order appoint in order that the registering authority may satisfy itself that the particulars contained in the application are true and that the vehicle complies with the requirements of this Act and of the rules made thereunder.

COMMENTS

Registering Authority may Refuse to Register Motor Cycle though Agency Granted Test Certificate – The registering authority before registering a motor-vehicle or renewing a certificate in respect of motor-vehicle may satisfy itself that the vehicle complies with the requirements of the Act and the Rules made thereunder. Thus, even where agencies mentioned in rule 126 of the Rules have tested the prototypes of the motor-cycles and have granted test certificates, the registering authority may refuse to register the motor cycle if it does not comply with the requirements of rule 123 of the Rules; *Gyan Prakash* v. *Union of India*, AIR 2009 MP 55: 2009 AIHC 315 (NOC): 2009 (2) ACC 501.

45. Refusal of registration or renewal of the certificate of registration.—The registering authority may, by order, refuse to register any motor vehicle, or renew the certificate of registration in respect of a motor vehicle (other than a transport vehicle), if in either case, the registering authority has reason to believe that it is a stolen motor vehicle or the vehicle is mechanically defective or fails to comply with the requirements of this Act or of the rules made thereunder, or if the applicant fails to furnish particulars of any previous registration of the vehicle or furnishes inaccurate particulars in the application for registration of the vehicle or, as the case may be, for renewal of the certificate or registration thereof and the registering authority shall furnish the applicant whose vehicle is refused registration, or whose application for renewal of the certificate of registration is refused, a copy of such order, together with the reasons for such refusal.

46. Effectiveness in India of registration.—Subject to the provisions of section 47, a motor vehicle registered in accordance with this Chapter in any State shall not require to be registered elsewhere in India and a certificate of registration issued or in force under this Act in respect of such vehicle shall be effective throughout India.

47. Assignment of new registration mark on removal to another State.—(1) When a motor vehicle registered in one State has been kept in another State, for a period exceeding twelve months, the owner of the vehicle shall, within such period and in such form containing such particulars as may be prescribed by the Central Government, apply to the registering authority, within whose jurisdiction the vehicle then is, for the assignment of a new registration mark and shall present the certificate of registration to that registering authority:

Provided that an application under this sub-section shall be accompanied—

(i) by the no objection certificate obtained under section 48, or

(ii) in a case where no such certificate has been obtained, by—

(a) the receipt obtained under sub-section (2) of section 48; or

(b) the postal acknowledgment received by the owner of the vehicle if he has sent an application in this behalf by registered post acknowledgment due to the registering authority referred to in section 48,

together with a declaration that he has not received any communication from such authority refusing to grant such certificate or requiring him to comply with any direction subject to which such certificate may be granted:

Provided further that, in a case where a motor vehicle is held under a hire-purchase, lease or hypothecation agreement, an application under this sub-section shall be accompanied by a no objection certificate from the person with whom such agreement has been entered into, and the provisions of section 51, so far as may be, regarding obtaining of such certificate from the person with whom such agreement has been entered into, shall apply.

(2) The registering authority, to which application is made under sub-section (1), shall after making such verification, as it thinks fit, of the returns, if any, received under section 62, assign the vehicle a registration mark as specified in sub-section (6) of section 41 to be displayed and shown thereafter on the vehicle and shall enter the mark upon the certificate of registration before returning it to the applicant and shall, in communication with the registering authority by whom the vehicle was previously registered, arrange for the transfer of the registration of the vehicle from the records of that registering authority to its own records.

(3) Where a motor vehicle is held under a hire-purchase or lease or hypothecation agreement, the registering authority shall, after assigning the vehicle a registration mark under sub-section (2), inform the person whose name has been specified in the certificate of registration as the person with whom the registered owner has entered into the hire-purchase or lease or hypothecation agreement (by sending to such person a notice by registered post acknowledgment due at the address of such person entered in the certificate of registration the fact of assignment of the said registration mark).

(4) A State Government may make rules under section 65 requiring the owner of a motor vehicle not registered within the State, which is brought into or is for the time being in the State, to furnish to the prescribed authority in the State such information with respect to the motor vehicle and its registration as may be prescribed.

(5) If the owner fails to make an application under sub-section (1) within the period prescribed, the registering authority may, having regard to the circumstances of the case, require the owner to pay, in lieu of any action that may be taken against him under section 177, such amount not exceeding one hundred rupees as may be prescribed under sub-section (7):

Provided that action under section 177 shall be taken against the owner where the owner fails to pay the said amount.

(6) Where the owner has paid the amount under sub-section (5), no action shall be taken against him under section 177.

(7) For the purposes of sub-section (5), the State Government may prescribe different amounts having regard to the period of delay on the part of the owner in making an application under sub-section (1).

48. No objection certificate.—(1) The owner of a motor vehicle when applying for the assignment of a new registration mark under sub-section (1) of section 47, or where the transfer of a motor vehicle is to be effected in a State other than the State of its registration, the transferor of such vehicle when reporting the transfer under sub-section (1) of section 50, shall make an application in such form and in such manner as may be prescribed by the Central Government to the registering authority by which the vehicle was registered for the issue of a certificate (hereafter in this section referred to as the no objection certificate), to the effect that the registering authority has no objection for assigning a new registration mark to the vehicle or, as the case may be, for entering the particulars of the transfer of ownership in the certificate of registration.

(2) The registering authority shall, on receipt of an application under sub-section (1), issue a receipt in such form as may be prescribed by the Central Government.

(3) On receipt of an application under sub-section (1), the registering authority may, after making such inquiry and requiring the applicant to comply with such directions as it deems fit and within thirty days of the receipt thereof, by order in writing, communicate to the applicant that it has granted or refused to grant the no objection certificate:

Provided that a registering authority shall not refuse to grant the no objection certificate unless it has recorded in writing the reasons for doing so and a copy of the same has been communicated to the applicant.

(4) Where within a period of thirty days referred to in sub-section (3), the registering authority does not refuse to grant the no objection certificate or does not communicate the refusal to the applicant, the registering authority shall be deemed to have granted the no objection certificate.

(5) Before granting of refusing to grant the no objection certificate, the registering authority shall obtain a report in writing from the police that no case relating to the theft of the motor vehicle concerned has been reported or is pending, verify whether all the amounts due to Government including road tax in respect of that motor vehicle have been paid and take into account such other factors as may be prescribed by the Central Government.

[1][(6) The owner of the vehicle shall also inform at the earliest, in writing, the registering authority about the theft of his vehicle together with the name of the police station where the theft report was lodged, and the registering authority shall take into account such report while disposing of any application for no objection certification, registration, transfer of ownership or issue of duplicate registration certificate].

49. Change of residence or place of business.—(1) If the owner of a motor vehicle ceases to reside or have his place of business at the address recorded in the certificate of registration of the vehicle, he shall, within thirty days of any such change of address, intimate in such form accompanied by such documents as may be prescribed by the Central Government, his new address, to the registering authority by which the certificate of registration was issued, or, if the new address is within the jurisdiction of another registering authority, to that other registering authority, and shall at the same time forward the certificate of registration to the registering authority or, as the case may be, to the other registering authority in order that the new address may be entered therein.

(2) If the owner of a motor vehicle fails to intimate his new address to the concerned registering authority within the period specified in sub-section (1), the registering authority may, having regard to the circumstances of the case, require the owner to pay, in lieu of any action that may be taken against him

1. Ins. by Act 54 of 1994, sec. 13 (w.e.f. 14-11-1994).

under section 177, such amount not exceeding one hundred rupees as may be prescribed under sub-section (4):

Provided that action under section 177 shall be taken against the owner where he fails to pay the said amount.

(3) Where a person has paid the amount under sub-section (2), no action shall be taken against him under section 177.

(4) For the purposes of sub-section (2), a State Government may prescribe different amounts having regard to the period of delay in intimating his new address.

(5) On receipt of intimation under sub-section (1), the registering authority may, after making such verification as it may think fit, cause the new address to be entered in the certificate of registration.

(6) A registering authority other than the original registering authority making any such entry shall communicate the altered address to the original registering authority.

(7) Nothing in sub-section (1) shall apply where the change of the address recorded in the certificate of registration is due to a temporary absence not intended to exceed six months in duration or where the motor vehicle is neither used nor removed from the address recorded in the certificate of registration.

COMMENTS

Rejection Order cannot be Passed without Notice to Party with Regard to Deficiencies – Rejection of application made for change of address in registration book, entails severe civil consequences and such rejection cannot be made without notice to the party. Any action which visits the citizens with adverse civil consequences may it be administrative has to be preceded by show cause notice in that regard and failure to issue notice would render all subsequent steps and proceedings *void ab initio*. Here, if a notice could have been issued to the petitioner with regard to some or any of the deficiencies which ultimately led the rejection of his application the petitioner could have met the deficiencies immediately and got the necessary change made saving him from five years of loss. Thus, the District, Transport Officer, abused his authority in not issuing any notice to the petitioner prior to rejection of his application; *Shashi Ranjan* v. *State of Bihar*, AIR 2008 Pat 175.

50. Transfer of ownership.—(1) Where the ownership of any motor vehicle registered under this Chapter is transferred,—

(a) the transferor shall,—

(i) in the case of a vehicle registered within the same State, within fourteen days of the transfer, report the fact of transfer, in such form with such documents and in such manner, as may be prescribed by the Central Government to the registering authority within whose jurisdiction the transfer is to be effected and shall simultaneously send a copy of the said report to the transferee; and

(ii) in the case of a vehicle registered outside the State, within forty-five days of the transfer, forward to the registering authority referred to in sub-clause (i)—

(A) the no objection certificate obtained under section 48; or

(B) in a case where no such certificate has been obtained,—

(I) the receipt obtained under sub-section (2) of section 48; or

(II) the postal acknowledgment received by the transferee if he has sent an application in this behalf by registered post acknowledgment due to the registering authority referred to in section 48,

together with a declaration that he has not received any communication from such authority refusing to grant such certificate or requiring him to comply with any direction subject to which such certificate may be granted;

(b) the transferee shall, within thirty days of the transfer, report the transfer to the registering authority within whose jurisdiction he has the residence or place of business where the vehicle is normally kept, as the case may be, and shall forward the certificate of registration to that registering authority together with the prescribed fee and a copy of the report received by him from the transferor in order that particulars of the transfer of ownership may be entered in the certificate of registration.

(2) Where—

(a) the person in whose name a motor vehicle stands registered dies, or

(b) a motor vehicle has been purchased or acquired at a public auction conducted by, or on behalf of, Government,

the person succeeding to the possession of the vehicle or, as the case may be, who has purchased or acquired the motor vehicle, shall make an application for the purpose of transferring the ownership of the vehicle in his name, to the registering authority in whose jurisdiction he has the residence or place of business where the vehicle is normally kept, as the case may be, in such manner, accompanied with such fee, and within such period as may be prescribed by the Central Government.

(3) If the transferor or the transferee fails to report to the registering authority the fact of transfer within the period specified in clause (a) or clause (b) of sub-section (1), as the case may be, or if the person who is required to make an application under sub-section (2) (hereafter in this section referred to as the other person) fails to make such application within the period prescribed, the registering authority may, having regard to the circumstances of the case, require the transferor or the transferee, or the other person, as the case may be, to pay, in lieu of any action that may be taken against him under section 177 such amount not exceeding one hundred rupees as may be prescribed under sub-section (5):

Provided that action under section 177 shall be taken against the transferor or the transferee or the other person, as the case may be, where he fails to pay the said amount.

(4) Where a person has paid the amount under sub-section (3), no action shall be taken against him under section 177.

(5) For the purposes of sub-section (3), a State Government may prescribe different amounts having regard to the period of delay on the part of the transferor or the transferee in reporting the fact of transfer of ownership of the motor vehicle or of the other person in making the application under sub-section (2).

(6) On receipt of a report under sub-section (1), or an application under sub-section (2), the registering authority may cause the transfer of ownership to be entered in the certificate of registration.

(7) A registering authority making any such entry shall communicate the transfer of ownership to the transferor and to the original registering authority, if it is not the original registering authority.

SYNOPSIS

1. Compensation for not Delivering Registration Certificate within Reasonable Time
2. Liability for Payment of Arrears of Tax
3. Mandatory Requirements of Transfer
4. Registration Number of Choice – Allotment of
5. Transfer of Ownership of Motor Vehicle
6. Entry in Registration Certificate not Condition Precedent for Ownership of Movable Property
7. Liability of Transferor to Pay Compensation
8. Auction Sale

COMMENTS

1. Compensation for not Delivering Registration Certificate within Reasonable Time – The authorities whose duty was to deliver the registration certificate to the petitioner after making the necessary changes, sat over the registration certificate for about 18 months, such a tendency must be curbed. The authorities are required to do their duty expeditiously without causing any undue delay and inconvenience to the person concerned. The public servants by discharging their duties are not doing any charity to the citizens. They are paid for their job and it is expected that they will discharge their duties efficiently, diligently and honestly. In the circumstances, the respondents must pay compensation to the petitioner for causing mental tension, physical inconvenience and harassment by not delivering the registration certificate after the requisite changes to the petitioner within reasonable time; *Archana Garg* v. *Rajpur Road Transport Authority*, AIR 1999 Del 95: 1999 (4) Civ LJ 582: 1999 (78) DLT 609.

2. Liability for Payment of Arrears of Tax – The liability for payment of arrears of Motor Vehicle Tax obviously would be on the part of the original owner. Like that registered owner until the transfer is statutorily effected and as mandated in section 50 read with rule 55(2) and also in light of the prescribed Form 29 and 30, until the entire process is, successfully, complied with the liability for payment of motor vehicle tax would be on the part of the original owner *i.e.*, registered owner and he cannot be permitted to avail the constitutional remedy enshrined in Article 226 of the Constitution of India; *Champakbhai Parsottambhai Patel* v. *State of Gujarat*, AIR 2001 Guj 200: 2001 (2) Guj LR 1814.

3. Mandatory Requirements of Transfer – The Act carves out only three exceptions and does not cover a case of sale of vehicle where the price is paid and the possession of the vehicle is delivered to the purchaser/transferee. Even if sale is effectuated in the absence of compliance of mandatory requirements of law, transfer does not take place and the transferor continues to be the registered owner. Therefore, the registered owner cannot be absolved of liability qua third party. Importantly, the person in whose name the vehicle is registered is considered to be the owner and unless the name of the transferee is registered he does not become the owner thereof; *Vinod Kumar* v. *Nirmala Devi*, AIR 2009 HP 37.

4. Registration Number of Choice – Allotment of – The petitioner has not been able to refer to any document from which it could be made out whether the Transport Officer, had accepted his request for the allotment of a registration number of his choice. In such a situation, mere deposit of the amount would not create any right in the petitioner to seek the assignment of a registration number of his choice; *Jagjit Singh* v. *State of Punjab*, AIR 2008 P&H 140.

5. Transfer of Ownership of Motor Vehicle – Rule 56 of the Central Rules can be invoked only in a case when the motor vehicle continues to be with the owner who dies and there is a successor, purchaser, or a person who acquires the vehicle by any other means other than under section 50(1) of the Act. When apparently the sale-cum-delivery receipt has been effected, there is no question of ownership being retained by erstwhile owner. On the date when the registration certificate was endorsed with regard to the transfer of ownership of the vehicle, the petitioner is the owner. When the authorities clearly accept that the sale-cum-delivery receipt was effected during the lifetime of erstwhile owner, it is a clear case of transfer of ownership in terms of section 50(1) of the Act. Thus the transfer of ownership in this case has taken place on the date of sale-cum-delivery receipt and the date of recording of transfer of ownership in the registration certificate is only a procedure prescribed under the Act and cannot be a ground to dispute the factum of transfer of ownership; *S.R. Ramakrishnan* v. *Deputy Transport Commissioner, Coimbatore*, AIR 2013 Mad 100: 2013 (3) ACC 406: 2013 Writ LR 59.

6. Entry in Registration Certificate not Condition Precedent for Ownership of Movable Property – The ownership of a movable property is not dependent upon the entries in the registration certificate. For the delay in seeking mutation of change in the registration certificate, the transferor or the transferee, as the case may be, can be penalized and proceeded against in terms of section 177 of the M.V. Act, 1988. Such default is again compoundable on payment of prescribed fee under sub-section (5) of section 50 of the M.V. Act, but the ownership of the movable property is not dependent upon the registration certificate. The act of transfer of owner in the registration certificate in terms of section 31 of the M.V. Act, 1939 or in terms of section 50 of the M.V. Act, 1988 is required to be performed by the transferee. If the transferee does not effect the ownership transferred in the registration certificate in his name, it may liable him for punishment in terms of section 112 of the M.V. Act, 1939 and 177 of the M. V. Act, 1988 but the property in the vehicle will stand transferred in terms of section 19 of the Sale of Goods Act, when it was intended, it being movable property. Thus, where appellant has admitted that both the parties have purchased the vehicle by contributing equal amount and are owner of the truck in equal shares, therefore, though the registration of the vehicle is in the name of the appellant alone but the title of the movable property would vest with the plaintiff as well and entry in the registration certificate would not be a condition precedent for ownership of the movable property; *Munni Ram* v. *Fakir Chand*, AIR 2010 P&H 50: 2011 (1) ACC 302: 2011 (2) ACJ 747.

7. Liability of Transferor to Pay Compensation – Unless the Registering Authority causes the transfer of ownership to be entered in the registration certificate, the person whose name appears in that certificate as such an owner would be deemed to be owner of the vehicle for all purposes. The transferor and transferee are jointly and severally liable to pay the compensation amount as awarded by the Tribunal; *Thangaraj* v. *Ameer Hussain*, AIR 2010 Mad 13: 2010 AIHC 287 NOC: 2011 (2) ACJ 1190.

8. Auction Sale – Transfer of ownership of vehicle free from encumbrances – Auction-purchaser not liable to pay tax and penalty for pre-auction period; *Ishwar Chandra Prusti* v. *R.T.O., Sambalpur*, AIR 2015 Ori 82.

51. Special provisions regarding motor vehicle subject to hire-purchase agreement, etc.—(1) Where an application for registration of a motor vehicle which is held under a hire-purchase, lease or hypothecation agreement (hereafter in this section referred to as the said agreement) is made, the registering authority shall make an entry in the certificate of registration regarding the existence of the said agreement.

(2) Where the ownership of any motor vehicle registered under this Chapter is transferred and the transferee enters into the said agreement with any person, the [1][last registering authority] shall, on receipt of an application in such form as the Central Government may prescribe from the parties to the said agreement, make an entry as to the existence of the said agreement in the certificate of registration [2][and an intimation in this regard shall be sent to the original registering authority if the last registering authority is not the original registering authority].

(3) Any entry made under sub-section (1) or sub-section (2), may be cancelled by the [1][last registering authority] on proof of the termination of the said agreement by the parties concerned on an application being made in such form as the Central Government may prescribe [2][and an intimation in this behalf shall be sent to the original registering authority if the last registering authority is not the original registering authority].

(4) No entry regarding the transfer of ownership of any motor vehicle which is held under the said agreement shall be made in the certificate of registration except with the written consent of the person whose name has been specified in the certificate of registration as the person with whom the registered owner has entered into the said agreement.

(5) Where the person whose name has been specified in the certificate of registration as the person with whom the registered owner has entered into the said agreement, satisfies the registering authority that he has taken possession of the vehicle [3][from the registered owner] owing to the default of the registered owner under the provisions of the said agreement and that the registered owner refuses to deliver the certificate of registration or has absconded, such authority may, after giving the registered owner an opportunity to make such representation as he may wish to make (by sending to him a notice by registered post acknowledgment due at his address entered in the certificate of registration) and notwithstanding that the certificate of registration is not produced before it, cancel the certificate and issue a fresh certificate of registration in the name of the person with whom the registered owner has entered into the said agreement:

Provided that a fresh certificate of registration shall not be issued in respect of a motor vehicle, unless such person pays the prescribed fee:

Provided further that a fresh certificate of registration issued in respect of a motor vehicle, other than a transport vehicle, shall be valid only for the remaining period for which the certificate cancelled under this sub-section would have been in force.

---

1. Subs. by Act 54 of 1994, sec. 14, for "original registering authority" (w.e.f. 14-11-1994).
2. Added by Act 54 of 1994. sec. 14 (w.e.f. 14-11-1994).
3. Ins. by Act 54 of 1994, sec. 14 (w.e.f. 14-11-1994).

(6) The registered owner shall, before applying to the appropriate authority, for the renewal of a permit under section 81 or for the issue of duplicate certificate of registration under sub-section (14) of section 41, or for the assignment of a new registration mark [1][under section 47, or removal of the vehicle to another State, or at the time of conversion of the vehicle from one class to another, or for issue of no objection certificate under section 48, or for change of residence or place of business under section 49, or for the alteration of the vehicle under section 52, make an application] to the person with whom the registered owner has entered into the said agreement, (such person being hereafter in this section referred to as the financier) for the issue of a no objection certificate (hereafter in this section referred to as the certificate).

Explanation.—For the purposes of this sub-section and sub-sections (8) and (9), "appropriate authority" in relation to any permit, means the authority which is authorised by this Act to renew such permit and, in relation to registration means the authority which is authorised by this Act to issue duplicate certificate of registration or to assign a new registration mark.

(7) Within seven days of the receipt of an application under sub-section (6) the financier may issue, or refuse, for reasons which shall be recorded in writing communicated to the applicant, to issue, the certificate applied for, and where the financier fails to issue the certificate and also fails to communicate the reasons for refusal to issue the certificate to the applicant within the said period of seven days, the certificate applied for shall be deemed to have been issued by the financier.

(8) The registered owner shall, while applying to the appropriate authority for the renewal of any permit under section 81, or for the issue of a duplicate certificate of registration under sub-section (14) of section 41, or while applying for assignment of a new registration mark under section 47, submit with such application the certificate, if any, obtained under sub-section (7) or, where no such certificate has been obtained, the communication received from the financier under that sub-section, or, as the case may be, a declaration that he has not received any communication from the financier within the period of seven days specified in that sub-section.

(9) On receipt of an application for the renewal of any permit or for the issue of duplicate certificate of registration or for assignment of a new registration mark in respect of a vehicle which is held under the said agreement, the appropriate authority may, subject to the other provisions of this Act,—

(a) in a case where the financier has refused to issue the certificate applied for, after giving the applicant an opportunity of being heard, either—

(i) renew or refuse to renew the permit, or

(ii) issue or refuse to issue the duplicate certificate of registration, or

(iii) assign or refuse to assign a new registration mark;

1. Subs. by Act 54 of 1994, sec. 14, for "under section 47, make an application" (w.e.f. 14-11-1994).

(b) in any other case,—

(i) renew the permit, or

(ii) issue duplicate certificate of registration, or

(iii) assign a new registration mark.

(10) A registering authority making an entry in the certificate of registration regarding—

(a) hire-purchase, lease or hypothecation agreement of a motor vehicle, or

(b) the cancellation under sub-section (3) of an entry, or

(c) recording transfer of ownership of motor vehicle, or

(d) any alteration in a motor vehicle, or

(e) suspension or cancellation of registration of a motor vehicle, or

(f) change of address,

shall communicate [1][by registered post acknowledgment due] to the financier that such entry has been made.

[2][(11) A registering authority registering the new vehicle, or issuing the duplicate certificate of registration or a no objection certificate or a temporary certificate of registration, or issuing or renewing, a fitness certificate or substituting entries relating to another motor vehicle in the permit, shall intimate the financier of such transaction.]

[2][(12) The registering authority where it is not the original registering authority, when making entry under sub-section (1) or sub-section (2), or cancelling the said entry under sub-section (3) or issuing the fresh certificate of registration under sub-section (5) shall communicate the same to the original registering authority.]

SYNOPSIS

COMMENTS

1. Refusal to Register Vehicle for want of Order from Court is not Proper – Once the society produced the necessary documents and the vehicle in support of its case that it had taken possession thereof in exercise of its right available under the hypothecation agreement, he was under the statutory obligation to register it in the name of the society. On the facts of the case the registering authority acted improperly by directing the society to obtain an order from the Court. An order from the court was not a requirement in terms of provisions in section 51(5). The registering authority should be directed to register the vehicle in the name of the society; *Contai Co-operative Bank Ltd.* v. *State of West Bengal,* AIR 2008 Cal 46: 2008 AIHC 306 (NOC): 2007 (56) All Ind Cas 660.

2. Right to Claim Status of Financier – Section 51(6) obliges the registered owner before applying to the appropriate authority for renewal of permit to approach the person with whom the registered owner has entered into an agreement (financier) for issuance of NOC. May be the owner of the vehicle has entered into more than one agreement

1. Ins. by Act 54 of 1994, sec. 14 (w.e.f. 14-11-1994).

2. Subs. by Act 54 of 1994, sec 14, for sub-section (11) (w.e.f. 14-11-1994).

with more than one person for purchase of the vehicle. But it is only that person with whom an agreement is stated to have been entered into for hire-purchase of the vehicle or hypothecation agreement, and so endorsed in the certificate of registration in terms of section 51(1) of the Act, who is entitled to claim the status of the financier for the purpose of section 51(6) of the Act. It is only such person who can claim the right to be involved in the procedure provided under sections 51(7) and 51(8) of the Act or the right to be heard in terms of section 51(9) of the Act. Right thereunder cannot be claimed by anyone other than the person with whom, existence of an agreement is endorsed in terms of section 51(1) of the Act; *Bindhu K.S.* v. *Secretary Regional Transport Authority, Kottayam,* AIR 2009 Ker 199.

3. Entries be made on Authentic Documents if Registration Required in Name of Financier – The Motor Vehicles Act is a Central Act which, of course, authorises the State Government also to frame/make/issue Circulars. However, whether the Circular issued is in terms of section 51 or the Rules framed under the Motor Vehicles Act is not made clear by the respondent authorities. The Circular is issued on the basis of the Government letter. Might be, the Government with a noble idea to regulate such money lending by persons who are not having Money Lending license and also to avoid exorbitant charging of interest, has issued such a direction. The hire purchase agreement is a sort of sub-contract and it is an executory contract. It is also noticed that the difference in the cash and hire purchase price is not interest to rather, it is a privilege being allowed to discharge the purchase price of goods by installments. In that view of the matter, when the hire purchase agreement is necessarily entered with a private financier or with a public institution like nationalised/non-nationalised banks, ultimately, the agreement is there in the form of a hire purchase contract. Necessarily that hire purchase agreement forms the basis on which the authorities are required to make an entry in the RC Books which is the mandate. But the restriction imposed by way of a Circular to make entries, if the registration of vehicles is required to be done in the name of the financier, only on producing authentic documents like Money Lenders License or the rate of interest charged, may not come within the purview of section 51(1) of the Act. However, under the Money Lenders Act if the license is made compulsory for money lending, for violation of the same, penal consequences could be invoked under the Act on coming to know of the illegal money lending and, it is open to the concerned Department under the Act to have recourse to law. Since already this Court has held that such imposing of conditions by way of a Circular, is extraneous to the Motor Vehicles Act, 1988 thereby violating the provisions provided under section 51 of the Motor Vehicles Act. The very idea behind the Circular though would be noble, it cannot be held as a regulatory measure by the RTO authorities. Thus the Circular and its implications would be implemented as per the provisions of the Money Lenders Act and not under the Motor Vehicles Act, 1988 or by the authorities under the Motor Vehicles Act; *K.H.P. Association* v. *Commissioner for Transport in Karnataka,* AIR 2011 Kant 101.

[1][**52. Alteration in motor vehicle.**—(1) No owner of a motor vehicle shall so alter the vehicle that the particulars contained in the certificate of registration are at variance with those originally specified by the manufacturer:

Provided that where the owner of a motor vehicle makes modification of the engine, or any part thereof, of a vehicle for facilitating its operation by different type of fuel or source of energy including battery, compressed natural gas, solar power, liquid petroleum gas or any other fuel or source of energy, by fitment of a conversion kit, such modification shall be carried out subject to such conditions as may be prescribed:

1. Subs. by Act 27 of 2000, sec. 2, for section 52 (w.e.f. 11-8-2000). Earlier section 52 was amended by Act 54 of 1994, sec. 15 (w.e.f. 14-11-1994).

Provided further that the Central Government may prescribe specifications, conditions for approval, retrofitment and other related matters for such conversion kits:

Provided also that the Central Government may grant exemption for alteration of vehicles in a manner other than specified above, for any specific purpose.

(2) Notwithstanding anything contained in sub-section (1), a State Government may, by notification in the Official Gazette, authorise, subject to such conditions as may be specified in the notification, and permit any person owning not less than ten transport vehicles to alter any vehicle owned by him so as to replace the engine thereof with engine of the same make and type, without the approval of registering authority.

(3) Where any alteration has been made in motor vehicle without the approval of registering authority or by reason of replacement of its engine without such approval under sub-section (2), the owner of the vehicle shall, within fourteen days of the making of the alteration, report the alteration to the registering authority within whose jurisdiction he resides and shall forward the certificate of registration to that authority together with the prescribed fee in order that particulars of registration may be entered therein.

(4) A registering authority other than the original registering authority making any such entry shall communicate the details of the entry to the original registering authority.

(5) Subject to the provisions made under sub-sections (1), (2), (3) and (4), no person holding a vehicle under a hire-purchase agreement shall make any alteration to the vehicle except with the written consent of the registered owner.

Explanation.—For the purposes of this section, "alteration" means a change in the structure of a vehicle which results in a change in its basic feature.].

SYNOPSIS

1. Modification of Engine
2. Mere Reduction of Seating Capacity not Alternation
3. Conversion of Gas Cylinder as Fuel
4. Conversion of Vehicle as a Goods Carriage
5. Permission for Reducing Seating Capacity of Contract Carriage Vehicles
6. Stipulation to Fix Maximum Number of Seats – Applicable
7. Permission to Reduce Number of Seats
8. Tata Mobile 207 with Cab and Body cannot be Converted into Sedan
9. Conversion was from Omni Bus to Goods Vehicle – Permissibility
10. Retrofitting LPG Kit
11. Conversion of Vehicle from Ambulance to Omni Bus – Permissibility

COMMENTS

1. Modification of Engine – The proviso appended to sub-section (1) of section 52 of the 1988 Act permits modification of the engine or any part thereof. Such modification of engine may be made for facilitating its operation by different types of fuel or source of energy as specified therein. But such modification has to be made only by fitting a conversion kit. Such modification is also required to be carried out subject to such conditions as may be prescribed. The proviso therefore, confines itself to the modification of engine and not the total change of the engine. The provisions of section 52(1) inserted by the Amendment Act, 2000 must be read as to fulfil the object and purpose of the Act. The changes in the structure of a vehicle resulting in change in its basic feature must not be at variance with the certificate of registration; *A. Chandra Sekhar Reddy* v. *Union of India,* AIR 2002 AP 148: 2002 AIHC 1307: 2002 (1) ACC 311 (FB).

2. Mere Reduction of Seating Capacity not Alternation – Alteration in motor vehicle can be permitted where the particulars contained in the certificate of registration are no longer accurate. Alteration means a change in the structure of a vehicle which results in change in its basic feature. Mere reduction of the seats cannot be said to amount to alteration of the seating capacity nor does it result in change of structure of the vehicle. The seating capacity has been fixed by the manufacturers which was entered in the certificate of registration and if the owner of the vehicle reduces the number of seats, no such permission is required under section 52 as by such reduction no alteration has to be made in the entry regarding the seating capacity in the certificate of registration. Seating capacity will continue to be the same irrespective of reduction in the number of actual seats by the vehicle owners; *O. Gangadhar* v. *Transport Commissioner, A.P.*, AIR 2000 AP 198: 2000 (2) ACC 668: 2000 (1) Andh LT 704.

The provisions of section 52 of the Act do not debar the owner of the vehicle to reduce the number of seats for the convenience of the passengers by paying taxes to the Government for the seating capacity. Further, by such reduction of seats no alteration has to be made in the entry regarding "seating capacity" in the certificate of registration inasmuch as the built-in seating capacity in such case would continue to remain the same irrespective of the reduction in the number of actual seats. Merely by reducing the number of seats for the convenience of the passengers, the "seating capacity" of the vehicle will not change. By the said process, the basic structure of the vehicle also will not be changed. Thus, no permission is required under section 52 of the Act to reduce number of seats; *Appasaheb V. Shinge* v. *Dy. Commr. for Transports, Belgaum,* AIR 2005 Kant 75: 2005 AIHC 582: 2005 (1) Civ LJ 903.

3. Conversion of Gas Cylinder as Fuel – Use of gas cylinder as fuel to run automobile vehicles in place of petrol is not permissible. Liquid petroleum gas cannot be used as a fuel for running the automobile vehicles. Thus an injunction was issued for restraining the user of liquid petroleum gas as a fuel by anybody to run any automobile vehicles; *Paper Clipping* v. *S.H.O., Karimnagar,* AIR 2000 AP 217: 2000 (1) ACC 543: 1999 (5) Andh LT 654.

4. Conversion of Vehicle as a Goods Carriage – There is no scope for conversion of a passenger vehicle as a goods carriage unless the prototype test of the same vehicle include the conversion of the vehicle to another type. Though the basic model of van mini bus etc. under Category VIII is the same the different items mentioned thereunder are approved prototypes under rule 126 of the Central Motor Vehicles Rules. Further section 52(1) of the Act does not permit any alteration of to the vehicle as the particulars in the registration certificate should not be in variance with the particular originally specified by the manufacturers. In view of section 52(1) of the Act no alteration can be effected converting the passenger vehicle as a goods carriage; *P.K. Baiju* v. *Joint Regional Transport Officer,* AIR 2003 Ker 26: 2002 (1) Ker LJ 802: ILR 2002 (2) Ker 231.

When a vehicle is manufactured and prototype test was conducted for the purpose of carriage of goods, the same cannot be used for carriage of passengers unless and until it is so certified. Insistence of conducting prototype testing is for the purpose of finding out whether a vehicle can be used for a particular purpose. Therefore when it was certified after undergoing prototype test that the use of the vehicle is for carriage of goods, the same cannot be altered by the registering authority as a passenger vehicle; *George Panakezham, Fr.* v. *Regional Transport Officer,* AIR 1999 Ker 133: 1998 (2) Ker LJ 638: 1999 (1) Civ LJ 346.

5. Permission for Reducing Seating Capacity of Contract Carriage Vehicles – For contract carriage vehicles with bodies manufactured by the manufacturers themselves and having a definite seating, no permission is necessary under section 52 for reducing the number of seats as by such reduction, no alteration has to be made in the entry regarding 'seating capacity' in the certificate of registration. 'Seating capacity' in such cases would continue to be the same irrespective of the reduction in the number of actual seats. There where no permission is necessary to reduce the number of seats in these type of vehicles as it would not amount to change in the 'seating capacity', the question of refusing a petition under section 52 for the reason that it would adversely affect the interest of revenue would not arise; *B. Mohandas* v. *Registering Authority, R.T.O., Trichur,* AIR 1998 Ker 300: 1998 AIHC 4165: 1998 (2) Ker LJ 168 (FB).

6. Stipulation to Fix Maximum Number of Seats – Applicable – The stipulation to fix maximum number of seats is applicable only in case the vehicle had undergone an alteration and reconstruction as contemplated under section 52 of the Act of 1988. Therefore, when the alteration alleged to have been effected by the owner of the vehicle registered in compliance with the provisions of Act of 1939 and Rules framed thereunder does not come under the scope and ambit of section 52 of the Act of 1988 the same would not attract the stipulation; *Poulose Mathai* v. *Joint Regional Transport Officer, Thalassery,* AIR 1996 Ker 225: 1996 (1) ACC 319: 1995 (2) Ker LT 778.

7. Permission to Reduce Number of Seats – Contract carriage vehicles with bodies manufactured by the manufacturers themselves and having a definite seating capacity as designed by the manufacturers, no permission is necessary under section 52 of the Act for reducing the number of seats as by such reduction, no alteration has to be made in the entry regarding seating capacity in the certificate of registration. Seating capacity in such cases would continue to be the same irrespective of the reduction in the number of actual seats; *B. Mohandas* v. *Registration Authority, Regional Transport Office, Trichur,* AIR 1998 Ker 300: 1998 AIHC 4165: 1999 (1) Civ LJ 103.

8. Tata Mobile 207 with Cab and Body cannot be Converted into Sedan – Tata Mobile 207 Passenger Version having a seating capacity of minimum 10 or 11 has to be classified as an Omnibus and it cannot be classified as a motor car with seating capacity of six. Similarly Tata Mobile 207 with cab and body can be used only a transport vehicles and it cannot be converted into a sedan; *Saramma Philipose* v. *Regional Transport Officer, Ernakulam,* AIR 1996 Ker 44: 1995 (2) Ker LJ 472: 1995 (2) Ker LT 450.

9. Conversion was from Omni Bus to Goods Vehicle – Permissibility – Under section 52 of the Act certain types of alteration of motor vehicle is permissible. What is not permitted is the variation of the original specification of the manufacturer. If the basic feature of the vehicle remains unchanged, then section 52 provides for alteration of the motor vehicle. In the present case, the conversion is from omni bus to goods vehicle. The only two changes the petitioner seeks are for removing the seats and the colour and type of the body for the purpose of modifying the omni buses as goods vehicles. The circular also emphasises that 'alteration' means, the basic feature of the vehicle should not be changed. It allows alteration from non-transport to transport *vice versa,* which means that a transport vehicle can become a non-transport vehicle. It may also include a goods vehicle. The only requirement is that the basic feature as specified by the manufacturer should not be changed. This proposition becomes clear on a reading of the circular, which clearly provides for certain alterations, namely, petrol to diesel or any engine to be used with source of energy including battery, compressed natural gas, solar power, liquified petroleum gas or any other fuel. This also amounts to conversion as against the original specification of the manufacturer. The horse power, cubic capacity, seating capacity, unladen weight, colour also can be altered. If the circular provides such an alteration which is contrary to the specification of the manufacturer, a mere change in removal of seats and removal of colour in the body or type of body for conversion into a goods vehicle can fall outside the scope of section 52. In any event, the provisions of section 52 are very clear and unambiguous. So long as the original specification of the manufacturer remains, the proviso enables the modification of the vehicle and that is what is sought to be done by the petitioner. Thus a *mandamus* is issued directing the authorities to consider the application for conversion of the omni buses in question to goods vehicles; *M. Abdul Rahman* v. *Transport Commissioner, Chepauk,* AIR 2013 Mad 92: 2013 (3) ACC 155.

10. Retrofitting LPG Kit – For registration of vehicle with LPG kit, the only requirement, which is relevant under the law is such that retrofitment of LPG kits on in-use vehicle shall be carried out by workshops authorized by the Kit Manufacturer/ Kit Supplier or Vehicle Manufacturer, as the case may be and for the purpose even the Central Government has categorically confirmed that there is no other statutory requirement for doing so, there is no reason for the present respondents to ask for any additional formalities or conditions except the conditions laid down in Central Motor Vehicles Rules, 1989 with reference to retrofitment of LPG kit and use of vehicle with said LPG kit. The documents produced by the petitioner also confirm such position. The petitioner has proved on record that it is authorized by several gas kit manufacturers/ kit suppliers and, therefore, they are entitled to retrofitting the LPG kit and there is no need to get them registered with the respondent or to get prior permission from the respondent for their activity and business as workshop for LPG kit installer; *Universal Auto Link* v. *State of Gujarat,* AIR 2013 Guj 203: 2013 (3) ACC 311.

11. Conversion of Vehicle from Ambulance to Omni Bus – Permissibility – Section 52(1) of the Act prohibits alteration of vehicles as regards the particulars contained in the Certificate of Registration which are at variance with those originally specified by the manufacturer. The Certificate of Registration contains many particulars including the type of body, seating capacity and class of vehicle. The class of the vehicle in question was shown as "ambulance". Similarly the type of body was shown as "closed" and the seating capacity was shown as "five in all". The alterations made by the petitioner have admittedly resulted in alteration of the above said particulars contained in the Certificate of Registration and apparently they are at variance with the particulars originally specified by the manufacturer. Thus the statutory prohibition under section 52(1) is attracted and consequently the respondent has rightly rejected the petitioner's request for registering the conversion of the vehicle from Ambulance to Omni Bus; *E. Dastagiri E. Papa Saheb* v. *Regional Transport Officer, Proddutur,* AIR 2011 AP 8.

53. Suspension of registration.—(1) If any registering authority or other prescribed authority has reason to believe that any motor vehicle within its jurisdiction—

(a) is in such a condition that its use in a public place would constitute a danger to the public, or that it fails to comply with the requirements of this Act or of the rules made thereunder, or

(b) has been, or is being, used for hire or reward without a valid permit for being used as such,

the authority may, after giving the owner an opportunity of making any representation he may wish to make (by sending to the owner a notice by registered post acknowledgment due at his address entered in the certificate of registration), for reasons to be recorded in writing, suspend the certificate of registration of the vehicle—

(i) in any case falling under clause (a), until the defects are rectified to its satisfaction; and

(ii) in any case falling under clause (b), for a period not exceeding four months.

(2) An authority other than a registering authority shall, when making a suspension order under sub-section (1), intimate in writing the fact of such

suspension and the reasons therefor to the registering authority within whose jurisdiction the vehicle is at the time of the suspension.

(3) Where the registration of a motor vehicle has been suspended under sub-section (1) for a continuous period of not less than one month, the registering authority, within whose jurisdiction the vehicle was when the registration was suspended, shall, if it is not the original registering authority, inform that authority of the suspension.

(4) The owner of a motor vehicle shall, on the demand of a registering authority or other prescribed authority which has suspended the certificate of registration of the vehicle under this section, surrender the certificate of registration.

(5) A certificate of registration surrendered under sub-section (4) shall be returned to the owner when the order suspending registration has been rescinded and not before.

COMMENTS

Cancellation of Registration of Vehicle – The seating arrangements of the vehicles are not as prescribed in the Rules. The over hang of the vehicles is 60% excess than the prescribed limit and with a view to provide more seats the chassis of the vehicles are welded and their length are increased. This is a finding of fact which is based on actual inspection of the vehicles by the competent Authority. Therefore, the authorities were justified in withdrawing the permission granted earlier and cancelling the registration certificate of vehicle; *Sri Durgamba Motors* v. *Dy. Commr. for Transport, Shimoga,* AIR 2005 Kant 72: 2004 AIR Kant HCR 3244.

54. Cancellation of registration suspended under section 53.—Where the suspension of registration of a vehicle under section 53 has continued without interruption for a period of not less than six months, the registering authority within whose jurisdiction the vehicle was when the registration was suspended, may, if it is the original registering authority, cancel the registration, and if it is not the original registering authority, shall forward the certificate of registration to that authority which may cancel the registration.

55. Cancellation of registration.—(1) If a motor vehicle has been destroyed or has been rendered permanently incapable of use, the owner shall, within fourteen days or as soon as may be, report the fact to the registering authority within whose jurisdiction he has the residence or place of business where the vehicle is normally kept, as the case may be, and shall forward to the authority the certificate of registration of the vehicle.

(2) The registering authority shall, if it is the original registering authority, cancel the registration and the certificate of registration, or, if it is not, shall forward the report and the certificate of registration to the original registering authority and that authority shall cancel the registration.

(3) Any registering authority may order the examination of a motor vehicle within its jurisdiction by such authority as the State Government may by order appoint and, if upon such examination and after giving the owner an opportunity to make any representation he may wish to make (by sending to the owner a notice by registered post acknowledgment due at his address entered in the certificate of registration), it is satisfied that the vehicle is in such a condition that it is incapable of being used or its use in a public place would constitute

a danger to the public and that it is beyond reasonable repair, may cancel the registration.

(4) If a registering authority is satisfied that a motor vehicle has been permanently removed out of India, the registering authority shall cancel the registration.

(5) If a registering authority is satisfied that the registration of a motor vehicle has been obtained on the basis of documents which were, or by representation of facts which was, false in any material particular, or the engine number or the chassis number embossed thereon are different from such number entered in the certificate of registration, the registering authority shall after giving the owner an opportunity to make such representation as he may wish to make (by sending to the owner a notice by registered post acknowledgment due at his address entered in the certificate of registration), and for reasons to be recorded in writing, cancel the registration.

(6) A registering authority cancelling the registration of a motor vehicle under section 54 or under this section shall communicate such fact in writing to the owner of the vehicle, and the owner of the vehicle shall forthwith surrender to that authority the certificate of registration of the vehicle.

(7) A registering authority making an order of cancellation under section 54 or under this section shall, if it is the original registering authority, cancel the certificate of registration and the entry relating to the vehicle in its records, and, if it is not the original registering authority, forward the certificate of registration to that authority, and that authority shall cancel the certificate of registration and the entry relating to the motor vehicle in its records.

(8) The expression "original registering authority" in this section and in sections 41, 49, 50, 52, 53 and 54 means the registering authority in whose records the registration of the vehicle is recorded.

(9) In this section "certificate of registration" includes a certificate of registration renewed under the provisions of this Act.

COMMENTS

Not Liable to Pay Tax on Surrender – The Uttar Pradesh Motor Vehicles Taxation Rules, 1998 really do not impose any burden on the owner or operator of the vehicle if he does not want to use or he keeps the vehicle not for use or does not use the vehicle on road, as he may surrender the registration certificate in accordance with the procedure prescribed under rule 22 of the Rules read with section 12 of the Act and in that event the owner shall not be liable to pay tax or additional taxes. What is required under the aforesaid provisions of the Act and Rules is that the owner or operator who intends not to use the vehicle shall surrender the vehicle according to the procedure prescribed and in that event he has not to pay tax or additional taxes and non compliance of the procedure for surrender as prescribed, shall really mean that the vehicle has not been surrendered; *Vidya Gupta* v. *State of Uttar Pradesh*, AIR 2003 All 1.

56. Certificate of fitness of transport vehicles.—(1) Subject to the provisions of sections 59 and 60, a transport vehicle shall not be deemed to be validly registered for the purposes of section 39, unless it carries a certificate of fitness in such form containing such particulars and information as may be prescribed by the Central Government, issued by the prescribed authority, or by an authorized testing station mentioned in sub-section (2), to the effect that the vehicle complies for the time being with all the requirements of this Act and the rules made thereunder:

Provided that where the prescribed authority or the "authorized testing station" refuses to issue such certificate, it shall supply the owner of the vehicle with its reasons in writing for such refusal.

(2) The "authorized testing station" referred to in sub-section (1) means a vehicle service station or public or private garage which the State Government, having regard to the experience, training and ability of the operator of such station or garage and the testing equipment and the testing personnel therein, may specify in accordance with the rules made by the Central Government for regulation and control of such stations or garages.

(3) Subject to the provisions of sub-section (4), certificate of fitness shall remain effective for such period as may be prescribed by the Central Government having regard to the objects of this Act.

(4) The prescribed authority may for reasons to be recorded in writing cancel a certificate of fitness at any time, if satisfied that the vehicle to which it relates no longer complies with all the requirements of this Act and the rules made thereunder; and on such cancellation the certificate of registration of the vehicle and any permit granted in respect of the vehicle under Chapter V shall be deemed to be suspended until a new certificate of fitness has been obtained:

[1][Provided that no such cancellation shall be made by the prescribed authority unless such prescribed authority holds such technical qualification as may be prescribed or where the prescribed authority does not hold such technical qualification on the basis of the report of an officer having such qualifications.]

(5) A certificate of fitness issued under this Act shall, while it remains effective be valid throughout India.

SYNOPSIS

1. Interference into Exclusive Power of Authorised Testing Stations
2. State Government cannot Regulate Role of Authorised Testing Stations
3. Fitness Certificate – Lapse of Period – Registration or Permit Issued would not Stand Cancelled
4. Renewal of Certificate
5. 'Authorised Testing Station'

COMMENTS

1. Interference into Exclusive Power of Authorised Testing Stations – The Authorised Testing Stations cannot be compelled to get the counter-signature of the Motor Vehicle Inspectors in the certificates of fitness, as it amounts to interference into the exclusive power of the Authorised Testing Stations to issue such certificates. Thus the State Government, by issuing the notification putting condition of getting the counter-signature from the Motor Vehicle Inspectors, cannot be allowed to indirectly take away the powers of the Authorised Testing Stations given by the Parliament to issue certificates of fitness; *Nag's Auto Testing Station* v. *State of Jharkhand,* AIR 2008 Jhar 42: 2008 AIHC 588: 2008 (2) ALJ (NOC) 507.

2. State Government cannot Regulate Role of Authorised Testing Stations – The State Government is not empowered under the Act and the Rules to restrict the role of an authorised testing station once a letter of authority has been issued in its favour

1. Ins. by Act 54 of 1994, sec. 16 (w.e.f. 14-11-1994).

by Registering Authority upon satisfaction of the parameters stipulated under the said Rules. Thus the State Government cannot regulate or control role of 'authorised testing stations; by incorporating rule 170(c) of the Rules for testing of headlight beams and brake system only. While the 'Authorised Testing Stations' can test headlight beams and brake system of the vehicles for the purposes of other tests, the transport operations shall have to necessarily approach the Inspecting Officer or the prescribed authority for grant of a certificate of fitness; *Kirpal Singh Sandhu* v. *State of Punjab,* AIR 2010 P&H 24: 2010 AIHC 425 NOC: 2010 (1) AKAR (NOC) 112.

3. Fitness Certificate – Lapse of Period – Registration or Permit Issued would not Stand Cancelled – No doubt the lapse of fitness certificate would constitute breach of provisions of Motor Vehicle Act or Rules; *V.M. Augustine, Vattakavumal* v. *Ayyapankutty,* AIR 2015 Ker 131.

4. Renewal of Certificate – Grant on basis of certificate of fitness issued by prescribed authority and not by authorised testing station; *Shekhar Bhushan Nag* v. *State of Jharkhand,* AIR 2015 Jhar 26.

5. 'Authorised Testing Station' – Not authority or that authority as mentioned in section 56(1) of Act; *Shekhar Bhushan Nag* v. *State of Jharkhand,* AIR 2015 Jhar 26.

57. Appeals.—[1][(1) Any person aggrieved by an order of the registering authority under section 41, 42, 43, 45, 47, 48, 49, 50, 52, 53, 55 or 56 may, within thirty days of the date on which he has received notice of such order, appeal against the order to the prescribed authority.]

(2) The appellate authority shall give notice of the appeal to the original authority and after giving an opportunity to the original authority and the appellant to be heard in the appeal pass such order as it thinks fit.

COMMENTS

Jurisdiction of Transport Commissioner to withhold Allotment of Fancy Registration Mark – The chronology of events suggest that the fourth respondent submitted a petition to the Regional Transport Officer on the afternoon offering a bid of Rs.1,01,000 much after the results were known. The fourth respondent also met the Transport Commissioner who orally directed the Regional Transport Officer to withhold the actual allotment of the fancy registration mark to the petitioner. This was followed by an appeal to the Transport Commissioner purporting to be under section 57 of the Act against the proceedings of the Regional Transport Officer. But no appeal is provided under section 57 of the Act against an order of the registering authority under section 39 of the Act read with rule 95 of the Rules. The Transport Commissioner had obviously no jurisdiction either to entertain the appeal under section 57 of the Act or to withhold the actual allotment of the fancy registration mark to the highest bidder; *Thambi T.G.* v. *State of Kerala,* AIR 2013 Ker 129: 2013 (1) Ker LJ 779: 2013 (1) Ker LT 730.

58. Special provisions in regard to transport vehicles.—(1) The Central Government may, having regard to the number, nature and size of the tyres attached to the wheels of a transport vehicle (other than a motor cab), and its make and model and other relevant considerations, by notification in the Official Gazette, specify, in relation to each make and model of a transport vehicle, the [2][maximum gross vehicle weight] of such vehicle and the maximum safe axle weight of each axle of such vehicle.

1. Subs. by Act 54 of 1994, sec. 17, for sub-section (1) (w.e.f. 14-11-1994).
2. Subs. by Act 54 of 1994, sec. 18, for "maximum safe laden weight" (w.e.f. 14-11-1994).

(2) A registering authority, when registering a transport vehicle, other than a motor cab, shall enter in the record of registration and shall also enter in the certificate of registration of the vehicle the following particulars, namely:—

(a) the unladen weight of the vehicle;

(b) the number, nature and size of the tyres attached to each wheel;

(c) the gross vehicle weight of the vehicle and the registered axle weights pertaining to the several axles thereof; and

(d) if the vehicle is used or adapted to be used for the carriage of passengers solely or in addition to goods, the number of passengers for whom accommodation is provided,

and the owner of the vehicle shall have the same particulars exhibited in the prescribed manner on the vehicle.

(3) There shall not be entered in the certificate of registration of any such vehicle any gross vehicle weight or a registered axle weight of any of the axles different from that specified in the notification under sub-section (1) in relation to the make and model of such vehicle and to the number, nature and size of the tyres attached to its wheels:

Provided that where it appears to the Central Government that heavier weights than those specified in the notification under sub-section (1) may be permitted in a particular locality for vehicles of a particular type, the Central Government may, by order in the Official Gazette direct that the provisions of this sub-section shall apply with such modifications as may be specified in the order.

[1][***]

(5) In order that the gross vehicle weight entered in the certificate of registration of a vehicle may be revised in accordance with the provisions of sub-section (3), the registering authority may require the owner of transport vehicle in accordance with such procedure as may be prescribed to produce the certificate of registration within such time as may be specified by the registering authority.

COMMENTS

Power of Self-correction – The authority has initially mentioned the wrong maximum gross vehicle weight, but subsequently corrected said the weight in conformity with the weight specified by the Central Government the notification. Regional Transport Officers have the power to correct their own mistakes. The power of self-correction cannot be denied to the statutory authorities, particularly, to prevent a wrong being committed to the public interest. It cannot be said that the concerned Regional Transport Officers lack legal authority to correct their own wrongs and mistakes; *Ravi Ranjan Kumar* v. *State of Chhattisgarh,* AIR 2006 Chhat 157: 2007 AIHC 403: 2006 (4) MPHT 1.

59. Power to fix the age limit of motor vehicle.—(1) The Central Government may, having regard to the public safety, convenience and objects of this Act, by notification in the Official Gazette, specify the life of a motor vehicle reckoned from the date of its manufacture, after the expiry of which the motor vehicle shall not be deemed to comply with the requirements of this Act and the rules made thereunder:

1. Sub-section (4) omitted by Act 27 of 2000, sec. 3 (w.e.f. 11-8-2000).

Provided that the Central Government may specify different ages for different classes or different types of motor vehicles.

(2) Notwithstanding anything contained in sub-section (1), the Central Government may, having regard to the purpose of a motor vehicle, such as, display or use for the purposes of a demonstration in any exhibition, use for the purposes of technical research or taking part in a vintage car rally, by notification in the Official Gazette, exempt, by a general or special order, subject to such conditions as may be specified in such notification, any class or type of motor vehicle from the operation of sub-section (1) for the purpose to be stated in the notification.

(3) Notwithstanding anything contained in section 56, no prescribed authority or authorized testing station shall grant a certificate of fitness to a motor vehicle in contravention of the provisions of any notification issued under sub-section (1).

COMMENTS

Imposition of Conditions should be Traceable to Provisions of Act – The provisions of section 59 and section 72 operate in two different fields and the authorities acting under both the provisions can impose conditions relevant thereto including as to date of manufacture of the motor vehicle. Even in the absence of rules, if conditions could be prescribed in the permit and such conditions are reasonable and such power to impose conditions is traceable to the provisions of the Act itself, it cannot be said that such power is exercised by the authority beyond its powers; *Bharath Kumar* v. *Karnataka State Transport Appellate Tribunal,* AIR 1995 Kant 264: 1995 (1) ACC 553: ILR (KANT) 1995 KAR 331.

60. Registration of vehicles belonging to the Central Government.—(1) Such authority as the Central Government may, by notification in the Official Gazette, specify, may register any motor vehicle which is the property or for the time being under the exclusive control of the Central Government and is used for Government purposes relating to the defence of the country and unconnected with any commercial enterprise and any vehicle so registered shall not, so long as it remains the property or under the exclusive control of the Central Government, require to be registered otherwise under this Act.

(2) The authority registering a vehicle under sub-section (1) shall assign a registration mark in accordance with the provisions contained in the rules made in this behalf by the Central Government and shall issue a certificate in respect of that vehicle to the effect that such vehicle complies for the time being with all the requirements of this Act and the rules made thereunder and that the vehicle has been registered under this section.

(3) A vehicle registered under this section shall carry the certificate issued under sub-section (2).

(4) If a vehicle registered under this section ceases to be the property or under the exclusive control of the Central Government, the provisions of sections 39 and 40 shall thereupon apply.

(5) The authority registering a vehicle under sub-section (1) shall furnish to any State Government all such information regarding the general nature, overall dimensions and axle weights of the vehicle as the State Government may at any time require.

61. Application of Chapter to trailers.—(1) The provisions of this Chapter shall apply to the registration of trailers as they apply to the registration of any other motor vehicle.

(2) The registration mark assigned to a trailer shall be displayed in such manner on the side of the drawing vehicle as may be prescribed by the Central Government.

(3) No person shall drive a motor vehicle to which a trailer is or trailers are attached unless the registration mark of the motor vehicle so driven is displayed on the trailer or on the last trailer in the train, as the case may be, in such manner as may be prescribed by the Central Government.

62. Information regarding stolen and recovered motor vehicles to be furnished by the police to the State Transport Authority.—The State Government may, if it thinks necessary or expedient so to do in the public interest, direct the submission by the Inspector General of Police (by whatever designation called) and such other police officers as the State Government may specify in this behalf, of such returns containing the information regarding vehicles which have been stolen and stolen vehicles which have been recovered of which the police are aware, to the State Transport Authority, and may prescribe the form in which and the period within which such returns shall be made.

63. Maintenance of State Registers of Motor Vehicles.—(1) Each State Government shall maintain in such form as may be prescribed by the Central Government a register to be known as the State Register of Motor Vehicles, in respect of the motor vehicles in that State, containing the following particulars, namely:—

(a) registration numbers;

(b) years of manufacture;

(c) classes and types;

(d) names and addresses of registered owners; and

(e) such other particulars as may be prescribed by the Central Government.

(2) Each State Government shall supply to the Central Government [1][[if so desired by it] a printed copy of the State Register of Motor Vehicles and shall also inform the Central Government without delay of all additions to and other amendments in such register made from time to time.

(3) The State Register of Motor Vehicles shall be maintained in such manner as may be prescribed by the State Government.

64. Power of Central Government to make rules.—The Central Government may make rules to provide for all or any of the following matters, namely:—

(a) the period within which and the form in which an application shall be made and the documents, particulars and information it shall accompany under sub-section (1) of section 41;

(b) the form in which the certificate of registration shall be made and the particulars and information it shall contain and the manner in which it shall be issued under sub-section (3) of section 41;

---

1. Ins. by Act 54 of 1994, sec. 19 (w.e.f. 14-11-1994).

(c) the form and manner in which the particulars of the certificate of registration shall be entered in the records of the registering authority under sub-section (5) of section 41;

(d) the manner in which and the form in which the registration mark, the letters and figures and other particulars referred to in sub-section (6) of section 41 shall be displayed and shown;

(e) the period within which and the form in which the application shall be made and the particulars and information it shall contain under sub-section (8) of section 41;

(f) the form in which the application referred to in sub-section (14) of section 41 shall be made, the particulars and information it shall contain and the fee to be charged;

(g) the form in which and the period within which the application referred to in sub-section (1) of section 47 shall be made and the particulars it shall contain;

(h) the form in which and the manner in which the application for "No Objection Certificate" shall be made under sub-section (1) of section 48 and the form of receipt to be issued under sub-section (2) of section 48;

(i) the matters that are to be complied with by an applicant before no objection certificate may be issued under section 48;

(j) the form in which the intimation of change of address shall be made under sub-section (1) of section 49 and the documents to be submitted along with the application;

(k) the form in which and the manner in which the intimation of transfer of ownership shall be made under sub-section (1) of section 50 or under sub-section (2) of section 50 and the document to be submitted along with the application;

(l) the form in which the application under sub-section (2) or sub-section (3) of section 51 shall be made;

(m) the form in which the certificate of fitness shall be issued under sub-section (1) of section 56 and the particulars and information it shall contain;

(n) the period for which the certificate of fitness granted or renewed under section 56 shall be effective;

(o) the fees to be charged for the issue or renewal or alteration of certificates of registration, for making an entry regarding transfer of ownership on a certificate of registration, for making or cancelling an endorsement in respect of agreement of hire-purchase or lease or hypothecation on a certificate of registration, for certificates of fitness for registration marks, and for the examination or inspection of motor vehicles, and the refund of such fees.

(p) any other matter which is to be, or may be, prescribed by the Central Government.

SYNOPSIS

1. Vehicle Owner cannot Seek Issuance of Duplicate Certificate of Registration
2. Power to Make Rules
3. Implementation of Scheme Regulating Issuance and Fixation of HSRP
4. Driving License – Automated Driving Test – Grant on Basis not Improper

COMMENTS

1. Vehicle Owner cannot Seek Issuance of Duplicate Certificate of Registration – After having voluntarily transferred the vehicle to a third party the erstwhile owner cannot validly claim for a duplicate certificate of registration. In view of the voluntary transfer of the vehicle to the appellant cannot contend that the certificate of registration was lost or destroyed or that it is not in his possession for reasons beyond his control. A vehicle owner who has transferred his vehicle and handed over the registration certificate to the transferee cannot claim duplicate registration certificate. As the appellant had transferred the vehicle to a third party and handed over the registration certificate to him, he cannot validly seek issuance of a duplicate registration certificate; *P.J. Shaji* v. *Joint Regional Transport Officer,* AIR 1995 Ker 388: 1996 (1) ACC 101: 1995 (2) Ker LJ 69.

2. Power to Make Rules – The purport and object of the amendment in the Rule is that nobody would be able to change the registration/number plates or the same cannot be tampered with and new high security registration number plates fixed in the cars cannot be removed from the vehicles. The impugned Rules seek to take into account all precautions, which the Executive found it necessary for fulfilling the object of the said Act, and thus, no exception thereto can be taken. Central government has the power to make rules; *D.R. Thadani* v. *Union of India,* AIR 2003 Del 10: 2003 (67) DRJ 477.

3. Implementation of Scheme Regulating Issuance and Fixation of HSRP – The State of Andhra Pradesh has decided to have a competitive bidding process by segregating the tender into different sections *i.e.,* one for manufacturing, another for embossing, hot stamping and printing of Higher Security Registration Plate (HSRP) and yet another to supply the same to the Corporation for installation. Again, the process adopted by the State of Andhra Pradesh is not only in violation of the directions contained in the judgment of this Court but is also contrary to the Notification which was issued under sub-section (3) of section 109 of the Motor Vehicles Act, 1988 and called the Motor Vehicles (New High Security Registration Plates) Order, 2001. This Order does not permit the completion of the HSRP scheme in the manner sought to be adopted by the State of Andhra Pradesh. The State was to award the contract but the same has not so far been awarded. Thus it is directed the State of Andhra Pradesh to issue fresh tender, award the contract and commence the implementation of the scheme by the time schedule; *Maninderjit Singh Bitta* v. *Union of India,* AIR 2012 SC 348: 2012 AIR SCW 193: (2012) 1 SCC 707.

The draft agreement provides that the supplier of the plate shall notify the purchaser in writing of all sub-contracts awarded under the contract. Neither rule 50 of the Motor Vehicles Rules, 1989, Motor Vehicles (New High Security Registration Plates) Order, 2011 nor the judgments of this Court permit sub-contracts to be awarded by the contractor to whom the award for manufacture and fixation of HSRP is awarded. The DIMTS when it is getting the HSRP manufactured from the contractor, such manufacture should be *firstly* from a single contractor and *secondly* it should, without fail, be under the direct supervision and control of DIMTS. They should not let the sub-contractors or other parties to have control over the manufacturing processing and fixation of HSRP in any manner, whatsoever. They should ensure that one single person is responsible for manufacturing, affixation of seals, imprinting of numbers and affixation of HSRP on the vehicles in the NCT of Delhi. The Government has prayed for extension of time. Thus the period for implementation of the scheme has been extend; *Maninderjit Singh Bitta* v. *Union of India,* AIR 2012 SC 348: 2012 AIR SCW 193: (2012) 1 SCC 707.

4. Driving License – Automated Driving Test – Grant on Basis not Improper – Automated Driving Test is in the interest of general public and not contrary to public interest; *Bhupendra Mangaldas Patel* v. *State of Gujarat*, AIR 2015 Guj 65.

65. Power of State Government to make rules.—(1) A State Government may make rules for the purpose of carrying into effect the provisions of this Chapter other than the matters specified in section 64.

(2) Without prejudice to the generality of the foregoing power, such rules may provide for—

(a) the conduct and hearing of appeals that may be preferred under this Chapter (the fees to be paid in respect of such appeals and the refund of such fees);

(b) the appointment, functions and jurisdiction of registering and other prescribed authorities;

(c) the exemption of road-rollers, graders and other vehicles designed and used solely for the construction, repair and cleaning of roads from all or any of the provisions of this Chapter and the rules made thereunder and the conditions governing such exemption;

(d) the issue or renewal of certificates of registration and fitness and duplicates of such certificates to replace the certificates lost, destroyed or mutilated;

(e) the production of certificates of registration before the registering authority for the revision of entries therein of particulars relating to the gross vehicle weight;

(f) the temporary registration of motor vehicles and the issue of temporary certificate of registration and marks;

(g) the manner in which the particulars referred to in sub-section (2) of section 58 and other prescribed particulars shall be exhibited;

(h) the exemption of prescribed persons or prescribed classes of persons from payment of all or any portion of the fees payable under this Chapter;

(i) the forms, other than those prescribed by the Central Government, to be used for the purpose of this Chapter;

(j) the communication between registering authorities of particulars of certificates of registration and by owners of vehicles registered outside the State of particulars of such vehicles and of their registration;

(k) the amount or amounts under sub-section (13) of section 41 or sub-section (7) of section 47 or sub-section (4) of section 49 or sub-section (5) of section 50;

(l) the extension of the validity of certificates of fitness pending consideration of applications for their renewal;

(m) the exemption from the provisions of this Chapter and the conditions and fees for exemption, of motor vehicles in the possession of dealers;

(n) the form in which and the period within which the return under section 62 shall be sent;

(o) the manner in which the State Register of Motor Vehicles shall be maintained under section 63;

(p) any other matter which is to be or may be prescribed.

COMMENTS

Mode of Reservation of Registration Members – When once a person applies for reservation by paying the prescribed fee, that number, in fact get reserved in his name, if more than one application is received on the same day, then only an auction is contemplated and allotment of the number to the highest bidder. When once that number is reserved on a particular day, it does not remain open for reservation on any other day. Sub-rule (5) specifies reservation of any number within the range of 250 numbers from the last number registered in the serial order and it cannot be held that the same number shall remain open for reservation on all other days; *B. Mahesh Jyothi* v. *State of Kerala,* AIR 2002 Ker 353: ILR 2002 (3) Ker 46.

CHAPTER V

CONTROL OF TRANSPORT VEHICLES

66. Necessity for permits.—(1) No owner of a motor vehicle shall use or permit the use of the vehicle as a transport vehicle in any public place whether or not such vehicle is actually carrying any passengers or goods save in accordance with the conditions of a permit granted or countersigned by a Regional or State Transport Authority or any prescribed authority authorising him the use of the vehicle in that place in the manner in which the vehicle is being used:

Provided that a stage carriage permit shall, subject to any conditions that may be specified in the permit, authorise the use of the vehicle as a contract carriage:

Provided further that a stage carriage permit may, subject to any conditions that may be specified in the permit, authorise the use of the vehicle as a goods carriage either when carrying passengers or not:

Provided also that a goods carriage permit shall, subject to any conditions that may be specified in the permit, authorise the holder to use the vehicle for the carriage of goods for or in connection with a trade or business carried on by him.

(2) The holder of a goods carriage permit may use the vehicle, for the drawing of any trailer or semi-trailer not owned by him, subject to such conditions as may be prescribed:

[1][Provided that the holder of a permit of any articulated vehicle may use the prime-mover of that articulated vehicle for any other semi-trailor.]

(3) The provisions of sub-section (1) shall not apply—

(a) to any transport vehicle owned by the Central Government or a State Government and used for Government purposes unconnected with any commercial enterprise;

(b) to any transport vehicle owned by a local authority or by a person acting under contract with a local authority and used solely for road cleansing, road watering or conservancy purposes;

1. Added by Act 54 of 1994, sec. 20 (w.e.f. 14-11-1994).

(c) to any transport vehicle used solely for police, fire brigade or ambulance purposes;

(d) to any transport vehicle used solely for the conveyance of corpses and the mourners accompanying the corpses;

(e) to any transport vehicle used for towing a disabled vehicle or for removing goods from a disabled vehicle to a place of safety;

(f) to any transport vehicle used for any other public purpose as may be prescribed by the State Government in this behalf;

(g) to any transport vehicle used by a person who manufactures or deals in motor vehicles or builds bodies for attachment to chassis, solely for such purposes and in accordance with such conditions as the Central Government may, by notification in the Official Gazette, specify in this behalf;

[1][***]

(i) to any goods vehicle, the gross vehicle weight of which does not exceed 3,000 kilograms;

(j) subject to such conditions as the Central Government may, by notification in the Official Gazette, specify, to any transport vehicle purchased in one State and proceeding to a place, situated in that State or in any other State, without carrying any passenger or goods;

(k) to any transport vehicle which has been temporarily registered under section 43 while proceeding empty to any place for the purpose of registration of the vehicle;

[2][***]

(m) to any transport vehicle which, owing to flood, earthquake or any other natural calamity, obstruction on road, or unforeseen circumstances, is required to be diverted through any other route, whether within or outside the State, with a view to enabling it to reach its destination;

(n) to any transport vehicle used for such purposes as the Central or State Government may, by order, specify;

(o) to any transport vehicle which is subject to a hire-purchase, lease or hypothecation agreement and which owing to the default of the owner has been taken possession of by or on behalf of the person with whom the owner has entered into such agreement, to enable such motor vehicle to reach its destination; or

(p) to any transport vehicle while proceeding empty to any place for purpose of repair.

(4) Subject to the provisions of sub-section (3), sub-section (1) shall, if the State Government by rule made under section 96 so prescribes, apply to any motor vehicle adapted to carry more than nine persons excluding the driver.

1. Clause (h) omitted by Act 27 of 2000, sec. 4 (w.e.f. 11-8-2000).
2. Clause (l) omitted by Act 39 of 2001, sec. 2 (w.e.f. 27-9-2001). Earlier clause (l) was substituted by Act 54 of 1994, sec. 20 (w.e.f. 14-11-1994).

SYNOPSIS

COMMENTS

1. Necessity of Permit for Vehicle Used by Institute – The petitioner is the owner of the vehicle and is a recognized educational institution and has produced the relevant documents showing the affiliation under the I.C.S.E. Board. Thus the respondent was not justified in insisting on permit under section 66(1) of the Act; *Catholic Diocese of Gorakhpur Education Society* v. *State of Uttar Pradesh,* AIR 2001 All 196: 2001 All LJ 1512: 2001 (1) All CJ 336.

2. Owner cannot Ply Vehicle Off Route though not Carrying Passengers – The owner cannot ply the vehicle off the route even it is not actually carrying any passenger as section 66 enjoins upon the permit holder to ply his vehicle in strict adherence to and observations of the conditions attached to the permit. Thus, if a vehicle is found whether stationary or moving at a place which does not fall on the route, it will be in contravention of the statutory provisions of the Act unless it falls under exceptions provided in section 66(3) of the Act, and this contravention amounts to plying the vehicle contrary to the condition attached to permit itself and thus it will be liable to be cancelled or suspended under the provisions of section 86 of the Act and action can be taken against the permit holder under the provisions of section 192 of the Act; *Rampati Jaiswal* v. *State of Uttar Pradesh,* AIR 1997 All 170: 1997 All LJ 827: 1998 (1) All CJ 447.

3. Exemption from Permits not Depend upon Realization of Conveyance Charge – The exemption from permit control comes as a matter of course if the requisite conditions are fulfilled and such exemption was or is not a matter of discretion of the Government. Once it is found that the educational institution is recognised by the Government and the transport vehicle of the school is used solely for the purposes of the school, the exemption from permit control is automatic and does not depend upon the discretion of the Government. In view of the fact that a bus of the school is solely and exclusively used for carrying the students of the school from their residences to school and back, such use cannot but be use solely for the purpose of the educational institution. The question whether conveyance charges are realized by the school from the students, is wholly immaterial. The question of conveyance charge is therefore wholly irrelevant whether the use of the bus is solely for the purpose of the educational institution; *Birla Vidya Vihar Trust* v. *State of West Bengal,* AIR 1994 Cal 245.

4. Words "within whose jurisdiction the vehicle then is" – In section 47 the Parliament has used the words "within whose jurisdiction the vehicle then is". The words "then is" are indicative of the fact that the owner of the vehicle can apply to the registering authority of the place, in whose jurisdiction the vehicle is kept. The owner of the vehicle may be a permanent resident of a particular place, but at the same time he can carry on his business at another place. There is no bar under any law that a owner of vehicle who is a permanent resident of a particular place, cannot ply his vehicle within the jurisdiction of different District Transport Officer and cannot keep his vehicle for business purposes; *Regional Transport Officer* v. *Pradeep Kumar Jain,* AIR 1995 Raj 145.

5. Necessity of Permits – Provisions of section 66, merely prevents use of the vehicle as a transport vehicle without a permit. It does not prohibit driving of such a vehicle on a public road. The vehicle can be driven on a public road so long as it is not used as a transport vehicle. The owner of such a vehicle may use that vehicle for taking his family out for a picnic. Section 66 will not bar such a use; *State of Orissa* v. *Bijaya C. Tripathy,* AIR 2005 SC 1431: 2004 AIR SCW 7327: 2005 (30) OCR 23: 2004 (7) SCC 139: 2004 (8) SCALE 39.

According to the Registration Certificate the unladen weight of the Tractor was 1680 kgs, and that of the Trolley was 1000 kgs. Thus, the total unladen weight of Tractor-Trolley comes to 2680 kgs. Since the total unladen weight of both the Tractor Trolley is 2680 kilograms, the same is well within the prescribed limit i.e. 7500 kilograms. Therefore, in the present case, the Tractor-Trolley comes within the purview of Light Motor Vehicles for which no permit endorsing the driver to drive the Tractor was required and as such the driver of the Tractor was having valid and effective driving license on the date of accident to driver the vehicle *i.e.,* LMV and there was no necessity of endorsement authorizing the driver especially to drive the Tractor or a transport vehicle; *Ramdheen Sahu* v. *Thanuram,* AIR 2011 Chht 158.

6. Stage Carriage Permit – Even after the Motor Vehicles Act, 1988 was enacted and brought into force, a person other than the registered owner of a vehicle can apply for a regular permit or a temporary permit. Stage carriage permit can be issued to person other than registered owner of vehicle. Thus person in lawful possession of vehicle under lease agreement with registered owner is entitled to stage carriage permit; *Anil Kumar S. Anupam* v. *Secretary, Regional Transport Authority, Kollam,* AIR 2010 Ker 94: 2010 (2) ACC 497: 2010 (1) Ker LT 758.

7. Legality of Agreements to Operate Vehicles on Notified Routes – The Corporation has entered into agreements with the outsourcing agents. For the purpose of running their vehicles, only the services of the outsourcing agents is availed with certain terms and conditions for a period of one year. It is indeed their vehicles which are being operated by outsourcing agents. The terms and conditions would clearly go to show that it is not the transfer of the permits in favour of the outsourcing agents, obtained from STA or RTA in respect of notified routes, upon which exclusive right is conferred upon the Corporation under section 100 of Chapter VI of the Act. The relevant clauses of the terms and conditions of one of the agreements show that the agreements with outsourcing agents to operate the services on the notified routes is not transfer of permits in favour of the outsourcing agents. The services are operated under the control, supervision and management of the Corporation through the second party outsourcing agent. Therefore, the same cannot be termed that there is a transfer of permits in favour of outsourcing agents to operate the vehicle or vehicles on the notified routes for which permission of either STA or RTA, is required under the provision of the 1939 Act. Thus the agreements with reference to the aforesaid provision, the agreements entered into between the Corporation and the outsourcing agents, is perfectly legal and valid. There is no arbitrary action on the part of the Corporation. There is also no statutory violation either under section 66 or 82 of the M.V. Act; *All Orissa Bus Owners Association* v. *Orissa State Road Transport Corporation,* AIR 2012 Ori 179.

8. Stage Carriage Permit – Grant of – Lease executed in favour of person – Can be deemed to be owner of vehicle; *Rishikesh Singh* v. *Seema Arora,* AIR 2015 MP 10.

9. Stage Carriage Permit – Rival Operators have no *locus standi* to challenge transport permit in favour of other operator; *Dinesh Mehta* v. *STA, Odisha,* AIR 2015 Ori 88.

10. Stage Carriage Permit – Cancellation at the Instance of Rival Operator – Amounts to deprivation of enjoyment of Fundamental Rights under Article 19(1)(g) of Constitution; *Dinesh Mehta* v. *STA, Odisha,* AIR 2015 Ori 88.

67. Power to State Government to control road transport.—(1) A State Government, having regard to—

(a) the advantages offered to the public, trade and industry by the development of motor transport,

(b) the desirability of co-ordinating road and rail transport,

(c) the desirability of preventing the deterioration of the road system, and

(d) the desirability of preventing uneconomic competition among holders of permits.

may, from time to time, by notification in the Official Gazette, issue directions both to the State Transport Authority and Regional Transport Authority—

(i) regarding the fixing of fares and freights (including the maximum and minimum in respect thereof) for stage carriages, contract carriages and goods carriages:

[1][***]

(ii) regarding the prohibition or restriction, subject to such conditions as may be specified in the directions, of the conveying of long distance goods traffic generally, or of specified classes of goods by goods carriages;

(iii) regarding any other matter which may appear to the State Government necessary or expedient for giving effect to any agreement entered into with the Central Government or any other State Government or the Government of any other country relating to the regulation of motor transport generally, and in particular to its coordination with other means of transport and the conveying of long distance goods traffic:

Provided that no such notification in respect of the matters referred to in clause (ii) or clause (iii) shall be issued unless a draft of the proposed directions is published in the Official Gazette specifying therein a date being not less than one month after such publication, on or after which the draft will be taken into consideration and any objection or suggestion which may be received has, in consultation with the State Transport Authority, been considered after giving the representatives of the interests affected an opportunity of being heard.

(2) Any direction under sub-section (1) regarding the fixing of fares and freights for stage carriages, contract carriages and goods carriages may provide that such fares or freights shall be inclusive of the tax payable by the passengers or the consignors of the goods, as the case may be, to the operators of the stage carriages, contract carriages or goods carriages under any law for the time being in force relating to tax on passengers and goods.

SYNOPSIS

1. Charging of Fares
2. Rules cannot Prevail Over Provisions of Act
3. Limiting Scope or Fixing Number of Permits is Inconsistent with Provisions of Act

---

1. Proviso omitted by Act 39 of 2001, sec. 3 (w.e.f. 27-9-2001). Earlier the proviso was inserted by Act 54 of 1994, sec. 21 (w.e.f. 14-11-1994).

COMMENTS

1. Charging of Fares – Delhi Transport corporation are bound to charge fare in terms of statutory notification or rules. It cannot charge any fare in violation of the said notification; *Atma Prakash Goel* v. *State of Transport Authority*, AIR 2003 Del 69: 2003 (1) ACC 142.

2. Rules cannot Prevail Over Provisions of Act – The Rules framed under the Act cannot prevail over provisions of the Act and thus the Rules cannot provide any guideline for interpreting the provisions of section 67 or section 71 of the Act; *Shiv Raj* v. *State*, AIR 1992 Raj 99.

3. Limiting Scope or Fixing Number of Permits is Inconsistent with Provisions of Act – The directions under section 67 can be issued by the State Government only in the administrative matters which fall to be dealt with by the State Transport Authority or the Regional Transport Authorities under the relevant provisions of the Act in their Administrative capacity but these directions cannot be issued to interfere in the exercise of quasi-judicial functions of the S.T.A. or the R.T.As. The State in its discretion of exercising the direction cannot control the *quasi*-judicial functions of the State Transport Authority or the Regional Transport Authorities and the issuance of such type of directions limiting the scope or fixing the number of permits will be completely inconsistent with the provisions of the Act unaccepted by the judicial norms. If such type of directions are issued by the State Government then these directions will be contrary to the object of the provisions of the Act; *Shiv Raj* v. *State*, AIR 1992 Raj 99.

68. Transport Authorities.—(1) The State Government shall by notification in the Official Gazette, constitute for the State a State Transport Authority to exercise and discharge the powers and functions specified in sub-section (3), and shall in like manner constitute Regional Transport Authorities to exercise and discharge throughout such areas (in this Chapter referred to as regions) as may be specified in the notification in respect of each Regional Transport Authority; the powers and functions conferred by or under this Chapter on such Authorities:

Provided that in the Union Territories, the Administrator may abstain from constituting any Regional Transport Authority.

(2) A State Transport Authority or a Regional Transport Authority shall consist of a Chairman who has had judicial experience or experience as an appellate or a revisional authority or as an adjudicating authority competent to pass any order or take any decision under any law and in the case of a State Transport Authority, such other persons (whether officials or not), not being more than four and, in the case of a Regional Transport Authority, such other persons (whether officials or not), not being more than two, as the State Government may think fit to appoint; but no person who has any financial interest whether as proprietor, employee or otherwise in any transport undertaking shall be appointed, or continue to be, a member of a State or Regional Transport Authority, and, if any person being a member of a any such Authority acquires a financial interest in any transport undertaking, he shall within four weeks of so doing, give notice in writing to the State Government of the acquisition of such interest and shall vacate office:

Provided that nothing in this sub-section shall prevent any of the members of the State Transport Authority or a Regional Transport Authority, as the case may be, to preside over a meeting of such Authority during the absence of the Chairman, notwithstanding that such member does not possess judicial experience or experience as an appellate or a revisional authority or as an adjudicating authority competent to pass any order or take any decision under any law:

Provided further that the State Government may,—

(i) where it considers necessary or expedient so to do, constitute the State Transport Authority or a Regional Transport Authority for any region so as to consist of only one member who shall be an official with judicial experience or experience as an appellate or a revisional authority or as an adjudicating authority competent to pass any order or take any decision under any law;

(ii) by rules made in this behalf, provide for the transaction of business of such authorities in the absence of the Chairman of any other member and specify the circumstances under which, and the manner in which, such business could be so transacted:

Provided also that nothing in this sub-section shall be construed as debarring an official (other than an official connected directly with the management or operation of a transport undertaking) from being appointed or continuing as a member of any such authority merely by reason of the fact that the Government employing the official has, or acquires, any financial interest in a transport undertaking.

(3) The State Transport Authority and every Regional Transport Authority shall give effect to any directions issued under section 67 and the State Transport Authority shall, subject to such directions and save as otherwise provided by or under this Act, exercise and discharge throughout the State the following powers and functions, namely:—

(a) to coordinate and regulate the activities and policies of the Regional Transport Authorities, if any, of the State;

(b) to perform the duties of a Regional Transport Authority where there is no such Authority and, if it thinks fit or if so required by a Regional Transport Authority, to perform those duties in respect of any route common to two or more regions;

(c) to settle all disputes and decide all matters on which differences of opinion arise between Regional Transport Authorities; and

[1][(ca) Government to formulate routes for plying stage carriages;]

(d) to discharge such other functions as may be prescribed.

(4) For the purpose of exercising and discharging the powers and functions specified in sub-section (3), a State Transport Authority may, subject to such conditions as may be prescribed, issue directions to any Regional Transport Authority, and the Regional Transport Authority shall, in the discharge of its functions under this Act, give effect to and be guided by such directions.

(5) The State Transport Authority and any Regional Transport Authority, if authorised in this behalf by rules made under section 96, may delegate such of its powers and functions to such authority or person subject to such restrictions, limitations and conditions as may be prescribed by the said rules.

---

1. Ins. by Act 54 of 1994, sec. 22 (w.e.f. 14-11-1994).

SYNOPSIS

COMMENTS

1. Permits in Absence of Application – The State Transport Authority over the jurisdiction under section 68(3)(b) and granted 48 permits on the same day. Taking over jurisdiction under section 68(3)(b) and the grant of stage carriage permit are two different functions. The power to grant stage carriage permit is a quasi-judicial power. It was found that some of the applications were found to have made much after the date of order of grant. Some of the files have been sent to the Vigilance Department for inquiry and were not made available. Out of 36 files, some of them were without application for grant of permits yet the permits were granted. The grants, therefore, were not bona fide specifically in view of the fact that all the grants were made on the same day when the route was taken over and were made in a *mala fide* exercise of power with ulterior motive. Thus the grant of permits by the authority quashed; *M.K. Jain* v. *State Transport Appellate Tribunal*, AIR 2004 All 33: 2004 All LJ 406.

2. Direction to Authorities for Implementation of Provisions – The State Road Transport Corporation had sought the direction to the authorities for implementation of the provisions of the Motor Vehicles Act on principal ground that inaction on the part of the transport authorities, resulting heavy losses by allowing the private operators to ply the vehicles unauthorisedly or in contravention of the permits granted to them. Though the authorities of transport department have a legal duty, but at the same time, the Corporation should have a legal right. The right to seek implementation of the provisions of a statute is a general right and it is not a specific right which is acquired by the Corporation. The Corporation is one of the operators in the motor transport filed except with some privileges. Since the Act is conceived of in the interest of the citizens the Corporation may bring it to the notice of the authorities, if any illegalities are committed by the rival operators and it is the discretion of the authorities to proceed to take action as per law. It cannot seek the authorities to be compelled to perform the legal duty in a particular manner, only with a view to ensure that it is saved from the heavy losses. The Motor Vehicles Act enjoins upon the authorities to grant permits and to check illegal operation of the transport vehicles. But it would be rather impossible for them to detect each and every illegal transportation. That would not constitute inaction on the part of the authorities in not discharging their legal duties. Even though the Corporation brought it to the notice of the authorities, the instances where the alleged illegal transportations are taking place, yet, it cannot be a ground to seek the direction; *A.P.S.R.T.C.* v. *Transport Commissioner, Government of A.P., Hyderabad,* AIR 2000 AP 252: 2000 (2) Andh LD 387: 2000 (2) Andh LT 465.

3. Jurisdiction of State Transport Authority – The State Transport Authority has the jurisdiction to perform the duties of a Regional Transport Authority 'if it thinks fit' or if so required by a Regional Transport Authority. The term 'if it thinks fit' cannot be further circumscribed that there must be a request from the Regional Transport Authority before the State Transport Authority to exercise the power of Regional Transport Authority. It also cannot be limited to cases where there is no Regional Transport Authority. It is undoubtedly expected that such authority would be exercised by the State Transport Authority in a reasonable manner, as such exercise would clearly be amenable to judicial review. The State Transport Authority had the jurisdiction to grant permit even in the presence of the two Regional Transport Authorities functioning in the districts; *Sanjit Chakraborty* v. *State of West Bengal*, AIR 2007 Cal 252: 2007 AIHC 3288: 2007 (3) Cal HN 859.

4. Overriding Effect of Delegation of Power to Secretary – The delegation empowers only the Secretary to discharge the functions of State Transport Authority. Such delegation has got overriding effect on section 68 of the Motor Vehicles Act or making it redundant. Such a power is not conferred upon the State Government under section 96 of the Act. The state Rules being subordinate legislation framed by the State Government cannot have the overriding effect on Act enacted by the Union of India. If the Chairman and other Members of the State Transport Authority are busy in their day-to-day affairs of the posts held by them and are unable to attend the meetings of State Transport Authority for considering the applications to be disposed of by it, the State Government should not have constituted the State Transport Authority comprising of such high-rank officers, who, sometimes, are unable to discharge their own duties and functions on account of busy schedule for various reasons. The Government should have brought suitable amendment so that the Chairman and members of State Transport Authority who are able to devote full time for its functioning without hampering their routine works; *K.S.R.T.C.* v. *K.S.T. Authority*, AIR 2005 Kant 205: 2005 AIHC 1364: 2005 (3) KCCR 1645.

5. Collector as RTA not Aggrieved Person – Where the State Transport Authority had constituted the Collector as Regional Transport Authority and the Tribunal has changed the order of the Collector refusing to grant permit or variation of conditions of permit, the Collector was not the aggrieved person and, hence, the writ petition to challenge the order of the Tribunal at his instance was not competent. Once the powers have been exercised by the Collector as Regional Transport Authority, he has become *functus officio*. Therefore, after exercising the powers under section 80, either by refusing or granting permit to an applicant, the function of the Regional Transport Authority has become complete and he has no power to deal with the matter thereafter; *Regional Transport Authority* v. *State Transport Appellate Tribunal*, AIR 1995 Mad 226: 1994 (1) Mad LW 509: 1994 Writ LR 316.

6. Appointment of Chairman – Prohibition Clause when Attracted – Third proviso to section 68(2) enables the Government to appoint an official as a member of such authority even though the Government employing the official has, or acquires, any financial interest in a transport undertaking. This is subject to the condition that the official to be appointed by the Government as member of the Judge or Regional Transport Authority shall not be connected directly with the management or operation of a transport undertaking. The prohibition contained in third proviso to section 68(2) is attracted only if the official to be appointed as member of the State or Regional Transport Authority is connected directly with the management or operation of a transport undertaking and not otherwise. The use of the expression "connected directly" in the said proviso is quite significant. It connotes the active involvement of the person in the day to day management or operation of a transport undertaking. Thus pecuniary interest of a person, would render him ineligible to be appointed as member in view of the prohibition contained in section 68(2) but the disability clause contained in the third proviso will be attracted only if it is shown that the official concerned is connected directly with the management or operation of a transport undertaking and not otherwise; *Haryana Co-op. Transport S.W. Assocn.* v. *State of Haryana*, AIR 2000 P&H 230: 2000 (126) Pun LR 180: 2000 (2) Rec Civ R 685.

7. Expression "person" means – Section 68 mandates that no person who has any financial interest, whether as proprietor, employee or otherwise in any transport undertaking shall be appointed or continue to be a member of a Regional Transport Authority. The person concerned may be a proprietor, or an employee, or he may otherwise have financial interest in the transport undertaking. Clearly a proprietory concern also comes within the ambit of sub-section (2) of section 68. Even applying the dictionary meaning of the word "undertaking," an entity such as the Haryana Roadways, which is engaged in the business of providing transport service to the people must be held be an "undertaking." The use of the words "any undertaking" also makes it abundantly clear that the undertaking may be either a private undertaking or a Government or public sector undertaking including a statutory Corporation; *M.M. Co-op. T.S. Ltd.* v. *Financial C. and S. to Government, Haryana,* AIR 2002 SC 2513: 2002 AIR SCW 2826: JT 2002 (5) SC 125: 2002 (6) SCC 269: 2002 (5) SCALE 145: 2002 (5) Supreme 55.

8. Expression "Financial Interest" – The expression "financial interest" is capable of a narrower as well as a wider meaning. In the narrower sense it implies direct personal benefit of an economic nature. In the wider sense it may include any interest direct or indirect which a person has in relation to the finances of the undertaking. Such an interest may be the interest of an official who manages the finances of the undertaking or on whom rests the burden of financial accountability. Section 68(2) in express terms refers to a person having "any financial interest" as proprietor, employee or otherwise in any transport undertaking. The words employed are of the widest amplitude and expressly include an "employee" of an undertaking. The wide sweep of the language employed in section 68(2) particularly the use of the word "any" before "financial interest" clearly shows that the financial interest of the person concerned need not be direct personal financial interest, but includes the financial interest which he may have even as an employee of the undertaking; *M.M. Co-op. T.S. Ltd.* v. *Financial C. and S. to Government, Haryana,* AIR 2002 SC 2513: 2002 AIR SCW 2826: JT 2002 (5) SC 125: 2002 (6) SCC 269: 2002 (5) SCALE 145: 2002 (5) Supreme 55.

9. Chairman of Regional Transport Authority – Appointment – The Transport Commissioner of the State of Haryana has financial interest within the meaning of section 68(2) of the Act in the Government undertaking so as to render him ineligible for appointment as Chairman of the Regional Transport Authority; *M.M. Co-op. T.S. Ltd.* v. *Financial C. and S. to Government, Haryana,* AIR 2002 SC 2513: 2002 AIR SCW 2826: JT 2002 (5) SC 125: 2002 (6) SCC 269: 2002 (5) SCALE 145: 2002 (5) Supreme 55.

10. Transport Commissioner not Jurisdiction to Interpret Permit Issued under Act – The Transport Commissioner has no jurisdiction to interpret or vary a permit issued under the Act, as it is not a competent authority under the 1988 Act. The permits are issued by either the Regional Transport Authority or the State Transport Authority, as the case may be, as provided under sections 68, 71, 74 and 80(3) of the Motor Vehicles Act, 1988 which clearly indicates that the permit was for the non-notified portion. Hence the findings recorded in the impugned order that the permit was only for a notified route is absolutely perverse and against the material on record. The petitioner corporation being the State Transport Undertaking has preferential right for grant of State permits under the first proviso of section 71(3) of the 1988 Act with respect to non-notified routes. Merely because the corporation was plying on non-notified route did not mean that the corporation could not be granted permit on a non-notified route. The permits had been issued to the corporation by the State Transport Authority and hence the question of interpretation of the line of travel could only be decided by the State Transport Authority or the Appellate Tribunal. Hence the restriction imposed by the Transport Commissioner restraining Corporation to ply bus on non-notified route is not proper, absolutely illegal and without jurisdiction; *U.P. State Road Transport Corporation* v. *State of Uttar Pradesh,* AIR 2012 All 95: 2012 (2) ADJ 176: 2012 (91) All LR 559.

11. Fixing of Age of Vehicles – Under section 68 (3) of the Act, 1988, the STA subject to the directions issued by the State Government under section 67 shall exercise and discharge throughout the State the functions and powers as enumerated in sub-section (3). One of the functions provided in sub-section (3) is to co-ordinate and regulate the activities and policies of the R.T.A. Keeping in view serious air pollution and traffic problem, the STA has fixed the age of vehicles for safety and benefit of the general public. The fixing of age of the vehicles by the STA is not improper. The STA is fully justified to put model condition regarding age of vehicles including three wheeler. Thus the Regional Transport Authority, while granting permits, can impose model condition for grant of permit *i.e.*, fixing of age of the vehicles; *Mahraj Uddin* v. *State of Uttar Pradesh*, AIR 2011 All 151: 2010 (4) ALJ 542: 2010 (83) All LR 701.

12. Putting of Model Condition Regarding Age of Vehicles – Earlier the maximum age fixed for vehicles was 7 years but by subsequent order STA has fixed the age to 5 years The decision of the STA which is the basis for putting model condition in the petitioners permit that vehicles are to be changed after 5 years, having been set-aside, the period of 5 years in the model condition in the permits of the petitioners shall stand substituted by the period of 7 years which was prevalent prior to prior to order of STA would hold field; *Mahraj Uddin* v. *State of Uttar Pradesh*, AIR 2011 All 151: 2010 (4) ALJ 542: 2010 (83) All LR 701.

13. State Government – Duty-bound to Consider Objections and Give Reasons to Accept or Reject – Mandatory Requirement – Non-compliance – State is supposed to be acting in public interest while exercising power under section 102 of Act; *B.A. Linga Reddy* v. *Karnataka State Transport Authority*, (2015) 4 SCC 515.

14. Compliance with P.O.N.J. – *Quasi*-judicial Function; *B.A. Linga Reddy* v. *Karnataka State Transport Authority*, (2015) 4 SCC 515.

15. Non-notified Route which Overlaps same Like of Travel as Portion of Notified Route – Permit can't be granted; *B.A. Linga Reddy* v. *Karnataka State Transport Authority*, (2015) 4 SCC 515.

69. General provision as to applications for permits.—(1) Every application for a permit shall be made to the Regional Transport Authority of the region in which it is proposed to use the vehicle or vehicles:

Provided that if it is proposed to use the vehicle or vehicles in two or more regions lying within the same State, the application shall be made to the Regional Transport Authority of the region in which the major portion of the proposed route or area lies, and in case the portion of the proposed route or area in each of the regions is approximately equal, to the Regional Transport Authority of the region in which it is proposed to keep the vehicle or vehicles:

Provided further that if it is proposed to use the vehicle or vehicles in two or more regions lying in different States, the application shall be made to the Regional Transport Authority of the region in which the applicant resides or has his principal place of business.

(2) Notwithstanding anything contained in sub-section (1), the State Government may, by notification in the Official Gazette, direct that in the case of any vehicle or vehicles proposed to be used in two or more regions lying in different States, the application under that sub-section shall be made to the State Transport Authority of the region in which the applicant resides or has his principal place of business.

SYNOPSIS

1. Jurisdiction to Grant Permit in Case of Inter-district Routes
2. Counter Signature not Necessary
3. Stage Carriage Permit

COMMENTS

1. Jurisdiction to Grant Permit in Case of Inter-district Routes – The jurisdiction of the RTA to grant the permit in respect of inter-district routes has to be decided on the basis of the use of vehicle. But not the route length; *Elias Mathai* v. *Regional Transport Authority, Malappuram,* AIR 2003 Ker 53: 2003 (1) ACC 204: 2002 (3) Ker LT 434.

2. Counter Signature not Necessary – When a new permit can be granted under the provisions of the Act without any counter-signature, no useful purpose would be served in insisting upon such counter-signature from the Regional Transport Authority of the neighboring District, while implementing the order made under the provisions of the repealed enactment. Therefore it is not necessary for the respondent to obtain counter-signature; *Anna Transport Corporation Ltd.* v. *N. Ramasamy,* AIR 1996 Mad 82: 1995 (2) Mad LW 584.

3. Stage Carriage Permit – Application can be filed before Regional Transport Authority where he resides or principal place of business; *Dinesh Mehta* v. *STA, Odisha,* AIR 2015 Ori 88.

70. Application for stage carriage permit.—(1) An application for a permit in respect of a stage carriage (in this Chapter referred to as a stage carriage permit) or as a reserve stage carriage shall, as far as may be, contain the following particulars, namely:—

(a) the route or routes or the area or areas to which the application relates;

(b) the type and seating capacity of each such vehicle;

(c) the minimum and maximum number of daily trips proposed to be provided and the time-table of the normal trips.

Explanation.—For the purposes of this section, section 72, section 80 and section 102, "trip" means a single journey from one point to another, and every return journey shall be deemed to be a separate trip;

(d) the number of vehicles intended to be kept in reserve to maintain the service and to provide for special occasions;

(e) the arrangements intended to be made for the housing, maintenance and repair of the vehicles, for the comfort and convenience of passengers and for the storage and safe custody of luggage;

(f) such other matters as may be prescribed.

(2) An application referred to in sub-section (1) shall be accompanied by such documents as may be prescribed.

SYNOPSIS

1. Grant or Renewal of Permit to Stage Carriage Operator is Saved under the Nationalised Scheme
2. Application for Stage Carriage Permit
3. Words "the route or routes"
4. Permits can be Granted to Various Parties in Absence of Provisions
5. Renewal of Permit after Enforcement of New Act
6. Permit Holder cannot Object Granting of New Permit
7. Furnishing of Particulars in Application Form
8. Word "Permit" includes Permits
9. Application for Permit can be made only after Route is Open
10. Grant of Stage Carriage Permit

COMMENTS

1. Grant or Renewal of Permit to Stage Carriage Operator is Saved under the Nationalised Scheme – No third party private operators are entitled to apply for permits on the same notified route or part thereof, nor are they entitled to compete with them for grant of permit, since the right of all other private operators to apply for and operate in the approved notified area, route or a part thereof, has been frozen. The right is reserved only in relation to the named operators and that too for specified permit, and none else. Along with the application under section 70 of New Act filed for grant of permit under section 72 or renewal under section 81 made by the named holder of a specified permit in an approved scheme, he should enclose an authenticated copy of the approved scheme, the details of the route on which he was plying his stage carriage with corridor restrictions on over lapping routes. The RTA or STA, as the case may be should verify the original under which the named operator, whose specified permit was saved, whether he is entitled to ply the stage carriage in the approved scheme with the condition of the corridor restrictions on the notified scheme and if so to what extent. The named stage carriage operators whose permits are granted under the old Act are saved under the nationalised scheme. The RTA or STA, as the case may be, should consider and may grant permits or renewal of permits as per law or rejection thereof for reasons to be recorded in that behalf; *Pancham Chand* v. *State of Himachal Pradesh,* 2008 AIR SCW 2111: 2008 (7) SCC 117: 2008 (3) SCALE 378.

2. Application for Stage Carriage Permit – Chief Minister of a State has no role to play in the matter of grant of stage carriage permit. Neither can he entertain any application nor can he pass any order thereon. Section 72 of empowers the Regional Transport Authority to grant stage carriage permit in respect of any route or the area specified in the application. The State, although, have a general control but such control must be exercised strictly in terms of article 162 of the Constitution of India. Having regard to the nature and the manner of the control specified therein, it may lay down a policy. Statutory authorities are bound to act in terms thereof, but per se the same does not authorize any Minister including the Chief Minister to act in derogation of the statutory provisions. Any such interference on the part of any authority upon whom the Act does not confer any jurisdiction, is wholly unwarranted in law; *Pancham Chand* v. *State of Himachal Pradesh,* 2008 AIR SCW 2111: 2008 (7) SCC 117: 2008 (3) SCALE 378.

3. Words "the route or routes" – The plain reading of the provisions of section 70 shows that the words "the route or routes" occurring in clause (a) of sub-section (1) of section 70 are very important. It clearly goes to show that an application for a permit can be moved for the route or routes. In other words, a single application, for a single permit can be moved for one or more routes; *Prem Narain Sharma* v. *State Transport Appellate Tribunal, Gwalior,* AIR 1998 MP 229: 1998 (2) Jab LJ 250: 1999 (1) MPLJ 185.

4. Permits can be Granted to Various Parties in Absence of Provisions – Under the new Act of the policy is for grant of free permit subject to any restriction imposed by the provisions of the Act. Thus the old concept of strength of the route as provided in the old Act has been done away with. Therefore, ordinarily all permits applied for any route are to be granted unless the route or part thereof is nationalised or there is some prohibition or restriction by any provision of the new Act. The provision of section 70 only relates to the speed at which the vehicle may be driven and that aspect has to be seen by the R.T.A. before granting a permit so that the prescribed speed may not be contravened. However, there is no provision which prohibits grant of permits to various parties who furnish the same time-table. In the absence of any such provision, the R.T.A. can grant permits to various parties who furnish the same time-table; *Aftab Ahmad* v. *State Transport Appellate Tribunal, Lucknow,* AIR 1997 All 176: 1997 All LJ 833: 1997 (31) All LR 326.

5. Renewal of Permit after Enforcement of New Act – For stage carriage permits granted under the Repealed Act, if they stand to expire or expired after the date of enforcement of new Act, without any pending application for renewal having been made under section 58 as on the date of enforcement of new Act, fresh application under section 70 should be filed and after consideration under section 71, permits be obtained as per law under section 72; *Nataraj Ukkund* v. *Karnataka State Transport Appellate Tribunal*, AIR 1998 Kant 58.

6. Permit Holder cannot Object Granting of New Permit – A permit holder cannot object to the granting of permit. His only right is to contest the timings; *Joseph Chacko* v. *Regional Transport Authority, Kottayam*, AIR 2000 Ker 356.

The existing operators have no right to object to the grant of new permit and their right is only confined to the objection regarding timings; *Ushakumari* v. *Abdul Azeez*, (2000) 1 Ker LJ 141: 2000 AIHC 1015; *Mithilesh Garg* v. *Union of India*, (1992) 1 Ker LJ 247: AIR 1992 SC 443: 1992 AIR SCW 41.

7. Furnishing of Particulars in Application Form – Even though it is not mandatory on the part of an applicant to furnish the particulars of the vehicle in the application when it is submitted, he is legally obliged to furnish all the particulars of the vehicle before the application is taken up for consideration by the Regional/State Transport Authority; *R. Natarajan* v. *State Transport Appellate Tribunal, Ernakulam*, AIR 1999 Ker 207.

8. Word "Permit" includes Permits – The provisions contained in section 70 of the Act, have to be interpreted not in a pedantic manner but taking into consideration the provisions contained in section 13 of the General Clauses Act, which provides that in all Central Acts and Regulations, unless there is anything repugnant in the subject or context, words in the singular shall include the plural, and vice versa. The word, 'permit'. Include permits; *Vivek Dwivedi* v. *Prem Narain*, AIR 1999 MP 1: 1998 (2) MPLJ 618: 1999 (1) Civ LJ 351.

9. Application for Permit can be made only after Route is Open – The application can be for the route in existence and not for the proposed route or the route which is under contemplation only. Thus the application for permit can be submitted only after the route is open. The application submitted prior to the opening of the route is incompetent and premature application; *Deva Ram* v. *State of Rajasthan*, AIR 2006 Raj 180: 2006 (5) ALJ (NOC) 1138: 2007 (1) ACC 617.

10. Grant of Stage Carriage Permit – Where the Scheme prohibits operation by a private operator no permit can be granted to operate on a notified route or a portion thereof. The only exception to that is where a private operator has to intersect a notified route, an intersection of a notified route does not amount to traversing or overlapping the notified route because the prohibition imposed applies to the whole or part of the route on the same line only. An intersection cuts across the notified route and does not permit traversing the same line of travel on a notified route. Thus though overlapping was for short length, permit could not be granted in view of the Scheme which prohibits such operation; *Kerala State Road Transport Corporation* v. *Regional Transport Authority, Kollam*, AIR 2013 Ker 120: 2013 (2) Ker LJ 384: 2013 (2) Ker LT 280.

71. Procedure of Regional Transport Authority in considering application for stage carriage permit.—(1) A Regional Transport Authority shall, while considering an application for a stage carriage permit, have regard to the objects of this Act.

[1][***]

(2) A Regional Transport Authority shall refuse to grant a stage carriage permit if it appears from any time-table furnished that the provisions of this

1. Proviso omitted by Act 54 of 1994, sec. 23 (w.e.f. 14-11-1994).

Act relating to the speed at which vehicles may be driven are likely to be contravened:

Provided that before such refusal an opportunity shall be given to the applicant to amend the time-table so as to conform to the said provisions.

(3) (a) The State Government shall, if so directed by the Central Government having regard to the number of vehicles, road conditions and other relevant matters, by notification in the Official Gazette, direct a State Transport Authority and a Regional Transport Authority to limit the number of stage carriages generally or of any specified type, as may be fixed and specified in the notification, operating on city routes in towns with a population of not less than five lakhs.

(b) Where the number of stage carriages are fixed under clause (a), the Government of the State shall reserve in the State certain percentage of stage carriage permits for the scheduled castes and the scheduled tribes in the same ratio as in the case of appointments made by direct recruitment to public services in the State.

(c) Where the number of stage carriages are fixed under clause (a), the Regional Transport Authority shall reserve such number of permits for the scheduled castes and the scheduled tribes as may be fixed by the State Government under sub-clause (b).

(d) After reserving such number of permits as is referred to in clause (c), the Regional Transport Authority shall in considering an application have regard to the following matters, namely:—

(i) financial stability of the applicant;

(ii) satisfactory performance as a stage carriage operator including payment of tax if the applicant is or has been an operator of stage carriage service; and

(iii) such other matters as may be prescribed by the State Government:

Provided that, other conditions being equal, preference shall be given to applications for permits from—

(i) State transport undertakings;

(ii) co-operative societies registered or deemed to have been registered under any enactment for the time being in force; [1][***]

(iii) ex-servicemen; [3][or]

[2][(iv) any other class or category of persons, as the State Government may, for reasons to be recorded in writing, consider necessary.]

[3][***]

Explanation.—For the purposes of this section "company" means any body corporate, and includes a firm or other association of individuals; and "director", in relation to a firm, means a partner in the firm.

1. The word "or" omitted by Act 54 of 1994, sec. 23 (w.e.f. 14-11-1994).
2. Ins. by Act 54 of 1994, sec. 23 (w.e.f. 14-11-1994).
3. Sub-sections (4) and (5) omitted by Act 54 of 1994, sec. 23 (w.e.f. 14-11-1994).

SYNOPSIS

COMMENTS

1. Determination of Town Service Routes – Only on the basis of the Transport Commissioner's permission the Regional Transport Authority can determine the town service routes. Hence the permission of the Transport Commissioner contemplated in rule 258(2) of the rules has to be obtained before an application for permit is filed for a route covered by a scheme notified under the Act. The grant of permit by the Tribunal before the grant of permission by the Transport Commissioner was therefore without jurisdiction; *A.P.S.R.T.C.* v. *State Transport Appellate Tribunal,* AIR 1998 SC 2621: 1998 AIR SCW 2663: JT 1998 (5) SC 417: 1998 (7) SCC 353: 1998 (3) SCR 1106: 1998 (4) SCALE 445: 1998 (6) Supreme 316.

2. Authority cannot Refuse Permit Merely of Number of Operators on Route – The primary duty for the Regional Transport Authority is to find out whether the issue of permit is necessary for the travelling public. Even though the Regional Transport Authority has stated that for the route a number of permits have been issued, it has not taken into account the fact that the route is one which is mostly frequented by the travelling public. If necessity exists, then the Regional Transport Authority cannot refuse to grant permits on the ground that there are number of operators on the route. The orders of the Regional Transport Authority have not considered these points. In a State which is thickly populated and the ordinary mode of transportation is by bus, the Regional Transport Authority should take more care when it takes a decision that it will not issue permits on the route, because it is oversaturated. Further, any decision taken regarding the non-grant of permit cannot be said to be permanent. Even if the Regional Transport Authority had taken a decision more than six months back that permit need not be issued, that decision would require reconsideration in the light of subsequent developments; *Joseph Chacko* v. *Regional Transport Authority, Kottayam,* AIR 2000 Ker 356.

3. Existing Operators do not have Right of being Heard at Time of Grant of Permits – The existing operators do not have a right of being heard at the time of grant of permits on their route. Every statutory authority knows its duty and function. Granting permits by the RTA is *quasi*-judicial function. There is a presumption that every Act of such an authority shall be regularly performed, *i.e.,* carried out in accordance with law. There is nothing on record to rebut the said presumption. The existing operators cannot have any grievance at this stage. The only remedy to the existing operators is to file a revision under section 90 of the Act, if they are aggrieved of any resolution passed by the RTA; *Jameela Begum* v. *State of Uttar Pradesh,* AIR 2006 All 144: 2006 AIHC 1600: 2006 (2) ALJ 267.

4. Policy of Grant of Permit – Social and economic status does not make a man different from any other person in the matter of grant of permits. Similarly, since the policy of grant of permit has been liberlised to attract open market force the question of economics in direction No.(3) cannot be a factor to be taken into account. Further the Regional transport, has no authority to limit the number of permits on the particular route. The question of limiting the number of 35 permits in the route cannot be sustained in view of section 71(3) of the said Act; *Shamim Haider* v. *Regional Transport Authority, Meerut*, AIR 1995 All 385: 1996 All LJ 27.

5. Granting of Permit on Basis of "First Come First Serve" not Proper – The permit shall not be granted on the basis of 'first come first serve'. In fact, every one has a right to apply for a permit from amongst whom the choice has to be made by the transport authority in accordance with the provisions contained in the Act itself and only suitable candidate in order of suitability or merit is to be selected; *Shamim Haider* v. *Regional Transport Authority, Meerut*, AIR 1995 All 385: 1996 All LJ 27.

6. Mere Submission of Application before Notification does not Confer any Right – Whereby the petitioner was not permitted to operate his vehicle on the route the operation of vehicle is in clear violation of the notification which prohibits not only formulation of new route but also grant of new permit for any vehicle which may pass through the central business district. No valuable right was accrued in favour of the petitioner though the petitioner submitted the application prior to issuance of the notification. As a matter of fact no right, can accrue in favour of an applicant by mere submission of an application for such grant. Right to obtain such permit matures into actionable right only when the applicant fulfils the conditions as mentioned in the offer letter; *State of West Bengal* v. *Prabir Chatterjee*, AIR 2008 Cal 217: 2008 AIHC 936 (NOC): 2008 (2) Cal LJ 496.

7. Authority cannot Adopt Unpublished Policy – Where in the advertisement inviting applications for stage carriage permit it was not mentioned whether there was any reservation for the Scheduled Caste or for that matter physically handicapped candidates, or any other reserved category or minority or otherwise, though the statute permitted the authorities to make reservation and the reservation policy was followed not only in case of Scheduled Caste candidates but also in case of ex-servicemen, physically handicapped and minority community, thus while taking decision the State Transport authority followed such norms and procedures, which were not published nor made known to the public in any manner whatsoever, Such decision of authorities could not be upheld because had there been proper publication, perhaps large number of physically handicapped and disabled persons and Scheduled Caste Candidates, Ex-service men candidates or minority community candidates could have come. The Statutory authority cannot exercise its jurisdiction adopting secret and unpublished policy or norms. Transparency in action either in executive field or *quasi*-judicial field is one of the facets of observance of principle of natural justice; *Rina Maity* v. *State of West Bengal*, AIR 2003 Cal 124.

8. No Bar to Grant more than Five Permits – For granting of stage carriage permit there is no such bar to grant more than five carriage stage permits to any individual, if otherwise eligible and succeeds. Therefore the decision of the State Transport Authority, imposing restrictions to grant more than one carriage permit to an individual for the same route is arbitrary, illegal and against the provisions of the Act; *Subodh Prasad* v. *State of Jharkhand*, AIR 2003 Jhar 72: 2003 (2) ACC 346: 2003 (3) JCR JHA 690.

9. Joint Survey Report not Necessary – As per the permit, the proposed route is from Coorg border to Somwarpet and back. But an error has crept in, in the resolution wherein it was noted that the application was from Coorg border to Kodlipet and back. Therefore, a corrigendum has been issued by the RTA correcting the mistake that has crept-in in its resolution. If the application of the petitioner is read along with the resolution, assignment of timing and the proposed route in the permit, it is clear that RTA has considered grant of permit on the route from Coorg border to Somwarpet. The Corrigendum has only corrected the mistake that had crept-in in the resolution. No prejudice, whatsoever has been caused to the contesting respondents by the correction of the mistake. It is not the case of the respondents that the route from Coorg border to Somwarpet traverses the notified routes. Therefore, securing a joint route survey report is unnecessary. RTA was justified in granting permit to the petitioner on the route from Coorg border to Somwarpet because it is in conformity with the application of the petitioner seeking grant of permit. The Tribunal has erred in holding that the RTA has considered the application for the route not applied for by the petitioner; *B.A. Bhavikumar* v. *Regional Transport Authority,* AIR 2006 Kant 160: 2006 AIHC 2232: 2006 (2) Kant LJ 191.

10. Advance Fixation of Time Schedule – Every citizen has a right to engage in stage carriage operation, in exercise of his fundamental rights guaranteed under article 19(1)(g) of the Constitution of India. The provisions of the Motor Vehicles Act impose reasonable restrictions on the said right. Any action, regulating a fundamental right guaranteed under article 19(1)(g) should be supported by relevant statutory provisions referable to article 19(6). An application for permit presented with a settled set of timings, is not contemplated. Settlement of time schedule is contemplated only after the grant of the permit and before issuing the same. Advance fixation of time schedule will be permissible, if only the provisions of the Act and the Rules expressly provide for it; *K.S. Somarajan* v. *Regional Transport Authority,* AIR 2007 Ker 75: 2007 AIHC 1278: 2006 (4) Ker LT 628.

11. Reservation of Permits for State Transport Undertaking – The State Government has been empowered to formulate and publish schemes for running of road transport services in any route or area by the State Road Transport undertaking in exclusion of others complete or partial. When such schemes are published, no permit can be issued to any private operator except as provided under the scheme itself. Thus, the law empowered the State to publish such schemes for monopolising the operation of services on such notified routes or area. But so far as section 71(3) of the Act was concerned, the law specifically granted a right of priority alone to the State Transport undertaking. The reservation of certain permits in favour of State Transport undertaking therefore was not in accordance with law and was beyond the powers conferred under the Statute and was ultra vires of the powers; *K.P. Ajith Kumar* v. *Regional Transport Authority, Kozhikode,* AIR 2002 Ker 178: 2002 (2) ACC 115: 2002 (1) Ker LT 775.

12. Not Applicable to Vehicles Owned by State Transport Undertaking – Vehicles of a specified type mentioned in the sections 71(3) and 74(3) cannot be taken as vehicles owned by the State Transport undertaking, when the right of preference in respect of the State Transport undertaking is specifically dealt with in the same sub-section. The vehicles of specified type mentioned therein can only be in respect of the nature or type or model of the vehicle and it can never be taken as the vehicles owned by a person or an undertaking. Hence, the stage carriages operated by the State Transport undertaking cannot be treated as "specified type" of stage carriages. The term specified type mentioned in section 71 is in respect of the nature or type or model of the vehicles and not in respect of the vehicles owned and operated by the State Transport undertaking; *K.P. Ajith Kumar* v. *Regional Transport Authority, Kozhikode,* AIR 2002 Ker 178: 2002 (2) ACC 115.

13. Computation of Number of Permits – A temporary permit is not a species or a kind of stage-carriage permit and also the object underlying the provision of ceiling contained in section 71(4), a temporary permit should not be taken into account while computing the number of stage carriage permits for which ceiling is fixed in section 71(4) of the Act; *Sushil Madan Bairagi* v. *State Transport Appellate Tribunal,* AIR 1993 MP 128.

14. Notification Deemed to be Issued under provisions of New Act – The Notification issued in terms of sub-section (1)(a) of section 47 conforms to the provision enacted in sub-section (3)(b) of section 71 of the new Act. The old and the new provisions, both envisage reservation in the matter of grant of stage carriage permit for Scheduled Castes and Scheduled Tribes and indeed, the two provisions are in *pari materia* achieving complete verbal congruence in the use of language. Thus the Notification though it is issued under the old Act, it is not inconsistent" with the provisions of the new Act and can be deemed to be issued under the correspondent provision of the new Act and is thereby saved; *Shivchand Amolakchand Bus Operator* v. *S.T. Appellate Tribunal,* AIR 1990 MP 300.

15. Consideration of Application through Lottery Process – In a lottery method, element of chance or luck is inherent and is within the boundaries of gambling. Its consequences are pernicious because by sheer luck an intending applicant whose financial stability is in the doldrums, or whose performance as a stage carriage operator is unsatisfactory or who is in arrears in the matter of payment of tax might come out as a successful applicant in the lottery process. The decision of the R.T.A. to consider all the applications for stage carriage permit through lottery process" is illegal and unauthorised; *Rajni Bala Das* v. *Regional Transport Authority, Cuttack,* AIR 2003 Ori 28: 2003 (1) Civ LJ 874: 2002 (94) Cut LT 572.

16. Considerations for Grant of Permit – The STA can take into consideration relevant materials or circumstances having bearing on the issue which may emerge during the period from the date of applications till it takes up the applications for consideration subject of course to the wholesome principles of natural justice. The experience gained by an applicant on the basis of temporary permit granted to him on the disputed route during post application period will be a plus point in favour of the applicant; *Samuel Pani* v. *Ramesh Chandra Mallick,* AIR 1994 Ori 231.

17. Trafficking in Permit – Where two stage carriage permits were granted on the same route in favour of the applicant and his son operating in opposite direction and the applicant's application for transfer of his permit in favour of his son was allowed on ground that convenience of travelling public would be better served if his permit was transferred in favour of his son, as otherwise lot of difficulties would be experienced by the public, such transfer of permit by applicant with permission of authority would not be trafficking in permit and would not be germane consideration for deciding his application for grant of stage carriage permit on different route, nor can it be held to be an inefficiency on the part of the applicant in operating a major portion of the route applied for and thereby would adversely affect his right of consideration for the applied for route; *Udayanath Pani* v. *State Transport Authority, Cuttack,* AIR 1993 Ori 14.

18. Person in Default as Regards Payment of Tax – Where an order of stay against the demand of tax under Orissa Motor Vehicles Taxation Act was passed by the Appellate Authority under section 18 of the said Act, it was not open to the State Transport Authority discharging the powers vested in him under section 71 of the Motor Vehicles Act to deny the grant of permit on the ground that the performance of the applicant was not satisfactory as a stage carriage operator as regards payment of tax. There is an order of stay in operation. Hence, until the stay order was vacated and the applicant was thereafter in default, it could not be held that he was a person in default as regards payment of tax within meaning of sub-clause (ii) of clause (d) of sub- section (3) of section 71 of the Motor Vehicles Act; *State Transport Authority, Orissa* v. *Presiding Officer, State Transport Appellate Tribunal,* AIR 1992 Ori 13: 1991 (72) Cut LT 157: 1991 (2) Ori LR 29.

19. Opportunity to an End Time – There is no provision in the Act for out-right rejection of an application for grant of stage carriage permit, if the time-table proposed in the application contravenes the provisions of the Act relating to speed at which the vehicle may be driven at a particular type of road. The Act provides for such a condition but the provisions of the Act are not mandatory in character. Even if it is treated that the provisions of the Act are mandatory in nature, they do not provide that if the time-table proposed in the permit contravenes the provisions of the Act relating to the speed, keeping in view the width, traffic and the nature of the road and vehicle plied on the route and other factors which are relevant for such a consideration, such an application for grant of stage carriage permit is liable to be rejected outrightly. In such circumstances, an opportunity will have to be granted to such an applicant to amend his time-table so as to conform to the said provisions; *Ramkumar* v. *Secretary, R.T.A., Bikaner,* AIR 1993 Raj 30: 1992 (1) Raj LR 314: 1992 (2) Raj LW 27.

20. Mere Proposal not Condition of Permit – The R.T.A. or its delegate has to be examined whether the time-table proposed in the application should be approved or some other time-table should be provided. If it is a case of grant of a totally new route, time-table proposed in the application can be approved provided it does not contravene the provisions of speed-limit provided by the Act but if it is a case of grant of a permit on the existing route where other vehicles are also running and their time-tables have been approved by the R.T.A. or his delegate then the R.T.A. has every power to accept or not to accept the proposed time-table. The proposed time-table does not become a condition of the permit even after the stage of modification or variation under the orders of the competent authority its sole purpose is that the vehicle or traffic on that route may be properly monitored and guided and every sort of conflict in plying of the buses may be avoided. The mere proposal does not become a condition of the permit and the R.T.A. is not obliged to accept that. He has every authority to prescribe a time-table for the running of the buses and, therefore and the Secretary, R.T.A. can vary that proposal; *Ramkumar* v. *Secretary, R.T.A., Bikaner,* AIR 1993 Raj 30.

21. State Transport Undertaking has Preferential Right for Grant of State Permits – The Transport Commissioner has no jurisdiction to interpret or vary a permit issued under the Act, as it is not a competent authority under the 1988 Act. The permits are issued by either the Regional Transport Authority or the State Transport Authority, as the case may be, as provided under sections 68, 71, 74 and 80(3) of the Motor Vehicles Act, 1988 which clearly indicates that the permit was for the non-notified portion. Hence the findings recorded in the impugned order that the permit was only for a notified route is absolutely perverse and against the material on record. The petitioner corporation being the State Transport Undertaking has preferential right for grant of State permits under the first proviso of section 71(3) of the 1988 Act with respect to non-notified routes; *U.P. State Road Transport Corporation* v. *State of Uttar Pradesh,* AIR 2012 All 95: 2012 (2) ADJ 176: 2012 (91) All LR 559.

22. Revision – Violation of Statutory Prohibitions – Existing permit-holder has no right to file revision under section 90; *M.C. Ratheesh* v. *The Secretary, Regional Transport Authority, Thrissur,* AIR 2015 Ker 86.

23. Stage Carriage Permit – Rival Operators have no *locus standi* to challenge transport permit in favour of other operator; *Dinesh Mehta* v. *STA, Odisha,* AIR 2015 Ori 88.

24. Stage Carriage Permit – Cancellation at the Instance of Rival Operator – Amounts to deprivation of enjoyment of Fundamental Rights under Article 19(1)(g) of Constitution; *Dinesh Mehta* v. *STA, Odisha,* AIR 2015 Ori 88.

72. Grant of stage carriage permit.—(1) Subject to the provisions of section 71, a Regional Transport Authority may, on an application made to it under section 70, grant a stage carriage permit in accordance with the application or with such modifications as it deems fit or refuse to grant such a permit:

Provided that no such permit shall be granted in respect of any route or area not specified in the application.

(2) The Regional Transport Authority, if it decides to grant a stage carriage permit, may grant the permit for a stage carriage of a specified description and may, subject to any rule that may be made under this Act, attach to the permit any one or more of the following conditions, namely:—

(i) that the vehicles shall be used only in a specified area, or on a specified route or routes;

(ii) that the operation of the stage carriage shall be commenced with effect from a specified date;

(iii) the minimum and maximum number of daily trips to be provided in relation to any route or area generally or on specified days and occasions;

(iv) that copies of the time-table of the stage carriage approved by the Regional Transport Authority shall be exhibited on the vehicles and at specified stands and halts on the route or within the area;

(v) that the stage carriage shall be operated within such margins of deviation from the approved time-table as the Regional Transport Authority may from time to time specify;

(vi) that within municipal limits and such other areas and places as may be prescribed, passengers or goods shall not be taken up or set down except at specified points;

(vii) the maximum number of passengers and the maximum weight of luggage that may be carried on the stage carriage, either generally or on specified occasions or at specified times and seasons;

(viii) the weight and nature of passengers' luggage that shall be carried free of charge, the total weight of luggage that may be carried in relation to each passenger, and the arrangements that shall be made for the carriage of luggage without causing inconvenience to passengers;

(ix) the rate of charge that may be levied for passengers' luggage in excess of the free allowance;

(x) that vehicles of a specified type fitted with body conforming to approved specifications shall be used:

Provided that the attachment of this condition to a permit shall not prevent the continued use, for a period of two years from the date of publication of the approved specifications, of any vehicle operating on that date;

(xi) that specified standards of comfort and cleanliness shall be maintained in the vehicles;

(xii) the conditions subject to which goods may be carried in the stage carriage in addition to or to the exclusion of passengers;

(xiii) that fares shall be charged is accordance with the approved fare table;

(xiv) that a copy of or extract from the fare table approved by the Regional Transport Authority and particulars of any special fares or rates of fares so approved for particular occasions shall be exhibited on the stage carriage and at specified stands and halts;

(xv) that tickets bearing specified particulars shall be issued to passengers and shall show the fares actually charged and that records of tickets issued shall be kept in a specified manner;

(xvi) that mails shall be carried on the vehicle subject to such conditions (including conditions as to the time in which mails are to be carried and the charges which may be levied) as may be specified;

(xvii) the vehicles to be kept as reserve by the holder of the permit to maintain the operation and to provide for special occasions;

(xviii) the conditions subject to which vehicle may be used as a contract carriage;

(xix) that specified arrangements shall be made for the housing, maintenance and repair of vehicle;

(xx) that any specified bus station or shelter maintained by Government or a local authority shall be used and that any specified rent or fee shall be paid for such use;

(xxi) that the conditions of the permit shall not be departed from, save with the approval of the Regional Transport Authority;

(xxii) that the Regional Transport Authority may, after giving notice of not less than one month,—

(a) vary the conditions of the permit;

(b) attach to the permit further conditions:

Provided that the conditions specified in pursuance of clause (i) shall not be varied so as to alter the distance covered by the original route by more than 24 kilometres, and any variation within such limits shall be made only after the Regional Transport Authority is satisfied that such variation will serve the convenience of the public and that it is not expedient to grant a separate permit in respect of the original route as so varied or any part thereof;

(xxiii) that the holder of a permit shall furnish to the Regional Transport Authority such periodical returns, statistics and other information as the State Government may from time to time prescribe;

(xxiv) any other conditions which may be prescribed.

SYNOPSIS

COMMENTS

1. Grant of Stage Carriage Permit to Private Vehicle Operators – Once a scheme is notified it prohibits the plying of private vehicle except as permitted by Scheme. In notified Scheme private operator can operate only as permitted by the Scheme. Both Schemes nowhere permit operation by private operators. No permit could have been granted on the route as both schemes are of total exclusion; *Uttar Pradesh State Road Transport Corporation* v. *Omaditya Verma,* AIR 2005 SC 2250: 2005 AIR SCW 2097: JT 2005 (4) SC 62: 2005 (4) SCC 424: 2005 (3) SCALE 636: 2005 (3) Supreme 521.

2. Grant of Stage Carriage Permit – Copy of the approved scheme or draft scheme, if any, has not been placed before the court. Whether the scheme excludes the private operators wholly or partly does not known to court. Further the State Transport Undertaking has not chosen to challenge the grant of permits to the appellants. It is only the Respondents who are operating on a route which partially overlaps the route concerned that have chosen to come forward. Thus the court has inclined to entertain the said objection at their instance, more particularly, when a copy of the scheme(s) even has not been filed. This aspect would become relevant if and when the State Transport Undertaking objects to the grant of permits to the appellants and the approved scheme or draft scheme, as the case may be, is placed before the Court in support of the said objection; *Mithilesh Rani* v. *Regional Transport Authority, Dehradun,* AIR 1994 SC 2229: 1994 AIR SCW 2037: JT 1994 (3) SC 34.

Where the Scheme prohibits operation by a private operator no permit can be granted to operate on a notified route or a portion thereof. The only exception to that is where a private operator has to intersect a notified route, an intersection of a notified route does not amount to traversing or overlapping the notified route because the prohibition imposed applies to the whole or part of the route on the same line only. An intersection cuts across the notified route and does not permit traversing the same line of travel on a notified route. Thus though overlapping was for short length, permit could not be granted in view of the Scheme which prohibits such operation; *Kerala State Road Transport Corporation* v. *Regional Transport Authority, Kollam,* AIR 2013 Ker 120: 2013 (2) Ker LJ 384: 2013 (2) Ker LT 280.

3. Extension of Period of Validity of after Letter – If the benefit of extension was given to the petitioner, then, in view of the provisions of rule 141, the offer letter could remain valid for six months when it was actually issued. Within that six months he did not produce the vehicle and seek the permit. He purchased a vehicle only after that period. Simply because it was registered by making a reference to the offer letter, it cannot be said that he acquired a right to seek extension of the period of validity of the offer letter beyond the statutory period of six months. At the date the vehicle was registered, the offer letter was not alive; *Chapal Kumar Gayen* v. *State of West Bengal,* AIR 2009 Cal 81: 2009 AIHC 403 (NOC): 2009 (3) ALJ (NOC) 554.

4. Authority can Impose any Condition while Granting Renewing Permit – The petitioner was earlier granted stage carriage permit. At the time of renewal of the said permit, the condition for replacing the existing model Bus by a higher model has been imposed. The law provides that conditions, can be imposed by the authority for granting stage carriage permit while granting permit to a person and. The authority can also impose a condition that the vehicles should be of a specified type fitted with body conforming to approved specification but for imposing the said condition the permit holder cannot be prevented from the continued use, for a period of two years from the date of publication of the approved specification of any vehicle operating on that date. No contrary provision has been placed in the matter of grant/renewal of stage carriage permit, under which the authority can impose any condition while granting/renewing of such permit without giving any prior notice particularly of a condition for replacing the Bus itself; *Giribala Jha* v. *State of Jharkhand,* AIR 2007 Jhar 47: 2007 (1) ACC 779: 2007 (2) Cur CC 482.

5. Renewal of Old Permit – The Regional Transport Authority, has acted in excess of the jurisdiction in passing the order of renewal of old permit which had been granted under the old Act by wrongly assuming the jurisdiction to grant renewal, on the basis of wrong interpretation and consideration of section 217A. Section 217A did not apply. The RTA has to consider the application above for fresh permit. The Regional Transport Authority ignoring that passed the order without jurisdiction. Therefore, the impugned order has been quashed; *Sathish Nayak* v. *Regional Transport Authority*, AIR 2001 Kant 214: 2001 AIR Kant HCR 984.

6. Scope of Powers of Regional Transport Authority – The Regional Transport Authority has power to vary or modify the conditions of stage carriage permit including the power to modify timings. Before exercising such power Regional Transport Authority is required to give a notice of not less than one month period. Giving of notice is not a mere formality. It means that notice should be given and if any party or permit holder, affected, files any objection, then his objections have also got to be considered and it is thereafter any order varying the condition of the permit or attaching any further conditions may be passed. When the law so provides, the manner for doing or exercising of this power, the intention of the legislature appears to be that power to vary condition or to attach further conditions shall not be exercised otherwise than the mode provided under the provision of the Act. In other words it can be said that power to modify the conditions vested in the authority is not exercisable without giving due notice of a period of not less than one month; *N. Muddappa* v. *Secretary, Regional Transport Authority, Bangalore,* AIR 1998 Kant 61: 1998 (1) ACC 56: 1997 (4) Kant LJ 409.

7. RTA has to Meet at Least once in a Month – The Rule authorises the Chairman to hold meeting on such other occasions for the dispatch of business would indicate that when there is business to be transacted, the RTA has to meet more than once in a month and thereby the business of the RTA cannot be unduly delayed. A consideration of the Rule would mandate that the RTA has to meet at least once in a month when there is business to be transacted. It is imperative and the duty of every RTA to meet once in a month when there is business to be transacted. The failure to meet every month when there was business to be transacted would defeat public interest. When as many as 198 items were scheduled for consideration the adjournment of the meeting without transacting any business for the last more than six months was unjustifiable; *Ajesh V. Kumar* v. *Regional Transport Authority, Kollam,* AIR 2003 Ker 51: 2003 (1) ACC 328: 2002 (3) Ker LT 491.

8. Principles to be followed while Considering Allotment of Time Chart – The authorities while considering the allotment of time chart should keep in mind among others the following principles:—

(i) The interest of travelling public should be the prime and overriding consideration. Thus where there are sufficient numbers of passengers requiring frequent bus service, the intervals between two buses can be very shorter.

(ii) Operators operating in different routes have no right to object to the timings of operators in other routes unless the objecting operator has common portion covering substantial portion of each other's route.

(iii) Whether there is real clash, it is to be considered with reference to the volume of passengers, number of common stoppages, if any, and the extent of common portion in case of the different routes.

(iv) The principle, that the prior permit holders should have priority over latter permit holders is to be normally followed but where application of such principle clashes with interest of the travelling public or the former permit holder does not suffer any real prejudice, the principle may be deviated from.

(v) Interval between two buses will be dependent upon the total volume of passengers available and normally 25 to 30 minutes interval should be regarded as reasonable.

(vi) If necessary and possible, the authorities may allot time to the rival operators on rotation basis, so that the advantages and disadvantages if any are equally shared by the rival operators; *Susil Kumar Panigrahi* v. *Commr.-cum-Chairman, S.T.A.*, AIR 2000 Ori 113: 2000 (89) Cut LT 788.

9. Attachment of Model Condition is Executive Duties – When RTA decides to grant a stage carriage permit, it acts as a quasi judicial authority. After this decision, the grant of permit is his executive function. Thus the attachment of model condition with it comes under his executive duties; *Regional Transport Authority, Jodhpur* v. *Sita Ram*, AIR 1993 Raj 76: 1992 (2) Raj LR 450: 1992 (2) Raj LW 344.

10. Proviso what Prohibits? – By the proviso to sub-section (1) of section 72 what is prohibited is granting of a permit in respect of any route or area not specified in the application. The said proviso does not prohibit curtailment in regard to portion of the route applied for any valid reason; *State of West Bengal* v. *S.K. Nuruj*, (2010) 6 SCALE 190.

11. Change of Condition of Permit – Clauses (iii) and (iv) of section 72(2) of the Act clearly provides that a time-table for the running of the vehicle has to be approved by the R.T.A. and that has to be exhibited on the vehicle and at specified stands and halts on the route or within the area and the permit should also specify the minimum and maximum number of daily trips to be provided in relation to any route or area generally or on specified days and occasions. If those trips to be provided in relation to any route or are a generally or on specified days and occasions. If those trips have to be increased or decreased than that would result in the; *Ramkumar* v. *Secretary, R.T.A., Bikaner*, AIR 1993 Raj 30: 1992 (1) Raj LR 314: 1992 (2) Raj LW 27.

12. Power to Vary or Modify Conditions of Permit – A perusal of clause (xxii) of sub-section (2) of section 72 *per se* reveals that Regional Transport Authority is empowered to vary or modify the conditions of permit which may include the time-table *vide* clause (vi) of sub-section (2) of section 72. He is also entitled to attach further conditions to the permit. It means as regards the power to vary conditions from rime to time, the power vests in the Regional Transport Authority and it cannot be said that Regional Transport Authority has no power to review its order or modify the timings or the conditions of the permit nor can it be said that no further conditions can be attached to the permit; *N. Muddappa* v. *Secretary, Regional Transport Authority, Bangalore*, AIR 1998 Kant 61: 1998 (1) ACC 56: 1998 (2) Civ LJ 300.

13. Variation in Stage Carriage Permit not Proper – The Regional Transport Authority while modifying the route permit of the respondent No.4 has changed the termini from Pathankot - Kahanphatt via Nagrota Bagwan to Pathankot-Palampur *via* Kangra-Nagrota Bagwan and Parour. The Regional Transport Authority has also not produced records before this Court that it was satisfied that the variation/extension would serve the convenience of public and it was not expedient to grant a separate permit in respect of the original permit. In the supplementary affidavit filed, stand of respondents Nos. 2 and 3 is that the route permit has been modified by Regional Transport Authority under the provisions of section 72(2) read with section 80(3) of the Act. However, the fact of the matter is that the case was to be considered under sub-section (3) of section 80 and not under sub-section (2) of section 72 of the Act. The Regional Transport Authority has over- looked the letter and spirit of section 80(3) of the Act while modifying the said route permit. Thus, the modification changing the termini of the route of respondent No. 4 by the Regional Transport Authority was without authority and jurisdiction. Respondent No.4 shall ply his bus on the old route, *i.e.*, Pathankot - Kahanphatt *via* Nagrota Bagwan; *Suboth Sharoti* v. *State of Himachal Pradesh*, AIR 2013 HP 55: 2013 (3) ACC 797: 2013 (1) Sim LC 355.

14. Tourist Vehicles cannot Carry Luggage on Roof of Vehicles – In a tourist vehicle, the permit holder should only provide luggage holds at the rear or at the sides or both, of the tourist vehicle with sufficient space and size. When the Rules specifically make a provision in regard to the place where luggage holds shall be provided by necessary implication, it goes to exclude all the other places of the tourist vehicle for being used as luggage holds. Rule 128 is a special provision for tourist vehicles which excludes General rule 93 to the extent of conflict between the former and the later. The plea that rule 93 in entirety gets incorporated in rule 128 and, therefore, operators could carry luggage on roof is not tenable. Rule 93(3) is applicable only to "an articulated vehicle or a tractor-trailer combination specially constructed and used for the conveyance of individual load of exceptional length" and sub-rule (3A) of rule 93 is applicable to "construction equipment vehicle". Only sub-rule (1) of rule 93, which is in reference to "a motor vehicle", will be incorporatd and read into rule 128 by virtue of sub-rule (1) of rule 128. The restriction imposed by the Rule is a reasonable restriction keeping in view the safety of the passengers in a tourist vehicle. Therefore, the Rule cannot be said either arbitrary or unreasonable or violative of Article 19(1)(g) of the Constitution; *Sharma Transports* v. *State of Maharashtra,* AIR 2011 SC 3279: 2011 AIR SCW 4688: (2011) 8 SCC 647.

15. Grant of Permit Curtailing Sum Portion of Route is Valid – Section 72(1) prohibits granting of a permit in respect of any route or area not specified in the application. The said proviso does not prohibit curtailment in regard to portion of the route applied for, for any valid reason. In fact section 72(1) specifically authorizes the Authority to grant the stage carriage permit with such modifications as it deems fit. Curtailment of a route would be a modification as contemplated under the section 72(1) of the Act. in the present case the appellant-State responded by contending that in view of the traffic congestion and automobile pollution in Kolkata reaching alarming proportions, entry of vehicles in Kolkata was being restricted in a phased manner as a matter of policy; that the State Government constituted a technical committee to examine inter alia the road space, availability of halting space, terminus and related matters; that in accordance with the recommendation of a Technical Committee, the State Government issued a notification directing the Authority and all Regional Transport Authorities to grant a stage carriage permit in accordance with the application or with such modifications as it deems fit. So long as the reason for the modification is not found to be arbitrary or unreasonable, the question of interfering with the order of the Authority does not arise. The grant of some permits to others for routes touching Kolkata during the pendency of these matters, would not affect the validity of the orders of the Authority, nor be a ground for interfering with the orders of the Authority, as appellants have explained the reason why in some cases, during the pendency of the matter it had to issue permits; *State of West Bengal* v. *S.K. Nurul Amin,* AIR 2010 SC 2271: 2010 AIR SCW 4075: (2010) 6 SCALE 190.

16. Stage Carriage Permit – Rival Operators have no *locus standi* to challenge transport permit in favour of other operator; *Dinesh Mehta* v. *STA, Odisha,* AIR 2015 Ori 88.

17. Stage Carriage Permit – Cancellation at the Instance of Rival Operator – Amounts to deprivation of enjoyment of Fundamental Rights under Article 19(1)(g) of Constitution; *Dinesh Mehta* v. *STA, Odisha,* AIR 2015 Ori 88.

73. Application for contract carriage permit.—An application for a permit in respect of a contract carriage (in this Chapter referred to as a contract carriage permit) shall contain the following particulars, namely:—

(a) the type and seating capacity of the vehicle;

(b) the area for which the permit is required;

(c) any other particulars which may be prescribed.

74. Grant of contract carriage permit.—(1) Subject to the provisions of sub-section (3), a Regional Transport Authority may, on an application made to it under section 73, grant a contract carriage permit in accordance with the application or with such modifications as it deems fit or refuse to grant such a permit:

Provided that no such permit shall be granted in respect of any area not specified in the application.

(2) The Regional Transport Authority, if it decides to grant a contract carriage permit, may, subject to any rules that may be made under this Act, attach to the permit any one or more of the following conditions, namely:—

(i) that the vehicles shall be used only in a specified area or on a specified route or routes;

(ii) that except in accordance with specified conditions, no contract of hiring, other than an extension or modification of a subsisting contract, may be entered into outside the specified area;

(iii) the maximum number of passengers and the maximum weight of luggage that may be carried on the vehicles, either generally or on specified occasions or at specified times and seasons;

(iv) the conditions subject to which goods may be carried in any contract carriage in addition to, or to the exclusion of, passengers;

(v) that, in the case of motorcabs, specified fares or rates of fares shall be charged and a copy of the fare table shall be exhibited on the vehicle;

(vi) that, in the case of vehicles other than motorcabs, specified rates of hiring not exceeding specified maximum shall be charged;

(vii) that in the case of motorcabs, a specified weight of passengers' luggage shall be carried free of charge, and that the charge, if any, for any luggage in excess thereof shall be at a specified rate;

(viii) that, in the case of motorcabs, a taximeter shall be fitted and maintained in proper working order, if prescribed;

(ix) that the Regional Transport Authority may, after giving notice of not less than one month,—

(a) vary the conditions of the permit;

(b) attach to the permit further conditions;

(x) that the conditions of permit shall not be departed from save with the approval of the Regional Transport Authority;

(xi) that specified standards of comfort and cleanliness shall be maintained in the vehicles;

(xii) that, except in the circumstances of exceptional nature, the plying of the vehicle or carrying of the passengers shall not be refused;

(xiii) any other conditions which may be prescribed.

(3) (a) The State Government shall, if so directed by the Central Government, having regard to the number of vehicles, road conditions and other relevant matters, by notification in the Official Gazette, direct a State Transport Authority and a Regional Transport Authority to limit the number of contract carriages generally or of any specified type, as may be fixed and specified in the

notification, operating on city routes in towns with a population of not less than five lakhs.

(b) Where the number of contract carriages are fixed under clause (a), the Regional Transport Authority shall, in considering an application for the grant of permit in respect of any such contract carriage, have regard to the following matters, namely:—

(i) financial stability of the applicant;

(ii) satisfactory performance as a contract carriage operator including payment of tax if the applicant is or has been an operator of contract carriages; and

(iii) such other matters as may be prescribed by the State Government:

Provided that, other conditions being equal, preference shall be given to applications for permits from—

(i) the India Tourism Development Corporation;

(ii) State Tourism Development Corporations;

(iii) State Tourism Departments;

(iv) State Transport Undertakings;

(v) co-operative societies registered or deemed to have been registered under any enactment for the time being in force;

(vi) ex-servicemen.

SYNOPSIS

1. Circulars in Contravention of Policy cannot be Sustained in Law
2. Fairness in Consideration
3. Permit Holders shall not put Luggage Carrier on Top of Jeep
4. Grant of Contract Carriage Permit
5. Conversion Contract Carriage Permits into Stage Carriage Permits
6. Words "if Prescribed"

COMMENTS

1. Circulars in Contravention of Policy cannot be Sustained in Law – The Commissioner cannot issue any circulars in contravention of the policy formulated by the Government. If, according to him, any change in the existing policy is warranted, the maximum he can do is, to address the Government and apprise it, of the necessity. The action of the Commissioner in issuing the circular, which has the effect of annulling the memo of the Government, cannot be sustained in law; *G. Nagabhushanam* v. *Government of Andhra Pradesh,* AIR 2007 AP 179: 2007 AIHC 2372: 2007 (4) Andh LT 101.

2. Fairness in Consideration – If a statutory authority receives more than one application for parting largesse of the State or for grant of permit, licence etc., equitable principles which flow from Article 14 postulates would mandate such statutory authority to club all such rival applications, consider them together and dispose of them by a common order in order to ensure fairness in consideration and also in order to appreciate relatives merits of the applicants together and to part with largesse of the State to a most suitable person amongst the applicants to subserve the public interest. Since the petitioner made application well before the respondent made application for grant of regular permit on the same route, in terms of priority as well as seniority, the petitioner's application should have been considered and decided earlier or at least it should have been clubbed with the application of the respondent. The ends of justice would be met by directing the respondent to club the application of the petitioner with that of the respondent; *Yakub Sarif* v. *State Transport Appellate Tribunal, Raipur,* AIR 2006 Chhat 46: 2006 AIHC 1976: 2006 (5) AIR Bom R 833 NOC.

3. Permit Holders shall not put Luggage Carrier on Top of Jeep – In public interest it is considered not to allow the luggage carrier on the top of the Jeep for the reason that it is put only on four iron pipes without any proper body which could support the luggage. Moreso only six passengers are permitted to be carried and for carrying the luggage of six passengers there is sufficient space inside the Jeep itself. The conditions imposed herein cannot be held to be illegal or invalid as the same has been imposed in public safety and public interest; *Taxi Vikas Karya Sanstha* v. *State of Rajasthan*, AIR 2002 Raj 151: 2001 (2) Raj LW 1003: 2001 WLC (Raj) (UC) 435.

4. Grant of Contract Carriage Permit – The restrictions can only be imposed on issuing contract carriage permits which are to be operated on any city route in a town in accordance with the conditions mentioned in the above statutory provisions. Any action contrary thereto amounts to sub-plantation of the statutory provision. Such an action cannot be sustained in law. The fact of non-production of any notification in support of imposing restrictions on issuing permits for contract carriage permits to be operated on city route in the districts has not been produced before this Court is taken note of. Therefore, the resolutions of the State Transport Authority with regard to taking decision for restricting the number of issuing contract carriage permits in respect of the aforesaid three districts cannot be sustained in law; *Alit Kumar Sarkar* v. *State*, AIR 2010 Cal 58: 2010 AIHC 609 NOC: 2010 (4) ACC 209.

5. Conversion Contract Carriage Permits into Stage Carriage Permits – Rule 120(4) provides that no auto-rickshaw shall be allowed to ply in any route other than the specified or fixed route allotted to it by the respective Regional Transport Authorities violation of which is punishable under the Motor Vehicles Act, 1988. Fare for autorickshaw shall be fixed or determined by the State Government. Any complaint of overcharging of fare shall render the permit to be suspended/cancelled. There shall be not metering system in the auto rickshaw. The Rules does not convert contract carriage permit into stage carriage permit. The section 72(2)(ii) and section 74(2)(i) dealing with stage carriage permit and contract carriage permit respectively, empower the RTO in respect of both the permits to impose a condition that the vehicle shall be used only in a specified area on a specified route or routes. Since section 72(2)(ii) and section 72(2)(i) themselves empower the RTO to impose a condition that the vehicle shall be used only in a specified area or on a specified route or routes there is no question of any conversion merely because the authority has imposed a condition in a contract carriage permit which could also have been imposed under section 72(2)(ii) in a stage carriage permit. Thus rule 120(4) does not convert contract carriage permits into stage carriage permits; *Calcutta Howrah Auto Rickshaws Owners Assocn.* v. *State of West Bengal*, AIR 2010 Cal 122: 2010 (2) Cal HN 630: 2010 (2) Cal LJ 118.

6. Words "if Prescribed" – Section 74(2)(viii) requires the owner of motor cabs to have such a taxi meter fitted on the motorcab if prescribed. The words "if prescribed" in section 74(4)(viii) make it clear that installation of a taxi meter would be mandatory only if the Rules so provide. Hence it is open to the rule making authority to mention in rule 120 that there shall be no metering system in the auto rickshaw; *Calcutta Howrah Auto Rickshaws Owners Assocn.* v. *State of West Bengal*, AIR 2010 Cal 122: 2010 (2) Cal HN 630: 2010 (2) Cal LJ 118.

75. Scheme for renting of motor cabs.—(1) The Central Government may, by notification in the Official Gazette, make a scheme for the purpose of regulating the business of renting of [1][motor cabs or motor cycles to persons desiring to drive either by themselves or through drivers, motor cabs or motor cycles] for their own use and for matters connected therewith.

1. Subs. by Act 54 of 1994, sec. 24, for "motor cabs to persons desiring to drive the cabs" (w.e.f. 14-11-1994).

(2) A scheme made under sub-section (1) may provide for all or any of the following matters, namely:—

(a) licensing of operators under the scheme including grant, renewal and revocation of such licences;

(b) form of application and form of licences and the particulars to be contained therein;

(c) fee to be paid with the application for such licences;

(d) the authorities to which the application shall be made;

(e) condition subject to which such licences may be granted, renewed or revoked;

(f) appeals against orders of refusal to grant or renew such licences and appeals against orders revoking such licences;

(g) conditions subject to which motor cabs may be rented;

(h) maintenance of records and inspection of such records;

(i) such other matters as may be necessary to carry out the purposes of this section.

76. Application for private service vehicle permit.—(1) A Regional Transport Authority may, on an application made to it, grant a private service vehicle permit in accordance with the application or with such modification as it deems fit or refuse to grant such permit:

Provided that no such permit shall be granted in respect of any area or route not specified in the application.

(2) An application for a permit to use a motor vehicle as a private service vehicle shall contain the following particulars, namely:—

(a) type and seating capacity of the vehicle;

(b) the area or the route or routes to which the application relates;

(c) the manner in which it is claimed that the purpose of carrying persons otherwise than for hire or reward or in connection with the trade or business carried on by the applicant will be served by the vehicle; and

(d) any other particulars which may be prescribed.

(3) The Regional Transport Authority if it decides to grant the permit may, subject to any rules that may be made under this Act, attach to the permit any one or more of the following conditions, namely:—

(i) that the vehicle be used only in a specified area or on a specified route or routes;

(ii) the maximum number of persons and the maximum weight of luggage that may be carried;

(iii) that the Regional Transport Authority may, after giving notice of not less than one month—

(a) vary the conditions of the permit;

(b) attach to the permit further conditions;

(iv) that the conditions of permit shall not be departed from, save with the approval of the Regional Transport Authority;

(v) that specified standards of comforts and cleanliness shall be maintained in the vehicle;

(vi) that the holder of the permit shall furnish to the Regional Transport Authority such periodical returns, statistics and other information as the State Government may, from time to time, specify; and

(vii) such other conditions as may be prescribed.

77. Application for goods carriage permit.—An application for a permit to use a motor vehicle for the carriage of goods for hire or reward or for the carriage of goods for or in connection with a trade or business carried on by the applicant (in this Chapter referred to as a goods carriage permit) shall, as far as may be, contain the following particulars, namely:—

(a) the area or the route or routes to which the application relates;

(b) the type and capacity of the vehicle;

(c) the nature of the goods it is proposed to carry;

(d) the arrangements intended to be made for the housing, maintenance and repair of the vehicle and for the storage and safe custody of the goods;

(e) such particulars as the Regional Transport Authority may require with respect to any business as a carrier of goods for hire or reward carried on by the applicant at any time before the making of the application, and of the rates charged by the applicant;

(f) particulars of any agreement, or arrangement, affecting in any material respect the provision within the region of the Regional Transport Authority of facilities for the transport of goods for hire or reward, entered into by the applicant with any other person by whom such facilities are provided, whether within or without the region;

(g) any other particulars which may be prescribed.

78. Consideration of application for goods carriage permit.—A Regional Transport Authority shall, in considering an application for a goods carriage permit, have regard to the following matters, namely:—

(a) the nature of the goods to be carried with special reference to their dangerous or hazardous nature to human life;

(b) the nature of the chemicals or explosives to be carried with special reference to the safety to human life.

79. Grant of goods carriage permit.—(1) A Regional Transport Authority may, on an application made to it under section 77, grant a goods carriage permit to be valid throughout the State or in accordance with the application or with such modifications as it deems fit or refuse to grant such a permit:

Provided that no such permit shall be granted in respect of any area or route not specified in the application.

(2) The Regional Transport Authority, if it decides to grant a goods carriage permit, may grant the permit and may, subject to any rules that may be made under this Act, attach to the permit any one or more of the following conditions, namely:—

(i) that the vehicle shall be used only in a specified area, or on a specified route or routes;

(ii) that the gross vehicle weight of any vehicle used shall not exceed a specified maximum;

(iii) that goods of a specified nature shall not be carried;

(iv) that goods shall be carried at specified rates;

(v) that specified arrangement shall be made for the housing, maintenance and repair of the vehicle and the storage and safe custody of the goods carried;

(vi) that the holder of the permit shall furnish to the Regional Transport Authority such periodical returns, statistics and other information as the State Government may, from time to time, prescribe;

(vii) that the Regional Transport Authority may, after giving notice of not less than one month,—

(a) vary the conditions of the permit;

(b) attach to the permit further conditions;

(viii) that the conditions of the permit shall not be departed from, save with the approval of the Regional Transport Authority;

(ix) any other conditions which may be prescribed.

(3) The conditions referred to in sub-section (2) may include conditions relating to the packaging and carriage of goods of dangerous or hazardous nature to human life.

COMMENTS

Multi-axle Goods Carriage Permit – The Rules make it apparent that multi-axle goods carriage can be permitted to be on the road for a period of 15 years. The period of 15 years is to be computed from the date of initial registration of the motor vehicle covered under the permit. This is also provided under the *Explanation* to rule 88; *Bhogiram Verma* v. *Regional Transport Authority, Morena,* AIR 1998 MP 142: 1998 (2) MPLJ 39: 1998 (4) Civ LJ 314.

80. Procedure in applying for and granting permits.—(1) An application for a permit of any kind may be made at any time.

(2) A [1][Regional Transport Authority, State Transport Authority or any prescribed authority referred to in sub-section (1) of section 66] shall not ordinarily refuse to grant an application for permit of any kind made at any time under this Act:

Provided that the [1][Regional Transport Authority, State Transport Authority or any prescribed authority referred to in sub-section (1) of section 66] may summarily refuse the application if the grant of any permit in accordance with the application would have the effect of increasing the number of stage carriages as fixed and specified in a notification in the Official Gazette under clause (a) of sub-section (3) of section 71 or of contract carriages as fixed and specified in a notification in the Official Gazette under clause (a) of sub-section (3) of section 74:

1. Subs. by Act 54 of 1994, sec. 25, for "Regional Transport Authority" (w.e.f. 14-11-1994).

Provided further that where a [1][Regional Transport Authority, State Transport Authority or any prescribed authority referred to in sub-section (1) of section 66] refuses an application for the grant of a permit of any kind under this Act, it shall give to the applicant in writing its reasons for the refusal of the same and an opportunity of being heard in the matter.

(3) An application to vary the conditions of any permit, other than a temporary permit, by the inclusion of a new route or routes or a new area or by altering the route or routes or area covered by it, or in the case of a stage carriage permit by increasing the number of trips above the specified maximum or by the variation, extension or curtailment of the route or routes or the area specified in the permit shall be treated as an application for the grant of a new permit:

Provided that it shall not be necessary so to treat an application made by the holder of stage carriage permit who provides the only service on any route to increase the frequency of the service so provided without any increase in the number of vehicles:

Provided further that,—

(i) in the case of variation, the termini shall not be altered and the distance covered by the variation shall not exceed twenty-four kilometres;

(ii) in the case of extension, the distance covered by extension shall not exceed twenty-four kilometres from the termini,

and any such variation or extension within such limits shall be made only after the transport authority is satisfied that such variation will serve the convenience of the public and that it is not expedient to grant a separate permit in respect of the original route as so varied or extended or any part thereof.

(4) A [1][Regional Transport Authority, State Transport Authority or any prescribed authority referred to in sub-section (1) of section 66] may, before such date as may be specified by it in this behalf, replace any permit granted by it before the said date by a fresh permit conforming to the provisions of section 72 or section 74 or section 76 or section 79, as the case may be, and the fresh permit shall be valid for the same route or routes or the same area for which the replaced permit was valid:

Provided that no condition other than a condition which was already attached to the replaced permit or which could have been attached thereto under the law in force when that permit was granted shall be attached to the fresh permit except with the consent in writing of the holder of the permit.

(5) Notwithstanding anything contained in section 81, a permit issued under the provisions of sub-section (4) shall be effective without renewal for the remainder of the period during which the replaced permit would have been so effective.

SYNOPSIS

1. Subs. by Act 54 of 1994, sec. 25, for "Regional Transport Authority" (w.e.f. 14-11-1994).

COMMENTS

1. Expression "any permit" – The expression "any permit" used in section 80 would obviously mean all kinds of permanent permits like Stage Carriage Permit, Contract Carriage Permit and the like. The reason is obvious, a temporary permit can only be for a temporary need and for a temporary period, and therefore to follow the procedures for grant of permanent permit may frustrate the purpose of grant of a temporary permit to meet a temporary need; *Sanjit Kumar Sardar* v. *State of West Bengal*, AIR 1996 Cal 135: 1996 (1) Cal LT 25: 1996 Cal WN 489.

2. Preference to Applicant Over Other – If any person has a right to apply *suo motu* under section 80(1) of the Act for grant of permit for a route, at any time, the authorities are bound to consider it. There cannot be a limitation to file such application or documents. Therefore, the date on which the Transport Authority considers the claim for grant of permit, it should be in accordance with law. If by the time applicant rectifies defect, if any, in accordance with law, it is open to the Transport Authority to consider such application along with others.

Under the statutory rule, if it is open to an applicant to give details of the vehicle or produce the documents relating to vehicle or the registration number of the vehicle within one month from the date of sanction, such right cannot be curtailed by any advertisement, nor any application can be rejected on the ground of non-production of documents relating to the vehicle or registration of vehicle. Under the Act, or Rules, there being no provision made to give preference over another, if equally situated, it is always open to the Transport Authority to prescribe a guideline to give preference to an applicant over the other; *Subodh Prasad* v. *State of Jharkhand*, AIR 2004 Jhar 42: 2004 AIR Jhar HCR 186: 2003 (4) JCR JHA 245: 2003 (4) JLJR 167.

3. Grant of Application for Permits for Mini Buses – The scheme did not mean that there was any contemplation by the State Transport Undertaking for operating on the routes linking one village with another village or a town or a Municipality in between the aforesaid two villages or a route linking a village with block head quarter or a Municipality or city, Consequently Regional Transport Authority cannot refuse to grant application for permits for mini-buses. It was moreso when grant of permit was not challenged by State Transport Undertaking or State Government but by operators who were already having such permits; *Subhash Chander* v. *State Transport Appellate Tribunal*, AIR 2002 SC 1562: 2002 AIR SCW 1457: JT 2002 (3) SC 239: 2002 (4) SCC 168: 2002 (3) SCALE 79: 2002 (2) Supreme 520.

4. Grant of Permit to Run Mini Buses – Under section 99 of the Act if the State Transport Undertaking is to operate on a particular route, then only the scheme could be made applicable. The Scheme does not provide that the routes mentioned in Clause are to be covered and operated completely or partially by the State Transport Undertaking. In such cases, section 80(2) would be applicable as under section 99, the State Government is not empowered to provide that only few private operators would operate on a particular route/routes and Regional Transport Authority or other prescribed authority cannot ordinarily refuse to grant an application for permit of any kind made at any time under the Act; *Jagdip Singh* v. *Jagir Chand*, AIR 2001 SC 3027: 2001 AIR SCW 4109: JT 2001 (8) SC 559: 2001 (8) SCC 437: 2001 (7) SCALE 109: 2001 (7) Supreme 473.

5. Permit without Holding Proceeding – Without holding proceedings to consider the merits and demerits of the application and also without assigning reasons granting of permit is illegal; *Thirumalai Transport Service* v. *P. Samiappa Gounder*, AIR 1997 SC 1029: 1997 AIR SCW 1011: JT 1997 (2) SC 105: 1997 (3) SCC 510: 1997 (1) SCALE 535.

6. Liberal Policy for Grant of Policy – The Act provides liberal policy for the grant of permits to those who intend to enter the motor transport business. The provisions of the Act are in conformity with article 19(1)(g). When the State has chosen not to impose any restriction under article 19(6) in respect of motor transport business and has left the citizens to enjoy their right under article 19(1)(g) there can be no cause for complaint by the existing operators. The three categories of permit-seekers *i.e.*, inter-region, intra region and inter-State cannot be considered to be belonging to the same class. Different criteria have been provided under the Act for granting permits in respect of each of the categories. Thus section 80 cannot be said to be violative of article 14 on ground that the imposition of limit for grant of inter-State permits is permissible under section 88(5) of the Act whereas no such limit can be imposed in respect of intra-region permits; *Mithilesh Garg* v. *Union of India*, AIR 1992 SC 443: 1992 AIR SCW 41: JT 1991 (4) SC 447: 1992 (1) SCC 168.

7. Existing as well as Temporary Permit Holders have No Right to Object Grant of Permit – An existing operator has no right to object to the grant of a permit to other persons and the authorities are entitled to increase the strength as provided under the Act and the Rules. The petitioners who are temporary permit holders also have no *locus standi* or any right to object to the grant of permit to respondents under the provisions of the Motor Vehicles Act; *Narayan Kumar Mitra* v. *State of West Bengal*, AIR 1995 Cal 119.

8. Person has Right to apply *Suo Motu* for Grant of Permit – If any person has a right to apply *suo motu* under section 80(1) of the Act for grant of permit for a route, at any time, the authorities are bound to consider it. There cannot be a limitation to file such application or documents. Therefore, the date on which the Transport Authority considers the claim for grant of permit, it should be in accordance with law. If by the time applicant rectifies defect, if any, in accordance with law, it is open to the Transport Authority to consider such application along with others. Under the statutory rule, if it is open to an applicant to give details of the vehicle or produce the documents relating to vehicle or the registration number of the vehicle within one month from the date of sanction, such right cannot be curtailed by any advertisement, nor any application can be rejected on the ground of non-production of documents relating to the vehicle or registration of vehicle. There being no provision made to give preference over another, if equally situated, it is always open to the Transport Authority to prescribe a guideline to give preference to an applicant over the other; *Subodh Prasad* v. *State of Jharkhand*, AIR 2004 Jhar 42: 2003 (4) JCR JHA 245: 2003 (4) JLJR 167.

9. Grant of Permit shall not be in Violation of any Scheme – A scheme duly published under section 100(3) of the Motor Vehicles Act, is the law and the violation of the same would be viewed in the same manner as the violation of any other provision of the Statutes. In terms of section 104 of the M.V. Act, the R.T.A. or the S.T.A. is disabled from issuing a permit except in accordance with the provisions of the Scheme published under section 100(3). For a proper exercise of its power under section 80 of the Act, the authority concerned shall have to keep in view the provisions of section 104 of the Act and make sure that the grant of permit by it is not in violation of any scheme duly published under section 100(3). Jurisdiction of the authority, to grant a permit would depend upon the existence or non-existence of a Scheme and the total or partial ban it may contain against any private operator, operating a service on a notified route. Determination of these facts, would be essential as the same are jurisdictional facts without which the authority concerned, cannot take a proper decision in the matter the failure on the part of the authority concerned, to address itself to the provisions of section 104, and to make an order consistent therewith would amount to failure on its part to exercise its jurisdiction properly and an error of law which would vitiate the order passed by it; *Karnataka State Road Transport Corporation* v. *Pauli Govis*, AIR 1996 Kant 247: ILR 1996 Kant 295.

10. Authority should Comply with Statutory Provision – When it is found that the application for permit was not considered in accordance with the provisions contained in the statute, the proper course is to set aside the decision and to direct the authority to consider the application afresh in accordance with the statutory provisions. It is neither proper nor prudent to justify the impugned decision by guessing or presuming what would have persuaded the authority to take such a decision. The authority should be made to comply with the statutory provision and State its own reasons for the decision. Since the Regional Transport Authority has not given any reasons for taking the decision and has not communicated the reasons for refusal of permit to the appellant and since it has not given him an opportunity of being heard in the matter, the decision is illegal and arbitrary and is liable to be set aside; *N. Vineetha* v. *Regional Transport Authority*, AIR 2004 Ker 24: 2004 (1) ACC 245: 2003 (3) Ker LT 714.

11. Always Open to Authority to Assess Comparative Merits – When Regional Transport Authority receives large number of applications, it is always open to the Authority to assess the comparative merits, if the Authority does not propose to grant permit for all the applicants. In a case where the Regional Transport Authority decides to grant few permits on the same route, and when large numbers of applications are received by it, it is open to the Authority to look into the comparative merits and make best judgment assessment of its own for granting the permit. In a given case, when an applicant who submitted application first offers old model vehicle, and the applicant who submitted application later, offers a latest model vehicle, it is always open to the Authority to grant permit to the latest model vehicles, which is more beneficial to the travelling public. Therefore the plea that even though a person who submitted his application later has got superior qualities is not a ground for not considering the earlier application and granting the same is not correct. Thus the Regional Transport Authority, being a quasi judicial authority, is always justified in assessing the comparative merits of all the applications when they come up for consideration; *Beena Rani* v. *Regional Transport Authority, Kollam*, AIR 1999 Ker 249: 1999 (3) Civ LJ 42: 1999 (1) Ker LT 716.

12. Permit Based on Bid not to be Allowed – System of granting permits by bid would not only create monopoly but would be detrimental to public interest, as those enjoying financial muscle shall usurp all route permits. Furthermore, the concern of State that an efficient and adequate transport system is evolved, will also be a casualty. It is incumbent upon State to determine merits of each applicant, taking into consideration antecedents and verification of past performance track. Punctuality, adherence to route, condition of vehicle, customer care, past satisfactory performance, financial stability, issuance of tickets and non evasion of tax, are various factors, which can be taken into consideration while allotting permit. These factors cannot be put in water tight jackets. Depending upon each area route, safety of passengers, amenities and facilities to be provided by operator ought to have been the concern of State, than to allot permit on basis of maximum bid without ensuring providing of better service to passengers. Since the sole criteria is, to give maximum bid, that being contrary to the provisions of the Act. Therefore, allotment of the route permits on the basis of bid alone, being bad, cannot be sustained; *Shivani Adarsh Co-op. Transport Society Ltd.* v. *State of Haryana*, AIR 2009 P&H 95.

13. Period of Limitation for Filing Appeal in Case of Non-communication of Order of Refusal – If a party does not know about the making of the order either actually or constructively it may claim that the period of limitation would start running from the date it acquires knowledge of the making of an order but one cannot understand how a party, who has acquired knowledge of the making an order either directly or constructively can ignore the same and belatedly seek redress just because the authority making the order had made a default in formally communicating the order to him. Allowing a party to do so would amount to placing a premium on the lack of diligence of a party, who is remiss in seeking a remedy that was available to it. Therefore, knowledge whether actual or constructive of the order passed by the State or Regional Transport Authority should result in commencement of the period of limitation. Thus, in cases where the State or Regional Transport Authority has not communicated the order of refusal passed to the persons concerned, the period of limitation for filing an appeal would commence from the date when the parties concerned acquire knowledge of passing of the said order; *Jagtar Singh* v. *State Transport Appellate Tribunal*, AIR 2009 P&H 114.

14. Application for Change of Trips Amounts to Application for New Permit – In the case of a stage carriage permit by increasing the number of trips above the specified maximum or by the variation, extension or curtailment of the route or routes or the area specified in the permit shall be treated as an application for the grant of a new permit. Thus, any application made for increasing or decreasing the number of trips would certainly result in the change of the condition of the permit and that application shall be treated as an application for grant of a new permit; *Ramkumar* v. *Secretary, R.T.A., Bikaner*, AIR 1993 Raj 30: 1992 (1) Raj LR 314: 1992 (2) Raj LW 27.

15. Grant of Permits to More and More Applicants is Public Interest – The public interest would be served by granting the permits to more and more applicants because the competition is the great regulative force which establishes the control over the economic activities and it is in the best interest of the society as it ensures salvation of the society. The competition in the present case is a competition for efficiency and not competition by interference with the business of the competitors. Prevention of monopoly and ensuring every competition on the route is in the interest of public and it is for the government to protect the common man from exploitation by the vested interest which can be done by providing number of services on the routes; *Shiv Raj* v. *State of Rajasthan*, AIR 1992 Raj 99: 1991 (1) Raj LR 642: 1991 (1) Raj LW 579.

16. Authority can Refuse Counter-Signature of Permit only after Hearing Parties – Sub-section (2) of section 80 is to the effect that where the R.T.A. refuses an application for grant of permit of any kind under the Act, it shall give to the applicant in writing its reasons for the refusal of the same and an opportunity of being heard in the matter. The order of the R.T.A. refusing the counter-signature is appealable under section 89(d) of the Act and thus it is not permissible for the R.T.A. to refuse the counter-signature of the permit of inter-State route by oral order. The R.T.A. can refuse counter-signature of the permit only after hearing the parties effected, by an order in writing, *Rai Sahib* v. *State of Haryana*, AIR 1996 Raj 83.

17. Authority has Discretion to Grant Permits both for Entire Route and for Shorter Route – The limit of twenty four kilometres as prescribed in clause (ii) of second proviso appended to sub-section (3) of section 80 applies only to extension and not to curtailment. The second proviso deals with the cases of variations and clause (ii) deals with the cases of extension. It, therefore, follows that so far as curtailment is concerned, there is embargo on the power exercised by the authorities and it lies totally in its discretion to grant the permits not only for the entire route but for a shorter route also; *State of Rajasthan* v. *Roshan Lal Inder Lal Choudhary,* AIR 1995 Raj 31: 1994 (2) Raj LR 593: 1994 (2) Raj LW 250.

18. Variation or Increase in Number of Trips – Once a Scheme stands published in relation to any route, be it in complete or partial exclusion of then existing routes, only the concerned State Transport Undertakings can operate services on the notified areas or routes, as per the Scheme itself. The permit originally granted to any person would be rendered ineffective. The permit holder cannot operate on any part or portion of the notified route or area merely on the ground that the permit as originally granted to him covered the notified route or area. If there is any need for protecting the travelling public from inconvenience, it was for the State Transport Undertaking and the Government to increase their own bus services. In the case in hand, the Appellant has no legal right to seek for any variation or increase in the number of trips by the Bellary Scheme. Thus the variation of conditions of the stage carriage permit granted by the KSTA was subsequently set aside by the KSTAT was proper; *Neelakanteshwara Motor Service* v. *Karnataka State Transport,* AIR 2013 Kant 7: 2013 (1) ACC 835.

19. Variation in Stage Carriage Permit not Proper – The Regional Transport Authority while modifying the route permit of the respondent No.4 has changed the termini from Pathankot - Kahanphatt *via* Nagrota Bagwan to Pathankot-Palampur *via* Kangra-Nagrota Bagwan and Parour. The Regional Transport Authority has also not produced records before this Court that it was satisfied that the variation/extension would serve the convenience of public and it was not expedient to grant a separate permit in respect of the original permit. In the supplementary affidavit filed, stand of respondents Nos. 2 and 3 is that the route permit has been modified by Regional Transport Authority under the provisions of section 72(2) read with section 80(3) of the Act. However, the fact of the matter is that the case was to be considered under sub-section (3) of section 80 and not under sub-section (2) of section 72 of the Act. The Regional Transport Authority has over- looked the letter and spirit of section 80(3) of the Act while modifying the said route permit. Thus, the modification changing the termini of the route of respondent No. 4 by the Regional Transport Authority was without authority and jurisdiction. Respondent No. 4 shall ply his bus on the old route, *i.e.,* Pathankot - Kahanphatt *via* Nagrota Bagwan; *Suboth Sharoti* v. *State of Himachal Pradesh,* AIR 2013 HP 55: 2013 (3) ACC 797: 2013 (1) Sim LC 355.

20. Application for Variation of Permit Conditions – If an existing operator on a particular route seeks variation of permit conditions involving curtailments, paramount consideration has to be interest of travelling public on entire existing route. A deviation from original route may be beneficial to travelling public on that route to which deviation is sought for. But, when it involves curtailment of route originally granted, such variation cannot be granted ignoring interest of travelling public on existing route. The variation sought for in instant case reveal that such curtailments will be adverse to interest of travelling public on existing route. In fact, it will affect late night passengers. The mere fact that said deviation will provide travelling facilities to another remote area cannot be a reason to allow variation affecting interest of travelling public on existing route; *Sani Xavier* v. *Regional Transport Authority,* AIR 2011 Ker 101.

21. Application for Grant of Permanent Permit – Dismissal of – While dismissing the application no reasons have been assigned. Only reason assigned is 'dismissed' thus directed to the concerned respondent to decide afresh the application of the petitioner under section 80 of the Act by a speaking order, within a period of four weeks from the date of receipt of a copy of the order of the Court; *Sarda Devi* v. *State of Jharkhand*, AIR 2012 Jhar 5: 2011 (4) AIR Jhar R 302.

It appears from the impugned order that no reasons have been assigned. Only one reason assigned is "dismissed". This is not a method in which an order should be passed by the respondent authorities. This is thoroughly a non-application of mind and it reveals absolute arbitrariness, which leads to inequality. By this type of attitude, authority may allow the application whereas in rest of the cases, he may dismiss by one word like the present impugned order. The impugned order is an appellable order under section 89 of the Motor Vehicles Act, 1988 and, therefore, also reasons ought to have been assigned by the concerned respondent authorities. Reasons are the soul of the order. Unless, the reasons are given, higher authorities cannot appreciate why the application was allowed or dismissed. This is a bare minimum requirement, which, the respondent authorities ought to have kept in mind. Not to assign any reasons and the application is dismissed, is a non-application of mind and arbitrariness. Therefore, it is directed that the concerned respondent authorities to decide afresh, the application of the petitioner and speaking order shall be passed under section 80 of the Motor Vehicles Act within a period of four weeks from the date of receipt of a copy of the order of the Court; *Dinesh Nand Jha* v. *State of Jharkhand*, AIR 2011 Jhar 6: 2010 AIHC 143: 2010 (3) ICC 193.

22. Variation of Conditions of Permit – Once a scheme is published in relation to any area or route or portion thereof, to the complete exclusion of other persons, no person other than the State Transport Undertaking may operate on the modified route. Thus the deviation granted by the Karnataka State Transport Authority from the non-monopoly route to the monopoly route to a saved operator was not permissible; *G.K. Venkatashiva Reddy* v. *Karnataka State Transport Appellate Tribunal, Bangalore*, AIR 2011 Kant 162.

23. Cut-off Date – Notice not in accordance with mandate of section 80 but in excess of authority of law; *Pawan Arora* v. *State of Madhya Pradesh*, AIR 2015 MP 36.

24. Writ Jurisdiction – Grant of Fresh Permits in Favour of New Operators – Writ Petition Challenging Maintainable – If the challenge is on the ground of illegality or arbitrariness or colourable exercise of power or otherwise being violative of Article 14 of the Constitution, notwithstanding that the action may be impelled by the commercial interests of the existing operator; provided that the substance of challenge is not founded only on the commercial interests of the existing operator being prejudiced by the acts complained of; *Prabhat Pan* v. *State of West Bengal*, AIR 2015 Cal 112.

25. Operators Plying Vehicles for Carrying Passengers in Violation of Statutory Provisions – Writ Petition by holders of permit maintainable; *Prabhat Pan* v. *State of West Bengal*, AIR 2015 Cal 112.

26. Stage Carriage Permit – Cancellation at the Instance of Rival Operator – Amounts to deprivation of enjoyment of Fundamental Rights under Article 19(1)(g) of Constitution; *Dinesh Mehta* v. *STA, Odisha*, AIR 2015 Ori 88.

27. Stage Carriage Permit – Rival Operators have no *locus standi* to challenge transport permit in favour of other operator; *Dinesh Mehta* v. *STA, Odisha*, AIR 2015 Ori 88.

81. Duration and renewal of permits.—(1) A permit other than a temporary permit issued under section 87 or a special permit issued under sub-section (8) of section 88 shall be effective [1][from the date of issuance or renewal thereof] for a period of five years:

Provided that where the permit is countersigned under sub-section (1) of section 88, such counter-signature shall remain effective without renewal for such period so as to synchronise with the validity of the primary permit.

1. Subs. by Act 54 of 1994, sec. 26 for "without renewal" (w.e.f. 14-11-1994).

(2) A permit may be renewed on an application made not less than fifteen days before the date of its expiry.

(3) Notwithstanding anything contained in sub-section (2), the Regional Transport Authority or the State Transport Authority as the case may be, entertain an application for the renewal of a permit after the last date specified in that sub-section if it is satisfied that the applicant was prevented by good and sufficient cause from making an application within the time specified.

(4) The Regional Transport Authority or the State Transport Authority, as the case may be, may reject an application for the renewal of a permit on one or more of the following grounds, namely:—

(a) the financial condition of the applicant as evidenced by insolvency, or decrees for payment of debts remaining unsatisfied for a period of thirty days, prior to the date of consideration of the application;

(b) the applicant had been punished twice or more for any of the following offences within twelve months reckoned from fifteen days prior to the date of consideration of the application committed as a result of the operation of a stage carriage service by the applicant, namely:—

(i) plying any vehicle—

(1) without payment of tax due on such vehicle;

(2) without payment of tax during the grace period allowed for payment of such tax and then stop the plying of such vehicle;

(3) on any unauthorised route;

(ii) making unauthorised trips:

Provided that in computing the number of punishments for the purpose of clause (b), any punishment stayed by the order of an appellate authority shall not be taken into account:

Provided further that no application under this sub-section shall be rejected unless an opportunity of being heard is given to the applicant.

(5) Where a permit has been renewed under this section after the expiry of the period thereof, such renewal shall have effect from the date of such expiry irrespective of whether or not a temporary permit has been granted under clause (d) of section 87, and where a temporary permit has been granted, the fee paid in respect of such temporary permit shall be refunded.

SYNOPSIS

1. Grant or Renewal of Permit to Stage Carriage Operator Saved
2. Renewal of Stage Carriage Permit
3. Rule Providing for Period of 9 Years is not Violative of Section 81
4. Grant of Renewal of Stage Carriage Permits
5. Application for Temporary Permit

COMMENTS

1. Grant or Renewal of Permit to Stage Carriage Operator Saved – No third party private operators are entitled to apply for permits on the same notified route or part thereof, nor are they entitled to compete with them for grant of permit, since the right of all other private operators to apply for and operate in the approved notified area, route or a part thereof, has been frozen. The right is reserved only in relation to the named operators and that too for specified permit, and none else. Along with the application under section 70 of New Act filed for grant of permit under section 72 or renewal under section 81 made by the named holder of a specified permit in an approved scheme, he should enclose an authenticated copy of the approved scheme, the details of the route on which he was plying his stage carriage with corridor restrictions on over lapping routes. The RTA or STA, as the case may be should verify the original under which the named operator, whose specified permit was saved, whether he is entitled to ply the stage carriage in the approved scheme with the condition of the corridor restrictions on the notified scheme and if so to what extent. The named stage carriage operators whose permits are granted under the old Act are saved under the nationalised scheme. The RTA or STA, as the case may be, should consider and may grant permits or renewal of permits as per law or rejection thereof for reasons to be recorded in that behalf; *Pancham Chand* v. *State of Himachal Pradesh,* 2008 AIR SCW 2111: 2008 (7) SCC 117: 2008 (3) SCALE 378.

2. Renewal of Stage Carriage Permit – State carriage permit granted under old Act not saved by the new Act 1988 and section 6 of General Clauses Act. The private operators are neither entitled to apply for permits on the same notified route or part thereof, nor are they entitled to compete with them for grant of permit, since the right of all other private operators to apply for and operate in the approved notified area, route or a part thereof, has been frozen. The right is reserved only in relation to the named operators and that too for specified permit, and none else. The authorities should consider their applications in accordance with the law and the prescribed procedure and may grant new permits under section 72 and later on before the expiry thereof, to renew it in accordance with the procedure prescribed in sections 80 and 81, that too on compliance with law, until the scheme is duly modified or cancelled in accordance with law; *Gajraj Singh* v. *State Transport Appellate Tribunal,* AIR 1997 SC 412: 1996 All LJ 1767.

3. Rule Providing for Period of 9 Years is not Violative of Section 81 – For a vehicle to run under national permit its age should not cross nine years, while the national permit can be granted for a period of five years at a time and renewal also is for five years at a time. If the permit as originally granted or renewed goes beyond the age of the vehicle, that national permit is deemed to be invalid so far as that vehicle is concerned. That does not mean that the petitioner is not entitled to replace that vehicle and run another vehicle of the same nature with the same permit for the unexpired period of the permit. The intention of the legislature is expressed in the sections as well as the rule. If they are so construed, the rule is not violative of section 81; *A. Rafeek* v. *Union of India,* AIR 1992 AP 331: 1992 (1) ALT 260.

It cannot be said that R. 88 providing for life span of vehicle for national permit is inconsistent with section 81 inasmuch as the duration of the permit has to be five years under section 81 and likewise the duration of renewal also has to be five years and if a permit is renewed for another period of five years then such permit shall be valid under section 81 up to the period of 10 years. But that permit cannot be availed for its full duration under sub-rule (2) of rule 88 as life span, provided for vehicle under rule 88 is only 9 years. If the incumbent wants to avail the permit for a full tenure he will have to employ a vehicle which has not spent the life span of nine years. Section 83 lays down that the incumbent can replace the vehicle by another vehicle of the same nature. Now, in case the incumbent wants to avail the full tenure of permit then in that case he can get the vehicle replaced by another vehicle which is not nine years old; *K. Rajendran* v. *K.S. Krishnadas,* AIR 1992 Ker 5: 1991 (2) Ker LJ 187: 1991 (2) KLT 203.

4. Grant of Renewal of Stage Carriage Permits – The grant of renewal of the stage carriage permits should necessarily be preceded by a grant of a permit to stage carriage under section 72, in accordance with the procedure laid down in sections 70 and 71. This should be made before the expiry of the period prescribed in the permit granted under the Act of 1939. Therefore, for stage carriage permits granted under Chapter IV of the Act of 1939, if they stand to expire or expired after 1st July, 1989, without after any pending application for renewal having been made under section 58 as on 1st July, 1989, fresh applications under section 70 should be filed and after consideration under section 71, permits may be obtained as per law under section 72 of the Motor Vehicles Act, 1988; *Gajraj Singh* v. *State Transport Appellate Tribunal,* AIR 1997 SC 412: 1996 All LJ 1767.

5. Application for Temporary Permit – The applications for temporary permit filed invoking section 87(1)(d) shall be considered only in cases where the applications for renewal of permit are filed within the period prescribed in section 81 and in case where the applications for renewal are filed out of time, the applications for temporary permit under section 87(1)(d) shall be considered only after the RTA or the STA, as the case may be, entertains such applications for renewal on being satisfied that the applicant was prevented by good and sufficient cause from making the application for renewal within the time specified. Thus, an application for renewal of a regular permit filed, beyond the time prescribed by law, along with an application for excusing the delay is not eligible to be treated as an application pending consideration, for the purpose of entertaining an application for temporary permit under section 87(1)(d); *C. Abdul Nasar* v. *Secretary, Regional Transport Authority,* AIR 2012 Ker 142.

82. Transfer of permit.—(1) Save as provided in sub-section (2), a permit shall not be transferable from one person to another except with the permission of the transport authority which granted the permit and shall not, without such permission, operate to confer on any person to whom a vehicle covered by the permit is transferred any right to use that vehicle in the manner authorised by the permit.

(2) Where the holder of a permit dies, the person succeeding to the possession of the vehicle covered by the permit may, for a period of three months, use the permit as if it had been granted to himself:

Provided that such person has, within thirty days of the death of the holder, informed the transport authority which granted the permit of the death of the holder and of his own intention to use the permit:

Provided further that no permit shall be so used after the date on which it would have ceased to be effective without renewal in the hands of the deceased holder.

(3) The transport authority may, on application made to it within three months of the death of the holder of a permit, transfer the permit to the person succeeding to the possession of the vehicles covered by the permit:

Provided that the transport authority may entertain an application made after the expiry of the said period of three months if it is satisfied that the applicant was prevented by good and sufficient cause from making an application within the time specified.

SYNOPSIS

1. Joint Application for Transfer of Permit
2. Transfer of Permits in Respect of Notified Routes
3. Right of Access And Access as of Right – Distinction between

COMMENTS

1. Joint Application for Transfer of Permit – Factum of death of Chandra Bhushan Sharma was not brought to the notice of the R.T.A. either by the petitioner or by the legal heirs of the deceased. The State Transport Appellate Tribunal after hearing both the parties on merits has set aside the order dated, passed by the R.T.A. and remanded the matter for proceeding in accordance with section 82(2) of the Act. the petitioner may take recourse to sub-section (3) of section 82 instead of sub-section (2) of section 82 of the Act.

The petitioner may prosecute his application for transfer of permit under section 82(3) of the Act; *Kishan Lal* v. *State Transport Appellate Tribunal*, AIR 2008 Uttra 58.

2. Transfer of Permits in Respect of Notified Routes – The Corporation has entered into agreements with the outsourcing agents. For the purpose of running their vehicles, only the services of the outsourcing agents is availed with certain terms and conditions for a period of one year. It is indeed their vehicles which are being operated by outsourcing agents. The terms and conditions would clearly go to show that it is not the transfer of the permits in favour of the outsourcing agents, obtained from STA or RTA in respect of notified routes, upon which exclusive right is conferred upon the Corporation under section 100 of Chapter VI of the Act. The relevant clauses of the terms and conditions of one of the agreements show that the agreements with outsourcing agents to operate the services on the notified routes is not transfer of permits in favour of the outsourcing agents. The services are operated under the control, supervision and management of the Corporation through the second party outsourcing agent. Therefore, the same cannot be termed that there is a transfer of permits in favour of outsourcing agents to operate the vehicle or vehicles on the notified routes for which permission of either STA or RTA, is required under the provision of the 1939 Act. Thus the agreements with reference to the aforesaid provision, the agreements entered into between the Corporation and the outsourcing agents, is perfectly legal and valid. There is no arbitrary action on the part of the Corporation. There is also no statutory violation either under section 66 or 82 of the M.V. Act; *All Orissa Bus Owners Association* v. *Orissa State Road Transport Corporation*, AIR 2012 Ori 179.

3. Right of Access And Access as of Right – Distinction between – It is also necessary to bear in mind distinction between the expression "right of access" and "access as of right". The latter expression denotes a place where members of public have a right of its use as members of public and as a matter of right, whether regulated, restricted or not. They cannot, however, be denied said right except on legal grounds. On other hand, where there is only a right of access, owner of place, if happens to be a private owner, may deny access to any members of public on any ground which he chooses. In other words in former case right of members of public to use place is restricted compared to their right to use in latter case. The definition under M.V. Act, uses expression "right of access" what is, therefore significant to note is that under present definition even a place right to use of which is restricted is a public place; *M.K. Bhaumik* v. *Sukura Singh*, AIR 2011 Ori 144.

83. Replacement of vehicles.—The holder of a permit may, with the permission of the authority by which the permit was granted, replace any vehicle covered by the permit by any other vehicle of the same nature.

COMMENTS

Permit Holder not Entitled to Seek Replacement of Vehicle without Paying Tax Dues – Under section 83 of the M.V. Act the holder of a permit is not entitled to replace any vehicle covered by the permit by any other vehicle of the same nature without paying the tax dues as on the date of the application on the vehicle to be replaced. Where an application is made for replacement of the vehicle under section 83 of the M.V. Act, the condition precedent for permission to replace the vehicle is, there should be a valid permit on the day the application is made, because it is the holder of a permit alone who is eligible to make such an application. The permit holder should possess a valid permit. In order to find out whether the permit holder has a valid permit or not, if the authorities insist on either payment of tax or proof of tax paid receipts in respect of the vehicle covered under the permit it cannot be found fault with. They are discharging statutory obligation as contained in section 14 of the Taxation Act. Only when it is shown that in respect of the vehicle covered under the permit, tax has been paid, the permit is valid. The replacement of a vehicle cannot be, granted if the permit is not valid. Therefore, when a person seeks replacement of the vehicle under a permit he must keep the permit effective as on the date of the said application is filed by paying tax due under the Taxation Act. Without paying the tax in respect of the vehicle covered under the permit, the permit holder is not entitled to seek replacement of the vehicle covered under the permit. Therefore, a person who has not performed his statutory obligation and who has not paid tax to the Government due under the enactment cannot have the benefit of replacement of the vehicle. If a person who has not paid the tax is still granted the benefit of replacement of the vehicle, it is nothing but a premium to the tax evasion which is not permissible in law; *Nafiza Sultana* v. *Secretary, R.T.A., Bangalore Rural, B.D.A. Complex,* AIR 2010 Kant 179: 2011 (1) Civ LJ 806: 2010 (6) Kant LJ 154.

84. General conditions attaching to all permits.—The following shall be conditions of every permit—

(a) that the vehicle to which the permit relates carries valid certificate of fitness issued under section 56 and is at all times so maintained as to comply with the requirements of this Act and the rules made thereunder;

(b) that the vehicle to which the permit relates is not driven at a speed exceeding the speed permitted under this Act;

(c) that any prohibition or restriction imposed any fares or freight fixed by notification made under section 67 are observed in connection with the vehicle to which the permit relates;

(d) that the vehicle to which the permit relates is not driven in contravention of the provisions of section 5 or section 113;

(e) that the provisions of this Act limiting the hours of work of drivers are observed in connection with any vehicle or vehicles to which the permit relates;

(f) that the provisions of Chapters X, XI and XII so far as they apply to the holder of the permit are observed; and

(g) that the name and address of the operator shall be painted or otherwise firmly affixed to every vehicle to which the permit relates on the exterior of the body of that vehicle on both sides thereof in a colour or colours vividly contrasting to the colour of the vehicle centred as high as practicable below the window line in bold letters.

SYNOPSIS

COMMENTS

1. Cancellation of Carriage Permit – An operator is not entitled to ply his bus in public place merely because it was registered and was having a fitness certificate unless the bus is sound and roadworthy. The operator shall maintain specified standards of comfort and cleanliness in the vehicle. Section 84 of the new Act have imposed a condition in every permit that the vehicle at all time is so maintained as to comply with' the requirement of Chapter V and Rules framed thereunder. The object of the Motor Vehicles Act and permits issued thereunder is to provide travelling facilities without exposing public to risk of human lives. If the vehicle is kept in a shabby condition incapable of giving reasonable comfortable travelling facilities to the public, the purpose for which permits are granted stands frustrated. Therefore, where the body of the petitioners bus was absolutely broken and shattered by constant use without repairs causing great hardship to travelling public and condition of the vehicle was definitely not roadworthy and pose risk for human lives and petitioner did not make good the deficiency despite earlier checking by the authority, the authority was justified in cancelling the carriage permit of petitioner even if the vehicle was having valid registration and fitness certificate; *Hindustani Bus Service, Moradabad* v. *State Transport Appellate Tribunal, U.P., Lucknow*, AIR 1991 All 382: (1991) 18 All LR 98: 1991 (1) All CJ 634.

2. Conversion of Permit – Merely for the convenience of the long distance passengers permit for ordinary service cannot be allowed to be converted into Fast Passenger Service; *P.K. Poulose* v. *State of Kerala*, AIR 1998 Ker 10: ILR 1997 (2) Ker 821.

85. General form of permits.—Every permit issued under this Act shall be complete in itself and shall contain all the necessary particulars of the permit and the conditions attached thereto.

86. Cancellation and suspension of permits.—(1) The transport authority which granted a permit may cancel the permit or may suspend it for such period as it thinks fit—

(a) on the breach of any condition specified in section 84 or of any condition contained in the permit, or

(b) if the holder of the permit uses or causes or allows a vehicle to be used in any manner not authorised by the permit, or

(c) if the holder of the permit ceases to own the vehicle covered by the permit, or

(d) if the holder of the permit has obtained the permit by fraud or misrepresentation, or

(e) if the holder of the goods carriage permit, fails without reasonable cause, to use the vehicle for the purposes for which the permit was granted, or

(f) if the holder of the permit acquires the citizenship of any foreign country:

Provided that no permit shall be suspended or cancelled unless an opportunity has been given to the holder of the permit to furnish his explanation.

(2) The transport authority may exercise the powers conferred on it under sub-section (1) in relation to a permit granted by any authority or person to whom power in this behalf has been delegated under sub-section (5) of section 68 as if the said permit was a permit granted by the transport authority.

(3) Where a transport authority cancels or suspends a permit, it shall give to the holder in writing its reasons for the action taken.

(4) The powers exercisable under sub-section (1) (other than the power to cancel a permit) by the transport authority which granted the permit may be exercised by any authority or person to whom such powers have been delegated under sub-section (5) of section 68.

(5) Where a permit is liable to be cancelled or suspended under clause (a) or clause (b) or clause (e) of sub-section (1) and the transport authority is of opinion that having regard to the circumstances of the case, it would not be necessary or expedient so to cancel or suspend the permit if the holder of the permit agrees to pay a certain sum of money, then, notwithstanding anything contained in sub-section (1), the transport authority may, instead of cancelling

or suspending the permit, as the case may be, recover from the holder of the permit the sum of money agreed upon.

(6) The powers exercisable by the transport authority under sub-section (5) may, where an appeal has been preferred under section 89, be exercised also by the appellate authority.

(7) In relation to a permit referred to in sub-section (9) of section 88, the powers exercisable under sub-section (1) (other than the power to cancel a permit) by the transport authority which granted the permit, may be exercised by any transport authority and any authority or persons to whom power in this behalf has been delegated under sub-section (5) of section 68, as if the said permit was a permit granted by any such authority or persons.

SYNOPSIS

1. Owner cannot Ply Vehicle Off Route though not Carrying Passengers
2. Compounding is not Automatic
3. Delegate cannot Reject Application Securing Replacement of Vehicle
4. Authority cannot Re-fix Compounding Fee Once Fixed by Delegated Authority
5. Power cannot be Exercised merely on Basis of Complaints
6. Availability of Vehicle is not Relevant for Grant of Permit
7. Provision Applies to Owner of Vehicle
8. Power to Cancel Permit
9. Decision of Judge or Tribunal must be Absolutely Unfettered by any Extraneous Guidance
10. Statutory Functionary Çannot Pressurise Another to Perform Act not Authorised by Statute
11. Clauses of Circular Enabling Refusal of Renewal of Permit are Arbitrary
12. Contract Carriage and Stage Carriage – Difference between
13. Cancellation of Permit – Validity

COMMENTS

1. Owner cannot Ply Vehicle Off Route though not Carrying Passengers – The owner cannot ply the vehicle off the route even it is not actually carrying any passenger as section 66 enjoins upon the permit holder to ply his vehicle in strict adherence to and observations of the conditions attached to the permit. Thus, if a vehicle is found whether stationary or moving at a place which does not fall on the route, it will be in contravention of the statutory provisions of the Act unless it falls under exceptions provided in section 66(3) of the Act, and this contravention amounts to plying the vehicle contrary to the condition attached to permit itself and thus it will be liable to be cancelled or suspended under the provisions of section 86 of the Act and action can be taken against the permit holder under the provisions of section 192 of the Act; *Rampati Jaiswal* v. *State of Uttar Pradesh,* AIR 1997 All 170: 1997 All LJ 827: 1998 (1) All CJ 447.

2. Compounding is not Automatic – Compounding is not automatic, and it is only in the event of cancellation or suspension under clause (a) or (b) or (e) of section 86(1). Even if the cancellation is in respect of clause (a) or (b) or (e) of sub-section (1), even then, the authorities are to form an opinion by applying their mind to the circumstances of the case, and, therefore, it is not automatic or mechanic as argued by the respondent; *Hanuman Transport Co. Pvt. Ltd.* v. *R.T.A., Shimoga,* AIR 2004 Kant 164: 2004 AIR Kant HCR 450.

3. Delegate cannot Reject Application Securing Replacement of Vehicle – The power delegated is restricted to the power to allow replacement of one vehicle by another. In other words, the secretary RTA as the delegatee is not empowered to reject an application under section 83 of the Act seeking replacement of one vehicle by another. He can consider the application. He can allow the same. It is open to him to place an application before the RTA which in course is competent to deal with it in terms of section 83 of the Act. But, he cannot reject the same; *Viswambaran Kovilparambil House* v. *State of Kerala,* AIR 2009 Ker 53: 2009 AIHC 313 (NOC): 2008 (3) Ker LJ 687.

4. Authority cannot Re-fix Compounding Fee Once Fixed by Delegated Authority – Once the delegated authority under sections 95 and 96 of the Act had already exercised the powers of framing the rules and fixed the quantum, though as a minimum under the Rules, it is not open for any Authority to re-fix or re-determine the amounts either as a maximum or otherwise. Even on a reading of section 86(5) of the Act and rule 217 of the Rules, the discretion is left with the authority to consider all the aspects in individual cases and then to arrive at a certain sum of money, but not to fix a sweeping uniform rates as sought to be done in the impugned resolutions. Therefore, the entire exercise of powers by the authorities in trying to fix the uniform rates, though in respect of various such offences and also at different stages, is totally beyond the powers conferred under the provisions of the Act and the Rules made thereunder. Further, where law specifically contemplates a discretion to be used in individual cases, the same cannot be curtailed or eroded in any such manner as sought to be done under the impugned resolutions, which fetters the discretion vested in the individual authority to come to a conclusion in a situation in regard to the different permit holders depending upon the facts of each case; *Jami Appala Swamy* v. *Regional Transport Authority,* AIR 2003 AP 265: 2003 (2) Andh LD 324: 2003 (2) Andh LT 270.

5. Power cannot be Exercised merely on Basis of Complaints – Before taking the decision to suspend the petitioner's route permit, the competent authority did not make any independent enquiry for ascertaining the veracity of the allegations contained in the written complaints. The allegations made in the written complaints were taken at their face value, and admittedly without examining any of the complainants. The procedure adopted by the Chairman of the State Transport Authority does not satisfy the basic requirements of rule of law that put an obligation on him to act fairly, and without leaving any scope to describe his action as arbitrary. Merely on the basis of complaints made by some persons, the Chairman, if he was the competent authority, should not have exercised the power under section 86, and before exercising the power he ought to have ascertained the correctness of the allegations made; and for the purpose he should have either made an independent enquiry or examined the complainants or some of them, and the first petitioner should have been given opportunity to lead evidence in support of its case; *Kalpana Travels* v. *Union of India,* AIR 2005 Cal 73.

6. Availability of Vehicle is not Relevant for Grant of Permit – The availability of a vehicle is not relevant for the grant but for the issuance of the permit. Section 86 does not provide the non-availability of vehicle as a ground for cancellation of permit. All that law requires is that the permit should be availed within the outer limit prescribed by the Act and the Rules. Section 86 does not provide non-replacement of a vehicle or the non-availability of a vehicle that is being plied under a permit as a ground for cancellation of permit. The embargo on the permit holder is that, a stage carriage, which would have become 15 years' old, could not be plied. This does not, by, itself, mean that the operator could not have brought a ready vehicle later on, during the currency of the permit. Therefore, the fact that the vehicle has attained the age of more than 15 years is not ground to cancel the permit and an operator, who has permit in his favour, is entitled to bring in another proper vehicle during the currency of the permit; *Aysha* v. *Regional Transport Authority, Kasaragod,* AIR 2006 Ker 360.

7. Provision Applies to Owner of Vehicle – The permit was issued in the name of the petitioner and since the vehicles were repossessed by the financier, petitioner sought for replacement by his own vehicle. The ownership of the vehicle is different from the grant of permit. The possession of the vehicle pursuant to a hire purchase agreement does not contemplate ownership of the vehicle as contemplated under section 86(1)(c) of the Act. The petitioner is only a permit holder, and in view of his default, the vehicles were repossessed by the financier. It is therefore, clear that the petitioner is not the owner of the vehicle and he does not claim so. Section 86(1)(c) of the Motor Vehicles Act, speaks about ownership of the vehicle. The petitioner ceased to have possession of the vehicles.

There is, a clear indication in section 86(1)(c) of the Act that it will apply with regard to persons who own the vehicle. Therefore section 86(1) cannot be applied to permit-holders who possess vehicles by virtue of hire-purchase agreement; *B.S. Chinnasamy Gounder* v. *Regional Transport Authority Dharmapuri*, AIR 2007 Mad 288: 2007 AIHC 567 (NOC): 2007 (2) Mad LJ 1104.

8. Power to Cancel Permit – Circular impinges upon the power of the Transport Authority to cancel or suspend a permit under section 86 of the Act read with rule 185 or 186 of the Rules. Only the State Transport Authority or the Regional Transport Authority as specified under section 68 of the Act is empowered to cancel the permit under section 86 of the Act and rule 185 or 186 of the Rules. The jurisdiction so vested in the Transport Authority cannot be tinkered with by the Transport Commissioner who is not a Transport Authority as specified under section 68 of the Act. The Transport Authority is exercising a *quasi* judicial function in the matter of suspension or cancellation of permit under section 86 of the Act and rule 185 or 186 of the Rules. The exercise of such *quasi*-judicial function should be left unfettered by any extraneous guidance by the executive or administrative wing of the State and the impugned clauses are clearly an affront in that regard; *Kerala Bus Transport Association* v. *Transport Commissioner, Thiruvananthapuram*, AIR 2013 Ker 140: 2013 (3) Civ LJ 255: 2013 (1) Ker LT 440.

9. Decision of Judge or Tribunal must be Absolutely Unfettered by any Extraneous Guidance – It is of the essence of fair and objective administration of law that the decision of the Judge or the Tribunal must be absolutely unfettered by any extraneous guidance by the executive or administrative wing of the State. If the exercise of discretion conferred on a quasi judicial Tribunal is controlled by any such direction, that forges fetters on the exercise of quasi judicial authority and the presence of such fetters would make the exercise of such authority completely inconsistent with the well accepted notion of judicial process; *B. Rajagopala Naidu* v. *The State Transport Appellate Tribunal*, AIR 1964 SC 1573: 1964 (2) SCJ 570: 1964 2 MLJ (SC) 131.

10. Statutory Functionary cannot Pressurise Another to Perform Act not Authorised by Statute – The Collector has evinced unjustified though possibly bona fide exuberance of enthusiasm while resorting to a recovery method not sanctioned by law. He cannot, by persuasion or by pressure, make another statutory functionary do an act which that authority does not possess under the statute under which it functions. Thus a statutory functionary cannot pressurise another to perform an act not authorised by statute; *Chairman, Calicut-Wyanad Motor Services (Pvt.) Ltd.* v. *State of Kerala*, 1986 KLT 1216: AIR 1987 Ker 21: (1987) 2 Civ LJ 390.

11. Clauses of Circular Enabling Refusal of Renewal of Permit are Arbitrary – The clauses of circular enabling the refusal of renewal of permit or declining the certificate of fitness because of the mere pendency of a 'check report' is wholly inequitable. The owner/permit holder cannot be kept on tenterhooks awaiting the culmination of the proceedings pursuant to a 'check report' for him to continue the service being operated. The clauses of circular would pressurise the owner/permit holder to part with Rs. 10,000 on receipt of a charge memo even in the absence of a prior decision of the Transport Authority as regards breach. The likelihood of a 'check report' being misused by a checking officer to extract money from the vehicles whose permit is on the verge of renewal cannot at all be overlooked. The clauses of circular are arbitrary and falls foul of article 14 of the Constitution of India besides offending the right guaranteed to the operators to carry on the business under article 19(1)(g) of the Constitution of India; *Kerala Bus Transport Association* v. *Transport Commissioner, Thiruvananthapuram*, AIR 2013 Ker 140: 2013 (3) Civ LJ 255: 2013 (1) Ker LT 440.

12. Contract Carriage and Stage Carriage – Difference between – The basic difference between contract carriage and stage carriage is that a contract carriage has to be hired together as a whole for the carriage of passengers from one point to another and without stopping to pick up and getting down passengers. On the other hand a stage carriage is one where separate fare from individual passengers can be charged and the journey can be undertaken by individual passengers in stages. Basically, a contract carriage can be hired as a whole by an individual or a group of persons and it must go from the starting point to the destination and should not permit the passengers to embark or alight from the vehicle at any station in between. On the other hand stage carriage is like a bus run by the HRTC where each individual pays separate fare for the whole or any part of the journey; *Manmohan Bedi* v. *State Transport Authority, Shimla,* AIR 2012 HP 78: 2012 (4) ACJ 317: 2012 (3) Sim LC 1403.

13. Cancellation of Permit – Validity – To prevent the unhealthy practice where tour operators having contract carriage permits actually ply buses like stage carriage buses, the permit holder of a contract carriage is required to maintain records showing the names, addresses and ages of the passengers and also required to issue a receipt to the hirer and the counterfoil of the same is to be kept with the permit holder. Neither before the authorities nor before us any material has been placed on record to show that the names and addresses of the passengers or hirers of the vehicles were ever noted. There are one or two stray entries by name but these are also incomplete. Some entries show that a group travelled together but no details of the passengers were given. No log books were maintained. Neither any receipt issued to the hirer nor any counterfoil(s) of the same have been produced. Thus the officer could not verify whether the bus was being run as a 'stage carriage' or a 'contract carriage', when no such document was maintained by the appellants. Once the operators were not maintaining these documents the authorities would be justified in taking a view that an adverse inference should be drawn against the transporters and it may be presumed that they are running their buses as stage carriage. Thus the cancellation of the permits of contract carriage is not improper; *Manmohan Bedi* v. *State Transport Authority, Shimla,* AIR 2012 HP 78: 2012 (4) ACJ 317: 2012 (3) Sim LC 1403.

A bare perusal of the Annexure shows non-application of mind. The reply filed by the petitioner and his statement ought to have been considered by the Regional Transport Authority before the decision was taken to cancel the permit. The necessity of issuing notice is to enable the person to explain his position. It is also the requirement under section 86 of the Act that the holder of the permit has to be given an opportunity to explain his position and thereafter the holder has to be informed of reasons for the action taken in writing. The Regional Transport Authority has not followed the mandatory provisions of section 86 of the Act in letter and spirit. Thus the cancellation of the permit is improper; *Happy Awasthi* v. *State of Himachal Pradesh,* AIR 2012 HP 90: 2012 (4) ACC 602.

87. Temporary permits.—(1) A Regional Transport Authority and the State Transport Authority may without following the procedure laid down in section 80, grant permits to be effective for a limited period which shall, not in any case exceed four months, to authorise the use of a transport vehicle temporarily—

(a) for the conveyance of passengers on special occasions such as to and from fairs and religious gatherings, or

(b) for the purposes of a seasonal business, or

(c) to meet a particular temporary need, or

(d) pending decision on an application for the renewal of a permit,

and may attach to any such permit such condition as it may think fit:

Provided that a Regional Transport Authority or, as the case may be, State Transport Authority may, in the case of goods carriages, under the circumstances of an exceptional nature, and for reasons to be recorded in writing, grant a permit for a period exceeding four months, but not exceeding one year.

(2) Notwithstanding anything contained in sub-section (1), a temporary permit may be granted thereunder in respect of any route or area where—

(i) no permit could be issued under section 72 or section 74 or section 76 or section 79 in respect of that route or area by reason of an order of a Court or other competent authority restraining the issue of the same, for a period not exceeding the period for which the issue of the permit has been so restrained;

(ii) as a result of the suspension by a Court or other competent authority of the permit of any vehicle in respect of that route or area, there is no transport vehicle of the same class with a valid permit in respect of that route or area, or there is no adequate number of such vehicles in respect of that route or area, for a period not exceeding the period of such suspension:

Provided that the number of transport vehicles in respect of which temporary permits are so granted shall not exceed the number of vehicles in respect of which the issue of the permits have been restrained or, as the case may be, the permit has been suspended.

SYNOPSIS

COMMENTS

1. Temporary Permit cannot be Granted Exceeding Period of Four Months – Since section 87 empowers the S.T.A. or the R.T.A. to grant temporary permit to be effective for a limited period not exceeding four months there cannot be any scope for granting permit exceeding the period of four months even when such permits are granted to meet temporary need in respect of any notified area or route under the approved Scheme in terms of section 104. The outer limit can never exceed four months when permit is granted under section 87, within the scope of the proviso to section 104, but however, such permit shall cease to be effective as soon as permits are obtained by the S.T.U. on such route though the period of temporary permit may not have expired. Therefore on the expiry of such permit a person may obtain fresh temporary permit subject to same conditions and go on repeating such obtaining of permit until S.T.U. obtains permit; *Ved Pal Singh* v. *State Transport Appellate Tribunal, Lucknow,* AIR 1999 All 136: 1999 All LJ 925: 1998 All CJ 694.

2. Disclose of Purpose for Obtaining Temporary Permit in Application – A temporary permit can be granted for the purposes indicated in the Act and the Rules, the purpose for obtaining the temporary permit is required to be indicated in the application for the same and non-disclosure of such purpose certainly entitles the Regional Transport Authority to reject the application for temporary permit. In the case the Regional Transport Authority, granted temporary permit though in the application the purpose for granting of such temporary permit was not indicated. But the same cannot create any right for the present writ petitioners to obtain a temporary permit without fulfilling the statutory requirement of indicating the purpose of the same in the application for the temporary permit, for the simple reason that once illegality committed by the Regional Transport Authority, cannot justify the commission of another illegality; *Sanjit Kumar Sardar* v. *State of West Bengal,* AIR 1996 Cal 135: 1996 (1) Cal LT 25: 1996 Cal WN 489.

3. Discretion of RTA in Granting Temporary Permit – The grant of a permit is a quasi-judicial function. The same has to be exercised in accordance with the satisfaction of the RTA or Secretary concerned. No superior authority can dictate, in what manner the power vested in the RTA or Secretary. If the temporary need is for a period of one month, the RTA should be conceded freedom to grant the permit for a period of one month. The STA has no authority to say that even if the temporary need exists for a period of one month, permit can be granted only for a period of five days. If the RTA, when it feels that the temporary need is for a longer period grants permit only for five days, the same will amount to acting under dictation; *Anoj Abraham* v. *State Transport Authority, Kerala,* AIR 2007 Ker 72: 2007 AIHC 1275: 2006 (3) Ker LJ 732.

4. Positive Finding of Temporary Need – The authorities, while granting a temporary permit should give a positive finding of a temporary need and the statement of reasons generally support that finding. It is necessary that the RTA should primarily apply its mind before granting a permit; *O.V. Manu Kurikkal* v. *Secretary, R.T.A., Malappuram,* AIR 2000 Ker 54: 1999 (2) Ker LJ 461: ILR (Ker) 1999 (3) KER 699.

5. Power of Granting Temporary Permit is Restricted Power – The order granting temporary permit must show how the temporary need had arisen. It cannot be granted merely for the convenience that may appeal to the granting authority. This power of issuing the temporary permit is not an uncontrolled or unrestricted power. While granting the permit, the interest of the public generally and the advantages flowing from the temporary provision to the public must be borne in mind. Ordinarily, however too frequent temporary permits for the same vehicle on the same route ought not be granted, specially when the provision for permanent permits is already there. Further, it cannot be said that once the number of stage carriage permits between the two states is exhausted, the transport authorities of the two states cannot issue fresh temporary permits beyond the said limit till there is a fresh agreement between the two states as it all depends on the exigencies of the situation and it is for meeting out such exigencies that a provision has been made under section 87(1) in the Act; *Hridyanand Tiwari* v. *State of Madhya Pradesh,* AIR 2001 MP 17: 2001 (1) MPLJ 466: 2001 (1) ACC 13.

6. Chairman cannot Interfere in Order Passed by Secretary – The State Transport Authority, delegate to its Chairman or Secretary, its power, to grant a temporary permit. The orders passed by them are appealable or revisable by S.T.A.'s Tribunal. The authorities thus exercise delegated concurrent powers. Though it is true that as per the Rule, Chairman can call records of matters in which Secretary is exercising delegated powers. But Chairman cannot call records once Secretary disposed the matter. Therefore as Chairman is not an appealable or revisable authority against the order of Secretary, he cannot interfere an order passed by Secretary; *Atanu Patnaik* v. *State Transport Authority, Orissa,* AIR 1999 Ori 30: 1999 (1) Civ LJ 329: 1998 (1) Ori LR 546.

7. Application for Temporary Permit – The applications for temporary permit filed invoking section 87(1)(d) shall be considered only in cases where the applications for renewal of permit are filed within the period prescribed in section 81 and in case where the applications for renewal are filed out of time, the applications for temporary permit under section 87(1)(d) shall be considered only after the RTA or the STA, as the case may be, entertains such applications for renewal on being satisfied that the applicant was prevented by good and sufficient cause from making the application for renewal within the time specified. Thus, an application for renewal of a regular permit filed, beyond the time prescribed by law, along with an application for excusing the delay is not eligible to be treated as an application pending consideration, for the purpose of entertaining an application for temporary permit under section 87(1)(d); *C. Abdul Nasar* v. *Secretary, Regional Transport Authority,* AIR 2012 Ker 142.

88. Validation of permits for use outside region in which granted.—(1) Except as may be otherwise prescribed, a permit granted by the Regional

Transport Authority of any one region shall not be valid in any other region, unless the permit has been countersigned by the Regional Transport Authority of that other region, and a permit granted in any one State shall not be valid in any other State unless countersigned by the State Transport Authority of that other State or by the Regional Transport Authority concerned:

Provided that a goods carriage permit, granted by the Regional Transport Authority of any one region, for any area in any other region or regions within the same State shall be valid in that area without the counter-signature of the Regional Transport Authority of the other region or of each of the other regions concerned:

Provided further that where both the starting point and the terminal point of a route are situate within the same State, but part of such route lies in any other State and the length of such part does not exceed sixteen kilometres, the permit shall be valid in the other State in respect of that part of the route which is in that other State notwithstanding that such permit has not been countersigned by the State Transport authority or the Regional Transport Authority of that other State:

Provided also that—

(a) where a motor vehicle covered by a permit granted in one State is to be used for the purposes of defence in any other State, such vehicle shall display a certificate, in such form, and issued by such Authority, as the Central Government may, by notification in the Official Gazette, specify, to the effect that the vehicle shall be used for the period specified therein exclusively for the purposes of defence; and

(b) any such permit shall be valid in that other State notwithstanding that such permit has not been countersigned by the State Transport Authority or the Regional Transport Authority of that other State.

(2) Notwithstanding anything contained in sub-section (1), a permit granted or countersigned by a State Transport Authority shall be valid in the whole State or in such regions within the State as may be specified in the permit.

(3) A Regional Transport Authority when countersigning the permit may attach to the permit any condition which it might have imposed if it had granted the permit and may likewise vary any condition attached to the permit by the authority by which the permit was granted.

(4) The provisions of this Chapter relating to the grant, revocation and suspension of permits shall apply to the grant, revocation and suspension of countersignatures of permits:

Provided that it shall not be necessary to follow the procedure laid down in section 80 for the grant of countersignatures of permits, where the permits granted in any one State are required to be countersigned by the State Transport Authority of another State or by the Regional Transport Authority concerned as a result of any agreement arrived at between the States after complying with the requirements of sub-section (5).

(5) Every proposal to enter into an agreement between the States to fix the number of permits which is proposed to be granted or countersigned in respect of each route or area, shall be published by each of the State Governments

concerned in the Official Gazette and in any one or more of the newspapers in regional language circulating in the area or route proposed to be covered by the agreement together with a notice of the date before which representations in connection therewith may be submitted, and the date not being less than thirty days from the date of publication in the Official Gazette, on which, and the authority by which, and the time and place at which, the proposal and any representation received in connection therewith will be considered.

(6) Every agreement arrived at between the States shall, in so far as it relates to the grant of countersignature of permits, be published by each of the State Governments concerned in the Official Gazette and in any one or more of the newspapers in the regional language circulating in the area or route covered by the agreement and the State Transport Authority of the State and the Regional Transport Authority concerned shall give effect to it.

(7) Notwithstanding anything contained in sub-section (1), a Regional Transport Authority of one region may issue a temporary permit under section 87 to be valid in another region or State with the concurrence, given generally or for the particular occasion, of the Regional Transport Authority of that other region or of the State Transport Authority of that other State, as the case may be.

(8) Notwithstanding anything contained in sub-section (1), but subject to any rules that may be made under this Act by the Central Government, the Regional Transport Authority of any one region or, as the case may be, the State Transport Authority may, for the convenience of the public, [1][grant a special permit to any public service vehicle including any vehicle covered] by a permit issued under section 72 (including a reserve stage carriage) or under section 74 or under sub-section (9) of this section for carrying a passenger or passengers for hire or reward under a contract, express or implied, for the use of the vehicle as a whole without stopping to pick up or set down along the line of route passengers not included in the contract, and in every case where such special permit is granted, the Regional Transport Authority shall assign to the vehicle, for display thereon, a special distinguishing mark in the form and manner specified by the Central Government and such special permit shall be valid in any other region or State without the countersignature of the Regional Transport Authority of the other region or of the State Transport Authority of the other State, as the case may be.

(9) Notwithstanding anything contained in sub-section (1) but subject to any rules that may be made by the Central Government under sub-section (14), any State Transport Authority may, for the purpose of promoting tourism, grant permits in respect of tourist vehicles valid for the whole of India, or in such contiguous States not being less than three in number including the State in which the permit is issued as may be specified in such permit in accordance with the choice indicated in the application and the provisions of sections 73, 74, 80, 81, 82, 83, 84, 85, 86 [2][clause (d) of sub-section (1) of section 87 and section 89] shall, as far as may be, apply in relation to such permits.

1. Subs. by Act 54 of 1994, see. 27, for "grant a special permit in relation to a vehicle covered" (w.e.f. 14-11-1994).
2. Subs. by Act 54 of 1994, sec. 27, for "and 89" (w.e.f. 14-11-1994).

[1][***]

(11) The following shall be conditions of every permit granted under sub-section (9), namely:—

(i) every motor vehicle in respect of which such permit is granted shall conform to such description, requirement regarding the seating capacity, standards of comforts, amenities and other matters, as the Central Government may specify in this behalf;

(ii) every such motor vehicle shall be driven by a person having such qualifications and satisfying such conditions as may be specified by the Central Government; and

(iii) such other conditions as may be prescribed by the Central Government.

(12) Notwithstanding anything contained in sub-section (1), but, subject to the rule that may be made by the Central Government under sub-section (14), the appropriate authority may, for the purpose of encouraging long distance inter-State road transport, grant in a State, national permits in respect of goods carriages and the provisions of sections 69, 77, 79, 80, 81, 82, 83, 84, 85, 86, [2][clause (d) of sub-section (1) of section 87 and section 89] shall, as far as may be, apply to or in relation to the grant of national permits.

[3][***]

(14) (a) The Central Government may make rules for carrying out the provisions of this section.

(b) In particular, and without prejudice to the generality of the foregoing power, such rules may provide for all or any of the following matters, namely:—

(i) the authorisation fee payable of the issue of a permit referred to in sub-sections (9) and (12);

(ii) the fixation of the laden weight of the motor vehicle;

(iii) the distinguishing particulars or marks to be carried or exhibited in or on the motor vehicle;

(iv) the colour or colours in which the motor vehicle is to be painted;

(v) such other matters as the appropriate authority shall consider in granting a national permit.

Explanation.—In this section,—

(a) "appropriate authority", in relation to a national permit, means the authority which is authorised under this Act to grant a goods carriage permit;

(b) "authorisation fee" means the annual fee, not exceeding one thousand rupees, which may be charged by the appropriate authority of a State to enable a motor vehicle, covered by the permit referred to in sub-sections (9) and (12) to be used in other States subject to the payment of taxes or fees, if any, levied by the States concerned;

1. Sub-section (10) omitted by Act 54 of 1994, sec. 27 (w.e.f. 14-11-1994).
2. Subs. by Act 54 of 1994, sec. 27, for "and 89" (w.e.f. 14-11-1994).
3. Sub-section (13) omitted by Act 54 of 1994, sec. 27 (w.e.f. 14-11-1994).

(c) "national permit" means a permit granted by the appropriate authority to goods carriages to operate throughout the territory of India or in such contiguous States, not being less than four in number, including the State in which the permit is issued as may be specified in such permit in accordance with the choice indicated in the application.

SYNOPSIS

COMMENTS

1. Power to Make Rules for Purposes of All-India Tourist Vehicles – The Central Government alone has been authorised to frame the Rules as well as to prescribe the conditions for the purposes of All-India tourist vehicles. The power to make rules under sections 95 and 96 would not include the power to frame rules applicable to All-India tourist permit which is exclusively vested in the Central Government. The power to frame rules and prescribe conditions for the All-India tourist permit is exclusively vested in the Central Government and the High Court was right in holding that the State Government would have no jurisdiction to either frame the Rules or prescribe conditions for the All-India tourist permits; *State of Andhra Pradesh* v. *B. Noorulla Khan,* AIR 2004 SC 2413: 2004 AIR SCW 2901: 2004 (6) SCC 194: 2004 (5) SCALE 618: 2004 (5) Supreme 660.

2. Grant of Inter-State Permit – The grant of inter-State permits are permissible under section 88(5) of the Act. The existence of a inter-State route is a condition precedent for exercise of the power under section 88(1) of the Act. Inter-State route under the scheme of the Act has to be reciprocal and cannot be unilaterally created by one State or an Authority in the State. Thus where the inter-State route for which permit was granted was found to be non-existent prior to the grant of permit and it was found that the inter-State route was opened for the first time by RTA of only one State and impugned permits were granted consequent upon opening of such route, the grant of permits was illegal; *Ashwani Kumar* v. *Regional Transport Authority, Bikaner,* AIR 1999 SC 3888: 1999 AIR SCW 3974: JT 1999 (7) SC 609: 1999 (8) SCC 364: 1999 (6) SCALE 219: 1999 (8) Supreme 279.

3. Number of Trips can be Increased only if Inter-State Agreement is Revised – Existence of a route and reciprocal agreement by two State fixing the ceiling of the permit or number of trips by each State are conditions precedent for considering the application for grant of permit on an inter-State route. The Transport Authority of either State is not competent to grant permit or counter signature over and above the strength fixed by the agreement. Similarly, number of trips provided in the agreement cannot be enhanced, as it would amount to variation of conditions of permit, in contravention of the terms and conditions incorporated in the inter-State agreement, and thus, such an order of the authority either granting permit or counter signature or increasing the number of trips would be without jurisdiction. However, in public interest if both the states come to the conclusion that number of vehicle or trips provided in the agreement are not sufficient to cater the need of the traveling public, the law permits the revision of the agreement by both the States adopting the similar procedure as had been adopted at the time of having the reciprocal agreement initially; *Mohd. Sajid Ansari* v. *State of Uttar Pradesh*, AIR 2006 All 308: 2006 AIHC 3029: 2007 (2) Civ LJ 253.

4. Model Condition is to be Considered while Granting National Permit – Section 88(14) does not expressly authorises the Government to frame rules prescribing model condition of a motor vehicle for operation under a national permit. It empowers the Government to frame rules providing for "such other matters as the appropriate authority shall consider in granting a national permit." By this clause Government can prescribe any relevant matter which should be considered by the transport authorities while granting national permit. Model condition is one of the relevant matters which is to be considered by the transport authorities while granting a national permit. The prescription of model condition as such, is implicit in sub-clause (v) of clause (b) of sub-section (14) of section 88; *Radhey Shyam Sharma* v. *Regional Transport Authority, Kathgodam, Nainital*, AIR 1991 All 158: 1991 All LJ 104.

5. Grant of Special Permit – The court direct the authority to consider the applications of the operators for grant of special permits on fulfilment of the following conditions.

1. The operator has to file an application seeking special permit with the contract entered into between him and the contractor duly enclosing the list of passengers, at least 24 hours before the commencement of journey, unless special circumstances exist. As and when special circumstances exist, it is always open to the authorities concerned to relax the time limit for submitting the application. After receipt of the application, the authorities concerned shall complete the enquiry as expeditiously as possible and see that permission is accorded to the operator at least three hours before commencement of the journey.
2. The commuters travelling in the vehicle should belong to one homogeneous group and they should undertake the journey for a common purpose.
3. The driver shall always keep the list of passengers along with the vehicle till the vehicle completes the trip as shown in the special permit.
4. The entire party shall travel point to point. Of course, if any of the passengers wants to get down enroute, it is always open to him to do so, but the operators shall not pick up any passenger in place of the person who got down; *S.M. Haneef* v. *Transport Commissioner, Government of A.P., Hyderabad*, AIR 1999 AP 446: 1999 (5) Andh LD 228: 1999 (3) Andh WR 250.

6. National Permit alone cannot make Vehicle Eligible for Use in Other States – National Permit alone does not make a vehicle eligible for use in other States. It naturally follows that in respect of the year or the States for which authorisation is not issued by the home State in respect of the vehicle, for the only reason that there was a national permit valid for a period of five years, the State is not entitled to collect authorisation fee and composite fee. The position is clear from of the Central Rules read with state Rules whereby the State is required to give periodic intimation of the authorisation already issued, to the States concerned. If the vehicle has been used outside the State without authorisation, it is for that State or the home State to take appropriate action for violating the Act and Rules and not for the home State to collect authorisation fee and composite fee for those States covered by the national permit; *M.C. Sunil* v. *Regional Transport Officer, Palakkad,* AIR 2005 Ker 221: 2005 (2) ACC 834: 2005 (1) Ker LJ 835.

7. Temporary Permit in Respect of Inter-State Route – An inter-State route as the terminii was created under the reciprocal agreement between the respective parties. Since the expression "route" has been defined under the Motor Vehicles Act as a line of travel which specifies the highway, which may be traversed by a Motor Vehicle between one terminus and another, any alteration made in a manner that it does not alter the numbers of the terminus will not render the route with the alteration keeping the terminii to be the same to be a different route. Any extra trip or partial return trip may sometimes in effect and substance constitute a separate route though on the part of the same Highway or line of travel as contemplated under the original route in case of altering the terminii but where no different terminii are either contemplated or created the stoppages at the intervening places of the route not constituting a terminii will not and cannot result in creating a different route with different terminii. Thus, taking into consideration the implications arising under the provisions contained in section 87(7) of the Act, there could be no impediment in permitting the plying of the stage carriage on the same route, that is to say, with the same terminii or even with a deviation keeping the terminii to be the same if the concerned States agreed to the deviation specially when the reciprocal agreement did not envisage the grant of a temporary permit for meeting out any extraordinary situation justifying the grant of a temporary permit for a specified period to meet any exigency for a short duration taking into consideration the convenience of the general public and providing them facility of transportation; *Hridyanand Tiwari* v. *State of Madhya Pradesh,* AIR 2001 MP 17: 2001 (1) MPLJ 466: 2001 (1) ACC 13.

8. Word "Route" Means Parent Route and not Modified Route – The section talks of the validation of a permit for use outside the region in which it was granted. By variation of a route, it is not uncommon that a terminus as per the original route, is changed, and in such cases, if both the terminal are within the same State, the proviso will come into operation. Even in common parlance nobody refers to a varied route having a starting point and a terminal point. Therefore, in the context in which the proviso is introduced, the word "a route" means only these, parent route or the route, which is sought to be modified. If so, it goes without anything that the said proviso will not come to the aid of the respondent; *K. Vaithianathan* v. *Union Territory of Pondicherry,* AIR 1995 Mad 197.

9. Agreement cannot be given Effect to before Publication – The section 88 of the Act provides for a proposal to enter into an agreement regarding fixing of number of permits which is proposed to be granted or countersigned. It provides the subsequent stage *i.e.,* after the publication of the proposed agreement. It provides the publication of the agreement in the Official Gazette as well as in the local newspaper. The authorities can give effect to such an agreement only when such agreement is published in Gazette as well as in the newspaper. Thus, an agreement can be effected only after the same is published in the Official Gazette as well as in the local newspapers. The R.T.A. cannot give effect to the agreement before its publication in the local newspapers; *Radhey Shyam* v. *State of Rajasthan,* AIR 2004 Raj 300.

10. Communication of Grant of Permit – The provisions of the Rules are mandatory for the reason that non-compliance of the conditions mentioned in the Resolution while granting the permit, if not communicated, would cause serious prejudice to the grantee as he would not be able to lift the permit in stipulated period nor he would be able to go in appeal under the provisions of section 89 of the Act, if he feels aggrieved by the resolution order; *R.S.R.T.C.* v. *State Transport Appellate Tribunal,* AIR 1999 Raj 111: 1999 (1) Raj LR 218: 1999 (1) Raj LW 91.

11. Increase in Number of Permits in Agreement – Increasing the number of permits in the agreement which are more than the proposal is not beyond the scope of section 88(5). A proposal become final only when a final shape is given to it and final shape is by way of an agreement in which proposal can be varied either way and as such the plea of the permit holders that the agreement entered into is not in accordance with the provisions of section 88(5) of the Act of 1988 has no substance. The right of the permit holders to make the representation in a case where the number is increased is not otherwise denied because it is an open fact that transport will never prefer increase of the number of the permits on their route. Their representations will only be either to reduce the number of the permit or to keep as minimum as possible so that their income is not affected. The grant of more permits does not effect legal rights but it is only a reasonable restriction contemplated by the Legislature so that more vehicles may be operated on a particular route or area. If after considering the representation, State Authorities come to the conclusion that number of the permits has to be increased, they are within their jurisdiction to do so; *Nirmal Kumar* v. *State of Rajasthan,* AIR 1998 Raj 189: 1997 (3) Raj LW 2086: 1998 (2) WLC 141.

12. For Plying Vehicle in another State Counter Signature of Authority of that other State is Necessary – From the perusal of the provisions of section 88 it is apparent that unless and until a specific permission is granted by the Authority of any one region, the same shall not be valid in another region unless and until the permit has been countersigned by the Authority of that particular region and a permit granted by any one State shall not be valid for plying vehicle in another State unless the same is countersigned by the Authority of that other State or by the Regional Transport Authority concerned. The said provision is mandatory requirement of the statute and its *vires* are not open to question by any aggrieved party; *Ajay Singh* v. *State Transport Appellate Tribunal, Rajasthan, Jaipur,* AIR 1998 Raj 266: 1999 (1) Civ LJ 260: 1998 (3) WLC 336.

A careful reading of section 88 clearly provides that the Regional Transport Authority of the State is empowered to grant permit on the inter-State route but that will not be valid in any other State unless the permit has been countersigned by the State Transport Authority of that State or Regional Transport Authority of that region; *Rajasthan State Road Transport Corporation, Jaipur* v. *R.T.A., Bikaner,* AIR 1996 Raj 11: 1995 (3) Civ LJ 769: 1995 (1) Raj LW 684.

13. Change of Condition of Permit – Any application made under section 80(3) for increasing or decreasing the number of trips would certainly result in the change of the condition of the permit and that application shall be treated as an application for grant of a new permit; *Ramkumar* v. *Secretary, R.T.A., Bikaner,* AIR 1993 Raj 30: 1992 (1) Raj LR 314: 1992 (2) Raj LW 27.

14. Increase of Number of Trips – Increasing the number of permits in the agreement 'which are more than the proposed is not beyond the scope of section 88(5) of the Act. A proposal becomes final only when a final shape is given to it and final shape is by way of any agreement in which proposal can be varied either way and as such the plea of the permit holders that the agreement entered into was not in accordance with the provisions or intention of this section is devoid of any substance. A reasonable restriction is contemplated by Legislature but if after consideration of the permit holders' representation, the State authorities conclude that the number of the permits needs to be increased, the authorities are within their jurisdiction to do so; *Nirmal Kumar* v. *State of Rajasthan,* AIR 1998 Raj 189: 1997 (3) Raj LW 2086: 1998 (2) WLC 141.

15. Refusal to Countersign Permits is Proper – Refusal to counter-sign the two permits in question by the Karnataka State Transport Authority cannot be said to be illegal. A State Transport Authority can countersign an inter-State route permit only for an authorised route specified in an inter-State agreement. In the present case, the inter-State routes, for which the counter-signatures were sought for, do not figure in any of the reciprocal agreements between the two States. Hence, Karnataka State Transport Authority's refusal to counter-sign the two permits cannot be faulted with; *S.A. Wahab*

v. *Karnataka State Transport Authority Bangalore,* AIR 2013 Kant 69: 2013 (2) AIR Kar R 253: 2013 (2) Kant LJ 692.

16. Temporary Inter-State Stage Carriage Permits – Though the State of West Bengal and the State of Bihar had entered into a reciprocal agreement in 1988 for issue of a certain number of permits, the State Transport Authority, Bihar exceeded the quota of permits for the inter-State route and there was no concurrence in general or for a particular occasion for issue of the temporary permit in favour of the respondent for the route from Motihari in Bihar to Siliguri in West Bengal. There was no counter-signature of the State Transport Authority, West Bengal, on the temporary permit issued by the State Transport Authority (Bihar), the respondent did not have a valid permit for the part of the route inside the State of West Bengal. The plying of the vehicle of the respondent in the Siliguri region within the State of West Bengal was thus in contravention of section 66(1) of the Motor Vehicles Act which provides that no owner of a vehicle shall use or permit use of the vehicle as a transport vehicle save in accordance with the conditions of a permit granted or counter-signed by the Regional or State Transport Authority. The appellants, therefore, were well within their powers to detain and seize the vehicle of the respondent under section 207 of the Motor Vehicles Act for contravention of section 66 of the said Act; *State of West Bengal* v. *Mani Bhushan Kumar,* AIR 2012 SC 184: 2011 AIR SCW 6366: (2011) 10 SCC 147.

17. Permits Granted to Ply Vehicles and Renewed from Time to Time would be Saved – When the permit was indisputably granted to the State Transport Undertaking (RSRTC) pursuant to earlier agreement and renewed from time to time and by virtue of latter final agreement, it was saved and the RSRTC was permitted to ply its vehicle on inter-State route impugned and no error was committed by the respondent. When the route was not available for private operators to ply on a nationalized route, and it being not incorporated in draft agreement, obviously there was no occasion for the State and the Committee constituted to still examine and give its detailed finding regarding objections raised under section 88(5) of MV Act; *Anmol Bus Service* v. *State,* AIR 2011 Raj 74: 2010 AIHC 769 (NOC): 2010 (2) Cur CC 382.

18. Writ Jurisdiction – Grant of Fresh Permits in Favour of New Operators – Writ Petition Challenging Maintainable – If the challenge is on the ground of illegality or arbitrariness or colourable exercise of power or otherwise being violative of Article 14 of the Constitution, notwithstanding that the action may be impelled by the commercial interests of the existing operator; provided that the substance of challenge is not founded only on the commercial interests of the existing operator being prejudiced by the acts complained of; *Prabhat Pan* v. *State of West Bengal,* AIR 2015 Cal 112.

19. Operators Plying Vehicles for Carrying Passengers in Violation of Statutory Provisions – Writ Petition by holders of permit maintainable; *Prabhat Pan* v. *State of West Bengal,* AIR 2015 Cal 112.

89. Appeals.—(1) Any person—

(a) aggrieved by the refusal of the State or a Regional Transport Authority to grant a permit, or by any condition attached to a permit granted to him, or

(b) aggrieved by the revocation or suspension of the permit or by any variation of the conditions thereof, or

(c) aggrieved by the refusal to transfer the permit under section 82, or

(d) aggrieved by the refusal of the State or a Regional Transport Authority to countersign a permit, or by any condition attached to such counter-signature, or

(e) aggrieved by the refusal of renewal of a permit, or

(f) aggrieved by the refusal to grant permission under section 83, or

(g) aggrieved by any other order which may be prescribed,

may, within the prescribed time and in the prescribed manner, appeal to the State Transport Appellate Tribunal constituted under sub-section (2), who shall, after giving such person and the original authority an opportunity of being heard, give a decision thereon which shall be final.

[1][(2) The State Government shall constitute such number of Transport Appellate Tribunals as it thinks fit and each such Tribunal shall consist of a judicial officer who is not below the rank of a District Judge or who is qualified to be a Judge of the High Court and it shall exercise jurisdiction within such area as may be notified by that Government.]

(3) Notwithstanding anything contained in sub-section (1) or sub-section (2), every appeal pending at the commencement of this Act, shall continue to be proceeded with and disposed of as if this Act had not been passed.

Explanation.—For the removal of doubts, it is hereby declared that when any order is made by the State Transport Authority or the Regional Transport Authority in pursuance of a direction issued by the Inter-State Transport Commission under clause (c) of sub-section (2) of section 63A of the Motor Vehicles Act, 1939 (4 of 1939), as it stood immediately before the commencement of this Act, and any person feels aggrieved by such order on the ground that it is not in consonance with such direction, he may appeal under sub- section (1) to the State Transport Appellate Tribunal against such order but not against the direction so issued.

SYNOPSIS

1. Writ Petition cannot be Invoked when Specific Provision Lay Down
2. Words "any person"
3. Object to Grant of Variation not to be Permitted First Time in Appeal
4. Unless Reasons Given Higher Authorities cannot Appreciate Application
5. Appeal Against Order Refusing Permission for Plying Vehicle – Condonation of Delay
6. Delay in Filing Appeal Against Order of Variation

COMMENTS

1. Writ Petition cannot be Invoked when Specific Provision Lay Down – Writ petition for executing orders of State Transport Appellate Tribunal under Motor Vehicles Act, is not maintainable. Tribunal is constituted under section 89(2) which is capable of implementing its own order under the rules framed governing the procedure before the S.T.A.T. Therefore it is capable of executing its own order and does not require any aid of any outside agency. When specific provision has been laid down; writ jurisdiction cannot be invoked to reduce the jurisdiction under Article 226 of the Constitution; *Ved Pal Singh* v. *State Transport Appellate Tribunal, Lucknow,* AIR 1999 All 136: 1999 All LJ 925: 1998 All CJ 694.

2. Words "any person" – the words "any person" in the context should undoubtedly include "every aggrieved person". Therefore, the appeal remedy provided in section 89 of the Act is available to any aggrieved person. Even according to the appellant, it is aggrieved by the order of the State Transport Appellate Tribunal impugned in the writ petition. Therefore, it cannot be said that the appellant does not fall within the expression

1. Subs. by Act 54 of 1994, sec. 28, for sub-section (2) (w.e.f. 14-11-1994).

"any person aggrieved" occurring in section 89 of the Act. The appellant is entitled to prefer an appeal to the State Transport Appellate Tribunal under section 89(b) of the Act; *Sree Gajanana Motor Transport Co. Ltd.* v. *K.S.T.A. Tribunal,* AIR 2003 Kant 326: 2004 (2) Kant LJ 87: 2003 AIR Kant HCR 1481.

3. Object to Grant of Variation not to be Permitted First Time in Appeal – When the State Transport Undertaking cannot object to the grant of variation, it cannot be permitted to object for the first time at the appellate stage by filing an appeal; *Tvl. Cholan Roadways Corpn. Ltd.* v. *Tvl. Ajantha Travels, Pondicherry,* AIR 1995 Mad 139: 1994 Writ LR 741.

4. Unless Reasons Given Higher Authorities cannot Appreciate Application – No reasons have been assigned in the impugned order. Only one reason assigned is "dismissed". This is not a method in which an order should be passed by the respondent authorities. This is thoroughly a non-application of mind and it reveals absolute arbitrariness, which leads to inequality. By this type of attitude, authority may allow the application whereas in rest of the cases, he may dismiss by one word like the present impugned order. The impugned order is an appealable order under section 89 of the Motor Vehicles Act, 1988 and, therefore, also reasons ought to have been assigned by the concerned respondent authorities. Reasons are the soul of the order. Unless, the reasons are given, higher authorities cannot appreciate why the application was allowed or dismissed. This is a bare minimum requirement, which, the respondent authorities ought to have kept in mind. Not to assign any reasons and the application is dismissed, is a non-application of mind and arbitrariness. Therefore, it is directed that the concerned respondent authorities to decide afresh, the application of the petitioner and speaking order shall be passed under section 80 of the Motor Vehicles Act within a period of four weeks from the date of receipt of a copy of the order of the Court; *Dinesh Nand Jha* v. *State of Jharkhand,* AIR 2011 Jhar 6: 2010 AIHC 143: 2010 (3) ICC 193.

5. Appeal Against Order Refusing Permission for Plying Vehicle – Condonation of Delay – The application for getting permission for plying a motor vehicle has been dismissed by the State Transport Authority. The appellant has caused thirteen days delay in preferring an appeal. The Transport Appellate Tribunal ought to have condoned the delay of thirteen days. The reason canvassed by the petitioner is a reasonable reason for condonation of delay. The Appellate Tribunal has passed the order mechanically and without any application of mind. Thirteen days delay caused by a citizen in preferring an appeal and that too because of sickness, ought to have been condoned by the Appellate Tribunal. The Appellate Tribunal has referred several decisions of criminal matters under section 302 of the Indian Penal Code etc., which are not at all useful and relevant. Looking to the provisions of rule 111(4) of the Bihar Motor Vehicles Rules, 1992 to be read with section 29(2) of the Limitation Act, 1963, section 4 to section 24 of the Limitation Act, 1963 are applicable to the transport appeal, preferred under section 89 of the Motor Vehicles Act, when application for getting permission for plying a motor vehicle has been dismissed by the State Transport Authority. Therefore the delay has been condoned in preferring Transport Appeal and directed to the State Transport Appellate Tribunal to hear and dispose of the Transport Appeal on its own merits; *Dineshanand Jha* v. *State of Jharkhand,* AIR 2010 Jhar 125: 2010 (93) All Ind Cas 881: 2011 (1) Civ LJ 473.

6. Delay in Filing Appeal Against Order of Variation – The appellants are running a Stage Carriage had applied for variation by curtailing the route. The said order was passed by the State Transport Authority (STA) on 30th March, 1998. If the respondents -Corporations have filed an appeal in 2005 questioning the grant of variation passed in 1998 without there being an application to condone the delay the appeal could not have been entertained. But unfortunately, on perusal of the order of the STA it is unable to make out whether there an application was filed to condone the delay. Such an application has been filed where the delay of 7 years was condoned by the STA. Therefore, if really there is no order passed to condone the delay by the State Appellate Tribunal (STAT), it is for the Tribunal to consider the said issue as a Preliminary Issue and then to hear all the appeals filed by the appellants and consider the order passed by the STA on merits and in accordance with law. On perusal of the order of the STAT, it is clear that none of the grounds urged by the appellants are considered by it. Thus where the Tribunal has allowed the appeals without considering grounds urged by the appellants, in all fairness, it was required to remand the matter to the STAT and not to the STA; *M. Krishna Murthy* v. *Karnataka State Transport Authority, Bangalore,* AIR 2012 Kant 188.

90. Revision.—The State Transport Appellate Tribunal may, on an application made to it, call for the record of any case in which an order has been made by a State Transport Authority or Regional Transport Authority against which no appeal lies, and if it appears to the State Transport Appellate Tribunal that the order made by the State Transport Authority or Regional Transport Authority is improper or illegal, the State Transport Appellate Tribunal may pass such order in relation to the case as it deems fit and every such order shall be final:

Provided that the State Transport Appellate Tribunal shall not entertain any application from a person aggrieved by an order of a State Transport Authority or Regional Transport Authority, unless the application is made within thirty days from the date of the order:

Provided further that the State Transport Appellate Tribunal may entertain the application after the expiry of the said period of thirty days, if it is satisfied that the applicant was prevented by good and sufficient cause from making the application in time:

Provided also that the State Transport Appellate Tribunal shall not pass an order under this section prejudicial to any person without giving him a reasonable opportunity of being heard.

SYNOPSIS

1. *Locus Standi* of Operator to File Revision
2. Refusal of Permit without Assigning Reasons not Justified
3. Revision will Lie where No Appeal Lies
4. Order can be Called in Question by Aggrieved Operator in Revision
5. Jurisdiction can be Exercised only when Person Aggrieved Filed Application
6. Revision – Violation of Statutory Prohibitions
7. "Person Aggrieved"

COMMENTS

1. *Locus Standi* of Operator to File Revision – An order granting permits may affect the working of the route. Therefore the existing operator has *locus standi,* being aggrieved person, to file a revision under section 90 of the Act before the Appellate Tribunal. The Appellate Tribunal should or not interfere is a matter for the tribunal itself to decide but the revision cannot be thrown out on the ground that it is not maintainable. As the Act gives the power of superintendence to the Tribunal so as to keep the transport authorities within check, it is the bounden duty of the Appellate Tribunal to interfere if it finds that the transport authorities have exercised their powers of granting permits erroneously or illegally. It is true that under the Act the existing operator cannot claim any legal right to file representation or right for hearing at the stage of the grant of permit on his route. Absence of legal right to file representation or to be heard may be relevant consideration for determining as to whether existing operator can be treated to be an aggrieved person for the purpose of filing revision under section 90 of the Act against the order of the R.T.A. granting permit, but this is not an exclusive test for determination of the *locus standi* of an operator to file a revision; *Surendra Rao* v. *State Transport Appellate Tribunal, U.P., Lucknow,* AIR 1992 All 211: 1992 All LJ 695: 1992 (1) All CJ 391.

2. Refusal of Permit without Assigning Reasons not Justified – The Tribunal has refuse permit on ground that no proper affidavits were filed in support of applications. The Tribunal has not specified any reason as to how the Regional Transport Authority has violated the provisions in granting the permit. The Tribunal was possessed of the whole record and if there was violation of any provisions of law or the grant of permit was not in the public interest in any manner, the specific reasons ought to have been assigned; *Manzoor Ahmad* v. *State Transport Appellate Tribunal, Lucknow,* AIR 1994 All 202: 1993 (22) All LR 329: 1993 (2) All WC 812.

3. Revision will Lie where No Appeal Lies – A revision will lie to the State Transport Appellate Tribunal where no appeal lies if the order of the State Transport Authority or Regional Transport Authority is improper or illegal. Use of the word 'improper' in section 90 of the Act implies that a revision will lie even on questions of facts and it is not limited to questions of law alone. Hence all questions which the petitioner wishes to agitate, both legal and factual, can be raised before the S.T.A.T. under section 90 of the Act; *Om Prakash Gupta* v. *R.T.A., Meerut,* AIR 1992 All 291: 1992 AWC 1610.

4. Order can be Called in Question by Aggrieved Operator in Revision – Any order of the Regional Transport Authority or the State Transport Authority, whether it be grant of a permit or assignment of timings, can be called in question by an aggrieved operator and the order can be demonstrated to be either illegal or improper. It follows that a rival operator on making allegations which prima facie demonstrates a grievance which calls for examination, is entitled to have his revision examined on merits in accordance with law and he cannot be thrown out at the threshold on the ground that he has no grievance; *D.L. Sadashiva Reddy* v. *P. Lala Sheriff,* AIR 1999 Kant 5: 1998 (6) Kant LJ 42: 1999 (2) Civ LJ 614.

5. Jurisdiction can be Exercised only when Person Aggrieved Filed Application – Section 90 does not confer power on the STAT to pass orders under that section merely for the reason that the order of the STA or RTA is improper or illegal. The jurisdiction will be exercised only when an application is filed by a person aggrieved. To hold otherwise will be to render the words "person aggrieved" in section 90 redundant and otiose. The scope of the expression "person aggrieved" occurring in section 90 shall conform to the scheme of the enactment whereas for the purpose of judicial review a different yardstick may be warranted so as to meet the ends of justice. The existing operator cannot invoke the revisional jurisdiction on the sole ground that the grant of permit to the opposite party prejudicially affects his rights. It is not as though he can impeach each and every order of the RTA or STA alleging illegality or impropriety. He can challenge only those orders against which he can have a legal grievance. He cannot be a person aggrieved in respect of every action or decision of RTA or STA; *Binu Chacko* v. *Regional Transport Authority, Pathanamthitta,* AIR 2006 Ker 177: 2006 AIHC 2259: 2006 (3) ICC 57.

6. Revision – Violation of Statutory Prohibitions – Existing permit-holder has no right to file revision under section 90; *M.C. Ratheesh* v. *The Secretary, Regional Transport Authority, Thrissur,* AIR 2015 Ker 86.

7. "Person Aggrieved" – Question to be decided in facts of each case; *M.C. Ratheesh* v. *The Secretary, Regional Transport Authority, Thrissur,* AIR 2015 Ker 86.

91. Restriction of hours of work of drivers.—[1][(1) The hours of work of any person engaged for operating a transport vehicle shall be such as provided in the Motor Transport Workers Act, 1961 (7 of 1961)].

(2) A State Government may, by notification in the Official Gazette, grant such exemptions from the provisions of sub-section (1) as it thinks fit, to meet cases of emergency or of delays by reason of circumstances which could not be foreseen.

1. Subs. by Act 54 of 1994, sec. 29, for sub-section (1) (w.e.f. 14-11-1994).

(3) A State Government or, if authorised in this behalf by the State Government by rules made under section 96, the State or a Regional Transport Authority may require persons employing any person whose work is subject to any of the provisions of sub-section (1) to fix beforehand the hours of work of such persons so as to conform to those provisions, and may provide for the recording of the hours so fixed.

(4) No person shall work or shall cause or allow any other person to work outside the hours fixed or recorded for the work of such persons under sub-section (3).

(5) A State Government may prescribe the circumstances under which and the period during which the driver of a vehicle although not engaged in work is required to remain on or near the vehicle may be deemed to be an interval for rest within the meaning of sub-section (1).

92. Voidance of contracts restrictive of liability.—Any contract for the conveyance of a passenger in a stage carriage or contract carriage, in respect of which a permit has been issued under this Chapter, shall, so far as it purports to negative or restrict the liability of any person in respect of any claim made against that person in respect of the death of, or bodily injury to, the passenger while being carried in, entering or alighting from the vehicle, or purports to impose any conditions with respect to the enforcement of any such liability, be void.

COMMENTS

Owner cannot Ply Vehicle Off Route though not Carrying Passengers – The owner cannot ply the vehicle off the route even it is not actually carrying any passenger as section 66 enjoins upon the permit holder to ply his vehicle in strict adherence to and observations of the conditions attached to the permit. Thus, if a vehicle is found whether stationary or moving at a place which does not fall on the route, it will be in contravention of the statutory provisions of the Act unless it falls under exceptions provided in section 66(3) of the Act, and this contravention amounts to plying the vehicle contrary to the condition attached to permit itself and thus it will be liable to be cancelled or suspended under the provisions of section 86 of the Act and action can be taken against the permit holder under the provisions of section 192 of the Act; *Rampati Jaiswal* v. *State of Uttar Pradesh*, AIR 1997 All 170: 1997 All LJ 827: 1998 (1) All CJ 447.

93. Agent or canvasser to obtain licence.—(1) No person shall engage himself—

(i) as an agent or a canvasser, in the sale of tickets for travel by public service vehicles or in otherwise soliciting customers for such vehicles, or

(ii) as an agent in the business of collecting, forwarding or distributing goods carried by goods carriages,

unless he has obtained a licence from such authority and subject to such conditions as may be prescribed by the State Government.

(2) The conditions referred to in sub-section (1) may include all or any of the following matters, namely:—

(a) the period for which a licence may be granted or renewed;

(b) the fee payable for the issue or renewal of the licence;

(c) the deposit of security—

(i) of a sum not exceeding rupees fifty thousand in the case of an agent in the business of collecting, forwarding or distributing goods carried by goods carriages,

(ii) of a sum not exceeding rupees five thousand in the case of any other agent or canvasser,

and the circumstances under which the security may be forfeited;

(d) the provision by the agent of insurance of goods in transit;

(e) the authority by which and the circumstances under which the licence may be suspended or revoked;

(f) such other conditions as may be prescribed by the State Government.

(3) It shall be a condition of every licence that no agent or canvasser to whom the licence is granted shall advertise in any newspaper, book, list, classified directory or other publication unless there is contained in such advertisement appearing in such newspaper, book, list, classified directory or other publication the licence number, the date of expiry of licence and the particulars of the authority which granted the licence.

COMMENTS

Company neither Sell Tickets for Travel by Public Service Vehicles nor Soliciting Customer for Use of Taxi – Company not agent or canvasser; *ANI Technologies Pvt. Ltd.* v. *State of Uttarakhand,* AIR 2015 Uttra 90.

94. Bar on jurisdiction of Civil Courts.—No Civil Court shall have jurisdiction to entertain any question relating to the grant of a permit under this Act, and no injunction in respect of any action taken or to be taken by the duly constituted authorities under this Act with regard to the grant of a permit, shall be entertained by any Civil Court.

COMMENTS

Jurisdiction of Civil Courts – Section 94 of the Act puts a bar on the jurisdiction of the civil Courts to entertain any question relating to grant of permit under the Act. It is noticed that section 3 of the Consumer Protection Act, 1986 provides that the said Act is not in derogation of the provisions of any other law. Therefore, if any person including a passenger, has any grievance, remedies are provided under the special Act itself and other civil Courts have no jurisdiction to usurp the functions of the RTA. Therefore, any grievance regarding anomalies in the fixation of fare stages have to be first raised before the RTA and then by way of revision before the STAT; *Malappuram Dist. Pvt. Bus Operators' Assocn.* v. *M.P. Mohan,* AIR 2000 Ker 192: 1999 (2) Ker LJ 306: 1999 (2) Ker LT 898.

95. Power of State Government to make rules as to stage carriages and contract carriages.—(1) A State Government may make rules to regulate, in respect of stage carriages and contract carriages and the conduct of passengers in such vehicles.

(2) Without prejudice to the generality of the foregoing provision, such rules may—

(a) authorise the removal from such vehicle of any person contravening the rules by the driver or conductor of the vehicle, or, on the request of the driver or conductor, or any passenger, by any police officer;

(b) require a passenger who is reasonably suspected by the driver or conductor of contravening the rules to give his name and address to a police officer or to the driver or conductor on demand;

(c) require a passenger to declare, if so demanded by the driver or conductor, the journey he intends to take or has taken in the vehicle and to pay the fare for the whole of such journey and to accept any ticket issued therefor;

(d) require, on demand being made for the purpose by the driver or conductor or other person authorised by the owners of the vehicle, production during the journey and surrender at the end of the journey by the holder thereof of any ticket issued to him;

(e) require a passenger, if so requested by the driver or conductor, to leave the vehicle on the completion of the journey the fare for which he has paid;

(f) require the surrender by the holder thereof on the expiry of the period for which it is issued of a ticket issued to him;

(g) require a passenger to abstain from doing anything which is likely to obstruct or interfere with the working of the vehicle or to cause damage to any part of the vehicle or its equipment or to cause injury or discomfort to any other passenger;

(h) require a passenger not to smoke in any vehicle on which a notice prohibiting smoking is exhibited;

(i) require the maintenance of complaint books in stage carriages and prescribe the conditions under which passengers can record any complaints in the same.

SYNOPSIS

COMMENTS

1. Town Service Route – Meaning – In the normal connotation, 'town service route' would mean a route within a town to enable passengers to go from one place to another in the town. But generally people in the peripheral and neighbouring areas would be frequenting the town and to serve them, buses have to ply between a place in the town and a place outside. Hence, the rule provides for an extension of 8 kms beyond the limits of the town or municipality; *A.P.S.R.T.C.* v. *State Transport Appellate Tribunal,* AIR 1998 SC 2621: 1998 AIR SCW 2663: JT 1998 (5) SC 417: 1998 (7) SCC 353: 1998 (3) SCR 1106: 1998 (4) SCALE 445: 1998 (6) Supreme 316.

2. Authority cannot Re-fix Compounding Fee once Fixed by Delegated Authority – Once the delegated authority under sections 95 and 96 of the Act had already exercised the powers of framing the rules and fixed the quantum, though as a minimum under the Rules, it is not open for any Authority to re-fix or re-determine the amounts either as a maximum or otherwise. Even on a reading of section 86(5) of the Act and rule 217 of the Rules, the discretion is left with the authority to consider all the aspects in individual cases and then to arrive at a certain sum of money, but not to fix a sweeping uniform rates as sought to be done in the impugned resolutions. Therefore, the entire exercise of powers by the authorities in trying to fix the uniform rates, though in respect of various such offences and also at different stages, is totally beyond the powers conferred under the provisions of the Act and the Rules made thereunder. Further, where law specifically contemplates a discretion to be used in individual cases, the same cannot be curtailed or eroded in any such manner as sought to be done under the impugned resolutions, which fetters the discretion vested in the individual authority to come to a conclusion in a situation in regard to the different permit holders depending upon the facts of each case; *Jami Appala Swamy* v. *Regional Transport Authority*, AIR 2003 AP 265: 2003 (2) Andh LD 324: 2003 (2) Andh LT 270.

3. Extent of Liability of Insurer to Indemnify Insured – Mere fact that the insured has taken a comprehensive policy, does not lead to an inference that the Insurance Company is liable of the entire awarded amount including the amount in excess of the statutory liability; *New India Assurance Co. Ltd.* v. *Chameli Devi*, AIR 2010 P&H 156: 2011 (1) ACJ 211: 2011 (2) Pun LR 454.

96. Power of State Government to make rules for the purposes of this Chapter.—(1) A State Government may make rules for the purpose of carrying into effect the provisions of this Chapter.

(2) Without prejudice to the generality of the foregoing power, rules under this section may be made with respect to all or any of the following matters, namely:—

(i) the period of appointment and the terms of appointment of and the conduct of business by Regional and State Transport Authorities and the reports to be furnished by them;

(ii) the conduct of business by any such authority in the absence of any member (including the Chairman) thereof and the nature of business which, the circumstances under which and the manner in which, business could be so conducted;

(iii) The conduct and hearing of appeals that may be preferred under this Chapter, the fees to be paid in respect of such appeals and the refund of such fees;

(iv) the forms to be used for the purposes of this Chapter, including the forms or permits;

(v) the issue of copies of permits in place of permits lost, destroyed or mutilated;

(vi) the documents, plates and marks to be carried by transport vehicles, the manner in which they are to be carried and the languages in which any such documents are to be expressed;

(vii) the fees to be paid in respect of applications for permits, duplicate permits and plates;

(viii) the exemption of prescribed person or prescribed classes of persons from payment of all or any or any portion of the fees payable under this Chapter;

(ix) the custody, production and cancellation on revocation or expiration of permits, and the return of permits which have been cancelled;

(x) the conditions subject to which, and the extent to which, a permit granted in another State shall be valid in the State without counter-signature;

(xi) the conditions subject to which, and the extent to which, a permit granted in one region shall be valid in another region within the State without counter-signature;

(xii) the conditions to be attached to permits for the purpose of giving effect to any agreement such as is referred to in clause (iii) of sub-section (1) of section 67;

(xiii) the authorities to whom, the time within which and the manner in which appeals may be made;

(xiv) the construction and fittings of, and the equipment to be carried by, stage and contract carriages, whether generally or in specified areas;

(xv) the determination of the number of passengers a stage or contract carriage is adapted to carry and the number which may be carried;

(xvi) the conditions subject to which goods may be carried on stage and contract carriages partly or wholly in lieu of passengers;

(xvii) the safe custody and disposal of property left in a stage or contract carriage;

(xviii) regulating the painting or marking of transport vehicles and the display of advertising matter thereon, and in particular prohibiting the painting or marking of transport vehicles in such colour or manner as to induce any person to believe that the vehicle is used for the transport of mails;

(xix) the conveyance in stage or contract carriages of corpses or persons suffering from any infectious or contagious disease or goods likely to cause discomfort or injury to passengers and the inspection and disinfection of such carriages if used for such purposes;

(xx) the provision of taxi meters on motor cabs requiring approval or standard types of taxi meters to be used and examining testing and sealing taxi meters;

(xxi) prohibiting the picking up or setting down of passengers by stage or contract carriages at specified places or in specified areas or at places other than duly notified stands or halting places and requiring the driver of a stage carriage to stop and remain stationary for a reasonable time when so required by a passenger desiring to board or alight from the vehicle at a notified halting place;

(xxii) the requirements which shall be complied with in the construction or use of any duly notified stand or halting place, including the provision of adequate equipment and facilities for the convenience of all users thereof; the fees, if any, which may be charged for the use of such facilities, the records which shall be maintained at such stands or places, the staff to be employed thereat, and the duties and conduct of such staff, and generally for maintaining such stands and places in a serviceable and clean condition;

(xxiii) the regulation of motor-cab ranks;

(xxiv) requiring the owners of transport vehicles to notify any change of address or to report the failure of or damage to any vehicle used for the conveyance of passengers for hire or reward;

(xxv) authorising specified persons to enter at all reasonable times and inspect all premises used by permit holders for the purposes of their business;

(xxvi) requiring the person in charge of a stage carriage to carry any person tendering the legal or customary fare;

(xxvii) the conditions under which and the types of containers or vehicles in which animals or birds may be carried and the seasons during which animals or birds may or may not be carried;

(xxviii) the licensing of and the regulation of the conduct of agents or canvassers who engage in the sale of tickets for travel by public service vehicles or otherwise solicit customers for such vehicles;

(xxix) the licensing of agents engaged in the business of collecting for forwarding and distributing goods carried by goods carriages;

(xxx) the inspection of transport vehicles and their contents and of the permits relating to them;

(xxxi) the carriage of persons other than the driver in goods carriages;

(xxxii) the records to be maintained and the returns to be furnished by the owners of transport vehicles; and

(xxxiii) any other matter which is to be or may be prescribed.

SYNOPSIS

1. Power of State to Regulate Painting of Transport
2. Personal Hearing
3. Power of State Government under Section 96
4. Grant of Permanent Stage Carriage Permit

COMMENTS

1. Power of State to Regulate Painting of Transport – The state is empowered to regulate painting or making of transport vehicles and in particular prohibiting the painting of vehicle identical with mail vehicle. The word "regulating" is to include power to prohibit. "Regulation" means control and control can only be done by imposing conditions. If it is presumed that "regulating painting" does not empower the State to suggest a particular colour for a particular class of vehicle then in what mode it can "regulate the painting" apart from prohibiting a particular colour to segregate the mail vehicles is not know. The State was entitled to impose conditions while grant of permit and one of such condition would be suggesting a particular colour for a particular class of vehicles. Such restriction was imposed in terms of the power conferred under section 96(2)(xviii) *i.e.*, regulation of painting; *State of West Bengal* v. *Burdwan District Bus Association*, AIR 2009 Cal 32: 2009 AIHC 124 (NOC): 2008 (3) Cal LT 489.

2. Personal Hearing – That the objections have been taken into consideration. The possibility that thousand of objections might have ushered in could not be ruled out. In that event it would not have been possible on the part of the State Government to give personal hearing to all the objectors and that is why perhaps the Act and Rules, framed thereunder are silent with regard to giving personal hearing to the objectors. So, only because no chance of hearing was given to the objectors, it cannot be said that the amended rules should be quashed; *Balasore Bus Association* v. *State of Orissa*, AIR 2006 Ori 163: 2007 AIHC 361.

3. Power of State Government under Section 96 – Section 96(1) is wide enough to empower the State Government to make the Rules for the purpose of carrying into effect the provisions of Chapter V of the Act regarding control of transport vehicles. The clauses in section 96(2) giving instances of the situations for which the State Government may make rules are without prejudice to the generality of the power of the State Government under sub-section (1) of section 96 to make rules for the purpose of carrying into effect provisions of Chapter V regarding control of transport vehicles; *Calcutta Howrah Auto Rickshaws Owners Assocn.* v. *State of West Bengal*, AIR 2010 Cal 122: 2010 (2) Cal HN 630: 2010 (2) Cal LJ 118.

4. Grant of Permanent Stage Carriage Permit – Offer letter has been issued by the STA in discharge of its statutory obligation. There is nothing to show that within the statutory life of the offer any decision was taken by the STA to issue the permit. Since the offer could not remain alive beyond six months from the date the permit was granted, even if the STA had wrongfully withheld the permit, it was for the petitioner to enforce her legal right created by the offer within the statutory life of the offer. She having not enforced her right created by the offer that, according to her, she had duly accepted, it is to be presumed that she consciously abandoned the right. Thus the Denial to grant of permit was proper; *Mita Ghosh* v. *State of West Bengal*, AIR 2013 Cal 123: 2013 (3) ACC 295.

CHAPTER VI

SPECIAL PROVISIONS RELATING TO STATE TRANSPORT UNDERTAKINGS

97. Definition.—In this Chapter, unless the context otherwise requires, "road transport service" means a service of motor vehicles carrying passengers or goods or both by road for hire or reward.

98. Chapter to override Chapter V and other laws.—The provisions of this Chapter and the rules and orders made thereunder shall have effect notwithstanding anything inconsistent therewith contained in Chapter V or in any other law for the time being in force or in any instrument having effect by virtue of any such law.

99. Preparation and publication of proposal regarding road transport service of a State transport undertaking.—[1][(1)] Where any State Government is of opinion that for the purpose of providing an efficient, adequate, economical and properly co-ordinated road transport service, it is necessary in the public interest that road transport services in general or any particular class of such service in relation to any area or route or portion thereof should be run and operated by the State transport undertaking, whether to the exclusion, complete or partial, of other persons or otherwise, the State Government may formulate a proposal regarding a scheme giving particulars of the nature of the services proposed to be rendered, the area or route proposed to be covered and other relevant particulars respecting thereto and shall publish such proposal in the Official Gazette of the State formulating such proposal and in not less than one newspaper in the regional language circulating in the area or route proposed to be covered by such scheme and also in such other manner as the State Government formulating such proposal deem fit.

[2][(2) Notwithstanding anything contained in sub-section (1), when a proposal is published under that sub-section, then from the date of publication of such proposal, no permit shall be granted to any person, except a temporary permit

1. Section 99 renumbered as sub-section (1) thereof by Act 54 of 1994, sec. 30 (w.e.f. 14-11-1994).
2. Ins. by Act 54 of 1994, sec. 30 (w.e.f. 14-11-1994).

during the pendency of the proposal and such temporary permit shall be valid only for a period of one year from the date of its issue or till the date of final publication of the scheme under section 100, whichever is earlier.]

SYNOPSIS

COMMENTS

1. Wants of Pre-publication – Sections 99 and 100 of the Act by themselves make complete provisions for preparation and finalisation of a scheme. No doubt the Government is empowered to frame Rules regarding the form and manner in which a scheme can be proposed and finalised. Nevertheless, section 100 also provides in brief regarding such matters. Being so, independently of the Rules framed under section 107, the Government is empowered to frame the scheme and finalise the same under sections 99 and 100 of the Act. Therefore, even if the Rules framed under section 107 of the Act may appear to be void for want of pre-publication, that itself would not render the scheme formulated in exercise of powers under sections 99 and 100, to be void; *Socorro N. Gracias* v. *State of Goa*, AIR 1999 Bom 436: 1999 (3) Bom CR 744.

2. Inconvenience to Public not Ground to Challenge Validity of Nationalisation Scheme – The purpose of nationalisation is to bring into being an efficient, adequate and properly co-ordinated passenger road transport service between two termini. Any inconvenience caused to the passengers performing a journey between the other points and the distance cannot afford a ground for challenging the scheme as invalid. It is a duty of the State Undertaking to arrange its service on the nationalised route that those passengers are subjected to the least inconvenience. The arguments of inconvenience to the public because of the natioanlisation is not a ground for invalidation; *Kasaragode District Bus Owners Association* v. *State of Kerala*, AIR 1991 Ker 139: (1990) 2 Ker LJ 845: (1990) 2 Ker LT 830.

3. Modifications of Scheme – The effect of 1959 Scheme and 1993 Scheme that the entire Saharanpur-Delhi route became fully nationalized for the exclusive operation by the STU *i.e.*, UPSRTC and no private operator could operate on the said route. As a matter of fact, the RTA cannot either renew the permit of such private operators or give any fresh permit in respect of a route which overlaps the notified route, the appellants' permits stood cancelled and in any case these permits lost its legal significance and sanctity. In this backdrop, the whole exercise undertaken by the State Government under sub-section (1) of section 102 of 1988 Act proposing to modify the 1993 Scheme relating to Saharanpur - Delhi notified route was misconceived as the permits specified in that Notification did not exist in law. In the absence of any proposal to modify the 1959 Scheme, the modification proposed in the 1993 Scheme vide the Notification was meaningless; *Rasid Javed* v. *State of Uttar Pradesh*, AIR 2010 SC 2275: 2010 AIR SCW 4079: (2010) 7 SCC 781.

4. Commencing Date of Period of One year – When prefatory words like 'Notwithstanding anything contained in this section', would occur, then it excludes the application of any other provision in that section. Therefore, the provisions of sub-section (4) of section 100 of the Act are not encumbered by any other provision of that section. It follows then that the period of one year is to commence from the date of publication of the proposal concerning Scheme in the official gazette. Where Scheme was published in the official gazette on 11-3-2010, the publication of corrigendum on 4-5-2010 with a few amendments in the notification dated 11-3-2010 would not amount to publication of draft Scheme. Its publication in the 'newspapers' on the same day would not have any impact. This time complete Scheme was not published and the official gazette only contained the extracts of the Scheme. The final Scheme was published on 3-5-2011. On the plain language of section 99 read with section 100(4), it could not be accepted that the period of one year would commence from the date of corrigendum published in the official gazette on 4-5-2010. *Firstly,* the corrigendum published only 'excerpts' of Scheme. *Secondly,* plea that after publication of the proposal concerning Scheme in the 'newspapers', the objections started pouring in could not be accepted because under section 100(1) of the Act, objections are to be filed by an objector within thirty days from the date of publication of the notice under section 99(1), in the official gazette. It does not talk of the date of publication of notice in the newspapers and counting of thirty days from that date. Thus the final scheme dated 3-5-2011, as published in official gazette had lapsed; *Rania Bratch Co-operative Transport Society Ltd.* v. *State of Haryana,* AIR 2012 P&H 81: 2012 (3) Ker LT 20 SN: 2012 (2) Pun LR 730.

5. **State Government – Duty-bound to Consider Objections and Give Reasons to Accept or Reject – Mandatory Requirement – Non-compliance** – State is supposed to be acting in public interest whiile exercising power under section 102 of Act; *B.A. Linga Reddy* v. *Karnataka State Transport Authority,* (2015) 4 SCC 515.

6. **Non-notified Route which Overlaps same Like of Travel as Portion of Notified Route** – Permit can't be granted; *B.A. Linga Reddy* v. *Karnataka State Transport Authority,* (2015) 4 SCC 515.

7. **Cut-off Dates for Validating Permits held on Different Cut-off Dates – Discriminatory** – Issue to be gone into by State Government while considering objections against modification of scheme; *B.A. Linga Reddy* v. *Karnataka State Transport Authority,* (2015) 4 SCC 515.

100. Objection to the proposal.—(1) On the publication of any proposal regarding a scheme in the Official Gazette and in not less than one newspaper in the regional language circulating in the area or route which is to be covered by such proposal any person may, within thirty days from the date of its publication in the Official Gazette, file objections to it before the State Government.

(2) The State Government may, after considering the objections and after giving an opportunity to the objector or his representatives and the representatives of the State transport undertaking to be heard in the matter, if they so desire, approve or modify such proposal.

(3) The scheme relating to the proposal as approved or modified under sub-section (2) shall then be published in the Official Gazette by the State Government making such scheme and in not less than one newspaper in the regional language circulating in the area or route covered by such scheme and the same shall thereupon become final on the date of its publication in the Official Gazette and shall be called the approved scheme and the area or route to which it relates shall be called the notified area or notified route:

Provided that no such scheme which relates to any inter-State route shall be deemed to be an approved scheme unless it has the previous approval of the Central Government.

(4) Notwithstanding anything contained in this section, where a scheme is not published as an approved scheme under sub-section (3) in the Official Gazette within a period of one year from the date of publication of the proposal

regarding the scheme in the Official Gazette under sub-section (1), the proposal shall be deemed to have lapsed.

Explanation.—In computing the period of one year referred to in this sub-section, any period or periods during which the publication of the approved scheme under sub-section (3) was held up on account of any stay or injunction by the order of any Court shall be excluded.

SYNOPSIS

1. Limitation for Publishing Scheme
2. Extension of Route Permits
3. Scope of Objection
4. Draft Nationalisation Scheme
5. Computation of Period of One Year
6. Validity of Grant of Stage Carriage Permits to Private Operators
7. Grant Temporary Permits to Private Operators – Validity
8. Agreements to Operate Vehicles on Notified Routes – *Locus Standi* to Challenge
9. Legality of Agreements to Operate Vehicles on Notified Routes
10. Commencing Date of Period of One Year

COMMENTS

1. Limitation for Publishing Scheme – A scheme which is not published or approved in the Official Gazette within a period of one year from the date of proposal regarding the scheme in the Official Gazette shall be deemed to have lapsed. Therefore, the last date on which the scheme could have lapsed is 30-6-1990. The scheme, was published on 29-12-1989, *i.e.*, well within the time stipulated under section 100(4).; *Kodali Kumara Swamy* v. *State of Andhra Pradesh*, AIR 1992 AP 170: 1991 (2) APLJ 351: 1991 (2) ALT 223.

2. Extension of Route Permits – If no scheme is prepared permits could be granted in a liberalised manner. However, when a scheme is prepared and approved, permits are to be granted in accordance with the scheme and the Regional Transport Authority would be within its powers to decline to entertain any application for grant of permit, which is not in accordance with the scheme approved, as provided under section 103(2) of the Act. The private operators cannot be allowed to operate on the monopoly route by extension of their routes, which are not Highway routes. It could only be done in the case of private operators to the extent the scheme permitted, *i.e.* on the Highway routes. Since the private respondents' routes, on which they were plying their buses under the permits granted are not State Highway routes the orders of extension of their route-permits violated provisions of the scheme; *PEPSU Road Transport Corporation, Patiala* v. *State*, AIR 1995 P&H 50: 1994 (2) Cur CC 450: 1995 (109) Pun LR 385.

3. Scope of Objection – That the objection which may be raised by any person to the proposed nationalisation scheme must relate to the matters about which the State Government is required to form an opinion under Statute *i.e.* for the purpose of providing an efficient, adequate, economical and proper transport service. Therefore, it follows that the object to be filed by an objector should be related to only these relevant factors and he is not entitled to raise any other objection which is irrelevant and extraneous to the provisions of the statute. The objection that in view of the loss suffered by them in operating the services under the permits granted to them, the proposed nationalisation scheme should be postponed is clearly outside the scope of considerations under the statute; *M. Madan Mohan Rao* v. *Union of India*, AIR 2002 SC 2647: 2002 AIR SCW 2972: JT 2002 (5) SC 230: 2002 (6) SCC 348: 2002 (5) SCALE 225: 2002 (5) Supreme 38.

4. Draft Nationalisation Scheme – On all the 39 routes, the State Road Transport Corporation is operating buses ever since 1993 and for that purpose it has made substantial investment by putting the buses on the routes and recruiting employees to conduct, oversee and maintain operation on such nationalised routes. While protecting the statutory right of the operators to be heard under section 100(2) of the 1988 Act, and also in view the public interest also the court has not quashed post haste the notification which has notified the draft scheme as the approved scheme; *Gajraj Singh* v. *State of Uttar*

Pradesh, AIR 2001 SC 2370: 2001 AIR SCW 2212: JT 2001 (5) SC 140: 2001 (5) SCC 762: 2001 (3) SCALE 631: 2001 (3) Supreme 598.

5. Computation of Period of One Year – A scheme published under the old Act pending on the date of commencement of the new Act could not be a scheme proposed under sub-section (1) of section 100, therefore, the rigour of period of one year as applicable to a scheme proposed under sub-section (1) of section 100 could not apply to a scheme under old Act pending on the date of commencement of the Act. If the rigour of one year contained in section 100(4) is applied to a pending scheme then section 217(2)(e) will become nugatory and no scheme published under old Act could be finalised under the new Act. It is settled principle of interpretation that where there appears to be inconsistency in two sections of the same Act, the principle of harmonious construction should be followed. Applying the Rule of harmonious construction section 100(4) has to be read as prescribing period of limitation of one year in respect of the scheme proposed under the provisions of the new Act, while in the case of a scheme under the old Act, pending on the date of enforcement of the new Act, the period of one year as prescribed under section 100(4) should be computed from the date of commencement of the new Act; *Krishan Kumar* v. *State of Rajasthan,* AIR 1992 SC 1789: 1992 AIR SCW 2004: JT 1991 (3) SC 470: 1991 (4) SCC 258.

The rigour of one year period provided under section 100(4) would apply to the draft scheme published under section 100(1) of the Act and it would not apply to the scheme framed under and pending as on the date of the commencement of the Act. On harmonious construction of section 217(2)(e) and 100(4) of the Act, the draft scheme published under the Repealed Act would stand lapsed only if it is not approved within one year from the date when the Act came into force; *Ram Krishna Verma* v. *State of Uttar Pradesh,* AIR 1992 SC 1888: 1992 AIR SCW 2141: JT 1992 (2) SC 545: 1992 (2) SCC 620: 1992 (2) SCR 378.

6. Validity of Grant of Stage Carriage Permits to Private Operators – Out of two stage carriage permits one permit for plying one return trip daily each was to be allotted in favour of the State Transport Undertaking and the private operators. The State Transport Undertaking having not even submitted an application for the grant of regular stage carriage permit on the route in question and thereafter having chosen not to even file an appeal against the order passed by the State Transport Commissioner granting both the regular stage carriage permits in favour of private operators, the State would not even have the *locus* to file the instant writ petition. Even otherwise on merits, the State Transport Commissioner in the order was alive to the ratio of 40:60 between the private operators and State Transport Undertaking as stipulated under the approved Transport Scheme and yet had granted both the stage carriage permits in favour of private operators keeping in view the fact that the State Transport Undertaking had not claimed the grant of a stage carriage permit on the route in question. While adopting such course of action, it had been observed that the share of mileage accruing to the State Transport Undertaking would be accordingly adjusted on some other route. Thus the grant of permits is proper; *State of Punjab* v. *State Transport Appellate Tribunal,* AIR 2013 P&H 40: 2013 (2) ACC 15.

7. Grant Temporary Permits to Private Operators – Validity – The State Transport Undertaking having not even submitted an application for the grant of regular stage carriage permit on the route in question and thereafter having chosen not to even file an appeal against the order passed by the State Transport Commissioner granting both the regular stage carriage permits in favour of private operators, the State would not even have the locus to file the instant writ petition. Even otherwise on merits, the State Transport Commissioner in the order was alive to the ratio of 40:60 between the private operators and State Transport Undertaking as stipulated under the approved Transport Scheme as modified vide the notification and yet had granted both the stage carriage permits in favour of private operators keeping in view the fact that the State Transport Undertaking had not claimed the grant of a stage carriage permit on the route in question. While adopting such course of action, it had been observed that the share of mileage accruing to the State Transport Undertaking would be accordingly adjusted on some other route. Such view stands affirmed by the State Transport Appellate Tribunal. Even under section 104 of the Act, it is clearly envisaged that where a scheme stands published under section 100 of the Act in respect of any notified area or notified route, the State Transport Commissioner shall not grant any permit except in accordance with the provisions of the Scheme but in terms of the proviso to section 104 of the Act in such a situation where no application for a permit has been made by the State Transport Undertaking. Thus the State Transport Commissioner can grant temporary permits to any person in respect of such notified area or notified route and the same would cease to be effective upon the issue of a permit to the State Transport Undertaking in respect of that area or route; *State of Punjab* v. *State Transport Appellate Tribunal*, AIR 2013 P&H 40: 2013 (2) ACC 15.

8. Agreements to Operate Vehicles on Notified Routes – *Locus Standi* to Challenge – The State Government has notified several routes under section 100 of Chapter VI of the Act. Those notified routes could not be opposed by the petitioner association or the other petitioners have no right to apply for grant of permits in respect of those routes. They can apply for grant of either permanent or temporary permits in respect of other routes which are not notified under section 100 of Chapter VI of the Act. It is not the case of the petitioners that the Corporation has entered into agreements with the outsourcing agents to operate the motor vehicle on the notified routes inter-region or inter-State affecting the public interest not following the procedure of inviting fresh tenders. The petitioners have no *locus standi* to question the action of the Corporation in entering into the agreements with the outsourcing agents for the purpose of operating their vehicles on the notified routes of inter-region or inter-State. It is on the basis of the terms and conditions which have been obtained by the Corporation as it has got the monopoly to operate their services in respect of such notified routes. Therefore, the petitioners have no *locus standi* to challenge or question the action of the Corporation in entering into the agreements with the outsourcing agents for the purpose of operating their vehicles on the notified routes; *All Orissa Bus Owners Association* v. *Orissa State Road Transport Corporation*, AIR 2012 Ori 179.

9. Legality of Agreements to Operate Vehicles on Notified Routes – The Corporation has entered into agreements with the outsourcing agents. For the purpose of running their vehicles, only the services of the outsourcing agents is availed with certain terms and conditions for a period of one year. It is indeed their vehicles which are being operated by outsourcing agents. The terms and conditions would clearly go to show that it is not the transfer of the permits in favour of the outsourcing agents, obtained from STA or RTA in respect of notified routes, upon which exclusive right is conferred upon the Corporation under section 100 of Chapter VI of the Act. The relevant clauses of the terms and conditions of one of the agreements show that the agreements with outsourcing agents to operate the services on the notified routes is not transfer of permits in favour of the outsourcing agents. The services are operated under the control, supervision and management of the Corporation through the second party outsourcing agent. Therefore, the same cannot be termed that there is a transfer of permits in favour of outsourcing agents to operate the vehicle or vehicles on the notified routes for which permission of either STA or RTA, is required under the provision of the 1939 Act. Thus the agreements with reference to the aforesaid provision, the agreements entered into between the Corporation and the outsourcing agents, is perfectly legal and valid. There is no arbitrary action on the part of the Corporation. There is also no statutory violation either under section 66 or 82 of the M.V. Act; *All Orissa Bus Owners Association* v. *Orissa State Road Transport Corporation*, AIR 2012 Ori 179.

10. Commencing Date of Period of One Year – When prefatory words like 'Notwithstanding anything contained in this section', would occur, then it excludes the application of any other provision in that section. Therefore, the provisions of sub-section (4) of section 100 of the Act are not encumbered by any other provision of that section. It follows then that the period of one year is to commence from the date of publication of the proposal concerning Scheme in the official gazette. Where Scheme was published in the official gazette on 11-3-2010, the publication of corrigendum on 4-5-2010 with a few amendments in the notification dated 11-3-2010 would not amount to publication of draft Scheme. Its publication in the 'newspapers' on the same day would not have any impact. This time complete Scheme was not published and the official gazette only contained the extracts of the Scheme. The final Scheme was published on 3-5-2011. On the plain language of section 99 read with section 100(4), it could not be accepted that the period of one year would commence from the date of corrigendum published in the official gazette on 4-5-2010. *Firstly,* the corrigendum published only 'excerpts' of Scheme. *Secondly,* plea that after publication of the proposal concerning Scheme in the 'newspapers', the objections started pouring in could not be accepted because under section 100(1) of the Act, objections are to be filed by an objector within thirty days from the date of publication of the notice under section 99(1), in the official gazette. It does not talk of the date of publication of notice in the newspapers and counting of thirty days from that date. Thus the final scheme dated 3-5-2011, as published in official gazette had lapsed; *Rania Bratch Co-operative Transport Society Ltd.* v. *State of Haryana,* AIR 2012 P&H 81: 2012 (3) Ker LT 20 SN: 2012 (2) Pun LR 730.

101. Operation of additional services by a State transport undertaking in certain circumstances.—Notwithstanding anything contained in section 87, a State transport undertaking may, in the public interest operate additional services for the conveyance of the passengers on special occasions such as to and from fairs and religious gatherings:

Provided that the State transport undertaking shall inform about the operation of such additional services to the concerned Transport Authority without delay.

102. Cancellation or modification of scheme.—(1) The State Government may, at any time, if it considers necessary, in the public interest so to do, modify any approved scheme after giving—

(i) the State transport undertaking; and

(ii) any other person who, in the opinion of the State Government, is likely to be affected by the proposed modification,

an opportunity of being heard in respect of the proposed modification.

(2) The State Government shall publish any modification proposed under sub-section (1) in the Official Gazette and in one of the newspapers in the regional languages circulating in the area in which it is proposed to be covered by such modification, together with the date, not being less than thirty days from such publication in the Official Gazette, and the time and place at which any representation received in this behalf will be heard by the State Government.

SYNOPSIS

1. Modification of Notified Route
2. Power to Cancel or Modify Scheme
3. Modifications of Scheme
4. Authority to Rescined Proposed Modification
5. *Quasi*-judicial Function while Modifying or Cancelling Scheme
6. State Government – Duty-bound to Consider Objections and Give Reasons to Accept or Reject – Mandatory Requirement – Non-compliance

7. Non-notified Route which Overlaps same Line of Travel as Portion of Notified Route
8. Cut-off Dates for Validating Permits held on Different Cut-off Dates – Discriminatory

COMMENTS

1. Modification of Notified Route – that the Government have approved the routes, have exercised the power under section 102(2) of the Act and given benefit by intersecting the approved routes only up to a distance of 25 kms. without picking up or setting down the passengers on the notified route, strictly subject to the terms and conditions mentioned therein. Under those circumstances, the writ petitioners cannot be given any relief. But if they have any right under the modified scheme, then that would be a matter appropriately to be gone into by the RTA or STA, after due notice to the State Transport Undertaking and all other interested persons; *Afsar Jahan Begum* v. *State of Madhya Pradesh*, AIR 1996 SC 3303: 1996 AIR SCW 2541: JT 1996 (1) SC 604: 1996 (8) SCC 38.

2. Power to Cancel or Modify Scheme – By virtue of section 102, the power to cancel the scheme or modify the scheme rests with the State Government and not with the Road Transport Authority and Tribunal; *Punjab Roadways, Moga* v. *Punja Sahib Bus and Transport Co.*, (2010) 5 SCC 235: JT 2010 (4) SC 495: (2010) 4 SCALE 444.

3. Modifications of Scheme – The effect of 1959 Scheme and 1993 Scheme that the entire Saharanpur-Delhi route became fully nationalized for the exclusive operation by the STU *i.e.*, UPSRTC and no private operator could operate on the said route. As a matter of fact, the RTA cannot either renew the permit of such private operators or give any fresh permit in respect of a route which overlaps the notified route, the appellants' permits stood cancelled and in any case these permits lost its legal significance and sanctity. In this backdrop, the whole exercise undertaken by the State Government under sub-section (1) of section 102 of 1988 Act proposing to modify the 1993 Scheme relating to Saharanpur - Delhi notified route was misconceived as the permits specified in that Notification did not exist in law. In the absence of any proposal to modify the 1959 Scheme, the modification proposed in the 1993 Scheme vide the Notification was meaningless; *Rasid Javed* v. *State of Uttar Pradesh*, AIR 2010 SC 2275: 2010 AIR SCW 4079: (2010) 7 SCC 781.

4. Authority to Rescined Proposed Modification – Even if an executive action not expressed to be made in the name of the Governor as contemplated under article 166(1) of the Constitution may not vitiate such action as nullity. But then there has to be some formal order by the State Government under section 102(1). Moreover, there is nothing on record even to indicate that the order of the Hearing Authority was communicated to the appellants or any of the affected parties. The order of hearing authority was not an order as contemplated under section 102(1) by the State Government approving the modification proposed in the Notifications. The State Government has therefore authority to rescined the proposed modification; *Rasid Javed* v. *State of Uttar Pradesh*, AIR 2010 SC 2275: 2010 AIR SCW 4079: (2010) 7 SCC 781.

5. *Quasi*-judicial Function while Modifying or Cancelling Scheme – State Government is duty-bound to consider the objections and to give reasons either to accept or reject them; *B.A. Linga Reddy* v. *Karnataka State Transport Authority*, AIR 2015 SC 767.

6. State Government – Duty-bound to Consider Objections and Give Reasons to Accept or Reject – Mandatory Requirement – Non-compliance – State is supposed to be acting in public interest while exercising power under section 102 of Act; *B.A. Linga Reddy* v. *Karnataka State Transport Authority*, (2015) 4 SCC 515.

7. Non-notified Route which Overlaps same Line of Travel as Portion of Notified Route – Permit can't be granted; *B.A. Linga Reddy* v. *Karnataka State Transport Authority*, (2015) 4 SCC 515.

8. Cut-off Dates for Validating Permits held on Different Cut-off Dates – Discriminatory – Issue to be gone into by State Government while considering objections against modification of scheme; *B.A. Linga Reddy* v. *Karnataka State Transport Authority*, (2015) 4 SCC 515.

103. Issue of permits to State transport undertakings.—(1) Where, in pursuance of an approved scheme, any State transport undertaking applies in such manner as may be prescribed by the State Government in this behalf for a stage carriage permit or a goods carriage permit or a contract carriage permit in respect of a notified area or notified route, the State Transport Authority in any case where the said area or route lies in more than one region and the Regional Transport Authority in any other case shall issue such permit to the State transport undertaking, notwithstanding anything to the contrary contained in Chapter V.

(2) For the purpose of giving effect to the approved scheme in respect of a notified area or notified route, the State Transport Authority or, as the case may be, the Regional Transport Authority concerned may, by order,—

(a) refuse to entertain any application for the grant or renewal of any other permit or reject any such application as may be pending;

(b) cancel any existing permit;

(c) modify the terms of any existing permit so as to—

(i) render the permit ineffective beyond a specified date;

(ii) reduce the number of vehicles authorised to be used under the permit;

(iii) curtail the area or route covered by the permit in so far as such permit relates to the notified area or notified route.

(3) For the removal of doubts, it is hereby declared that no appeal shall lie against any action taken, or order passed, by the State Transport Authority or any Regional Transport Authority under sub-section (1) or sub-section (2).

STATE AMENDMENTS

Karnataka.—In section 103, after sub-section (1), insert the following sub-section, namely:—

"(1A) It shall be lawful for the State Transport Undertaking to operate on any route as stage carriage, under any permit issued therefor to such Undertaking under sub-section (1), any vehicle placed at the disposal and under the control of such Undertaking by the owner of such vehicle under any arrangement entered into between such owner and the Undertaking for the use of the said vehicle by the Undertaking."

[Karnataka Act 11 of 1996, sec. 2 (w.r.e.f. 8-7-1996)]

Uttar Pradesh.—In section 103, after sub-section (1), the following sub-section shall be inserted, namely:—

"(1A) It shall be lawful for a State transport undertaking to operate on any route as stage carriage, under any permit issued therefor to such undertaking under sub-section (1), any vehicle placed at the disposal and under the control of such undertaking by the owner of such vehicle under any arrangement entered into between such owner and the undertaking for the use of the said vehicle by the undertaking."

[Uttar Pradesh Act 5 of 1993, sec. 2 (w.r.e.f. 16-1-1993)].

SYNOPSIS

COMMENTS

1. Extension of Route Permits – If no scheme is prepared permits could be granted in a liberalised manner. However, when a scheme is prepared and approved, permits are to be granted in accordance with the scheme and the Regional Transport Authority would be within its powers to decline to entertain any application for grant of permit, which is not in accordance with the scheme approved, as provided under section 103(2) of the Act. The private operators cannot be allowed to operate on the monopoly route by extension of their routes, which are not Highway routes. It could only be done in the case of private operators to the extent the scheme permitted, *i.e.* on the Highway routes. Since the private respondents' routes, on which they were plying their buses under the permits granted are not State Highway routes the orders of extension of their route-permits violated provisions of the scheme. The period of one year has to be counted from the date of the publication of the proposal, if any period has been spent on account of stay or injunction order passed by any competent court then such period shall be excluded for computing the period of one year; *PEPSU Road Transport Corporation, Patiala* v. *State*, AIR 1995 P&H 50: 1994 (2) Cur CC 450: 1995 (109) Pun LR 385.

2. Where Approved Scheme Already Exist – Where there is an approved scheme already existing in respect of a notified area or notified route, the Regional. Transport Authority may refuse to entertain the application for grant of permit or reject any such application. Thus, as there is an approved scheme already existing in respect of the notified route, the Regional Transport Authority has rejected the application of the appellant for grant of permit, which cannot be found fault with; *R. Mageswari* v. *A. Sengoda Gounder*, AIR 2009 Mad 87: 2009 AIHC 546 (NOC): 2009 (2) Mad LJ 513.

3. Right to Challenge Grant of Permit – Mere failure to challenge granting of licence by the Road Transport Corporation before the tribunal does not affect its right to challenge grant of permit on the ground that it is in violation of the scheme. Thus the plea that Corporation cannot be aggrieved party as the permits granted in favour of licencee were not challenged by the Roadways Transport Corporation by preferring an appeal and as it is not operating any service on the routes of the approved schemes cannot be sustained; *Tvl. Cholan Roadways Corpn. Ltd.* v. *PLA Annamalai Chettiar*, AIR 1995 Mad 205.

104. Restriction on grant of permits in respect of a notified area or notified route.—Where a scheme has been published under sub-section (3) of section 100 in respect of any notified area or notified route, the State Transport Authority or the Regional Transport Authority, as the case may be, shall not grant any permit except in accordance with the provisions of the scheme:

Provided that where no application for a permit has been made by the State Transport Undertaking in respect of any notified area or notified route in pursuance of an approved scheme, the State Transport Authority or the Regional Transport Authority, as the case may be, may grant temporary permits to any person in respect of such notified area or notified route subject to the condition that such permit shall cease to be effective on the issue of a permit to the State transport undertaking in respect of that area or route.

SYNOPSIS

1. Temporary Permits on Failure to Provide Vehicles for Maximum Strength Fixed
2. Route Exclusively for Town Service
3. Variation of Existing Permit
4. Scheme of Total Exclusion
5. No Prohibition for Grant of Permit if Scheme is not Finalised
6. Grant of Permit shall not be in Violation of any Scheme
7. Totally not Forbidden to Grant Temporary Permits to Private Operators
8. Obligatory to Provide All Services Specified in Scheme
9. Validity of Grant of Stage Carriage Permits to Private Operators
10. Grant Temporary Permits to Private Operators – Validity
11. Variation or Increase in Number of Trips

COMMENTS

1. Temporary Permits on Failure to Provide Vehicles for Maximum Strength Fixed – When a scheme is framed for providing efficient, adequate, economical and properly co-ordinated road transport service on a route, it is obligatory on the State Transport Undertaking to provide all services specified in the scheme. If it fails to provide vehicles for the maximum strength fixed under the scheme then proviso to section 104 is attracted and the concerned transport authority has to grant temporary permits to private operators against the remaining services. Proviso to section 104 states that temporary permit can be granted to private operators on notified route if no application for permit in pursuance of approved scheme, has been made by state transport undertaking. But this proviso cannot be read in isolation. According to sections 99, 100 routes are nationalised "for the purpose of providing on efficient, adequate, economical and properly co-ordinated transport service". If the state transport undertaking fails to do so, the purpose of scheme will be frustrated. The proviso to section 104 has therefore to be interpreted in same way the provision of section 68F(1C) were interpreted; *Sanjeev Kumar* v. *State Transport Authority, Uttar Pradesh,* AIR 1995 All 294: 1995 (1) All CJ 585: 1995 (2) All LR 410.

2. Route Exclusively for Town Service – A route which is exclusively for town service cannot, for the reason that a mofussil service stage carriage shall traverse it for a longer distance, become a route falling under the nationalization scheme for town service; *A.P.S.R.T.C.* v. *State Transport Appellant Tribunal,* AIR 2001 AP 335: 2001 (3) Andh LD 235: 2001 (2) Andh LT 532.

3. Variation of Existing Permit – The petitioner holds a stage carriage permit to ply on an inter-state route. Under the permit issued to him, he is authorised to make two single trips a day *i.e.,* one round trip. The same route with the road length of 225 Kms is covered by the approved scheme notified by the State Government under section 68D(2) of the Motor Vehicles Act, 1939 the route attained the character of an inter-state route. The petitioner filed an application before the Secretary (STA) to grant two more additional single trips by inclusion of one more vehicle in the existing permit and to frame revised timings. The said application does not fall within the purview of the saving clause of the Scheme. If the application is granted, it would amount to substantial modification of the scope and ambit of the existing permit. The character and amplitude of the existing permit will be materially altered. By allowing the amendment to the existing permit as sought for by the petitioner, the efficacy of nationalisation scheme might be whittled down and it may result in detriment to public interest. The saving clause authorises such a type of modification of the permit. Therefore it cannot be said that the terms of the existing scheme do not preclude, nay, permit the variation of the existing permit to such an extent as to allow additional trips with an additional vehicle on the very same notified route; *B. Satyam* v. *Secretary, State Transport Authority, Andhra Pradesh, Hyderabad,* AIR 1994 AP 327: 1994 (2) Andh LT 385.

4. Scheme of Total Exclusion – The date, on which the variation was granted by the State Transport Appellate Tribunal, the scheme must be deemed to have been in force. As per section 104 of the Act, after the scheme is published in respect of a notified area of notified route, the State Transport Authority or the Regional Transport Authority, shall not grant any permit except in accordance with the provisions of the scheme. When the scheme does not provide for any such variation of the conditions of the permit, and it is the scheme of total exclusion, there is a bar for granting such variation; *Tvl. Jeeva Transport Corpn. Ltd.* v. *Regional Transport Authority, Salem,* AIR 1998 Mad 292: 1997 Writ LR 407.

5. No Prohibition for Grant of Permit if Scheme is not Finalised – Under section 104 of the Motor Vehicles Act, 1988 what is prohibited is grant of a permit on a notified area or notified route. The Act of 1988 vide Proviso to section 104 has gone a step further that even on a notified route a permit can be granted to a private operator if the State Transport Undertaking had not applied for permit. That shows that the Motor Vehicles

Act, 1988 does not prohibit the grant of a permit on the route for which a scheme has been framed but it has not been finalised by the State Government and the area or route or portion thereof has not been notified. The cancellation of the permit granted to the petitioner on ground that the route covered by permit overlaps the draft scheme is not proper; *P.R.T. Corpn.* v. *State Transport Appellate Tribunal,* AIR 2008 P&H 155.

6. Grant of Permit shall not be in Violation of any Scheme – A scheme duly published under section 100(3) of the Motor Vehicles Act, is the law and the violation of the same would be viewed in the same manner as the violation of any other provision of the Statutes. In terms of section 104 of the M.V. Act, the R.T.A. or the State T.A. Is disabled from issuing a permit except in accordance with the provisions of the Scheme published under section 100(3). For a proper exercise of its power under section 80 of the Act, the authority concerned shall have to keep in view the provisions of section 104 of the Act and make sure that the grant of permit by it is not in violation of any scheme duly published under section 100(3). Jurisdiction of the authority, to grant a permit would depend upon the existence or non-existence of a Scheme and the total or partial ban it may contain against any private operator, operating a service on a notified route. Determination of these facts, would be essential as the same are jurisdictional facts without which the authority concerned, cannot take a proper decision in the matter the failure on the part of the authority concerned, to address itself to the provisions of section 104, and to make an order consistent therewith would amount to failure on its part to exercise its jurisdiction properly and an error of law which would vitiate the order passed by it; *Karnataka State Road Transport Corporation* v. *Pauli Govis,* AIR 1996 Kant 247: ILR 1996 Kant 295.

7. Totally not Forbidden to Grant Temporary Permits to Private Operators – The State Transport Authority or the Regional Transport Authority are not totally forbidden to grant temporary permits to private operators to ply their stage carriages in the notified routes if no application for a permit has been made by the State transport undertakings in respect of any notified route in pursuance of the approved scheme: *Kerala State Road Transport Corporation* v. *Regional Transport Authority, Ernakulam,* AIR 1998 Ker 46: 1997 (2) Ker LJ 131: 1997 (2) Ker LT 330.

8. Obligatory to Provide All Services Specified in Scheme – When a scheme is framed for providing efficient, adequate, economical and properly co-ordinated road transport service on a route it is obligatory on the State transport undertaking to provide all services specified in the scheme. If it is unable to provide vehicles for maximum strength fixed by the scheme, proviso to section 104 is attracted and the concerned transport authority has to grant temporary permits to private operator against the remaining series; *Sanjeev Kumar* v. *State Transport Authority, Uttar Pradesh,* AIR 1995 All 294: 1995 (1) All CJ 585: 1995 (2) All LR 410.

9. Validity of Grant of Stage Carriage Permits to Private Operators – Out of two stage carriage permits one permit for plying one return trip daily each was to be allotted in favour of the State Transport Undertaking and the private operators The State Transport Undertaking having not even submitted an application for the grant of regular stage carriage permit on the route in question and thereafter having chosen not to even file an appeal against the order passed by the State Transport Commissioner granting both the regular stage carriage permits in favour of private operators, the State would not even have the locus to file the instant writ petition. Even otherwise on merits, the State Transport Commissioner in the order was alive to the ratio of 40:60 between the private operators and State Transport Undertaking as stipulated under the approved Transport Scheme and yet had granted both the stage carriage permits in favour of private operators keeping in view the fact that the State Transport Undertaking had not claimed the grant of a stage carriage permit on the route in question. While adopting such course of action, it had been observed that the share of mileage accruing to the

State Transport Undertaking would be accordingly adjusted on some other route. Thus the grant of permits is proper; *State of Punjab* v. *State Transport Appellate Tribunal,* AIR 2013 P&H 40: 2013 (2) ACC 15.

10. Grant Temporary Permits to Private Operators – Validity – The State Transport Undertaking having not even submitted an application for the grant of regular stage carriage permit on the route in question and thereafter having chosen not to even file an appeal against the order passed by the State Transport Commissioner granting both the regular stage carriage permits in favour of private operators, the State would not even have the *locus* to file the instant writ petition. Even otherwise on merits, the State Transport Commissioner in the order was alive to the ratio of 40:60 between the private operators and State Transport Undertaking as stipulated under the approved Transport Scheme as modified vide the notification and yet had granted both the stage carriage permits in favour of private operators keeping in view the fact that the State Transport Undertaking had not claimed the grant of a stage carriage permit on the route in question. While adopting such course of action, it had been observed that the share of mileage accruing to the State Transport Undertaking would be accordingly adjusted on some other route. Such view stands affirmed by the State Transport Appellate Tribunal. Even under section 104 of the Act, it is clearly envisaged that where a scheme stands published under section 100 of the Act in respect of any notified area or notified route, the State Transport Commissioner shall not grant any permit except in accordance with the provisions of the Scheme but in terms of the proviso to section 104 of the Act in such a situation where no application for a permit has been made by the State Transport Undertaking. Thus the State Transport Commissioner can grant temporary permits to any person in respect of such notified area or notified route and the same would cease to be effective upon the issue of a permit to the State Transport Undertaking in respect of that area or route; *State of Punjab* v. *State Transport Appellate Tribunal,* AIR 2013 P&H 40: 2013 (2) ACC 15.

11. Variation or Increase in Number of Trips – Once a Scheme stands published in relation to any route, be it in complete or partial exclusion of then existing routes, only the concerned State Transport Undertakings can operate services on the notified areas or routes, as per the Scheme itself. The permit originally granted to any person would be rendered ineffective. The permit holder cannot operate on any part or portion of the notified route or area merely on the ground that the permit as originally granted to him covered the notified route or area. If there is any need for protecting the travelling public from inconvenience, it was for the State Transport Undertaking and the Government to increase their own bus services. In the case in hand, the Appellant has no legal right to seek for any variation or increase in the number of trips by the Bellary Scheme. Thus the variation of conditions of the stage carriage permit granted by the KSTA was subsequently set aside by the KSTAT was proper; *Neelakanteshwara Motor Service* v. *Karnataka State Transport,* AIR 2013 Kant 7: 2013 (1) ACC 835.

105. Principles and method of determining compensation and payment thereof.—(1) Where, in exercise of the powers conferred by clause (b) or clause (c) of sub-section (2) of section 103, any existing permit is cancelled or the terms thereof are modified, there shall be paid by the State transport undertaking to the holder of the permit, compensation, the amount of which shall be determined in accordance with the provisions of sub-section (4) or sub-section (5), as the case may be.

(2) Notwithstanding anything contained in sub-section (1), no compensation shall be payable on account of the cancellation of any existing, permit or any modification of the terms thereof, when a permit for an alternative route or area in lieu thereof has been offered by the State Transport Authority or the Regional Transport Authority, as the case may be and accepted by the holder of the permit.

(3) For the removal of doubts, it is hereby declared that no compensation shall be payable on account of the refusal to renew a permit under clause (a) of sub-section (2) of section 103.

(4) Where, in exercise of the powers conferred by clause (b) or sub-clause (i) or sub-clause (ii) of clause (c) of sub-section (2) of section 103, any existing permit is cancelled or the terms thereof are modified so as to prevent the holder of the permit from using any vehicle authorised to be used thereunder for the full period from which the permit, would otherwise have been effective, the compensation payable to the holder of the permit for each vehicle affected by such cancellation or modification shall be computed as follows:—

(a) for every complete month or part of a month exceeding fifteen days of the unexpired period of the permit: Two hundred rupees;

(b) for part of a month not exceeding fifteen days of the unexpired period of the permit; One hundred rupees:

Provided that the amount of compensation shall, in no case, be less than four hundred rupees.

(5) Where, in exercise of the powers conferred by sub-clause (iii) of clause (c) of sub-section (2) of section 103, the terms of an existing permit are modified so as to curtail the area or route of any vehicle authorised to be used thereunder, the compensation payable to the holder of the permit on account of such curtailment shall be an amount computed in accordance with the following formula, namely:—

$$\frac{Y \times A}{R}$$

Explanation.—In this formula,—

(i) "Y" means the length or area by which the route or area covered by the permit is curtailed;

(ii) "A" means the amount computed in accordance with sub-section (4);

(iii) "R" means the total length of the route or the total area covered by the permit.

(6) The amount of compensation payable under this section shall be paid by the State transport undertaking to the person or persons entitled thereto within one month from the date on which the cancellation or modification of the permit becomes effective:

Provided that where the State transport undertaking fails to make the payment within the said period of one month, it shall pay interest at the rate of seven per cent. per annum from the date on which it falls due.

106. Disposal of article found in vehicles.—Where any article found in any transport vehicle operated by the State transport undertaking is not claimed by its owner within the prescribed period, the State transport undertaking may sell the article in prescribed manner and the sale proceeds thereof, after deducting the costs incidental to sale, shall be paid to the owner on demand.

107. Power of State Government to make rules.—(1) The State Government may make rules for the purpose of carrying into effect the provisions of this Chapter.

(2) In particular and without prejudice to the generality of the foregoing power, such rules may provide for all or any of the following matters, namely:—

(a) the form in which any proposal regarding a scheme may be published under section 99;

(b) the manner in which objections may be filed under sub-section (1) of section 100;

(c) the manner in which objections may be considered and disposed of under sub-section (2) of section 100;

(d) the form in which any approved scheme may be published under sub-section (3) of section 100;

(e) the manner in which application under sub-section (1) of section 103 may be made;

(f) the period within which the owner may claim any article found left in any transport vehicle under section 106 and the manner of sale of such article;

(g) the manner of service of orders under this Chapter;

(h) any other matter which has to be, or may be, prescribed.

SYNOPSIS

1. Emblem on Registration Plates of Vehicles
2. Extension of Time Never be more than Original Period
3. Prohibition of Use of Tinted Safety Glasses
4. Safety Requirement in Motor Vehicle
5. Use of Multi-toned Horns

COMMENTS

1. Emblem on Registration Plates of Vehicles – Use of hologram of Ashok Chakra' on registration plates is not permissible. All motor manufacturing companies including respondent restrained from using hologram of Ashok Chakra'; *Poonam Singh* v. *Union of India*, AIR 2003 Del 163: 2003 (1) ACC 52: 2002 (101) DLT 429.

2. Extension of Time Never be more than Original Period – When the statute prescribes 30 days as the time within which the applicant does not possess the vehicle has to be produced the documents of the vehicle after sanction of permit to get a permit and in a given case the authority has been vested with the power to prescribe a longer period than 30 days and in the absence of specifying any prescribed time, the question of extending the time at the instance of the applicant for producing the documents would not arise. At any rate, time to be extended can never be more than the original period. In a case like this where even after 8 years if the petitioner is unable to acquire the vehicle, the question of granting any extension of time would not arise; *Rathnakala* v. *Secretary, R.T.A., Mysore*, AIR 2005 Kant 24: 2004 (3) KCCR 1883: 2004 (5) Kant LJ 282.

3. Prohibition of Use of Tinted Safety Glasses – There shall be guidelines as to what constitute 'tinted safety glasses'. The phrase 'safety glasses' means glass conforming to the specifications of the Bureau of Indian Standards or any international standards as certified by the Automobile Research Association of India, Pune, the Bureau of Indian Standards and so manufactured or treated that if fractured it does not fly or break into fragments capable of causing severe cut. It also means any windscreen or window at the front of the vehicle, the inner surface of which is at an angle extending to thirty degrees to the longitudinal axis of the vehicle shall be deemed to face to the front. The above meaning given to safety glasses may not be same meaning for the words 'tinted safety glasses'. The glass of the wind screen and rear window of every motor vehicle shall be such and shall be maintained in such a condition that the visual transmission of light is not less than 70%. The glasses used for side windows are such and shall be maintained in such condition that the visual transmission of light is not less than 50% and conforms to Indian Standards IS : 2553 Part 2. All these cannot be treated as prohibition of the use of safety glasses unless a proper definition or meaning is supplied to the words 'tinted safety glasses' in view of the wide meaning of the word 'tint'. It is, therefore, quite possible to argue that there is no proper guidelines as to the use of tinted safety glasses or the prohibition as to its use. The definiteness or certainty is required while imposing prohibition or restriction on persons against the enjoyment they already had. There is no indication given of the Rules as to what actually means by the words 'tinted safety glasses' or as to the manner, they have to be used on the motor vehicles. It cannot therefore be said that there is a total prohibition of the use of tinted safety glasses. Fact that section 110(1)(d) authorises the Central Government to frame rules with regard to prohibition of the use of tinted safety glasses, does not mean that there is a total prohibition of the use of tinted safety glasses till the rule is framed in that behalf. Therefore without a rule, direction or order by the Central or State Government or by any competent authority, the petitioners cannot be restrained from doing so; *M.K. Chandran* v. *Commissioner of Police, Kochi,* AIR 1998 Ker 347: 1998 (2) Ker LJ 263: 1998 (2) Ker LT 468.

4. Safety Requirement in Motor Vehicle – A permanent hand-grip for the pillion rider has to be fitted on the side or behind driver's seat and not behind seat of pillion rider. IS : 14495-1998 also requires that pillion hand-hold system shall be so fitted that it is convenient for pillion rider to make use of it in his normal sitting position irrespective of whether he is sitting side or cross-saddled. Hand-grip or pillion hand-hold system at the back of the seat of the pillion rider may be convenient for pillion rider if he is sitting side behind the driver but will not at all be convenient for the pillion rider if he sits cross-saddled behind the driver and not every pillion rider sits side, rather many pillion riders sit cross-saddled. Thus, fitting hand-grip for the pillion rider behind the pillion rider's seat is in violation of both the CMV Rules as well as IS : 14495-1998; *Gyan Prakash* v. *Union of India,* AIR 2009 MP 55: 2009 AIHC 315 (NOC): 2009 (2) ACC 501.

5. Use of Multi-toned Horns – Constant use of devices producing unduly harsh, shrill, loud or alarming noise is bound to cause disturbance and distraction to the students who are not able to concentrate fully due to irritation caused by such devices. It is also causing adverse effect on infants, sick and elderly persons and is generally causing inconvenience, as persons like the petitioner are not able to concentrate on their work because of constant sound pollution. Thus, it is an addition to the already existing sound pollution and appropriate steps are required to be taken for controlling the same. But, as the use of such type of horns is not permitted by the rules, the question of issuing any direction prohibiting such use does not arise. However, it to be a fit case in which some directions (are) to be issued. Accordingly, would be appropriate, if at regular intervals announcement is made through the medium of All India Radio and Doordarshan and the Press that the use of multi-toned horns or such other devices creating unduly harsh, shrill, loud or alarming noise is prohibited. It will be advisable if notices are exhibited at the bus stops, and at the R.T.O. offices regarding the prohibition on the use of multi-toned horns and similar devices; *Nayan Behari Das* v. *State of Orissa,* AIR 1998 Ori 39: 1997 (2) Ori LR 406.

108. Certain powers of State Government exercisable by the Central Government.—The powers conferred on the State Government under this Chapter shall, in relation to a corporation or company owned or controlled by the Central Government or by the Central Government and one or more State Governments, be exercisable only by the Central Government in relation to an inter-State route or area.

CHAPTER VII

CONSTRUCTION, EQUIPMENT AND MAINTENANCE OF MOTOR VEHICLES

109. General provision regarding construction and maintenance of vehicles.—(1) Every motor vehicle shall be so constructed and so maintained as to be at all times under the effective control of the person driving the vehicle.

(2) Every motor vehicle shall be so constructed as to have right hand steering control unless it is equipped with a mechanical or electrical signalling device of a prescribed nature.

[1][(3) If the Central Government is of the opinion that it is necessary or expedient so to do in public interest, it may by order published in the Official Gazette, notify that any article or process used by a manufacturer shall conform to such standard as may be specified in that order.]

COMMENTS

Implementation of Scheme regulating issuance and fixation of HSRP – The State of Andhra Pradesh has decided to have a competitive bidding process by segregating the tender into different sections *i.e.*, one for manufacturing, another for embossing, hot stamping and printing of Higher Security Registration Plate (HSRP) and yet another to supply the same to the Corporation for installation. Again, the process adopted by the State of Andhra Pradesh is not only in violation of the directions contained in the judgment of this Court but is also contrary to the Notification which was issued under sub-section (3) of section 109 of the Motor Vehicles Act, 1988 and called the Motor Vehicles (New High Security Registration Plates) Order, 2001. This Order does not permit the completion of the HSRP scheme in the manner sought to be adopted by the State of Andhra Pradesh. The State was to award the contract but the same has not so far been awarded. Thus it is directed the State of Andhra Pradesh to issue fresh tender, award the contract and commence the implementation of the scheme by the time schedule; *Maninderjit Singh Bitta* v. *Union of India*, AIR 2012 SC 348: 2012 AIR SCW 193: (2012) 1 SCC 707.

The draft agreement provides that the supplier of the plate shall notify the purchaser in writing of all sub-contracts awarded under the contract. Neither rule 50 of the Motor Vehicles Rules, 1989, Motor Vehicles (New High Security Registration Plates) Order, 2011 nor the judgments of this Court permit sub-contracts to be awarded by the contractor to whom the award for manufacture and fixation of HSRP is awarded. The DIMTS when it is getting the HSRP manufactured from the contractor, such manufacture should be *firstly* from a single contractor and *secondly* it should, without fail, be under the direct supervision and control of DIMTS. They should not let the sub-contractors or other parties to have control over the manufacturing processing and fixation of HSRP in any manner, whatsoever. They should ensure that one single person is responsible for manufacturing, affixation of seals, imprinting of numbers and affixation of HSRP on the vehicles in the NCT of Delhi. The Government has prayed for extension of time. Thus the period for implementation of the scheme has been extend; *Maninderjit Singh Bitta* v. *Union of India*, AIR 2012 SC 348: 2012 AIR SCW 193: (2012) 1 SCC 707.

110. Power of Central Government to make rules.—(1) The Central Government may make rules regulating the construction, equipment and maintenance of motor vehicles and trailers with respect to all or any of the following matters, namely:—

1. Ins. by Act 54 of 1994, sec. 31 (w.e.f. 14-11-1994).

(a) the width, height, length and overhand of vehicles and of the loads carried;

[1][(b) the size, nature, maximum retail price and condition of tyres, including embossing thereon of date and year of manufacture, and the maximum load carrying capacity;]

(c) brakes and steering gear;

(d) the use of safety glasses including prohibition of the use of tinted safety glasses;

(e) signalling appliances, lamps and reflectors;

(f) speed governors;

(g) the emission of smoke, visible vapour, sparks, ashes, grit or oil;

(h) the reduction of noise emitted by or caused by vehicles;

(i) the embossment of chassis number and engine number and the date of manufacture;

(j) safety belts, handle bars of motor cycles, auto-dippers and other equipments essential for safety of drivers, passengers and other road user;

(k) standards of the components used in the vehicle as inbuilt safety devices;

(l) provision for transportation of goods of dangerous or hazardous nature to human life;

(m) standards for emission of air pollutants;

[2][(n) installation of catalytic convertors in the class of vehicles to be prescribed;]

[2][(o) the placement of audio-visual or radio or tape recorder type of devices in public vehicles;]

[2][(p) warranty after sale of vehicle and norms therefor:]

Provided that any rules relating to the matters dealing with the protection of environment, so far as may be, shall be made after consultation with the Ministry of the Government of India dealing with environment.

(2) Rules may be made under sub-section (1) governing the matters mentioned therein, including the manner of ensuring the compliance with such matters and the maintenance of motor vehicles in respect of such matters, either generally in respect of motor vehicles or trailers or in respect of motor vehicles or trailers of a particular class or in particular circumstances.

(3) Notwithstanding anything contained in this section,—

(a) the Central Government may exempt any class of motor vehicles from the provisions of this Chapter;

(b) a State Government may exempt any motor vehicle or any class or description of motor vehicles from the rules made under sub-section (1) subject to such conditions as may be prescribed by the Central Government.

1. Subs. by Act 54 of 1994, sec. 32, for clause (b) (w.e.f. 14-11-1994).
2. Ins. by Act 54 of 1994, sec. 32 (w.e.f. 14-11-1994).

SYNOPSIS

COMMENTS

1. Words "from any person" – The words from any person are referable to persons other than the driver/owner or insurer of the motor vehicle; *Union of India* v. *United India Insurance Co. Ltd.*, AIR 1998 SC 640: 1998 AIR SCW 245: JT 1997 (8) SC 653: 1997 (8) SCC 683: 1997 (9) Supreme 69.

2. Tribunal is Alternative Forum – The Tribunal under Motor Vehicles Act is clearly an alternative forum in substitution for the Civil Court for adjudicating upon claims for compensation arising out of the "use of motor vehicles". This is further made clear from S. 110-F of the Act which states that no Civil Court shall entertain any question "relating to any claims for compensation which may be adjudicated upon by the Claims Tribunal". When one is concerned only with section 110(1) and when section 110B does not and cannot control section 110(1), a claim is entertainable by the Tribunal, if it arises out of the use of a motor vehicle and if it is claimed against persons or agencies other than the driver, owner or insurer of the vehicle provided in tort, such other persons or agencies are also claimed to be liable as joint tort-feasors. It is obvious that prior to the constitution of the Tribunal, such compensation could be decreed by the Civil Court not only against the owner/driver and insurer of the motor vehicle but also against others who are found to be joint tort feasors; *Union of India* v. *United India Insurance Co. Ltd.*, AIR 1998 SC 640: 1998 AIR SCW 245: JT 1997 (8) SC 653: 1997 (8) SCC 683: 1997 (9) Supreme 69.

3. Emission Norms – The notification which was issued for the purpose of controlling pollution within the National Capital Region in phased manner, makes it quite clear that the vehicles manufactured prior to the given date being permitted to ply does not anyway militate or discriminate against the prohibition of plying vehicles manufactured after that date. Further, the other notification which inter alia inserts proviso to rule 90(7) clarifies that where such vehicle is registered in the National Capital Region, it shall not pick up or set down goods between two points situated in the National Capital Region unless it conforms to the mass emission standards. The said classification is essential in view of the fact that all vehicles could not have been prohibited from plying on road in one stroke. Therefore, there is a clear nexus of the classification with the objects sought to be achieved by the legislation. The rationale behind the said notification is to phase out the older vehicles automatically in due course in order to gradually increase the emission norms thereby curbing air pollution; *Bharat Petroleum Corporation Ltd.* v. *Sunil Bansal*, AIR 2010 SC (Supp) 175: 2010 AIR SCW 13.

111. Power of State Government to make rules.—(1) A State Government may make rules regulating the construction, equipment and maintenance of motor vehicles and trailers with respect to all matters other than the matters specified in sub-section (1) of section 110.

(2) Without prejudice to the generality of the foregoing power, rules may be made under this section governing all or any of the following matters either generally in respect of motor vehicles or trailers or in respect of motor vehicles or trailers of a particular class or description or in particular circumstances, namely:—

(a) seating arrangements in public service vehicles and the protection of passengers against the weather;

(b) prohibiting or restricting the use of audible signals at certain times or in certain places;

(c) prohibiting the carrying of appliances likely to cause annoyance or danger;

(d) the periodical testing and inspection of vehicles by prescribed authorities [1][and fees to be charged for such test];

(e) the particulars other than registration marks to be exhibited by vehicles and the manner in which they shall be exhibited;

(f) the use of trailers with motor vehicles; and

[2][***]

COMMENTS

Increasing of Seating Capacity of Carriage will not Jeopardize Right of Livelihood – The right of livelihood of the petitioner is not jeopardized by increasing the seating capacity of the stage carriage or contract carriage. On the contrary, by increasing the seating capacity, it does not deprive the petitioners of the means of their livelihood. The submission that there would be deprivation of livelihood of the petitioners as, is totally without substance. By increasing maximum seating capacity, the petitioners are not put to any monetary loss and further there is no deprivation of means of livelihood. No legislation or delegated legislation can be declared invalid solely on the ground that Directive Principles of State Policy have not been followed or there has been violation of the same unless the requirement under the said Article which is meant for good governance, establishment of a welfare state, Social and economic revolution and such other aspects read in consonance with the fundamental rights are really infringed and further some facet of fundamental rights are played foul with. Discrimination solely on the ground of sex, as regards pay despite similar work is impermissible being irrational but one cannot be oblivious of the fact that it is also a part of the fundamental rights. But once no facet of fundamental right is abridged, the challenge exclusively on the ground of non-following the provisions contained in Chapter IV of the Constitution would make a statutory provision or a rule *ultra vires* is devoid of merit. Thus the Rules cannot be declared violative of article 39(a) unless the requirement of the said Article read in consonance with the fundamental rights are infringed; *Uma Devi Sharma* v. *State of Madhya Pradesh,* AIR 2008 MP 110: 2008 AIHC 326 (NOC): 2008 (2) AIR Jhar (NOC) 412.

CHAPTER VIII

CONTROL OF TRAFFIC

112. Limits of speed.—(1) No person shall drive a motor vehicle or cause or allow a motor vehicle to be driven in any public place at a speed exceeding the maximum speed or below the minimum speed fixed for the vehicle under this Act or by or under any other law for the time being in force:

Provided that such maximum speed shall in no case exceed the maximum fixed for any motor vehicle or class or description of motor vehicles by the Central Government by notification in the Official Gazette.

(2) The State Government or any authority authorised in this behalf by the State Government may, if satisfied that it is necessary to restrict the speed of motor vehicles in the interest of public safety or convenience or because of the nature of any road or bridge, by notification in the Official Gazette, and by causing appropriate traffic signs to be placed or erected under section 116 at suitable places, fix such maximum speed limits or minimum speed limits as it thinks fit for motor vehicles or any specified class or description of motor

1. Ins. by Act 54 of 1994 sec. 33 (w.e.f. 14-11-1994).
2. Clause (g) omitted by Act 54 of 1994 sec. 33 (w.e.f. 14-11-1994).

vehicles or for motor vehicles to which a trailer is attached, either generally or in a particular area or on a particular road or roads:

Provided that no such notification is necessary if any restriction under this section is to remain in force for not more than one month.

(3) Nothing in this section shall apply to any vehicle registered under section 60 while it is being used in the execution of military manoeuvres within the area and during the period specified in the notification under sub-section (1) of section 2 of the Manoeuvres, Field Firing and Artillery Practice Act, 1938 (5 of 1938).

SYNOPSIS

1. Suitable Speed Control Device Necessity to Fit with
2. Extension of Time for Fitting Speed Governors
3. Fixing of Speed Governors in Transport Vehicles

COMMENTS

1. Suitable Speed Control Device Necessity to Fit with – No heavy and medium transport vehicles, and light goods vehicles being four wheelers would be permitted to operate on the roads of the NCR and NCT, Delhi, unless they are fitted with suitable speed control devices to ensure that they do not exceed the speed limit of 40 KMPH. This will not apply to transport vehicles operating on Inter-State permits and national goods permits. Such exempted vehicles would, however, be confined to such routes and such timings during day and night as the police/transport authorities may publish; *M.C. Mehta* v. *Union of India*, AIR 1999 SC 301: 1998 AIR SCW 3822: JT 1998 (8) SC 341: 1999 (1) SCC 413: 1998 (6) SCALE 384: 1998 (9) Supreme 142.

2. Extension of Time for Fitting Speed Governors – The Government showing indulgence and granting time for practical reasons like the difficulty to fix Speed Governors in all the transport vehicles all of a sudden. But Annexure B Notification was issued about 12 years after Rule came into force. Even after three years of issuing Annexure B Notification, the operators of the vehicles do not want to fit Speed Governors in their vehicles. The object of fitting Speed Governors is to strictly enforce the speed limits imposed under section 112 of the Act. The attitude of the operators reflects their lack of concern for the safety and the lives of the passengers and the public. None of the respondents has advanced any valid legal contention against the statutory provisions or against the requirement of fitting Speed Governors. The main thrust of their argument is the alleged non-availability of Speed Governors and the financial burden in fitting Speed Governors. There is no factual basis for the allegation that sufficient number of Speed Governors are not available in the market. Of course there will be some financial burden for fitting Speed Governors. But it cannot be a valid ground of indefinitely postpone the enforcement of a statutory provision incorporated with the object of protecting the lives of passengers and public. The private interest of the operators should yield to the public interest in ensuring public safety. There must be an end to the extensions of time to fit Speed Governors; *Y.N. Nanjappa* v. *State of Karnataka*, AIR 2008 Kant 199: 2008 (6) AIR Kar R 106.

3. Fixing of Speed Governors in Transport Vehicles – Section 112 of the Act, provide that no person shall drive a motor vehicle or cause or allow a motor vehicle to be driven in any public place at a speed exceeding the maximum speed or below the minimum speed fixed for the vehicle under the Act or by or under any other law for the time being in force. Maxi cabs also are motor vehicles governed by the provisions contained in section 112 of the Act. Rule 118 providing for Speed Governors was made for enforcing the provisions contained in section 112 of the Act. Hence there is no logic in contending that Maxi Cabs should be exempted from fitting Speed Governors. It cannot be contended that Speed Governors are not available in the market; *Raghupathy Bhat* v. *State of Karnataka,* AIR 2008 Kant 203: 2008 (6) AIR Kar R 102.

113. Limits of weight and limitations on use.—(1) The State Government may prescribe the conditions for the issue of permits for [1][transport vehicles] by the State or Regional Transport Authorities and may prohibit or restrict the use of such vehicles in any area or route.

(2) Except as may be otherwise prescribed, no person shall drive or cause or allow to be driven in any public place any motor vehicle which is not fitted with pneumatic tyres.

(3) No person shall drive or cause or allow to be driven in any public place any motor vehicle or trailer—

(a) the unladen weight of which exceeds the unladen weight specified in the certificate of registration of the vehicle, or

(b) the laden weight of which exceeds the gross vehicle weight specified in the certificate of registration.

(4) Where the driver or person in charge of a motor vehicle or trailer driven in contravention of sub-section (2) or clause (a) of sub-section (3) is not the owner, a Court may presume that the offence was committed with the knowledge of or under the orders of the owner of the motor vehicle or trailer.

SYNOPSIS

1. Laden Weight and Unladen Weight
2. Initiation of Proceedings by Police Officer is Illegal
3. Police Officers are not Authorised to Book Cases for Overloading

COMMENTS

1. Laden Weight and Unladen Weight – Non-compliance of the provisions relating to "laden weight" and "unladen weight" being penal in nature must be held to be imperative in character. For the purpose of construction of the provisions of the Act the Courts will have to take into consideration the freedom on the part of the citizens as also non citizens to carry out trade and business in terms of article 301 of the Constitution of India, subject of course to the other provisions thereof; *J.H. Truck Owners Assocn.* v. *S.A. Coal Dealer and Truck Owner Assocn.,* AIR 2009 SC 3041: 2009 AIR SCW 4881: 2009 (8) SCC 492: 2009 (9) SCALE 469.

2. Initiation of Proceedings by Police Officer is Illegal – Only the Officers of the Motor Vehicles Department are authorised or empowered by the State Government to proceed against the persons who contravenes section 113 of the Act. In other words, the Police Officers are not authorised to book cases for overloading; *Bhalchandra Transport Co., Hubli* v. *State of Karnataka,* AIR 1998 Kant 213: 1998 (3) Kant LJ 278: ILR 1998 Kant 1794.

3. Police Officers are not Authorised to Book Cases for Overloading – In case of overloading of transport vehicles, only the officers of the Motor Vehicles Department are authorised or empowered by the State Government to proceed against such persons who contravenes section 113 of the Act. In other words the police officers are not authorised to book cases for overloading; *Bhalchandra Transport Co., Hubli* v. *State of Karnataka,* AIR 1998 Kant 213: 1998 (3) Kant LJ 278: ILR 1998 Kant 1794.

114. Power to have vehicle weighed.—(1) [2][Any officer of the Motor Vehicles Department authorised in this behalf by the State Government shall, if he has

1. Subs. by Act 54 of 1994, sec. 34, for "heavy goods vehicles or heavy passenger motor vehicles" (w.e.f. 14-11-1994).
2. Subs. by Act 54 of 1994, sec. 35, for certain words (w.e.f. 14-11-1994).

reason to believe that a goods vehicle or trailer is being used in contravention of section 113,] require the driver to convey the vehicle to a weighing device, if any, within a distance of ten kilometres from any point on the forward route or within a distance of twenty kilometres from the destination of the vehicle for weighment; and if on such weighment the vehicle is found to contravene in any respect the provisions of section 113 regarding weight, he may, by order in writing, direct the driver to off-load the excess weight at his own risk and not to remove the vehicle or trailer from that place until the laden weight has been reduced or the vehicle or trailer has otherwise been dealt with so that it complies with section 113 and on receipt of such notice, the driver shall comply with such directions.

(2) Where the person authorised under sub-section (1) makes the said order in writing, he shall also endorse the relevant details of the overloading on the goods carriage permit and also intimate the fact of such endorsement to the authority which issued that permit.

115. Power to restrict the use of vehicles.—The State Government or any authority authorised in this behalf by the State Government, if satisfied that it is necessary in the interest of public safety or convenience, or because of the nature of any road or bridge, may by notification in the Official Gazette, prohibit or restrict, subject to such exceptions and conditions as may be specified in the notification, the driving of motor vehicles or of any specified class or description of motor vehicles or the use of trailers either generally in a specified area or on a specified road and when any such prohibition or restriction is imposed, shall cause appropriate traffic signs to be placed or erected under section 116 at suitable places:

Provided that where any prohibition or restriction under this section is to remain in force for not more than one month, notification thereof in the Official Gazette shall not be necessary, but such local publicity as the circumstances may permit, shall be given of such prohibition or restriction.

SYNOPSIS

COMMENTS

1. Restriction on Entry of Vehicles in Interest of Public – Section 115 of the Act, in fact, gives power to the Collector/Competent Authority to prohibit or restrict entry of the Motor Vehicles on road or roads in the interest of public at large. However, he has to exercise this power only on being satisfied on the basis of the material available before him that it is necessary to do so in the interest of public safety or convenience. Thus in the facts and circumstances, the impugned Notification issued by Collector prohibiting plying of Pvt. Luxury Buses/heavy vehicles on roads, is undoubtedly in the public interest and stands the test of reasonableness and can be construed as reasonable restriction on the fundamental rights. The same is, therefore, not violative of article 19(1)(d) and (g) of the Constitution of India. The impugned Notification cannot be declared *mala fide* merely because the Collector did not invite objections by issuing proclamation before issuing the impugned Notification. There is no such requirement under section 115 of the Act. The only requirement under section 115 of the Act is whether there is a requisite material or circumstances existing before the Competent Authority to reach the necessary satisfaction in order to issue prohibitory order in the interest of public safety or convenience. In the instant case, it cannot be said that there was no material available before the Collector to reach the necessary satisfaction contemplated under section 115 of the Act; *Zakir Hussain* v. *State of Maharashtra,* AIR 2001 Bom 21: 2001 (1) Mah LJ 442: 2001 (1) ACC 219.

2. Power of Shifting Bus Stand – If an authority has power to set up a bus stand or if an authority has the power to decide which will be the halting place of the buses, then it is implied that the authority can also exercise the power of shifting the bus stand; *Girimallappa* v. *Chairman, Regional Transport Authority, Bellary,* AIR 1998 Kant 182: 1998 (1) Kant LJ 320.

3. Public Notice for Shifting of Bus Stand – The authority has power to decide which will be the halting places for buses It implies that the authority can exercise the power of shifting of the bus stand. There is no rigid requirement of law that public notice be given or that objections should be invited. Thus no public notice is necessary; *Girimallappa* v. *Chairman, Regional Transport Authority, Bellary,* AIR 1998 Kant 182: 1998 (1) Kant LJ 320.

4. Order Regulating Route – No Gazette notification has been made with regard to the order regulating route at Annexure A/14. Thus, the notification shall have no legal effect. In other words, the same may not be given effect to. Again, regarding the exercise of the power under section 117 also such power, determining parking and halting places can only be made in consultation with the local authority having jurisdiction in the area concerned and regarding this also nothing is mentioned in the notification itself regarding the consultation with the local authority. Some exercise have been made by the State authorities in this regard. Attention was drawn to Annexure A/16 in which the matter is found to have been discussed as Agenda No. 9. Thus, it is proper for the authorities to regulate the matter in accordance with the provisions contained under sections 115 and 117 of the Act; *Ch. Ibomcha Singh* v. *State of Manipur,* AIR 2004 Gau 125: 2004 (1) ACC 487: 2004 (2) Civ LJ 224.

116. Power to erect traffic signs.—(1) (a) The State Government or any authority authorised in this behalf by the State Government may cause or permit traffic signs to be placed or erected in any public place for the purpose of bringing to public notice any speed limits fixed under sub-section (2) of section 112 or any prohibitions or restrictions imposed under section 115 or generally for the purpose of regulating motor vehicle traffic.

(b) A State Government or any authority authorised in this behalf by the State Government may, by notification in the Official Gazette or by the erection at suitable places of the appropriate traffic sign referred to in Part A of the Schedule, designate certain roads as main roads for the purposes of the driving regulations made by the Central Government.

(2) Traffic signs placed or erected under sub-section (1) for any purpose for which provision is made in the Schedule shall be of the size, colour and type and shall have the meanings set forth in the Schedule, but the State Government or any authority empowered in this behalf by the State Government may make or authorise the addition to any sign set forth in the said Schedule, of transcriptions of the words, letters or figures thereon in such script as the State Government may think fit provided that the transcriptions shall be of similar size and colour to the words, letters or figures set forth in the Schedule.

(3) Except as provided by sub-section (1), no traffic sign shall, after the commencement of this Act, be placed or erected on or near any road; but all traffic signs placed or erected prior to the commencement of this Act by any competent authority shall for the purpose of this Act by any competent authority

shall for the purpose of this Act be deemed to be traffic signs placed or erected under the provisions of sub-section (1).

(4) A State Government may, by notification in the Official Gazette, empower any police officer not below the rank of a Superintendent of Police to remove or cause to be removed any sign or advertisement which is so placed in his opinion as to obscure any traffic sign from view or any sign or advertisement which in his opinion is so similar in appearance to a traffic sign as to be misleading or which in his opinion is likely to distract the attention or concentration of the driver.

(5) No person shall wilfully remove, alter, deface, or in any way tamper with, any traffic signs placed or erected under this section.

(6) If any person accidentally causes such damage to a traffic sign as renders it useless for the purpose for which it is placed or erected under this section, he shall report the circumstances of the occurrence to a police officer or at a police station as soon as possible, and in any case within twenty four hours of the occurrence.

(7) For the purpose of bringing the signs set forth in [1][the First Schedule] in conformity with any International Convention relating to motor traffic to which the Central Government is for the time being a party, the Central Government may, by notification in the Official Gazette, make any addition or alteration to any such sign and on the issue of any such notification, [1][the First Schedule] shall be deemed to be amended accordingly.

117. Parking places and halting stations.—The State Government or any authority authorised in this behalf by the State Government may, in consultation with the local authority having jurisdiction in the area concerned, determine places at which motor vehicles may stand either indefinitely or for a specified period of time, and may determine the places at which public service vehicles may stop for a longer time than is necessary for the taking up and setting down of passengers.

SYNOPSIS

1. Levy of Fee without any Service is Unauthorised
2. Competent Authority to Designate Bus-stand and Prescribes Fees
3. Order Regulating Route

COMMENTS

1. Levy of Fee without any Service is Unauthorised – Where there was no town bus stand in existence still fee was sought to be collected from every vehicles that was crossing the town on pretext that they were using the parking and halting facility of the town bus stand, which was non-existent, such collection of fee without even there being commensurate service capable of being rendered, even to the group of people possessing commercial vehicle would render the realization not only contrary to the provisions of the Motor Vehicle Act and the Rules framed thereunder but would render the same ultra vires the Constitution itself. There being no dispute that no services were even capable of being provided, the realization of fee becomes ipso facto unauthorized, then the settlement for realization thereof had no legs to stand on, the settlement thus was rendered void; *Punam Singh* v. *State of Bihar,* AIR 2009 Pat 95: 2009 AIHC 604 (NOC): 2009 (4) ALJ (NOC) 682.

---

1. Subs. by Act 54 of 1994, sec. 36, for "the Schedule" (w.e.f. 14-11-1994).

2. Competent Authority to Designate Bus-stand and Prescribes Fees – The provision of section 117 deals with designating parking zones in crowded market places and busy areas in a city or town with a view to facilitate smooth and un-obstructed flow of traffic. It must be borne in mind that a parking zone or a bus stop in a city or town is quite different from a bus stand. A parking zone or a bus stop are internal to a city and are set up primarily for the control of traffic inside the town and to save the crowded market areas and other busy centres of the city or town from further pressure of vehicles being parked there haphazardly, leading to further congestion. A bus stand on the other hand is primarily set up for stage carriage vehicles coming from and going to places outside the city or town. The Act and the Rules maintain this clear distinction. While section 96(2)(xxii) along with rule 191 deals with the setting up of bus stands and empowers the Regional Transport Authority to designate the bus stand and to prescribe fees etc. section 117 read with rule 187 empowers the District Magistrate to designate parking zones and issue directions on matters allied thereto. The setting up of a bus stand, as distinct and separate from a parking zone or a bus stop, is dealt with under rule 191 of the Rules which empowers the Regional Transport Authority to designate a bus stand and to prescribe fees etc. The setting up of a parking zone or a bus stop for controlling the internal traffic of a city and town is dealt with under section 117 read with rules 187 and 214 which empower the District Magistrate to identify parking zones/places. The power to designate a bus stand and to prescribe the fees to be paid by the owners of public service vehicle vests in the Regional Transport Authority and not with the District Magistrate; *Dinesh Kumar Yadav* v. *State of Bihar,* AIR 1999 Pat 213: 1999 (3) BLJ 752: 1999 (3) Pat LJR 130.

3. Order Regulating Route – No Gazette notification has been made with regard to the order regulating route at Annexure A/14. Thus, the notification shall have no legal effect. In other words, the same may not be given effect to. Again, regarding the exercise of the power under section 117 also such power, determining parking and halting places can only be made in consultation with the local authority having jurisdiction in the area concerned and regarding this also nothing is mentioned in the notification itself regarding the consultation with the local authority. Some exercise have been made by the State authorities in this regard. Attention was drawn to Annexure A/16 in which the matter is found to have been discussed as Agenda No. 9. Thus, it is proper for the authorities to regulate the matter in accordance with the provisions contained under sections 115 and 117 of the Act; *Ch. Ibomcha Singh* v. *State of Manipur,* AIR 2004 Gau 125: 2004 (1) ACC 487: 2004 (2) Civ LJ 224.

118. Driving regulations.—The Central Government may, by notification in the Official Gazette, make regulations for the driving of motor vehicles.

119. Duty to obey traffic signs.—(1) Every driver of a motor vehicle shall drive the vehicle in conformity with any indication given by mandatory traffic sign and in conformity with the driving regulations made by the Central Government, and shall comply with all directions given to him by any police officer for the time being engaged in the regulation of traffic in any public place.

(2) In this section "mandatory traffic sign" means a traffic sign included in Part A of †[the First Schedule], or any traffic sign of similar form (that is to say, consisting of or including a circular disc displaying a device, word or figure and having a red ground or border) placed or erected for the purpose of regulating motor vehicle traffic under sub-section (1) of section 116.

† **Ed.**—For the words "the Schedule" the words "the First Schedule" have been substituted as the Schedule has been renumbered as the First Schedule by Act 54 of 1994, sec. 63 (w.e.f. 14-11-1994).

120. Vehicles with left hand control.—No person shall drive or cause or allow to be driven in any public place any motor vehicle with a left-hand steering control unless it is equipped with a mechanical or electrical signalling device of a prescribed nature and in working order.

121. Signals and signalling devices.—The driver of a motor vehicle shall make such signals and on such occasions as may be prescribed by the Central Government:

Provided that the signal of an intention to turn to the right or left or to stop—

(a) in the case of a motor vehicle with a right-hand steering control, may be given by a mechanical or electrical device of a prescribed nature affixed to the vehicle; and

(b) in the case of a motor vehicle with a left hand steering control, shall be given by a mechanical or electrical device of a prescribed nature affixed to the vehicle:

Provided further that the State Government may, having regard to the width and condition of the roads in any area or route, by notification in the Official Gazette, exempt subject to such conditions as may be specified therein any motor vehicle or class or description of motor vehicles from the operation of this section for the purpose of plying in that area or route.

122. Leaving vehicle in dangerous position.—No person in charge of a motor vehicle shall cause or allow the vehicle or any trailer to be abandoned or to remain at rest on any public place in such a position or in such a condition or in such circumstances as to cause or likely to cause danger, obstruction or undue inconvenience to other users of the public place or to the passengers.

123. Riding on running board, etc.—(1) No person driving or in charge of a motor vehicle shall carry any person or permit any person to be carried on the running board or otherwise than within the body of the vehicle.

(2) No person shall travel on the running board or on the top or on the bonnet of a motor vehicle.

124. Prohibition against travelling without pass or ticket.—No person shall enter or remain in any stage carriage for the purposes of travelling therein unless he has with him a proper pass or ticket:

Provided that where arrangements for the supply of tickets are made in the stage carriage by which a person has to travel, a person may enter such stage carriage but as soon as may be after his entry therein, he shall make the payment of his fare to the conductor or the driver who performs the functions of a conductor and obtain from such conductor or driver, as the case may be, a ticket for his journey.

Explanation.—In this section,—

(a) "pass" means a duty, privilege or courtesy pass entitling the person to whom it is given to travel in a stage carriage gratuitously and includes a pass issued on payment for travel in a stage carriage for the period specified therein;

(b) "ticket" includes a single ticket, a return ticket or a season ticket.

125. Obstruction of driver.—No person driving a motor vehicle shall allow any person to stand or sit or to place anything in such a manner or position as to hamper the driver in his control of the vehicle.

126. Stationary vehicles.—No person driving or in charge of a motor vehicle shall cause or allow the vehicle to remain stationary in any public place, unless there is in the driver's seat a person duly licensed to drive the vehicle or unless the mechanism has been stopped and a brake or brakes applied or such other measures taken as to ensure that the vehicle cannot accidentally be put in motion in the absence of the driver.

127. Removal of motor vehicles abandoned or left unattended on a public place.—[1][(1) Where any motor vehicle is abandoned or left unattended on a public place for ten hours or more or is parked in a place where parking is legally prohibited, its removal by a towing service or its immobilisation by any means including wheel clamping may be authorised by a police officer in uniform having jurisdiction.]

(2) Where an abandoned, unattended, wrecked, burnt or partially dismantled vehicle is creating a traffic hazard, because of its position in relation to the [2][public place], or its physical appearance is causing the impediment to the traffic, its immediate removal from the [2][public place] by a towing service may be authorised by a police officer having jurisdiction.

(3) Where a vehicle is authorised to be removed under sub-section (1) or sub-section (2) by a police officer, the owner of the vehicle shall be responsible for all towing costs, besides any other penalty.

128. Safety measures for drivers and pillion riders.—(1) No driver of a two-wheeled motor cycle shall carry more than one person in addition to himself on the motor cycle and no such person shall be carried otherwise than sitting on a proper seat securely fixed to the motor cycle behind the driver's seat with appropriate safety measures.

(2) In addition to the safety measures mentioned in sub-section (1), the Central Government may, prescribe other safety measures for the drivers of two-wheeled motor cycles and pillion riders thereon.

SYNOPSIS

1. Wearing of Protective Headgear
2. Permitted to Carry Only Two Individuals

COMMENTS

1. Wearing of Protective Headgear – Provisions under sections 128, 129 makes it compulsory for every person driving or riding two wheeler motor-cycle in public place to wearing of protective headgear. There has been no implementation of the sections 128 and 129 of the Act, since the Act came in force, therefore, direction is issued to the Police Commissioner of Delhi that this decision shall be given adequate publicity by media and also through local Doordarshan programme, indicating that henceforth these provisions of the Act shall be strictly implemented and violators shall be punished. The Commissioner of Police shall ensure compliance of these provisions after giving adequate publicity of this order; *Pt. Parmanand Katara* v. *Union of India*, AIR 1998 Del 200.

2. Permitted to Carry Only Two Individuals – A motorcycle or a motor-scooter or a moped conventionally answering to the description of two wheelers is permitted under

1. Subs. by Act 54 of 1994, sec. 37, for sub-section (1) (w.e.f. 14-11-1994).
2. Subs. by Act 54 of 1994, sec. 37, for "highway" (w.e.f. 14-11-1994).

the law to carry only two individuals regardless of the age or size of those persons. Secondly, the law postulates that the person other than the driver can only be carried in a position behind the driver and the police and the traffic control authorities reminded that it is totally and completely impermissible to permit the second person travelling on that vehicle to be in any other position. The entire legislative intent behind incorporating this provision in section 128 of the Act is directed towards incorporating the safety angle because apart from the aspect of the vision, the stability of the vehicle and the possibility of serious injury to the child are something which the law desires to eliminate. This is the reason why section 128 of the Act postulates that the second passenger even if it is a child can only travel in a position behind the rider and secondly, that the passenger, irrespective of again of the age is only permitted to travel sitting on a proper seat securely fixed to the motorcycle behind the driver's seat with appropriate safety measures. The Act postulates that only one other individual regardless of the age can occupy this seat and the customary practice of 3 adults or two adults and children or as has happened in the present case one adult and 3 children and the like, is totally prohibited by law. The result of these breaches is obvious insofar as the stability of the vehicle is seriously affected and secondly, in the unfortunate eventuality of an accident taking place the number of injured or dead persons gets multiplied. It is very necessary that steps be taken in order to put a full stop to the reckless practice of operating two-wheelers in breach of provisions of section 128 of the Act; *P.S. Somaiah* v. *Director, Bangalore Diary,* AIR 2003 Kant 258: 2004 (1) Kant LJ 498: 2005 (2) ACJ 1359.

A motor bike with seating capacity for two is obviously designed to carry only two passengers. In the first place, there is no space in the bike to be shared by any other person. If the rider sacrifices his comfortable seat at least in part to accommodate a third passenger, certainly, he will not be able to control the bike. Besides this, since the bike is designed to carry only two passengers, additional weight on account of third passenger will affect its stability. However, in violation of section 128 of the M.V. Act, three passengers and very often children are taken in two wheelers along with rider and pillion rider as in this case. Even though section 128 of the M.V. Act bars the driver of a motor bike from taking more then one pillion rider and though the provision is more often violated than observed, the Motor Vehicle and the police authorities do not take serious note of this. May be petty traffic cases are booked against such people and matter is settled on payment of paltry sum of fine. Therefore in the public interest, the Government authorities should be ordered to enforce the law strictly. No purpose will be served by booking petty cases and releasing the offenders on collection of small amounts of fine. Even though strict enforcement of law involves absolute prohibition against the rider of the motor bike taking more than one pillion rider, considering ground realities a small baby can be permitted to be carried in the lap of the pillion rider without sacrificing any seating space in the bike which is only for two passengers. The Director General of Police and the Transport Commissioner to instruct the police and the motor vehicle authorities to seize two wheelers taking more than one pillion rider and at the maximum a small baby and take stern action against those committing violation of section 128 of the M.V. Act; *Pournami* v. *Sandhya Sudheer, Sougandhikam,* AIR 2009 Ker 31: 2009 AIHC 210 (NOC): 2009 (2) ACJ 1291.

129. Wearing of protective headgear.—Every person driving or riding (otherwise than in a side car, on a motor cycle of any class or description) shall, while in a public place, wear [1][protective headgear conforming to the standards of Bureau of Indian Standards]:

Provided that the provisions of this section shall not apply to a person who is a Sikh, if he is, while driving or riding on the motor cycle, in a public place, wearing a turban:

1. Subs. by Act 54 of 1994, sec. 38, for certain words (w.e.f. 14-11-1994).

Provided further that the State Government may, by such rules, provide for such exceptions as it may think fit.

Explanation.—"Protective headgear" means a helmet which,—

(a) by virtue of its shape, material and construction, could reasonably be expected to afford to the person driving or riding on a motor cycle a degree of protection from injury in the event of an accident; and

(b) is securely fastened to the head of the wearer by means of straps or other fastenings provided on the headgear.

SYNOPSIS

1. Order Making Wearing of Helmet Optional is *Ultra Vires*
2. Non-compliance of Provisions would Result in Imposition of Fine and Prosecution
3. Exception to Person to wear Helmet who Normally Wear Turban
4. Provisions Neither Discriminatory nor Vitiated
5. Bureau of Indian Standard for Protective Headgears
6. No Discrimination amongst Road Users
7. Wearing of Helmet is Mandatory
8. Sikh Ladies who do not Wear Turban are Bound to Wear Helmet
9. Central Government is not Empowered to Grant Exemption from Wearing Helmet
10. Matter Provided under Section 129 is not Specific Matters
11. Wearing of Protective Headgear
12. Power of State Government to Exempt Person from Wearing Helmet is Limited

COMMENTS

1. Order Making Wearing of Helmet Optional is *Ultra Vires* – The proviso to section 129 does not authorise the State Government to make rules providing for total exemption from the requirement of wearing of protective headgears. The said proviso merely authorises the State Government to make rules providing for such exceptions as it may think fit. But under no circumstances, the State Government can grant a total exemption or exception from the operation of provisions of section 129. The proviso does not confer any such power to grant wholesale exemption from the operation of the section itself. Order issued in exercise of the power conferred by the second proviso to section 129 and making wearing of protective headgear (helmet) optional in respect of every person driving or riding on a motorcycle including scooter and moped is *ultra vires; C.S. Subba Rao* v. *Secretary to Government of A.P. Transport Deptt.*, AIR 2003 AP 59: 2002 (6) Andh LD 447: 2002 (6) Andh LT 458.

2. Non-compliance of Provisions would Result in Imposition of Fine and Prosecution – The provisions of the Act are intended for the prevention of fatal and serious accidents and the State must ensure that the provisions of the said Act are strictly adhered to. People must be made aware of the benefit of using Helmet during the period in which the law is being implemented in a phased manner. People must be informed that this piece of legislation is designed entirely for their own safety and well being. These provisions have been incorporated for the benefit, welfare and the safe journey of the driver and pillion-rider of a two wheeled vehicle. Wearing Helmet helps the driver to drive the vehicle in exercise of his freedom of movement without being subjected to a constant apprehension of a fatal head injury, if any accident takes place. State and the Helmet Manufacturers Association directed to inform them that they must wholeheartedly support this piece of legislation. These provisions have been incorporated for the welfare and benefit of the public at large. Therefore, it is all the more essential that these provisions have to be strictly implemented in the larger interest of public. The State also undertakes to paste notices at the prominent places in the city that it is compulsory to wear helmets and non-compliance of the Act would result in imposition of fine and prosecution; *Free Legal Aid Cell (NGO)* v. *Government of Maharashtra*, AIR 2005 Bom 271: 2005 (6) Bom CR 429.

3. Exception to Person to wear Helmet who Normally Wear Turban – The State Government has been conferred limited power under section 129 is concerned is to make an exception in respect of similar categories of persons who for reasons of religion or custom normally wear a turban and in whose case therefore, the wearing of a helmet would not be feasible. It would be a misconception of the law if the proviso to section 129 were to be understood to empower the State Government to dilute the compulsory and mandatory requirements of section 129 by exemption of the whole or greater class of motorised two wheelers. This would be doing violence to the law and which is something that is wholly impermissible. It would be wholly outside the legislative competence of the State Government. The proviso to the Rule granting exemption from wearing headgear to a person driving motor cycle with not more than three metric brake horse power is *ultra vires* section 129 of the Act; *S.R. Bhat* v. *State of Karnataka,* AIR 1998 Kant 153: 1998 (2) Kant LJ 92: 1999 (1) TAC 40.

4. Provisions Neither Discriminatory nor Vitiated – Wearing of Helmet is made compulsory for purposes of protection from injury, and heat and pollution, Rules and Regulations alone cannot be panacea since human error is considered as the major cause for road accidents. Accusations regarding the causes of the accident as being due to carelessness, drunkenness, rashness, negligence, over-speeding arrogance, incompetence etc., are of secondary line of thinking since often riders might not be there as a living witness to explain the causes. In this modern society one should not speak through, rules and regulations but must visualies their moral commitment to the Society at large. Rider must realise that woman who is widowed because of the road accident may be his own wife or *vice versa*. Thus the Rules in making wearing of helmet compulsory to two wheeler riders is based on rational basis taking into consideration the alarming proportion of the road accidents involving two wheeler riders, such policy is not only rational but is also in the interest of larger public interests, since statistics revealed that more number of two wheelers are on the road having in view of transport problems and economics of the cost. The Rule making authority has merely given effect to the intention of the legislature whereby separate treatment to two wheeler has been provided to have riders, from accidents resulting in fatal injuries. If the rules could be validly framed then there is no reason as to why rule making authority could not be held to have the power to frame a rule which is in consonance with the legislative intent as envisaged under the Act. Any classification which is founded on an intelligible differentia having a rational relation to the purpose of the Act concerned being permissible, classification excluding persons belonging to Sikh community does not violate article 14 of the Constitution; *K. Veeresh Babu* v. *Union of India,* AIR 1994 Kant 56: ILR 1993 Kant 2939.

5. Bureau of Indian Standard for Protective Headgears – The State Government is now bound to follow the specification laid down by the Bureau of Indian Standards for protective headgears; *Kerala Auto Two Wheelers Association* v. *S.S. Sathjith,* AIR 2000 Ker 118: 2000 (1) ACC 478: 2000 (1) Ker LJ 208.

6. No Discrimination amongst Road Users – The provisions of section 129 of the Act is challenged on grounds that it creates discrimination amongst the road users namely motor cyclists or any class of vehicles of that description and others inasmuch as the said provision is not applicable to the pedestrians or vehicles of other categories. The classification has a rational basis inasmuch as a person who is driving a motorcycle stands on a different footing than the person travelling in a side car or any other vehicle. A motorcyclist of any class or description is more prone to get injured in an accident because his head is open, whereas the person travelling in other kind of vehicle, which is covered, is protected. A pedestrian and a person who is driving or riding motorcycle cannot be equated. A pedestrian, who walks on the road cannot be conceived to stand on equal footing of that class of motorcyclist. Hence, he is excluded from wearing a helmet. Thus, the classification made is on rational basis and has a nexus for the purpose of which legislation has made and no fault can be found with it; *Rajneesh Kapoor* v. *Union of India,* AIR 2007 MP 204: 2007 AIHC 509 (NOC).

7. Wearing of Helmet is Mandatory – Section 129 of the Act has made mandatory for wearing of helmet. The proviso to such section contains an enabling provision under which the State can make rules providing for any exemption. Such law has been enacted by the Parliament in its wisdom. The assertion that such provisions have been made with a view to help the helmet manufacturers, has been rejected. Moreover, any imputation relating to collective *mala fides* against the Parliament, cannot be countenanced; *Accident Victims Association* v. *State of Tamil Nadu,* AIR 2008 Mad 86: 2008 AIHC 383 (NOC): 2008 (1) Mad LJ 968.

8. Sikh Ladies who do not Wear Turban are Bound to Wear Helmet – As per rule 201 enacted under section 129 of new Act, only persons who are wearing turban are exempted from wearing a protective headgear while driving a motor cycle, scooter or moped. Since Sikh women admittedly do not wear turban, they are bound to wear protective headgear in compliance with section 129 of the Motor Vehicles Act, 1988 and rule 201 of the Uttar Pradesh Motor Vehicles Rules, 1998; *Uttaranchal Sikh Federation* v. *State of Uttaranchal,* AIR 2006 Uttra 67.

9. Central Government is not Empowered to Grant Exemption from Wearing Helmet – Section 129 of the Motor Vehicles Act, has not empowered to the Central Government to make any rules providing for exceptions to the provisions contained in the said section. On the other hand, as per the second proviso to section 129 such power has been conferred only on the State Government. Merely because there is a provision under section 129 of the Motor Vehicles Act, 1988 empowering the State Government to make rules providing for exception to the provision of section 129, it does not mean that rule 3 of the Motor Vehicles (Protective Headgears) Rules, 1980 issued under section 85A of the Motor Vehicles Act, 1939 providing for exception to the provisions of the said section 85A, can be deemed to be valid and operative even now. Any provision contained in the Motor Vehicles (Protective Headgears) Rules, 1980, which is inconsistent with the provisions contained in section 129 of the Motor Vehicles Act, 1988 cannot be operative or applicable after the commencement of Motor Vehicles Act, 1988. Thus no person can be given exemption from the application of section 129 of the Motor Vehicles Act, 1988 otherwise than by the Rules made by the State Government under the second proviso to section 129; *Uttaranchal Sikh Federation* v. *State of Uttaranchal,* AIR 2006 Uttra 67.

10. Matter Provided under Section 129 is not Specific Matters – Under section 27(q), the Central Government is not competent to make rules providing for exception to the provisions of section 129. Clauses (a) to (p) of section 27 confer power on the Central Government to make rules regarding the specific matters mentioned therein. The matter dealt with in section 129 is not covered by clauses (a) to (p) of section 27. Even under clause (q) Central Government can exercise the power to make rules only regarding a "matter which is, or has to be, prescribed by the Central Government". Any exception to the provisions of section 129 is not a matter which is, or has to be, prescribed by the Central Government. It is a matter which is, or has to be, prescribed by the Central Government; *Uttaranchal Sikh Federation* v. *State of Uttaranchal,* AIR 2006 Uttra 67.

11. Wearing of Protective Headgear – Provisions under sections 128, 129 makes it compulsory for every person driving or riding two wheeler motor-cycle in public place to wearing of protective headgear. There has been no implementation of the sections 128 and 129 of the Act, since the Act came in force, therefore, direction is issued to the Police Commissioner of Delhi that this decision shall be given adequate publicity by media and also through local Doordarshan programme, indicating that henceforth these provisions of the Act shall be strictly implemented and violators shall be punished. The Commissioner of Police shall ensure compliance of these provisions after giving adequate publicity of this order; *Pt. Parmanand Katara* v. *Union of India,* AIR 1998 Del 200.

12. Power of State Government to Exempt Person from Wearing Helmet is Limited – The limited power conferred on the State Government, as far as section 129 is concerned, is to make an exception in respect of similar categories of persons who for reasons of religion or custom normally wear a turban and in whose case therefore, the wearing of a helmet would not be feasible. It would be a misconception of the law if this proviso were to be understood to empower the State Government to dilute the compulsory and mandatory requirements of section 129 by exemption of the whole or greater class of motorised two wheelers. This would be doing violence to the law and which is something that is wholly impermissible. It would be wholly outside the legislative competence of the State Government; *S.R. Bhat* v. *State of Karnataka,* AIR 1998 Kant 153: 1998 (2) Kant LJ 92: 1999 (1) TAC 40.

130. Duty to produce licence and certificate of registration.—(1) The driver of a motor vehicle in any public place shall, on demand by any police officer in uniform, produce his licence for examination:

Provided that the driver may, if his licence has been submitted to, or has been seized by, any officer or authority under this or any other Act, produce in lieu of the licence a receipt or other acknowledgment issued by such officer or authority in respect thereof and thereafter produce the licence within such period, in such manner as the Central Government may prescribe to the police officer making the demand.

[1][(2) The conductor, if any, of a motor vehicle on any public place shall on demand by any officer of the Motor Vehicles Department authorised in this behalf, produce the licence for examination.]

[2][(3) The owner of a motor vehicle (other than a vehicle registered under section 60), or in his absence the driver or other person in charge of the vehicle, shall, on demand by a registering authority or any other officer of the Motor Vehicles Department duly authorised in this behalf, produce the certificate of insurance of the vehicle and, where the vehicle is a transport vehicle, also the certificate of fitness referred to in section 56 and the permit; and if any or all of the certificates or the permit are not in his possession, he shall, within fifteen days from the date of demand, submit photo copies of the same, duly attested in person or send the same by registered post to the officer who demanded it.

Explanation.—For the purposes of this sub-section, "certificate" of insurance" means the certificate issued under sub-section (3) of section 147.]

(4) If the licence referred to in sub-section (2) or the certificates or permit referred to in sub-section (3), as the case may be, are not at the time in the possession of the person to whom demand is made, it shall be a sufficient compliance with this section if such person produces the licence or certificates or permit within such period in such manner as the Central Government may prescribe, to the police officer or authority making the demand:

Provided that, except to such extent and with such modifications as may be prescribed, the provisions of this sub-section shall not apply to any person required to produce the certificate of registration or the certificate of fitness of a transport vehicle.

1. Subs. by Act 54 of 1994, sec. 39, for sub-section (2) (w.e.f. 14-11-1994).
2. Subs. by Act 54 of 1994, sec. 39, for sub-section (3) (w.e.f. 14-11-1994).

COMMENTS

Power to Demand Production of Documents – The power to demand productions of and to examine the documents cannot be divorced from the purpose behind the conferment of the said power. The purpose is to enable the Police Officers concerned to check such vehicles for the commission of any violation of the provisions of the Act and to take such follow up action as may be necessary. Therefore the power to demand the production of the documents including the permit and the power to impound the same in certain situations preferred to in section 206 as also the power to seize the vehicle in the circumstances mentioned in section 207 are all exercisable by a Police Officer. The very fact that there is an amendment to section 130, sub-section (2) and (3) of the Act, by which the power to ask the conductor to produce his licence has been taken away and conferred upon an officer of the Motor Vehicles Department does not in the least affect the powers of the Police Officers under the aforesaid three provisions. The exercise of power under sections 158, 206 and 207 was in no way dependent upon the availability of the power under section 130(2) so as to make the former redundant in the absence of the later. The Amendment of section 130 sub-section (2) has a very limited effect and does not render the other provisions of the Act particularly sections 158, 206 and 207 nugatory. The power exercisable under the later provisions continues to be available to he Police Officers and could have been therefore legitimately exercised by them; *M.S. Palaksha* v. *Union of India,* AIR 1996 Kant 209: 1996 (2) Kant LJ 256: ILR 1996 Kant 1582.

131. Duty of the driver to take certain precautions at unguarded railway level crossings.—Every driver of a motor vehicle at the approach of any unguarded railway level crossing shall cause the vehicle to stop and the driver of the vehicle shall cause the conductor or cleaner or attendant or any other person in the vehicle to walk up to the level crossing and ensure that no train or trolley is approaching from either side and then pilot the motor vehicle across such level crossing, and where no conductor or cleaner or attendant or any other person is available in the vehicle, the driver of the vehicle shall get down from the vehicle himself to ensure that no train or trolley is approaching from either side before the railway track is crossed.

132. Duty of driver to stop in certain cases.—(1) The driver of a motor vehicle shall cause the vehicle to stop and remain stationary so long as [1][may for such reasonable time as may be necessary, but not exceeding twenty-four hours],—

[2][(a) when required to do so by any police officer not below the rank of a Sub-Inspector in uniform, in the event of the vehicle being involved in the occurrence of an accident to a person, animal or vehicle or of damage to property, or]

(b) when required to do so by any person in charge of an animal if such person apprehends that the animal is, or being alarmed by the vehicle will become, unmanageable, or;

[3][***]

and he shall give his name and address and the name and address of the owner of the vehicle to any person affected by any such accident or damage who demands it provided such person also furnishes his name and address.

1. Subs. by Act 54 of 1994, sec. 40, for "may reasonably be necessary" (w.e.f. 14-11-1994).
2. Subs. by Act 54 of 1994, sec. 40, for clause (a) (w.e.f. 14-11-1994).
3. Clause (c) omitted by Act 54 of 1994, sec. 40 (w.e.f. 14-11-1994).

(2) The driver of a motor vehicle shall, on demand by a person giving his own name and address and alleging that the driver has committed an offence punishable under section 184 give his name and address to that person.

(3) In this section the expression "animal" means any horse, cattle, elephant, camel, ass, mule, sheep or goat.

133. Duty of owner of motor vehicle to give information.—The owner of a motor vehicle, the driver or conductor of which is accused of any offence under this Act shall, on the demand of any police officer authorised in this behalf by the State Government, give all information regarding the name and address of, and the licence held by, the driver or conductor which is in his possession or could by reasonable diligence be ascertained by him.

134. Duty of driver in case of accident and injury to a person.—When any person is injured or any property of a third party is damaged, as a result of an accident in which a motor vehicle is involved, the driver of the vehicle or other person in charge of the vehicle shall—

(a) unless it is not practicable to do so on account of mob fury or any other reason beyond his control, take all reasonable steps to secure medical attention for the injured person, [1][by conveying him to the nearest medical practitioner or hospital, and it shall be the duty of every registered medical practitioner or the doctor on duty in the hospital immediately to attend to the injured person and render medical aid or treatment without waiting for any procedural formalities], unless the injured person or his guardian, in case he is a minor, desires otherwise;

(b) give on demand by a police officer any information required by him, or, if no police officer is present, report the circumstances of the occurrence, including the circumstances, if any, for not taking reasonable steps to secure medical attention as required under clause (a), at the nearest police station as soon as possible, and in any case within twenty-four hours of the occurrence;

[2][(c) give the following information in writing to the insurer, who has issued the certificates of insurance, about the occurrence of the accident, namely:—

(i) insurance policy number and period of its validity;

(ii) date, time and place of accident;

(iii) particulars of the persons injured or killed in the accident;

(iv) name of the driver and the particulars of his driving licence.

Explanation.—For the purposes of this section the expression "driver" includes the owner of the vehicle.]

COMMENTS

Driver Holding American Driving Licence – In India, the driver is always on the defensive due to various reasons. Pedestrians in India seldom use footpaths nor respect

1. Subs. by Act 54 of 1994, sec. 41, of "and, if necessary, convey him to the nearest hospital" (w.e.f. 14-11-1994).
2. Ins. by Act 54 of 1994, sec. 41 (w.e.f. 14-11-1994).

Zebra lines or traffic lights, two wheelers, auto rickshaws, cyclists and street vendors are common sights on Indian roads. A driver on Indian roads should expect the unexpected always, therefore, the plea that the accused has an American driving licence is not an answer for driving in Indian roads unless it is recognized in India or that person is having a driving licence issued by the Licensing Authority in India; *State Tr. P.S. Lodhi Colony, New Delhi* v. *Sanjeev Nanda*, AIR 2012 SC 3104: 2012 Cr LJ 4174: 2012 AIR SCW 4506.

135. Schemes to be framed for the investigation of accident cases and wayside amenities, etc.—(1) The State Government may, by notification in the Official Gazette, make one or more schemes to provide for—

(a) an in-depth study on causes and analysis of motor vehicle accidents;

(b) wayside amenities on highways;

(c) traffic aid posts on highways; and

(d) truck parking complexes along highways.

(2) Every scheme made under this section by any State Government shall be laid, as soon as may be after it is made, before the State Legislature.

136. Inspection of vehicle involved in accident.—When any accident occurs in which a motor vehicle is involved, any person authorised in this behalf by the State Government may, on production if so required of his authority, inspect the vehicle and for that purpose may enter at any reasonable time any premises where the vehicle may be, and may remove the vehicle for examination:

Provided that the place to which the vehicle is so removed shall be intimated to the owner of the vehicle and the vehicle shall be returned [1][after completion of the formalities to the owner, driver or the person in charge of the vehicle within twenty-four hours].

137. Power of Central Government to make rules.—The Central Government may make rules to provide for all or any of the following matters, namely:—

(a) the occasions on which signals shall be made by drivers of motor vehicles and such signals under section 121;

(b) the manner in which the licences and certificates may be produced to the police officer under section 130.

COMMENTS

Use of Red Lights in Front of Vehicles – As long as the notification wherein the list of dignitaries entitled to use red lights in front of the car and the vehicles escorting such vehicles have been identified and specified, has not violated any service condition or caused deprivation of any statutory rights of the members of the petitioner's Indian Forest Service Association. The notification which was issued specifying the office/posts of dignitaries of the State, is beyond the scope of judicial review and, moreso, when the petitioners have failed to point out any arbitrariness or violation of any service condition or statutory rights of the members of the petitioner. The use of red lights by dignitaries specified by the Government, differs from State to State, and it is a settled position of law that pay/scale cannot be the criteria for equation of posts and entitlement thereto. As such, inclusion of the members of the IAS/IPS officers in the list of dignitaries specified under notification dated while excluding the IFS Officers, is not arbitrary; *State of Tripura* v. *Indian Forest Service Association, Tripura Unit, Agartala,* AIR 2008 Gau 132: 2008 (6) ALJ (NOC) 1188: 2008 (3) Gau LT 207.

1. Subs. by Act 54 of 1994, sec. 42, for "without unnecessary delay" (w.e.f. 14-11-1994).

138. Power of State Government to make rules.—(1) The State Government may make rules for the purpose of carrying into effect the provisions of this Chapter other than the matters specified in section 137.

(2) Without prejudice to the generality of the foregoing power, such rules may provide for—

(a) the removal and the safe custody of vehicles including their loads which have broken down or which have been left standing or have been abandoned on roads;

(b) the installation and use of weighing devices;

(c) the maintenance and management of wayside amenities complexes;

(d) the exemption from all or any of the provisions of this Chapter of fire brigade vehicles, ambulances and other special classes or descriptions of vehicle, subject to such conditions as may be prescribed;

(e) the maintenance and management of parking places and stands and the fees, if any, which may be charged for their use;

(f) prohibiting the driving downhill of a motor vehicle with the gear disengaged either generally or in a specified place;

(g) prohibiting the taking hold of or mounting of a motor vehicle in motion;

(h) prohibiting the use of foot-paths or pavements by motor vehicles;

(i) generally, the prevention of danger, injury or annoyance to the public or any person, or of danger or injury to property or of obstruction to traffic; and

(j) any other matter which is to be, or may be, prescribed.

COMMENTS

Eligibility to Apply for Reservation of Number – The applicant should produce the vehicle within a period of three months, either he owned or proposed to be purchased at the time of making the application. It was the intention of the rule making authority that the applicant should have taken any concrete step for purchase of the vehicle to be eligible to apply for reservation of the number. Therefore, if an applicant proposes to purchase a vehicle and has furnished the details of the vehicle he proposed to purchase, he satisfies the requirement of rule 95 to make an application for reservation of fancy number in his favour. If that be the purport of the Rule, it cannot be said that the other two applicants who too had submitted their applications with the details of the vehicles they proposed to purchase, were ineligible to apply for the same. If that be so, the interpretation placed on the terms of rule 95 cannot be upheld; *Joint Regional Transport Officer, Koyilandy* v. *P.K. Sathiapalan*, AIR 2011 Ker 117.

CHAPTER IX

MOTOR VEHICLES TEMPORARILY LEAVING OR VISITING INDIA

139. Power of Central Government to make rules.—(1) The Central Government may, by notification in the Official Gazette, make rules for all or any of the following purposes, namely:—

(a) the grant and authentication of travelling passes, certificates or authorisations to persons temporarily taking motor vehicles out of India to any place outside India or to persons temporarily proceeding out of India to any place outside India and desiring to drive a motor vehicle during their absence from India;

(b) prescribing the conditions subject to which motor vehicles brought temporarily into India from outside India by persons intending to make a temporary stay in India may be possessed and used in India; and

(c) prescribing the conditions subject to which persons entering India from any place outside India for a temporary stay in India may drive motor vehicles in India.

(2) For the purpose of facilitating and regulating the services of motor vehicles operating between India and any other country under any reciprocal arrangement and carrying passengers or goods or both by road for hire or reward, the Central Government may, by notification in the Official Gazette, make rules with respect to all or any of the following matters, namely:—

(a) the conditions subject to which motor vehicles carrying on such services may be brought into India from outside India and possessed and used in India;

(b) the conditions subject to which motor vehicles may be taken from any place in India to any place outside India;

(c) the conditions subject to which persons employed as drivers and conductors of such motor vehicles may enter or leave India;

(d) the grant and authentication of travelling passes, certificates or authorisations to persons employed as drivers and conductors of such motor vehicles;

(e) the particulars (other than registration marks) to be exhibited by such motor vehicles and the manner in which such particulars are to be exhibited;

(f) the use of trailers with such motor vehicles;

(g) the exemption of such motor vehicles and their drivers and conductors from all or any or the provisions of this Act [other than those referred to in sub-section (4)] of the rules made thereunder;

(h) the identification of the drivers and conductors of such motor vehicles;

(i) the replacement of the travelling passes, certificates or authorisations, permits, licences or any other prescribed documents lost or defaced, on payment of such fee as may be prescribed;

(j) the exemption from the provisions of such laws as relate to customs, police or health with a view to facilitate such road transport services;

(k) any other matter which is to be, or may be, prescribed.

(3) No rule made under this section shall operate to confer on any person any immunity in any State from the payment of any tax levied in that State on motor vehicles or their users.

(4) Nothing in this Act or in any rule made thereunder by a State Government relating to—

(a) the registration and identification of motor vehicles, or

(b) the requirements as to construction, maintenance and equipment of motor vehicles, or

(c) the licensing and the qualifications of drivers and conductors of motor vehicles,

shall apply—

(i) to any motor vehicle to which or to any driver of a motor vehicle to whom any rules made under clause (b) or clause (c) of sub-section (1) or under sub-section (2) apply; or

(ii) to any conductor of a motor vehicle to whom any rules made under sub-section (2) apply.

CHAPTER X

LIABILITY WITHOUT FAULT IN CERTAIN CASES

140. Liability to pay compensation in certain cases on the principle of no fault.—(1) Where death or permanent disablement of any person has resulted from an accident arising out of the use of a motor vehicle or motor vehicles, the owner of the vehicle shall, or, as the case may be, the owners of the vehicles shall, jointly and severally, be liable to pay compensation in respect of such death or disablement in accordance with the provisions of this section.

(2) The amount of compensation which shall be payable under sub-section (1) in respect of the death of any person shall be a fixed sum of [1][fifty thousand rupees] and the amount of compensation payable under that sub-section in respect of the permanent disablement of any person shall be a fixed sum of [2][twenty-five thousand rupees].

(3) In any claim for compensation under sub-section (1), the claimant shall not be required to plead and establish that the death or permanent disablement in respect of which the claim has been made was due to any wrongful act, neglect or default of the owner or owners of the vehicle or vehicles concerned or of any other person.

(4) A claim for compensation under sub-section (1) shall not be defeated by reason of any wrongful act, neglect or default of the person in respect of whose death or permanent disablement the claim has been made nor shall the quantum of compensation recoverable in respect of such death or permanent disablement be reduced on the basis of the share of such person in the responsibility for such death or permanent disablement.

[3][(5) Notwithstanding anything contained in sub-section (2) regarding death or bodily injury to any person, for which the owner of the vehicle is liable to give compensation for relief, he is also liable to pay compensation under any other law for the time being in force:

1. Subs. by Act 54 of 1994, sec. 43, for "twenty-five thousand rupees" (w.e.f. 14-11-1994).
2. Subs. by Act 54 of 1994 sec. 43, for "twelve thousand rupees" (w.e.f. 14-11-1994).
3. Ins. by Act 54 of 1994, sec. 43 (w.e.f. 14-11-1994).

Provided that the amount of such compensation to be given under any other law shall be reduced from the amount of compensation payable under this section or under section 163A.]

SYNOPSIS

COMMENTS

1. Quantum of Compensation cannot be Lees on Ground Claimant is Legal Representative – The liability under section 140 of the Act does not cease because there is absence of dependency. The right to file a claim application has to be considered in the background of right to entitlement. While assessing the quantum, the multiplier system is applied because of deprivation of dependency. Where a legal representative who is not dependent files an application for compensation, the quantum cannot be less than the liability referable to section 140 of the Act. Therefore, even if there is no loss of dependency the claimant if he or she is a legal representative will be entitled to compensation, the quantum of which shall be not less than the liability flowing from section 140 of the Act; *New India Assurance Co. Ltd.* v. *Jasinta Kujur,* AIR 2007 Chhat 107: 2007 AIHC 2652: 2007 (5) AKAR (NOC) 621.

2. Liability is not Retrospective – A statute is presumed to be prospective unless held to be retrospective, either expressly or by necessary implication. A substantive law is presumed to be prospective. It is one of the facets of rule of law. Section 140 of the 1988 Act does not contain any procedural provisions so as to construe it to have retrospective effect. Section 140 as amended in 1994 providing sum of Rs. 50,000 as no fault liability is not retrospective; *State of Punjab* v. *Bhajan Kaur,* AIR 2008 SC 2276: 2008 AIR SCW 4073: 2008 (8) SCALE 475.

3. Owner Primarily Liable to Pay Compensation – On a bare reading of section 140 it appears that the owner is responsible to pay Rs. 50,000 under the said proceeding to the claimant and under the statute the Insurance Company is not bound to pay and also could not be made responsible to pay such amount. As such, no liability could be fixed upon the Insurance Company directly by any Motor Accident Claims Tribunal. While adjudicating the application under section 140 of the Motor Vehicles Act, the liability of the owner is fixed which also could be revealed on a comparison of section 163A of the said Act, wherein the legislature at their wisdom not only had used the word 'the owner of the motor vehicle' but also added the word 'or the authorized insurer', while fixing the liability of the payment of compensation under the structured formula basis. Furthermore, it appears that under no fault liability, the Motor Vehicles Act identified by section 140 of the Act, fixed liability of limited amount of Rs. 50,000 to the owner concerned whereas under the structured formula higher amount has been fixed by putting the liability upon the owner or authorized insurer under section 163A of the Act. Both the aforesaid two provisions are under 'no fault liability', which means the claimant need not to prove rash and negligent driving of the offending vehicle as the cause of accident. Thus under section 140 of the Motor Vehicles Act, when the legislature at their wisdom did not saddle the Insurance Company with any liability by using the word 'authorized insurer' similar to section 163A of the said Act, the Insurance Company neither could be made a party in proceeding under section 140 of the said Act nor any liability could be fixed upon their shoulder.

Section 140 makes, primarily the owner of the vehicle liable to pay compensation on the principle of 'No fault', that is, irrespective of the fact as to whether the accident took place due to wrongful act, neglect or default of the person, who drove the vehicle, or not. Section 140 does not *per se* make the insurer liable. The insurer is required to indemnify the owner for the liability, which the owner may incur, under section 140, to pay compensation on the principle of 'No fault'; *New India Assurance Co. Ltd.* v. *Lohit Distt. Legal Service Authority,* AIR 2008 Gau 166: 2008 (68) All Ind Cas 471: 2008 (3) Gau LT 824.

4. Order is Appealable – An order, made under section 140, is also an award and it is appealable under section 173 of the M.V. Act; *New India Assurance Co. Ltd.* v. *Lohit Dist. Legal Service Authority,* AIR 2008 Gau 166.

5. Plea as to Validity of Policy only be decided in Regular Proceeding – The question as to whether the insurance policy, was a valid one or not is really a plea raised by the petitioner and such a plea can be decided only in a regular proceeding and not at the interim stage, when the Tribunal is considering the question of No Fault liability in terms of section 140(2) of the MV Act. Until proved to be forged, the insurance policy, shall have to be treated as valid; *National Insurance Co. Ltd.* v. *Amiya Borbora,* AIR 2004 Gau 22.

6. Recovery of Interim Compensation from Claimant – Thus the liability under section 140 of the Act, is based on the principle of "no fault liability" and even if ultimately the negligence of the driver in driving of the vehicle is not proved or for other reasons the driver or owner is exonerated, the amount paid by way of interim compensation cannot be recovered from the claimants but this principle may not be applicable to the cases where the insurance company made good of the liability of the owner of the vehicle and cannot realise this amount ultimately on their exoneration from the liability; *Harishbhai Chamanlal Panchal* v. *Dahyaben Jayantilal Panchal,* AIR 1999 Guj 33: 1999 (2) ACC 58: 2000 (2) ACJ 957.

7. Section 166 of Act has No Overriding Effect Over Section 140 – Lodging of a petition for compensation under section 166 is not a condition precedent to filing of a petition for interim compensation on the principle of no fault liability. The Legislature has advisedly therefore nowhere stated in section 140 that application for interim compensation can be made only if a substantive petition under section 166 is filed. Chapter XII which deals with the Claims Tribunal and section 166 which finds its place in Chapter XII, cannot have overriding effect over section 140 in light of the clear statutory provision enacted by section 144 of the said Act. Therefore, where main claim petition under section 166 was dismissed on ground of bar of limitation, application under section 140 for interim compensation, cannot be dismissed on that ground; *Munshiram D. Anand* v. *Pravinsinh Prabhatsinh Anand Society, Navagam Gedh, Jamnagar,* AIR 1997 Guj 60: 1997 ACJ 206: 1996 (3) Civ LJ 844.

8. Immediate Aid Available before Adjudication of Claim on Merits – The object underlying enactment of section 140 is to make available to the claimant compensation amount to the extent of Rs. 12,000 in case of permanent disablement as expeditiously as possible and the said award has to be made before adjudication of the claim under section 168 of the Act. Provision of section 140 is a piece of beneficial and ameliorative legislation providing for an immediate aid to the hapless and helpless victims of the motor vehicle. The objects for which section 140 of the Act is enacted would be defeated if the claims Tribunal is required to hold regular trial in the same manner as for adjudicating a claim made in a petition filed under section 168 of the Act. Having regard to the purpose underlying the enactment of the said provision, the defences raised by the insurer or other objections of the insurer or the owner should be examined later when the claims petition is decided on merits; *New India Assurance Co. Ltd.* v. *Mithakhan Dinakhan Netiyar,* AIR 1995 Guj 126: 1996 ACJ 155: 1995 (2) Guj LR 1111.

9. Provision is not Applicable for All Injuries – The injuries mentioned in the petition do not come within the definition of the disability mentioned in section 142 and as such section 140 of the Act cannot be attracted. Claim under section 140 cannot be put forward for all injuries sustained in motor accident; *K.P. Muhammed* v. *Devassia,* AIR 2003 Ker 354: 2003 (2) Ker LJ 479: 2004 (2) ACJ 1341.

10. Nature of Enquiry is very Limited – Nature of enquiry contemplated under section 140 is very limited. In order to sustain a claim under section 140, there is no necessity for the claimant to plead or establish that the death or permanent disablement was due to wrongful act, neglect or default of the owner or owners of the vehicles. There is no question of fixation of negligence on any person, while determining a claim under section 140. The only question to be considered by the Tribunal at that stage was whether the accident had occurred and whether it resulted in death or permanent disablement. Question as to whether the accident occurred due to negligence of victim is not a matter to be gone into by the Tribunal. Further the approach of the Tribunal in adjudicating claim under sections 140 and 166 of the Act is different. Tribunal is required to satisfy itself that the accident has arisen out of the use of the motor vehicle, that the accident has resulted in permanent disablement of the person who is making the claim or death of the person, whose legal representatives are making the claim, a claim is made against the owner and insurer of the vehicle involved in the accident. These informations are to be furnished by the claimants in their claim petition. Once these particulars are furnished the Tribunal is bound to order compensation, irrespective of the fact whether the claim is made by a third party or not; *Oriental Insurance Co. Ltd.* v. *Santha,* AIR 2000 Ker 49: 2000 (1) ACC 306: 1999 (2) Ker LJ 760 (FB).

11. Provisions Deals with Substantive Law – The provisions contained under section 140(2) are not procedural in nature. Section 140(2) deals with substantive law; *Oriental Insurance Co. Ltd.* v. *Sheela Ratnan,* AIR 1997 Ker 109: 1996 (2) Ker LJ 393: 1996 ACJ 1298 (FB).

12. Scope of word "Use" – The expression employed by the Legislature is "accident arising out of the use of a motor vehicle" in the place of "accident caused by the use of a motor vehicle". Evidently the Legislature wanted to enlarge the scope of the word 'use' and not to restrict it for denying compensation in deserving cases. The test should be whether the accident was reasonably proximate to the use of a motor vehicle, whether or not the motor vehicle was in motion then; *"Babu* v. *Remesan,* AIR 1996 Ker 95: 1995 (2) Ker LJ 337: 1996 (0) ACJ 988.

13. Liability is Joint and Several – The liability of owner or owners of the vehicle or vehicles under section 140 is joint and several. This section contemplates involvement of two or more motor vehicles. In an accident involving two motor vehicles, liability to pay compensation is upon both the owners of the vehicles. In such cases, when an owner of one vehicle is identified he is liable to pay compensation because the liability is joint and several. The claim under section 140 cannot be defeated in such cases on the ground that owner of other vehicle is not detected; *Theethi* v. *Motor Accidents Claims Tribunal, Palakkad,* AIR 1996 Ker 237: 1995 (2) Ker LJ 751: 1996 ACJ 609.

14. Interim Compensation – On the date and time of the accident said truck was insured with the respondent. The Tribunal has obviously committed the error in rejecting the interim compensation to the appellants when it was prayed for by them in view of the provisions of section 140 of the Act. Thus appellants are entitled to receive interim compensation in view of the provisions of section 140 of the M.V. Act; *Shivlal* v. *Girish Kumar,* AIR 1999 MP 52: 1999 (2) MPLJ 519: 1999 (3) TAC 815.

15. Fixed Amount of Compensation – The legislative intent to provide fixed compensation on no fault principle is only in certain cases including permanent disability to the accident victim of the nature described in section 142. Such compensation was not naturally awardable mechanically in all cases of injury irrespective of whether these resulted in permanent disablement or not. Where the injury was minor causing only partial disability and not a permanent one the injured cannot claim the fixed amount of compensation as a matter of right; *Rajesh* v. *Dalip,* AIR 1999 MP 66: 1999 (2) MPLJ 182: 1999 (4) Civ LJ 39.

16. Compensation Payable is not by way of Interim Measure – A combined reading of section 140 and 166 of the Act would not suggest that the compensation payable under section 140 of the Act is by way of interim measure. The same would only become by way of interim measure, when a larger claim is awarded or at least to the extent as mentioned in section 140 of the Act, the liability whereunder is fixed; *Ratan Kumar* v. *Naveen Kumar,* AIR 2008 Pat 171: 2008 (71) All Ind Cas 681: 2008 (3) TAC 16.

17. To Attract Liability under Section – To attract the liability under section 140, all that is required is an accident arising out of the use of a motor vehicle leading to death or a permanent disability of any person; *Eshwamppa* v. *C.S. Gurushanthappa,* AIR 2010 SC 2967: (2010) 8 SCC 620: JT 2010 (8) SC 508.

18. Fracture should be Permanent Disablement – To award compensation under section 140 of the Act, the resultant effect of the fracture should be permanent disablement which is the *sine que non* for award of compensation. If the injury is simple fracture only without anything more as contemplated in section 142 of the Act, person receiving such injury would not be entitled to compensation under section 20 of the Act; *Saurabh Kumar Shukla* v. *Hukum Chand,* AIR 1998 MP 144: 1998 (1) ACJ 523: 1999 (1) Civ LJ 94.

19. To Limit Operation of Section – To control or limit operation of section 140 to these cases where a substantiative petition under section 166 of the Act is filed and is pending would tantamount to giving a very limited scope to a beneficial piece of legislation which is enacted for the benefit of the class of claimants, either heirs and legal representatives of the deceased or injured persons in vehicular accident. The Legislature has advisedly, therefore, nowhere stated in section 140 that application for interim compensation can be made only if a substantive petition under section 166 is filed; *Munshiram D. Anand* v. *Pravinsinh Prabhatsinh Anand Society, Navagam Gedh, Jamnagar,* AIR 1997 Guj 60: 1997 ACJ 206: 1996 (3) Civ LJ 844.

20. Determination of Claim – A decision under section 140 of the Act is a decision on a claim for compensation thereunder. It must be passed after following the procedure contemplated in section 160(2) of the; Act. It must indicate the findings and the reasons, at least briefly. These attributes of "determination" of a claim under section 140 would certainly make the "determination" an award for the purpose of section 166 as well as section 173 of the Act; *Oriental Insurance Company Ltd., New Delhi* v. *Chitaman,* AIR 1995 MP 229: 1995 (1) ACJ 225: 1995 (2) Civ LJ 440.

21. Proof of Negligence of Deceased – The witness for the claimants asserted, that while giving way to a bus coming from opposite side, the motorcycle being ridden by the deceased, hit a large laterite stone lying on the tar road, whereupon, the motorcycle overturned, and the rider and the pillion-rider suffered injuries. The petitioner-insurance company did not produce any witness before the Tribunal. In the absence of evidence to contradict the aforesaid factual position, it is not possible to conclude, that the deceased was "negligent" at the time when the accident occurred. Since no pleading or evidence has been brought to our notice, it is not possible for us to conclude, that the inverse *onus* which has been placed on the shoulders of the petitioner under section 163A of the Act to establish negligence, has been discharged by it; *National Insurance Company Ltd.* v. *Sinitha,* AIR 2012 SC 797: 2012 AIR SCW 10: (2012) 2 SCC 356.

22. Compensation under Section 140 is Governed by No-fault Liability Principle – The burden of "pleading and establishing", whether or not "wrongful act", "neglect" or "default" was committed by the person (for or on whose behalf) compensation is claimed under section 140, would not rest on the shoulders of the claimant. In other words the onus of proof of "wrongful act", "neglect" or "default" is not on the claimant. The matter, however, does not end with this. Further the claim of compensation under section 140 of the Act cannot be defeated because of any of the "fault" grounds ("wrongful act", "neglect" or "default"). This additional negative bar precluding the defence from defeating a claim for reasons of a "fault", is of extreme significance, for the consideration of the issue in hand. It is apparent, that both sides are precluded in a claim raised under section 140 of the Act from entering into the arena of "fault" ("wrongful act" or "neglect" or "default"). There can be no doubt, therefore, that the compensation claimed under section 140 is governed by the "no-fault" liability principle; *National Insurance Company Ltd.* v. *Sinitha,* AIR 2012 SC 797: 2012 AIR SCW 10: (2012) 2 SCC 356.

23. Distinction between Section 140 and Section 163A – Section 163A(2) is in *pari materia* with section 140(3). In other words, just as in section 140 of the Act, so also under section 163A of the Act, it is not essential for a claimant seeking compensation to "plead or establish", that the accident out of which the claim arises suffers from "wrongful act" or "neglect" or "default" of the offending vehicle. But then, there is no equivalent of section 140(4) in section 163A of the Act. Whereas, under section 140(4), there is a specific bar, whereby the concerned party (owner or insurance company) is precluded from defeating a claim raised under section 140 of the Act, by "pleading and establishing", "wrongful act", "neglect" or "default", there is no such or similar prohibiting clause in section 163A of the Act. The additional negative bar, precluding the defence from defeating a claim for reasons of a "fault" ("wrongful act", "neglect" or "default"), as has been expressly incorporated in section 140(4) of the Act, having not been embodied in section 163A of the Act, has to have a bearing on the interpretation of section 163A of the Act. The presence of section 140(4), and the absence of a similar provision in section 163A, leaves no room for any doubt, that the only object of the Legislature in doing so was that the Legislature desired to afford liberty to the defence to defeat a claim for compensation raised under section 163A of the Act, by pleading and establishing "wrongful act", "neglect" or "default". Thus, it is open to a concerned party (owner or insurer) to defeat a claim raised under section 163A of the Act, by pleading and establishing anyone of the three "faults", namely, "wrongful act", "neglect" or "default". The object for incorporating section 163A(2) of the Act is, that the burden of pleading and establishing proof of "wrongful act", "neglect" or "default" would not rest on the shoulders of the claimant. The absence of a provision similar to section 140(4) of the Act from section 163A of the Act, is for shifting the *onus* of proof on the grounds of "wrongful act", "neglect" or "default" onto the shoulders of the defence (owner or the insurance company). A claim which can be defeated on the basis of any of the aforesaid considerations, regulated under the "fault" liability principle. Hence section 163A of the Act is founded on the "fault" liability principle; *National Insurance Company Ltd.* v. *Sinitha,* AIR 2012 SC 797: 2012 AIR SCW 10: (2012) 2 SCC 356.

24. Principles of *Res Judicata* – The award was passed on the principle of no fault under section 140 of the Act. No appeal has been preferred against the award passed either by the owner or the insurer. At the instance of either the owner or the insurer that cannot again be reopened in proceedings under section 166 of the Act. Principles of *res judicata* shall apply. Further from the admitted facts appearing on record are sufficient to invoke at least the doctrine of estoppel and acquiescence against both the Insurance Company and the owner of the vehicle in question; *Prakash Chandra Biswas* v. *New India Assurance Co. Ltd.*, AIR 2010 Cal 19: 2011 (1) ACC 159: 2011 (1) ACJ 622.

25. Compensation on Principle of No Fault Liability – The auto driver has suffered injury in the accident. He had to remain out of work for two days. He had to spend money for treatment in the hospital. Unfortunately, the said Act of 1988 does not recognise any claim unless and until such eventuality brings a permanent disability in his life impairing his regular ability to work and earn his livelihood. Thus though the doctor did not specifically certified that injuries were beyond repair or that he had permanent disablement and certified only 10% disablement, award of Rs. 5000 as general damage is not improper in absence of any cross-objection filed by the Insurance Company. *Madhai Naskar* v. *New India Assurance Co. Ltd.*, AIR 2010 Cal 23: 2009 (2) Cal LJ 410: 2009 (3) Cal LT 210.

26. Refund of Amount of 'no Fault Compensation' Not Proper – The marginal heading to section 140 describes it as based 'on the principle of no fault'. As the expression 'no fault' suggests the compensation under section 140 is regardless of any wrongful act, neglect or default of the person in respect of whose death the claim is made. The Tribunal was patently in error, in directing for the refund of the amount of 'no fault compensation' already paid to the claimants, to the insurance company. The order of the Tribunal insofar as it permits the insurance company to recover the amount of interim compensation along with the interest from the claimants/appellants is set aside; *Indra Devi* v. *Bagada Ram*, AIR 2010 SC 2913: 2010 AIR SCW 4924: (2010) 8 SCALE 312.

27. Delay in Lodging FIR – Where the victim child aged 8 years was seriously injured in accident and it was more important for his father to get him treated first and he was not aware of niceties of law that lodging of FIR was condition precedent before filing claim petition and other persons in locality pressurized him that matter could be sorted out amicably since driver of vehicle was his neighbour, the delay in lodging FIR cannot be held fatal to the claim case. Even the police had arrived at the hospital, where injury report was prepared in which it was mentioned that injuries were caused on account of road accident and there was categorical admission by owner of the truck, that vehicle in question was involved in the accident when the same was being driven by his driver and this information was conveyed to him on phone the very same day. The cumulative effect of the aforesaid events would establish that accident had taken place on stated date on account of rash and negligent reversing of the truck by the driver. Therefore, delay in lodging the FIR was fatal to the claim case; *Ravi* v. *Badrinarayan*, AIR 2011 SC 1226: 2011 AIR SCW 1530: (2011) 4 SCC 693.

28. Compensation under No Fault Liability – Though there is no loss of dependency, yet the claimants being legal representatives are entitled to inherit the estate of the deceased persons, therefore, the appellants are entitled to receive compensation under no fault liability in terms of section 140(2) of the Act; *Joy Minocha* v. *Vijay Kumar*, AIR 2011 Chht 166.

29. Contributory Negligence – No direct evidence shows negligence on part of deceased – Apportionment by courts below on part of deceased set aside; *Ashvinbhai Jayantilal Modi* v. *Ramkaran Ramchandra Sharma*, (2015) 2 SCC 180.

141. Provisions as to other right to claim compensation for death or permanent disablement.—(1) The right to claim compensation under section 140 in respect of death or permanent disablement of any person shall be in addition to [1][any other right, except the right to claim under the scheme referred to in section 163A (such other right hereafter] in this section referred to as the right on the principle of fault) to claim compensation in respect thereof under any other provision of this Act or of any other law for the time being in force.

(2) A claim for compensation under section 140 in respect of death or permanent disablement of any person shall be disposed of as expeditiously as possible and where compensation is claimed in respect of such death or permanent disablement under section 140 and also in pursuance of any right on the principle of fault, the claim for compensation under section 140 shall be disposed of as aforesaid in the first place.

(3) Notwithstanding anything contained in sub-section (1), where in respect of the death or permanent disablement of any person, the person liable to pay compensation under section 140 is also liable to pay compensation in accordance with the right on the principle of fault, the person so liable shall pay the first-mentioned compensation and—

(a) if the amount of the first-mentioned compensation is less than the amount of the second-mentioned compensation, he shall be liable to pay (in addition to the first-mentioned compensation) only so much of the second-mentioned compensation as is equal to the amount by which it exceeds the first mentioned compensation;

(b) if the amount of the first-mentioned compensation is equal to or more than the amount of the second-mentioned compensation, he shall not be liable to pay the second-mentioned compensation.

COMMENTS

While Claiming Fault Compensation One may Claim No Fault Compensation – Section 141(1) makes the compensation under section 140 independent of any claim of compensation based on the principle of fault under any other provision of the Motor Vehicles Act or under any other law but subject to any claim of compensation under section 163A of the Act. Section 141(2) and (3) further provide that even while claiming compensation under the principle of fault one may claim no fault compensation under section 140. Section 144 gives overriding effect to the provisions of Chapter X of the Act; *Eshwarappa* alias *Maheshwarappa* v. *C.S. Gurushanthappa,* AIR 2010 SC 2907: 2010 AIR SCW 4918: (2010) 8 SCC 620.

142. Permanent disablement.—For the purposes of this Chapter, permanent disablement of a person shall be deemed to have resulted from an accident of the nature referred to in sub-section (1) of section 140 if such person has suffered by reason of the accident, any injury or injuries involving—

(a) permanent privation of the sight of either eye or the hearing of either ear, or privation of any member or joint; or

(b) destruction or permanent impairing of the powers of any member or joint; or

(c) permanent disfiguration of the head or face.

SYNOPSIS

1. Fracture to Term as Privation of Member of Joint
2. Award for No Fault Liability
3. Ist Proviso, Engaged in Driving the Vehicle – Coverage – Employee only be Engaged in Driving Vehicle Irrespective of Employed as Driver or Not

1. Subs. by Act 54 of 1994, sec. 44, for "any other right (hereafter" (w.e.f. 14-11-1994).

COMMENTS

1. Fracture to Term as Privation of Member of Joint – Fracture of bone simpliciter in an accident through a motor vehicle cannot be termed as privation of any member of joint, unless it is proved by the medical evidence that after union of bones disability has occurred or on account of mal-union injury has suffered permanent or partial disability. In the absence of any evidence, each fracture cannot be termed as privation of any member or joint. However, fracture in a joint where union of bones is not possible or where union of bone may cause permanent or partial disability, then interim compensation under section 140 of the Act can be awarded. In other cases for the purposes of permanent disability, Claims Tribunal has to record findings at the time of final adjudication of the case, and loss of income should be determined on the basis of evidence on record. If the evidence about permanent or partial disability is insufficient, the Courts can certainly refer to the Schedule of Workmen's Compensation Act to determine loss of earning capacity or percentage of loss of partial disability or permanent disability, as the case may be, and determine the quantum of compensation; *Kamal Kumar Jain* v. *Tazuddin*, AIR 2004 MP 212: 2004 AIHC 4430: 2004 (2) MPLJ 472 (FB).

2. Award for No Fault Liability – Section 144 of the Act provides that all other provisions of the Act or any other law must yield to the provisions contained in Chapter X of the Act. Therefore, the award for no fault liability in a motor accident which occurred prior to the coming into force of Act should be in tune with the amount fixed by the Act; *Mosmi* v. *Ram Kumar*, I (1991) ACC 187.

3. Ist Proviso, Engaged in Driving the Vehicle – Coverage – Employee only be Engaged in Driving Vehicle Irrespective of Employed as Driver or Not – This, therefore, means that to claim coverage of clause (a) to the proviso to section 147 of the Act, the employee need only be engaged in driving the vehicle, irrespective of whether he was employed as driver or not. Needless to say that such coverage would be available only if the accident arose out of and in the course of his employment and only if the other requirements of the Workmen's Compensation Act are also satisfied; *United India Insurance Company Ltd., Kochi* v. *P.R. Surendran*, AIR 2015 Ker 36.

143. Applicability of Chapter to certain claims under Act 8 of 1923.—The provisions of this Chapter shall also apply in relation to any claim for compensation in respect of death or permanent disablement of any person under the Workmen's Compensation Act, 1923 (8 of 1923) resulting from an accident of the nature referred to in sub-section (1) of section 140 and for this purpose, the said provisions shall, with necessary modifications, be deemed to form part of that Act.

144. Overriding effect.—The provisions of this Chapter shall have effect notwithstanding anything contained in any other provision of this Act or of any other law for the time being in force.

CHAPTER XI

INSURANCE OF MOTOR VEHICLES AGAINST THIRD PARTY RISKS

145. Definitions.—In this Chapter,—

(a) "authorised insurer" means an insurer for the time being carrying on general insurance business in India under the General Insurance Business (Nationalisation) Act, 1972 (57 of 1972), and any Government insurance fund authorised to do general insurance business under that Act;

(b) "certificate of insurance" means a certificate issued by an authorised insurer in pursuance of sub-section (3) of section 147 and includes a cover note complying with such requirements as may be prescribed, and where more than one certificate has been issued in connection with a policy, or where a copy of a certificate has been issued, all those certificates or that copy, as the case may be;

(c) "liability", wherever used in relation to the death of or bodily injury to any person, includes liability in respect thereof under section 140;

(d) "policy of insurance" includes "certificate of insurance";

(e) "property" includes goods carried in the motor vehicle, roads, bridges, culverts, causeways, trees, posts and mile-stones;

(f) "reciprocating country" means any such country as may on the basis of reciprocity be notified by the Central Government in the Official Gazette to be a reciprocating country for the purposes of this Chapter;

(g) "third party" includes the Government.

COMMENTS

Expression Third Party – The definition appearing in section 145(g) is only inclusive; yet there may not be any difficulty in discerning the expression third party, as contemplated by the Legislature, in that, the Policy of Insurance being an agreement between first and the second party, *i.e.*, the insurer and the insured, rest all others, who suffer because of the use of Motor Vehicles, and whose risks, the Legislature intended to cover by introduction of sections 146 and 149 appearing in Chapter XI of the Act, would fall within the definition of third party. The third party includes persons who suffer loss or damage, by use of Motor Vehicle, either as occupants thereof or while travelling on road, or in any other vehicle. The persons travelling in a Goods Vehicle, would therefore fall within the definition of third party in terms of the provisions appearing in section 146 of the Act; *United India Insurance Co. Ltd.* v. *Karam Chand*, AIR 2012 J&K 20: 2012 (2) ACC 366: 2012 (3) ACJ 1661.

146. Necessity for insurance against third party risk.—(1) No person shall use, except as a passenger, or cause or allow any other person to use, a motor vehicle in a public place, unless there is in force in relation to the use of the vehicle by that person or that other person, as the case may be, a policy of insurance complying with the requirements of this Chapter:

[1][Provided that in the case of a vehicle carrying, or meant to carry, dangerous or hazardous goods, there shall also be a policy of insurance under the Public Liability Insurance Act, 1991 (6 of 1991).]

Explanation.—A person driving a motor vehicle merely as a paid employee, while there is in force in relation to the use of the vehicle no such policy as is required by this sub-section, shall not be deemed to act in contravention of the sub-section unless he knows or has reason to believe that there is no such policy in force.

(2) Sub-section (1) shall not apply to any vehicle owned by the Central Government or a State Government and used for Government purposes unconnected with any commercial enterprise.

1. Ins. by Act 54 of 1994, sec. 45 (w.e.f. 14-11-1994).

(3) The appropriate Government may, by order, exempt from the operation of sub-section (1) any vehicle owned by any of the following authorities, namely:—

(a) the Central Government or a State Government, if the vehicle is used for Government purposes connected with any commercial enterprise;

(b) any local authority;

(c) any State transport undertaking:

Provided that no such order shall be made in relation to any such authority unless a fund has been established and is maintained by that authority in accordance with the rules made in that behalf under this Act for meeting any liability arising out of the use of any vehicle of that authority which that authority or any person in its employment may incur to third parties.

Explanation.—For the purposes of this sub-section, "appropriate Government" means the Central Government or a State Government, as the case may be, and—

(i) in relation to any corporation or company owned by the Central Government or any State Government, means the Central Government or that State Government;

(ii) in relation to any corporation or company owned by the Central Government and one or more State Governments, means the Central Government;

(iii) in relation to any other State transport undertaking or any local authority, means that Government which has control over that undertaking or authority.

SYNOPSIS

1. Whether Accident Took Place in Public Place
2. To Cover Third Party Risk
3. Insurance Company is State
4. Expression "Third Party"
5. Provision meant to Create Large Pool of Money for Payments of No Fault Compensation
6. Hypothecation Agreement – Financier, not Owner of Vehicle – Not Liable to Pay Compensation
7. Violation of Statutory Provision
8. Rights of Victims of Vehicular Accidents

COMMENTS

1. Whether Accident Took Place in Public Place – Therefore, the motor accident of the offending gas tanker took place when the offending gas tanker was parked at the road side which is undisputedly a public place. Therefore accident can be said to have been taken at a 'public place'. Insurance company is be liable to indemnify the damages arising out of the motor accident of the offending gas tanker caused by or arising out of the use of the offending gas tanker in a 'Public place'; *New India Assurance Co. Ltd.* v. *Biman Prasad Barkakati*, AIR 2009 Gau 7: 2009 AIHC 136 (NOC): 2009 (2) ACJ 974.

2. To Cover Third Party Risk – The owner of vehicle is statutorily obligated to obtain an insurance for the vehicle to cover the third party risk; *National Insurance Co. Ltd.* v. *Geeta Bhat*, AIR 2008 SC 1837: (2008) 5 SCR 734: JT 2008 (4) SC 425.

3. Insurance Company is State – The insurance company being State within the meaning of article 12 of the Constitution cannot discriminate and deny or refuse third party insurance cover to State run vehicles as their actions are guided by article 14 of the Constitution; *Kerala State Road Transport Corporation* v. *General Insurance Corporation of India,* AIR 1998 Ker 184.

4. Expression "Third Party" – Other than the contracting parties to the insurance policy, the expression "third party" therefore, should include everyone, be it a person travelling in another vehicle, one walking on the road or a passenger in the vehicle itself which is the subject-matter of the insurance policy; *National Insurance Co. Ltd.* v. *Faqir Chand,* AIR 1995 J&K 91: 1996 ACJ 111: 1995 Kash LJ 162.

The definition appearing in section 145(g) is only inclusive; yet there may not be any difficulty in discerning the expression third party, as contemplated by the Legislature, in that, the Policy of Insurance being an agreement between first and the second party, *i.e.,* the insurer and the insured, rest all others, who suffer because of the use of Motor Vehicles, and whose risks, the Legislature intended to cover by introduction of sections 146 and 149 appearing in Chapter XI of the Act, would fall within the definition of third party. The third party includes persons who suffer loss or damage, by use of Motor Vehicle, either as occupants thereof or while travelling on road, or in any other vehicle. The persons travelling in a Goods Vehicle, would therefore fall within the definition of third party in terms of the provisions appearing in section 146 of the Act; *United India Insurance Co. Ltd.* v. *Karam Chand,* AIR 2012 J&K 20: 2012 (2) ACC 366: 2012 (3) ACJ 1661.

5. Provision meant to Create Large Pool of Money for Payments of No Fault Compensation – Section 146 forbids the use of the vehicle in a public place unless there is in force, in relation to the use of the vehicle, a policy of insurance complying with the provisions of that chapter. Section 147 contains the provisions that are commonly referred to as 'Act only insurance'. The provisions of sections 146 and 147 are meant to create the large pool of money for making payments of no fault compensation. Thus the liability arising from section 140 would almost invariably be passed on to the insurer to be paid off from the vast fund created by virtue of sections 146 and 147 unless the owner of the vehicle causing accident is guilty of some flagrant violation of the law; *Eshwarappa* alias *Maheshwarappa* v. *C.S. Gurushanthappa,* AIR 2010 SC 2907: 2010 AIR SCW 4918: (2010) 8 SCC 620.

6. Hypothecation Agreement – Financier, not Owner of Vehicle – Not Liable to Pay Compensation – The High Court has erroneously opined that the financier had the responsibility to get the vehicle insured, if the borrower failed to insure it. Term in hypothecation agreement does not convey that the appellant-financier had become the owner and was in control and possession of the vehicle. It was the absolute fault of the respondent No. 2 to take the vehicle from the dealer without full payment of the insurance. Nothing has been brought on record that this fact was known to the appellant financier or it was done in collusion with the financier. When the intention of the Legislature is quite clear to the effect, a registered owner of the vehicle should not be held liable if the vehicle is not in his possession and control and there is evidence on record that respondent No. 2, without the insurance plied the vehicle in violation of the statutory provision contained in section 146 of the 1988 Act, the High Court could not have mulcted the liability on the financier; *HDFC Bank Ltd.* v. *Kumari Reshma,* AIR 2015 SC 290.

7. Violation of Statutory Provision – Plying vehicle without insurance – Liability not mulcted on financier; *HDFC Bank Limited* v. *Reshma,* (2015) 3 SCC 679.

8. Rights of Victims of Vehicular Accidents – Not defeated on flimsy grounds; *United India Insurance Company Limited* v. *Brijbala,* AIR 2015 HP 34.

147. Requirements of policies and limits of liability.—(1) In order to comply with the requirements of this Chapter, a policy of insurance must be a policy which—

(a) is issued by a person who is an authorised insurer; and

(b) insures the person or classes of persons specified in the policy to the extent specified in sub-section (2)—

(i) against any liability which may be incurred by him in respect of the death of or bodily [1][injury to any person, including owner of the goods or his authorised representative carried in the vehicle] or damage to any property of a third party caused by or arising out of the use of the vehicle in a public place;

(ii) against the death of or bodily injury to any passenger of a public service vehicle caused by or arising out of the use of the vehicle in a public place:

Provided that a policy shall not be required—

(i) to cover liability in respect of the death, arising out of and in the course of his employment, of the employee of a person insured by the policy or in respect of bodily injury sustained by such an employee arising out of and in the course of his employment other than a liability arising under the Workmen's Compensation Act, 1923 (8 of 1923) in respect of the death of, or bodily injury to, any such employee—

(a) engaged in driving the vehicle, or

(b) if it is a public service vehicle engaged as conductor of the vehicle or in examining tickets on the vehicle, or

(c) if it is a goods carriage, being carried in the vehicle, or

(ii) to cover any contractual liability.

Explanation.—For the removal of doubts, it is hereby declared that the death of or bodily injury to any person or damage to any property of a third party shall be deemed to have been caused by or to have arisen out of, the use of a vehicle in a public place notwithstanding that the person who is dead or injured or the property which is damaged was not in a public place at the time of the accident, if the act or omission which led to the accident occurred in a public place.

(2) Subject to the proviso to sub-section (1), a policy of insurance referred to in sub-section (1), shall cover any liability incurred in respect of any accident, up to the following limits, namely:—

(a) save as provided in clause (b), the amount of liability incurred;

(b) in respect of damage to any property of a third party, a limit of rupees six thousand:

Provided that any policy of insurance issued with any limited liability and in force, immediately before the commencement of this Act, shall continue to be effective for a period of four months after such commencement or till the date of expiry of such policy whichever is earlier.

(3) A policy shall be of no effect for the purposes of this Chapter unless and until there is issued by the insurer in favour of the person by whom the policy is effected a certificate of insurance in the prescribed form and containing the

1. Subs. by Act 54 of 1994, sec. 46, for "injury to any person" (w.e.f. 14-11-1994).

prescribed particulars of any condition subject to which the policy is issued and of any other prescribed matters; and different forms, particulars and matters may be prescribed in different cases.

(4) Where a cover note issued by the insurer under the provisions of this Chapter or the rules made thereunder is not followed by a policy of insurance within the prescribed time, the insurer shall, within seven days of the expiry of the period of the validity of the cover note, notify the fact to the registering authority in whose records the vehicle to which the cover note relates has been registered or to such other authority as the State Government may prescribe.

(5) Notwithstanding anything contained in any law for the time being in force, an insurer issuing a policy of insurance under this section shall be liable to indemnify the person or classes of persons specified in the policy in respect of any liability which the policy purports to cover in the case of that person or those classes of persons.

SYNOPSIS

COMMENTS

1. Liability Towards Employees of Insured – The proviso does not carve out the employees of the insured as an exception to a liability arising in respect of death of or bodily injury to any person as contemplated under sub-section (1) of section 147. It only limits the liability to the extent that would arise under the provision of the Workmen's Compensation Act in respect of the three specified categories of the employees namely; driver, conductor or ticket examiner, and those who are carried in a goods carriage. It does not deal with the question of the liability arising in respect of the other categories of employees who would fall under the expression "any person" occurring in section 147(1) (b)(i). The employees other than those falling in the said three specified categories are simply not dealt with in the proviso. If all the employees of the insured were intended to be covered, there was no need to specify these three categories of employees in proviso (i). The statutory liability of the insurer in respect of these three specified categories of the employees seems to have been limited due to the nature of their employment as driver, conductor or as an employee carried in a goods carriage and it could not be the intention of the legislature to exclude a large number of the employees who fall outside these three categories and would be covered under the main provision of section 147(1) (b)(i) since they would fall in the expression "any person". Therefore barring those three categories of the employees in respect of all other employees, the extent of the liability of the Insurance Company will be the "amount of liability incurred"; *New India Assurance Co. Ltd.* v. *Jyotikaben Bhupendrabhai Maniyar,* AIR 1999 Guj 292: 2000 (1) ACJ 622: 1999 (4) Civ LJ 480.

2. Injury to any Person Includes Owner or his Representative – The evidence led by the respondents-claimants has conclusively proved on record that the victims and the injured persons were travelling in the goods vehicle as owners of their goods. There is no rebuttal to the evidence of the respondents-claimants led either by the owners of the truck in question or the appellant-Company. Therefore, the victims and the injured persons were travelling in the truck in question as owners of their goods. The word 'injury' to any person including owner of the goods or his authorised representative carried in the vehicle. The appellant-Company is under statutory obligation to pay the amount of compensation and it cannot take the shelter that such passengers are not covered under the Insurance Policy as it has failed to prove the Policy, its exclusions and breach thereof to show that the appellant-Company is exempted from such liability; *Oriental Insurance Co.* v. *Sukh Pal,* AIR 1999 HP 98: 2001 (1) ACJ 890: 2000 (1) Civ LJ 212.

3. *Onus* to Prove Insurer's Liability is Unlimited is on Insured – Liability of the insurer is to indemnify the insured in accordance with the terms of the policy. In order to escape liability to pay compensation to the victim of the accident, it is for the insured to prove that insurer's liability is unlimited. The Insurance Company in this case has pleaded limited liability by producing a copy of the Insurance Policy, but the owner/insured neither controverted this plea nor produced any evidence to the contrary. So there was no reason to hold that the liability of the insurer was unlimited; *Kewal Krishan* v. *Krishna Devi,* AIR 2000 J&K 89: 2001 (1) ACJ 1029: 2000 (3) TAC 506.

4. Liability to Indemnify Insured – The appellant has to prove specifically that the insured had intentionally committed the breach of the insurance contract either directly or impliedly. There is not even an iota of evidence on the record which lends assurance to this view. Therefore the appellant cannot absolve itself from the liability to indemnify the insured; *United India Insurance Co. Ltd.* v. *Mst. Sharief Jan,* AIR 1998 J&K 76: 1999 (2) ACC 474: 1998 (1) ACJ 317: 1998 (2) TAC 323.

5. Disclaim of Liability with Respect to Particular Class of Person or Kind of Vehicles – Section 147 it is quite comprehensive in scope and meaning. It has to be given wider, effective and practical meaning. The legislature clearly intended that every policy of insurance statutorily required to cover the risk of liability in respect of classes of persons relating to all types of vehicles without exception and with no defence to the Insurance Company disclaiming the liability with respect to particular class of persons or particular kind of vehicles. Thus the deceased being a labourer travelling in the truck, engaged by either of the parties, is covered under section 147 of the Motor Vehicles Act, and the liability to pay the compensation has to fall on the insurance company; *New India Assurance Company* v. *Smt. Shakuntla Devi,* AIR 1997 J&K 40: 1998 (2) ACC 418: 1998 (1) ACJ 195.

6. Occupants shall Cover under Policy – The occupants deceased and her son died when the jeep fell down from the bridge. There is nothing on the record to show that the owner and the occupants of the vehicle were covered under the policy. The appellant-Insurance Company is not liable to pay compensation for the death and injury caused to the occupants of the vehicle; *Branch Manager, Oriental Insurance Co. Ltd.* v. *Kunti Devi,* AIR 2009 Jhar 74: 2009 AIHC 2172: 2009 (4) ACJ 2795.

7. No Liability of Insurer if Private Vehicle given on Hire – The vehicle was taken on hire by the claimants for going to hospital and on the way the vehicle met with an accident. Admittedly, the vehicle was insured as a private car and not as a commercial vehicle. Hence the insurance company has no liability for payment of compensation. The owner of the vehicle is liable to pay the compensation amount; *United India Insurance Co. Ltd.* v. *Sukhni Mahto,* AIR 2009 Jhar 127: 2009 (4) ACJ 2545: 2009 (3) TAC 158.

8. Mere Violation of Condition shall not Exonerate Insurer from its Liability – The road permit was issued in respect of the offending vehicle. The owner of the vehicle categorically deposed that because of the obstruction and traffic the route of the truck was diverted by the police. No evidence was led to contradict the evidence adduced by the owner of the vehicle. Therefore, merely violation of condition of permit the Insurance Company shall not be exonerated from its liability for payment of compensation; *Kiran Singh* v. *Sarju Verma,* AIR 2009 Jhar 134: 2009 AIHC 3561: 2009 (4) Civ LJ 422.

9. Once No Liability on Registered Owner – The bus in question was hired by the State Road Transport Corporation from the registered owner *qua* agreement. The bus was run by the driver under the instructions and directions given by the corporation and as such, the question of the registered owner of the bus having anything to do with the manner of driving the bus or the road in which the bus was to be driven or had any control whatsoever over the driver concerned, therefore does not arise. Once no liability is there on the registered owner of the vehicle, calling upon the insurer to satisfy the award, also cannot be construed as a possibility in law having regard to the provisions of Act. Insurer is not liable to satisfy the award corporation. Cannot avoid liability to pay compensation both on facts and in law; *North West Karnataka Road Transport Corporation* v. *D. Kenchappa*, AIR 2009 Kant 186: 2009 AIHC 2981: 2009 (4) AIR Kar R 284.

10. Wider Liability in Policy – The insurance company has not placed detailed terms and conditions of the policy. Therefore, it is not proper to assume that the policy was only Act policy and it did not cover wider liability particularly when the cover note itself refers to "important notice" which refers to "Avoidance of certain terms and rights of recovery" clause. Thus the policy contained a wider liability. Since the accident has occurred not on account of the rash and negligent driving of the deceased insurer cannot avoid its liability; *United India Insurance Co. Ltd.* v. *Kirloskar Electric Co. Ltd.*, AIR 2008 Kant 184: 2008 AIHC 3675: 2008 (5) AIR Kar R 472.

11. Insurer not Liable where Deceased a Passenger in Goods Vehicle without Goods – As there were no goods being carried in the vehicle in question by the deceased at the time of accident, the conclusion that the deceased travelled as a passenger becomes inevitable. Once it is held that the deceased was a passenger in the goods vehicle, the question of liability on the part of the insurance company will not arise. Therefore, the deceased not travelled as a owner of the goods. The liability will have to be borne by the owner of the vehicle; *National Insurance Co. Ltd.* v. *Aishabi*, AIR 2007 Kant 155: 2007 AIHC 2954: 2007 (6) Kant LJ 482.

12. Liability of Insurer Towards Third Party where vehicle is Transferred – The essence of contract of insurance is to indemnify insured against the claim of third party. The expression 'third party' means a person who is not a party to the contract, but beneficiary of the contract and has right to enforce the terms of the contract against the insurer and the insured. Section 147 of the Act mandates that there should be compulsory coverage of insurance for (1) passengers in public transport vehicle, (2) passengers travelling in goods vehicle along with goods and 3) the workmen under the Workmen Compensation Act, employed in connection with the motor vehicle, etc. The statutory policy issued under section 147 of the Act in common parlance is called as 'Act Policy'. In the case, the deceased was working as a cleaner and the risk of the deceased was to be compulsorily covered under the Act Policy. Whether or not the deceased was employed by the insured, by deeming effect of section 157 of the Act, there is automatic transfer of policy along with the vehicle whether or not there is intimation to the insurer under sub-section (2) of section 157 of the Act. In the case of transfer of the vehicle even without transfer of policy, the liability of the insurer shall not cease in so far as the third party is concerned. The insurer, however, has right of recovery from the insured or from the transferee; *United India Assurance Co. Ltd., Mysore* v. *M.N. Ravikumar*, AIR 2007 Kant 179: 2007 AIHC 3706: 2007 (6) Kant LJ 272.

13. Employer Liable where Workmen not Engaged by Insured – There is no serious dispute that the workmen on the lorry at the time of the accident were not the workmen engaged to load or unload the goods, nor were they engaged by the insured. The admitted circumstance that they were all workmen engaged by a person other than the insured and were being carried as passengers to their work place, did not cover any such risk. The accident however, had occurred during and in the course of employment and the claimants may have been entitled to claim compensation against the employer under the provisions of the Workmen's Compensation Act. Thus the insurer is not liable to pay compensation in respect of such workmen; *National Insurance Co. Ltd.* v. *Shankar Baburao Gavade*, AIR 2007 Kant 191: 2008 (1) ALJ (NOC) 207: 2007 (4) Cur CC 467.

14. Term 'any person' Covers Pillion Rider – The policy one issueable by the Insurance Company must cover as against any liability which may be incurred by the owner of the vehicle in respect of the death or bodily injury to any person and must include the death or bodily injury or injuries likely to be suffered by the third parties too. The term 'any person' used in the section also covers the pillion rider, for in the Explanation below the proviso thereto, it is clarified that the death or bodily injury to any person or damage to any property of a third person shall be deemed to have been caused by or to have arisen out of the use of the vehicle in a public place at the point of time of accident that occurred in a public place. Therefore, it is obvious that section 147 of the Act contemplates coverage of risk of the third parties too, who suffered either bodily injury or death as the case may be; *Oriental Insurance Co. Ltd.* v. *Minaxi*, AIR 2000 Kant 73: 1999 (5) Kant LJ 573: 2000 (1) ACJ 385.

15. Liability of Insurer with Respect to Death of Gratuitous Passenger – Under the Act, the insurer is required to cover the risk to "any person" who is a victim of the motor accident, whether or not the victim was a gratuitous passenger in any insured vehicle - either it be a private car or a private jeep vehicle, or a goods truck or even a two wheeler. The insurer of a vehicle covered by 'Act only' policy *i.e.*, statutory policy would be liable to indemnify the insured owner against any liability to pay compensation incurred by him for death of or bodily injury to a gratuitous passenger travelling in the offending vehicle, be it a private car, a private jeep or a goods vehicle or even a two wheeler; *New India Assurance Co. Ltd.* v. *Rajendra Singh*, AIR 2000 Kant 202: 2000 (2) ACC 392: 2000 (2) Kant LJ 207.

16. Liability of Insurer Towards Pillion Rider – When there is an express term in the policy excluding the liability for the death or injury caused to a person carried on the motor cycle unless he is being carried by reason of or in pursuance of a contract of employment, it cannot be contended that because the policy is comprehensive and no separate tariff is prescribed to cover the risk of a pillion rider, it must be held that the policy covers such risk. It is only by virtue of the circular issued by the Tariff Advisory Committee that the liability is undertaken by the insurer to cover the risk of pillion rider also. The circular makes it clear that a decision had been taken to cover the liability to pillion passengers treating them as occupants. The policy was issued prior to the circular of the Tariff Advisory Committee does not cover liability for pillion rider. Further there is nothing in circular to indicate that retrospective effect has to be given to the new liability undertaken; *New India Assurance Co. Ltd.* v. *Nagarathna*, AIR 1996 Kant 396: 1997 (1) ACC 648: 1997 ACJ 376.

17. Insurance Policy Covered Accident Occurring in 'Public Places' – Public place does not have a restricted meaning in as much as it is not to be taken as a place where public have uncontrolled access at all times. "Public place" for the purpose of the Act has to be understood with reference to the places to which a vehicle has access. It is specifically mentioned in the definition that any place of stand at which passengers are picked up or set down by a stage carriage is a public place. The private premises of a house where goods vehicle is allowed entry, is a public place for the purpose of section 2(34) of the Motor Vehicles Act which leads to liability for the Insurance Company subject to satisfying other conditions of the policy; *Rajan P. Pullan* v. *K.J. John*, AIR 2009 Ker 136: 2009 AIHC 719 (NOC): 2009 (1) Ker LJ 618.

18. Liability of Insurer Towards Third Party – The insured who is a party to the insurance is not a third party for the purpose Chapter XI of the Act, particularly section 147 thereof. Thus, any person other than the insurer and the insured who are parties to the insurance policy is a 'third party'. The insurer, however, would not be liable for any bodily injury or death of a third party in an accident unless the liability is fastened on the insurer under the provisions of section 147 of the Act or under the terms and conditions of the policy of insurance. Hence, the mere fact that a passenger is a third party would not fasten liability on the insurer unless such liability arises under section 147 of the Act or under the terms and conditions of the insurance policy. An employee is a third party inasmuch as he is not a party to the insurance policy. But merely because an employee is a third party, the insurance company would not be liable to compensate in case such employee suffers bodily injury or dies in an accident in which the motor vehicle is involved unless section 147 of the Act fixes such liability on the insured or unless the terms and conditions of the contract of insurance fixes liability on the insurer. Even if an employee is a passenger or a person travelling in a motor vehicle which is insured the insurer will not be liable to cover any liability in respect of death or bodily injury of such employee unless such employee falls in one of the categories mentioned in sub-clauses (a), (b) and (c) of clause (i) of the Proviso to sub-section (1) of section 147 of the Act and further in cases where such employees fall under categories mentioned in sub-clauses (a), (b) and (c) of clause (i) of the Proviso to sub-section (1) of section 147 of the Act, the insurer is liable only for the liability under the Workmen's Compensation Act; *Bhav Singh* v. *Savirani,* AIR 2008 MP 1: 2008 AIHC 386: 2008 (1) MPLJ 72.

19. Liability of Insurance Company – The insurer's liability is not limited in case of claim made by the legal representatives of the deceased or the injured employee who approaches the Tribunal to claim compensation to the extent of liability arising under the W.C. Act; *Ramji Porte* v. *Premabai Patel,* AIR 1998 MP 257: 1998 (2) MPLJ 442: 2000 (2) ACJ 1359.

20. Liability of Insurer where Driver has No Valid Licence – Merely because a driver is without a valid licence the insurance company cannot escape liability. The driver had a licence but all that has been stated is that this was not meant for a commercial vehicle. There was authorisation to drive a vehicle and merely because there was some insertion or deletion prohibiting the driver from driving a transport vehicle would not absolve the insurance company; *National Insurance Co.* v. *Prem Narain Sahu,* AIR 1997 MP 66: 1996 MPLJ 399: 1996 (2) Civ LJ 222.

21. Expression "Arising Out of Use of Vehicle" – Expression, "arising out of use of motor vehicle" has to be given a wider meaning. In the instant case, vehicle was parked in the road side workshop for doing some welding work. Deceased was vulcanising a tube which got punctured. Due to the processing of welding by another person, the diesel tank caught fire. Thereby the deceased who was doing work of vulcanising the tube, involved in the fire accident and sustained fatal injuries. It could therefore be inferred that the death of deceased "arose out of the use of motor vehicle". The owner and the insurer of the vehicle would be liable to pay compensation to the claimants for the death of their deceased son; *United India Insurance Company Ltd.* v. *Amir Basha,* AIR 2003 Mad 237: 2003 (2) ACJ 1386: 2003 (2) Civ LJ 313.

22. Owner cannot Challenge Attested Copy of Policy – Where the Insurance Company had taken the stand that the goods vehicle in question was not permitted to convey any passenger either for hire or for reward, it was the Insurance Company which had to produce the policy, and in such a case, an office copy or an attested copy was certainly permissible in evidence and when once an attested copy was filed through a witness it should clearly be admitted and accepted. But if the owner or the claimant seeks to dispute its genuineness, then the burden would be on the owner to produce the original since he was bound to have the original. The owner in such a case, could not be allowed to suppress the original which should be available with him and be heard to challenge the correctness of the certified copy available with the Insurance Company. Therefore, if the genuineness or the truth of the copy of the policy produced by the Insurance Company is challenged, it is for the owner to disprove the same by producing the original; *National Insurance Company Ltd.* v. *V. Velammal,* AIR 2000 Mad 476: 2001 (1) ACC 709: 2002 (1) ACJ 706.

23. Mere Non-issuance of Badge would not Render Licence Invalid – The driving licence indicates driver was authorised to drive a transport vehicle. Mere non-issuance of public service vehicle badge to the driver would not render the driving licence invalid. Therefore, insurer cannot escape its liability on the ground that the driver had no valid driving licence; *National Insurance Co. Ltd.* v. *Raisa Bibi,* AIR 1999 Ori 78: 2000 (1) ACJ 600: 1999 (2) TAC 298.

24. Third Party Policy is Wider than Act Policy – Act Policy means an insurance policy which is issued by an insurer and obtained by the assured under a mandatory provision of the Act. Third party policy is, wider than the Act policy; it covers liabilities arising from injury to person or property of a third party or from death of a third party arising out of the use of a motor vehicle insured; *Jabanananda Mohanty* v. *Artatrana Misra,* AIR 1992 Ori 110: 1992 (2) ACC 294: 1992 (2) ACJ 851.

25. Words "any person" does not include Owner – The owner of the vehicle, who dies, cannot be included in the term "in respect of death or bodily injury to any person". Obviously the term "any person" would have to be different from "the owner". Moreover, he cannot be included as a "third party" as the contract is between the insurer-company and the insured, who are the first and second party. Therefore, under the provisions of section 147, the Insurance Company would not be liable to pay any compensation for any bodily injury to or death of the owner of the vehicle; *Oriental Insurance Company Ltd.* v. *Charu Agrawal,* AIR 2007 Raj 153: 2007 AIHC 2655: 2007 (3) Raj LW 1990.

26. Policy when becomes Effective – An insurance policy becomes operative from the previous midnight, when bought during the day following, but, in cases where there is a mention of the specific time for the purchase of the policy, then a special contract comes into being and the policy becomes effective from the time mentioned in the cover note/the policy itself; *New India Assurance Co. Ltd.* v. *Sita Bai,* AIR 1999 SC 3577: 1999 AIR SCW 3586: JT 1999 (6) SC 616: 1999 (7) SCC 575: 1999 (5) SCALE 495: 1999 (7) Supreme 637.

27. Liability to Pay Compensation – Pillion rider is a gratuitous passenger died in accident. Insurance company would not be liable to pay compensation; *General Manager, United Insurance Co. Ltd.* v. *M. Laxmi,* AIR 2009 SC 626: 2008 AIR SCW 7786: 2008 (14) SCALE 474.

28. Liability of Insurer – The deceased and other injured members of the marriage party were returning back from marriage in the goods vehicle. The deceased and others could not have become the representatives of the owner of the goods. The insurance company was not liable; *National Insurance Co. Ltd.* v. *Rattani,* AIR 2009 SC 1499: 2009 AIR SCW 992: 2009 (2) SCC 75: 2009 (1) SCALE 379.

Licence having been granted for a period of 20 years, a presumption, arises that it was meant for the purpose of a vehicle other than a transport vehicle. If the driving licence had been granted for transport vehicle, the tenure thereof could not have exceeded to three years. Thus the driver of the offending vehicle did not hold a valid and effective driving licence for driving a goods vehicle. Breach of conditions of the insurance is, therefore, apparent on the face of the records. The fact that the Vehicle in question was not proved to be a goods vehicle is not correct as the driving licence had been granted for a period of 20 years and not for a period of 3 years. The insurer therefore the directed to deposit the compensation amount with liberty to the claimants to withdraw the same and recover the same from the owner and the driver of the vehicle; *Oriental Insurance Co. Ltd.* v. *Angad Kol,* AIR 2009 SC 2151: 2009 AIR SCW 2747: 2009 (3) SCALE 749.

The injured had shared the seat of driver at the time of accident such travel is in violation of the conditions of the insurance Policy. Thus the insurer cannot be held liable. However, considering the fact that injured was coolie worker the insurer has been directed to pay the claimant and realise the same from owner; *United India Insurance Co. Ltd.* v. *Suresh K.K.,* AIR 2008 SC 2871: 2008 AIR SCW 4739: 2008 (6) SCALE 589.

Driving licence of the deceased driver had expired four months prior to the date of accident the Claimant had also not claiming that the driver had applied for renewal of the licence within 30 days of the date of its expiry. The deceased driver was not even permitted to drive the insured vehicle in a public place. The claimant not only committed breach of the terms of the policy, he also violated the provisions of section 5 of the Act by entrusting the vehicle to a person who did not hold a valid licence on the date of the accident. Since deceased had no valid and effective driving licence on date of accident, the insurer is not liable to indemnify the claimant for the loss suffered by him in the accident of the insured vehicle; *New India Assurance Co. Ltd.* v. *Suresh Chandra Aggarwal,* AIR 2009 SC 2987: 2009 AIR SCW 4801: 2009 (9) SCALE 449.

The expression "goods carriage" is solely used for the "carriage of goods". Carrying of passengers in a goods carriage is not contemplated in the Act. There is no reference to any passenger in "goods carriage". The inevitable conclusion, therefore, is that provisions of the Act do not enjoin any statutory liability on the owner of a vehicle to get his vehicle insured for any passenger travelling in a goods carriage and the insurer would have no liability therefore; *Thokchom Ongoi Sangeeta* v. *Oriental Insurance Co. Ltd.,* AIR 2008 SC 245: 2007 AIR SCW 6665: 2007 (11) SCC 750: 2007 (12) SCALE 448.

Abourers are traveling in tractor trollies. The Insurance Company has no liability; *United India Insurance Co. Ltd.* v. *Serjerao,* AIR 2008 SC 460: 2007 AIR SCW 7280: 2008 (7) SCC 425: 2007 (13) SCALE 80: 2007 (8) Supreme 25: 2008 (1) WLC (SC) CVL 570.

There is no proof that the deceased was traveling in lorry along with the driver or cleaner, as the owner of goods. The goods carriage carrying passengers met with accident. Traveling with goods itself does not entitle anyone to protection under section 147. The deceased was gratuitous passenger and policy would not cover his life; *National Insurance Co. Ltd.* v. *Cholleti Bharatamma,* AIR 2008 SC 484: 2007 AIR SCW 7337: (2008) 1 SCC 423.

The owner of taxi while driving it met with an accident and died. Insurance policy covers only risk of paid driver Considering the fact that the deceased was only a bread earner of his family and the claimants have lost their only breadwinner, the court has not interfered with the concurrent orders of the court below; *New India Assurance Co. Ltd.* v. *Kendra Devi,* AIR 2008 SC 490: 2007 AIR SCW 7352: 2007 (12) SCALE 718: 2007 (8) Supreme 174.

If a vehicle is 'Light Motor Vehicle', but falls under the category of Transport Vehicle, the driving licence has to be duly endorsed under section 3 of the Act. If it is not done, a person holding driving licence to ply Light Motor Vehicle cannot ply transport vehicle. In the case. The licence was not endorsed as required and hence, the deceased could not have driven Tata 709 in absence of requisite endorsement and Insurance Company could not be held liable; *New India Assurance Co. Ltd.* v. *Prabhu Lal,* AIR 2008 SC 614: 2007 AIR SCW 7677: 2008 (1) SCC 696: 2007 (13) SCALE 588: 2008 (1) SCC (Cri) 308: 2007 (8) Supreme 343.

Where the policy of insurance is issued by an authorized insurer on receipt of cheque towards payment of premium and such cheque is returned dishonoured, the liability of authorized insurer to indemnify third parties in respect of the liability which that policy covered subsists and it has to satisfy award of compensation by reason of the provisions of sections 147(5) and 149(1) of the Act unless the policy of insurance is cancelled by the authorized insurer and intimation of such cancellation has reached the insured before the accident. In other words, where the policy of insurance is issued by an authorized insurer to cover a vehicle on receipt of the cheque paid towards premium and the cheque gets dishonoured and before the accident of the vehicle occurs, such insurance company cancels the policy of insurance and sends intimation thereof to the owner, the insurance company's liability to indemnify the third parties which that policy covered ceases and the insurance company is not liable to satisfy awards of compensation in respect thereof;

United India Insurance Co. Ltd. v. *Laxmamma,* AIR 2012 SC 2817: 2012 AIR SCW 2657: (2012) 5 SCC 234.

29. Term "person"- Purview of – Whosoever becomes victim of an accident arising out of the use of two wheelers would not come within the purview of the term "a person" If they all come within the purview, then to a large extent, the provisions of the Insurance Act become otiose. By reason of such an interpretation the insurer would be liable to cover risk of not only a third party but also others who would not otherwise come within the purview thereof; *New India Assurance Company Ltd.* v. *Sadanand Mukhi,* AIR 2009 SC 1788: 2009 AIR SCW 1372: 2009 (2) SCC 417: 2009 (1) SCALE 252.

30. Statutory Liability under Contract of Insurance – The statutory liability of the Insurance Company *vis-a-vis* a third party in the context of sections 147 and 149 of the Act, arising under a contract of insurance would have to be met if the contract is valid. If the contract of insurance has been cancelled and all concerned have been intimated thereabout, the insurance company would not be liable to satisfy the claim. A beneficial legislation as is well known should not be construed in such a manner so as to bring within its ambit a benefit which was not contemplated by the legislature to be given to the party; *Deddappa* v. *Branch Manager, National Insurance Co. Ltd.,* AIR 2008 SC 767: 2007 AIR SCW 7948: 2008 (2) SCC 595: 2007 (14) SCALE 257.

31. Liability where Insurance Covers Risk of Third Party – Where the contract of insurance covered risk of third party but not that of owner or pillion rider of two wheeler, the liability of the Insurance Company in a case of this nature was not extended to a pillion rider of the motor vehicle unless the requisite amount of premium is paid for covering his/her risk. The pillion rider in a two wheeler was not to be treated as a third party when the accident has taken place owing to rash and negligent riding of the scooter and not on the part of the driver of another vehicle; *Oriental Insurance Co. Ltd.* v. *Sudhakaran K.V.,* AIR 2008 SC 2729: 2008 AIR SCW 4549: 2008 (7) SCC 428: 2008 (8) SCALE 402.

32. Liability of Insurer to Indemnify Owner – In a case of accident, the primary liability under law for payment of compensation is that of the driver. The owner of the vehicle also becomes vicariously liable therefor. In a case involving a third-party to the contract of insurance in terms of section 147 of the Act, providing for a compulsory insurance, the insurer becomes statutorily liable to indemnify the owner. Therefore, where the liability is fastened upon the insurer, the insurer would be bound to indemnify the insured unless the exceptions contained in section 149 of the Act are attracted; *Samundra Devi* v. *Narendra Kaur,* AIR 2008 SC 3205: 2008 AIR SCW 5416: 2008 (9) SCC 100.

33. Third Party Risk – If the insured cannot be fastened with any liability under the provisions of the Act, the question of the insurer being liable to indemnify insured, does not arise. The additional premium was not paid in respect of the entire risk of death or bodily injury of the owner of the vehicle. If that be so, section 147(b) of the Act which in no uncertain terms covers a risk of a third party only would be attracted in the present case; *Oriental Insurance Co. Ltd.* v. *Jhuma Saha,* AIR 2007 SC 1054: 2007 AIR SCW 859: 2007 (2) ACJ 818.

34. Liability of Insurer in Case of Injury or Death of Passengers – Because the expression 'goods carriage' is solely for the carriage of goods. Carrying of passengers in a goods carriage is not contemplated in the Act. Section 147 of the Act mandates compulsory coverage against death of or bodily injury to any passenger of 'public service vehicle'. The proviso makes it further clear that compulsory coverage in respect of drivers and conductors of public service vehicles and employees carried in goods vehicle would be limited to liability under Workmen's Compensation Act, 1923. There is no reference to passengers. Thus, provisions of the Act do not enjoin any statutory liability on the owner of a vehicle to get his vehicle insured for any passenger travelling in goods carriage and the insurer would have no liability therefore; *New India Assurance Co. Ltd.* v. *Vedwati,* AIR 2007 SC 1334: 2007 AIR SCW 1505: (2007) 3 SCALE 397.

The deceased a labourer, was slipped down from the trolley attached to a the tractor was insured that to for carrying out agricultural work which would not include digging of earth and taking it in trolley to brick kiln the deceased being a mere passenger and as not the owner or driver, his claim petition has not been allowed but considering that he was a poor labourer and had become disabled, the insurer is directed to satisfy the award reserving right to realise the same from the owner of the tractor; *Oriental Insurance Co. Ltd.* v. *Brij Mohan,* AIR 2007 SC 1971: 2007 AIR SCW 3734: 2007 (7) SCC 56: 2007 (7) SCALE 753.

35. Liability Limited to Number of Passengers Authorised – The extent of liability of the insurance company in respect of the passengers of a stage carriage insured is limited only to the number of passengers authorised to be carried in the vehicle. Section 149 cannot bind the insurer to pay amount outside the contract of insurance; *National Insurance Co. Ltd.* v. *Anjana Shyam,* AIR 2007 SC 2870: 2007 AIR SCW 5237: 2007 (7) SCC 445: 2007 (10) SCALE 116.

36. Liability of Insurance Company *Qua* Employees of Owner – An insurance policy, which covers only the liability arising under the Workmen's Compensation Act in respect of death or bodily injury to any employee as described in sub-clauses (a) or (b) or (c) to proviso (1) to section 147(1)(b) of the Act is perfectly valid and permissible under the Act. Therefore, where any such policy has been taken by the owner of the vehicle, the liability of the insurance company will be confined to that arising under the Workmen's Compensation Act. In case the owner of the vehicle wants the liability of the insurance company in respect of death or bodily injury to any such employee should not be restricted to that under the Workmen's Compensation Act but should be more or unlimited, he must take such a policy by making payment of extra premium and the policy should also contain a clause to that effect. However, where the policy mentions "a policy for Act Liability" or "Act Liability", the liability of the insurance company qua the employees as aforesaid would not be unlimited but would be limited to that arising under the Workmen's Compensation Act; *National Insurance Co. Ltd.* v. *Prembai Patel,* AIR 2005 SC 2337: 2005 AIR SCW 2254: JT 2005 (4) SC 399: 2005 (6) SCC 172: 2005 (4) SCALE 185: 2005 (3) Supreme 587.

37. Owner can Claim only when Insurance has Taken Out – An insurance policy covers the liability incurred by the insured in respect of death of or bodily injury to any person (including an owner of the goods or his authorized representative) carried in the vehicle or damage to any property of a third party caused by or arising out of the use of the vehicle. Section 147 does not require an Insurance Company to assume risk for death or bodily injury to the owner of the vehicle. An owner of a vehicle can only claim provided a personal accident insurance has been taken out. In this case, there is no such insurance; *Dhanraj* v. *New India Assurance Co. Ltd.,* AIR 2004 SC 4767: 2004 AIR SCW 5438: JT 2004 (8) SC 604: 2004 (8) SCC 553: 2004 (8) SCALE 229: 2004 (7) Supreme 164.

38. Comprehensive Insurance Policy does not Cover All Third Party Risks – An insurance policy only covers the person or classes of persons specified in the policy. A comprehensive policy merely means that the loss sustained by such person/persons will be payable up to the insured amount irrespective of the actual loss suffered; *Ramashray Singh* v. *New India Assurance Co. Ltd.,* 2003 AIR SCW 3601: JT 2003 (6) SC 97: 2003 (10) SCC 664: 2003 (5) SCALE 377: 2003 (5) Supreme 118.

39. Passenger in Goods Vehicle – Liability of Insurer – The expression "goods carriage" "is solely for the carriage of goods". Carrying of passengers in a goods carriage is not contemplated in the Act. Thus insurance company is not liable to pay compensation; *National Insurance Co. Ltd.* v. *Ajit Kumar,* AIR 2003 SC 3093: 2003 AIR SCW 4120: JT 2003 (7) SC 520: 2003 (9) SCC 668: 2003 (7) SCALE 136: 2003 (6) Supreme 436.

40. Licence to Drive Tractor does not Disqualify to Drive Tractor when Trailer is Attached – Merely because a trailer is added either to a tractor or to a motor vehicle by itself does not make that tractor or motor vehicle a transport vehicle. The tractor or motor vehicle remains a tractor or motor vehicle. If a person has a valid driving licence to drive a tractor or a motor vehicle he continues to have a valid licence to drive that tractor or motor vehicle even if a trailer is attached to it and some goods are carried in it. In other words a person having a valid driving licence to drive a particular category of vehicle does not become disabled to drive that vehicle merely because a trailer is added to that vehicle; *Nagashetty* v. *United India Insurance Co. Ltd.*, AIR 2001 SC 3356: 2001 AIR SCW 3099: JT 2001 (6) SC 482: 2001 (8) SCC 56: 2001 (5) SCALE 322: 2001 (6) Supreme 171.

41. Liability Towards Owner of Goods or his Representative or Gratuitous Passengers – The claimants have confined their claim only for the owner or his representative who were travelling in a goods vehicle and not for the gratuitous passenger. Right over gratuitous passengers is not claimed by any of the claimants thus the right over gratuitous passenger is not required to be considered; *Ramesh Kumar* v. *National Insurance Co. Ltd.*, AIR 2001 SC 3363: 2001 AIR SCW 3291: JT 2001 (6) SC 657: 2001 (6) SCC 713: 2001 (5) SCALE 370: 2001 (6) Supreme 353.

42. Liability of Insurer not Limited to Extent Specified in Policy of Insurance – Proviso to section 147(2) of Act 1988 does not limit the liability of Insurance Companies to payment of compensation to the extent specified in the policy of insurance in terms of section 95(2) of the Old Act. The policy issued under of Old Act and which is in force before the commencement of the New Act for a period of four months after commencement of the New Act or till the date of expiry of such a policy, whichever is earlier, is kept alive within that period by the proviso to section 147(2) of the New Act, but said proviso does not limit the liability of Insurance Company to the amount mentioned in the policy in accordance with terms of section 95(2) of Old Act; *National Insurance Company Ltd.* v. *Behari Lal*, AIR 2000 SC 3053: 2000 AIR SCW 3352: JT 2000 (10) SC 39: 2000 (7) SCC 137: 2000 (5) Supreme 747.

43. Light Motor Vehicle cannot always mean Light Goods Carriage – Definition of "light motor vehicle" as given in clause (21) of section 2 of the Act can apply only to a "light goods vehicle" or a "light transport vehicle". A light motor vehicle cannot always mean a light goods carriage. Light motor vehicle can be non-transport vehicle as well; *Ashok Gangadhar Maratha* v. *Oriental Insurance Co. Ltd.*, AIR 1999 SC 3181: 1999 AIR SCW 3142: JT 1999 (6) SC 423: 1999 (6) SCC 620: 1999 (5) SCALE 346: 1999 (9) Supreme 478.

44. Extent of Liability – The insurance policy between the insurer and the insured represents a contract between the parties. Since the insurer undertakes to compensate the loss suffered by the insured on account of risks covered by the insurance policy, the terms of the agreement have to be strictly construed to determine the extent of liability of the insurer. The insured cannot claim anything more than what is covered by the insurance policy. That being so, the insured has also to act strictly in accordance with the statutory limitations or terms of the policy expressly set out therein. Where there was, a specific prohibition operating against the respondent from carrying a hazardous, and that too, flammable substance in his vehicle which, under the 'permit' granted to him, could be utilised only for carrying unhazardous goods under the Motor Vehicles Act, and truck of respondent carrying Ether solvent which is flammable substance caught fire, the claim of respondent is liable to be dismissed on grounds that it was not covered by terms of insurance policy; *Oriental Insurance Co. Ltd.* v. *Sony Cheriyan*, AIR 1999 SC 3252: 1999 AIR SCW 3226: JT 1999 (6) SC 149: 1999 (6) SCC 451: 1999 (5) SCALE 114: 1999 (7) Supreme 195.

45. Liability in Respect of Third Party where Policy Issued without Receiving Premium – The insurer has issued policy to cover the bus without receiving the premium. By reason of the provisions of sections 147(5) and 149(1) of the Motor Vehicles Act, the became liable to indemnify third parties in respect of the liability which that policy covered and to satisfy awards of compensation in respect thereof notwithstanding its entitlement to avoid or cancel the policy for the reason that the cheque issued in payment of the premium thereon had not been honoured; *Oriental Insurance Co. Ltd.* v. *Inderjit Kaur,* AIR 1998 SC 588: 1998 AIR SCW 183: 1998 (1) SCC 371: 1997 (7) SCALE 488: 1997 (10) Supreme 289.

46. Insurer Liable to make Good Principal Amount and Liable for Interest if Commissioner Ordered – Workmen's when an employee suffers from a motor accident injury while on duty on the motor vehicle belonging to the insured employer, the claim for compensation payable under the Compensation Act along with interest thereon, if any, as imposed by the Commissioner sections 3 and 4A(3)(a) of the workmen's Compensation Act will have to be made good by the insurance company jointly with the insured employer. But so far as the amount of penalty imposed on the insured employer under contingencies contemplated by section 4A(3)(b) is concerned as that is on account of personal fault of the insured not backed up by any justifiable cause, the insurance company cannot be made liable to reimburse that part of the penalty amount imposed on the employer. The latter because of his own fault and negligence will have to bear the entire burden of the said penalty amount with proportionate interest thereon if imposed by the Workmen's Commissioner. Therefore the insurance companies will be liable to make good not only the principal amounts of compensation payable by insured employers but also interest thereon if ordered by the Commissioner to be paid by the insured employers. However they would not be liable to pay the penalty imposed under section 4A(3)(b); *Ved Prakash Garg* v. *Premi Devi,* AIR 1997 SC 3854: 1997 AIR SCW 3775: JT 1997 (8) SC 229: 1997 (8) SCC 1: 1997 (6) SCALE 238: 1997 (8) Supreme 412.

47. Lifting more Person than Permitted – Liability of Insurer not to be Avoided Altogether – The insured vehicle was entitled to carry 6 workmen, excluding the driver. If those 6 workmen when travelling in the vehicle, are assumed not to have increased any risk from the point of view of the Insurance Company on occurring of an accident, how could those added persons be said to have contributed to the causing of it is the poser, keeping apart the load it was carrying. It was not alleged that the driver of the insured vehicle was responsible for the accident. The coming vehicle had collided head-on against the insured vehicle, which resulted in the damage. Merely by lifting a person or two, or even three, by the driver or the cleaner of the vehicle, without the knowledge of owner, cannot be said to be such a fundamental breach that the owner should; in all events, be denied indemnification. The misuse of the vehicle was somewhat irregular though but not so fundamental in nature so as to put an end to the contract, unless some factors existed which, by themselves, had gone to contribute to the causing of the accident; *B.V. Nagaraju* v. *Oriental Insurance Co. Ltd., Divisional Office, Hassan,* AIR 1996 SC 2054: 1996 AIR SCW 2466: JT 1996 (6) SC 32: 1996 (4) SCC 647.

48. No Liability if No Valid Licence on Date of Accident – The vehicle was being driven by the minor whose was aged about fifteen years. The minor did not hold any valid licence on the date of accident. Thus the insurance company released from its liablility; *United India Insurance Co. Ltd.* v. *Rakesh Kumar Arora,* AIR 2009 SC 24: 2008 AIR SCW 6872: 2008 (13) SCC 298: 2008 (13) SCALE 35.

Driving licence of the driver of offending vehicle was not in force on the date of accident thus the insurance company, is released from its liability; *National Insurance Co. Ltd.* v. *Vidhyadhar Mahariwala,* AIR 2009 SC 208: 2008 AIR SCW 7145: 2008 (12) SCC 701: 2008 (12) SCALE 577.

49. Insurer Duty Bound to Inform Authorities about Cancellation – Insurance company is not merely under contractual obligation but also under statutory obligation to pay compensation. Insurer is also duty bound to inform transport authorities about cancellation, to prevent vehicle from plying on road. In absence of the same an insurance company cannot be discharged from their liability to make payment of compensation to a third party even as a stop gap arrangement. Facilities under the statute cannot be frustrated by means of solitary intimation of the insurer to the insured about cancellation of insurance contract for dishonourment of requisite cheques. It is "strict liability" of the insurer under the law. An insurance company is doing business about risk as per its own policy. Therefore, if the insurance company is allowed to avoid the risk, the same will go against their own policy of business particularly when they are entitled to get back their money even by way of land revenue in case the contract does not seem to be in existence for any reason. There is, in general, no duty for the sufferer to anticipate that another will be negligent and to avoid the effects of that negligent by anticipation; *National Insurance Co. Ltd.* v. *Jitendra Kumar,* AIR 2009 All 70: 2009 AIHC 1568: 2009 (3) Civ LJ 405.

50. Insurer cannot Avoid Liability if Notices not Served on Insured – When the insurance company failed to prove that notices were served on the insured informing that it cancelled the policy, the insurance company cannot avoid liability as it failed to give opportunity to the insured of the vehicle to remit the premium for the cheque dishonoured. In these circumstances, subsequent cancellation of insurance policy on the ground that the cheque through which premium was paid was dishonoured would not effect the rights of the third party; *National Insurance Co. Ltd.* v. *Sk. Ahmedunnisa,* AIR 2008 AP 278.

51. Words "any person" – Chapters X, XI and XII of the 1988 Act were introduced with a view to benefit more number of victims of the road accidents by suitably extending the liability of the insurer in that regard and the words 'any person' occurring in the pre-amended provisions of section 147 of the new Act, even though appear to be identical to those which were used in the old Act, must be construed liberally and, especially in the light of the scheme of the new Act and if so construed, the said words shall be understood to mean "owner of the goods" also and merely because identical set of expressions are used in the new enactment, it is not necessary to interpret the word or words used in the new enactment in the case way in which the word in the old enactment was interpreted. Thus the words "any person" used in the pre-amending provisions of section 147 of the new Act shall be interpreted to mean and include 'owner of the goods' and that under section 147 of the pre-amending provisions of the new Act, the insurer is liable to pay compensation in the event of death or bodily injury to the owner of the goods also; *New India Assurance Co. Ltd.* v. *Thanichintala Venkaiah,* AIR 2001 AP 371: 2001 (2) ACC 152: 2002 (1) ACJ 485.

52. Insurer not Liable if No Extra Premium Taken – In case of death or bodily injury to a gratuitous passenger travelling as a pillion rider in a Motorbike, he, may be treated as a third party if another vehicle is found to be responsible for his injury or death, but in case of death or injury for the negligence of the driver of the selfsame Motorbike, he cannot, at any rate, be described as a third party so as to cover the liability of compensation by an ordinary third party risk coverage. In such a situation, unless it is established that the Insurance Company took extra premium for covering the liability of such pillion rider as well, the claimants cannot bind the Insurance Company of the said Motorbike to pay the compensation for the loss suffered by the victim. The Insurance Company is not liable to pay the amount assessed by the Tribunal though the owner of the vehicle will be liable to pay such amount; *National Insurance Company Ltd.* v. *Shyamali Guhathakurta,* AIR 2008 Cal 155: 2008 AIHC 611 (NOC): 2008 (2) TAC 844.

53. Scope of Recovery of Amount from Owner – During the pendency of the appeal, the Court permitted the claimants to withdraw a portion of the awarded amount. But then court set aside the award, and the claimants are directed to pay back the said amount to the Insurance Company. In default, the Insurance Company will be free to realise the amount from the claimants. That the gratuitous passenger of a private vehicle was actually driving the car at the time of accident and that for his own rash and negligent driving, the gratuitous passenger died. The owner of the vehicle should be held responsible for the compensation only to the extent of Rs. 50,000 as provided in section 140 of the Act. Since the Insurance Company has not preferred any appeal against the order passed in the proceedings under section 140 of the Act, there is no scope of giving any liberty to the Insurance Company to recover that amount from the owner in this appeal preferred against an award passed in the proceedings under section 166 of the Act; *New India Assurance Co. Ltd.* v. *Putul Nazir,* AIR 2008 Cal 189: 2008 (6) ALJ (NOC) 1183: 2008 (6) AKAR (NOC) 931.

54. Liability to Indemnify Third Parties – Once the certificate of insurance has been issued by the insurer under sub-section (3) of section 147 of the Act, 1988 in favour of the person by whom the policy has been effected despite compliance of sub-section (1) of section 64VB of the Act, 1938, then as regards the liability towards third parties is concerned, the insurance company shall be liable notwithstanding that it may be entitled to avoid or cancel or may have actually avoided or cancelled the policy of insurance. The policy of insurance that the appellant/insurer issued was a representation upon which the authorities and third parties were entitled to act and, therefore, the appellant/insurer was not absolved of its obligations towards third parties under the policy of insurance merely because it did not receive the premium, its remedies in this behalf lay against the insured; *National Insurance Company Ltd.* v. *Rajendra Mourya,* AIR 2007 Chhat 138: 2008 AIHC 9 (NOC): 2008 (62) All Ind Cas 915.

Appellant, an authorised insurer, issued a policy of insurance to cover the bus without receiving the premium therefor. By reason of the provisions of sections 147(5) and 149(1) of the Act, the appellant became liable to indemnify third parties in respect of the liability which that policy covered and to satisfy awards of compensation in respect thereof notwithstanding its entitlement to avoid or cancel the policy for the reason that the cheque issued in payment of the premium thereon had not been honoured; *Oriental Insurance Co. Ltd.* v. *Inderjit Kaur,* AIR 1998 SC 588: 1998 AIR SCW 183: (1998) 1 SCC 371.

55. Liability of Insurer not be Fastened with Insured – The owner of a vehicle, not being a third parry, is not entitled to be indemnified, by his insurer for the damage caused to his own vehicle in an accident irrespective of the fact as to whether the accident took place, because of his own fault or fault of some one else, particularly, when no special premium has been paid by such an owner for damage, which may be sustained by his vehicle in such an accident. Liability of insurer is limited to indemnifying the insured against liability which insured may incur towards third persons or in respect of damage to property of third party. It is, therefore, clear that when the owner of a vehicle himself sustains injury, or when his own vehicle gets damaged, he cannot be said to be liable to pay compensation to any one and since the owner, incurs no liability to pay compensation to a third party, the insurer can also not be fastened with any liability to indemnify such an insured. In such a case, it is really not material whether it was the owner himself, who was driving the vehicle, when the accident had taken place, or not; *United India Insurance Co. Ltd.* v. *Dipen Nath,* AIR 2009 Gau 12: 2009 AIHC 137 (NOC): 2009 (3) ACJ 2030.

56. Limits of Liability for Third Party – The phrase 'Limits of Liability for Third Party' refers to pecuniary limits of the liability of the insurer and does not refer to liability of insurer towards third party *qua* third party, and even if a pillion rider or a gratuitous passenger were not covered by the expression 'third party' or 'any person'. Liability of the insurer could arise under special conditions of the policy to cover any risk by way of contractual liability. Even otherwise, the condition contained in section II of Two Wheeler Package Policy in the instant case to indemnify the insured against all liabilities in respect of death of or bodily injury to occupants carried in the insured vehicle cannot be read as having been cancelled or excluded on account of the occupant not being treated as a "third party". Therefore, the plea that while undertaking the liability to indemnify the insured in respect of the liability arising out of death of or bodily injury to occupant is subject to limits of liability to third party under the Act and a gratuitous passenger was not a third party has to be rejected as disingenuous and circuitous. That condition of the policy and the mention of Motor Vehicles Act, 1988 against the column "Limits of Liability" in the Schedule to the Policy has to be read in the context of the provisions of section 147 of the Act, more particularly sub-section (2) of section 147. That sub-section requires cover of liability upto the amount of liability incurred and the only pecuniary limit is in respect of damage to any property of a third party. Therefore, by necessary implication, the insurer undertakes to indemnify the insured to the extent of liability incurred by him in respect of death of or bodily injury to the occupants carried in the insured vehicle. The language of the clauses for liability to third parties and the exceptions as prescribed in the standard Form for "Liability Only Policy" and in the Standard Form for "Two Wheeler Package Policy" also clearly show that a wider coverage to include the risk of occupants of the vehicle is clearly intended. Therefore in view of legal implications of the conditions of Two Wheeler Package Policy, the insurer is held to be liable to indemnify the insured in respect of the claim of compensation arising out of the death of or bodily injury to the occupants carried in the vehicle, including the pillion rider; *ICICI Lombard General Insurance Co. Ltd.* v. *A.G. Vala,* AIR 2008 Guj 158: 2008 AIHC 951 (NOC): 2008 (6) ALJ (NOC) 1237.

57. Limits of Statutory Liability Deemed to have been Extended – By introduction of section 163A, the liability arising thereunder the must now be deemed to have been covered under statutory liability regardless of the pecuniary limit in that regard is specified in policy, or premium charged. In other words, the limits of statutory liability should be deemed to have been extended or enlarged appropriately so as to cover the liability that arises under section 163A. For the said liability, extra premium is not to be charged or specific contract is not required to be entered into. When that is so, it cannot be said that the Insurance Company will have to pay more. However, in some cases, where third party does not come in picture if the Court directs the Insurance Company to pay more than its statutory or contractual liability, as the case may be, it would be open to the Insurance Company under the terms of the contract to recover, from the insured, the excess amount paid pursuant to the order or in execution and discharge of the order of the Court/Tribunal. In case the Insurance Company has to pay more than its liability or risk covered under the policy, to a third party, it can invoke sections 147 and 149(4) or (5) of the Act for the recovery of the amounts paid in excess of the liability; *New India Assurance Co. Ltd.* v. *Muna Maya Basant,* AIR 2001 Guj 304: 2001 (2) ACC 589: 2001 (1) ACJ 940.

58. Reimbursement to Owner of Vehicle – Only because the driving licence was fake, the same would not absolve the insurer to reimburse the owner of vehicle in respect of amount awarded in fvaour of third party; *National Insurance Co. Ltd.* v. *Geeta Bhat,* AIR 2008 SC 1837: (2008) 5 SCR 734: JT 2008 (4) SC 425.

59. Comprehensive in Scope and Meaning – A bare reading of section 147 demonstrated plainly that it is quite comprehensive in scope and meaning. It has to be given wider, effective and practical meaning so that the object of the Legislature which was faced with divergent views of various courts of the country giving different interpretation to the provisions of section 95 of the 1939 Act causing immense harm to many categories of persons by disentitling them from claiming compensation either from the insurer or the insured or both, in the facts and circumstances of the case. New provision therefore, covers such kind of cases as well; *New India Assurance Company* v. *Smt. Shakuntla Devi,* AIR 1997 J&K 40: 1998 (2) ACC 418: 1998 (1) ACJ 195.

60. Person in Vehicle is Third Person – Even a person who is in the vehicle may fall in the category of third person; *National Insurance Company Ltd.* v. *V.S.R. Kumaresan,* I (1991) ACC 204.

61. Private Carrier cannot be Used for Carrying any Passenger or Goods for Hire or Reward – The vehicle involved in the accident which is admitted to be a private carrier and registered as such in R.T.O. and also in the insurance policy, cannot, therefore, be used for carrying any passenger or goods for hire or reward. In any case, if the employees of a party hiring a private carrier belonging to the insured, are injured in the accident the Insurance Company will not at all be liable for compensating them for the injuries caused to them, either under the statute or under the insurance policy, *Dattu Nathu Kudekar* v. *National Insurance Co.,* (1991) 2 ACC 8: AIR 1991 Guj 126: 1991 (2) ACJ 743.

62. Liability of Owner to Claimant – The owner of the goods, who accompanies his goods in the lorry transporting the same, cannot be said to be person employed by the person insured by the policy and that either the injury or death arose out of and in the course of his employment, Therefore, the Insurance Company is not liable. This will not in any way affect the liability of the owner of the lorry to the claimant; *New India Assurance Co. Ltd.* v. *B. Saraswathi Ammal,* II (1991) ACC 512.

63. Liability of Insurer where Driver not Holding Valid Driving Licence at Time of Accident – The Insurance Company cannot be made liable to pay compensation if the offending vehicle was being driven by a person not holding a valid driving licence at the time of accident; *United India Insurance Company Ltd.* v. *K. Subramaniun,* II (1991) ACC 520.

64. Liability of Insurer in Case of Theft of Vehicle – The offenders have assaulted the driver and fled away with the impugned vehicle. The insurance company plead that there was violation of terms of Insurance Policy as vehicle was being used for hire. The trial Court as well as the appellate Court have thoroughly and independently assessed and appraised the oral and documentary evidences and have come to the concurrent findings of fact that there was no violation of terms of Insurance Policy and that the plaintiff has been able to establish his claim against the insurance company. Thus the insurance company cannot deny its liability *Jagdish Chand Sharma* v. *Bachan Singh,* AIR 2010 HP 49: 2011 (1) ACC 144: 2010 (2) ACJ 1229.

65. Provision meant to Create Large Pool of Money for Payments of No Fault Compensation – Section 146 forbids the use of the vehicle in a public place unless there is in force, in relation to the use of the vehicle, a policy of insurance complying with the provisions of that chapter. Section 147 contains the provisions that are commonly referred to as 'Act only insurance'. The provisions of sections 146 and 147 are meant to create the large pool of money for making payments of no fault compensation. Thus the liability arising from section 140 would almost invariably be passed on to the insurer to be paid off from the vast fund created by virtue of sections 146 and 147 unless the owner of the vehicle causing accident is guilty of some flagrant violation of the law; *Eshwarappa* alias *Maheshwarappa* v. *C.S. Gurushanthappa,* AIR 2010 SC 2907: 2010 AIR SCW 4918: (2010) 8 SCC 620.

66. Owner is Liable to Pay Compensation to Gratuitous Passengers – The deceased was engaged in the offending vehicle as a labour and was allowed to sit and travel in the vehicle and as such, his status in the said vehicle was of gratuitous passenger and as per section 147 of the Act the gratuitous passengers sitting in a goods vehicle are not required to be covered under the statutory policy. Further, the Tribunal has held that the owner and driver have breached the policy conditions and the driver of the vehicle was not having valid and effective driving license. Therefore, the impugned award of the Tribunal directing the Insurance Company to first pay the compensation to claimants and thereafter recover from the owner, is erroneous. Thus the Appellant Insurance Company is not liable to pay compensation to the claimants and the same shall be paid by the owner of the vehicle in question; *Iffco Tokio General Insurance Co. Ltd.* v. *Subhni,* AIR 2011 Chht 115.

When a person sends his goods by a goods vehicle, he enters into a contract with the owner of the goods vehicle and, therefore, the owner of the goods vehicle becomes contractually liable to transport the goods in a safe condition. This is a contractual liability covered under the Carriers Act and not a tortious liability covered under the Motor Vehicles Act. In section 147(b)(i) as well as section 165, the legislature in its wisdom has specifically used the phrase 'property of a third party'. If a gratuitous passenger in a vehicle is not a third party, it is obvious that the goods being carried in a vehicle cannot be said to be the goods of a third party. The owner of the goods cannot by any stretch of imagination be said to be a third party vis-a-vis, the insured. It is a contracting party with the insured and in our view, the risk cannot be said to be that of a third party. The goods of a consignor/consignee being carried in a goods vehicle cannot be termed to be property of a third party; *Jagdish Chand Sharma* v. *Bachan Singh,* AIR 2010 HP 49: 2011 (1) ACC 144: 2010 (2) ACJ 1229.

67. Phrase "any Property of Third Party" – Meaning – The phrase "Any property of a third party" occurring in sections 147 and 165 of the Motor Vehicles Act will mean property which is outside the goods vehicle and not being carried in the goods vehicle; *Jagdish Chand Sharma* v. *Bachan Singh,* AIR 2010 HP 49: 2011 (1) ACC 144: 2010 (2) ACJ 1229.

68. Record of Findings without Verifying Certificate Improper – When the tribunal chose to enter into the correctness and validity of the driving license, it was duty bound to ensure that the certificate in regard to the driving license of the driver should correctly be verified. The certificate issued by the RTO submitted by the respondents-Insurance Company on the face of it, suffers from grave discrepancy as to the name of the driver of the vehicle which ought to have been scrutinized with accuracy. It was clearly the duty of the Insurance Company, to ensure that the certificate in regard to the driving license should have been produced before the Tribunal, but it is sufficiently clear that the certificate was not produced in regard to the driver but it was in regard to a driver who had nothing to do with the accident. Thus the finding recorded by the Tribunal to the effect that the vehicle was driven by a driver without a valid driving license and the same was forged and fabricated, suffers from perversity even on prima facie reading of the finding in this regard. Hence recording of findings by the Tribunal without verifying the said certificate is not proper; *Sewak Singh* v. *D.M. National Insurance Co.,* AIR 2010 Jhar 90: 2010 AIHC 2654: 2011 (2) ACJ 826.

69. Policy does Not Cover Risk of Insured Not Proved – Insurer Liable to Pay Compensation – In order to save life of the calf the owner of the vehicle has dashed the vehicle against the tree on the road side which results in death of him. The insurance company has taken plea that the policy does not cover the risk of insured as he had not paid the additional premium amount. However, no evidence has been adduced by the insurance company before the Tribunal to prove the fact that the policy does not cover the risk of the insured. Therefore, it is not open for the insurance Company to urge the factual aspect in support of legal plea urged for the first time that it is not liable to pay compensation to the claimants for the reason that the insured had not paid additional premium amount towards his risk for setting aside the judgment and award in fastening the liability upon it; *New India Assurance Co. Ltd.* v. *Tulsi Rout,* AIR 2012 Ori 1: 2012 (2) Lab LN 265: 2012 (3) TAC 571.

70. Cover Note – Cancellation – Mandatory to Convey to Insured by Insurer – Insurer Liable to Pay Compensations; *United India Insurance Company Ltd.* v. *Mohan Lal,* AIR 2015 HP 15.

71. 'Persons Employed in Connection with Operation of Motor Vehicle' – Operation of Clause – Not restricted to persons employed in connection with loading/unloading of motor vehicle; *Hanumanagouda* v. *United India Insurance Co. Ltd.,* AIR 2015 SC 1467.

148. Validity of policies of insurance issued in reciprocating countries.—Where, in pursuance of an arrangement between India and any reciprocating country, the motor vehicle registered in the reciprocating country operates on any route or within any area common to the two countries and there is in force in relation to the use of the vehicle in the reciprocating country, a policy of insurance complying with the requirements of the law of insurance in force in that country, then, notwithstanding anything contained in section 147 but subject to any rules which may be made under section 164, such policy of insurance shall be effective throughout the route or area in respect of which, the arrangement has been made, as if the policy of insurance had complied with the requirements of this Chapter.

149. Duty of insurers to satisfy judgments and awards against persons insured in respect of third party risks.—(1) If, after a certificate of insurance has been issued under sub-section (3) of section 147 in favour of the person by whom a policy has been effected, judgment or award in respect of any such liability as is required to be covered by a policy under clause (b) of sub-section (1) of section 147 (being a liability covered by the terms of the policy) [1][or under the provisions of section 163A] is obtained against any person insured by the policy, then, notwithstanding that the insurer may be entitled to avoid or cancel or may have avoided or cancelled the policy, the insurer shall, subject to the provisions of this section, pay to the person entitled to the benefit of the decree any sum not exceeding the sum assured payable thereunder, as if he were the judgment debtor, in respect of the liability, together with any amount payable in respect of costs and any sum payable in respect of interest on that sum by virtue of any enactment relating to interest on judgments.

(2) No sum shall be payable by an insurer under sub-section (1) in respect of any judgment or award unless, before the commencement of the proceedings in which the judgment or award is given the insurer had notice through the Court or, as the case may be, the Claims Tribunal of the bringing of the proceedings, or in respect of such judgment or award so long as execution is stayed thereon pending an appeal; and an insurer to whom notice of the bringing of any such proceedings is so given shall be entitled to be made a party thereto and to defend the action on any of the following grounds, namely:—

(a) that there has been a breach of a specified condition of the policy, being one of the following conditions, namely:—

(i) a condition excluding the use of the vehicle—

(a) for hire or reward, where the vehicle is on the date of the contract of insurance a vehicle not covered by a permit to ply for hire or reward, or

(b) for organised racing and speed testing, or

(c) for a purpose not allowed by the permit under which the vehicle is used, where the vehicle is a transport vehicle, or

(d) without side-car being attached where the vehicle is a motor cycle; or

---

1. Ins. by Act 54 of 1994, sec. 47 (w.e.f. 14-11-1994).

(ii) a condition excluding driving by a named person or persons or by any person who is not duly licensed, or by any person who has been disqualified for holding or obtaining a driving licence during the period of disqualification; or

(iii) a condition excluding liability for injury caused or contributed to by conditions of war, civil war, riot or civil commotion; or

(b) that the policy is void on the ground that it was obtained by the non- disclosure of a material fact or by a representation of fact which was false in some material particular.

(3) Where any such judgment as is referred to in sub-section (1) is obtained from a Court in a reciprocating country and in the case of a foreign judgment is, by virtue of the provisions of section 13 of the Code of Civil Procedure, 1908 (5 of 1908) conclusive as to any matter adjudicated upon by it, the insurer (being an insurer registered under the Insurance Act, 1938 (4 of 1938) and whether or not he is registered under the corresponding law of the reciprocating country) shall be liable to the person entitled to the benefit of the decree in the manner and to the extent specified in sub-section (1), as if the judgment were given by a Court in India:

Provided that no sum shall be payable by the insurer in respect of any such judgment unless, before the commencement of the proceedings in which the judgment is given, the insurer had notice through the Court concerned of the bringing of the proceedings and the insurer to whom notice is so given is entitled under the corresponding law of the reciprocating country, to be made a party to the proceedings and to defend the action on grounds similar to those specified in sub-section (2).

(4) Where a certificate of insurance has been issued under sub-section (3) of section 147 to the person by whom a policy has been effected, so much of the policy as purports to restrict the insurance of the persons insured thereby by reference to any condition other than those in clause (b) of sub-section (2) shall, as respects such liabilities as are required to be covered by a policy under clause (b) of sub-section (1) of section 147, be of no effect:

Provided that any sum paid by the insurer in or towards the discharge of any liability of any person which is covered by the policy by virtue only of this sub-section shall be recoverable by the insurer from that person.

(5) If the amount which an insurer becomes liable under this section to pay in respect of a liability incurred by a person insured by a policy exceeds the amount for which the insurer would apart from the provisions of this section be liable under the policy in respect of that liability, the insurer shall be entitled to recover the excess from that person.

(6) In this section the expression "material fact" and "material particular" means, respectively a fact or particular of such a nature as to influence the judgment of a prudent insurer in determining whether he will take the risk and, if so, at what premium and on what conditions, and the expression "liability covered by the terms of the policy" means a liability which is covered by the policy or which would be so covered but for the fact that the insurer is entitled to avoid or cancel or has avoided or cancelled the policy.

(7) No insurer to whom the notice referred to in sub-section (2) or sub-section (3) has been given shall be entitled to avoid his liability to any person entitled to the benefit of any such judgment or award as is referred to in sub-section (1) or in such judgment as is referred to in sub-section (3) otherwise than in the manner provided for in sub-section (2) or in the corresponding law of the reciprocating country, as the case may be.

Explanation.—For the purposes of this section, "Claims Tribunal" means a Claims Tribunal constituted under section 165 and "award" means an award made by that Tribunal under section 168.

SYNOPSIS

COMMENTS

1. Notice before Insurer Making Liable – When a direction under section 140, can be passed against an insurer, the insurer must be inferred to have the right to refute its liability in terms of the defences available to an insurer under sub-section (2) of section 149. Even the owner of the vehicle may deny his liability on the ground that his vehicle was not involved in the accident, for, when a vehicle is not involved in an accident, its owner cannot be saddled with the liability to pay compensation on the principle of even 'No fault'. When any of the defences available to the insurer, under section 149(2), is taken by an insurer in a proceeding under section 140, the Motor Accidents Claims Tribunal has the duty to adjudicate upon the same and decide the issue as regards the liability of the insurer to indemnify the owner under section 140 of the Act. Hence, when a separate application is filed under section 140 of the M.V. Act, an insurer has to be served with a notice before any order is passed making it liable to pay compensation under section 140 and, upon receiving such a notice, an insurer may take such defence as may be statutorily available to the insurer under section 149(2) of the M.V. Act; *New India Assurance Co. Ltd.* v. *Lohit Dist. Legal Service Authority,* AIR 2008 Gau 166: 2008 (68) All Ind Cas 471: 2008 (3) Gau LT 824.

2. Insurer cannot Escape its Liability once Cover Note Issued – The Insurance Company is liable to pay compensation on the basis of cover note issued by its agent and the negligence or error of agent does not affect the liability of the insurer and even if he has been removed from service, it is for the Insurance Company to take suitable action against him; *Oriental Insurance Company Ltd.* v. *White Rose,* AIR 2002 All 117: 2002 AIHC 2677: 2002 (2) ACJ 1061.

3. *Onus* to Adduce Evidence that Driver not having Valid Licence – No evidence was led or adduced by the insurer to establish that the driver who was driving the truck was not having a valid licence. The owner of the truck and the driver did not appear in the proceeding before the Tribunal and, therefore, the onus was on the appellant insurance company to adduce sufficient evidence which could establish and prove that the driver who was driving the vehicle at the time of accident had no valid licence. The appellant having failed to adduce any evidence to the effect that the vehicle at the time of accident was being driven by a person who was not authorized and had no valid licence to drive the vehicle, insurer is liable to pay compensation he did not discharge the *onus* to prove the aforesaid fact. Multiplier of 17 is applied on consideration of the young age of the deceased; *Oriental Insurance Co. Ltd.* v. *Manju Gupta,* AIR 2001 All 158: 2001 All LJ 1217: 2002 (3) ACJ 1969.

4. Insurer cannot be Heard other than Grounds Contained in Section – Normally the insurance company cannot be heard on the grounds other than those contained in section 149(2) of the Act on which it can contest the proceedings or the claim petition. However, in exceptional circumstances where actually the tort-feasers or the owner of the vehicle had not colluded with the claimants or the Tribunal committed grave error of law in assessing the amount of compensation, the insurer can bring such facts to the notice of the appellate Court and the appellate Court can certainly look into and consider such submissions. Where though there was no specific evidence that driver and owner of vehicle had colluded with claimants, however, they could be said neglected or failed to contest claim, inasmuch as even though the owner filed his written statement, but did not contest the proceedings and the driver of the vehicle even did not file his written statement and allowed the claim petition to proceed *ex parte* against him, the appellate Court can go into such question relating to illegality or arbitrariness in computing the amount of compensation awarded by the Tribunal; *United India Insurance Co. Ltd.* v. *Manisa Porwar,* AIR 1999 All 142: 1999 All LJ 932: 2000 (1) ACJ 30.

5. Enforcement of Indemnity under Insurance Policy – A contract of insurance is akin to contract of indemnity. Parties to a policy of insurance are bound by mutual obligations and promises, the underlying aspect being that one party believes that other party would keep up his promises. When owner of vehicle fails to fulfil promise of entrusting the insured vehicle only to a person having valid driving licence and it is found due to effort of insurer that the vehicle was used at the relevant time by a person not having valid driving licence or a person having a fake driving licence or a person having invalid driving licence, the law can always infer that such thing happened with connivance of insured. It would be altogether different case if it is proved by owner of vehicle that he entrusted the vehicle to a person having valid driving licence but without his knowledge vehicle was driven by another person; *National Insurance Co. Ltd.* v. *Dupati Singaiah,* AIR 2009 AP 142: 2009 AIHC 641 (NOC): 2009 (4) ACC 28.

6. Liability of Insurer to Pay Compensation – The burden to prove that the driver of offending track was not having valid driving license is on owner but no evidence has been led by the owner of the offending Track in respect of proof of the factum of having a driving license in the name of driver on relevant point of time. It can be inferred that at time of accident, the driver of track did not have a valid driving license Insurer not liable to pay compensation; *Oriental Insurance Company Ltd.* v. *Kitbokson War,* AIR 2008 Gau 77: 2008 AIHC 492 (NOC): 2008 (2) Gau LT 496.

7. Right of Insurer to Raise Defences – The insurer can raise only those defences which are permitted under section 149 of the 1988 Act. If restriction is imposed on the right of the party to raise contentions in the trial forum, the restrictions must necessarily operate an the right of the party in the appellate forum also; otherwise it would mean that such a limited right of a party to raise defences in the trial forum would become enlarged and extended in the appellate forum; *United India Insurance Co. Ltd.*•v. *Member, M.A.C.T., Lakhimpur,* AIR 1993 Gau 28: 1993 (2) ACJ 828: 1994 (79) Com Cas 188 (FB); *National Insurance Co. Ltd.* v. *Sh. Kapoor Chand,* AIR 2009 HP 93.

8. Insurer has to Satisfy Award at First Instance in Case of Breach of Condition of Policy – The policy has specifically excluded from using of the vehicle for hire or reward. But the deceased is found to be travelling as a gratuitous passenger in the vehicle. This is a breach of condition of the policy. Insurance Company is not liable to indemnify insured. Insurance Company has to satisfy award at first instance and then it can recover awarded amount from owner. This finding, does not mean that the appellant-Insurance Company cannot be ordered to pay the compensation to the third party, *i.e.* the claimants. As a matter of fact, in a case where breach of condition of policy, which can be taken as a ground of defence, under section 149(2) of the Act, is successfully set up by the insurer, the Insurance Company has to satisfy the award at the first instance and then it can recover the awarded amount from the owner; *New India Assurance Co.* v. *Shri Kant,* AIR 2007 HP 27: 2007 (2) ACJ 1058: 2007 AIHC 1262.

9. Breach of Condition of Policy – Burden to prove breach of condition of policy is on the insurer. But how and in what manner breach is to be proved, is a matter to be decided on the facts and circumstances of each case; *National Insurance Co.* v. *Amar Chand,* AIR 2006 HP 49.

10. Where Vehicle not Insured on Relevant Date – Merely because on the relevant date the vehicle was not insured, the respondent-State cannot disowned its liability for payment of compensation. Respondent-State is liable to pay compensation; *Gray Hound Transport Co.* v. *Union of India,* AIR 2002 Jhar 47: 2003 (2) ACJ 869: 2002 (1) BLJ 427.

11. Liability of Insurer to Pay Interest – Under section 149(1) there is a statutory liability on the part of the insurer even to pay the interest which is awarded in pursuance of any enactment and even the parties cannot contract out of this liability. It is not shown as to how the insurer can avoid its liability to pay interest in view of specific provision in section 149(1). Thus the insurer is liable for the interest awarded under section 4A(3) of the Workmens Compensations Act; *United India Insurance Co. Ltd.* v. *Gangawwa,* AIR 1997 Kant 168: 1997 (1) Kant LJ 142: 1997 ACJ 825.

12. Absence of Badge cannot be Ground to Deny Statutory Liability to Third Party – The driver was having a valid driving licence to drive the type of vehicle which he was driving but he has no badge on the date of accident. There is no contention for the insurance company, even in the appeal, that absence of the badge is a fundamental breach of police condition and it is a cause for the accident. Merely because driver of the vehicle who was duly licensed was not having a badge will not enable the insurance company to shirk its liability as per section 149 of the Motor Vehicles Act, moreso when, insurance company also failed to prove that insured has committed a fundamental breach of the policy conditions resulting in the accident. Section 149(2) also speaks only about driving licence, but, not badge. Absence of badge in driving a commercial vehicle will attract penal consequences, but, it cannot be a ground to deny statutory liability to third party compensation; *P.T. Moidu* v. *Oriental Insurance Co. Ltd.,* AIR 2008 Ker 43: 2008 AIHC 217 (NOC): 2008 (1) Ker LJ 378.

13. Liability of Insurer to Third Party – The Act makes insurance of motor vehicles against third party risks compulsory and no vehicle can be put on the road without a valid policy of insurance covering risks that may occur to third parties out of use of such motor vehicle. The Insurance Company while issuing policy of insurance receiving cheque towards premium, enables the owner of the motor vehicle to ply the motor vehicle on the public roads. Whether the cheque is cashed and if not whether the policy is cancelled are all matters within the knowledge of the contracting parties namely insurer and insured. Thus insurer who has issued a policy of insurance for a motor vehicle receiving cheque towards payment of premium cannot be allowed to disown liability to third party. Their remedies have to be worked out against the insured. The liability of Insurance Company in damages for third party risks continues for entire period covered by policy in spite of the cheque issued towards payment of premium was dishonoured and consequently policy was cancelled by the Insurance Company. The remedy of the Insurance Company lies against the "insured" to have the amount paid by them by way of compensation for third party risks to be got reimbursed; *Oriental Insurance Co. Ltd.* v. *A.B. Sivankuty,* AIR 2006 Ker 20: 2006 AIHC 1: 2005 (3) Ker LJ 574.

14. When Accident Occur before Commencement of Policy – The accident occurred at 2 p.m.. The insurance policy was taken at 4.15 p.m. of the day. In the policy itself it is written that commencement of the policy is only from 4.15 p.m. of the day and, therefore, Insurance Company is not liable to pay compensation. The claimant will free to recover the amount from the owner and driver of the vehicle, as they are jointly and severely liable to pay the compensation; *New India Assurance Co. Ltd.* v. *M.P. Parvathi,* AIR 2004 Ker 159: 2004 (1) ACC 610: 2005 ACJ 1785: 2004 (1) ACC 610.

15. Mere Sitting Near Driver would not Exonerate Insurer – The deceased was an employee under the owner of the tractor. The tractor with a trolley is a goods vehicle and it would cover an employees. A tractor-trailer is a goods vehicle and it is constructed for the purpose of carriage of goods and when it is pulled by a tractor, both together constitute a vehicle. The deceased was sitting next to the driver of the tractor. Once it is held and accepted that he was an employee, mere sitting near the driver would not exonerate the Insurance Company from indemnifying the owner; *National Insurance Co. Ltd.* v. *Rainki Bai,* AIR 1998 MP 112: 1997 (2) MPLJ 455: 1998 (1) Civ LJ 81.

16. Expression "Manner" – The expression 'manner' means an insurer can avoid its liability only in accordance with what has been provided for in section 149(2). It, therefore, shows that the insurer can avoid its liability only on the statutory defences expressly provided in section 149(2) of 1988 Act. The Parliament, while enacting section 149(2) only specified some of the defences which are based on conditions of the policy and, therefore, any other breach of conditions of the policy by the insured which does not find place in section 149(2) cannot be taken as a defence by the insurer. Permitting the insurer to take any other defence other than those specified in section 149(2) would mean adding more defences to insurer in the statute which is neither found in the Act nor was intended to be included; *National Insurance Co. Ltd.* v. *Nicolletta Rohtagi,* AIR 2002 SC 3350: JT 2002 (7) SC 251: 2002 (7) SCC 456: 2002 (6) SCALE 569: 2002 (6) Supreme 362.

17. Insurance Company not Bound to Reimburse Owner – Filing of an application and grant thereof are pre-requisite for holding a valid and effective licence. The driver was not duly licensed as his learner's licence expired before a accident took place. He filed an application for grant of licence much later. Insurance Company, therefore, was not bound to reimburse him in terms of the Contract of Insurance; *Bhuwan Singh* v. *M/s. Oriental Insurance Co. Ltd.,* AIR 2009 SC 2177: 2009 AIR SCW 2865: 2009 (5) SCC 136: 2009 (3) SCALE 798.

18. Liability where Accident took place before Cover Note Take Effect – The cover note of the insurance had been issued on a date which was to take effect from a future date and the accident have taken place before that future date therefore the insurer was not liable to pay compensation. In view of peculiar facts directions issued to insurer not to recover amount from the claimant but from the owner and the driver of the vehicle; *Balbir Kaur* v. *New India Assurance Co. Ltd.,* AIR 2009 SC 2460: 2009 AIR SCW 4583: 2009 (6) SCALE 257.

19. Different Considerations in Different Forum – Different considerations would arise depending on the forum approached, as the Consumer Forum established under the Consumer Protection Act, was concerned only with a question as to whether there was deficiency of service on the part of the appellant or not. A right on the part of the Insurance Company not to pay the amount of insurance would depend upon the facts and circumstances of each case. It in certain situation may be bound to pay the claim made by the third party; if the same is filed before a forum created under the Motor Vehicles Act. But defence may be held to be justified before a different forum where the question raised is required to be considered in a different manner; *United India Insurance Co. Ltd.* v. *Davinder Singh,* AIR 2008 SC 329: 2007 AIR SCW 6866: 2007 (8) SCC 698: 2007 (12) SCALE 359.

20. Insurer Liable unless Proved Knowledge of Owner about Fake Licence – When the owner after verification satisfied himself that the driver has a valid licence and driving the vehicle in question competently at the time of the accident there would be no breach of a specified condition of the policy in that event, the Insurance Company would not then be absolved of liability. Further even in the case that the licence was fake, the Insurance Company would continue to remain liable unless they prove that the owner was aware or noticed that the licence was fake and still permitted him to drive; *Premkumari* v. *Prahlad Dev,* AIR 2008 SC 1073: 2008 AIR SCW 682: 2008 (3) SCC 193: 2008 (1) SCALE 531.

21. Return of Amount Deposited where Insurer has No Liability – Pursuant to the orders passed by the Court, the entire amount awarded was deposited in the Court. As the appellant-Insurance Company has no liability, the amount deposited be returned to the Insurance Company with accrued interest, if any; *Oriental Insurance Co. Ltd.* v. *Prithvi Raj,* AIR 2008 SC 1408: 2008 AIR SCW 888: 2008 (2) SCC 338: 2008 (1) SCALE 727.

22. Owner not Expected to Verify Genuineness of Licence from Transport Office – An owner of the vehicle is bound to make reasonable enquiry as to whether the person who is authorized to drive the vehicle holds a licence or not. Such a licence not only must be an effective one but should also be a valid one. Indisputably, in a case where the terms of the contract of insurance are found to have been violated by the insured, the insurer may not be held to be liable for reimbursing the insured. So far as a driving licence of a professional driver is concerned, the owner of the vehicle, despite taking reasonable care, might have not been able to find out as to whether the licence was a fake one or not. He is not expected to verify the genuineness thereof from the Transport Offices. Therefore, though the license possessed by the driver is a fake one, the insurer would not be absolved from the liability to reimburse the owner of a vehicle in respect of the amount awarded in favour of a third party; *National Insurance Co. Ltd.* v. *Geeta Bhat,* AIR 2008 SC 1837: 2008 AIR SCW 2534: 2008 (4) SCALE 757.

23. Insurer Deemed to be Judgment-Debtor in Respect of Liability – Section 149 casts a liability upon the insurer to pay to the person entitled to the benefit of the decree "as if he was the judgment debtor", that is, the statute raises a legal fiction to the effect that for the said purpose the insurer would be deemed to be a judgment-debtor in respect of the liability of the insurer in respect of third party risks; *Oriental Insurance Co. Ltd.* v. *Zaharulnisha,* AIR 2008 SC 2218: 2008 AIR SCW 3251: 2008 (3) ACJ 1928.

24. Insurer would not be absolved from Liability for Violation of Act in Case of Third Party – Where the insurers, relying upon the provisions of violation of law by the assured, take an exception to pay the assured or a third party, they must prove a wilful violation of the law by the assured. In some cases, violation of criminal law, particularly violation of the provisions of the MV Act, may result in absolving the insurers but, the same may not necessarily hold good in the case of a third party. In any event, the exception applies only to acts done intentionally or 'so recklessly as to denote that the assured did not care what the consequences of his act might be'. The provisions of section 149(4) and (5) of the MV Act may be considered as to the liability of the insurer to satisfy the decree at the first instance. The liability of the insurer is a statutory one. The liability of the insurer to satisfy the decree passed in favour of a third party is also statutory; *Oriental Insurance Co. Ltd.* v. *Zaharulnisha,* AIR 2008 SC 2218: 2008 AIR SCW 3251: 2008 (3) ACJ 1928.

25. Liability when Deceased not Traveling in Truck as Owner of Goods – The deceased was not travelling in the truck as owner of the goods *viz.* the vegetables. He was travelling in the truck for a purpose other than the one for which he was entitled to travel in a public carriage goods vehicle. The driver of track was also not holding a valid licence to drive the goods carriage therefore the owner alone was liable to pay compensation for causing death by rash and negligent driving on the part of the driver of the truck; *National Insurance Co. Ltd.* v. *Kaushalya Devi,* AIR 2008 SC 2252: 2008 AIR SCW 4025: 2008 (8) SCC 246: 2008 (8) SCALE 500.

26. Logic of Fake Licence to be considered Differently – The liabilities and the obligations relatable to third parties are created only by fiction of sections 147 and 149 of the Act. That there is no contractual relation between the insurance company and the third party. Section 149 is beneficial one *qua* the third party. But that benefit cannot be extended to the owner of the offending vehicle. The logic of fake license has to be considered differently in respect of third party and in respect of own damage claims. The restrictions relating to appeal in terms of section 173(2) does not also apply to own damage cases; *National Insurance Co. Ltd.* v. *Laxmi Narain Dhut,* AIR 2007 SC 1563: 2007 AIR SCW 2279: 2007 (3) SCC 700: 2007 (4) SCALE 36: 2007 (2) Supreme 721.

27. Liability though Breach of Condition of Policy – The offending vehicle was being used as taxi and is, therefore, commercial vehicle. The driver was holder of licence to drive a light motor vehicle only and does not possessing any licence to drive commercial vehicle. Thus there was breach of condition of contract of insurance. Insurance Company though not liable to pay compensation, in view fact that the victim was of 12 years of age and the claimants are from poor background, the Insurance Company is held liable to pay compensation. However, Insurance Company is directed to recover amount from the owner; *National Insurance Co. Ltd.* v. *Kusum Rai,* AIR 2006 SC 3440: 2006 AIR SCW 1649: 2006 (4) SCC 250: 2006 (3) SCALE 519: 2006 (3) Supreme 272.

28. Right to Raise Defence of Validity of Licence of Driver of Offending Vehicle – The insurer can take a defence that the driver did not have the requisite driving licence to drive a particular type of vehicle. Such defence can be raised and it will be for the insurer to prove that the insured did not take adequate care and caution to verify genuineness or otherwise of the licence held by the driver. The effect of the evidence in this regard has to be considered by the concerned Tribunal; *National Insurance Corporation Ltd.* v. *Kanti Devi,* AIR 2005 SC 2850: 2005 AIR SCW 3282: 2005 (5) SCC 789: 2005 (5) SCALE 69: 2005 (4) Supreme 1.

29. Duly Licensed does not mean Effective Licence – In section 3 the words used are 'effective licence,' it has been differently worded in section 149(2) *i.e.* 'duly licensed.' If a person does not hold an effective licence as on the date of the accident, he may be liable for prosecution in terms of section 141 of the Act but section 149 pertains to insurance as regard third party risks. A provision of a statute which is penal in nature *vis-a-vis* a provision which is beneficent to a third party must be interpreted differently. It is also well known that the provisions contained in different expressions are ordinarily construed differently. The words 'effective licence' used in section 3, therefore, cannot be imported for sub-section (2) of section 149 of the Motor Vehicles Act; *National Insurance Co. Ltd.* v. *Swaran Singh,* AIR 2004 SC 1531: 2004 AIR SCW 663: JT 2004 (1) SC 109: 2004 (3) SCC 297: 2004 (1) SCALE 180: 2004 (1) Supreme 243.

30. Third Party Risk – The liability is of the insurance company to satisfy the decree passed in favour of third party at the first instance and to recover the awarded amount from the owner or driver thereof. The liability of the insurer is a statutory one. The liability of the insurer to satisfy the decree passed in favour of a third party is also statutory. The insurance company cannot shake off its liability to pay the compensation only by saying that the relevant point of time the vehicle was driven by a person having no licence; *National Insurance Co. Ltd.* v. *Swaran Singh,* AIR 2004 SC 1531: 2004 AIR SCW 663: JT 2004 (1) SC 109: 2004 (3) SCC 297: 2004 (1) SCALE 180: 2004 (1) Supreme 243.

31. Liability of Insurer where Owner Consciously Allowed Driver not Holding Licence – The owner of a motor vehicle in terms of section 5 of the Act has a responsibility to see that no vehicle is driven except by a person who does not satisfy the provisions of section 3 or 4 of the Act. In a case, therefore, where the driver of the vehicle admittedly did not hold any licence and the same was allowed consciously to be driven by the owner of the vehicle by such person, the insurer is entitled to succeed in its defence and avoid liability. The matter, however, may be different where a disputed question of fact arises as to whether the driver had a valid licence or where the owner of the vehicle committed a breach of the terms of the contract of insurance as also the provisions of the Act by consciously allowing any person to drive a vehicle who did not have a valid driving licence; *National Insurance Co. Ltd.* v. *Swaran Singh,* AIR 2004 SC 1531: 2004 AIR SCW 663: JT 2004 (1) SC 109: 2004 (3) SCC 297: 2004 (1) SCALE 180: 2004 (1) Supreme 243.

32. Plying Vehicle without Valid Permit is Infraction of Law – A person without permit to ply a vehicle cannot be placed at a better pedestal *vis-a-vis* one who has a permit, but has violated any condition thereof. Plying of a vehicle without a permit is an infraction. Therefore, in terms of section 149(2) defence is available to the insurer on that aspect. The acceptability of the stand is a matter of adjudication. The insurer would not be liable to pay compensation; *National Insurance Co. Ltd.* v. *Challa Upendra Rao,* AIR 2004 SC 4882: 2004 AIR SCW 5301: JT 2004 (7) SC 519: 2004 (8) SCC 517: 2004 (8) SCALE 90: 2004 (7) Supreme 1.

33. For Recovery of Amount Paid from Owner, Insurer not Required to File Suit – Considering the beneficial object of the Act, it would be proper for the insurer to satisfy the award, though in law it has no liability. In some cases the insurer has been given the option and liberty to recover the amount from the insured. For the purpose of recovering the amount paid from the owner, the insurer shall not be required to file a suit. It may initiate a proceeding before the concerned Executing Court as if the dispute between the insurer and the owner was the subject matter of determination before the Tribunal and the issue is decided against the owner and in favour of the insurer. Before release of the amount to the claimants, owner of the offending vehicle shall furnish security for the entire amount which the insurer will pay to the claimants. The offending vehicle shall be attached, as a part of the security. If necessity arises the Executing Court shall take assistance of the concerned Regional Transport Authority. The Executing Court shall pass appropriate orders in accordance with the law as to the manner in which the owner of the vehicle shall make payment to the insurer. In case there is any default it shall be open to the Executing Court to direct realization by disposal of the securities to be furnished or from any other property or properties of the owner of the vehicle *i.e.* the insured; *National Insurance Co. Ltd.* v. *Challa Upendra Rao,* AIR 2004 SC 4882: 2004 AIR SCW 5301: JT 2004 (7) SC 519: 2004 (8) SCC 517: 2004 (8) SCALE 90: 2004 (7) Supreme 1.

34. No Breach of Condition when Owner Satisfied Driver has Licence and Driving Competently – When an owner is hiring a driver he will therefore have to check whether the driver has a driving licence. If the driver produces a driving licence which on the face of it looks genuine, the owner is not expected to find out whether the licence has in fact been issued by a competent authority or not. The owner would then take the test of the driver. If he finds that the driver is competent to drive the vehicle, he will hire the driver. It is rather strange that Insurance Companies expect owners to make enquiries with RTO's which are spread all over the country, whether the driving licence shown to them is valid or not. Thus where the owner has satisfied himself that the driver has a licence and is driving competently there would be no breach of section 149(2)(a)(ii). The Insurance Company would not then be absolved of liability. If it ultimately turns out that the licence was fake the Insurance Company would continue to remain liable unless then prove that the owner/insured was aware or had noticed that the licence was fake and still permitted that person to drive. More importantly even in such a case the Insurance Company would remain liable to the innocent third party, but it may be able to recover from the insured; *United India Insurance Co. Ltd.* v. *Lehru,* AIR 2003 SC 1292: 2003 AIR SCW 1695: JT 2003 (2) SC 595: 2003 (3) SCC 338: 2003 (3) SCALE 181: 2003 (2) Supreme 768.

35. Remedy of Appeal in Limited Ground – The right of appeal is a statutory right and where the law provides remedy by filing an appeal on limited grounds, the grounds of challenge cannot be enlarged by filing a petition under article 226/227 of the Constitution on the premises that the insurer has limited grounds available for challenging the award given by the Tribunal. Section 149(2) of the Act limits the insurer to file an appeal on those enumerated grounds and the appeal being a product of the statute it is not open to an insurer to take any plea other than those provided under section 149(2) of the Act; *Sadhana Lodh* v. *National Insurance Co. Ltd.,* AIR 2003 SC 1561: 2003 AIR SCW 930: JT 2003 (6) SC 126: 2003 (3) SCC 524: 2003 (1) SCALE 739: 2003 (3) Supreme 189.

36. Insurer cannot Repudiate Claim Solely on Ground Driver not have Valid Licence – The Insurance Company cannot repudiate any and every claim of the insured merely because he had engaged in driver who did not have a valid licence. Law does not empower the Insurance Company to repudiate a claim for damages which has occurred due to acts to which the driver has not. The fire which caused damage to the vehicle occurred due to mechanical failure and not due to any fault or act or omission of the driver. Insurance Company could not have repudiated the claim of the insured solely on the ground that the driver did not have a valid licence at the time of the incident; *Jitendra Kumar* v. *Oriental Insurance Co. Ltd.,* AIR 2003 SC 4161: 2003 AIR SCW 3739: JT 2003 (5) SC 538: 2003 (6) SCC 420: 2003 (5) SCALE 288: 2003 (5) Supreme 69.

37. Subsequent Cancellation of Policy would not Affect Rights of Third Party – Any contract of insurance under Chapter 11 of the Motor Vehicles Act, 1988 contemplates a third party who is not a signatory or a party to the contract of insurance but is, nevertheless, protected by such contract. The rights of the third party to get indemnified can be exercised only against the insurer of the vehicle. It is thus clear that the third party is not concerned and does not come into the picture at all in the matter of payment of premium. Whether the premium has been paid or not is not the concern of the third party who is concerned with the fact there was a policy issued in respect of the vehicle involved in the accident and it is on the basis of this policy that the claim can be maintained by the third party against the insurer. If, on the date of accident, there was a Policy of Insurance in respect of the vehicle in question, the third party would have a claim against the Insurance Company and the owner of the vehicle would have to be indemnified in respect of the claim of that party. Subsequent cancellation of Insurance Policy on the ground of non-payment of premium would not affect the rights already accrued in favour of the third party; *New India Assurance Co. Ltd.* v. *Rula,* AIR 2000 SC 1082: 2000 AIR SCW 788: JT 2000 (3) SC 37: 2000 (3) SCC 195: 2000 (2) SCALE 255: 2000 (2) Supreme 158.

38. Liability Arises Only when Liability of Insured Upheld – The liability of the insurer arises only when the liability of the insured has been upheld for the purpose of indemnifying the insured under the contract of insurance. Thus finding of Court, without assigning any reason, that the owner of the vehicle was not liable and that the insurer alone was liable is erroneous; *Oriental Insurance Co. Ltd.* v. *Sunita Rathi,* AIR 1998 SC 257: 1997 AIR SCW 4228: 1998 (1) SCC 365: 1997 (7) SCALE 469: 1998 (1) Supreme 52.

39. When Liability of Insurer Arise – The liability of the insurer arises only when the liability of the insured has been upheld for the purpose of indemnifying the insured under the contract of insurance; *Oriental Insurance Co. Ltd.* v. *Sunita Rathi,* AIR 1998 SC 257: 1997 AIR SCW 4228: 1998 (1) SCC 365: 1997 (7) SCALE 469: 1998 (1) Supreme 52.

40. Where Certificate of Insurance is Wrongly Granted – If the certificate of insurance is wrongly granted either by reason of any mistake or fraud committed by either of the parties or by its officers, the remedy may be to initiate a separate proceeding for realisation of the amount so paid by it from the owner of the vehicle, but keeping in view the letter and spirit of the Motor Vehicles Act a third party claimant should not suffer therefor; *V. Ravi* v. *New India Assurance Company Ltd.,* AIR 1997 Cal 242: 1998 (1) ACJ 598: 1997 (2) TAC 693.

41. Not Open to Insurer to Question Quantum of Compensation – An insurer cannot take plea beyond the scope of section 149 of the Act. It is not open to the Insurance Company to question the quantum of a compensation; *United India Insurance Co. Ltd.* v. *Shai Sibaqtulla,* I (1992) ACC 472.

42. Person Holding Learner's Licence is also 'Duly Licensed' – A person who is holding a learner's licence is also 'duly licensed' within the meaning of section 149(2)(a)(ii) of the Act. A person holding a learner's licence is also entitled to drive the vehicle, and there has been no violation of the condition in the policy of insurance; *New India Assurance Co. Ltd.* v. *Latha Jayaraj,* II (1991) ACC 303.

43. Defences Available to Insured – The defence that there was sale of the vehicle during the period of cover and the policy had lapsed, is not one of the defences available to the insured under section 149(2) as against the third party claim; *Ghisalal* v. *Nihal Singh,* II (1991) ACC 358.

44. Liability of Insurer Towards Third Party – An Insurance Company is liable to pay compensation in respect of the injury to or death of a third party, caused by a motor accident by a motor vehicle, which is a stage vehicle while plying or being used lawfully otherwise than a stage carriage, at a public place, even if such public place does not lie on the route in respect of which it is permitted to operate as a stage carriage; *K.V. Thimmagowda* v. *Kamalamma,* I (1992) ACC 477.

Even if there is a breach of policy condition, even then the Insurance Company is liable to satisfy the decree at the first instance. But of course, the Insurance Company shall have the right to recover the compensation amount from the owner and/or driver of the offending vehicle; *Oriental Insurance Co. Ltd.* v. *Puran,* AIR 2011 Raj 104.

45. Liability of Insurer – The limit of liability as per the Motor Vehicles Act is as mentioned in the certificate of insurance policy. The certificate of insurance is, therefore, an Act Policy or what is called a policy for Act Liability. The said certificate of insurance has no mention about payment of extra premium by the insured. The effect of non-payment of extra premium is that the insurer cannot be saddled with any extra liability to pay the entire amount of compensation as awarded by the Tribunal in favour of the claimant. The appellant as insurer is not liable to pay the entire compensation amount awarded by the Tribunal but only to the extent under the terms and conditions laid down in the contract between the appellant-insurer and owner-insured, because of the accepted position that the certificate of insurance is an Act Policy only without covering the entire liability of the insured. The impugned judgment and award suffers from infirmity insofar as it has saddled the appellant-insurance company with the entire liability which is not permissible under the law. The matter stands remitted to the Tribunal for determination of the amount of compensation to be born by the appellant-insurance company as per the contract of insurance *i.e.,* the Act Policy under the M.V. Act; *New India Assurance Co.* v. *Nazma Begum,* AIR 2012 Gau 42: 2012 (4) ACJ 216: 2011 (5) Gau LT 287.

Where the policy of insurance is issued by an authorized insurer on receipt of cheque towards payment of premium and such cheque is returned dishonoured, the liability of authorized insurer to indemnify third parties in respect of the liability which that policy covered subsists and it has to satisfy award of compensation by reason of the provisions of sections 147(5) and 149(1) of the Act unless the policy of insurance is cancelled by the authorized insurer and intimation of such cancellation has reached the insured before the accident. In other words, where the policy of insurance is issued by an authorized insurer to cover a vehicle on receipt of the cheque paid towards premium and the cheque gets dishonoured and before the accident of the vehicle occurs, such insurance company cancels the policy of insurance and sends intimation thereof to the owner, the insurance company's liability to indemnify the third parties which that policy covered ceases and the insurance company is not liable to satisfy awards of compensation in respect thereof; *United India Insurance Co. Ltd.* v. *Laxmamma,* AIR 2012 SC 2817: 2012 AIR SCW 2657: (2012) 5 SCC 234.

Since the licence has been granted for a period of 20 years, it can be safely said that the same has been issued for the purpose of a vehicle other than a transport vehicle, as had it been granted for transport vehicle, the tenure thereof could not have exceeded to three years, as per section 14(2)(a) of the Act and since the driver had no licence to drive transport vehicle, in absence of necessary endorsement in his licence to that effect, he could not have driven the offending vehicle and when that vehicle met with an accident, the appellant Insurance company could not be made liable to pay compensation. Thus the appellant-Insurance Company is not liable to pay compensation and that part of the impugned award is hereby set aside. Further it is directed that the liability to pay the compensation involved in the award is of the owner of the offending vehicle. In case any amount deposited by the appellant Insurance Company has been withdrawn by the injured claimants, it will be open for it to recover the same from the owner of the vehicle. However, if the amount, so deposited, has not been withdrawn so far, the appellant shall be allowed to withdraw the same. The claimants are free to execute the award against the owner of the vehicle; *Oriental Insurance Company Ltd.* v. *Shivratan Singh,* AIR 2011 Chht 107.

All places where members of public have an access, for whatever reasons, whether as of right or controlled in any manner whatsoever, would be covered by definition of 'public place' in section 2(34) of the Act. In instant case evidence on record shows that land in question was recorded as 'Nayanjori', abutting public road, to which public had free and easy access same does not cease to be a public place, merely because land stood recorded in name of a private individual. Thus, conclusion is irresistible that land in question, on which accident took place, was a 'public place' and therefore, insurer is liable to pay compensation; *M.K. Bhaumik* v. *Sukura Singh,* AIR 2011 Ori 144.

There was no permit relating to the vehicle and the Insurance Company cannot be held liable for compensation even if the policy was operative at the time of accident. The Insurance Company is exonerated from its liability to pay compensation; *Ram Kumar* v. *Nistor Kindo,* AIR 2011 Chht 126.

The insurance company has felt contended with mere pleading that the driver of offending vehicle did not have effective driving license without any proof to establish such pleadings before the Tribunal. While there can be no dispute with the legal prepositions that the insurance company to be saddled with the liability to indemnify the insured, the driver of the offending vehicle must have a valid and effective driving license, yet in absence of reliable and credit-worthy evidence that the offending vehicle was of a type of different from the vehicle, the respondent was competent to drive, the insurance company cannot wriggle out of its responsibility to indemnify the insured and pay compensation assessed by the Tribunal to the respondents; *National Insurance Co. Ltd.* v. *Fatima,* AIR 2011 J&K 125.

Tractor Trolley is 2680 kilograms, is well within the prescribed limit *i.e.* 7500 kilograms. Therefore, the Tractor-Trolley comes within the purview of Light Motor Vehicles for which no permit endorsing the driver to drive the Tractor was required and as such the driver of the Tractor was having valid and effective driving license on the date of accident to driver the vehicle *i.e.,* LMV and there was no necessity of endorsement authorizing the driver especially to drive the Tractor or a transport vehicle. Thus the Claims Tribunal has committed manifest error of law in exonerating the insurance company and fastening liability upon the owner and driver to pay the compensation. Therefore, it is directed that the owner and driver of the Tractor-Trolley in question, appellants herein, are exonerated from their liability to pay compensation and the Insurance Company is liable to pay compensation. It will be open for the claimants to realize the amount of compensation from the Insurance Company; *Ramdheen Sahu* v. *Thanuram,* AIR 2011 Chht 158.

The accident had occurred before the victim could reach the destination point to purchase their buffaloes. The vehicle had been hired by them only for transporting the goods and they were travelling in this vehicle for this purpose which was the transportation of their goods; even though the goods were not in the vehicle when the vehicle met with the accident but the vehicle was proceeding to reach the place of its destination, in such a scenario it cannot be said that the victims were gratuitous or paid passengers. The vehicle *i.e.,* the canter had been hired by them only for transporting the goods; in such a situation if their vehicle had met with an accident, it had to be deemed that the goods were with them. Liability of insurer extends to the person travelling in vehicle with goods. Thus the insurer is liable to pay compensation; *Oriental Insurance Co. Ltd.* v. *Hazara,* AIR 2012 Del 26.

46. Comprehensive/package Policy Fastened Liability on Insurer – A "comprehensive/package policy" would cover the liability of the insurer for payment of compensation for the occupant in a car. There is no cavil that an "Act Policy" stands on a different footing from a "Comprehensive/Package Policy". As the circulars have made the position very clear and the IRDA, which is presently the statutory authority, has commanded the insurance companies stating that a "Comprehensive/Package Policy" covers the liability, there cannot be any dispute in that regard. The earlier pronouncements were rendered in respect of the "Act Policy" which admittedly cannot cover a third party risk of an occupant in a car. But, if the policy is a "Comprehensive/Package Policy", the liability would be covered. In the case at hand, the policy is an "Act Policy" or "Comprehensive/Package Policy". The policy issued by the insurer only mentions the policy to be a "comprehensive policy" but we are inclined to think that there has to be a scanning of the terms of the entire policy to arrive at the conclusion whether it is really a "package policy" to cover the liability of an occupant in a car. The policy in question is a "Comprehensive/Package Policy", the liability would be fastened on the insurer; *National Insurance Company Ltd.* v. *Balakrishnan,* AIR 2013 SC 473: 2012 AIR SCW 6286: (2013) 1 SCC 731.

47. Liability of Insurer would Depend on Nature of Policy – The policy has not been brought on record. The insurer submit that it is an "Act Policy" while the respondent submit that it may be a "Comprehensive/Package Policy". When Certificate of Insurance is filed but the policy is not brought on record it only conveys that the vehicle is insured. The nature of policy cannot be discerned from the same. Thus, the matter remitted to the tribunal to enable the insurer to produce the policy and grant liberty to the parties to file additional documents and also lead further evidence as advised. The liability of insurer would depend upon the nature of the policy when it is brought on record in a manner as required by law; *Oriental Insurance Company Ltd.* v. *Surendra Nath Loomba,* AIR 2013 SC 483: 2012 AIR SCW 6296: (2012) 11 SCALE 134.

48. Once a Party Insurer Can Raise All Contentions Available to Resist Claim – Where the insurer is a party either on account of being impleaded as a party by the Tribunal under section 170 or being impleaded as a party-respondent by the claimants in the claim petition voluntarily, it will be entitled to contest the matter by raising all grounds, without being restricted to the grounds available under section 149(2). The claim petition is maintainable against the owner and driver without impleading the insurer as a party. When a statutory notice is issued under section 149(2) by the Tribunal, it is clear that such notice is issued not to implead the insurer as a party but merely to put it on notice that a claim has been made in regard to a policy issued by it and that it will have to bear the liability as and when an award is made in regard to such claim. Therefore, it cannot, as of right, require that it should be impleaded as a party. But it can, however, be made a party either by the claimants voluntarily in the claim petition or by the direction of the Tribunal under section 170. Whatever be the reason or ground for the insurer being impleaded as a party, once it is a party, it can raise all contentions that are available to resist the claim; *United India Insurance Co. Ltd.* v. *Shila Datta,* AIR 2012 SC 86: 2011 AIR SCW 6541: (2011) 10 SCC 509.

49. Extent of Liability of Insurer to Indemnify Insured – Mere fact that the insured has taken a comprehensive policy, does not lead to an inference that the Insurance Company is liable of the entire awarded amount including the amount in excess of the statutory liability; *New India Assurance Co. Ltd.* v. *Chameli Devi,* AIR 2010 P&H 156: 2011 (1) ACJ 211: 2011 (2) Pun LR 454.

50. Liability of Insurer to Reimburse Owner of Vehicle – The owner of the vehicle did not come forward to contest the claim petition, but the driver of the offending truck has been held to be guilty of rash and negligent driving which resulted in the death of the deceased. Therefore, the owner of the offending truck is vicariously liable to pay the compensation. The driver of the offending vehicle did not have a valid driving license at the time of the accident. A clear case of breach of policy condition by the owner of the offending vehicle has been established to the hilt by the insurer. Consequently, the insurer is not liable to reimburse the compensation payable by the owner of the vehicle. The Tribunal nevertheless directed the insurer to pay the compensation to the claimant and then recover the same from the insurer; *New India Assurance Co. Ltd.* v. *Smt. Alaka Dutta Baruah,* AIR 2010 Gau 1: 2010 (3) ACC 199: 2010 (2) ACJ 934.

51. Insurer not Liable to Pay Compensation to Pillion Rider – Under the comprehensive policy no separate premium has been paid for covering the pillion passenger paid. Thus the benefit of the notification cannot be availed of in respect of an accident occurred earlier. The benefit should be availed of only in respect of accident occurred after the issue of such notification by addition of the clause mentioned above. There was no intention reflected from the notification to give retrospective effect either expressly or by necessary implication. Therefore, the Insurance Company has no liability to pay the compensation to the pillion rider; *National Insurance Co. Ltd.* v. *Koli Bhayabhai Rajsibhai*, AIR 2012 Guj 109: 2012 (3) ACC 681: 2012 (3) Ker LT 64 (SN).

52. Liability only Coverage of Rider Included in Policy or Rider takes Position of Owner – In terms of the insurance policy the insurance company undertook to indemnify the owner, in case the vehicle which met with an accident was driven by a person with the consent of the owner. This undertaking of the company to indemnify the owner cannot and would not mean that even for the death of such rider or driver, the company would be liable to pay compensation. In other words, what it says is, if a vehicle handed over to a person by consent of the owner results in an accident, then the claims of the 3rd parties against the owner would be indemnified by the insurer. Only in case where the coverage of rider is included in the policy or where the owner of the policy is covered and the permitted rider takes the position of an owner by virtue of terms of contract then alone the insurer would be liable to pay compensation. By virtue of section 149(4), Court has to see whether there has to be a direction to pay and recover. If there are violations of the terms of the policy, the question of pay and recover would arise. When the case of the deceased is not covered under the policy, the question of pay and recover would not arise; *Oriental Insurance Co. Ltd., Kochi* v. *Joseph V.V.*, AIR 2012 Ker 116: 2012 (2) Ker LJ 195: 2012 (2) Ker LT 132.

53. Right of Recovery of Awarded Amount – The insurance policy was valid on the date of the accident and also the driver of the vehicle had a valid driving license to drive the vehicle. Thus the insurance company cannot be granted right of recovery of the awarded amount from the owner of the vehicle; *Divisional Manager, Oriental Insurance Co. Ltd.* v. *Narasingha Mohanta*, AIR 2012 Ori 141.

54. Statutory Obligation to Satisfy Judgments and Awards in Respect of Third Party Risks – To achieve the intended object of ensuring compensation of third party for the loss or damage caused to it or its property, section 149 requires the insurer to satisfy judgments and awards against person in respect of third party risks notwithstanding insurers right to avoid or cancel the Insurance Policy, *inter alia*, because of the breach of specified conditions of policy. Once a Motor Vehicle was found to have been insured against third party risks, the insurer is under a statutory obligation to satisfy judgments and awards against the insured in respect of third party risks. Thus the direction issued by the Tribunal requiring the appellant-Insurance Company to satisfy the Awards and thereafter recover the amount paid to the claimants in terms of the Awards from the insured, cannot be found to suffer from any error of law; *United India Insurance Co. Ltd.* v. *Karam Chand*, AIR 2012 J&K 20: 2012 (2) ACC 366: 2012 (3) ACJ 1661.

55. Third Party Risk – Vehicles Used for Permitted Purpose – Accident when Fitness Certificate Ceased to Exist – Technical Violation – Insurance Company not entitled to take up defence under section 149(2)(a)(i)(c) of the Act, *V.M. Augustine, Vattakavumal* v. *Ayyapankutty*, AIR 2015 Ker 131.

56. 'Duly Licensed' – Driving License Expired on Date of Road Accident and not Renewed Subsequently within Statutory Period – Requirement of 'duly licensed' not fulfilled; *Oriental Insurance Company Limited, Chalakudy, Kochi* v. *Poulose*, AIR 2015 Ker 148.

150. Rights of third parties against insurers on insolvency of the insured.—(1) Where under any contract of insurance effected in accordance with the provisions of this Chapter, a person is insured against liabilities which he may incur to third parties, then—

(a) in the event of the person becoming insolvent or making a composition or arrangement with his creditors, or

(b) where the insured person is a company, in the event of a winding-up order being made or a resolution for a voluntary winding-up being passed with respect to the company or of a receiver or manager of the company's business or undertaking being duly appointed, or of possession being taken by or on behalf of the holders of any debentures secured by a floating charge of any property comprised in or subject to the charge,

if, either before or after that event, any such liability is incurred by the insured person, his rights against the insurer under the contract in respect of the liability shall, notwithstanding anything to the contrary in any provision of law, be transferred to and vest in the third party to whom the liability was so incurred.

(2) Where an order for the administration of the estate of a deceased debtor is made according to the law of insolvency, then, if any debt provable in insolvency is owing by the deceased in respect of a liability to a third party against which he was insured under a contract of insurance in accordance with the provisions of this Chapter, the deceased debtor's rights against the insurer in respect of that liability shall, notwithstanding anything to the contrary in any provision of law, be transferred to and vest in the person to whom the debt is owing.

(3) Any condition in a policy issued for the purposes of this Chapter purporting either directly or indirectly to avoid the policy or to alter the rights of the parties thereunder upon the happening to the insured person of any of the events specified in clause (a) or clause (b) of sub-section (1) or upon the making of an order for the administration of the estate of a deceased debtor according to the law of insolvency shall be of no effect.

(4) Upon a transfer under sub-section (1) or sub-section (2), the insurer shall be under the same liability to the third party as he would have been to the insured person, but—

(a) if the liability of the insurer to the insured person exceeds the liability of the insured person to the third party, nothing in this Chapter shall affect the rights of the insured person against the insurer in respect of the excess, and

(b) if the liability of the insurer to the insured person is less than the liability of the insured person to the third party, nothing in this Chapter shall affect the rights of the third party against the insured person in respect of the balance.

151. Duty to give information as to insurance.—No person against whom a claim is made in respect of any liability referred to in clause (b) of sub-section (1) of section 147 shall on demand by or on behalf of the person making the claim refuse to state whether or not he was insured in respect of that liability by any policy issued under the provisions of this Chapter, or would have been so insured if the insurer had not avoided or cancelled the policy, nor shall he refuse, if he was or would have been so insured, to give such particulars with respect to that policy as were specified in the certificate of insurance issued in respect thereof.

(2) In the event of any person becoming insolvent or making a composition or arrangement with his creditors or in the event of an order being made for the administration of the estate of deceased person according to the law of insolvency, or in the event of a winding up order being made or a resolution for a voluntary winding-up being passed with respect to any company or of a receiver or manager of the company's business or undertaking being duly appointed or of possession being taken by or on behalf of the holders of any debentures secured by a floating charge on any property comprised in or subject to the charge, it shall be the duty of the insolvent debtor, personal representative of the deceased debtor or company, as the case may be, or the official assignee or receiver in insolvency, trustee, liquidator, receiver or manager, or person in possession of the property to give at the request of any person claiming that the insolvent debtor, deceased debtor or company is under such liability to him as is covered by the provisions of this Chapter, such information as may reasonably be required by him for the purpose of ascertaining whether any rights have been transferred to and vested in him by section 150, and for the purpose of enforcing such rights, if any; and any such contract of insurance as purports whether directly or indirectly to avoid the contract or to alter the rights of the parties thereunder upon the giving of such information in the events aforesaid, or otherwise to prohibit or prevent the giving thereof in the said events, shall be of no effect.

(3) If, from the information given to any person in pursuance of sub-section (2) or otherwise, he has reasonable ground for supporting that there have or may have been transferred to him under this Chapter rights against any particular insurer, that insurer shall be subject to the same duty as is imposed by the said sub-section on the persons therein mentioned.

(4) The duty to give the information imposed by this section shall include a duty to allow all contracts of insurance, receipts for premiums, and other relevant documents in the possession or power of the person on whom the duty is so imposed to be inspected and copies thereof to be taken.

152. Settlement between insurers and insured persons.—(1) No settlement made by an insurer in respect of any claim which might be made by a third party in respect of any liability of the nature referred to in clause (b) of sub-section (1) of section 147 shall be valid unless such third party is a party to the settlement.

(2) Where a person who is insured under a policy issued for the purposes of this Chapter has become insolvent, or where, if such insured person is a company, a winding- up order has been made or a resolution for a voluntary winding-up has been passed with respect to the company, no agreement made between the insurer and the insured person after the liability has been incurred to a third party and after the commencement of the insolvency or winding-up, as the case may be, nor any waiver, assignment or other disposition made by or payment made to the insured person after the commencement aforesaid shall be effective to defeat the rights transferred to the third party under this Chapter,

but those rights shall be the same as if no such agreement, waiver, assignment or disposition or payment has been made.

153. Saving in respect of sections 150, 151 and 152.—(1) For the purposes of sections 150, 151 and 152 a reference to "liabilities to third parties" in relation to a person insured under any policy of insurance shall not include a reference to any liability of that person in the capacity of insurer under some other policy of insurance.

(2) The provisions of sections 150, 151, and 152 shall not apply where a company is wound-up voluntarily merely for the purposes of reconstruction or of an amalgamation with another company.

154. Insolvency of insured persons not to affect liability of insured or claims by third parties.—Where a certificate of insurance has been issued to the person by whom a policy has been effected, the happening in relation to any person insured by the policy of any such event as is mentioned in sub-section (1) or sub-section (2) of section 150 shall, notwithstanding anything contained in this Chapter, not affect any liability of that person of the nature referred to in clause (b) of sub-section (1) of section 147; but nothing in this section shall affect any rights against the insurer conferred under the provisions of sections 150, 151 and 152 on the person to whom the liability was incurred.

155. Effect of death on certain causes of action.—Notwithstanding anything contained in section 306 of the Indian Succession Act, 1925 (39 of 1925), the death of a person in whose favour a certificate of insurance had been issued, if it occurs after the happening of an event which has given rise to a claim under the provisions of this Chapter, shall not be a bar to the survival of any cause of action arising out of the said event against his estate or against the insurer.

SYNOPSIS

1. Though Owner Died Cause of Action for Claim Survives
2. Death of Insured – Effect on Cause of Action – Claim Petition would not Abate
3. Death of Insured – Effect on Cause of Action – Section 306, Indian Succession Act cannot Affect Claim Petitions or Appeals if Insured Died after Happening of Event

COMMENTS

1. Though Owner Died Cause of Action for Claim Survives – Abatement of the appeal against the driver on account of his death will not effect the maintainability of appeal in view of the fact that substantive responsibility of payment of compensation awarded is of owner of vehicle and along with that it will be of Insurance Company. Even if the insured (owner) would have died cause of action for claim or enhancement of claim against the estate of insured and against the Insurance Company would have survived under section 155 of the Act; *Suresh* v. *Lokeshagauda,* AIR 1998 Kant 17: 1999 (1) ACJ 165: 1997 (3) Kant LJ 216.

2. Death of Insured – Effect on Cause of Action – Claim Petition would not Abate – Order XXII of the CPC deals with abatement and the provisions of said Order have not been made applicable. Only on this count, the argument of the learned counsel for the appellant merits to be turned down; *United India Insurance Company Limited* v. *Brijbala,* AIR 2015 HP 34.

3. Death of Insured – Effect on Cause of Action – Section 306, Indian Succession Act cannot Affect Claim Petitions or Appeals if Insured Died after Happening of Event – Section 155 of the Motor Vehicles Act provides what is the effect of death of the insured on cause of action. It specifically provides that section 306 of the Indian Succession Act,

1925 (39 of 1925) cannot affect the claim petitions or appeals if the insured has died after the happening of the event; *United India Insurance Company Limited* v. *Brijbala*, AIR 2015 HP 34.

156. Effect of certificate of insurance.—When an insurer has issued a certificate of insurance in respect of a contract of insurance between the insurer and the insured person, then—

(a) if and so long as the policy described in the certificate has not been issued by the insurer to the insured, the insurer shall, as between himself and any other person except the insured, be deemed to have issued to the insured person a policy of insurance conforming in all respects with the description and particulars stated in such certificate; and

(b) if the insurer has issued to the insured the policy described in the certificate, but the actual terms of the policy are less favourable to persons claiming under or by virtue of the policy against the insurer either directly or through the insured than the particulars of the policy as stated in the certificate, the policy shall, as between the insurer and any other person except the insured, be deemed to be in terms conforming in all respects with the particulars stated in the said certificate.

157. Transfer of certificate of insurance.—(1) Where a person in whose favour the certificate of insurance has been issued in accordance with the provisions of this Chapter transfers to another person the ownership of the motor vehicle in respect of which such insurance was taken together with the policy of insurance relating thereto, the certificate of insurance and the policy described in the certificate shall be deemed to have been transferred in favour of the person to whom the motor vehicle is transferred with effect from the date of its transfer.

[1][*Explanation*.—For the removal of doubts, it is hereby declared that such deemed transfer shall include transfer of rights and liabilities of the said certificate of insurance and policy of insurance.]

(2) The transferee shall apply within fourteen days from the date of transfer in the prescribed form to the insurer for making necessary changes in regard to the fact of transfer in the certificate of insurance and the policy described in the certificate in his favour and the insurer shall make the necessary changes in the certificate and the policy of insurance in regard to the transfer of insurance.

SYNOPSIS

1. Liability of Insurer on Failure to Notify Insurer of Fact of Transfer
2. Fiction Limited to Third Party Only
3. Agreement between Insurer and Transferee
4. Intimation Regarding Transfer

COMMENTS

1. Liability of Insurer on Failure to Notify Insurer of Fact of Transfer – The failure of the transferor to notify the insurer of the fact of transfer of ownership of the insured vehicle would hardly affect a third party's claim for compensation. Thus the liability of insurer towards the third party does not get absolved; *United India Insurance Co. Ltd.*,

1. Ins. by Act 54 of 1994, sec. 48 (w.e.f. 14-11-1994).

Shimla v. *Tilak Singh,* AIR 2006 SC 1576: 2006 AIR SCW 1822: 2006 (4) SCC 404: 2006 (4) SCALE 67: 2006 (3) Supreme 332.

2. Fiction Limited to Third Party Only – The fiction of section 157 of the Act is limited to third party risks only. The certificate of insurance to be issued in the prescribed form must, therefore, relate to third party risks. The transferee of the vehicle could not be said to be a third party *qua* the vehicle in question. It is only in respect of third party risks that section 157 of the Act provides that the certificate of insurance together with the policy of insurance described therein "shall be deemed to have been transferred in favour of the person to whom the motor is transferred". If the policy of insurance covers other risks as well, *e.g.*, damage caused to the vehicle of the insured himself, that would be a matter falling outside the provision of the Act *i.e.*, insurance against third party rises and in the realm of contract for which there must be an agreement between the insurer and the transferee, the former undertaking to cover the risk or damage to the vehicle; *Complete Insulations (P) Ltd.* v. *New India Assurance Company Ltd.,* AIR 1996 SC 586: 1995 AIR SCW 4520: 1996 (1) SCC 221.

3. Agreement between Insurer and Transferee – It is only in respect of third party risks that section 157 of the Act provides that the certificate of insurance together with the policy of insurance described therein "shall be deemed to have been transferred in favour of the person to whom the motor vehicle is transferred". If the policy of insurance covers other risks as well, *e.g.*, damage caused to the vehicle of the insured himself, that would be a matter falling outside Chapter XI of the Act and in the realm of contract for which there must be an agreement between the insurer and the transferee, the former undertaking to cover the risk or damage to the vehicle; *Cor plete Insulations (P) Ltd.* v. *New-India Assurance Company Ltd.,* AIR 1996 SC 586: 1995 AIR SCW 4520: (1996) 1 SCC 221.

4. Intimation Regarding Transfer – When vehicle which met with an accident was sold prior to the date of accident and neither the transferor nor the transferee gave any intimation to the Insurance Company about the transfer of the vehicle, the Insurance Company will not be liable. It is only after the Insurance Company is informed of the transfer of vehicle, if anything is not done by the insurer in the matter of effecting transfer of policy, then only the Insurance Company can be made liable; *New India Insurance Co.* v. *V. Parwathy Ammal,* 1989 ACJ 114.

158. Production of certain certificates, licence and permit in certain cases.—(1) Any person driving a motor vehicle in any public place shall, on being so required by a police officer in uniform authorised in this behalf by the State Government, produce—

(a) the certificate of insurance;

(b) the certificate of registration;

(c) the driving licence; and

(d) in the case of a transport vehicle, also the certificate of fitness referred to in section 56 and the permit,

relating to the use of the vehicle.

(2) If, where owing to the presence of a motor vehicle in a public place an accident occurs involving death or bodily injury to another person, the driver of the vehicle does not at the time produce the certificates, driving licence and permit referred to in sub-section (1) to a police officer, he shall produce the said certificates, licence and permit at the police station at which he makes the report required by section 134.

(3) No person shall be liable to conviction under sub-section (1) or sub-section (2) by reason only of the failure to produce the certificate of insurance if, within seven days from the date on which its production was required under sub-section (1), or as the case may be, from the date of occurrence of the accident, he produces the certificate at such police station as may have been specified by him to the police officer who required its production or, as the case may be, to the police officer at the site of the accident or to the officer-in-charge of the police station at which he reported the accident:

Provided that except to such extent and with such modifications as may be prescribed, the provisions of this sub-section shall not apply to the driver of a transport vehicle.

(4) The owner of a motor vehicle shall give such information as he may be required by or on behalf of a police officer empowered in this behalf by the State Government to give for the purpose of determining whether the vehicle was or was not being driven in contravention of section 146 and on any occasion when the driver was required under this section to produce his certificate of insurance.

(5) In this section, the expression "produce his certificate of insurance" means produce for examination the relevant certificate of insurance or such other evidence as may be prescribed that the vehicle was not being driven in contravention of section 146.

[1][(6) As soon as any information regarding any accident involving death or bodily injury to any person is recorded or report under this section is completed by a police officer, the officer incharge of the police station shall forward a copy of the same within thirty days from the date of recording of information or, as the case may be, on completion of such report to the Claims Tribunal having jurisdiction and a copy thereof to the concerned insurer, and where a copy is made available to the owner, he shall also within thirty days of receipt of such report, forward the same to such Claims Tribunal and Insurer.]

SYNOPSIS

1. Forwarding of Information of Accident to Tribunal
2. Expression as soon as Possible – Means
3. Power to Demand Production of Documents
4. Mandatory for Registration of Motor Accident Claim within One Month

COMMENTS

1. Forwarding of Information of Accident to Tribunal – Forwarding of information regarding accident involving death or bodily injury by the Police to the Tribunal is mandatory. Since there is a mandatory requirement to act in the manner provided in section 158(6) there is no justifiable reason as to why the requirement is not being followed. It is, therefore, directed that all the State Governments and the Union Territories shall instruct, if not already done, all concerned police officers about the need to comply with the requirement of section 158(6) keeping in view the requirement indicated in rule 159 and in Form 54; *General Insurance Council* v. *State of Andhra Pradesh*, AIR 2007 SC 2696: 2007 AIR SCW 4873: (2007) 9 SCALE 165.

2. Expression as soon as Possible – Means – Use of the expression 'as soon as' implies that there has to be promptitude in action. To do a thing 'as soon as possible' means to do it within a reasonable time, with an understanding to do it within the shortest

1. Subs. by Act 54 of 1994, sec. 49, for sub-section (6) (w.e.f. 14-11-1994).

possible time. 'As and when' and 'as soon as' are almost synonymous. Whenever these expressions are used in respect of time and place, they denote contemporaneous notion. 'As soon as' and 'forthwith' both are to be normally understood as allowing reasonable time, but latter is more peremptory than the former. But urgency is the hallmark of both expressions. Expression 'as soon as' may be stretched to mean 'as soon as' practicable. It has to be forwarded with promptitude; *General Insurance Council* v. *State of Andhra Pradesh,* AIR 2007 SC 2696: 2007 AIR SCW 4873: (2007) 9 SCALE 165.

3. Power to Demand Production of Documents – The power to demand productions of and to examine the documents cannot be divorced from the purpose behind the conferment of the said power. The purpose is to enable the Police Officers concerned to check such vehicles for the commission of any violation of the provisions of the Act and to take such follow up action as may be necessary. Therefore the power to demand the production of the documents including the permit and the power to impound the same in certain situations preferred to in section 206 as also the power to seize the vehicle in the circumstances mentioned in section 207 are all exercisable by a Police Officer. The very fact that there is an amendment to section 130, sub-section (2) and (3) of the Act, by which the power to ask the conductor to produce his licence has been taken away and conferred upon an officer of the Motor Vehicles Department does not in the least affect the powers of the Police Officers under the aforesaid three provisions. The exercise of power under sections 158, 206 and 207 was in no way dependent upon the availability of the power under section 130(2) so as to make the former redundant in the absence of the later. The Amendment of section 130 sub-section (2) has a very limited effect and does not render the other provisions of the Act particularly sections 158, 206 and 207 nugatory. The power exercisable under the later provisions continues to be available to he Police Officers and could have been therefore legitimately exercised by them; *M.S. Palaksha* v. *Union of India,* AIR 1996 Kant 209: 1996 (2) Kant LJ 256: ILR 1996 Kant 1582.

4. Mandatory for Registration of Motor Accident Claim within One Month – By virtue of sub-section (6) of section 158 of the Act, the Legislature tried to reduce the period of pendency of claim case and quicken the process of determination of compensation by making it mandatory for registration of a motor accident claim within one month of receipt of first information of accident without the claimants having to file a claim petition; *Jai Prakash* v. *National Insurance Co. Ltd.,* (2010) 2 SCC 607: JT 2009 (15) SC 443: (2010) 1 SCALE 8.

159. Production of certificate of Insurance on application for authority to use vehicle.—A State Government may make rules requiring the owner of any motor vehicle when applying whether by payment of a tax or otherwise for authority to use the vehicle in a public place to produce such evidence as may be prescribed by those rules to the effect that either—

(a) on the date when the authority to use the vehicle comes into operation there will be in force the necessary policy of insurance in relation to the use of the vehicle by the applicant or by other persons on his order or with his permission, or

(b) the vehicle is a vehicle to which section 146 does not apply.

160. Duty to furnish particulars of vehicle involved in accident.—A registering authority or the officer-in-charge of a police station shall, if so required by a person who alleges that he is entitled to claim compensation in respect of an accident arising out of the use of a motor vehicle, or if so required by an insurer against whom a claim has been made in respect of any motor vehicle, furnish to that person or to that insurer, as the case may be, on payment of the prescribed fee any information at the disposal of the said authority or the said police officer relating to the identification marks and other particulars of the vehicle and the name and address of the person who was using the vehicle at the time of the accident or was injured by it and the property, if any, damaged in such form and within such time as the Central Government may prescribe.

161. Special provisions as to compensation in case of hit and run motor accident.—(1) For the purposes of this section, section 162 and section 163—

(a) "grievous hurt" shall have the same meaning as in the Indian Penal Code, 1860 (45 of 1860);

(b) "hit and run motor accident" means an accident arising out of the use of a motor vehicle or motor vehicles the identity whereof cannot be ascertained in spite of reasonable efforts for the purpose;

(c) "scheme" means the scheme framed under section 163.

(2) Notwithstanding anything contained in the General Insurance Business (Nationalisation) Act, 1972 (57 of 1972) or any other law for the time being in force or any instrument having the force of law, the General Insurance Corporation of India formed under section 9 of the said Act and the insurance companies for the time being carrying on general insurance business in India shall provide for paying in accordance with the provisions of this Act and the scheme, compensation in respect of the death of, or grievous hurt to, persons resulting from hit and run motor accidents.

(3) Subject to the provisions of this Act and the scheme, there shall be paid as compensation—

(a) in respect of the death of any person resulting from a hit and run motor accident, a fixed sum of [1][twenty-five thousand rupees];

(b) in respect of grievous hurt to any person resulting from a hit and run motor accident, a fixed sum of [2][twelve thousand and five hundred rupees].

(4) The provisions of sub-section (1) of section 166 shall apply for the purpose of making applications for compensation under this section as they apply for the purpose of making applications for compensation referred to in that sub-section.

SYNOPSIS

COMMENTS

1. Case of "Hit-and-Run Motor Accident" – In a claim under section 161 of the Act there must be proof that the identity of the vehicle or vehicles cannot be ascertained in spite of the reasonable efforts in that behalf.. When identity of the vehicle is ascertained it may not *be a* case of "hit-and-run motor accident"; *Theethi* v. *Motor Accidents Claims Tribunal, Palakkad,* AIR 1996 Ker 237: 1995 (2) Ker LJ 751: 1996 ACJ 609.

2. Hit and Run Case – Minimum Compensation – The petition could not have been dismissed in totality. Presuming it to be a hit and run case, the appellants were entitled to at least Rs. 25,000 as per the provisions of section 161(3)(a) of the Motor Vehicles Act.

---

1. Subs. by Act 54 of 1994, sec. 50, for "eight thousand and five hundred rupees" (w.e.f. 14-11-1994).
2. Subs. by Act 54 of 1994, sec. 50, for "two thousand rupees" (w.e.f. 14-11-1994).

Therefore, both the Courts below have obviously failed to note this provision. Both the Courts below have completely erred in giving the finding that it was a hit and run case and that the concerned vehicle belonging to the respondent-owner was not involved in the accident. Insofar as that finding is concerned, the vehicle was involved in an accident with the motorcycle and secondly, the said vehicle was being driven by the respondent-driver. The admission in the pleadings in the order was itself sufficient to hold that the concerned vehicle belonging to the respondent-owner was involved in the accident; *Saroj v. Het Lal*, AIR 2011 SC 671: (2011) 1 SCC 388: 2011 (1) ACJ 552.

162. Refund in certain cases of compensation paid under section 161.—(1) The payment of compensation in respect of the death of, or grievous hurt to, any person under section 161 shall be subject to the condition that if any compensation (hereafter in this sub-section referred to as the other compensation) or other amount in lieu of or by way of satisfaction of a claim for compensation is awarded or paid in respect of such death or grievous hurt under any other provision of this Act or any other law or otherwise so much of the other compensation or other amount aforesaid as is equal to the compensation paid under section 161 shall be refunded to the insurer.

(2) Before awarding compensation in respect of an accident involving the death of, or bodily injury to, any person arising out of the use of a motor vehicle or motor vehicles under any provision of this Act (other than section 161) or any other law, the Tribunal, Court or other authority awarding such compensation shall verify as to whether in respect of such death or bodily injury compensation has already been paid under section 161 or an application for payment of compensation is pending under that section, and such Tribunal, Court or other authority shall,—

(a) if compensation has already been paid under section 161, direct the person liable to pay the compensation awarded by it to refund to the insurer, so much thereof as is required to be refunded in accordance with the provisions of sub-section (1);

(b) if an application for payment of compensation is pending under section 161 forward the particulars as to the compensation awarded by it to the insurer.

Explanation.—For the purpose of this sub-section, an application for compensation under section 161 shall be deemed to be pending—

(i) if such application has been rejected, till the date of the rejection of the application, and

(ii) in any other case, till the date of payment of compensation in pursuance of the application.

163. Scheme for payment of compensation in case of hit and run motor accidents.—(1) The Central Government may, by notification in the Official Gazette, make a scheme[1] specifying, the manner in which the scheme shall be administered by the General Insurance Corporation, the form, manner and the time within which applications for compensation may be made, the officers or authorities to whom such applications may be made, the procedure to be

1. Solatium Scheme, 1989 *vide* S.O. 440 (E), dated 12th June, 1989, published in the Gazette of India, Extra., Pt. II, sec. 3(ii) dated 12th June, 1989. *See Universal's Central Motor Vehicles Rules, 1989 along with allied material.*

followed by such officers or authorities for considering and passing orders on such applications, and all other matters connected with, or incidental to, the administration of the scheme and the payment of compensation.

(2) A scheme made under sub-section (1) may provide that—

(a) a contravention of any provision thereof shall be punishable with imprisonment for such term as may be specified but in no case exceeding three months, or with fine which may extend to such amount as may be specified but in no case exceeding five hundred rupees or with both;

(b) the powers, functions or duties conferred or imposed on any officer or authority by such scheme may be delegated with the prior approval in writing of the Central Government, by such officer or authority to any other officer or authority;

(c) any provision of such scheme may operate with retrospective effect from a date not earlier than the date of establishment of the Solatium Fund under the Motor Vehicles Act, 1939 (4 of 1939) as it stood immediately before the commencement of this Act:

Provided that no such retrospective effect shall be given so as to prejudicially affect the interests of any person who may be governed by such provision.

[1][**163A. Special provisions as to payment of compensation on structured formula basis.**—(1) Notwithstanding anything contained in this Act or in any other law for the time being in force or instrument having the force of law, the owner of the motor vehicle or the authorised insurer shall be liable to pay in the case of death or permanent disablement due to accident arising out of the use of motor vehicle, compensation, as indicated in the Second Schedule, to the legal heirs or the victim, as the case may be.

Explanation.—For the purposes of this sub-section, "permanent disability" shall have the same meaning and extent as in the Workmen's Compensation Act, 1923 (8 of 1923).

(2) In any claim for compensation under sub-section (1), the claimant shall not be required to plead or establish that the death or permanent disablement in respect of which the claim has been made was due to any wrongful act or neglect or default of the owner of the vehicle or vehicles concerned or of any other person.

(3) The Central Government may, keeping in view the cost of living by notification in the Official Gazette, from time to time amend the Second Schedule.]

SYNOPSIS

1. Limits of Statutory Liability Deemed to have been Extended
2. Where Loss of Future Earning Claimed
3. Option to Prefer Claim when Remedy is also in Other Laws
4. Both Owner and Authorised Insurer Liable to Pay Compensation
5. Deduction of 1/3rd Amount from Total Income not always Insisted upon
6. Owner could not be Recipient of Compensation
7. Reference to Workmen's Compensation Act by Incorporation
8. Compensation on Structured Formula Basis
9. Claimants have Option to Proceed under Section 166 or Section 163A
10. Claimants can not Pursue Claims both under Section 163A and Section 166

1. Ins. by Act 54 of 1994, sec. 51 (w.e.f. 14-11-1994).

COMMENTS

1. Limits of Statutory Liability Deemed to have been Extended – By introduction of section 163A, the liability arising thereunder the must now be deemed to have been covered under statutory liability regardless of the pecuniary limit in that regard is specified in policy, or premium charged. In other words, the limits of statutory liability should be deemed to have been extended or enlarged appropriately so as to cover the liability that arises under section 163A. For the said liability, extra premium is not to be charged or specific contract is not required to be entered into. When that is so, it cannot be said that the Insurance Company will have to pay more. However, in some cases, where third party does not come in picture if the Court directs the Insurance Company to pay more than its statutory or contractual liability, as the case may be, it would be open to the Insurance Company under the terms of the contract to recover, from the insured, the excess amount paid pursuant to the order or in execution and discharge of the order of the Court/Tribunal. In case the Insurance Company has to pay more than its liability or risk covered under the policy, to a third party, it can invoke sections 147 and 149(4) or (5) of the Act for the recovery of the amounts paid in excess of the liability; *New India Assurance Co. Ltd.* v. *Muna Maya Basant,* AIR 2001 Guj 304: 2001 (2) ACC 589: 2001 (1) ACJ 940.

2. Where Loss of Future Earning Claimed – If a claim for compensation is made under section 163A by an injured alleging disability, and if the quantum of loss of future earning claimed, falls under the second Schedule to the Act, the Tribunal, may have to apply the principles laid down in Note (5) of the Second Schedule to the Act to determine compensation; *Rai Kumar* v. *Ajay Kumar,* JT 2010 (13) SC 38: (2010) 12 SCALE 265.

3. Option to Prefer Claim when Remedy is also in Other Laws – As per section 163A notwithstanding any thing contained in the Act or in any other law for the time being in force, the owner and insurer of the motor vehicle are made liable to pay the compensation as per the structured formula given in Second Schedule. The words "in any other law for the time being in force" in their sweep certainly cover the Workmen's Compensation Act, 1923. Section 163A therefore permits the employee who is the victim of motor accident in the discharge of his duty or his heirs to claim compensation despite the fact that likewise remedy is available under Workmen's Compensation Act, 1923. The employee has his remedy under both the Acts namely M.V. Act and Workmen's

Compensation Act. Section 167 of the Act in clear terms and unambiguously provides that without prejudice to the provisions of sections 140 to 144, it is open to the victim having the remedy for claim under both the Acts to exercise option either to file the claim petition in M.A.C. Tribunal constituted under the Act or before the Commissioner under the Workmen's Compensation Act, 1923. Section 163A does not fall within the provisions of sections 140 to 144 of the Act. The respondent victims having the right to claim under both the Acts were therefore free to make the choice. When they have as per their right opted to claim under the Act and thereby preferred to have permissible remedial measure available, they cannot be directed to prefer the claim before the Commissioner under Workmen's Compensation Act. To do so would be highly unjust, improper and illegal; "*New India Assurance Co. Ltd.* v. *Muna Maya Basant*, AIR 2001 Guj 304: 2001 (2) ACC 589: 2001 (1) ACJ 940.

4. Both Owner and Authorised Insurer Liable to Pay Compensation – On a bare reading of section 140 it appears that the owner is responsible to pay Rs. 50,000 under the said proceeding to the claimant and under the statute the Insurance Company is not bound to pay and also could not be made responsible to pay such amount. As such, no liability could be fixed upon the Insurance Company directly by any Motor Accident Claims Tribunal. While adjudicating the application under section 140 of the Motor Vehicles Act, the liability of the owner is fixed which also could be revealed on a comparison of section 163A of the said Act, wherein the legislature at their wisdom not only had used the word 'the owner of the motor vehicle' but also added the word 'or the authorized insurer', while fixing the liability of the payment of compensation under the structured formula basis. Furthermore, it appears that under no fault liability, the Motor Vehicles Act identified by section 140 of the Act, fixed liability of limited amount of Rs. 50,000 to the owner concerned whereas under the structured formula higher amount has been fixed by putting the liability upon the owner or authorized insurer under section 163A of the Act. Both the aforesaid two provisions are under 'no fault liability', which means the claimant need not to prove rash and negligent driving of the offending vehicle as the cause of accident. Thus under section 140 of the Motor Vehicles Act, when the legislature at their wisdom did not saddle the Insurance Company with any liability by using the word 'authorized insurer' similar to section 163A of the said Act, the Insurance Company neither could be made a party in proceeding under section 140 of the said Act nor any liability could be fixed upon their shoulder; *National Insurance Co. Ltd.* v. *Krishna Biswas*, AIR 2007 Cal 122: 2007 (4) ALJ (NOC) 604: 2007 (3) TAC 862.

5. Deduction of 1/3rd Amount from Total Income not always Insisted upon – The amount of compensation arrived in the case of fatal accident claims is required to be reduced by one-third in consideration of the expenses which the victim would have incurred towards maintaining himself had he been alive. A person, although alive, but when he is not in a position to move and even for every small thing he has to depend upon the services of another, in our opinion, a direction to deduct 1/3rd of the amount from his total income need not always be insisted upon; *Oriental Insurance Co. Ltd.* v. *Ram Prasad Varma*, AIR 2009 SC 1831: 2009 AIR SCW 1430: 2009 (2) SCC 712: 2009 (1) SCALE 598.

6. Owner could not be Recipient of Compensation – If it is proved that the driver is the owner of the motor vehicle, in that case the owner could not himself be a recipient of compensation as the liability to pay the same is on him. In the case, the deceased was not the owner of the vehicle. He borrowed the said motorbike from its real owner. The deceased cannot be held to be employee of the owner of the motorbike although he was authorised to drive the vehicle by its owner, and therefore, he would step into the shoes of the owner of the motorbike. Accordingly, the legal representatives of the deceased who have stepped into the shoes of the owner of the motor vehicle could not have claimed compensation under section 163-A; *Ningamma* v. *United India Insurance Co. Ltd.*, AIR 2009 SC 3056: 2009 AIR SCW 4916: 2009 (8) SCALE 244.

7. Reference to Workmen's Compensation Act by Incorporation – The reference to Workmen's Compensation Act by incorporation was only for the purpose of sub-section (1) of section 163A. It was not meant to apply in a case falling under section 166 of the Act; *Rajesh Kumar* v. *Yudhvir Singh,* AIR 2008 SC 2396: 2008 AIR SCW 3967: 2008 (7) SCC 305: 2008 (8) SCALE 497.

8. Compensation on Structured Formula Basis – In determining an application for grant of compensation under section 166 of the Act, the Tribunal may be entitled to find out actual loss of damages suffered by the claimants. The formula having not envisaged such a contingency, ordinarily one-third should be deducted from the income of the deceased and not the half thereof; *Mg. Dir. Bangalore Metropolitan Tpt. Corpn.* v. *Sarojamma,* AIR 2008 SC 3244: 2008 AIR SCW 5480: 2008 (5) SCC 142: 2008 (7) SCALE 242.

9. Claimants have Option to Proceed under Section 166 or Section 163A – The victim of an accident or his dependants have an option either to proceed under section 166 or under section 163A. Once they approach the Tribunal under section 166, they have necessarily to take upon themselves the burden of establishing the negligence of the driver or owner of the vehicle concerned. But if they proceed under section 163A, the compensation will be awarded in terms of the Schedule without calling upon the victim or his dependants to establish any negligence or default on the part of the owner of the vehicle or the driver of the vehicle; *Oriental Insurance Co. Ltd.* v. *Meena Variyal,* AIR 2007 SC 1609: 2007 AIR SCW 2362: 2007 (5) SCC 428: 2007 (5) SCALE 269.

10. Claimants can not Pursue Claims both under Section 163A and Section 166 – Section 166 of the Act provides for a complete machinery for laying a claim on fault liability, the question of giving an option to the claimant to pursue their claims either under section 163A or section 166 does not arise. Remedy for payment of compensation both under sections 163A and 166 being final and independent of each other as statutorily provided, a claimant cannot pursue his remedies thereunder simultaneously. One, thus, must opt/to go either for a proceeding under section 163A or under section 166 of the Act, but not under both; *Deepal Girishbhai Soni* v. *United Insurance Co. Ltd., Barod,* AIR 2004 SC 2107: 2004 AIR SCW 1864: JT 2004 (4) SC 83: 2004 (5) SCC 385: 2004 (3) Supreme 602.

11. Assessment of Compensation in Fatal Accident Cases – Even if the formulae for assessment of compensation in Fatal Accident Cases, as indicated in the second Schedule under section 163A of the Motor Vehicles Act, 1988, had to be applied to assess the compensation payable to the petitioners, taking monthly income of the Cleaner at Rs. 4,000, the compensation awardable under the Motor Vehicles Act, would have been in the neighbourhood of Rs. 2.5 lac with suitable adjustment of the multiplier indicated in the second Schedule, in the facts and circumstances of the case. But as the petitioners have been held entitled to compensation not only under the Law of Torts but also for deprivation of the quality of their own life with injured emotions, so the compensation which would have been payable to them under the Motor Vehicles Act, would require suitable increase to compensate them for deprivation of their fundamental right to life too. The respondents are, accordingly, held liable to pay Rs. 3.40 lac to the petitioners as compensation; *S. Prem Singh* v. *State of Jammu and Kashmir,* AIR 2011 J&K 50.

12. Assessment of Compensation by Tribunal – Deceased were aged about 47 and 50 years. Assessment of compensation by adopting multiplier of 13 and 10 is perfectly in accordance with Second Schedule of the Motor Vehicles Act. The compensation assessed and awarded by the Tribunal is proper; *New India Assurance Co. Ltd.* v. *Richa Singh Katiyar,* AIR 2011 All 107.

13. Petition under Section 163A can be Treated as Application under Section 166 – When section 166(4) of the Act envisages that the Tribunal shall treat any report of accidents forwarded to it under section 158(6) of the Act as an application for compensation under the Act, there is nothing wrong in treating an application filed under section 163A of the Act as an application under section 166 of the Act. Considering the object of the Act, the petition filed under section 163A of the Act can be treated as an application under section 166 of the Act. Once it is held that petitions have to be treated under section 166 of the Act, necessarily, the petitioners have to prove that the accident occurred due to rash and negligent driving of the vehicle or that the respondents were negligent in using the vehicle; *Bhupathi Prameela* v. *Superintendent of Police, Vizianagaram*, AIR 2010 AP 189: 2011 (1) ACC 812: 2011 (2) ACJ 861.

14. Determination of Multiplier – The Respondents preferred Miscellaneous Appeal before the High Court for enhancement of amount of compensation stating that the income of the deceased was Rs. 4,500 and not Rs. 3,000 as determined by the Tribunal, and a multiplier of 16 instead of 9 was supposed to be applied. The High Court enhanced the multiplier to 18 instead of 9 and granted expenses to the tune of Rs. 15,000 under conventional heads. Accordingly, the High Court enhanced the amount of compensation from Rs. 1,72,000 to Rs. 3,39,000. It is held that the Tribunal had rightfully applied the multiplier by taking the average age of the parents of the deceased who were 55 and 56 years; *National Insurance Co. Ltd.* v. *Shyam Singh*, AIR 2011 SC 3231: 2011 AIR SCW 4126: (2011) 7 SCC 65.

15. Future Loss of Earning not to be Determined on Basis of any Legal Principle – The claimant was a child at time of accident. She had no earning. What amount could be awarded towards future loss of earning or prospective loss of earning could not have been determined on the basis of any legal principle. Compensation for the injuries suffered by a person in a motor vehicle accident can be determined either on the basis of the actual damages suffered or upon application of the structured formula. The amount of compensation of Rs. 1,20,000 granted by the High Court was adequate even as per structural formula in absence of any evidence having brought on record as to the actual damages; *Priya Vasant Kalgutkar* v. *Murad Shaikh*, AIR 2010 SC 40: 2009 AIR SCW 5492: (2009) 15 SCC 54.

16. Proper Multiplier – According to the Second Schedule appended to the Act for the age of the deceased not exceeding 40 years, the multiplier given is 16. Accordingly the compensation shall be calculated applying the multiplier of 16 and the impugned judgment is modified to this extent. The entire amount of compensation, after adjusting the amount already paid, shall be paid to the appellants with interest at the rate of 7% per annum; *Pushpa* v. *National Insurance Co. Ltd*, AIR 2011 SC 1165: 2011 AIR SCW 3935: 2011 (3) ACJ 2140.

17. Claimant cannot Pursue Remedies under Section 163A and Section 166 Simultaneously – The respondents having obtained compensation, finally determined under section 163A of the Act are precluded from proceeding further with the petition filed under section 166 of the Act. The exception mentioned by the High Court that a petition under section 166 of the Act can be proceeded further if it is filed before passing of an award passed under section 163A of the Act is not supported by the scheme envisaged under sections 163A and 166 of the Act and is contrary to the principles of law laid down by the Supreme Court. Therefore the remedy for payment of compensation both under sections 163A and 166 being final and independent of each other as statutorily provided, a claimant cannot pursue his remedies thereunder simultaneously. Thus a claimant must opt to go either for a proceeding under section 163A or under section 166 of the Act, but he cannot proceed under both of the section; *Oriental Insurance Co. Ltd.* v. *Dhanbai Kanji Gadhvi*, AIR 2011 SC 1138: 2011 AIR SCW 1269: (2011) 2 SCALE 39.

18. Murder is not Accident and Murder is Accident – Difference Between – The difference between a "murder" which is not an accident and a "murder" which is an accident, depends on the proximity of the cause of such murder and if the dominant intention of the act or felony is to kill any particular person then such killing is not an accidental murder but is a murder simpliciter, while if the cause of murder or act of murder was originally not intended and the same was caused in furtherance of any other felonious act then such murder is an accidental murder; *Rita Devi* v. *New India Assurance Company Ltd.*, 2000 (2) GLT (SC) 1: AIR 2000 SC 1930: 2000 AIR SCW 1579.

19. Accidental Murder or Accident – The murder took place while the deceased, as driver has been using the said vehicle and the same is remaining untraced and it reflects that the murder of the deceased driver was not originally intended but it was caused in furtherance of any other felonious act of the person who intended to steal the vehicle and in furtherance of such act, the incident took place and this is an accidental murder. No other view can be taken to brush aside the claim of the respondents under the M.V. Act; *New India Assurance Co.* v. *Nazma Begum*, AIR 2012 Gau 42: 2012 (4) ACJ 216: 2011 (5) Gau LT 287.

20. Re-computation of Income of Deceased – As the Central Government has failed in amending the Second Schedule as provided in sub-section (3) of section 163A of the Act, the Courts/Tribunal can take judicial notice of increase in the prices of essential commodities and the cost of living during the period between the introduction of the Second Schedule in the year 1994 and the date of accident in the given case. The unfortunate accident wherein the claimants' son lost his life took place in the year 2003. If the increase in the prices of the essential commodities and the cost of living between the year 1994 and the year 2003 are taken into consideration, the notional income of Rs. 15,000 prescribed in the Second Schedule in the year 1994 would certainly come to Rs. 30,000 in the year 2003. Therefore, the compensation has been recomputed taking the income of the deceased at Rs. 30,000 per annum; *Jagannath Budhram* v. *Nandlal Prasad Gupta*, AIR 2012 Chht 136.

21. Section 163A does not Apply wherein Owner of Vehicle is Involved – The deceased was driving a motorcycle which was borrowed from its real owner and met with an accident without involving any other vehicle. Since the deceased had stepped into shoes of owner of the vehicle, section 163A of the Act cannot apply wherein owner of the vehicle is involved. Hence the legal representatives of the deceased could not have claimed compensation under section 163A; *Sakun Kushwaha* v. *Dhaniram*, AIR 2011 Chht 103.

22. Section 163A is Founded on Fault Liability Principle – Section 163A(2) is in *pari materia* with section 140(3). In other words, just as in section 140 of the Act, so also under section 163A of the Act, it is not essential for a claimant seeking compensation to "plead or establish", that the accident out of which the claim arises suffers from "wrongful act" or "neglect" or "default" of the offending vehicle. But then, there is no equivalent of section 140(4) in section 163A of the Act. Whereas, under section 140(4), there is a specific bar, whereby the concerned party (owner or insurance company) is precluded from defeating a claim raised under section 140 of the Act, by "pleading and establishing", "wrongful act", "neglect" or "default", there is no such or similar prohibiting clause in section 163A of the Act. The additional negative bar, precluding the defence from defeating a claim for reasons of a "fault" ("wrongful act", "neglect" or "default"), as has been expressly incorporated in section 140(4) of the Act, having not been embodied in section 163A of the Act, has to have a bearing on the interpretation of section 163A of the Act. The presence of section 140(4), and the absence of a similar provision in section 163A, leaves no room for any doubt, that the only object of the legislature in doing so was that the legislature desired to afford liberty to the defence to defeat a claim for compensation raised under section 163A of the Act, by pleading and establishing "wrongful act", "neglect" or "default". Thus, it is open to a concerned party (owner or insurer) to defeat a claim raised under section 163A of the Act, by pleading and establishing anyone of the three "faults", namely, "wrongful act", "neglect" or "default". The object for incorporating section 163A(2) of the Act is, that the burden of pleading and establishing proof of "wrongful act", "neglect" or "default" would not rest on the shoulders of the claimant. The absence of a provision similar to section 140(4) of the Act from section 163A of the Act, is for shifting the *onus* of proof on the grounds of "wrongful act", "neglect" or "default" onto the shoulders of the defence (owner or the insurance company). A claim which can be defeated on the basis of any of the aforesaid considerations, regulated under the "fault" liability principle. Hence section 163A of the Act is founded on the "fault" liability principle; *National Insurance Company Ltd.* v. *Sinitha,* AIR 2012 SC 797: 2012 AIR SCW 10: (2012) 2 SCC 356.

The heading of section 163A reads as "Special Provisions as to Payment of Compensation on Structured Formula Basis". It is abundantly clear that section 163A, introduced a different scheme for expeditious determination of accident claims. Expeditious determination would have reference to a provision wherein litigation was hitherto before (before the insertion of section 163A of the Act) being long drawn. The only such situation (before the insertion of section 163A of the Act) wherein the litigation was long drawn was under Chapter 9 of the Act. Since the provisions under Chapter 9 are structured under the "fault" liability principle, its alternative would also inferentially be founded under the same principle. Section 163A of the Act, catered to shortening the length of litigation, by introducing a scheme regulated by a pre-structured formula to evaluate compensation. It provided for some short-cuts, as for instance, only proof of age and income, need to be established by the claimant to determine the compensation in case of death. There is also not much discretion in the determination of other damages, the limits whereof are also provided for. All in all, one cannot lose sight of the fact, that claims made under section 163A can result in substantial compensation. When taken together the liability may be huge. It is difficult to accept, that the legislature would fasten such a prodigious liability under the "no-fault" liability principle, without reference to the "fault" grounds. When compensation is high, it is legitimate that the insurance company is not fastened with liability when the offending vehicle suffered a "fault" ("wrongful act", "neglect", or "defect") under a valid Act only policy. Even the instant process of reasoning, leads to the inference, that section 163A of the Act is founded under the "fault" liability principle; *National Insurance Company Ltd.* v. *Sinitha,* AIR 2012 SC 797: 2012 AIR SCW 10: (2012) 2 SCC 356.

23. Distinction between Section 163A and Section 140 – Section 163A(2) is in *pari materia* with section 140(3). In other words, just as in section 140 of the Act, so also under section 163A of the Act, it is not essential for a claimant seeking compensation to "plead or establish", that the accident out of which the claim arises suffers from "wrongful act" or "neglect" or "default" of the offending vehicle. But then, there is no equivalent of section 140(4) in section 163A of the Act. Whereas, under section 140(4), there is a specific bar, whereby the concerned party (owner or insurance company) is precluded from defeating a claim raised under section 140 of the Act, by "pleading and establishing", "wrongful act", "neglect" or "default", there is no such or similar prohibiting clause in section 163A of the Act. The additional negative bar, precluding the defence from defeating a claim for reasons of a "fault" ("wrongful act", "neglect" or "default"), as has been expressly incorporated in section 140(4) of the Act, having not been embodied in section 163A of the Act, has to have a bearing on the interpretation of section 163A of the Act. The presence of section 140(4), and the absence of a similar provision in section 163A, leaves no room for any doubt, that the only object of the legislature in doing so was that the legislature desired to afford liberty to the defence to defeat a claim for compensation raised under section 163A of the Act, by pleading and establishing "wrongful act", "neglect" or "default". Thus, it is open to a concerned party (owner or insurer) to defeat a claim raised under section 163A of the Act, by pleading and establishing anyone of the three "faults", namely, "wrongful act", "neglect" or "default". The object for incorporating section 163A(2) of the Act is, that the burden of pleading and establishing proof of "wrongful act", "neglect" or "default" would not rest on the shoulders of the claimant. The absence of a provision similar to section 140(4) of the

Act from section 163A of the Act, is for shifting the onus of proof on the grounds of "wrongful act", "neglect" or "default" onto the shoulders of the defence (owner or the insurance company). A claim which can be defeated on the basis of any of the aforesaid considerations, regulated under the "fault" liability principle. Hence section 163A of the Act is founded on the "fault" liability principle; *National Insurance Company Ltd.* v. *Sinitha,* AIR 2012 SC 797: 2012 AIR SCW 10: (2012) 2 SCC 356.

24. Section 163A of Act has Overriding Effect – Section 163A of the Act has an overriding effect on all other provisions of the Act. In other words, none of the provisions of the Motor Vehicles Act which is in conflict with section 163A of the Act will negate the mandate contained in section 163A of the Act. Therefore, section 163A of the Act shall stand on its own, without being diluted by any provision; *National Insurance Company Ltd.* v. *Sinitha,* AIR 2012 SC 797: 2012 AIR SCW 10: (2012) 2 SCC 356.

25. Compensation under Section 163A of Act not Based on Showing of Absence of Wrongful Act – A claim for compensation raised under section 163A of the Act, need not be based on pleadings or proof at the hands of the claimants showing absence of "wrongful act", being "neglect" or "default". But that is not sufficient to determine that the provision falls under the "fault" liability principle. To decide whether a provision is governed by the "fault" liability principle the converse has also to be established, *i.e.,* whether a claim raised thereunder can be defeated by the concerned party (owner or insurance company) by pleading and proving "wrongful act", "neglect" or "default". Therefore, it is open to the owner or insurance company to defeat a claim under section 163A of the Act by pleading and establishing through cogent evidence a "fault" ground ("wrongful act" or "neglect" or "default"); *National Insurance Company Ltd.* v. *Sinitha,* AIR 2012 SC 797: 2012 AIR SCW 10: (2012) 2 SCC 356.

26. Proof of Negligence of Deceased – The witness for the claimants asserted, that while giving way to a bus coming from opposite side, the motorcycle being ridden by the deceased, hit a large laterite stone lying on the tar road, whereupon, the motorcycle overturned, and the rider and the pillion-rider suffered injuries. The petitioner-insurance company did not produce any witness before the Tribunal. In the absence of evidence to contradict the aforesaid factual position, it is not possible to conclude, that the deceased was "negligent" at the time when the accident occurred. Since no pleading or evidence has been brought to our notice, it is not possible for us to conclude, that the inverse onus which has been placed on the shoulders of the petitioner under section 163A of the Act to establish negligence, has been discharged by it; *National Insurance Company Ltd.* v. *Sinitha,* AIR 2012 SC 797: 2012 AIR SCW 10: (2012) 2 SCC 356.

27. Deceased whether Third Party – The other witnesses, who could have brought out the relationship between the owner and the deceased, were not produced by the petitioner before the Tribunal. The petitioner has, therefore, not discharged the *onus* which rested on its shoulders. Since the relationship between the deceased and the owner has not been established, nor the capacity in which he was riding the vehicle has been brought out, it is not possible to conclude, that the deceased while riding the motorcycle on the fateful day, was an agent, employee or representative of the owner. It was open to the petitioner to defeat the claim for compensation raised by the respondents by establishing, that the rider-deceased represented the owner. Therefore, the claim for compensation cannot be defeated by the insurer stating that the deceased cannot be treated as a third party; *National Insurance Company Ltd.* v. *Sinitha,* AIR 2012 SC 797: 2012 AIR SCW 10: (2012) 2 SCC 356.

28. Difference in Principles in Paying Compensation under Section 163A and Section 166 – The principles relating to determination of liability and quantum of compensation are different for the claims under section 163A and claims made under section 166. The structured formulas as prescribed under Second Schedule and the multiplier mentioned therein is not binding for claims under section 166 of the Act; *Puttamma* v. *K.L. Narayana Reddy,* AIR 2014 SC 706.

29. Necessity of Amending Second Schedule – In view of the fact that the cost of living has gone up manifold and no amendment has been made in the Second Schedule for more than 19 years, specific direction issued to the Central Government through Secretary, Ministry of Road Transport and Highways to make proper amendments to Second Schedule keeping in view the present cost of living, subject to amendment of Second Schedule as proposed by Parliament. Till such amendment is made by Central Government in exercise of power under section 163A(3) of the Act. Children up to age of 5 years shall be entitled to a fixed compensation of Rs. 1 lac and persons more than 5 years of age shall be entitled to a fixed compensation of Rs. 1.50 lacs or such amount as determined in terms of Second Schedule whichever is higher; *Puttamma* v. *K.L. Narayana Reddy*, AIR 2014 SC 706.

30. Compensation – Permanent Disability – Enormity of suffering, pain and agony, loss of enjoyment of life of appellant to be considered; *Kiran* v. *Sajjan Singh*, (2015) 1 SCC 539.

31. Special Food and Nutrition – Non-fatal – Permanent Disability – Compensation enhanced to Rs. 10,000 from Rs. 3,000; *Kiran* v. *Sajjan Singh*, (2015) 1 SCC 539.

32. Future Loss of Income – Non-fatal – Permanent Disability – Child's notional income cannot be ascertained as per figure for non-earning individuals – Award of Rs. 1 lac towards shock, pain and suffering (non-pecuniary head) in place of future income due to permanent disability; *Kiran* v. *Sajjan Singh*, (2015) 1 SCC 539.

33. Non-fatal – Permanent Disability 30% and 20% Due to Shortening of Right Leg by 1 Inch – Age just over 10 and 15 years. Rs. 25,000 awarded each towards agony to parents and Rs. 25,000 each towards future medical expenses; *Kiran* v. *Sajjan Singh*, (2015) 1 SCC 539.

34. Driving License – Valid license to Drive Light Motor Vehicle – Driver authorised to drive light goods vehicle; *Ashvinbhai Jayantilal Modi* v. *Ramkaran Ramchandra Sharma*, (2015) 2 SCC 180.

35. Driving License – No Breach of any Condition of Insurance Policy – Insurance company cannot disown liability; *Ashvinbhai Jayantilal Modi* v. *Ramkaran Ramchandra Sharma*, (2015) 2 SCC 180.

[1][**163B. Option to file claim in certain cases.**—Where a person is entitled to claim compensation under section 140 and section 163A, he shall file the claim under either of the said sections and not under both.]

164. Power of Central Government to make rules.—(1) The Central Government may make rules for the purpose of carrying into effect the provisions of this Chapter, other than the matters specified in section 159.

(2) Without prejudice to the generality of the foregoing power, such rules may provide for—

(a) the forms to be used for the purposes of this Chapter;

(b) the making of applications for and the issue of certificates of insurance;

(c) the issue of duplicates to replace certificates of insurance lost, destroyed or mutilated;

(d) the custody, production, cancellation and surrender of certificates of insurance;

(e) the records to be maintained by insurers of policies of insurance issued under this Chapter;

(f) the identification by certificates or otherwise of persons or vehicles exempted from the provisions of this Chapter;

1. Ins. by Act 54 of 1994, sec. 51 (w.e.f. 14-11-1994).

(g) the furnishing of information respecting policies of insurance by insurers;

(h) adopting the provisions of this Chapter to vehicles brought into India by persons making only a temporary stay therein or to vehicles registered in a reciprocating country and operating on any route or within any area in India by applying those provisions with prescribed modifications;

(i) the form in which and the time limit within which the particulars referred to in section 160 may be furnished; and

(j) any other matter which is to be, or may be, prescribed.

CHAPTER XII

CLAIMS TRIBUNALS

165. Claims Tribunals.—(1) A State Government may, by notification in the Official Gazette, constitute one or more Motor Accidents Claims Tribunals (hereafter in this Chapter referred to as Claims Tribunal) for such area as may be specified in the notification for the purpose of adjudicating upon claims for compensation in respect of accidents involving the death of, or bodily injury to, persons arising out of the use of motor vehicles, or damages to any property of a third party so arising, or both.

Explanation.—For the removal of doubts, it is hereby declared that the expression "claims for compensation in respect of accidents involving the death of or bodily injury to persons arising out of the use of motor vehicles" includes claims for compensation under section 140 [1][and section 163A].

(2) A Claims Tribunal shall consist of such number of members as the State Government may think fit to appoint and where it consists of two or more members, one of them shall be appointed as the Chairman thereof.

(3) A person shall not be qualified for appointment as a member of a Claims Tribunal unless he—

(a) is, or has been, a Judge of a High Court, or

(b) is, or has been a District Judge, or

(c) is qualified for appointment as a High Court Judge [1][or as a District Judge].

(4) Where two or more Claims Tribunals are constituted for any area, the State Government, may by general or special order, regulate the distribution of business among them.

SYNOPSIS

1. Jurisdiction of Claims Tribunal
2. Tribunal is Alternative Forum
3. Option Lies with Claimant to Refer Claim to Civil Court
4. Jurisdiction to Award Compensation against Joint Tortfeasor
5. Jurisdiction to Decide Claims Arising Out of Negligence
6. Tribunal once Concluded Accident by Use of Vehicle has to Award Compensation
7. Claims Tribunal is Civil Court of Limited Jurisdiction
8. Phrase "any Property of Third Party" – Meaning
9. Claims Tribunal is not Civil Court

1. Added by Act 54 of 1994, sec. 52 (w.e.f. 14-11-1994).

COMMENTS

1. Jurisdiction of Claims Tribunal – The Claims Tribunal constituted under section 165 read with section 168 is empowered to adjudicate all claims in respect of the accidents involving death or of bodily injury or damage to property of third party arising in use of motor vehicle. The said power of the Tribunal is not restricted to decide the claims inter se between claimant or claimants on one side and insured, insurer and driver on the other. In the course of adjudicating the claim for compensation and to decide the availability of defence or defences to the insurer, the Tribunal has necessarily the power and jurisdiction to decide disputes *inter se* between insurer and the insured. The decision rendered on the claims and disputes inter se between the insurer and insured in the course of adjudication of claim for compensation by the claimants and the award made thereon is enforceable and executable in the same manner as provided in section 174 of the Act for enforcement and execution of the award in favour of the claimants; *National Insurance Co. Ltd.* v. *Swaran Singh,* AIR 2004 SC 1531: 2004 AIR SCW 663: JT 2004 (1) SC 109: 2004 (3) SCC 297: 2004 (1) SCALE 180: 2004 (1) Supreme 243.

2. Tribunal is Alternative Forum – The Tribunal under Motor Vehicles Act is clearly an alternative forum in substitution for the Civil Court for adjudicating upon claims for compensation arising out of the "use of motor vehicles". This is further made clear from section 110F of the Act which states that no Civil Court shall entertain any question "relating to any claims for compensation which may be adjudicated upon by the Claims Tribunal". When one is concerned only with section 110(1) and when section 110B does not and cannot control section 110(1), a claim is entertainable by the Tribunal, if it arises out of the use of a motor vehicle and if it is claimed against persons or agencies other than the driver, owner or insurer of the vehicle provided in tort, such other persons or agencies are also claimed to be liable as joint tort-feasors. It is obvious that prior to the constitution of the Tribunal, such compensation could be decreed by the Civil Court not only against the owner/driver and insurer of the motor vehicle but also against others who are found to be joint tort feasors; *Union of India* v. *United India Insurance Co. Ltd.,* AIR 1998 SC 640: 1998 AIR SCW 245: JT 1997 (8) SC 653: 1997 (8) SCC 683: 1997 (9) Supreme 69.

The claim for compensation is maintainable before the Tribunal against other persons or agencies which are held to be guilty of composite negligence or are joint tort feasors, and if arising out of use of the motor vehicle. The Tribunal under the Act is clearly an alternative forum in substitution for the Civil Court for adjudicating upon claims for compensation arising out of the "use of motor vehicles". This is further made clear from section 110F of the Act which states that no Civil Court shall entertain any question "relating to any claims for compensation which may be adjudicated upon by the Claims Tribunal"; *Union of India* v. *United India Insurance Co. Ltd.,* AIR 1998 SC 640: 1998 AIR SCW 245: JT 1997 (8) SC 653: 1997 (8) SCC 683: 1997 (9) Supreme 69.

3. Option Lies with Claimant to Refer Claim to Civil Court – Option lies with the claimant to refer his claim to a civil court for adjudication where the claim relates to damages to property exceeding Rs. 2000 and where such reference has been made, the Tribunal ceases to have jurisdiction in respect of such claim; *National Insurance Co. Ltd.* v. *Union of India,* 1989 ACJ 307 (J&K).

4. Jurisdiction to Award Compensation against Joint Tortfeasor – Where an application is filed before a Claims Tribunal for compensation in respect of accidents involving the death or bodily injury to persons arising out of the use of Motor Vehicle and the claims is made both against the insurer, owner and driver of the motor vehicle as well as the other joint tortfeasors, if a finding on hearing is reached that it is solely the negligence of the joint tortfeasor and not the driver of the motor vehicle the Tribunal would not loose the jurisdiction to award compensation against the joint tortfeasor; *Union of India* v. *Bhagwati Prasad,* AIR 2002 SC 1301: 2002 AIR SCW 1112: JT 2002 (3) SC 10: 2002 (3) SCC 661: 2002 (2) SCALE 487: 2002 (2) Supreme 272.

5. Jurisdiction to Decide Claims Arising Out of Negligence – The jurisdiction of the Tribunal is not restricted to decide claims arising out of negligence in the use of motor vehicles. Negligence is only one of the species of the causes of action for making a claim for compensation in respect of accidents arising out of the use of motor vehicles. Where deceased was knocked down by jeep when its front tyre burst and consequently the vehicle became dis-balanced and turned turtle, the owner can be made vicariously liable for damages to dependants of victim even if there is no negligence on part of driver or owner of motor vehicle. Even apart from section 140 which envisages no fault liability claim for compensation can be sustained by applying Rule in *Rylands* v. *Fletcher,* (1861-73) All ER (Reprint) 1 unless any one of exceptions to Rule can be applied; *S. Kaushnuma Begum* v. *New India Assurance Co. Ltd.,* 2001 AIR SCW 85: AIR 2001 SC 485: 2001 AIR SCW 85: JT 2001 (1) SC 375: 2001 (2) SCC 9: 2001 (1) SCALE 1: 2001 (1) Supreme 5.

6. Tribunal once Concluded Accident by Use of Vehicle has to Award Compensation – The driver of the vehicle alone need not be rash and negligent in driving the vehicle, but if there is any negligent act on the part of the owner of the vehicle or on the part of the persons responsible for plying the vehicle, it also amounts to rash and negligent driving. For example, when a river is flowing and if the owner or conductor of a vehicle asks the driver of the vehicle to pass through the river and the vehicle capsized in the middle of the river, then the owner or the manager of the vehicle cannot escape from liability as it also amounts to rash and negligent driving of the vehicle. To be more clear, for example, if a road is under repair or a bridge is about to collapse, knowing very well the condition of the road or bridge, asking the driver to pass through such road or bridge also amounts to rash and negligent driving. In the present case the higher police officials had taken a bus with police personnels into forest area where extremists were moving. Taking a bus with police personnel into the forest area where extremists are moving without proper care and precaution is nothing but a negligent act by the police higher officials. Normally, the practice is to do combing operation by walk or by motorcycles. The Act of the superior police officers, without visualizing the consequences and asking the police personnel to travel by bus into the forest area, is nothing but a 'negligent act'. What is required to be seen is whether the claimants are entitled for compensation or not and what is just and reasonable compensation to be awarded. Under the circumstances of the case, if once the Tribunal comes to a conclusion that the accident occurred by use of vehicle in public place and if the claimants are entitled for compensation, the Tribunal has a point to award compensation. Thus, when death of driver and police constable took place due to blasting of vehicle by extremists, the Police Department would be liable to pay compensation; *Bhupathi Prameela* v. *Superintendent of Police, Vizianagaram,* AIR 2010 AP 189: 2011 (1) ACC 812: 2011 (2) ACJ 861.

7. Claims Tribunal is Civil Court of Limited Jurisdiction – A Motor Accident Claims Tribunal constituted under the Motor Vehicles Act, 1988 is a Civil Court of limited jurisdiction, and is certainly not a Court of Record. Therefore, the principle of sanctity of recitals in court proceedings is available to a Court of Record. This principle cannot be stretched to the proceedings of a Tribunal; *Oriental Insurance Co. Ltd.* v. *Vithabai,* AIR 2011 SC 2838: 2011 AIR SCW 4235: (2011) 7 SCALE 1.

8. Phrase "any Property of Third Party" – Meaning – The phrase "Any property of a third party" occurring in sections 147 and 165 of the Motor Vehicles Act will mean property which is outside the goods vehicle and not being carried in the goods vehicle; *Jagdish Chand Sharma* v. *Bachan Singh,* AIR 2010 HP 49: 2011 (1) ACC 144: 2010 (2) ACJ 1229.

9. Claims Tribunal is not Civil Court – Neither the language of the relevant provisions of the Motor Vehicles Act nor the Rules framed thereunder suggest that the Claims Tribunal was constituted as a civil Court. In fact it is constituted as an Administrative Authority and has no trappings or attributes of a civil Court. It, therefore, follows that the Claims Tribunal is not a civil Court subordinate to the High Court or subject to its revisional jurisdiction; *Abdul Gaffar Gujree* v. *Mohammad Phaphoo,* AIR 1985 J&K 26: 1984 Kash LJ 310: 1985 ACJ 556.

The Claims Tribunal is not constituted as a civil Court. It is constituted as an Administrative Authority and has no trappings or attributes of a civil Court. Therefore, the Claims Tribunal is not a civil Court subordinate to the High Court or subject to its revisional jurisdiction. Thus even if section 115 of Code of Civil Procedure (CPC) would be applicable still revision against such order is barred. Section 115(2) of CPC provides that High Court shall not under this section vary or reverse any order against which appeal lies to the High Court; *Hans Raj Bhagat* v. *State,* AIR 2013 J&K 15: 2013 (3) ACJ 1834: 2013 (1) TAC 679.

166. Application for compensation.—(1) An application for compensation arising out of an accident of the nature specified in sub-section (1) of section 165 may be made—

(a) by the person who has sustained the injury; or

(b) by the owner of the property; or

(c) where death has resulted from the accident, by all or any of the legal representatives of the deceased; or

(d) by any agent duly authorised by the person injured or all or any of the legal representatives of the deceased, as the case may be:

Provided that where all the legal representatives of the deceased have not joined in any such application for compensation, the application shall be made on behalf of or for the benefit of all the legal representatives of the deceased and the legal representatives who have not so joined, shall be impleaded as respondents to the application.

[1][(2) Every application under sub-section (1) shall be made, at the option of the claimant, either to the Claims Tribunal having jurisdiction over the area in which the accident occurred, or to the Claims Tribunal within the local limits of whose jurisdiction the claimant resides or carries on business or within the local limits of whose jurisdiction the defendant resides, and shall be in such form and contain such particulars as may be prescribed:

Provided that where no claim for compensation under section 140 is made in such application, the application shall contain a separate statement to that effect immediately before the signature of the applicant.]

[2][***]

[3][(4) The Claims Tribunal shall treat any report of accidents forwarded to it under sub-section (6) of section 158 as an application for compensation under this Act.]

SYNOPSIS

1. Just Compensation in Absence of Evidence
2. Prove of Negligence on Part of Driver
3. Legal Representatives are Entitled to Payment of Compensation
4. Application of Multiplier Method
5. Manner of Arriving Damages
6. Who can Claim Compensation
7. Claim Petition not Maintainable as Availed Benefits under ESI Act

1. Subs. by Act 54 of 1994, sec. 53, for sub-section (2) (w.e.f. 14-11-1994).
2. Sub-section (3) omitted by Act 53 of 1994, sec. 53 (w.e.f. 14-11-1994).
3. Subs. by Act 54 of 1994, sec. 53, for sub-section (4) (w.e.f. 14-11-1994).

COMMENTS

1. Just Compensation in Absence of Evidence – All the claimants appearing before the MACT should act promptly in prosecuting their matters so that expeditious disposal of the compensation cases can take place. However, at the same time, the Tribunals dealing with the compensation cases needs to be cautioned for not showing any kind of undue haste in disposing such matters. The compensation cases are to be dealt with not merely keeping in view the sound legal principles but with human compassion as well. In the instant case, a death of young boy has taken place and the Tribunal in utter haste has dismissed the compensation petition in the absence of evidence led by the appellants. The hasty approach of the Tribunal deserves to be deprecated. The Act being a beneficent legislation deserves a liberal construction and the remedy to the claimants against tortfeasor for obtaining just compensation cannot be taken away on account of the fact that the appellants failed to lead any evidence; *Kapur Chand* v. *Raj Kumar Yadav*, AIR 2008 Del 74: 2007 (4) ACC 586: 2008 AIHC 365 (NOC).

2. Prove of Negligence on Part of Driver – Before allowing conversion of the petition under section 166 to section 163A of the Motor Vehicles Act, the tribunal had framed issues arising out of the pleading of the parties, wherein the first issue framed by the tribunal relates to the aspect of rash and negligent driving of the offending bus. The tribunal while taking into account the evidence adduced by the parties as well as FIR came to the conclusion that the accident had occurred due to the rash and negligent driving of the bus. At the time of passing the award, tribunal had perhaps lost sight of the fact that once the petition was converted from section 166 to section 163A of the Act, there was no requirement to prove the rash and negligent act of the driver of the offending vehicle. After the conversion of the petition from section 166 to section 163A of the Act, the negligence on the part of the driver of the offending vehicle was not required to be proved; *Delhi Transport Corpn.* v. *Kamla Devi*, AIR 2008 Del 157: 2008 AIHC 830 (NOC): 2008 (5) ALJ (NOC) 1135.

3. Legal Representatives are Entitled to Payment of Compensation – The contention raised by the appellant that the brothers of the deceased not being dependent have no right to file a claim in share in the compensation awarded by the MACT cannot be accepted. The respondent brothers of the deceased are legal representatives within the definition given under section 2(11) of the CPC and also section 2(1)(g) of the Arbitration and Conciliation Act, 1966. Accordingly, such legal representatives would be entitled to make a claim for compensation under section 166 of the Act and the Tribunal was right to declare them as persons entitled to payment of compensation although they were not dependents of the deceased; *Hafizun Begum* v. *Member, Motor Accident Claims Tribunal*, AIR 2009 Gau 4: 2009 (4) ACJ 2329: 2009 AIHC 135 (NOC).

4. Application of Multiplier Method – The multiplier method involves the ascertainment of the loss of dependency or the multiplicand having regard to the circumstances of the case and capitalizing the multiplicand by an appropriate multiplier. The choice of the multiplier is determined by the age of the deceased or that of the claimants whichever is higher and by the calculation as to what capital sum, if invested at a rate of interest appropriate to a stable economy, would yield the multiplicand by way of annual interest. In ascertaining this, regard should also be had to the fact that ultimately the capital sum should also be consumed-up over the period for which the dependency is expected to last; *General Manager, Punjab Roadways, Nangal Depot* v. *Santosh Chadha*, AIR 1997 HP 36: 1998 (1) ACJ 608: 1997 (2) LJR 592.

5. Manner of Arriving Damages – For assessment of damages to compensate the dependants, it has to take into account many imponderables, e.g., the life expectancy of the deceased and the dependants, the amount that the deceased would have earned during the remainder of his life, the amount that he would have contributed to the dependants during that period, the chances that the deceased may not have lived or the dependants may not live up to the estimated remaining period of their life expectancy, the chances that the deceased might have got better employment or income or might have lost his employment or income altogether. The manner of arriving at the damages is to ascertain the net income of the deceased available for the support of himself and his dependants, and to deduct therefrom such part of his income as the deceased was accustomed to spend upon himself, as regards both self-maintenance and pleasure, and to ascertain what part of his net income the deceased was accustomed to spend for the benefit of the dependants. Then that should be capitalised by multiplying it by a figure representing the proper number of year's; *General Manager, Punjab Roadways, Nangal Depot* v. *Santosh Chadha*, AIR 1997 HP 36: 1998 (1) ACJ 608: 1997 (2) LJR 592.

6. Who can Claim Compensation – The sisters and brother of a person, who dies in a motor vehicle accident, are entitled to maintain a petition under section 166 of the Act, if they are legal representatives of the deceased. Under section 166(1)(a) of the Act, a claim can be made by any person, who suffered on account of accident arising out of the use of a motor vehicle. Such person would include those who lost dependency, consortium and any other kind of support as a consequence of death of the person in the accident. Section 166(1)(c) relates to claim of legal representatives of the person killed in the accident in respect of the loss or damages ensured to the estate of the deceased; *Gian Singh* v. *Ram Krishan Kohli*, AIR 2002 J&K 82: 2004 (2) ACC 90: 2003 (3) ACJ 1914.

7. Claim Petition not Maintainable as Availed Benefits under ESI Act – The petitioner met with an accident during the course of his employment and the injury sustained being an employment injury he availed benefit of obtaining treatment in the ESI Hospital and he has received certain monetary benefits from the ESI Corporation. As per under sections 53 and 61 of the ESI Act, the petitioner cannot received or recover any compensation or damages, under any other law, other than those available to him under ESI Act. Thus the claim petition under section 166 of M.V. Act is not maintainable for want of jurisdiction; *S.G. Pandu* v. *United India Insurance Company Ltd.*, AIR 2009 Kant 33: 2009 AIHC 889: 2009 (2) ALJ (NOC) 361.

8. Damage to Goods in Transit Claim under MV Act not Maintainable – The tempo met with an accident and the grape load of the petitioner was damaged. The petitioner has to make a claim as per the provisions of the Common Carrier Act. The provisions of section 147 obligates the insurer with liability in respect the damage to third party property, death or personal injuries to the third party and to the inmates of the vehicle but not with respect of the damage to goods in transit. The remedy for the petitioner would be under the Common Carriers Act and before the Civil Court. The provisions of section 166 do not permit a claim before the Tribunal under the M.V. Act in respect of property in transit; *Oriental Fire and General Insurance Co. Ltd.* v. *S. Rasheed Ahammad*, AIR 2006 Kant 158: 2006 AIHC 129 (NOC): 2006 (2) Kant LJ 473.

9. Claim by Second Wife whose Marriage is Void not Maintainable – The subsequent marriage being void, the second wife would not be entitled to succeed to the estate of the deceased under the Hindu Succession Act and therefore could not be termed as legal representatives representing the estate of the deceased. Thus claim petitions for grant of compensation would not be maintainable under section 166(c) of the Motor Vehicles Act on their behalf; *Parvathamma* v. *C. Subramanyam*, AIR 2000 Kant 309: 2000 (6) Kant LJ 322: 2001 (1) ACJ 876.

10. Depression Consequent to Injuries Resulted in Suicide: Legal Representative Entitled to Claim – Before the accident, the deceased had no depression. There is no evidence to the effect that the deceased has suffered depression leading to suicide or any other psychological disorder before the accident. He was a happy family man before the dreadful accident. His severe depression and worthless-ness and helplessness came after the accident in view of the accidental injuries. In his severe depressed state, he felt that he was a greater burden to his relative's life. His depression, resulted in the suicide.

Therefore, compensation should be given to the legal representative for the death as death was caused due to the mental depression developed consequent to the injuries, but, on the facts and circumstances of this case, a reduction has been given; *Venugopal Narayanan Nair* v. *T.L. Paulson,* AIR 2009 Ker 86: 2009 AIHC 537 (NOC0: 2008 (3) Ker LJ 817.

11. No Negligence on Part of Owner or Driver – Not Liable to Pay Compensation – The bus was blocked by persons armed with weapons and bombs and because of bomb blast passengers were injured. There is no negligence on the part of the driver or owner. By applying the rule of strict liability, the driver or owner cannot be held liable to pay compensation. *Onus* to prove negligence on part of driver or owner was rests upon the claimant but not proved. Thus claim petition under section 166 is not maintainable, but claimant are entitled to claim under sections 163A, 140; *Shaju* v. *A.V. Babu,* AIR 2008 Ker 79: 2008 AIHC 323 (NOC): 2008 (2) ACJ 1228.

12. Who are Legal Representative – Ordinarily, heirs of the deceased are the persons who represent the estate of the deceased and must be taken to be his legal representatives. A legal representative in a given case need not necessarily be the wife, husband, parent and child. Thus in case of death of a person in a motor vehicle accident, compensation can be claimed only by the legal representatives. They may claim besides special damages etc., compensation for economic loss and loss to the estates. A brother of the deceased may be a legal representative of the deceased in the absence of preferential heirs under the personal law governing the parties and if so, he can claim compensation. But he cannot do so, if he is not a legal representative entitled to succeed to the estate of the deceased. This is so even if as a matter of fact they were dependent on the deceased for financial help; *P.N. Unni* v. *Baby John,* AIR 2008 Ker 157: 2008 AIHC 522 (NOC): 2008 (1) Ker LJ 678.

13. Remedy when Claim Dismissed for Default – When the claim is dismissed for default, parties will be free to approach the Tribunal to set aside such orders by filing application under Order IX, rule 9. But, if the Tribunal decides the matter on merit *suo motu* collecting evidence, the only remedy open to the claimant will be to file an appeal before the High Court as provided under section 173 of the Act; *Jacob Thomas* v. *C. Pandian,* AIR 2006 Ker 77: 2006 AIHC 1265: 2006 (3) ALJ 199: 2005 (3) Ker LJ 331.

14. Word "Injury" – Meaning – The word 'injury' cannot be confined to bodily injury or physical injury alone. If the word 'injury' is intended to be understood as bodily injury alone the Legislature would have used the expression "bodily injury" in the section 166(1) (a) of the Act, especially when such an expression has been used in section 165(1). The meaning of the word "injury" in section 166(1)(a) cannot be restricted to physical injury alone particularly since such an interpretation would not be congenial to the interest of those who, though not legal representatives, are entitled to compensation on account of death of the victim of the motor accidents. Thus a claim can be made by any person who suffered on account of accident arising out of the use of a motor vehicle. Such person would include those who lost dependency, consortium and any other kind of support as a consequence of death of the victim in the accident; *Kallidukkil Cheriyakutty Mammi* v. *Thoniyadath Ummer Kutty,* AIR 1996 Ker 182: 1995 (2) Ker LJ 399: 1995 (2) Ker LT 555.

15. Brother of Deceased can Claim Compensation – The words 'legal representative' that occurred in section 110A of the Act have wider meaning. Thus, a brother can maintain an application for grant of compensation and at his instance the claim petition is entertainable; *Mahant Shyamdas Guru Mohandas* v. *Lalaram M. Kori,* AIR 2008 MP 47: 2008 AIHC 220 (NOC): 2008 (3) ACJ 1783.

16. Dependent brother of Deceased Entitled to Compensation – If the bread winner of the family dies on account of motor accident other person in the family who are dependent upon him entitled to claim compensation. The younger brother of the deceased is a handicapped person dependent upon the earning of the deceased. Accordingly, it has to be held that he was dependent upon his elder brother, it was the deceased who was maintaining him and because of the accident he has suffered adversely on account of death of his brother and therefore, is entitled to seek compensation; *Amna* v. *Royal Transport Services*, AIR 2008 MP 213: 2008 AIHC 745 (NOC): 2008 (1) MPLJ 334.

17. Legal Representative Entitled to Claim if Death Resulted from Accident – Section 166 of the Act provides that a legal representative of the deceased can also file claim where death has resulted from the accident. Thus, in a case of personal injury not resulting in death the legal representative of such person who was injured and who dies subsequently not on account of accident but for some other reason cannot maintain an application for compensation for personal injury sustained in an accident under sub-section (1) of section 166 of the Act. Therefore, a claim for personal injury filed under section 166 of the Act would abate on the death of the claimant and would not survive to his legal representatives except as regards the claim for pecuniary loss to the estate of the claimant; *Bhagwati Bai* v. *Bablu*, AIR 2007 MP 38: 2007 AIHC 849: 2006 (4) MPLJ 579.

18. Widow even after Remarriage Entitled to Get Compensation – Any of the legal representatives can file the claim petition. Widow even after remarriage continues to be the legal representative of her husband as there is no provision under the Hindu Succession Act or any other law which lays down that after remarriage she does not continue right of succession accrues immediately on the death of husband and in the absence of any provision she cannot be divested from the property vested in her due to remarriage; *Vimla* v. *Dinesh Kumar Sharma*, AIR 2007 MP 47: 2007 (2) ALJ (NOC) 254: 2007 (3) All MR 22 JS.

19. Claimants Need not be Sole Dependant – The requirement under the Motor Vehicles Act is that all the Legal Representatives or any one of the legal representatives or the agents authorised by them, can make an application for compensation arising out of an motor vehicle accident and it is suffice, if the claimants prove that they are dependants on the income of the deceased. Motor Vehicles Act being a beneficial legislation, does not contemplate any stringent condition that the claimants should be 'solely dependant' on the income of the deceased. The husband of the deceased, had deserted the deceased, married another woman and is living separately. Though the claimants parents of deceased have not impleaded the husband as party respondent in the claim petition, that by itself would not disentitle the parents of the deceased to claim compensation; *Minor Shyamala* v. *A. Madheswaran*, AIR 2008 Mad 1: 2008 AIHC 404: 2007 (6) Mad LJ 1182.

20. Contributory Negligence – When the disabled vehicle was being pulled by another vehicle and during the process bounced upon its retriever, it cannot be said that there was no fault on the part of the truck driver for the occurrence. When the vehicle had already suffered mechanical breakdown and was in the process of being pulled by another vehicle, it was required of the truck driver to have taken extra care and caution to guard against any mishap and it cannot be said that for such occurrence of the truck ramming into and bouncing upon the tractor, the truck driver was not responsible. Even in an ordinary use of vehicle, the user owes a duty to ensure safety of others. In this cases where the truck was being towed by the tractor on the request of truck driver and on a downward slope the truck suddenly gathered speed and truck driver was unable to control his vehicle that climbed upon the tractor and tractor driver died on the spot on being crushed beneath the wheels of tractor. Thus, there is no question of applying any contributory negligence on the tractor driver and therefore the persons related with the truck would be liable for the loss caused to the claimants; *National Insurance Company Ltd.* v. *Kur Singh*, AIR 2007 Raj 162: 2007 AIHC 2659: 2007 (5) ALJ (NOC) 772.

21. Claim by Widow and Minor Son of Driver is Maintainable – The owner of the vehicle was driving and driver was an occupant though in course of and arising out of his duty. The car met with an accident and they sustained total injuries. Claim for compensation by the widow and minor son of the driver under the Act is maintainable. The insurer is liable to compensate a workman driver to the extent provided under the

Workmen's Compensation Act. It comes to Rs. 1,27,074. Otherwise also under the Act just compensation would be near about the said amount; *New India Assurance Company Ltd.* v. *Raj Kumari,* AIR 1995 All 1: 1995 All LJ 47: 1994 (2) ACJ 1110.

22. Determination of Compensation – Merely by approaching to Tribunal under Motor Vehicles Act he could not be given more compensation than he would be entitled under another statute since both the statutes should be read together. The award of compensation of Rs. 85,000 would be the just compensation. In case this amount is invested in some security appellant would be able to earn Rs. 750 per month from out of the amount. This is also one of the methods of determining the compensation; *State of Uttar Pradesh* v. *Suresh Chandra,* AIR 1995 All 253: 1995 (1) ACC 177: 1995 (1) ACJ 245.

23. Amendment of Claim to Enhance Compensation – When there is no limitation prescribed for filing the claim petition, no reasons need be assigned for seeking such an amendment. Thus the claimants are entitled to seek amendment of a claim so as to enhance the claim of compensation not only before the primary Tribunal but also before the appellate authority; *Pochamma* v. *Mirza Dawood Bagi,* AIR 1998 AP 337: 1998 (2) APLJ 267: 1999 (2) ACJ 1006.

24. Accident must not Cause Due to Self Acquired Act of Victim – An accident within the meaning of the Act may occur not only from the negligent act but also from the positive or intended act. As per the explanation to section 147(1) of the Act, the accident within the meaning of the Act may cause either due to "omission" or "an act" of a person and such omission or the act need not be unintentional as would appear from the fact that in the proceedings under sections 140, 163A or 163B of the Act, the Tribunal is not required to consider whether there was rash or negligent driving on the part of the driver of the offending vehicle or whether there was contributory negligence on the part of the victim. However, in order to invoke section 166 of the Act, accident must not cause due to the self-incurred act on the part of the victim. But if the driver of the offending vehicle with the intention of killing the victim deliberately runs over the victim, the case will attract the provision of section 166. In order to maintain an application under section 166 of the Act, from the point of view of the victim who suffers from it, the event, in order to be accident, must be unexpected and without design on his part, although it might be caused intentionally by the author of the act. For the purpose of granting relief under section 140 or 163A of the Act or in the cases under the category of 'hit and run', however, even the intentional act of the victim resulting in the accident is inconsequential; *Dipa Ganguly* v. *New India Assurance Company Limited,* AIR 2009 Cal 122: 2009 AIHC 518 (NOC): 2009 (4) ALJ (NOC) 648.

25. Quantum of Compensation can not be Less on Ground Claimant is Legal Representative – The liability under section 140 of the Act does not cease because there is absence of dependency. The right to file a claim application has to be considered in the background of right to entitlement. While assessing the quantum, the multiplier system is applied because of deprivation of dependency. Where a legal representative who is not dependent files an application for compensation, the quantum cannot be less than the liability referable to section 140 of the Act. Therefore, even if there is no loss of dependency the claimant if he or she is a legal representative will be entitled to compensation, the quantum of which shall be not less than the liability flowing from section 140 of the Act; *New India Assurance Co. Ltd.* v. *Jasinta Kujur,* AIR 2007 Chhat 107: 2007 AIHC 2652: 2007 (5) AKAR (NOC) 621.

26. Section 166 of Act has No Overriding Effect Over Section 140 – Lodging of a petition for compensation under section 166 is not a condition precedent to filing of a petition for interim compensation on the principle of no fault liability. The Legislature has advisedly therefore nowhere stated in section 140 that application for interim compensation can be made only if a substantive petition under section 166 is filed. Chapter XII which deals with the Claims Tribunal and section 166 which finds its place in Chapter XII, cannot have overriding effect over section 140 in light of the clear statutory provision enacted by section 144 of the said Act. Therefore, where main claim petition under section 166 was dismissed on ground of bar of limitation, application under section 140 for interim compensation, cannot be dismissed on that ground; *Munshiram D. Anand* v. *Pravinsinh Prabhatsinh Anand Society, Navagam Gedh, Jamnagar,* AIR 1997 Guj 60: 1997 ACJ 206: 1996 (3) Civ LJ 844.

27. Territorial Jurisdiction – The jurisdiction of the Tribunal is wider than the civil court. Claimant a Resident of the State of Uttar Pradesh residing in the State of Uttaranchal at the time of accident Tribunal in the State of Uttaranchal has jurisdiction to try the claim; *Mantoo Sarkar* v. *Oriental Insurance Co. Ltd.,* AIR 2009 SC 1022: 2009 AIR SCW 136: 2009 (2) SCC 244: 2008 (16) SCALE 197.

28. Allegations in FIR though not Admissible can be made Part of Claim Petition – Ordinarily an allegation made in the first information would not be admissible in evidence per se but as the allegation made in the first information report had been made a part of the claim petition, there is no doubt whatsoever that the Tribunal and consequently the appellate courts would be entitled to look into the same; *National Insurance Co. Ltd.* v. *Rattani,* AIR 2009 SC 1499: 2009 AIR SCW 992: 2009 (2) SCC 75: 2009 (1) SCALE 379.

29. Just Compensation to be Awarded though No Specific Claim in Pleading – Even if in the pleadings no specific claim was made under section 166 a party should not be deprived from getting "Just Compensation" in case the claimant is able to make out a case under any provision of law. Needless to say, the M.V. Act is beneficial and welfare legislation. In fact, the Court is duty bound and entitled to award "Just Compensation" irrespective of the fact whether any plea in that behalf was raised by the claimant or not. However, whether or not the claimants would be governed with the terms and conditions of the Insurance Policy and whether or not the provisions of section 147 of the Act would be applicable in the instant case and also whether or not there was rash and negligent driving on the part of the deceased, who was driving the vehicle borrowed from the real owner, are essentially a matter of fact which was required to be considered and answered at least by the High Court; *Ningamma* v. *United India Insurance Co. Ltd.,* AIR 2009 SC 3056: 2009 AIR SCW 4916: 2009 (8) SCALE 244.

30. Driver is a Necessary Party – To make a finding on negligence without involving the driver as at least a witness would vitiate the proceedings not only on the basis of the fact that the driver has not been given an opportunity to make a representation, but also because the evidence to make a finding regarding negligence would necessarily be inadequate. On this basis, a driver should be made a 'party' to the proceedings; *Machindranath Kernath Kasar* v. *D.S. Mylarappa,* AIR 2008 SC 2545: 2008 AIR SCW 3546: 2008 (7) SCALE 496.

31. Married Daughter is Legal Representative – Claim petition filed by married daughter of a motor accident victim is maintainable. She cannot be denied compensation on ground that she is not dependant on deceased. Married daughter of deceased though not dependant on deceased is entitled to compensation - She is 'legal representative' under S. 166 of the Act; *Manjuri Bera* v. *Oriental Insurance Co. Ltd.,* AIR 2007 SC 1474: 2007 AIR SCW 1962: 2007 (5) SCALE 193: 2007 (3) Supreme 620.

32. Enhanced Compensation can be Claimed at Appellate Stage – where there is evidence on record justifying the enhanced compensation for the medical treatment which is required because of the injury caused to a claimant due to the accident, there is no reason why such amendment or enhanced compensation should not be granted. In such cases, there is no question of introducing a new or inconsistent cause of action. Cause of action and evidence remain the same. Thus there is no bar for the Claims Tribunal to award the compensation in excess of what is claimed, particularly when the evidence which is brought on record is sufficient to pass such award; *Nagappa* v. *Gurudayal Singh,* AIR 2003 SC 674: 2002 AIR SCW 5348: 2003 AIR Kant HCR 242: 2003 (2) SCC 274: 2002 (9) SCALE 37: 2002 (8) Supreme 497.

33. Periodical Medical Expenses – Where injury to a victim requires periodical medical expenses, fresh award cannot be passed or previous award cannot be reviewed when the medical expenses are incurred after finalisation of the compensation proceedings. Hence, only alternative is that at the time of passing of final award, Tribunal/Court should consider such eventuality and fix compensation accordingly. No one can suggest that it is improper to take into account expenditure genuinely and reasonably required to be incurred for future medical expenses. Further medical expenses required to be incurred can be determined only on the basis of fair guess-work after taking into account increase in the cost of medical treatment. Therefore it would be difficult to hold that for future medical expenses which are required to be incurred by a victim, fresh award could be passed. However, for such medical treatment, Court has to arrive at a reasonable estimate on the basis of the evidence brought on record; *Nagappa* v. *Gurudayal Singh,* AIR 2003 SC 674: 2002 AIR SCW 5348: 2003 (2) SCC 274: 2002 (9) SCALE 37: 2002 (8) Supreme 497.

34. Deviation from Structured Formula in Exceptional Cases – The payment of compensation on the basis of structured formula as provided for under the Second Schedule should not ordinarily be deviated from. Section 168 of the Act lays down the guidelines for determination of the amount of compensation in terms of section 166 thereof. Deviation of the structured formula, however, may be resorted to in exceptional cases. Furthermore, the amount of compensation should be just and fair in the facts and circumstances of each case. The victim at the relevant time was 40 years of age. Applying the multiplier of 15 is proper; *Abati Bezbaruah* v. *Dy. Director General, Geological Survey of India:* AIR 2003 SC 1817: 2003 AIR SCW 1266: JT 2003 (5) SC 205: 2003 (3) SCC 148: 2003 (2) SCALE 120: 2003 (2) Supreme 178.

35. Limitation for Filing Claim Petition – Though period of limitation has been prescribed by the Legislature for filing claim petition under M.V. Act, article 137 of the Limitation Act cannot be invoked. The Parliament, in its wisdom, realised the grave injustice and injury being caused to the heirs and legal representatives of the victims who suffer bodily injuries/die in accidents, by rejecting their claim petitions at the threshold on the ground of limitation, and purposely deleted section 166(3) which provided the period of limitation for filing the claim petitions and this being the intendment of the Legislature to give effective relief to the victims and the families of the motor accidents untrammelled by the technicalities of the limitation, invoking of article 137 of the Limitation Act would defeat the intendment of the Legislature; *New India Assurance Co. Ltd.* v. *C. Padma,* AIR 2003 SC 4394: 2003 AIR SCW 5027: 2003 (7) SCC 713: 2003 (7) SCALE 445: 2003 (6) Supreme 701.

There is no limitation for filing claims before the Tribunal in respect of any accident. The Parliament realised the grave injustice and injury which was being caused to the heirs and legal representatives of the victims who died in accidents by rejecting their claims petitions only on ground of limitation. It is a matter of common knowledge that majority of the claimants for such compensation are ignorant about the period during which such claims should be preferred. After the death due to the accident, of the bread earner of the family, in many cases such claimants are virtually on the streets. Even in cases where the victims escape death some of such victims are hospitalised for months if not for years. Thus the Parliament, rightly thought that prescribing a period of limitation and restricting the power of Tribunal to entertain any claim petition beyond the period of twelve months from the date of the accident was harsh, inequitable and in many cases was likely to cause injustice to the claimants; *Dhannalal* v. *D.P. Vijayvargiya,* AIR 1996 SC 2155: 1996 AIR SCW 2617: JT 1996 (5) SC 601: 1996 (4) SCC 652.

36. Sum Awarded must be Fair and Reasonable – The determination of the quantum of compensation must answer what contemporary society "would deem to be a fair sum such as would allow the wrong doer to hold up his head among his neighbours and say with their approval that he has done the fair thing". The amount awarded must not be niggardly since the "law values life and limb in a free society in generous scales". All this means that the sum awarded must be fair and reasonable by accepted legal standards; *General Manager, Punjab Roadways, Nangal Depot* v. *Santosh Chadha*, AIR 1997 HP 36: 1998 (1) ACJ 608: 1997 (2) LJR 592.

37. Not Necessary for Claimant to Plead Evidence in Petition – In case of application for compensation, it is not necessary for the claimant to plead evidence in the petition. It is suffice for claimant to convey to the respondents that it was due to their act that the victim met with an accident which killed him. Thus when the rashness causing accident is made the basis for claiming compensation, the nondisclosure of manner of accident does not make the petition incomplete nor leads to the conclusion that the cause of action had not been disclosed in the petition; *Uttar Pradesh State Roadways Transport Corporation*, v. *Shanti Devi*, AIR 1997 Del 342: 1997 (1) ACC 423: 1998 (2) Civ LJ 570.

38. Limitation for Filing Claims before Tribunal – Sub-section (3) of section 166 has been omitted by the Motor Vehicles (Amendment) Act, 1994 w.e.f. 14-11-1994. The effect of amendment is that w.e.f. 14-11-1994. There is no limitation for filing claims before the tribunal in respect of any accident; *Dhannalal* v. *D.P. Vijayvargiya*, AIR 1996 SC 2155: 1996 (1) ACC 603: 1996 (0) ACJ 1013.

39. Condonation of Delay in Making Application for Compensation – Section 29(2) of the Limitation Act, 1963 makes section 5 of the said Act applicable in the case of an application for compensation filed before a Claims Tribunal for a period of twelve months from the date of the occurrence of the accident. Proviso to sub-section (3) of section 166 of Motor Vehicles Act, 1988 in so many terms provides that a Claims Tribunal can entertain an application for compensation not above the period of 12 months from the date of occurrence of the accident provided sufficient cause is shown. This clearly means that if an application for compensation is filed beyond a period of 12 months from the date of the occurrence of the accident, the Claims Tribunal shall not be entitled to entertain it or in other words, it shall have no power to condone the delay. There is thus an express provision in proviso to sub-section (3) of section 166 that delay in making an application for compensation shall be condonable only if it is not beyond 12 months from the date of the occurrence of the accident and that proviso expressly excludes the applicability of section 5 in cases 'where an application for compensation is delayed by more than 12 months from the date of the occurrence of the accident. Thus the Claims Tribunal acting under the Act of 1988 has no jurisdiction to condone the delay beyond the period of 12 months from the date of the occurrence of the accident; *Mer Ramda Vejunandbhai* v. *Hardasbhai Parbatbhai*, (1992) 1 ACC 717: AIR 1992 Guj 122: 1992 (1) ACJ 399.

40. Period of Limitation for Filing a Claim Petition – The period of limitation for filing a claim petition both under the old Act and the new Act is six months from the date of the accident. The difference in the two Acts is in regard to the provisions relating to condonation of delay. In view of the proviso to sub-section (3) of section 166 of the new Act, the maximum period of delay which can be condoned is six months. "Sufficient cause" as a ground of condonation of delay in filing the claim is distinct from "cause of action" for the claim itself. The question of delay must, therefore, be governed by the new law; *Vinod Gurudas Raikar* v. *National Insurance Co. Ltd.*, AIR 1991 SC 2156: 1991 AIR SCW 2503: 1991 (2) ACC 4449 (SC).

41. Dependants of Deceased are Entitled to Compensation – When husband dies in accident and her widow remarries, she is not entitled to compensation; *Chandan* v. *Kanwarlal*, 1989 ACJ 1816: (1989) 1 ACC 451 (Del).

When claim petition filed by widow and married daughter, married daughter not being dependant upon deceased is not entitled for compensation, only widow is entitled; *Nathi Singh* v. *Vimlesh Gupta*, 1989 ACJ 1128 (All).

42. Jurisdiction of Motor Accident Claim Tribunal – In order to decide the maintainability of the application, the Tribunal has to consider whether the applicant is a legal representative of the deceased. MACT has the authority to decide this issue because without deciding as to who are the legal representatives of the deceased, the maintainability of the application cannot be decided at all. It is also to be noted that jurisdiction of the Civil Courts are specifically excluded and the Motor Vehicles Act confers exclusive jurisdiction to the Accidents Claims Tribunals to decide all matters pertaining to award and disbursement of compensation to the eligible claimants. Therefore, the MACT has full powers to decide as to who are the legal representatives and if there is any contest among parties to decide it also. The Tribunals should demand convincing evidence from the claimants to prove that they are the legal representatives, even though no other rival party has made the claim. The section 8 of the Family Courts Act conferring jurisdiction under section 7 to the Family Court is exclusive and no other Court has power to decide the matter cannot override section 175 of the Motor Vehicles Act which provides for award of compensation to legal heirs for the death of a person in Motor Accident; *Clara* v. *Yasoda,* AIR 2010 Ker 34: 2009 (4) ACJ 2706: 2009 (1) Ker LT 984.

43. Award in Favour of Married Sisters is not Illegal – When a claim petition is made by a married son or daughter, or in the absence of any other Class-I heir and if the claimants adduce evidence that they are the legal representatives and that the deceased during his lifetime, had contributed a portion of his income to them and if the said contention is disputed, it is the burden of the objector to lead strong rebuttal evidence to dislodge the claim of dependency. If the contention of contribution by the deceased to the legal representatives is not rebutted by any acceptable evidence, the inevitable conclusion of the Tribunal should be in favour of the claimants. Thus the award made in favour of the married sisters and others, cannot be said to be without any legal principles; *M.D., T.N. State Transport Corpn. Ltd.* v. *M. Shanthi,* AIR 2011 Mad 118.

44. Legal Representatives – Certainly when the claimants were depending upon their widow sister by all means and she was living with them in the maternal home, it would be deemed that they represent the estate of the deceased and intermeddle with the estate of the deceased and therefore, are legal representatives of the deceased. The earning of the widow sister is the main source of livelihood of the claimants who were dependent on the deceased and if she was feeding her brother who is handicapped and unable to walk as also the unmarried sister and in case of her death by a motor accident, her dependents that is unmarried sister and physically handicapped brother are entitled to file claim petition in the capacity of legal representatives; *Durgaram* v. *Yadavram,* AIR 2011 Chht 84.

45. Period of Limitation for Filing Claim Petition – The period of limitation for filing the claim petition was provided under section 166(3) of the Act but was omitted in the year 1994. Thus there is no limitation prescribed for filing the claim petition after omission of sub-section (3) of section 166 of the Act; *Ketki Kumari* v. *Inder Prasad,* AIR 2011 Chht 160.

46. Claim Petitions by Legal Representatives – Maintainability – Though there is no loss of dependency, yet the claimants being legal representatives are entitled to inherit the estate of the deceased persons, therefore, the appellants are entitled to receive compensation under no fault liability in terms of section 140(2) of the Act. Hence the claim petitions were maintainable as filed by the legal representatives of the deceased; *Joy Minocha* v. *Vijay Kumar,* AIR 2011 Chht 166.

47. Claimant cannot Pursue Remedies under Section 163A and Section 166 Simultaneously – The respondents having obtained compensation, finally determined under section 163A of the Act are precluded from proceeding further with the petition filed under section 166 of the Act. The exception mentioned by the High Court that a petition under section 166 of the Act can be proceeded further if it is filed before passing of an award passed under section 163A of the Act is not supported by the scheme envisaged under sections 63A and 166 of the Act and is contrary to the principles of law laid down by the Supreme Court. Therefore the remedy for payment of compensation both under sections 163A and 166 being final and independent of each other as statutorily provided, a claimant cannot pursue his remedies thereunder simultaneously. Thus a claimant must opt to go either for a proceeding under section 163A or under section 166 of the Act, but he cannot proceed under both of the section; *Oriental Insurance Co. Ltd.* v. *Dhanbai Kanji Gadhvi,* AIR 2011 SC 1138: 2011 AIR SCW 1269: (2011) 2 SCALE 39.

48. Delay in Lodging FIR – Where the victim child aged 8 years was seriously injured in accident and it was more important for his father to get him treated first and he was not aware of niceties of law that lodging of FIR was condition precedent before filing claim petition and other persons in locality pressurized him that matter could be sorted out amicably since driver of vehicle was his neighbour, the delay in lodging FIR cannot be held fatal to the claim case. Even the police had arrived at the hospital, where injury report was prepared in which it was mentioned that injuries were caused on account of road accident and there was categorical admission by owner of the truck, that vehicle in question was involved in the accident when the same was being driven by his driver and this information was conveyed to him on phone the very same day. The cumulative effect of the aforesaid events would establish that accident had taken place on stated date on account of rash and negligent reversing of the truck by the driver. Therefore, delay in lodging the FIR was fatal to the claim case; *Ravi* v. *Badrinarayan*, AIR 2011 SC 1226: 2011 AIR SCW 1530: (2011) 4 SCC 693.

49. No Fault Compensation Though not Raised in Beginning Door would not Close Permanently – Normally a claim under section 140 is made at the threshold of the proceeding and the payment of compensation under section 140 is directed to be made by an interim award of the Tribunal which may be adjusted if in the final award the claimants are held entitled to any larger amounts. But that does not mean, that in case a claim under section 140 is not made at the beginning of the proceedings due to the ignorance of the claimant or no direction to make payment of the compensation under section 140 was issued due to the over-sight of the Tribunal, the door would be permanently closed. Such a view would be contrary to the legal provisions and would be opposed to the public policy. Section 140 of the Act is intended to provide immediate succour to the injured or the heirs and legal representatives of the deceased; *Eshwarappa* alias *Maheshwarappa* v. *C.S. Gurushanthappa,* AIR 2010 SC 2907: 2010 AIR SCW 4918: (2010) 8 SCC 620.

50. Compromise – Oral Statement Cannot be Accepted – While acting as a Claims Tribunals, its proceedings are summary in nature but in exercising its summary jurisdiction the Tribunal must follow principles of justice, equity and good conscience and must be aware that its summary enquiry is in connection with a legislation which is meant for social welfare. Therefore, when a representation is made before the Tribunal that a claim of Rs. 15 lacs by way of consent is reduced to Rs. 6 lacs and odd, the Tribunal must insist on production of some material either, an affidavit of claimant or statement of claimant before the MACT in support of such lowering down of claim. The MACT cannot accept said representation on mere oral statement of counsel since such settlement is purely a question of fact. In fact no leave was obtained from the Tribunal to enter into a compromise between parties in respect of the settlement. In absence of all these materials, when an affidavit was filed by advocate who appeared before the Tribunal, contending that no such settlement was ever entered into by consent of parties, the High Court fell into an error by discarding same only on ground that same was filed belatedly before the High Court and was an afterthought; *Oriental Insurance Co. Ltd.* v. *Vithabai,* AIR 2011 SC 2838: 2011 AIR SCW 4235: (2011) 7 SCALE 1.

51. Refund of Amount of 'no Fault Compensation' not Roper – The marginal heading to section 140 describes it as based 'on the principle of no fault'. As the expression 'no fault' suggests the compensation under section 140 is regardless of any wrongful act, neglect or default of the person in respect of whose death the claim is made. The Tribunal was patently in error, in directing for the refund of the amount of 'no fault compensation' already paid to the claimants, to the insurance company. The order of the Tribunal insofar as it permits the insurance company to recover the amount of interim compensation along with the interest from the claimants/appellants is set aside; *Indra Devi* v. *Bagada Ram,* AIR 2010 SC 2913: 2010 AIR SCW 4924: (2010) 8 SCALE 312.

52. Principles of *Res Judicata* – The award was passed on the principle of no fault under section 140 of the Act. No appeal has been preferred against the award passed either by the owner or the insurer. At the instance of either the owner or the insurer that cannot again be reopened in proceedings under section 166 of the Act. Principles of *res judicata* shall apply. Further from the admitted facts appearing on record are sufficient to invoke at least the doctrine of estoppel and acquiescence against both the Insurance Company and the owner of the vehicle in question; *Prakash Chandra Biswas* v. *New India Assurance Co. Ltd.,* AIR 2010 Cal 19: 2011 (1) ACC 159: 2011 (1) ACJ 622.

53. Claimant not Required to Prove Case Beyond Shadow of Reasonable Doubt – The claimant is not required to prove his case beyond shadow of reasonable doubt. It would suffice, if he has proved his case on the basis of preponderance of probabilities. The claim of the appellant could not have been dismissed merely because the name of the appellant did not find place in the FIR as well as in the relevant column of the witness list of the charge sheet. From such omission, on the part of the investigating officer in criminal case, an inference cannot be drawn that the claim petition is baseless and frivolous. The object of the FIR from the point of view of the informant is to set the criminal law in motion. The FIR does not constitute substantive evidence. It can be used only for the purpose contemplated under section 157 or section 145 of the Evidence Act that is for corroborating or contradicting its maker only and not of other witnesses; *Prakash Chandra Biswas* v. *New India Assurance Co. Ltd.,* AIR 2010 Cal 19: 2011 (1) ACC 159: 2011 (1) ACJ 622.

54. Claim Petition – *Locus* of Legal Representative – Only if there is justification in consonance with principles of justice, equity and good conscience, dependent of deceased may be denied right to claim compensation. Claim petition cannot be held to be not maintainable because of provisions of the Fatal Accidents Act; *Montford Brothers of S.t. Gabriel* v. *United India Insurance,* AIR 2014 SC 1550.

55. Objection Against Legal Representative – Issues of facts cannot be decided by High Court for the first time in writ petition which could only be entertained under article 227 of the Constitution for limited purpose; *Montford Brothers of S.t. Gabriel* v. *United India Insurance,* AIR 2014 SC 1550.

56. Difference in Principles in Paying Compensation under Section 163A and Section 166 – The principles relating to determination of liability and quantum of compensation are different for the claims under section 163A and claims made under section 166. The structured formulas as prescribed under Second Schedule and the multiplier mentioned therein is not binding for claims under section 166 of the Act; *Puttamma* v. *K.L. Narayana Reddy,* AIR 2014 SC 706.

57. Compensation – Permanent Disability – Enormity of suffering, pain and agony, loss of enjoyment of life of appellant to be considered; *Kiran* v. *Sajjan Singh,* (2015) 1 SCC 539.

58. Special Food and Nutrition – Non-fatal – Permanent Disability – Compensation enhanced to Rs. 10,000 from Rs. 3,000; *Kiran* v. *Sajjan Singh,* (2015) 1 SCC 539.

59. Future Loss of Income – Non-fatal – Permanent Disability – Child's notional income cannot be ascertained as per figure for non-earning individuals – Award of Rs. 1 lac towards shock, pain and suffering (non-pecuniary head) in place of future income due to permanent disability; *Kiran* v. *Sajjan Singh,* (2015) 1 SCC 539.

60. Non-fatal – Permanent Disability 30% and 20% Due to Shortening of Right Leg by 1 Inch – Age just over 10 and 15 years. Rs. 25,000 awarded each towards agony to parents and Rs. 25,000 each towards future medical expenses; *Kiran* v. *Sajjan Singh*, (2015) 1 SCC 539.

61. Contributory Negligence – Negligence wholly on Part of Driver of Offending Vehicle – Apportionment of 25% on part of appellant erroneous; *Kiran* v. *Sajjan Singh*, (2015) 1 SCC 539.

62. Compensation – Pain and Suffering – Enhancement from Rs. 5000 to Rs. 50,000; *Kiran* v. *Sajjan Singh*, (2015) 1 SCC 539.

63. Driving License – Valid license to Drive Light Motor Vehicle – Driver authorised to drive light goods vehicle; *Ashvinbhai Jayantilal Modi* v. *Ramkaran Ramchandra Sharma*, (2015) 2 SCC 180.

64. Driving License – No Breach of any Condition of Insurance Policy – Insurance company cannot disown liability; *Ashvinbhai Jayantilal Modi* v. *Ramkaran Ramchandra Sharma*, (2015) 2 SCC 180.

65. Monthly Income of Deceased – Computation on basis of I.T. return correct; *Kalpanaraj* v. *Tamil Nadu State Transport Corporation*, (2015) 2 SCC 764.

66. Deduction under Various Heads to Arrive at Net Income – Erroneous – Instead High Court to ascertain the gross income of deceased out of annual income earned from his occupation mentioned in I.T. return submitted for the relevant financial year 1994-95; *Kalpanaraj* v. *Tamil Nadu State Transport Corporation*, (2015) 2 SCC 764.

67. Future Prospects – Deceased 46 Years, Multiplier of 13 Applied – 30% increase in future prospects of income warranted; *Kalpanaraj* v. *Tamil Nadu State Transport Corporation*, (2015) 2 SCC 764.

68. Damage to Motor Cycle – Claim not rebutted with evidence – Grant of Rs. 10,000; *Kalpanaraj* v. *Tamil Nadu State Transport Corporation*, (2015) 2 SCC 764.

69. Loss of Dependency – Fatal – Deceased 25 years of age, driver – Skilled job – Loss of dependency calculated at Rs. 10,36,800, taking monthly income at Rs. 9,000 per month; *Kala Devi* v. *Bhagwan Das Chauhan*, (2015) 2 SCC 771.

70. Private or Self-employment – Fatal – Compensation – Minimum wages notified in Act relied in absence of salary slip; *Rajiv Chowdhrie Huf* v. *Union of India*, (2015) 3 SCC 541.

71. Violation of Statutory Provision – Plying vehicle without insurance – Liability not mulcted on financier – Appreciation by Single Judge in appeal under section 173 of Motor Vehicle Act, both on facts and law is wholly erroneous; *HDFC Bank Limited* v. *Reshma*, (2015) 3 SCC 679.

72. Death of House Wife – Self-employed *i.e.*, Embroidery, Tailoring – Hard to monetise domestic work – Income fixed at Rs. 3000 per month reasonable; *Jitendra Khimshankar Trivedi* v. *Kasam Daud Kumbhar*, (2015) 4 SCC 237.

73. Just and Reasonable Compensation – House Wife and Self-employed – Total Compensation Awarded at Rs. 6,47,000 – Age of deceased 22 years. Proper multiplier to be applied is 18. Loss of dependency calculated at Rs. 4,32,000, Rs. 1 lakh awarded for loss of love and affection, Rs. 1 lakh for loss of consortium, Rs. 15,000 for loss of estate and funeral expenses; *Jitendra Khimshankar Trivedi* v. *Kasam Daud Kumbhar*, (2015) 4 SCC 237.

167. Option regarding claims for compensation in certain cases.—Notwithstanding anything contained in the Workmen's Compensation Act, 1923 (8 of 1923) where the death of, or bodily injury to, any person gives rise to a claim for compensation under this Act and also under the Workmen's Compensation

Act, 1923, the person entitled to compensation may without prejudice to the provisions of Chapter X claim such compensation under either of those Acts but not under both.

SYNOPSIS

COMMENTS

1. Multiplier – The deceased was holding the post of Supervisor at the time of her death and she was aged about 48 years at that time. The salary drawn by the deceased, was Rs. 2,570 p.m. the multiplier of 10 was rightly taken; *Rejendra Kumar* v. *Rambhai,* AIR 2003 SC 2095: 2003 AIR SCW 92: 2002 (1) JT (Supp) 549: 2002 (7) Supreme 205.

2. Jurisdiction where Accident Solely Attributable to Negligence of Railway – Motor Accidents Claims Tribunal has no jurisdiction if the accident is solely attributable to the negligence of the Railway and observed that where there is no vehicle but the accident is only due to the sole negligence of the other parties the claim would go out of section 110(1) of the Act because the case would then become one of the exclusive negligence of Railways. Again if the accident has arisen only on account of the negligence of persons other than the driver/owner of the motor vehicle, the claim would not be maintainable before the Tribunal. The victims of this accident are entitled to compensation from the Railways at any rate, and compensation has been awarded to them; *G.M., N.F. Railway, Malegaon, Guwahati* v. *Jitendra Shah,* AIR 2000 SC 3398: 2000 (4) Supreme 523: 2000 (4) Andh LD 102.

3. Once Option Exercised in Other Law not Open to Claimants to Avail Remedy under Motor Vehicles Act – Once option was exercised and an award was passed under Workmen's Compensation Act, 1923, it is not open to claimants to avail the remedy under the Motor Vehicles Act; *Shaik Iman Bai* v. *Oriental Fire and General Insurance Co. Ltd.,* 1989 ACJ 291 (AP).

4. Claimant not entitled to Claim in both Alternative Forums – A claimant has no right to approach both the forums prescribed by the M.V. Act of 1988 as well as WC Act. He can opt for the benefit under either of the Acts and his option must be a conscious option, *i.e.* free choice. Not only that the claimant is not bound by the act of the employer of the deceased workman, *i.e.* even if the third party deposits the compensation in discharge of its statutory obligation under the WC Act that cannot debar the claimant from choosing the forum under the Act of 1988 as the claimant is the best person to exercise his option. The claimant has the right before adjudication of claim to exercise choice by way of abandoning his claim in one forum and may proceed with the other forum; *Abul Khayer* v. *Union of India,* AIR 2008 Gau 134: 2008 (6) ALJ (NOC) 1189: 2008 (3) Gau LT 119.

5. Words "May Claim Compensation" – The words "may claim compensation" used in both the Acts show that person entitled to compensation must take conscious decision and opt for compensation under one of the statutes; *Oriental Insurance Co. Ltd.* v. *Gouribai,* AIR 1998 MP 104: 1998 (1) MPLJ 121: 1999 (2) ACJ 1056.

168. Award of the Claims Tribunal.—(1) On receipt of an application for compensation made under section 166, the Claims Tribunal shall, after giving notice of the application to the insurer, and after giving the parties (including the insurer) an opportunity of being heard, hold an inquiry into the claim or, as the case may be, each of the claims and, subject to the provisions of section 162 may make an award determining the amount of compensation which appears to it to be just and specifying the person or persons to whom compensation shall be paid and in making the award the Claims Tribunal shall specify the amount which shall be paid by the insurer or owner or driver of the vehicle involved in the accident or by all or any of them, as the case may be:

Provided that where such application makes a claim for compensation under section 140 in respect of the death or permanent disablement of any person, such claim and any other claim (whether made in such application or otherwise) for compensation in respect of such death or permanent disablement shall be disposed of in accordance with the provisions of Chapter X.

(2) The Claims Tribunal shall arrange to deliver copies of the award to the parties concerned expeditiously and in any case within a period of fifteen days from the date of the award.

(3) When an award is made under this section, the person who is required to pay any amount in terms of such award shall, within thirty days of the date of announcing the award by the Claims Tribunal, deposit the entire amount awarded in such manner as the Claims Tribunal may direct.

SYNOPSIS

COMMENTS

1. Mere Driving without License would not Tantamount to Contributory Negligence – The offending vehicle, was coming in a great speed with one head light and dashed against the motorcycle. No evidence has been adduced to establish that the motorcyclist had acted in any manner due to which the accident was caused. Thus, in essence, there was absolutely no negligence on the part of the motorcyclist. Violation of statutory requirement *per se* would not tantamount to contributory negligence. There is no shadow of doubt that there has to be casual relationship between violation and accident caused. There has to be some act done by the person concerned in causing the accident. The commission or omission must have some nexus with the accident. In the case at hand, nothing has been brought on record that the accident had occurred due to some act caused by the motorcyclist as he was driving the vehicle without licence. His presence alone at the place of accident would not tantamount to contributory negligence. The statutory violation per se would not usher in the concept of contributory negligence; *Vidya Soni* v. *Pushpesh Dwivedi*, AIR 2008 MP 319.

2. Contributory Negligence – The bus had hit with a lamp post stands admitted. The nature of the injury, suggests that the upper arm of his body had hit the body of the bus. If he had put his hand out, his upper arm would not have broken into two pieces by way of crush injury. The injury would have been confined to the wrist or the arm upto the elbow. Therefore, the appellant was not guilty of any contributory negligence; *G. Gnanam* v. *Metropolitan Transport Corporation*, AIR 2009 SC 1166: 2009 AIR SCW 407: 2009 (2) SCC 71: 2008 (16) SCALE 362.

Even if the driver of the passenger vehicle was negligent, the Railways, if its negligence was otherwise proved - could not plead contributory negligence on the part of the passengers of the vehicle. What is clear is that qua the passengers of the bus who were innocent, the driver and owner of the bus and, if proved, the railways - can all be joint tort-feasors; *Union of India* v. *United India Insurance Co. Ltd.*, AIR 1998 SC 640: 1998 AIR SCW 245: JT 1997 (8) SC 653: 1997 (8) SCC 683: 1997 (9) Supreme 69.

The evidence shows that the truck was coming in high speed. It was the truck, which hit the Car and not vice versa. The Maruti Car was going on its own side. There was absolutely no evidence to suggest that there was any failure on the part of the Car driver to take any particular care or that he had breached his duty in any manner. Redaction of the compensation payable to the deceased-car driver by 50% of the assessed amount of compensations is not proper; *Usha Rajkhowa* v. *Paramount Industries*, AIR 2009 SC 1951: 2009 AIR SCW 1576: 2009 (2) SCALE 725.

On account of the motor cycle touching the road-median the deceased fell on the other side of the road and that the vehicle which was coming from the opposite direction though was brought to halt by its driver, on account of the car which was coming behind the van dashing against the van, the van ran over the deceased resulting in the death of the claimants' son. The van which was stationed moved further and ran over the deceased only shows the velocity with which the car has dashed against the van. The Motor Vehicles Inspector's report reveals the damages caused to the car. The brakes were in order. Considering the extent of damages caused to the cars, the car was at a great speed and its driver didn't make any attempt to stop the vehicle. Therefore, there is contributory negligence on the part of the driver of the Car which can be assessed at 25%. Accordingly, the driver of the Car was also responsible in causing the accident and his contribution is assessed at 25%; *Girijesh Vyas* v. *G. Vishnuvardhan*, AIR 2012 Kant 44: 2012 AAC 46: 2012 (4) ACJ 2326.

The Tribunal reduced the 50 per cent. of the compensation allowed on the ground of contributory negligence on the part of the driver of the motorcycle in question for the reason that the motorcycle and the tempo met head on collision and *secondly*, applicant did not produce the driving license of the motorcycle driver. As regards the second ground, the contention of the learned counsel for the appellant is that the applicant witness widow of the motorcycle driver has deposed that her husband was possessing the driving license but the same could not be located after the accident from the spot. The Insurance Company except for stating in the written statement that the driver of the motorcycle was not having the license as the applicant did not produce the same, neither any material has been produced nor the widow was cross-examined on this point. The motorcycle driver has not possessed any driving license but non-possession of such licence does not amount to contributory negligence on the part of the deceased. The motorcycle was on the eastern side of the road and going from North to South whereas the tempo was coming from South to North, both vehicles met head on collision. Thus contributory negligence could not be attributed to the deceased as he was on the extreme left of the road therefore, the deduction of 50% towards contributory negligence is improper; *Binny Sharma* v. *Om Prakash,* AIR 2012 Pat 74: 2012 (119) All Ind Cas 702.

3. Expression "which appears to be just" – The expression "which appears to be just" vests a wide discretion in the Tribunal in the matter of determination of compensation. Nevertheless, the wide amplitude of such power does not empower the Tribunal to determine the compensation arbitrarily, or to ignore settled principles relating to determination of compensation. Similarly, although the Act is a beneficial legislation, it can neither be allowed to be used as a source of profit, nor as a windfall to the persons affected nor should it be punitive to the person(s) liable to pay compensation. The determination of compensation must be based on certain data, establishing reasonable nexus between the loss incurred by the dependents of the deceased and the compensation to be awarded to them; *Syed Basheer Ahamed* v. *Mohd. Jameel,* AIR 2009 SC 1219: 2009 AIR SCW 493: 2009 (2) SCC 225: 2009 (1) SCALE 222.

4. Cogent Evidence to Determine Income of Deceased – Though the entries in the current account of the deceased and his transactions with his client, may not *per se* be cogent evidence to determine the yearly or monthly income of the deceased from the business(s) he was carrying on, yet these are some indicators in support of the appellants' plea that the business income of the deceased in the succeeding years could be more than what was declared; *Syed Basheer Ahamed* v. *Mohd. Jameel,* AIR 2009 SC 1219: 2009 AIR SCW 493: 2009 (2) SCC 225: 2009 (1) SCALE 222.

5. Proper Multiplier – The Second Schedule as such may not have any application as the maximum annual income of a deceased or an injured which could be taken into consideration therefor is Rs. 40,000 per annum. However, keeping in view the peculiar factual circumstances of the case, the proper multiplier which, in our opinion, should be adopted is eight for the purpose of determining fair compensation; *Oriental Insurance Co. Ltd.* v. *Ram Prasad Varma,* AIR 2009 SC 1831: 2009 AIR SCW 1430: 2009 (2) SCC 712: 2009 (1) SCALE 598.

Although the Second Schedule is applicable only in respect of the claim petitions filed under section 163A of the Act, indisputably, the same provides for some guidelines. In a case where the deceased was above 25 years but not exceeding 30 years, in terms of the said Second Schedule, the multiplier of 18 is to be applied. In the case of the deceased whose age was above 30 years but not exceeding 35 years, the multiplier of 17 in terms of the Second Schedule is required to be applied. The quantum of multiplicand, is not in question. In a case of this nature, it is not necessary to go into the larger question, *viz.,* as to whether the courts should apply the multiplier specified in the Second Schedule in a proceeding under section 166 of the Act; *Mohan Singh* v. *Kashi Bai,* AIR 2009 SC 2006: 2009 AIR SCW 1664: 2009 (4) SCC 507: 2009 (1) SCALE 539.

Where there is so much of disparity in the economic conditions and affluence of the two places *viz.,* the place to which the victim belongs and the place where the compensation is to be paid, a golden balance must be struck somewhere, to arrive at a reasonable and fair mesne. Looking by the Indian standards they may not be much too over compensated and similarly not very much under compensated as well, in the background of the country where most of the dependent beneficiaries reside. Two of the dependents namely, parents aged 69/73 years live in India, but four of them are in the United States. Considering all the facts and factors it appears that application of multiplier of 7 is definitely on the lower side. Some deviation in the figure of multiplier would not mean that there may be a wide difference between the multiplier applied and he scheduled multiplier which in this case is 13. The difference between 7 and 13 is too wide. Looking to the high amount of multiplicand and the ages of the dependents and the fact that parents are residing in India, application of multiplier of 10 would be reasonable and would provide a fair compensation; *United India Insurance Co. Ltd.* v. *Patricia Jean Mahajan,* AIR 2002 SC 2607: 2002 AIR SCW 2920: JT 2002 (5) SC 74: 2002 (6) SCC 281: 2002 (5) SCALE 56: 2002 (4) Supreme 518.

The deceased was 35 years old. The claimants are his wife and four minor daughters. Even as per the Second Schedule the multiplier in case of the persons between 35 to 40 years is 16. In the case the rate of interest granted is only 6% considering the general rate of interest prevalent therefore, the proper multiplier would be 14 as the value of the notional income has been increased. It was nobody's case that the deceased was not working at all; *Laxmi Devi* v. *Mohammad Tabbar,* AIR 2008 SC 1858: 2008 AIR SCW 2605: 2008 (4) SCALE 683.

Though the deceased was aged about 25 years, considering the age of his mother about 65 years and of father more than 65 years at relevant time, the multiplier of 5 would be appropriate. Taking into account the monthly contribution at Rs. 3,500 the entitlement of the claim would be Rs. 2,10,000. The same shall bear interest @7.5% p.a. from the date of the application for compensation. Payment already made shall be adjusted from the amount due; *New India Assurance Co. Ltd.* v. *Shanti Pathak,* AIR 2007 SC 2649: 2007 AIR SCW 4779: 2007 (9) SCALE 216: 2007 (5) Supreme 460.

At the time of accident, the age of the deceased was 36 years. Therefore, the Tribunal and the High Court were not right in applying the multiplier of 10. They should have adopted the multiplier of 15 for the purpose of determining the amount of compensation; *New India Assurance Co. Ltd.* v. *Gopali,* AIR 2012 SC 3381: 2012 AIR SCW 4330: 2012 (4) ACJ 2131.

6. Multiplier Method – Multiplier method involves ascertainment of loss of dependency or multiplicand the choice of multiplier is determined by the age of the deceased and by the calculation as to what capital sum would yield the multiplicand by way of annual interest; *Uttaranchal Transport Corpn. Ltd.* v. *Vimla Devi,* AIR 2009 SC 2146: 2009 AIR SCW 2740: 2009 (4) SCC 377.

The claimant must be paid a capital sum, which would yield sufficient interest to provide material benefits of the same standard and duration as the deceased would have provided for the dependents, if the deceased had lived and earned. The multiplier method is based upon the assessment that yearly loss of dependency should be equal to interest that could be earned in normal course on the capital sum invested. The capital sum would be the compensation for loss of dependency or the pecuniary loss suffered by the dependents. Needless to say, uniform application of the multiplier method ensures consistency and certainty and prevents different amounts being awarded in different cases. The multiplier is decided and determined on the basis of length of dependency, which must be estimated. This has to be necessarily discounted for contingencies and uncertainties; *R.K. Malik* v. *Kiran Pal,* AIR 2009 SC 2506: 2009 AIR SCW 4381: 2009 (8) SCALE 451.

7. Plea of Owner Some Other Person Driving Vehicle is within his Special Knowledge – The plea of the owner of tractor is that he was not driving the tractor, some other person was driving the same. The burden of proof ordinarily would be on Insurance Company to establish that there has been a breach of conditions of the contract of insurance. In this case, however, the burden in terms of section 106 of the Evidence Act was on the appellant. He failed to discharge the said burden; *Bhuwan Singh* v. *Oriental Insurance Co. Ltd.,* AIR 2009 SC 2177: 2009 AIR SCW 2865: 2009 (5) SCC 136: 2009 (3) SCALE 798.

8. Fair Amount of Compensation – The deceased was offered job in USA at annual salary of Rs. 18 lacs but he has not accepted the same. He was not working when his accident took place in India. The cost of living in the western countries would be higher. The standard of living in the western countries cannot be followed; in the absence of any material placed before this Court it should not be followed in India. Even in a case where the victim of an accident was earning salary in U.S. Dollars, a lower multiplier should be applied. The fair amount of compensation should have been calculated at Rs. 25,000 per month being about 1/3rd of the amount which he was receiving in U.K. Indisputably, deduction of 1/3rd towards personal expenses is the ordinary rule in India; *Oriental Insurance Co. Ltd.* v. *Deo Patodi,* AIR 2009 SC 2442: 2009 AIR SCW 4559: 2009 (8) SCALE 194.

9. Requirement for Determining Compensation – Section 168 empowers the Claims Tribunal to "make an award determining the amount of compensation which appears to it to be just". Therefore, only requirement for determining the compensation is that it must be 'just'. There is no other limitation or restriction on its power for awarding just compensation; *Nagappa* v. *Gurudayal Singh,* AIR 2003 SC 674: 2002 AIR SCW 5348: 2003 (2) SCC 274: 2002 (9) SCALE 37: 2002 (8) Supreme 497.

10. Determination of Compensation – The widow of the deceased said that her husband's income was Rs. 1,500 per month. The brother of the deceased also supported the same version. No contra evidence has been adduced in regard to that aspect. It is, therefore, reasonable to believe that the monthly income of the deceased was Rs. 1,500. In calculating the amount of compensation in this case the court adopted the structured formula provided in the Second Schedule to the Act. Though it was formulated for the purpose of section 163A of the Act, the court finds it a safer guidance for arriving at the amount of compensation than any other method so far as the case is concerned. The age of the deceased at the time of accident was said to be 35 years plus. But when that is taken along with the annual income of Rs. 18,000 figure indicated in the structured formula is Rs. 2,70,000. When 1/3 is deducted the balance would be Rs. 1,80,000. Therefore, it is just and proper to fix the said amount as total compensation payable to the appellants as on the date of their claim; *S. Kaushnuma Begum* v. *New India Assurance Co. Ltd.,* AIR 2001 SC 485: 2001 AIR SCW 85: JT 2001 (1) SC 375: 2001 (2) SCC 9: 2001 (1) SCALE 1: 2001 (1) Supreme 5.

Where there was no certainty that the victim after his retirement would have increased his income or not, the award of compensation under the head of future income after retirement was unjustified. Likewise, the future income may diminish with a recession in trade or he might have had spells of unemployment. Therefore, the award of compensation under the head of future income after retirement was unjustified; *United India Insurance Co. Ltd.* v. *Manisa Porwar,* AIR 1999 All 142: 1999 All LJ 932: 2000 (1) ACJ 30.

Determination of the amount of compensation arising out of loss of life of a person, who was the earning member of the family, would depend upon a large number of factors; one of them being the nature of job or business he was doing. For the said purpose, an average gross future monthly income must be arrived at by adding the actual gross income at the time of his death to the maximum which he might have got, had he not met a pre-mature death. Average life expectancy in India also is one of the factors which must be taken into consideration for the purpose of calculating the average gross future monthly income. The average life expectancy in India is now 60-61 years. It is necessary to subtract personal and living expenses and other statutory liabilities like payment of income-tax etc. Deduction of 1/3rd of income of deceased is the ordinary rule. In a case of permanent disability, where the injured even for a very small thing would have to depend on the services of another, a direction to deduct the said amount may not be insisted upon; *Sarla Verma* v. *Delhi Transport Corporation,* AIR 2009 SC 3104: 2009 AIR SCW 4992: 2009 (6) SCC 121: 2009 (6) SCALE 129.

The deceased-claimants' son was unmarried at the time of death in motor accident. His income was Rs.2,00,000 per annum. If he was getting an income of Rs. 2,00,000 per annum 50% of his income has to be deducted towards personal expenditure. Therefore, the annual dependency has to be assessed at Rs. 1,00,000 per annum. Out of which 75% has to be deducted towards contributory negligence of the deceased. Therefore, the loss of dependency per annum has to be assessed at Rs. 25,000. Considering the age of the mother of the deceased, it is applied the multiplier of 13. Then the loss of dependency has to be assessed at Rs. 3,25,000. In addition, the claimants would be entitled to a sum of Rs. 30,000. Thus, the claimants are entitled to total compensation of Rs. 3,55,000 which shall be payable by the owner of the offending car and its insurer; *Girijesh Vyas* v. *G. Vishnuvardhan*, AIR 2012 Kant 44: 2012 AAC 46: 2012 (4) ACJ 2326.

The deceased was aged about 25 years at the time of his death. The deceased was not holding any driving license for driving a Road Roller. In fact, he was holding a driving license of the motorcycle only. Section 10 of the Motor Vehicles Act requires a separate license or endorsement for driving a Road Roller. Thus is difficult to believe that the deceased was a Road Roller Operator. The assessment of the income of the deceased by the Tribunal on its own estimate at Rs. 3,000 per month and Rs. 36,000 per annum, therefore, cannot be found fault with; *Shahnaj Khatun* v. *Suleman*, AIR 2012 Chht 174.

11. Assessment of Compensation in Infant or Child Death Case – The High Court has issued following guidelines to Tribunals and Courts regarding assessment of compensation in motor accident infant or child death cases:—

1. The items of compensation in cases of death of children should not be different from the items of compensation for the death of adults;.
2. While awarding the conventional sum for the death of the children, all the factors should be taken into consideration including the age of the deceased, the age of the parents or the dependents, the possibility of the deceased growing up and contributing to the family in future in an orderly life etc.;.
3. The monetary loss to the claimants should also be awarded subject to proof as special damages in each case;.
4. No precedent should be taken in such a question as the conclusion in the matter as each case has to be considered on its own merits subject to the general principles;.
5. No amount of compensation as conventional sum should be taken as fixed;.
6. The minimum amount of compensation awardable for the case of death of children as in the case of adults shall be as follows:
   (i) Rs. 15,000 for the death of children in respect of the accidents occurred on or after the date when section 92A of 1939 Act was brought on the statute book *i.e.* 1-10-1982;.
   (ii) Rs. 25,000 for the death of children in respect of the accidents occurred on or after the date when section 140 of 1988 Act was brought into force i.e. 1-7-1989; and.
   (iii) Rs. 50,000 for the death of children in respect of the accidents occurred on or after the date on which section 140 of 1988 Act was amended by Act No. 54 of 1994 *i.e.* 14-11-1994; *Amati Hymavathi* v. *Nissankararao Srikrishnamurthy*, AIR 1998 AP 345: 2000 (1) ACJ 350: 1998 (4) Andh LT 26.

12. Deduction Due to Lump Sum Payment – What should be the deduction due to lump-sum payment, depends on facts and circumstances of each case. There could not be any hard and fast rule that in all cases where lumpsum amount is awarded, there could be no deduction or if at all deduction is to be made, at what rate. The deductions on account of lump-sum payment also vary from case to case. In some cases, 10% of the deduction has been found to be just and proper while in other cases, deduction of

20%,25% and even 30% has been found to be justified; *Krishna* v. *Deepak Chhabra*, AIR 1995 Bom 130: 1995 (2) ACJ 1192: 1995 (1) TAC 640.

13. Deduction Towards Personal Expenses – The deceased left behind him a large family who were entirely dependents upon his income. Although in normal circumstances, in the case of unmarried man dying, half of the income is deducted towards his personal expenses for the purpose of computing loss of dependency, there is no hard and fast rule that that norm should be strictly adhered to in each and every case. It all depends upon who are dependents and to what extent they were depending upon the income of the deceased for their livelihood. The brother of the deceased was 15 years and sister was 20 years aged on the date of the accident. Therefore, the deceased had responsibility to educate the brother and to marry and settle the sister apart from supporting the aged parents. In that view of the matter, the court not taken any exception to the award of the M.A.C.T. in deducting only 1/3rd of the income towards personal expenses of the deceased; *National Insurance Co. Ltd.* v. *Gendram Sahu*, AIR 2006 Chhat 82: 2006 AIHC 309 (NOC): 2006 (4) ACC 566.

14. Directions to be followed by Tribunal – To ensure expeditious payments of compensation payable as per the award of Tribunal in accordance with mandate of section 168(3) High Court issued following directions to be followed by all Motor Accident Claims Tribunal—

(a) While filing the written statement, the concerned insurance company is required to furnish details of its Bank account and the Bank to the Court. In case a written statement has already been filed in an existing claim, all insurance companies are required to furnish the name of the concerned Bank and their account numbers within 3 months from today.

(b) Within a period of 30 days of the award, which is the period prescribed for depositing the amount under section 168(3) to the High Court, the insurance company is required to tender the payment awarded by the MACT by issuing cheques in the name of the claimant(s) unless and until a stay order has been obtained from the High Court. The names of the claimants who are to be paid the amounts along with the amount payable is required to be stated in the award.

(c) If after the expiry of 90 days which is the prescribed period for preferring an appeal under section 173(1) payment of the amount awarded by the MACT has not been made, notice must be issued to the Bank named by the Insurance Company directing such Bank to deposit the cheque drawn in the name of the claimant/claimants legally entitled as per the award covering the amount(s) as per the MACT award within a week of receipt of such orders and cheques should be retained for being given to the claimant.

(d) Once the amount is deposited by cheque as per the aforesaid procedure the MACT is required to ensure that within a period of six weeks thereafter the amount is disbursed to the claimants under the supervision of the Presiding Officer by issuing the said cheque to the claimant so that the claimants are not put to undue harassment.

(e) In case for some reason it is not possible to make the payment to the claimant within six months of the issue of the cheques in the name of the claimant, then the MACT should ensure that such cheques are returned to the Insurance Companies in lieu of fresh cheques drawn in favour of the appropriate account of the MACT which are required to be deposited in an interest bearing short term fixed deposit for a six monthly period by the MACT.

(f) In case the MACT has to resort to the procedure prescribed under sub-para (c) above which requires it to secure the amount through the banks upon a failure of the insurance company to deposit the amount within the time stipulated by section 168(3) and the above procedure, cost of Rs. 5000 payable to the claimant is required to be imposed on the Insurance Companies.

(g) If directions given by the MACT to the Banks are not complied with, the MACT may order freezing of Bank Accounts to the extent covered by the award; *New India Assurance Co. Ltd.* v. *Kashmiri Lal,* AIR 2006 Del 112: 2006 AIHC 1848: 2007 (1) ACJ 688.

15. Steps to Determine Compensation – To have uniformity and consistency, Tribunals should determine compensation in cases of death, by the following well settled steps:

Step 1: Ascertaining the multiplicand: The income of the deceased per annum should be determined. Out of the said income a deduction should be made in regard to the amount which the deceased would have spent on himself by way of personal and living expenses. The balance which is considered to be the contribution to the dependent family, constitutes the multiplicand.

Step 2: Ascertaining the multiplier: Having regard to the age of the deceased and period of active career, the appropriate multiplier should be selected. This does not mean ascertaining the number of years he would have lived or worked but for the accident. Having regard to several imponderable in life and economic factors, a table of multipliers with reference to the age has been identified by Supreme Court. The multiplier should be chosen from the said table with reference to the age of the deceased.

Step 3: Actual calculation: The annual contribution to the family (multiplicand) when multiplied by such multiplier gives the 'loss of dependency' to the family.

Thereafter, a conventional amount in the range of Rs. 5000 to Rs. 10,000 may be added as loss of estate. Where the deceased is survived by his widow, another conventional amount in the range of Rs. 5000 to Rs. 10,000 should be added under the head of loss of consortium. But no amount is to be awarded under the head of pain, suffering or hardship caused to the legal heirs of the deceased. The funeral expenses, cost of transportation of the body (if incurred) and cost of any medical treatment of the deceased before death (if incurred) should also added; *Sarla Verma* v. *Delhi Transport Corporation,* AIR 2009 SC 3104: 2009 AIR SCW 4992: 2009 (6) SCC 121: 2009 (6) SCALE 129.

16. Use of Multiplier – The multiplier to be used should be as which starts with an operative multiplier of 18 (for the age groups of 15 to 20 and 21 to 25 years), reduced by one unit for every five years, that is M-17 for 26 to 30 years, M-16 for 31 to 35 years, M-15 for 36 to 40 years, M-14 for 41 to 45 years, and M-13 for 46 to 50 years, then reduced by two units for every five years, that is, M-11 for 51 to 55 years, M-9 for 56 to 60 years, M-7 for 61 to 65 years and M-5 for 66 to 70 years; *Sarla Verma* v. *Delhi Transport Corporation,* AIR 2009 SC 3104: 2009 AIR SCW 4992: 2009 (6) SCC 121: 2009 (6) SCALE 129.

17. Deduction for Personal and Living Expenses – Where the deceased was married, the deduction towards personal and living expenses of the deceased, should be one-third where the number of dependent family members is 2 to 3, one-fourth where the number of dependent family members is 4 to 6, and one-fifth where the number of dependent family members exceed six. Where the deceased was a bachelor and the claimants are the parents, the deduction follows a different principle. In regard to bachelors, normally, 50% is deducted as personal and living expenses, because it is assumed that a bachelor would tend to spend more on himself. Even otherwise, there is also the possibility of his getting married in a short time, in which event the contribution to the parents and siblings is likely to be cut drastically. Further, subject to evidence to the contrary, the father is likely to have his own income and will not be considered as a dependent and the mother alone will be considered as a dependent. In the absence of evidence to the contrary, brothers and sisters will not be considered as dependents, because they will either be independent and earning, or married, or be dependent on the father. Thus, even if the deceased is survived by parents and siblings, only the mother would be considered to be a dependent, and 50% would be treated as the personal and living expenses of the bachelor and 50% as the contribution to the family. However, where family of the bachelor is large and dependent on the income of the deceased, as in a case where he has a widowed mother and large number of younger non-earning sisters or brothers, his personal and living expenses may be restricted to one-third and contribution to the family will be taken as two-third; *Sarla Verma* v. *Delhi Transport Corporation,* AIR 2009 SC 3104: 2009 AIR SCW 4992: 2009 (6) SCC 121: 2009 (6) SCALE 129.

18. Quantum of Compensation for Death of Seven Years Old Child – There are some aspects of human life which are capable of monetary measurement, but the totality of human life is like the beauty of sunrise or the splendor of the stars, beyond the reach of monetary tape-measure. The determination of damages for loss of human life is an extremely difficult task and it becomes all the more baffling when the deceased is a child and/or a non-earning person. The future of a child is uncertain. A child, is earning nothing but has a prospect to earn. Therefore, neither the income of the deceased child is capable of assessment on estimated basis nor the financial loss suffered by the parents is capable of mathematical computation. Thus, where child aged about 7 years died in an accident, Award of Rs. 51,500 by the Tribunal is not liable to be interfered with; *Oriental Insurance Co. Ltd.* v. *Syed Ibrahim,* AIR 2008 SC 103: 2007 AIR SCW 6197: 2007 (11) SCC 512: 2007 (11) SCALE 184: 2007 (6) Supreme 574.

19. Computation income of Victim – The term "income" has different connotations for different purposes. A Court of law, having regard to the change in societal conditions must consider the question not only having regard to pay packet the employee carries home at the end of the month but also other perks which are beneficial to the members of the entire family. In determining what constitutes income it cannot be lost sight that the private sector companies in place of introducing a pension scheme takes recourse to payment of contributory Provident Fund, Gratuity and other perks to attract the people who are efficient and hard working. If some facilities are being provided whereby the entire family stands to benefit, the same, must be held to be relevant for the purpose of computation of total income on the basis whereof the amount of compensation payable for the death of the kith and kin of the applicants is required to be determined; *National Insurance Co. Ltd.* v. *Indira Srivastava,* AIR 2008 SC 845: 2008 AIR SCW 143: 2008 (2) SCC 763: 2007 (14) SCALE 461.

20. Award Enhancing Compensation – There is no restriction that the Tribunal/ Court cannot award compensation amount exceeding the claimed amount. The function of the Tribunal/Court is to award "just" compensation which is reasonable on the basis of evidence produced on record. Further, in such cases there is no question of claim becoming time-barred or it cannot be contended that by enhancing the claim there should be change of cause of action; *A.P.S.R.T.C.* v. *M. Ramadevi,* AIR 2008 SC 1221: 2008 AIR SCW 1213: 2008 (3) SCC 379: 2008 (2) SCALE 10.

21. Income of Deceased on Date Retirement not Relevant Factor – Salary of the deceased has not been revised with retrospective effect on the date of death of the him only because such salary was revised at a later point of time, the same by itself would not have been a factor which could have been taken into consideration for determining the amount of compensation. What would have been the income of the deceased on the date of retirement was not a relevant factor in the light of peculiar facts of this case; *Oriental Insurance Company Ltd.* v. *Jashuben,* AIR 2008 SC 1734: 2008 AIR SCW 2393: 2008 (4) SCC 162: 2008 (2) SCALE 474.

22. Just and Fair Rate of Compensation – What would, be just and fair amount of compensation is required to be determined having regard to the facts and circumstances of the case involved. The Courts may deviate from the structured formula. In terms of the Second Schedule, where the deceased or injured were not having any income, the statute presumes an income of or about 15,000 per month. If having regard to the age of the appellant, the multiplier of 15 is applied, a sum of Rs. 2,25,000 would be payable. Besides the said sum, not only some amount of compensation should be awarded under the heading of mental agony but also some provision should be made for future treatment. What would be the genuine and reasonable expenditure likely to be incurred by the appellant towards her future treatment is not borne out from the records. It would require serious consideration for the purpose of award of damages. When a person becomes completely incapable to do any work and virtually has no enjoyment for life, the same form relevant factors and, thus, requires consideration for the purpose of determining a fair and reasonable amount of compensation. Future treatment for the appellant would be necessary. If future treatment is necessary, some provision should be made therefor. She may require another operation. She may require to be provided with an artificial limb; *Sapna* v. *United India Insurance Co. Ltd.,* AIR 2008 SC 2281: 2008 AIR SCW 4080: 2008 (7) SCC 613: 2008 (8) SCALE 622.

23. Driving without Licence may not Lead to Finding of Negligence – If a person drives a vehicle without a licence, he commits an offence. The appellant was not possessing any licence but no finding of fact has been arrived at that he was driving the two-wheeler rashly and negligently. If he was not driving rashly and negligently which contributed to the accident, only because he was not having a licence, he would not be held to be guilty of contributory negligence; *Sudhir Kumar Rana* v. *Surinder Singh,* AIR 2008 SC 2405: 2008 AIR SCW 3981: 2008 (8) SCALE 594.

24. Driver and Owner are Jointly Liable but not Joint Tort-feasors – When a law is enacted to consolidate and amend the law, the Legislature not only takes into consideration the law as it has then been existing but also the law which was prevailing prior thereto. A suit for damages arises out of a tortuous action. For the purpose of such an action, although, there is no statutory definition of negligence, ordinarily, it would mean omission of duty caused either by omission to do something which a reasonable man guided upon those considerations, who ordinarily by reason of conduct of human affairs would do or be obligated to, or by doing something which a reasonable or prudent man would not do. When a damage is caused upon act of negligence on the part of a person, the said person is primarily held to be liable for payment of damages. The owner of the vehicle would be liable as he has permitted the use thereof. To that effect only under the Motor Vehicles Act, both driver and owner would be jointly liable. This, however, would not mean that they are joint tort-feasors in the strict sense of the term. There exists a distinction between the liability of the owner of a vehicle which was used in commission of the accident and that of the driver for whose negligence the accident was caused, but the same would not mean that the owner and the driver are joint tort-feasors in the sense as it is ordinarily understood; *Machindranath Kernath Kasar* v. *D.S. Mylarappa,* AIR 2008 SC 2545: 2008 AIR SCW 3546: 2008 (7) SCALE 496.

25. Distinction between Composite Negligence and Contributory Negligence – 'Composite negligence' refers to the negligence on the part of two or more persons. Where a person is injured as a result of negligence on the part of two or more wrongdoers, it is said that the person was injured on account of the composite negligence of those wrongdoers. In such a case, each wrongdoer, is jointly and severally liable to the injured for payment of the entire damages and the injured person has the choice of proceeding against all or any of them. In such a case, the injured need not establish the extent of responsibility of each wrongdoer separately, nor is it necessary for the Court to determine the extent of liability of each wrong-doer separately. On the other hand where a person suffers injury, partly due to the negligence on the part of another person or persons, and partly as a result of his own negligence, then the negligence on the part of the injured which contributed to the accident is referred to as his contributory negligence. Where the injured is guilty of some negligence, his claim for damages is not defeated merely by reason of the negligence on his part but the damages recoverable by him in respect of the injuries stands reduced in proportion to his contributory negligence; *E.O. Antony* v. *Karvanan,* AIR 2008 (Supp) SC 1646.

26. Extent of Contributory Negligent – When two vehicles are involved in an accident, and one of the drivers claims compensation from the other driver alleging negligence, and the other driver denies negligence or claims that the injured claimant himself was negligent, then it becomes necessary to consider whether the injured claimant was negligent and if so, whether he was solely or partly responsible for the accident and the extent of his responsibility, that is his contributory negligence. Therefore where the injured is himself partly liable, the principle of 'composite negligence' will not apply nor can there be an automatic inference that the negligence was 50 : 50. Manner of the accident as deposed by the claimant's witnesses indicate that the deceased was partially responsible for the accident. There was contributory negligence. The proportion can be fixed at 1 : 4; *A.P.S.R.T.C.* v. *K. Hemalatha,* AIR 2008 SC 2851: 2008 AIR SCW 4712: 2008 (6) SCC 767: 2008 (8) SCALE 604.

27. Loss of Dependency – Assessment – The incumbent was a bachelor and he could not have spent more than 1/3rd of his total income for personal use and rest of the amount earned by him would certainly go to the family kitty. Therefore, determining the loss of dependency by 50% was not correct. Therefore, it is assessed that he must be spending 1/3rd towards personal use and contributing 2/3rd of his income to his family. Therefore, the loss of dependency was Rs. 20,000 it is 2/3rd of his income (Rs. 30000). As per schedule appended to the Act applying the multiplier of 12 the total loss of dependency will be Rs. 20,000 x 12 = Rs. 2,40,000 and Rs. 10,000 towards loss of estate and funeral expenses, the total compensation comes to Rs. 2,50,000 and incumbent is entitled for interest @ 9/% per annum from the date of the petition; *Bilkish* v. *United India Insurance Co. Ltd.,* AIR 2008 SC 2989:2008 AIR SCW 5040: 2008 (4) SCC 259: 2008 (4) SCALE 25.

28. Determination of Damages in Cases of Death of Child of Tender Age – The determination of damages for loss of human life is an extremely difficult task and it becomes all the more baffling when the deceased is a child and/or a non earning person. The future of a child is uncertain. Where the deceased was a child, he was earning nothing but had a prospect to earn. The question of assessment of compensation, therefore, becomes stiffer. The figure of compensation in such cases involves a good deal of guesswork. In cases, where parents are claimants, relevant factor would be age of parents. In cases of young children of tender age, in view of uncertainties abound, neither their income at the time of death nor the prospects of the future increase in their income nor chances of advancement of their career are capable of proper determination on estimated basis. The reason is that at such an early age, the uncertainties in regard to their academic pursuits, achievements in career and thereafter advancement in life are so many that nothing can be assumed with reasonable certainty. Therefore, neither the income of the deceased child is capable of assessment on estimated basis nor the financial loss suffered by the parents is capable of mathematical computation; *New India Assurance Co. Ltd.* v. *Satender,* AIR 2007 SC 324: 2006 AIR SCW 6139: 2006 (11) SCALE 589.

29. Determination of Compensation by Multiplier Method – The multiplier method involves the ascertainment of the loss of dependency or the multiplicand having regard to the circumstances of the case and capitalizing the multiplicand by an appropriate multiplier. The choice of the multiplier is determined by the age of the deceased (or that of the claimants whichever is higher) and by the calculation as to what capital sum, if invested at a rate of interest appropriate to a stable economy, would yield the multiplicand by way of annual interest. In ascertaining this, regard should also be had to the fact that ultimately the capital sum should also be consumed-up over the period for which the dependency is expected to last. In the case, the deceased was of 33 years of age and was driving a taxi. However in the absence of any definite material about the income, monthly contribution to the family, after deduction for personal expenses was fixed at Rs. 3,000 per month *i.e.* annually Rs. 36,000 and applying the multiplier of 13 as the age of deceased was 33 years, the compensation worked out to Rs. 4,68,000 which shall carry interest @ 6% p.a. from the date of claim till the date of actual payment; *New India Assurance Co. Ltd.* v. *Kalpana,* AIR 2007 SC 1243: 2007 AIR SCW 1316: 2007 (3) SCC 538: 2007 (2) SCALE 227: 2007 (1) Supreme 514.

30. Compensation in Case of Permanent Disabled – The claimant was 38 years and was working as carpenter and earning Rs. 4,500. He became permanently disabled and lost his earning capacity. Minimum compensation payable in a case of this nature should be considered from the sufferings of disability undergone by the victim. In certain situations, the multiplier specified in the Second Schedule cannot and should not be altered but therefor there must exist strong circumstances. Application of multiplicative factor should also be considered from that angle; *Chief Law Officer, A.P.S.R.T.C.* v. *M. Pentaiah Chary,* AIR 2007 SC 3141: 2007 AIR SCW 5689: 2007 (10) SCALE 495: 2007 (6) Supreme 237.

31. Multiplier Method – The multiplier method involves the ascertainment of the loss of dependency or the multiplicand having regard to the circumstances of the case and capitalizing the multiplicand by an appropriate multiplier. The choice of the multiplier is determined by the age of the deceased or that of the claimants whichever is higher and by the calculation as to what capital sum, if invested at rate of interest appropriate to a stable economy, would yield the multiplicand by way of annual interest. In ascertaining this, regard should also be had to the fact that ultimately the capital sum should also be consumed up over the period for which the dependency is expected to last. The multiplier method involves the ascertainment of the loss of dependency or the multiplicand having regard to the circumstances of the case and capitalizing the multiplicand by an appropriate multiplier. The choice of the multiplier is determined by the age of the deceased (or that of the claimants whichever is higher) and by the calculation as to what capital sum, if invested at a rate of interest appropriate to a stable economy, would yield the multiplicand by way of annual interest. In ascertaining this, regard should also be had to the fact that ultimately the capital sum should also be consumed up over the period for which the dependency is expected to last; *Managing Director, T.N.S.T.C.* v. *Sripriya,* AIR 2007 SC (Supp) 19: (2007) 4 SCALE 222.

32. Quantum of Compensation – The claimant was deriving income from agriculture. Normal rule about the deprivation of income is directly not applicable to cases where agricultural income is the source of deceased's or injured's income. In that case other circumstances have to be considered. Taking the totality of the circumstances, on the basis of the various factors, the quantum of compensation is fixed at Rs. 3,50,000. The amount shall carry interest @ 7.5% per annum from the date of filing of the claim application up to the date of payment; *New India Assurance Co. Ltd.* v. *Charlie,* AIR 2005 SC 2157: 2005 AIR SCW 1801: 2005 (10) SCC 720: 2005 (3) SCALE 541: 2005 (3) Supreme 262.

The deceased was a child aged about 7 years at the time of accident. The Tribunal, has awarded a sum of Rs. 60,000 as compensation to the parents of the deceased with interest at the rate of 10% per annum from the date of filing of the claim petition till realization. Thus the quantum of compensation awarded by the Claims Tribunal is not liable to be interfered with; *Ram Kumar* v. *Nistor Kindo,* AIR 2011 Chht 126.

33. Highest and Lowest Multiplier – The appropriate highest multiplier to be applied while determining compensation in motor accident cases would be 18. The highest multiplier has to be for the age group of 21 years to 25 years when an ordinary Indian

Citizen starts independently earning and the lowest would be in respect of a person in the age group of 60 to 70, which is the normal retirement age; *New India Assurance Co. Ltd.* v. *Charlie,* AIR 2005 SC 2157: 2005 AIR SCW 1801: 2005 (10) SCC 720: 2005 (3) SCALE 541: 2005 (3) Supreme 262.

34. Deduction for Personal Expenditure – What would be the percentage of deduction for personal expenditure while determining compensation in motor accident cases, cannot be governed by any rigid rule or formula by universal application. It would depend upon circumstances of each case. In the case the claimant was nearly 37 years of age and was married. Therefore, 1/3rd deduction has to be made for personal expenditure; *New India Assurance Co. Ltd.* v. *Charlie,* AIR 2005 SC 2157: 2005 AIR SCW 1801: 2005 (10) SCC 720: 2005 (3) SCALE 541: 2005 (3) Supreme 262.

35. Contributory Negligent – No reasons have been recorded for disbelieving the statement of eye witness. He has been disbelieved only on the ground that had the driver been negligent he himself would not have taken the injured to the hospital. This by itself is no reason to either disbelieve. Thus the finding arrived at by the High Court that the appellant himself contributed to the extent of 50 per cent in causing the accident cannot be accepted; *Suresh Yallappa Patil* v. *General Manager, K.S.R.T.C.,* AIR 2003 SC 85: 2002 AIR SCW 4489: JT 2002 (8) SC 484: 2002 (8) SCC 406: 2002 (8) SCALE 175: 2002 (7) Supreme 399.

36. Vicarious Liability – Where an accident took place due to collision of two buses and in a claim petition filed by driver of one of buses who was injured in the accident, only the Insurance Company and proprietor of other bus were made parties and proprietor of bus *i.e.* employer of claimant driver was not impleaded, the order of High Court *suo motu* impleadings the employee of the claimant and imposing liability to the extent of 50% on the employer of claimant driver, on finding contributory negligence of drivers of both buses was not justified. The employer cannot be held to be vicariously liable for the negligence of the claimant himself. Since the proprietor was not at fault and the accident was caused because of the contributory negligence of the drivers of both the buses, the proprietor could not be held liable under the provision of Act. Moreover, the claimant was given compassionate appointment on suitable alternative job and he never desired to obtain any other compensation from his employer; *Tamil Nadu State Transport Corporation, M/s. Tanjore* v. *Natarajan,* AIR 2003 SC 2232: 2003 AIR SCW 2680: JT 2003 (4) SC 446: 2003 (6) SCC 137: 2003 (4) SCALE 527: 2003 (3) Supreme 698.

37. Just Compensation – Every method or mode adopted for assessing compensation has to be considered in the background of "just" compensation which is the pivotal consideration. Though by use of the expression "which appears to it to be just" a wide discretion is vested on the Tribunal, the determination has to be rational, to be done by a judicious approach and not the outcome of whims, wild guesses and arbitrariness. The expression "just" denotes equitability, fairness and reasonableness, and non-arbitrary. If it is not so it cannot be just; *State of Haryana* v. *Jasbir Kaur,* AIR 2003 SC 3696: 2003 AIR SCW 4198: 2003 (7) SCC 484: 2003 (6) SCALE 113: 2003 (6) Supreme 206.

There can be no golden rule applicable to all cases for measuring the value of human life or a limb. Measure of damages cannot be arrived at by precise mathematical calculations. It would depend upon the particular facts and circumstances, and attending peculiar or special features, if any. Every method or mode adopted for assessing compensation has to be considered in the background of 'just' compensation which is the pivotal consideration. Though by use of the expression 'which appears to it to be just' a wide discretion is vested on the Tribunal, the determination has to be rational, to be done by a judicious approach and not the outcome of whims, wild guesses and arbitrariness. The expression 'just' denotes equitability, fairness and reasonableness, and non-arbitrary. If it is not so it cannot be just. A person not only suffers injuries on account of accident but also suffers in mind and body on account of the accident throughout his life and a feeling is developed that he is no more a normal man and cannot enjoy the amenities of life as another normal person can. While fixing compensation for pain and suffering as also for loss of amenities of life the features like his age, marital status and unusual deprivation he has undertaken in his life has to be reckoned; *Divisional Controller, K.S.R.T.C.* v. *Mahadeva Shetty,* AIR 2003 SC 4172: 2003 AIR SCW 3797: JT 2003 (6) SC 519: 2003 (7) SCC 197: 2003 (6) SCALE 16: 2003 (5) Supreme 266.

Just compensation even if the same is more than the amount claimed, can be awarded; *Oriental Fire & General Insurance Co. Ltd.* v. *Masi Ram,* 1989 ACJ 1120 HP.

The deceased was the sole bread winner and supporting the claimant. At the time of accident, the deceased was aged 42 years. The monthly income of the deceased was taken at Rs. 2500 per month, by applying "10" multiplier and after deducting 1/3 towards personal and living expenditure of the deceased, the Tribunal has awarded a sum of Rs. 2,04,540 as dependency compensation. In addition to the above, the Tribunal has awarded a sum of Rs. 2000 towards funeral expenses and Rs. 2500 for loss of estate. Under section 168 of the Motor Vehicles Act, the Tribunal/Court may make an award determining the amount of compensation, which appears to it to be just and specifying the person or persons, to whom compensation shall be paid. The sole dependent wife has lost her husband and is now left with no support. Applying the principles of just compensation, this Court is of the considered view that the application of "10" multiplier for the purpose of computing dependency compensation is not manifestly illegal; *Metropolitan Transport Corpn., Chennai* v. *D. Pappa Susaiammal,* AIR 2011 Mad 184.

38. Liability in Case of Act of God – The expression 'act of God' signifies the operation of natural forces free from human intervention, such as lightening, storm etc. It may include such unexpected occurrences of nature as severe gale, snowstorms, hurricanes, cyclones, tidal waves and the like. But every unexpected wind and storm does not operate as an excuse from liability, to pay compensation if there is a reasonable possibility of anticipating their happening. An act of God provides no excuse unless it is so unexpected that no reasonable human foresight could be presumed to anticipate the occurrence, having regard to the conditions of time and place known to be prevailing at. For instance, where by experience of a number of years, preventive action can be taken; *Divisional Controller, K.S.R.T.C.* v. *Mahadeva Shetty,* AIR 2003 SC 4172: 2003 AIR SCW 3797: JT 2003 (6) SC 519: 2003 (7) SCC 197: 2003 (6) SCALE 16: 2003 (5) Supreme 266.

39. Act to be Negligent – To determine whether an act would be or would not be negligent, it is relevant to determine if any reasonable man would foresee that the act would cause damage or not. The omission to do what the law obligates or even the failure to do anything in a manner, mode or method envisaged by law would equally and *per se* constitute negligence on the part of such person. If the answer is in the affirmative, it is a negligent act. Where an accident is due to negligence of both parties, substantially there would be contributory negligence and both would be blamed. In a case contributory negligence, the crucial question on which liability depends would be whether either party could, by exercise of reasonable care, have avoided the consequence of other's negligence. Whichever party could have avoided the consequence of other's negligence would be liable for the accident. If a person's negligent act or omission was the proximate and immediate cause of death, the fact that the person suffering injury was himself negligent and also contributed to the accident or other circumstances by which the injury was caused would not afford a defence to the other. Contributory negligence is applicable solely to the conduct of plaintiff. It means that there has been an act or omission on the part of the plaintiff which has materially contributed to the damage, the act or omission being of such a nature that it may properly be described as negligence, although negligence is not given its usual meaning. It is now well settled that in the case of contributory negligence, Courts have power to apportion the loss between the parties as seems just and equitable. Apportionment in that context means that damage are reduced to such an extent as the Court thinks just and equitable having regard to the claim shared in the responsibility for the damage. But in a case where there has been no contributory negligence on the part of the victim, the question of apportionment does not arise. Where a person is injured without any negligence on his part but as a result of combined effect of the negligence of two other persons, it is not a case of contributory negligence in that sense; *Municipal Corpn. of Greater Bombay* v. *Laxman Iyer,* AIR 2003 SC 4182: 2003 AIR SCW 5505: JT 2003 (8) SC 108: 2003 (8) SCC 731: 2003 (9) SCALE 2: 2003 (7) Supreme 492.

40. Loss of Earning Capacity cannot be Calculated in Terms of Percentage Only – Three bones of the appellant were fractured and surgery had to be performed. Appellant's right hand became irregular in shape and its movement became restrained and he cannot lift heavy articles with the right hand. The normal movement will be painful. However, the disability sustained was assessed at 20 per cent. The loss of earning capacity on account of permanent partial disability suffered by the appellant cannot be calculated in terms of percentage only. It will have serious repercussions on his studies and prospects of earning. He will have to face other handicaps in life. Taking inter alia the table in the 2nd Schedule as guiding factor, the compensation on account of disability incurred by the appellant is enhanced; *Kapil Kumar* v. *Kudrat Ali,* AIR 2002 SC 1813: 2002 AIR SCW 1785: JT 2002 (4) SC 8: 2002 (4) SCC 337: 2002 (3) SCALE 396: 2002 (3) Supreme 241.

41. Deviation from Multiplier – Ordinarily while awarding compensation, the provisions contained in the second schedule may be taken as a guide including the multiplier, but there may arise some cases which may fall in the category having special feature or facts calling for deviation from the multiplier usually applicable. By applying a multiplier other than the schedule multiplier does not mean that any method other than multiplier method has been applied. For some special reasons some deviation from the scheduled multiplier can be made. The amount of multiplicand shall surely be relevant and in case it is a high amount, a lower multiplier can appropriately be applied. The Court cannot be totally oblivion to the realities. The 2nd Schedule while prescribing the multiplier, had maximum income of Rs. 40,000 p.a. in mind, but it is considered to be a safe guide for applying prescribed multiplier in cases of higher income also. But in cases where the gap in income is wide it cannot be said that some deviation in the multiplier, would be impermissible; *United India Insurance Co. Ltd.* v. *Patricia Jean Mahajan,* AIR 2002 SC 2607: 2002 AIR SCW 2920: JT 2002 (5) SC 74: 2002 (6) SCC 281: 2002 (5) SCALE 56: 2002 (4) Supreme 518.

42. Criminal Negligence – Merely because a passenger fell down from the bus while boarding it, presumption of negligence cannot be drawn against the bus driver. A passenger might fall down from a moving vehicle due to one of the following causes : it could be accidental; it due to the negligent taking off of the bus by the driver. However, to fasten the liability with the driver for negligent driving in such a situation there should be the evidence that he moved the bus suddenly before the passenger could get into the vehicle or that the driver moved the vehicle even before getting any signal from the rear side. In the case no witnesses has said, that the driver moved the vehicle before getting signal to move forward. The evidence is therefore too scanty to fasten the driver with criminal negligence; *Mohammed Aynuddin* v. *State of Andhra Pradesh,* AIR 2000 SC 2511: 2000 AIR SCW 2679: JT 2000 (8) SC 317: 2000 (7) SCC 72: 2000 (5) SCALE 311: 2000 (5) Supreme 308.

43. Determination of Income of Deceased – The evidence of the doctor who has treated the deceased after the accident, to the effect that at the time of admission to the hospital the patient has given his income as Rs. 1,000 has to be weighed against that evidence of deceased's employer who had testified that deceased was employed on monthly salary of Rs. 3,000 and the evidence of widow of the deceased who had testified that she was receiving Rs. 3,000 p.m. from her husband; *Gurmit Kaur* v. *State of Haryana,* AIR 2000 SC 3465: 2000 AIR SCW 2213: 1999 (9) SCC 212.

44. Multiplier System – The multiplier system is sound in computing compensation is now well settled but what multiplier should be applied would depend on various circumstances. The age of deceased, the age of dependants, not only existing salary when he did if any additional sum payable to the deceased depending upon the nature of job in which he was working, his chances of promotion, the life expectancy etc. Hence multiplier is bound to change to some degree; *Jyoti Kaul* v. *State of Madhya Pradesh,* AIR 2000 SC 3582: 2000 AIR SCW 3789: JT 2000 (7) SC 367: 2002 (6) SCC 306: 2000 (6) Supreme 243.

45. Explosion Inside Bus Negligence of Owner or Driver – The explosion took place inside the bus is an admitted fact and the usual police escort was not there. The atmosphere during the period of accident was so polluted requiring care on the part of the conductor and driver of the bus. There cannot be any doubt that the accident arose out of the use of the motor vehicle justifying the claim of the appellant. The assessment in quantifying the compensation with interest at the rate of 12% is proper; *Samir Chanda* v. *Managing Director, Assam State Transport Corporation,* AIR 1999 SC 136: 1998 AIR SCW 3491: JT 1998 (6) SC 40: 1998 (6) SCC 605: 1998 (5) SCALE 25: 1998 (7) Supreme 66.

46. Additional Sum by Way of Compensation – Permanent partial disability was suffered by the appellant who was a pillion rider on the motor cycle and was earning Rs. 500 per month from his photography business. He has suffered prolonged period of medical treatment and hospitalisation in different hospitals and looking to the future economic loss he would suffer because of permanent partial disability which would affect his future photography business, interest of justice will be served if an additional amount of Rs. 1 lac is granted to the appellant by way of compensation both on the heads of pain, shock and sufferings as well as for future economic loss awarding an additional amount of Rs. 4 lacs to the motor cycle driver; *Swatantra Kumar* v. *Qamar Ali,* AIR 1999 SC 1500: 1998 AIR SCW 3859: 1998 (8) JT 247: 1998 (5) SCC 308.

47. Enhancement of Compensation – The appellant has been awarded Rs. 94,037 as expenses incurred on medical care, Rs. 20,000 for special diet and expenses for attendant during treatment. For his becoming permanently disabled and paraplegic on account of the injury and damages caused to his spinal cord, the appellant, who admittedly has been held permanently incapacitated has been granted only Rs. 1,00,000. The appellant was right in claiming his income at Rs. 2,000 per month while working with his father at the time of the accident and even if we apply the multiplier of 16, he is entitled to the claim of Rs. 3,84,000 on account of loss of expectation to life besides disappointment, frustration and mental stress particularly when he has to keep a permanent attendant to look after him in his rest of life. Adding this amount to the amount of Rs. 1,14,000 to which the appellant has rightly been held entitled on account of expenses incurred on medical care and for the pain suffering during the period of treatment, the appellant is entitled to a total sum of Rs. 4,98,000 which round up to Rs. 5,00,000 inclusive of costs of litigation. The aforesaid amount is liable to be paid by the respondent-Insurance Company; *Ashwani Kumar Mishra* v. *P. Muniam Babu,* AIR 1999 SC 2260: 1999 AIR SCW 2301: JT 1999 (2) SC 619: 1999 (4) SCC 22: 1999 (2) SCALE 479: 1999 (4) Supreme 24.

The deceased was unmarried on the date of accident. Thus 50% of income of the deceased is deducted towards his personal expenses. The claimants of deceased were parents. Their dependency, therefore, assessed at Rs. 15,000 p.a. and multiplier of 10 would be appropriate. By multiplying the annual dependency of Rs. 15,000 with the multiplier of 10, the compensation works out to Rs. 1,50,000. The claimants are further entitled to receive Rs. 5,000 towards funeral expenses; and Rs. 5,000 for loss of estate. The claimants, thus, become entitled to receive a total sum of Rs. 1,60,000 as compensation for the death of their son in the motor accident. However, as the appeal filed by the claimants for enhancement of the compensation is allowed in part and the income of the deceased is re-computed at Rs. 30,000 p.a., the compensation of Rs. 1,00,000 awarded by the Tribunal is enhanced to Rs. 1,60,000 with further quantified amount of interest of

Rs. 10,000 on the enhanced amount of compensation of Rs. 60,000; *Jagannath Budhram* v. *Nandlal Prasad Gupta*, AIR 2012 Chht 136.

So far as the compensation of Rs. 22,300 and Rs. 7,000 awarded by the Tribunal for the injuries sustained by the claimants are concerned, the claimants for the reasons best known to them did not examine any doctor before the Tribunal for establishing the number and nature of the injuries said to have been sustained by the claimants in the motor accident and the fact that those injuries resulted in any permanent disability. Thus compensation cannot be enhanced as there is no proof of the fact that the injuries resulted in any permanent disability; *Sunder Bai* v. *Loop Singh*, AIR 2011 Chht 174.

The deceased was aged about 24 years and he was working as tailor died due to injuries sustained in the motor accident. The Tribunal has taken the income of deceased as Rs. 60 per day. Taking income of the deceased as Rs. 60 per day is lower side thus compensation was enhanced by taking his income as Rs. 70 per day even by working as an unskilled labour. By deducting the usual 1/3rd of Rs. 24,000 towards the personal expenses of the deceased, the claimants dependency is assessed at Rs. 16,000 per annum. Considering the age of the deceased, his widow and their son, multiplier of 17 selected by the Tribunal, is appropriate in the present case. By multiplying the annual dependency of Rs. 16,000 with the multiplier of 17, the compensation works out to Rs. 2,72,000. The claimants are further entitled to receive Rs. 5,000 towards funeral expenses; Rs. 5,000 for loss of estate; and Rs. 5,000 for loss of consortium to the widow. The claimants, thus, become entitled to receive a total sum of Rs. 2,87,000 as compensation for the death of the deceased in the motor accident; *Anusuiya* v. *Saiuddinkaji*, AIR 2011 Chht 136.

The claimant was 20 years of age at the time of accident. Multiplier of 18 deserves to be applied for the purpose of determining the compensation payable to the appellant in lieu of the loss of earning. Thus, under this head the appellant will be entitled to a sum of Rs.1,62,000. Although, the appellant had suffered temporary disablement, the evidence of the doctor shows that he will require treatment in future. Future treatment necessarily include doctor's fee, cost of medicine, transportation, diet, etc. Keeping in view the high cost of living, a lump sum amount of Rs. 2 lacs has been awarded for future treatment; *Sanjay Batham* v. *Munnalal Parihar*, AIR 2012 SC 459: 2012 AIR SCW 93: (2011) 10 SCC 665.

The claimants cannot have any legitimate grievance about the assessment of the income of the deceased by the Tribunal as they themselves pleaded and proved that their son used to earn Rs. 80 per day as labour and the Tribunal assessed the income of the deceased at Rs. 80 per day and Rs. 2000 per month assuming that the deceased was getting work only for 20 days in a month. The claimants' dependency also has been rightly assessed by the Tribunal by deducting 50% of the income of the deceased towards his personal expenses. The multiplier of 12 selected by the Tribunal is rather on the higher side considering that the claimants are parents of the deceased. Where the claimants are parents of the deceased, the multiplier should never exceed 10. For the for going reasons, there is not any scope of enhancement of the compensation either on account of the assessment of the income of the deceased or the claimants' dependency by the Tribunal or the multiplier selected; *Basanti Bai* v. *Ishwar Kumar Sahu*, AIR 2011 Chha 86; *Syed Basheer Ahamed* v. *Mohammed Jameel*, (2009) 2 SCC 225: AIR 2009 SC 1219: 2009 AIR SCW 493; *Municipal Corporation of Greater Bombay* v. *Shri Laxman Iyer*, (2003) 8 SCC 731: AIR 2003 SC 4182: 2003 AIR SCW 5505.

In the light of this evidence, the *onus* has shifted to the appellant-claimant to establish that his disablement is permanent, partial or otherwise. Having not discharged this burden, it is difficult to hold that the appellant is suffering from permanent disablement. Notwithstanding the findings of the Tribunal in respect of the nature of injuries sustained by the claimant, the amount of compensation awarded to the appellant by the Tribunal appears to be somewhat low considering the temporary demotion of the appellant and the associated mental agony and also of the loss of status which can only be attributed to the accident. The possibility of his posting abroad at least for one year cannot be entirely ruled out when his colleagues could admittedly also go there. He would have been selected and earned considerable additional income apart from his normal salary in India. Thus the compensation has been enhanced by adding 1 lakh to the amount already awarded by the tribunal; *Ajay Kumar Singh* v. *Kyrshan Lamare Taliang*, AIR 2012 Gau 1: 2012 (3) Gau LR 159: 2011 (5) Gau LT 250.

The deceased was aged about 48 years. He could have easily earned Rs. 70-75 per day even by working as an unskilled labour. Therefore, the compensation has been recomputed taking the income of the deceased at Rs. 2,000 per month and Rs. 24,000 per annum. By deducting the usual 1/3rd of Rs. 24,000 towards the personal expenses of the deceased, the claimants' dependency is assessed at Rs. 16,000 per annum. The multiplier of 8 selected by the Tribunal considering the age of the deceased and the claimants is appropriate and does not call for any interference. By multiplying the annual dependency of Rs. 16,000 with the multiplier of 8 the compensation works out to Rs. 1,28,000. The claimants are further entitled to receive Rs. 5,000 towards funeral expenses; Rs. 5,000 for loss of estate; and Rs. 5,000 for loss of consortium to the widow. The claimants, thus, become entitled to receive a total sum of Rs. 1,43,000 as compensation for the death of the deceased in the motor accident; *Gomti Bai* v. *Laxminarayan Vishal Sahu*, AIR 2011 Chht 76.

Even if the income of the appellant is taken to be Rs. 2,000, the loss of income during the period of treatment, which continued till the judgment of the High Court would be Rs. 1,47,000 approximately. As per the disability certificate, the appellant had virtually become vegetative and, therefore, she is not in a position to look after herself what to say of discharging her functions as partner of the enterprises. Therefore, by applying the multiplier of 17, the future loss of earning would come to Rs. 3,67,200. Assuming the claimant's life expectancy to be 55 years, it is appropriate to award attendant charges at the rate of Rs. 2000 per month and physiotherapy expenses at the rate of Rs.3000 per month. With regard to the head of physical and mental pains the amount is enhanced to Rs. 3,00,000 and another Rs. 3,00,000 is awarded under the heads of loss of amenities and loss of life expectancy; *Kavita* v. *Deepak*, AIR 2012 SC 2893: 2012 AIR SCW 4771: (2012) 8 SCC 604.

The deceased was unmarried on the date of the accident. Thus it is appropriate to deduct 50% of the income of the deceased towards his personal expenses. The claimant's dependency, therefore, is assessed at Rs. 18,000 per annum by deducting 50% of Rs. 36,000 towards the personal expenses of the deceased. By multiplying the annual dependency of Rs. 18,000 with the multiplier of 10 the compensation works out to Rs. 1,80,000. The claimants are further entitled to receive Rs. 5,000 towards funeral expenses and Rs. 5,000 for loss of estate. The claimants, thus, become entitled to receive a total sum of Rs. 1,90,000 as compensation for the death of the deceased in the motor accident; *Mohd. Ramzan Khan* v. *Virendra Singh*, AIR 2012 Chha 182; *Syed Basheer Ahamed* v. *Mohammed Jameel*, (2009) 2 SCC 225: AIR 2009 SC 1219: 2009 AIR SCW 493; *Sarla Verma* v. *Delhi Transport Corporation*, (2009) 6 SCC 121: AIR 2009 SC 3104: 2009 AIRSCW 4992.

So far as the compensation of Rs. 31,500 awarded by the Tribunal for the death of the claimants' minor daughter is concerned, the Tribunal has certainly lost sight of the fact that under the provisions of the Motor Vehicles Act minimum amount awardable as compensation for the death in the motor accident is Rs. 50,000. The Tribunal, therefore, was legally bound to award at least Rs. 50,000 as compensation to the claimants for the death of their daughter in the motor accident. Thus the compensation has been enhanced by Rs. 20,000; *Sunder Bai* v. *Loop Singh*, AIR 2011 Chht 174.

The High Court has directed application of multiplier of 16 as the deceased was thirty five years of age at the time of his death. The compensation works out to

Rs. 3,84,000 by multiplying the annual dependency of Rs. 24,000 with the multiplier of 16. The claimants are further entitled to receive Rs. 5,000 towards funeral expenses; Rs. 5,000 towards loss of consortium to the widow; and Rs. 5,000 for loss of estate. The claimants become entitled to receive a total sum of Rs. 3,99,000 as compensation for the death of the deceased in the motor accident. Thus the compensation of Rs. 2,92,000 awarded by the Tribunal is enhanced to Rs. 3,99,000 with further quantified amount of interest of Rs. 13,000 on the enhanced amount of compensation of Rs. 1,07,000; *Kunti Bai* v. *Mahadeo Vishwakarma,* AIR 2012 Chht 160.

48. Appropriate Method of Assessment of Compensation – The appropriate method of assessment of compensation is the method of capitalisation of net income choosing a multiplier appropriate to the age of the deceased or the age of the defendants whichever multiplier is lower. It is no doubt, true that as a rough and ready measure, the method of aggregating the total expected income for the remainder of a life expectancy with appropriate deductions towards uncertainties of life and for lump sum payments is also resorted to. But this method is now considered unscientific and is virtually obsolete. At all events wherever it is resorted to it would require to be cross-checked with the results of the appropriate and the more scientific method of capitalisation of the loss of dependency; *National Insurance Co. Ltd.* v. *Swaranlata Das,* AIR 1993 SC 1259: 1993 AIR SCW 245: 1993 (2) ACJ 748.

49. Tribunal/Court is to Determine Fair Amount of Compensation – It is well settled that the Tribunal/Court is to determine the fair amount of compensation awardable to the victim of any accident or to the dependant of the deceased which must be proportionate to the injuries caused to him or for the cause of his death and the Tribunal/Court cannot go by the ready reckoner; *Panna Singh* v. *Himangshu Karmakar,* AIR 1997 Gau 112: 1998 (1) Civ LJ 123: 1997 (2) Gau LR 55.

50. Tribunal not Bound to Confine Amount of Compensation to Schedule in Workmen's Compensation Act – Claims Tribunal is not bound to confine amount of compensation to Schedule in Workmen's Compensation Act while determining compensation under Motor Vehicles Act; *Orissa State Road Transport Corporation* v. *Shanker Sahit,* 1989 ACJ 867 (Ori).

51. Application of Doctrine of *Res Ipsa Loquitur* – Jeep dashed against a tree and overturned and then covered a distance of 150 ft. resulting in the death of one passenger and injuries to others. The presumption that the vehicle was being driven rashly and negligently was not rebutted by the defendants. Under such circumstances, the doctrine of *res ipsa loquitur* is attracted and driver of the jeep can be held rash and negligent in causing the accident; *State of Orissa* v. *Nalini Kumar Patnaik,* 1989 ACJ 126 Ori.

52. While Distributing Compensation Tribunal shall Consider Dependency of Claimants – While distributing compensation amount between claimant's father, mother and widow of the deceased, Tribunal is not guided by personal law but consider dependency of claimants; *Abdul Rahman* v. *Daya Ram,* 1989 ACJ 806 (Bom).

53. Quantum of Compensation – Prove of Death of Deceased Beyond Reasonable Doubts – The Tribunal has proceeded to decide the claim case like that of a contested criminal trial case. Although he discussed the evidence but held that the claimants-appellants failed to prove beyond all reasonable doubts that the person died in the accident was not the person who was named in the FIR. The procedure adopted by the Tribunal is absolutely erroneous in law. The Tribunal in fact misdirected himself in holding that the claimants failed to prove the death of the deceased in the said accident beyond all reasonable doubts. The impugned judgment of the Tribunal, therefore, cannot be sustained in law. The claimants have proved the death of the deceased in the said accident. Therefore, the matter remitted back to the Tribunal to decide the issue of quantum of compensation which the claimants are entitled to get on account of death of deceased; *Satya Devi* v. *Shanti and Co., Ranchi,* AIR 2010 Jhar 52: 2010 AIHC 2593: 2011 (1) Civ LJ 373.

54. Death of Third Party – Accident Claim – The insurance Company has plead that the vehicle was carrying petroleum product which falls in the class of hazardous goods, so extra premium ought to have been paid by the owner of the vehicle. The accident caused the death of a third party and it was mandatory for the insurance company to issue at least third party policy. Admittedly the vehicle was insured with the insurance company. The Tribunal has awarded of Rs. 1 Lakh. The judgment and award passed by the Tribunal needs no interference by this Court; *New India Assurance Co. Ltd.* v. *Smt. Nebura Bibi,* AIR 2010 Jhar 98: 2010 AIHC 3469: 2011 (2) ACJ 772.

55. Composite Negligence – Tata Sumo was carrying passengers out of which 7 died. In the cross examination, it was not the suggestion of the insurance company that the accident occurred because of rash and negligent driving of the bus. On the contrary, cross examination is on the point that in fact he was not travelling and he has not seen the accident. In the written statement filed by the insurance company, case of it is that the accident occurred because of rash and negligent driving of both the drivers. Therefore, it was a case of composite negligence. When the Insurance Company has come with a case that the accident occurred because of composite negligence then at the stage of appeal insurance company has no right to say that the accident occurred because of rash and negligent driving of another vehicle, which has not been insured to avoid liability; *K.P. Nayer* v. *Pitamberdas Dawani,* AIR 2011 MP 218.

56. Driver of Offending Bus Responsible for Accident in Absence of Examination of Driver – A case was registered on the Police Station. The witness stated to have witnessed the accident has deposed that when he was in the bus-stop, the offending bus was started by its driver suddenly when the deceased was alighting from the bus and fell down. His further evidence is that immediately after the accident, the injured was taken to Government General Hospital. The conductor of the bus has deposed that when the bus was proceeded to halt at bus stop, the deceased was attempting to alight from the moving bus and fell down and sustained injuries. However, during the cross-examination, the witness-conductor has admitted that the employer transport corporation has taken disciplinary action against the driver of the bus and that he was also dismissed from service. On the principles of *"res ipsa loquitur"* it has to be presumed that in the absence of examination of the driver of the offending vehicle, the driver of the bus was responsible for the accident and accordingly quantified the compensation. Rash and negligent driving is a personal act attributed to the cause of accident. When an allegation is made against the driver of the vehicle, rebuttal evidence has to be let in by him and in the case on hand, admittedly the driver of the Transport Corporation bus has not been examined. Thus it could be presumed that the driver of the offending vehicle was responsible for the accident; *Metropolitan Transport Corpn., Chennai* v. *D. Pappa Susaiammal,* AIR 2011 Mad 184; *Ramchandran* v. *Valliammal,* 1992 (1) MLJ 188.

57. Loss of Future Earning – The appellant-claimant was about 32 years of age at the time of the accident therefore, the Tribunal was right in applying the multiplier of 16 to determine the compensation. Once the income is considered at Rs.8,500 per month it comes to Rs.1,02,000 per annum, 90% of the same comes to Rs.91,800. If the same is multiplied by 16 it comes to Rs.91,800 x 16 = Rs.14,68,800. Therefore, it is proper to award Rs. 14,68,800 towards "loss of future earning". So far as loss of income during the treatment is concerned, the Tribunal has noticed the nature of injuries and treatment taken by the appellant to come to the conclusion that the appellant might not have worked at least for six months. Even if such minimum period for treatment is accepted as six months, the appellant is entitled for a just and proper award of Rs.51,000 under the head of "loss of income during the treatment"; *N. Suresh* v. *Yusuf Shariff,* AIR 2012 SC 3431: 2012 AIR SCW 4193: 2012 (4) ACJ 2572.

The claimant has sustained serious head injuries in the accident which lead to weakness of his right hand and leg. Weakening of his right hand would adversely affect his ability to perform his occupation as he had been doing before the accident. As a result, the disability of the victim to earn in future is assessed at 30% as against 25% assessed by the High Court. Thus, loss of future income amounts to Rs. 2,01,600 (30% of Rs. 6,72,000). We also enhance the compensation awarded for future medical expenses to Rs.10,000. The compensation awarded by the High Court under the remaining heads is sustained. Thus, it comes to Rs. 3,17,100, which we round off to Rs. 3,20,000. Interest will be payable on the enhanced amount at 6% from the date of the claim petition till date of realization; *C. Mohanraju* v. *Divisional Manager, United India Assurance Co. Ltd.*, AIR 2011 SC 1897: 2011 AIR SCW 2662: 2011 (3) ACJ 1959.

The doctor stated that the appellant could not work as a coolie and could not also do any other manual work. The doctor assessed permanent residual physical disability of the upper limb at 68% and 22-23% of the whole body. The appellant is working as a manual labourer, for which he requires the use of both his hands. The fact that the accident has left him with one useless hand will severely affect his ability to perform his work as a coolie or any other manual work, and this has also been certified by the doctor. Thus, while awarding compensation it has to be kept in mind that the appellant is to do manual work for the rest of his life without full use of his left hand, and this is bound to affect the quality of his work and also his ability to find work considering his disability. Hence, while computing loss of future income, disability should be taken to be 68% and not 20% as was done by the Tribunal and the High Court. The appellant is severely hampered and perhaps forever handicapped from performing his occupation as a coolie; *Nagarajappa* v. *Divisional Manager, Oriental Insurance Co. Ltd.*, AIR 2011 SC 1785: 2011 AIR SCW 2609: (2011) 4 SCALE 515.

58. Determining Compensation by Granting 100% Increase in Income – The court was justified in determining the amount of compensation by granting 100% increase in the income of the deceased. In the normal course, the deceased would have served for 22 years and during that period his salary would have certainly doubled because the employer was paying 20% of his salary as bonus per year; *New India Assurance Co. Ltd.* v. *Gopali,* AIR 2012 SC 3381: 2012 AIR SCW 4330: 2012 (4) ACJ 2131.

59. Rule of 1/3rd Deduction Towards Personal Expenses – What may not apply to rich people living in urban areas who can afford to spend a substantial amount of their income in clubs, hotels and on drinks parties. In those cases, there may be a semblance of justification in applying the rule of 1/3rd deduction but it would be wholly unrealistic to universally apply that rule in all cases. In this case the victim is earning less than Rs. 3000 p.m. and who has nine family members. Thus the rule of 1/3rd deduction towards the personal expenses of the deceased cannot be applied. Thus the court below did not commit any error by not following the rule of 1/3rd deduction towards the personal expenses of the deceased; *New India Assurance Co. Ltd.* v. *Gopali,* AIR 2012 SC 3381: 2012 AIR SCW 4330: 2012 (4) ACJ 2131.

60. Loss of Earning Capacity – Determination of – While making assessment, there is element of guesswork, but that guesswork again must have reasonable nexus to available material/evidence and quantification made. It is not that under all circumstances, Court has to blindly accept Disability Certificate produced by claimant. Gourt has discretion to accept either totally or partially or reject Certificate so produced and marked in trial but, that can be done only by assigning cogent and acceptable reasons. Where the doctor assessed disability suffered by claimant at 75% and nothing adverse to interest of claimant was elicited though doctor was cross-examined at length by the insurance company, taking 50% disability into account while calculating loss of income was not proper. Thus the loss of earning capacity of claimant was calculated to be Rs. 6,12,000 by taking disability suffered by claimant at 75%; *D. Sampath* v. *United India Insurance Co. Ltd.*, AIR 2012 SC 544: 2012 AIR SCW 287: 2011 (4) ACJ 2466.

The claim is based on the assertion that the deceased owned agricultural land apart from the three mini-buses. The High Court rejected the claim insofar as it is based on the income from the land, on the ground that the income would still continue to accrue to the benefit of the family. Unfortunately, the High Court failed to see that the same logic would be applicable even to the income from the above-mentioned three buses. The asset (three mini-buses) would still continue with the family and fetch income. The only difference, perhaps, would be that during his life time the deceased was managing the buses, but now, the claimants may have to engage some competent person to manage the asset, which, in turn, would require some payment to be made to such a manager. To the extent of such payment, there would be a depletion in the net income accruing to the claimants out of the asset. Therefore, the amount required for engaging the service of a manager and the salary payable to a driver - as it is asserted that the deceased himself used to drive one of the three buses - would be the loss to the claimants. In the normal course the claimants are expected to adduce evidence as to what would be the quantum of depletion in the income from the above-mentioned asset on account of the above-mentioned factors. Unfortunately, no such evidence was led by the claimants. If somebody to be employed for the purpose of managing the business of the three mini-buses, he would certainly demand a higher salary than a driver, Thus it is reasonable to notionally fix the salary of such manager at Rs. 10,000 per month. The said amount coupled with the salary of one driver, *i.e.*, Rs. 3,900 would be the loss sustained by the family from the income arising out of the asset; *New India Assurance Co. Ltd.* v. *Yogesh Devi*, AIR 2012 SC 945: 2012 AIR SCW 1519: (2012) 2 SCALE 409.

61. Computation of Loss of Future Earning – In the context of loss of future earning, any physical disability resulting from an accident has to be judged with reference to the nature of work being performed by the person suffering the disability. This is the basic premise and once that is grasped, it clearly follows that the same injury or loss may affect two different persons in different ways. Take the case of a marginal farmer who does his cultivation work himself and ploughs his land with his own two hands; or the puller of a cycle-rickshaw, one of the main means of transport in hundreds of small towns all over the country. The loss of one of the legs either to the marginal farmer or the cycle-rickshaw-puller would be the end of the road insofar as their earning capacity is concerned. But in case of a person engaged in some kind of desk work in an office, the loss of a leg may not have the same effect. The loss of earning capacity of the appellant may be as high as 100% but in no case it would be less than 90%. Thus the compensation for the loss of appellant's future earnings must be computed on that basis. On calculation on that basis, the amount of compensation would come to Rs. 3,56,400and after addition of a sum of Rs. 30,000 and Rs. 15,000 the total amount would be Rs. 4,01,400. The additional compensation amount would carry interest at the rate of 9% per annum from the date of filing of the claim petition till the date of payment; *Mohan Soni* v. *Ram Avtar Tomar*, AIR 2012 SC 782: 2012 AIR SCW 555: (2012) 2 SCC 267.

62. Compensation is more Comprehensive than Damage – The expression compensation may include a claim for damage but compensation is more comprehensive. Normally damages are given for an injury which is suffered, whereas compensation stands on a slightly higher footing. It is given for the atonement of injury caused and the intention behind grant of compensation is to put back the injured party as far as possible in the same position, as if the injury has not taken place, by way of grant of pecuniary relief. Thus, in the matter of computation of compensation, the approach will be slightly more broad based than what is done in the matter of assessment of damages. At the same time it is true that there cannot be any rigid or mathematical precision in the matter of determination of compensation; *Yadava Kumar* v. *Divisional Manager, National Insurance Co. Ltd.*, AIR 2010 SC 3741: 2010 (3) ACC 869: 2010 (4) ACJ 2713.

63. Adequate Compensation – While determining the quantum of compensation payable to the victims of accident, who are disabled either permanently or temporarily, efforts should always be made to award adequate compensation not only for the physical injury and treatment, but also for the loss of earning and inability to lead a normal life and enjoy amenities, which would have been enjoyed but for the disability caused due to the accident. The amount awarded under the head of loss of earning capacity is distinct and do not overlap with the amount awarded for pain., suffering and loss of enjoyment of life or the amount awarded for medical expenses; *Kavita* v. *Deepak*, AIR 2012 SC 2893: 2012 AIR SCW 4771: (2012) 8 SCC 604.

64. Enhancement of Compensation for Future Treatment, Further Studies and Diminution of Marriage Prospects – The claimant had produced substantive evidence to prove that as a result of accident he had suffered 8 grievous injuries including fracture of pelvis and he had to remain in the hospital for one month and a half and that on account of grievous injuries he was unable to continue his studies. Deposition of doctor who treated claimant categorically stated that the claimant will have to undertake life-long treatment for recurrence of urethral strictures and consequential dysfunction due to fracture of pelvis. Unfortunately, neither the Tribunal nor the High Court adverted to this part of the evidence and omitted to award compensation for the expenses likely to be incurred by the appellant for future treatment. One can reasonably except that the claimant who was only 18 years old at the time of accident would live for at least next 50 years. The Tribunal awarded Rs. 20,340 for expenses incurred by the appellant for treatment taken by him in the hospital. Although, doctor did not indicate the approximate expenditure likely to be incurred by the claimant and his family for future treatment, keeping in view the nature of injuries and the fact that he will have to take treatment for the remaining life, it will be reasonable to infer that he will be required to spend a minimum of Rs. 1,000 per month for future treatment, which would necessarily include fees of the doctors, medicines, transportation, etc. In the absence of concrete evidence about the anticipated expenditure, to meet ends of justice claimant entitled to be awarded a sum of Rs. 2 lacs which, if deposited in a fixed deposit, would earn an interest of Rs. 14,000 to 16,000 per annum. Further on account of the injuries suffered by him, the prospects of the claimant's, marriage also considerably reduced. Rather, they are extremely bleak. In any case, on account of the fracture of pelvis, he will not be able to enjoy the matrimonial life. Therefore, the award of Rs. 50,000 under this head was wholly inadequate. Hence facts and circumstances of the case, claimant entitled for a sum of Rs. 2 lacs for loss of marriage prospects and enjoyment of life. Furthermore the consequences following from accident would be extremely grave inasmuch as he would lose all opportunities for making a career in future. The prospects of the claimant's marriage are extremely bleak. Therefore, sum of Rs. 2 lacs to be awarded to the claimant under these heads. Hence in these circumstances considering the fact that although claimant had filed petition for a claim of Rs. 3 lacs only and he was awarded a compensation of Rs. 1,89,440 but claimant had to suffer serious consequences in future because of accident, award of compensation liable to be enhanced to Rs. 6 lacs; *Ibrahim* v. *Raju*, AIR 2012 SC 534: 2012 AIR SCW 413: (2011) 10 SCC 634.

65. Compensation for Future Treatment – Multiplier of 18 deserves to be applied for the purpose of determining the compensation payable to the appellant in lieu of the loss of earning. Thus, under this head the appellant will be entitled to a sum of Rs.1,62,000. Although, the appellant had suffered temporary disablement, the evidence of the doctor shows that he will require treatment in future. Future treatment necessarily include doctor's fee, cost of medicine, transportation, diet, etc. Keeping in view the high cost of living, a lump sum amount of Rs. 2 lacs has been awarded for future treatment; *Sanjay Batham* v. *Munnalal Parihar*, AIR 2012 SC 459: 2012 AIR SCW 93: (2011) 10 SCC 665.

66. Deduction Towards Personal Expenses – Determination – The deduction of 1/3rd of the income of the deceased by the Tribunal towards the personal expenses of the deceased requires reconsideration, as there are as many as five claimants in the case and at least four of them *i.e.*, widow, the two minor daughters and mother were dependent on the income of the deceased. Therefore, the Tribunal ought to have deducted only 1/4th of the income of the deceased towards his personal expenses. We, therefore, assess the claimants' dependency at Rs. 27,000 per annum by deducting 1/4th of Rs. 36,000 towards the personal expenses of the deceased. The claimants cannot have any legitimate grievance about the selection of multiplier of 18 selected by the Tribunal as it is the highest multiplier prescribed in the Second Schedule under section 163A of the Motor Vehicles Act; *Shahnaj Khatun* v. *Suleman*, AIR 2012 Chht 174.

67. Words "Legal Representative" – The word "legal representative" occurring in section 166 of the MV Act, has the same meaning as defined under section 2(11) of CPC. The appellant, admittedly was not dependent upon the deceased, is neither a person who in law represents the estate of the deceased, nor is a successor in interest of the deceased. Therefore, if the definition of legal representative as provided under section 2(11) of CPC is taken in its widest amplitude even then appellant cannot be termed as a legal representative of the deceased entitled to file claim petition before the Tribunal under the MV Act and thus, the Tribunal has not committed any illegality in dismissing the claim petition; *Heeralal Giri* v. *Ramratan*, AIR 2011 Chht 22.

68. Reconsideration of Income and Re-compute of Compensation – The claimants have pleaded that their son used to earn Rs. 4,000 per month by working in the shop of his elder brother, but no reliable and clinching evidence was led before the Tribunal to establish the income of the deceased to that extent. Even the elder brother of the deceased in whose shop the deceased was said to be working was not examined before the Tribunal. In this state of evidence, it is not fault in the approach of the Tribunal in discarding the claimants' evidence about the income of the deceased. However, the income of the deceased assessed by the Tribunal at Rs. 15,000 per annum in the year 2003 is certainly on the lower side and requires reconsideration. The deceased was aged about 21 years on the date of the accident. He could have easily earned Rs. 80-90 per day even by working as an unskilled labour in the year 2003. Therefore, the compensation has been recomputed taking the income of the deceased at Rs. 2,500 per month and Rs. 30,000 per annum; *Ramgopal Rathore* v. *Rattan Lal*, AIR 2011 Chht 59.

69. Re-computation of Income of Deceased – The claimants pleaded that the deceased used to earn Rs. 4,000 per month by working as Turner in the Steel Plant but the evidence led in that behalf was not of clinching nature. Neither any salary certificate was produced by the claimants from the said company nor any Manager or other worker of the said company was examined before the Tribunal to establish that the deceased was working in the said factory at all and was getting salary to the extent of Rs. 4,000 per month. In this state of evidence, it is not any fault in the approach of the Tribunal in discarding the claimants' evidence about the income of the deceased. However, the income of the deceased assessed by the Tribunal at Rs. 15,000 per annum in the year 2001 is certainly on the lower side and requires reconsideration. As the deceased was aged about 48 years, he could have easily earned Rs. 70-75 per day even by working as an unskilled labour. Therefore, the compensation has been recomputed taking the income of the deceased at Rs. 2,000 per month and Rs. 24,000 per annum; *Gomti Bai* v. *Laxminarayan Vishal Sahu*, AIR 2011 Chht 76.

70. Assessment of Compensation by Tribunal – Deceased were aged about 47 and 50 years. Assessment of compensation by adopting multiplier of 13 and 10 is perfectly in accordance with Second Schedule of the Motor Vehicles Act. The compensation assessed and awarded by the Tribunal is proper; *New India Assurance Co. Ltd.* v. *Richa Singh Katiyar*, AIR 2011 All 107.

71. Compensation for Negligent Act – The driver of the vehicle alone need not be rash and negligent in driving the vehicle, but if there is any negligent act on the part of the owner of the vehicle or on the part of the persons responsible for plying the vehicle, it also amounts to rash and negligent driving. For example, when a river is flowing and if the owner or conductor of a vehicle asks the driver of the vehicle to pass through the river and the vehicle capsized in the middle of the river, then the owner or the manager of the vehicle cannot escape from liability as it also amounts to rash and negligent driving of the vehicle. To be more clear, for example, if a road is under repair or a bridge is about to collapse, knowing very well the condition of the road or bridge, asking the driver to pass through such road or bridge also amounts to rash and negligent driving. In the present case the higher police officials had taken a bus with police personnels into forest area where extremists were moving. Taking a bus with police personnel into the forest area where extremists are moving without proper care and precaution is nothing but a negligent act by the police higher officials. Normally, the practice is to do combing operation by walk or by motorcycles. The Act of the superior police officers, without visualizing the consequences and asking the police personnel to travel by bus into the forest area, is nothing but a 'negligent act'. What is required to be seen is whether the claimants are entitled for compensation or not and what is just and reasonable compensation to be awarded. Under the circumstances of the case, if once the Tribunal comes to a conclusion that the accident occurred by use of vehicle in public place and if the claimants are entitled for compensation, the Tribunal has a point to award compensation. Thus, when death of driver and police constable took place due to blasting of vehicle by extremists, the Police Department would be liable to pay compensation; *Bhupathi Prameela* v. *Superintendent of Police, Vizianagaram*, AIR 2010 AP 189: 2011 (1) ACC 812: 2011 (2) ACJ 861.

72. *Ex Gratia* and Other Allowances – The *ex gratia* and other allowances paid to the legal heirs of the deceased cannot be taken into consideration for determining the compensation under the provisions of the Act; *Bhupathi Prameela* v. *Superintendent of Police, Vizianagaram*, AIR 2010 AP 189: 2011 (1) ACC 812: 2011 (2) ACJ 861.

73. Assessment of Compensation – The deceased was employed as a Police Constable and his age was about 34 years on the date of the accident and was having further 24 years of service. The future prospects of increase in salary and promotions etc., should be taken into consideration. 50% of the actual salary of the deceased has to be added towards future prospects of the deceased, where the deceased is having a permanent job and is aged below 40 years. Therefore, if the income of the deceased is taken as Rs. 5,000 per month and 50% of the same is added to it towards future prospects, the income of the deceased can be determined at Rs. 7,500 per month. In total, the amount to be awarded comes to Rs. 10,97,000. The claimants are also entitled to interest at the rate of 7.5% per annum for the date of petition till the date of realization; *Bhupathi Prameela* v. *Superintendent of Police, Vizianagaram*, AIR 2010 AP 189: 2011 (1) ACC 812: 2011 (2) ACJ 861.

The deceased was working as a driver in the Police Department and earning Rs.5,000 per month. His age was aged about 55 years at the time of the accident. He was having another five years of service from the date of the accident. The claimants are also entitled Rs. 5,000 towards loss of estate, the first claimant is entitled for Rs. 5,000 towards loss of consortium and the claimants are also entitled for Rs. 2,000towards last rituals of the deceased. Hence, the total amount to be awarded comes to Rs. 5,07,000; *Bhupathi Prameela* v. *Superintendent of Police, Vizianagaram*, AIR 2010 AP 189: 2011 (1) ACC 812: 2011 (2) ACJ 861.

The deceased was shown to be 58 years of age in his post-mortem report. The multiplier of 9 is to be applied for the age group between 56-60 years. The Tribunal, therefore, ought to have applied the multiplier of 9 in place of 7. By multiplying the annual dependency of Rs. 24,000 with the multiplier of 9, the compensation works out to Rs. 2,16,000. The claimants are further entitled to receive Rs. 5,000 towards funeral expenses, Rs. 5,000 for loss of estate and Rs. 5,000 for loss of consortium to the widow. The claimants, thus, become entitled to receive a total sum of Rs. 2,31,000 as compensation for the death of deceased Besahu Ram Gond in the motor accident; *Ratko Besahu Ram* v.

Bhajan Ram, AIR 2012 Chhat 89; *Sarla Verma* v. *Delhi Transport Corporation,* (2009) 6 SCC 121: AIR 2009 SC 3104: 2009 AIR SCW 4992.

The deceased was shown to be 38 years of age in his postmortem report. The multiplier of 15 is to be applied for the age group between 36-40 years. By multiplying the annual dependency of Rs. 16,000 with the multiplier of 15 the compensation works out to Rs. 2,40,000. The claimants are further entitled to receive Rs. 5,000 towards funeral expenses; Rs. 5,000 for loss of estate; and Rs. 5,000 for loss of consortium to the widow. The claimants, thus, become entitled to receive a total sum of Rs. 2,55,000 as compensation for the death of deceased in the motor accident. Thus the compensation of Rs. 1,75,000 awarded by the Tribunal is enhanced to Rs. 2,55,000 with further quantified amount of interest of Rs. 12,000 on the enhanced amount of compensation of Rs. 80,000; *Jhuniya Bai* v. *Ashok Kumar Dhruvanshi,* AIR 2012 Chhattisgarh 134; *Sarla Verma* v. *Delhi Transport Corporation,* (2009) 6 SCC 121: AIR 2009 SC 3104: 2009 AIRSCW 4992.

The claimant was aged about 30 years at the time of accident and sustained 100% disability of permanent nature with no sign of recovery from disability. She has two children and they are solely dependant on her and her husband had died prior to the accident. Merely because she was homemaker compensation would not be assessed miserly for her. Compensation ought to be so assessed that interest accruing therefrom would be sufficient for the maintenance of her family members. Thus compensation has been assessed Rs. 15 lacs to which she is entitled; *Oriental Insurance Co. Ltd.* v. *Vithabai,* AIR 2011 SC 2838: 2011 AIR SCW 4235: (2011) 7 SCALE 1.

The High Court increased the multiplier from '8' to '11', as the age of the deceased was 56 years. After considering the submission made by the learned counsel and looking to the law laid down by this Court and in view of the fact that the age of the deceased was 56 and taking notice of the multiplier indicated in the Second Schedule of Motor Vehicles Act, the High Court was not justified in increasing the multiplier From '8' to '11'. Therefore, instead of '11', the multiplier of '8' should be used while calculating the amount of compensation. In view of the said fact, a sum of Rs. 1,20,000 shall be reduced on account of reduction in multiplier. While considering '11' as the multiplier, the High Court had determined the amount of compensation towards loss of dependency as Rs. 4,40,000 which is hereby reduced to Rs. 3,20,000 as multiplier has been reduced from '11' to '8'; *Urviben Chiragbhai Sheth* v. *Vijaybhai Shambhubhai Joranputra,* AIR 2011 SC 2502: 2011 AIR SCW 3172: 2011 (3) ACJ 1445.

74. Claim for Compensation – The driver, who continued to take a stand that vehicle being driven by him was not involved in the accident. This defence of the respondent is understandable as admittedly he is facing the prosecution for causing the accident and the death thereby of deceased. The owner of the vehicle has admitted in the written statement that the vehicle owned by him was involved in the accident. Thus the said admission in the pleadings is sufficient to hold that the concerned vehicle was involved in the accident. The matter remitted back to the Tribunal to decide the liability of the respondents on account of the accident caused by the vehicle with motorcycle and the death of the deceased in the same. The appellants have not received any compensation, therefore, the Tribunal shall be well advised to dispose of the matter within six months from the date on which this order is received by the Tribunal; *Saroj* v. *Het Lal,* AIR 2011 SC 671: (2011) 1 SCC 388: 2011 (1) ACJ 552.

75. Assessment of Compensation in Case of Permanent Disability – The permanent disability certificate issued by the Medical Board establishes that the appellant had sustained permanent disability to his own body to the extent of 50% and even after several surgeries; he was not able to control his urination. The young boy aged 16 years is not able to control his urination and spoils his clothes even while attending school. He is required to go with additional sets of clothings so that he could change the same, in case they are spoiled. This is the state of affairs even as on date. There is not any doubt of the genuineness and correctness of the said certificate. Even otherwise, Respondents have also not contended that this certificate is forged or fabricated and has been obtained with an intention to get compensation. Thus, it is clearly established that in the said accident, appellant had suffered severe injuries of permanent nature which have not been cured till date despite several surgeries. Looking into the nature of injuries which are permanent in nature, a total amount of Rs. 2,50,000 (Rs. 2.5 Lakhs) to be awarded to the appellant payable by the respondents jointly and severally which would meet the ends of justice. The amount would also carry interest @ 6% p.a. from the date of filing of petition till the same is actually paid; *Ravi* v. *Badrinarayan*, AIR 2011 SC 1226: 2011 AIR SCW 1530: (2011) 4 SCC 693.

76. Prospect of Future Income while Computing Compensation – Consideration of – The consistent evidence before the Tribunal was that if the deceased would have been alive he would have reached the gross salary of Rs. 20,000 per month. In view of this evidence the Tribunal should have considered the prospect of future income while computing compensation but the Tribunal has not done that. The High Court has also not considered the clear and corroborative evidence about the prospect of future increment of the deceased. When the age of the deceased is between 51 and 55 years the multiplier is 11, which is specified in the II Column in the II Schedule in the Motor Vehicles Act, and the Tribunal has not committed any error by accepting the said multiplier. The income of the deceased will be taken to be Rs. 20,000 p.m. which amounts to Rs. 2,40,000 p.a. After deduction of 1/3rd amount for personal expenses, the loss of notional income will be Rs.1,60,000. The multiplier of 11 will be applied, from which the loss of dependency will amount to Rs. 17,60,000. Also awarded Rs. 10,000 for funeral and transport expenses, Rs. 6,000 for medical expenses prior to death and Rs. 25,000 for loss of love and affection. Thus, the total compensation awarded amounts to Rs.18,01,000 which is round off to Rs.18,00,000; *K.R. Madhusudhan* v. *Administrative Officer*, AIR 2011 SC 979: 2011 AIR SCW 1390: (2011) 4 SCC 689.

77. Contributory Negligence – The minor person came from behind on the motorcycle and hit the scooter of the deceased from behind. The responsibility in causing the accident was, therefore, found to be solely that of the minor. However, since he was a minor and it was the responsibility of the petitioner to ensure that his motorcycle was not misused and that too by a minor who had no licence to drive the same, the Motor Accident Claims Tribunal quite rightly saddled the liability for payment of compensation on the petitioner and, accordingly, directed the Insurance Company to pay the awarded amount to the awardees and, thereafter, to recover the same from the Petitioner. Thus there is no case of contributory negligence on the part of the deceased; *Jawahar Singh* v. *Bala Jain*, AIR 2011 SC 2436: 2011 AIR SCW 3625: (2011) 6 SCC 425.

78. Future Loss of Earning not to be Determined on Basis of any Legal Principle – The claimant was a child at time of accident. She had no earning. What amount could be awarded towards future loss of earning or prospective loss of earning could not have been determined on the basis of any legal principle. Compensation for the injuries suffered by a person in a motor vehicle accident can be determined either on the basis of the actual damages suffered or upon application of the structured formula. The amount of compensation of Rs. 1,20,000 granted by the High Court was adequate even as per structural formula in absence of any evidence having brought on record as to the actual damages; *Priya Vasant Kalgutkar* v. *Murad Shaikh*, AIR 2010 SC 40: 2009 AIR SCW 5492: (2009) 15 SCC 54.

79. Compromise – Oral Statement cannot be Accepted – While acting as a Claims Tribunals, its proceedings are summary in nature but in exercising its summary jurisdiction the Tribunal must follow principles of justice, equity and good conscience and must be aware that its summary enquiry is in connection with a legislation which is meant for social welfare. Therefore, when a representation is made before the Tribunal that a claim of Rs. 15 lacs by way of consent is reduced to Rs. 6 lacs and odd, the Tribunal must insist on production of some material either, an affidavit of claimant or statement of claimant before the MACT in support of such lowering down of claim. The MACT cannot accept said representation on mere oral statement of counsel since such settlement is purely a question of fact. In fact no leave was obtained from the Tribunal to enter into a compromise between parties in respect of the settlement. In absence of all these materials, when an affidavit was filed by advocate who appeared before the Tribunal, contending that no such settlement was ever entered into by consent of parties, the High Court fell into an error by discarding same only on ground that same was filed belatedly before the High Court and was an afterthought; *Oriental Insurance Co. Ltd.* v. *Vithabai,* AIR 2011 SC 2838: 2011 AIR SCW 4235: (2011) 7 SCALE 1.

80. Enhancement of Compensation Awarded under Head Love and Affection – The deceased was 40 years of age; his minimum wages have been taken into account; benefit of future prospects has been given. He had a wife, two minor children and an old aged mother; in view of the enhancement of the awarded amount under the head of 'loss of love and affection' in the claim petition 'loss of love and affection' in this case is also enhanced from Rs. 10,000 to Rs. 1,00,000. This is the only modification made. In another claim petition No. 262/2010 the deceased was also 40 years of age; his minimum wages have been taken into account; benefit of future prospects has been granted. In this case also the victim was married and he had a wife, two minor children. In view of the enhancement of the awarded amount under the head of 'loss of love and affection' in the said claim petition, 'loss of love and affection' in this case is also enhanced from Rs. 10,000 to Rs. 1,00,000. This is the only modification made; *Oriental Insurance Co. Ltd.* v. *Hazara,* AIR 2012 Del 26.

81. Ascertainment of Loss of Dependency and Compensation – The deceased left behind both the parents and two minor non-earning brother and sister. The father of the deceased is a Government servant and contributed Rs. 7,000 to the family. It is also not the case of the claimant that the two minor brother and sister of the deceased were dependent on the income of the deceased. Thus this case cannot be an exception to the general rule of deduction of 50% from the monthly income of the deceased, who was a bachelor, towards his personal and living expenses, for the purpose of ascertaining the loss of dependency. Therefore, the claimant would be entitled to Rs. 2,70,000 towards the loss of dependency (50% of Rs. 3,000 x 12 x the appropriate multiplier, *i.e.* 15). The claimant would also be entitled to a further sum of Rs. 5,000 towards the loss of estate and another sum of Rs. 5,000 towards the funeral expenses. The claimant is thus entitled to a sum of Rs. 2,80,000, which amount shall carry simple interest @ 9% per annum from the date of filing of the application till the date of realization. There being no dispute relating to the contract of insurance between the Insurance Company and the owner of the offending vehicle (Truck), the Insurance Company is directed to satisfy the award by depositing the amount before the Tribunal within a period of two months from today, after deducting the amount, if any, already paid; *National Insurance Co. Ltd., Kolkata* v. *F. Lalthanpuii,* AIR 2011 Gau 160.

82. Doctrine of *Res Ipsa Loquitur* – Both the deceased and the offending truck were lying in the middle of the road shows that the truck was tried to overtake the scooter in the middle of the road. In absence of any unexpected development, it is for driver to explain how accident happened. The driver did not enter witness box to tender his evidence. Thus the doctrine of *res ipsa loquitur* clearly applies; *New India Assurance Co. Ltd.* v. *Smt. Alaka Dutta Baruah,* AIR 2010 Gau 1: 2010 (3) ACC 199: 2010 (2) ACJ 934.

83. Determination of Quantum of Compensation – The age of the deceased being 54 years at the time of the accident, there is no infirmity in applying a multiplier of 11 for determination of the quantum of compensation payable to the claimant. Therefore, the compensation is assessed at Rs. 86,168 x 11 + Rs. 9,47,848 to which shall be added Rs. 2,000 for funeral expenses, Rs. 5,000 for loss of consortium and Rs. 2,500 for loss of estate. Thus, the total amount of compensation payable to the claimant comes to

Rs. 9,59,348 (Rupees nine lakhs fifty-nine thousand three hundred forty-eight) only. The claimant will also be entitled to interest at the rate of six per centum per annum with effect from the date of filing the claim petition; *New India Assurance Co. Ltd.* v. *Smt. Alaka Dutta Baruah*, AIR 2010 Gau 1: 2010 (3) ACC 199: 2010 (2) ACJ 934.

84. Vicarious Liability of Owner to Pay Compensation – The age of the deceased being 54 years at the time of the accident, there is no infirmity in applying a multiplier of 11 for determination of the quantum of compensation payable to the claimant. Therefore, the compensation is assessed at Rs. 86,168 x 11 + Rs. 9,47,848 to which shall be added Rs. 2,000 for funeral expenses, Rs. 5,000 for loss of consortium and Rs. 2,500 for loss of estate. Thus, the total amount of compensation payable to the claimant comes to Rs. 9,59,348 (Rupees nine lakhs fifty-nine thousand three hundred forty-eight) only. The claimant will also be entitled to interest at the rate of six per centum per annum with effect from the date of filing the claim petition. The owner of the offending truck is vicariously liable to pay the compensation. The insurer is not liable to reimburse the compensation payable by the owner of the vehicle; *New India Assurance Co. Ltd.* v. *Smt. Alaka Dutta Baruah*, AIR 2010 Gau 1: 2010 (3) ACC 199: 2010 (2) ACJ 934.

85. Imposition of Condition of Deposit of Decretal Amount – Validity – As the owner of the offending vehicle has remained absent and did not contest the case, *ex parte* award was passed exonerating the insurance company from its liability to pay compensation but directions were issued to insurance company to deposit the amount of compensation and later on recover the same from the owner of the vehicle. The amount was deposited by the insurance company and also disbursed to the original claimants. However, subsequently the owner of the vehicle approached the Tribunal for setting aside of the *ex parte* award and restoration of the claim petitions. The insurance company had already deposited the amount and that amount has already been disbursed by the claims tribunal to the respective claimants and thereafter the execution proceedings have been initiated by the insurance company for recovering the said amount as per award passed by the Claims Tribunal from the owner. Therefore, if any other condition would have been imposed by Claims Tribunal and if these conditions would not have been imposed by Claims Tribunal, then, it would have nullified execution proceedings which have been initiated by insurance company against the owner. Sufficient care had been taken by the Claims Tribunal while granting an opportunity to the owner with such condition considering interest of the Insurance Company and the lapse committed by the petitioner owner. Claims Tribunal had also taken sufficient care that whatever amount is deposited by petitioner, same would be required to be invested in FDR and such FDR had to be kept in the custody of the Nazir of District Court. Thus the Claims Tribunal had rightly imposed condition for testing bona fides of petitioner whether it was genuine proceedings initiated by the petitioner or not or whether it was just to avoid execution proceedings initiated by insurance company or not; *Harendrakumar Ratilal Thaker* v. *New India Assurance Co.*, AIR 2010 Guj 173.

86. Claimant not Required to Prove Case Beyond Shadow of Reasonable Doubt – The claimant is not required to prove his case beyond shadow of reasonable doubt. It would suffice, if he has proved his case on the basis of preponderance of probabilities. The claim of the appellant could not have been dismissed merely because the name of the appellant did not find place in the FIR as well as in the relevant column of the witness list of the charge sheet. From such omission, on the part of the investigating officer in criminal case, an inference cannot be drawn that the claim petition is baseless and frivolous. The object of the FIR from the point of view of the informant is to set the criminal law in motion. The FIR does not constitute substantive evidence. It can be used only for the purpose contemplated under section 157 or section 145 of the Evidence Act that is for corroborating or contradicting its maker only and not of other witnesses; *Prakash Chandra Biswas* v. *New India Assurance Co. Ltd.*, AIR 2010 Cal 19: 2011 (1) ACC 159: 2011 (1) ACJ 622.

87. Liability of Insurer to Pay Compensation for Injuries of Pillion-rider – By virtue of the Circular issued by the IRDA, the insurer of the motorcycle has been held liable to pay compensation to the claimant/claimants for the injuries/death of the pillion-rider on a two-wheeler if the said two-wheeler is insured under a package/comprehensive policy. In the present case, the offending Motorcycle was insured with the National Insurance Company Limited under a package/comprehensive policy and the deceased was travelling on the said motorcycle as a pillion-rider. Thus the finding recorded by the Tribunal exonerating the insurer of the motorcycle from its liability to pay compensation to the claimants cannot be sustained. Thus the insurer of the offending Motorcycle liable to pay compensation to the claimants for the death of the deceased in the motor accident; *Vinay Shaha* v. *Harvilas Hajarilal Mistri,* AIR 2012 Chht 14.

88. Compensation in Cases of Total Disabilities – Taking into account the age of claimant victim (25 years) and fact that he had steady income, as evidenced by I.T. Returns an addition of 50% to the income that the claimant was earning at the time of accident would be justified. Adoption of 17 as multiplier would be appropriate; *Sanjay Varma* v. *Haryana Roadways,* AIR 2014 SC 995.

89. Compensation to Manual Labourer – Labourer involved in an unorganized sector doing his own business is not expected to produce documents to prove his monthly income. This Court is required to be sensitive while dealing with manual labour case where loss of limb is often equivalent to loss of livelihood. Appellant sustained injuries to lower end of right femur and his right leg was amputated. Considering that appellant/claimant is still capable to fend for his livelihood once he is brought in the market place, his disability is determined at 85% to determine loss of income. Going by the present state of economy and rising prices in agricultural products, this court is inclined to believe that vegetable vendor is reasonably capable of earning Rs. 6500 per month. Appellant claimant was 24 years old at the time of occurrence of the accident. Appellant claimant was entitled to the multiplier of 18. Considering that appt. might have to change his artificial leg from time to time, amount of Rs. 10000 allotted under the head of medical cost and incidental expenses to include future medical costs. Total amount awarded under the head "loss of future income" including 50% increment in the future works out to be Rs. 17, 90100. Along with the compensation under constitutional heads, appellant/claimant is also entitled to the cost of litigation as per legal principle laid down in Balram Pd. case *i.e.,* Rs. 25000; *Syed Sadiq* v. *Divisional Manager, United India Insurance Company,* AIR 2014 SC 1052.

90. Compensation for Future Loss of Income – Appellant claimant was cleaner of Lorries. He sustained fracture on middle 1/3rd of right humerus and comminuted fracture at the junction of upper 1/3rdand middle 1/3rd of right tibia. Functional disability to the extent of 85% suffered by Appellant/claimant. Based on Karnataka state Minimum Wages Rule 2012-13 appellant/Claimant is entitled to Rs. 4246 per month. Amount of Rs. 700 added as daily barter charges. His monthly income rounded to Rs. 5000. Age of appellant/claimant 22 years. Multiplier of 18 applied. He is entitled to 50 % increment in future loss of income and total amount of Rs. 13,77,000 with interest @ 9% per annum from date of application till payment; *Syed Sadiq* v. *Divisional Manager, United India Insurance Company,* AIR 2014 SC 1052.

91. Contributory Negligence – Evidence of – Where the fact of contributory negligence on the part of appellant/claimant in the accident was not proved by the respondent by producing evidence, finding of Tribunal regarding contributory negligence as upheld by the High Court is set aside. Tribunal arrived at said conclusion only on the basis of the fact that the accident took place in the middle of the road in absence of any evidence to prove the same; *Syed Sadiq* v. *Divisional Manager, United India Insurance Company,* AIR 2014 SC 1052.

92. Compensation for Disability of Children – Though it is difficult to have an accurate assessment of compensation in the case of children suffering disability on account of motor vehicle accident, appropriate compensations to be fixed having regard to relevant factors, precedent and approach of various High Courts. Claimant will be entitled to total compensation of Rs. 3.75 lacs along with interest @ 6% per annum from date of petition; *Master Mallikarjun* v. *Divisional Manager, The National Insurance Company Ltd.*, AIR 2014 SC 736.

93. Compensation in Cases of 100% Disability – High Court without good reasons treated monthly income of appellant to be Rs. 3000 in place of Rs. 5000. No good reason assigned even for reducing the compensation of Rs. 2 lacs for pain and suffering to Rs. 1 lac and Rs. 4 lacs for permanent disability to Rs 3 lacs. Tribunal was quite justified in allowing Rs. 14.20 lacs as total compensation on the basis of monthly income of Rs. 5000. Judgement of High Court under appeal set aside and that of Tribunal restored. Interest awarded @ 9 % per annum from date of petition; *M.D. Jacob* v. *United India Insurance Ltd.*, AIR 2014 SC 988.

94. English Courts and Indian Courts – Difference of Approach in Awarding Compensation – According to English Law compensation/damages were payable according to the proportionate loss, whereas, in India that much compensation is payable which appears to the Tribunal to be just. Indian Law recognises just compensation whereas English Law required compensation proportionate to the loss suffered. In India, the concept of culture and family life is totally distinct from the culture and family life in England and in other foreign countries; *Puttamma* v. *K.L. Narayana Reddy*, AIR 2014 SC 706.

95. Choosing of Multiplier – The Court/Tribunal has to take into consideration the rising inflation, increasing salaries and increasing cost of living; *Puttamma* v. *K.L. Narayana Reddy*, AIR 2014 SC 706.

96. Split Multiplier – Not a Routine Course – In absence of any specific reason and evidence on record the Tribunal or the Court should not apply split multiplier in routine course but as per decision of this Court in *Sarla Varma* v. *DTC*, (2009) 6 SCC 121 as affirmed in *Reshma Kumari* v. *Madan Mohan*, (2013) 9 SCC 65; *Puttamma* v. *K.L. Narayana Reddy*, AIR 2014 SC 706.

97. Copy of Judgment or Award – Issuance of by Court – Not for Purpose of Filing Appeal – Such interpretation will not be in any way beneficial to the parties, as the period of limitation runs from the date of receipt of the copy; *Sunitha* v. *Ranju*, AIR 2015 Ker 24.

98. Contributory Negligence – Erroneous Finding – Accident caused on account of negligence on part of driver of offending vehicle of Corporation; *Yerramma* v. *G. Krishnamurthy*, AIR 2015 SC 1145.

99. Dependency – Loss of – Gross income of deceased to be considered; *Yerramma* v. *G. Krishnamurthy*, AIR 2015 SC 1145.

100. Interest – Award of – @ 9 % per annum and not @ 6% per annum as awarded by Courts below; *Yerramma* v. *G. Krishnamurthy*, AIR 2015 SC 1145.

101. Compensation – Permanent Disability – Enormity of suffering, pain and agony, loss of enjoyment of life of appellant to be considered; *Kiran* v. *Sajjan Singh*, (2015) 1 SCC 539.

102. Contributory Negligence – Negligence wholly on Part of Driver of Offending Vehicle – Apportionment of 25% on part of appellant erroneous; *Kiran* v. *Sajjan Singh*, (2015) 1 SCC 539.

103. Compensation – Pain and Suffering – Enhancement from Rs. 5000 to Rs. 50,000; *Kiran* v. *Sajjan Singh*, (2015) 1 SCC 539.

104. Monthly Income of Deceased – Computation on basis of I.T. return correct; *Kalpanaraj* v. *Tamil Nadu State Transport Corporation,* (2015) 2 SCC 764.

105. Deduction under Various Heads to Arrive at Net Income – Erroneous – Instead High Court to ascertain the gross income of deceased out of annual income earned from his occupation mentioned in I.T. return submitted for the relevant financial year 1994-95; *Kalpanaraj* v. *Tamil Nadu State Transport Corporation,* (2015) 2 SCC 764.

106. Future Prospects – Deceased 46 Years, Multiplier of 13 Applied – 30% increase in future prospects of income warranted; *Kalpanaraj* v. *Tamil Nadu State Transport Corporation,* (2015) 2 SCC 764.

107. Damage to Motor Cycle – Claim not rebutted with evidence – Grant of Rs. 10,000; *Kalpanaraj* v. *Tamil Nadu State Transport Corporation,* (2015) 2 SCC 764.

108. Loss of Dependency – Fatal – Deceased 25 years of age, driver-Skilled job – Loss of dependency calculated at Rs. 10,36,800, taking monthly income at Rs. 9,000 per month; *Kala Devi* v. *Bhagwan Das Chauhan,* (2015) 2 SCC 771.

109. Private or Self-employment – Fatal – Compensation – Minimum wages notified in Act relied in absence of salary slip; *Rajiv Chowdhrie Huf* v. *Union of India,* (2015) 3 SCC 541.

110. Violation of Statutory Provision – Plying vehicle without insurance – Liability not mulcted on financier – Appreciation by Single Judge in appeal under section 173 of Motor Vehicle Act, both on facts and law is wholly erroneous; *HDFC Bank Limited* v. *Reshma,* (2015) 3 SCC 679.

111. Just and Reasonable Compensation – House Wife and Self-employed – Total Compensation Awarded at Rs. 6,47,000 – Age of deceased 22 years. Proper multiplier to be applied is 18. Loss of dependency calculated at Rs. 4,32,000, Rs. 1 lakh awarded for loss of love and affection, Rs. 1 lakh for loss of consortium, Rs. 15,000 for loss of estate and funeral expenses; *Jitendra Khimshankar Trivedi* v. *Kasam Daud Kumbhar,* (2015) 4 SCC 237.

112. Interest on Amount of Compensation – To be paid @ 9% per annum from date of filing of claim petition; *Amresh Kumari* v. *Niranjan Lal Jagdish,* (2015) 4 SCC 433.

113. Interest – Grant of – Rs. 50,000 for loss of consortium with interest @ 9% per annum from date of filing of petition; *Mohinder Kaur* v. *Hira Nand Sindhi (Ghoriwala),* (2015) 4 SCC 434.

169. Procedure and powers of Claims Tribunals.—(1) In holding any inquiry under section 168, the Claims Tribunal may, subject to any rules that may be made in this behalf, follow such summary procedure as it thinks fit.

(2) The Claims Tribunal shall have all the powers of a Civil Court for the purpose of taking evidence on oath and of enforcing the attendance of witnesses and of compelling the discovery and production of documents and material objects and for such other purposes as may be prescribed; and the Claims Tribunal shall be deemed to be a Civil Court for all the purposes of section 195 and Chapter XXVI of the Code of Criminal Procedure, 1973 (2 of 1974).

(3) Subject to any rules that may be made in this behalf, the Claims Tribunal may, for the purpose of adjudicating upon any claim for compensation, choose one or more persons possessing special knowledge of and matter relevant to the inquiry to assist it in holding the inquiry.

SYNOPSIS

4. Fact Recorded by Tribunal on Manner of Accident cannot be Disturbed
5. Procedural Wrangles and Tangles, Hyper-technicalities

COMMENTS

1. Detail Pleading – When the issue framed by the trial Court is wide and parties understood the scope thereof and adduced such evidence as they wanted to, then there can be no prejudice and a contention regarding absence of a detailed pleading cannot be countenanced; *Union of India* v. *United India Insurance Co. Ltd.*, AIR 1998 SC 640: 1998 AIR SCW 245: JT 1997 (8) SC 653: 1997 (8) SCC 683: 1997 (9) Supreme 69.

2. Tribunal cannot Decide Issues in Piecemeal – The object of summary procedure is to ensure that claim application is heard and decided by the Claims Tribunal expeditiously. The inquiry under section 168 and the summary procedure that the Claims Tribunal has to follow do not contemplate the controversy arising out of claim application being decided in piecemeal. The Claims Tribunal is required to dispose of all issues one way or the other in one go while deciding the claim application. The objection raised by the Insurance Company about maintainability of claim petition is intricately connected with its liability which in the facts and circumstances of the case is dependent on determination of the effect of the additional premium paid by the insured to cover the risk of the driver and other terms of the policy. Since all issues are required to be considered by the Claims Tribunal together in light of the evidence that may be let in by the parties and not in piecemeal, it would not be proper to consider the rival contentions on merits at this stage; *Bimlesh* v. *New India Assurance Co. Ltd.*, AIR 2010 SC 2591: 2010 AIR SCW 4581: (2010) 8 SCC 591.

3. Claims Tribunal can Accept Affidavit of Witness Permitting Other Side for Cross Examination – The purpose of statutory provisions is for due compliance of the principle of natural justice. The Rules provide for the examination of applicant in case present (rule 205) and in case parties contest then witness be examined orally. However, it is silent whether there should be examination-in-chief in every case. Rules provide that the oral evidence may be recorded with regard to facts in dispute. In case a party had filed an affidavit and liberty is given to the other side to cross-examine the witness and other side accepts the proposal and cross-examines such witness, then no objection may be raised at later stage with regard to violation of principle of natural justice or statutory provisions, more so when the statute is silent. In absence of any repugnancy, inference may be drawn to regulate the proceedings of the Tribunal by applying the provisions of C.P.C. The Order XVIII, rule 4, C.P.C. since provides for adducing evidence by filing affidavit, there appears to be no illegality on the part of the Motor Accident Claims Tribunal while accepting the affidavit and permit the appellant to cross-examine the witness. Thus the Tribunal can accept the affidavit of witness and permit other side to cross examine such witness; "*New India Assurance Co. Ltd.* v. *Richa Singh Katiyar*, AIR 2011 All 107.

4. Fact Recorded by Tribunal on Manner of Accident cannot be Disturbed – The deceased pedestrian sustained head injury and died before reaching the hospital. The report of the Investigator cannot be relied upon on the sole ground that two years after the accident took place, the Insurance Company deputed one Investigator to visit the spot where the accident took place and submit a report. The report submitted by the Investigator is not admissible in evidence for deciding the question as to which vehicles were involved in the accident. Further it will appear from the impugned judgment that the Tribunal has discussed and analyzed the entire evidence of the witnesses and also considered the First Information Report lodged against the driver of the auto-rickshaw immediately after the accident. A criminal case was also registered against the auto-rickshaw driver. The manner in which the accident took place as narrated in the F.I.R. is fully supported by the witnesses who had seen the occurrence. Hence, the finding of fact recorded by the Tribunal on the factum and the manner of the accident cannot be disturbed. The insurer and the owner both are liable to pay compensation; *United India Insurance Company Ltd.* v. *Revathy*, AIR 2012 Mad 25.

5. Procedural Wrangles and Tangles, Hyper-technicalities – No ground to dismiss claim petition; *United India Insurance Company Limited* v. *Brijbala*, AIR 2015 HP 34.

170. Impleading insurer in certain cases.—Where in the course of any inquiry, the Claims Tribunal is satisfied that—

(a) there is collusion between the person making the claim and the person against whom the claim is made, or

(b) the person against whom the claim is made has failed to contest the claim,

it may, for reasons to be recorded in writing, direct that the insurer who may be liable in respect of such claim, shall be impleaded as a party to the proceeding and the insurer so impleaded shall thereupon have, without prejudice to the provisions contained in sub-section (2) of section 149, the right to contest the claim on all or any of the grounds that are available to the person against whom the claim has been made.

SYNOPSIS

1. Defenses Available to Insurer
2. Fact of Contributory Negligence has to be taken Note of by Tribunal *Suo Motu*
3. Tribunal Required to give its Finding on Probabilities
4. Choice of Multiplier
5. Insurer cannot Challenge Awarded Compensation in Absence of Permission by Tribunal
6. Once a Party Insurer can Raise All Contentions Available to Resist Claim
7. Driving License – Valid License to Drive Light Motor Vehicle
8. Driving License – No Breach of any Condition of Insurance Policy

COMMENTS

1. Defenses Available to Insurer – The Insurance Company when impleaded as a party by the Court can be permitted to contest the proceeding on merits only if the conditions precedent mentioned in the section are found to be satisfied and for that purpose the Insurance Company has to obtain order in writing from the Tribunal and which should be a reasoned order by the Tribunal. Unless that procedure is followed the Insurance company cannot have a wider defence on merits than what is available to it by way of statutory defence. It is true that the claimants themselves had Insurance Company in the Petition but that was done with a view to thrust the statutory liability on the Insurance Company on account of the contract of the insurance. That was not an order of the Court itself permitting the Insurance Company which was impleaded to avail of a larger defence on merits on being satisfied on the aforesaid two conditions mentioned in section 170; *Shankarayya* v. *United India Insurance Co. Ltd.*, AIR 1998 SC 2968: 1998 AIR SCW 2819: JT 1998 (4) SC 300: 1998 (3) SCC 140.

2. Fact of Contributory Negligence has to be taken Note of by Tribunal *Suo Motu* – The fact of contributory negligence whether pleaded, or not has to be taken note of by the Tribunal *sno motu* and a finding regarding that aspect should be given; *P. Rnjesioari* v. *Hotel Impend,* 1989 ACJ 454 (Mad).

3. Tribunal Required to give its Finding on Probabilities – The Tribunal is required in law to give its finding on probabilities and not on proving the offence beyond reasonable doubt as is done by a criminal court; *Radha* v. *Ashok Kumar,* 1989 ACJ 379 (All).

4. Choice of Multiplier – The High Court increased the multiplier From '8' to '11', as the age of the deceased was 56 years. After considering the submission made by the learned counsel and looking to the law laid down by this Court and in view of the fact that the age of the deceased was 56 and taking notice of the multiplier indicated in the

Second Schedule of Motor Vehicles Act, the High Court was not justified in increasing the multiplier From '8' to '11'. Therefore, instead of '11', the multiplier of '8' should be used while calculating the amount of compensation; *Urviben Chiragbhai Sheth* v. *Vijaybhai Shambhubhai Joranputra*, AIR 2011 SC 2502: 2011 AIR SCW 3172: 2011 (3) ACJ 1445.

5. Insurer cannot Challenge Awarded Compensation in Absence of Permission by Tribunal – The appellant/Insurance Company neither sought nor was granted permission by the Tribunal under section 170 of the Motor Vehicles Act to contest the claim on all available defences, the Insurance Company cannot be permitted to challenge the quantum of compensation awarded by the Tribunal in this appeal; *Oriental Insurance Co. Ltd.* v. *Raju Kesharwani*, AIR 2009 Chht 13: 2009 AIHC 130 NOC: 2009 (2) AIR Bom R 293 (NOC).

6. Once a Party Insurer can Raise All Contentions Available to Resist Claim – Where the insurer is a party either on account of being impleaded as a party by the Tribunal under section 170 or being impleaded as a party-respondent by the claimants in the claim petition voluntarily, it will be entitled to contest the matter by raising all grounds, without being restricted to the grounds available under section 149(2). The claim petition is maintainable against the owner and driver without impleading the insurer as a party. When a statutory notice is issued under section 149(2) by the Tribunal, it is clear that such notice is issued not to implead the insurer as a party but merely to put it on notice that a claim has been made in regard to a policy issued by it and that it will have to bear the liability as and when an award is made in regard to such claim. Therefore, it cannot, as of right, require that it should be impleaded as a party. But it can, however, be made a party either by the claimants voluntarily in the claim petition or by the direction of the Tribunal under section 170. Whatever be the reason or ground for the insurer being impleaded as a party, once it is a party, it can raise all contentions that are available to resist the claim; *United India Insurance Co. Ltd.* v. *Shila Datta*, AIR 2012 SC 86: 2011 AIR SCW 6541: (2011) 10 SCC 509.

7. Driving License – Valid License to Drive Light Motor Vehicle – Driver authorised to drive light goods vehicle; *Ashvinbhai Jayantilal Modi* v. *Ramkaran Ramchandra Sharma*, (2015) 2 SCC 180.

8. Driving License – No Breach of any Condition of Insurance Policy – Insurance company cannot disown liability; *Ashvinbhai Jayantilal Modi* v. *Ramkaran Ramchandra Sharma*, (2015) 2 SCC 180.

171. Award of interest where any claim is allowed.—Where any Claims Tribunal allows a claim for compensation made under this Act, such Tribunal may direct that in addition to the amount of compensation simple interest shall also be paid at such rate and from such date not earlier than the date of making the claim as it may specify in this behalf.

SYNOPSIS

1. Interest on Compensation
2. Challenges to Interest Awarded
3. Interest on Compensation Amount
4. Compensation – Permanent Disability
5. Loss of Dependency – Fatal
6. Just and Reasonable Compensation – House Wife and Self-employed – Total Compensation Awarded at Rs. 6,47,000
7. Interest on Amount of Compensation
8. Interest – Grant of

COMMENTS

1. Interest on Compensation – The accident in the present case had taken place on 1-9-2004 and the Tribunal had passed the award on 18-5-2005. Rate at which the interest is to be awarded would normally depend upon the bank rate prevailing at the relevant time. Since in the month of April, 2005, the prevailing rate of interest on bank deposits was found and held to be 7.5% per annum, it was considered appropriate to award the same rate of interest, as the same was the prevailing rate of interest on the date of the passing of the award in the present case. The appellants would be entitled to be paid interest at the rate of 7.5% from the date of application till the date of payment; *Dharampal* v. *Uttar Pradesh State Road Transport Corporation,* AIR 2008 SC 2312: 2008 AIR SCW 3947: 2008 (7) SCALE 360.

Interest awarded at the rate of 12% per annum is payable on the entire amount awarded from the date of filing of application till realisation. Interest is to be awarded even on the amount awarded by the Tribunal and deposited by the insurer although the same could not be withdrawn by the claimants, because they could not furnish security as ordered in appeal filed by the insurer; *Chandra Devi* v. *Jit Singh,* 1989 ACJ 41 (Del).

Tribunal should grant interest from date of application unless claimant is responsible for causing delay in final disposal of the case; *Vidhya Kakkar* v. *D.T.C.,* 1989 ACJ 1088 (Del).

2. Challenges to Interest Awarded – Though the petitioner may have a point on the issue of interest but having regard to the facts and circumstances of the case and that the accident took place seventeen years ago, the court refused to interfere with the impugned order in exercise of powers under article 136 of the Constitution of India; "*National Insurance Co. Ltd.* v. *Swaroopa,* AIR 2006 SC 2472: 2006 AIR SCW 3227: 2005 (11) SCC 419.

3. Interest on Compensation Amount – Tribunals and Courts to decide the rate of interest after taking into consideration the rate of interest allowed by this court in similar cases, inflation, change in economy, policy adopted by R.B.I from time to time and period since when the case is pending; *Puttamma* v. *K.L. Narayana Reddy,* AIR 2014 SC 706.

4. Compensation – Permanent Disability – Enormity of suffering, pain and agony, loss of enjoyment of life of appellant to be considered; *Kiran* v. *Sajjan Singh,* (2015) 1 SCC 539.

5. Loss of Dependency – Fatal – Deceased 25 years of age, driver-Skilled job – Loss of dependency calculated at Rs. 10,36,800, taking monthly income at Rs. 9,000 per month; *Kala Devi* v. *Bhagwan Das Chauhan,* (2015) 2 SCC 771.

6. Just and Reasonable Compensation – House Wife and Self-employed – Total Compensation Awarded at Rs. 6,47,000 – Age of deceased 22 years. Proper multiplier to be applied is 18. Loss of dependency calculated at Rs. 4,32,000, Rs. 1 lakh awarded for loss of love and affection, Rs. 1 lakh for loss of consortium, Rs. 15,000 for loss of estate and funeral expenses; *Jitendra Khimshankar Trivedi* v. *Kasam Daud Kumbhar,* (2015) 4 SCC 237.

7. Interest on Amount of Compensation – To be paid @ 9% per annum from date of filing of claim petition; *Amresh Kumari* v. *Niranjan Lal Jagdish,* (2015) 4 SCC 433.

8. Interest – Grant of – Rs. 50,000 for loss of consortium with interest @ 9% per annum from date of filing of petition; *Mohinder Kaur* v. *Hira Nand Sindhi (Ghoriwala),* (2015) 4 SCC 434.

172. Award of compensatory costs in certain cases.—(1) Any Claims Tribunal adjudicating upon any claim for compensation under this Act, may in any case where it is satisfied for reasons to be recorded by it in writing that—

(a) the policy of insurance is void on the ground that it was obtained by representation of fact which was false in any material particular, or

(b) any party or insurer has put forward a false or vexatious claim or defence,

such Tribunal may make an order for the payment, by the party who is guilty of misrepresentation or by whom such claim or defence has been put forward of special costs by way of compensation to the insurer or, as the case may be, to the party against whom such claim or defence has been put forward.

(2) No Claims Tribunal shall pass an order for special costs under sub-section (1) for any amount exceeding one thousand rupees.

(3) No person or insurer against whom an order has been made under this section shall, by reason thereof be exempted from any criminal liability in respect of such mis-representation, claim or defence as is referred to in sub-section (1).

(4) Any amount awarded by way of compensation under this section in respect of any misrepresentation, claim or defence, shall be taken into account in any subsequent suit for damages for compensation in respect of such misrepresentation, claim or defence.

173. Appeals.—(1) Subject to the provisions of sub-section (2) any person aggrieved by an award of a Claims Tribunal may, within ninety days from the date of the award, prefer an appeal to the High Court:

Provided that no appeal by the person who is required to pay any amount in terms of such award shall be entertained by the High Court unless he has deposited with it twenty-five thousand rupees or fifty per cent. of the amount so awarded, whichever is less, in the manner directed by the High Court:

Provided further that the High Court may entertain the appeal after the expiry of the said period of ninety days, if it is satisfied that the appellant was prevented by sufficient cause from preferring the appeal in time.

(2) No appeal shall lie against any award of a Claims Tribunal if the amount in dispute in the appeal is less than ten thousand rupees.

SYNOPSIS

COMMENTS

1. Maintainability of Appeal – The Plea of the insurer that application filed by the claimant under section 173 of the Act was not maintainable in view of section 53 of the ESI Act which creates bar against receiving or recovering any compensation. The appeal deserves to be allowed. The entitlement shall be worked out by the concerned Motor Accident Claim Tribunal (MACT) by taking note of section 53 of the Act; *National Insurance Co. Ltd.* v. *Hamida Khatoon*, AIR 2009 SC 2599: 2009 AIR SCW 4520: 2009 (2) ACC 462.

2. Failure to Pass Reasoned Order would not Prejudices Insurer – The Tribunal, while passing its orders on the petition filed under section 170 of the Act only stated that the prayer was granted, though the mandate of section 170(b) of the Act states that the Tribunal while passing an order shall record its reasons. But it is very much evident in this case that the driver and the owner of the motor vehicle did not file the written statement and failed to contest the proceedings. The Tribunal could have merely recorded that fact while allowing the application. In a situation contemplated by clause (b) of section 170, nothing more was required than recording that indisputable fact. For failure to do so, the appellant shall not suffer prejudice. Therefore, the appellant-Insurance Company was justified in contesting the proceedings on the grounds other than those enumerated under sub-section (2) of section 149 of the Act, pursuant to the permission granted by Court. For the same reason, the Insurance Company can be legitimately considered to be 'person aggrieved' within the meaning of section 173 of the Act. Dismissal of the appeal filed by insurance company on the sole ground that the appellant had not obtained reasoned order permitting it to contest under section 170 of the Act was improper; *United India Insurance Co. Ltd.* v. *Jyotsnaben S. Patel*, AIR 2003 SC 3127: 2003 AIR SCW 4111: JT 2003 (6) SC 547: 2003 (7) SCC 212: 2003 (6) SCALE 288: 2003 (5) Supreme 529.

3. Appeal Entertainable if Appellant Suffered any Prejudice – An appeal against the Tribunal lies before the High Court. The High Court, while exercising its appellate power, would follow the provisions contained in Civil P.C. or akin thereto. It is obligatory on the part of the appellate Court to pose unto itself the right question, *viz.*, whether the appellant has been able to show sufferance of any prejudice. If it has not suffered any prejudice or otherwise no failure of justice had occurred, the High Court should not have entertained the appeal on that ground alone. A decision rendered without jurisdiction would be *coram non juris*. A distinction, however, must be made between a jurisdiction with regard to subject-matter of the suit and that of territorial and pecuniary jurisdiction. Whereas in the case falling within the former category the judgment would be a nullity, in the latter it would not be. It is not a case where the Tribunal had no jurisdiction in relation to the subject-matter of claim. As a matter of fact the civil Court had no jurisdiction to entertain the suit. If the Tribunal had the jurisdiction to entertain a claim petition, the Court should not have, in absence of any finding of sufferance of any prejudice on the part of the appellant entertained the appeal; *Mantoo Sarkar* v. *Oriental Insurance Co. Ltd.*, AIR 2009 SC 1022: 2009 AIR SCW 136: 2009 (2) SCC 244: 2008 (16) SCALE 197.

4. Joint Appeal – Section 173 of the Act confers a right on any aggrieved person to prefer an appeal from an award. The owner of the bus was an aggrieved person. He could maintain an appeal of his own. Appeal even in absence of insurer is maintainable; *V. Subbulakshmi* v. *S. Lakshmi*, AIR 2008 SC 1256: 2008 AIR SCW 1270: 2008 (4) SCC 224: 2008 (2) SCALE 218.

There is no bar to the filing of joint appeal by owner of the vehicle and insurer, *The Oriental Fire & General Insurance Co. Ltd.* v. *Rajendra Kaur*, 1989 ACJ 961 (All).

5. Order Awarding Compensation on No Fault Liability is Appealable – An order of the Tribunal awarding compensation under section 140 of the Act is appealable under section 173 as it amounts to an award under section 173. Chapter X of the Act provides for no forum for enforcement of the right under section 140. The only forum available is in Chapter XII. The right under section 140 can only be enforced under section 168 as an award. An appeal, therefore, lies under section 173 against such an award seeking to enforce the right under section 140. Furthermore, there can be more than one award particularly when a sum paid may have to be adjusted from the final award. Keeping in view the provisions of section 168 of the Act, there cannot be any doubt whatsoever that an award for enforcing the right under section 140 of the Act is also required to be passed under section 168 only after the parties concerned have filed their pleadings and have been given a reasonable opportunity of being heard. A Claims Tribunal, thus, must be satisfied that the conditions precedent specified in section 140 of the Act have been substantiated, which is the basis for making an award. Furthermore, evidently, the amount directed to be paid even in terms of Chapter X of the Act must as of necessity, in the event of non-compliance of directions has to be recovered in terms of section 174 of the Act. There is no other provision in the Act which takes care of such a situation. Therefore, even when objections are raised by the insurance company in regard to its liability, the Tribunal is required to render a decision upon the issue, which would attain finality and, thus, the same would be an award within the meaning of section 173 of the Act; *Yallwwa* v. *National Insurance Co. Ltd.*, AIR 2007 SC 2582: 2007 AIR SCW 4590: 2007 (6) SCC 657: 2007 (8) SCALE 77: 2007 (5) Supreme 144.

6. Writ Petition Challenging Award not Maintainable – The right of appeal is a statutory right to the parties and where the law provides a remedy by filing an appeal on limited grounds, the grounds of challenge cannot be enlarged by filing a petition under articles 226/227 of the Constitution on the premise that the insurer has limited grounds available for challenging the Award given by the Tribunal. Under section 173 of the Act, an insurer has a right to file an appeal before the High Court on limited grounds available under section 149(2). The appeal being a product of the statute it is not open to an insurer to take any plea other than those provided under section 149(2) of the Act. However, in a situation where there is collusion between the claimant and the insurer or the insured does not contest the claim and further, if the Tribunal does not implead the Insurance Company to contest the claim, in such a situation it is open to the insurer to seek permission of the Tribunal to contest the claim on the ground available to the insured or to a person against whom the claim has been made. If permission is granted and the insurer is allowed to contest the claim on merit, in that case it is open to the insurer to file an appeal against the Award of the Tribunal on merits. Thus, in such a situation, the insurer can question the quantum of compensation awarded by the Tribunal. In the case, the insurer made a challenge to the Award of the Tribunal before the High Court in the writ petition on the ground of its liability to pay the interest on the amount of compensation for a specified period without obtaining the permission of the Tribunal as contemplated under the statute. Thus, since the insurer has a remedy by filing an appeal before the High Court on the available defences envisaged under the statute, writ petition under article 226/227 of the Constitution by an insurer challenging the Award of the Tribunal is not maintainable; *Bijoy Kumar Dugar* v. *Bidyadhar Dutta*, AIR 2006 SC 1255: 2006 AIR SCW 1116: 2006 (3) SCC 242: 2006 (2) Supreme 374.

7. Insurer has No Right to file Appeal Challenging Award Unless Conditions Satisfied – Even if no appeal is preferred under section 173 of Act by an insured against the award of a Tribunal, it is not permissible for an insurer to file an appeal questioning the quantum of compensation as well as finding as regard negligence or contributory negligence of the offending vehicle, unless the conditions precedent specified in section 170 of Act is satisfied. The legislature has ensured by enacting section 149 of the Act that the victims of motor vehicle are fully compensated and protected. It is for that reason the insurer cannot escape from its liability to pay compensation on any exclusionary clause in the insurance policy except those specified in section 149(2) of the Act or where the condition precedent specified in section 170 is satisfied; *National Insurance Co. Ltd.* v. *Nicolletta Rohtagi*, AIR 2002 SC 3350: JT 2002 (7) SC 251: 2002 (7) SCC 456: 2002 (6) SCALE 569: 2002 (6) Supreme 362.

8. Joint Appeal Maintainable only if Permitted Defences Available – The insurer by associating the owner or the driver in the appeal when the owner or the driver is not an aggrieved person cannot be allowed to mock at the law which prohibit the insurer from filing any appeal except on the limited grounds on which it could defend the claims petition. Provision of law cannot be undermined in this way Court has to give effect to the real purpose of the provisions of law relating to the award of compensation in respect of accident arising out of the use of the motor vehicles and cannot permit the insurer to give him right to defend or appeal on grounds not permitted by law by a backdoor method. As such an insurer cannot maintain a joint appeal along with the owner or the driver if defence on any ground under section 149(2) is not available to it; *Chinnama George* v. *N.K. Raju,* AIR 2000 SC 1565: 2000 AIR SCW 1321: JT 2000 (4) SC 207: 2000 (4) SCC 130: 2000 (3) SCALE 106: 2000 (3) Supreme 136.

9. Condonation of Delay – The petitioners was claimed as compensation in respect of a motor accident in which brother of the petitioners died. Dissatisfied with the amount awarded, petitioners filed an appeal before the High Court. The appeal was barred by limitation and there was no explanation for an inordinate delay of 416 days. Consequently, the appeal was dismissed; *Prakash* v. *Managing Director, K.S.R.T.C.,* AIR 2000 SC 3419: 2000 AIR SCW 1886: JT 2000 (1) SC 183: 2000 (4) Supreme 663.

10. Ruling on Supposition is Obiter not Binding – The offending vehicle was driven by a driver who had a valid licence and it stood renewed on the date of the accident. There was thus no occasion for the High Court to have ruled on suppositions to the contrary in order to interpret the law and that too on a fact situation not available to it. Thus, the entire exercise of the High Court in that direction was obiter, not at all a binding precedent; *National Insurance Co. Ltd.* v. *Santro Devi,* AIR 1998 SC 1485: 1998 AIR SCW 346: JT 1997 (9) SC 197: 1998 (1) SCC 219: 1997 (7) SCALE 104: 1997 (9) Supreme 458.

11. Right of Appeal Accrued under Old Act Survives though Repealed by New Act – Unless the New Act expressly or by necessary implication makes the provision applicable retrospectively, the right to appeal will crystallise in the appellant on the institution of the application in the Tribunal of first instance and that vested right of appeal would not be dislodged by the enactment of the new Act. In other words, the appellant would be entitled to file the appeal without being required to make the deposit under the proviso to section 173 of the New Act. Right of appeal which accrued under the old Act survives even after its repeal by the New Act; *Ramesh Singh* v. *Cinta Devi,* AIR 1996 SC 1560: 1996 AIR SCW 1661: JT 1996 (5) SC 543: 1996 (3) SCC 142.

12. Appeal against Order Based No Fault Liability – Appeal against order passed on the basis of no fault liability is maintainable under section 173 of the Act; *United India Insurance Co. Ltd.* v. *Serjerao,* AIR 2008 SC 460: 2007 AIR SCW 7280: 2008 (7) SCC 425: 2007 (13) SCALE 80: 2007 (8) Supreme 25.

13. Where Court Decides Suit Barred by Time is Appealable – If a suit is barred by time and yet the court decides it, the Court would be committing an illegality but the aggrieved party would be entitled to have the degree set aside on the plea of limitation by preferring an appeal against it; *New India Assurance Co. Ltd.* v. *Lalita Harijan,* AIR 1996 Ori 61.

14. Deposit of Specific Amount – On a plain reading of the proviso to sub-section (1) of section 173, any person' who is required to pay any amount under an award passed by the Claims Tribunal prefers an appeal, his appeal can be entertained by the High Court only if he makes deposit of a specific amount as required by the said proviso and he cannot claim exemption from making the deposit on the ground that a co-respondent' before the Tribunal has filed an appeal and has made the requisite deposit; *Sohan Singh* v. *Kushla Devi,* AIR 1996 P&H 256: 1998 (1) ACJ 472: 1996 (3) Civ LJ 199.

Under section 173 of the Act, the High Court cannot refuse to take an appeal, which is not backed by deposit of twenty five thousand rupees or fifty per cent, of the amount awarded against the appellant whichever is less but it cannot judicially consider such appeals either for admission or for disposal of the stay application; *Rajasthan State Road Transport Corporation* v. *Santosh,* AIR 1995 Raj 2:1 1996 (1) ACC 73: 1995 (2) ACJ 721.

15. Aggrieved Person entitled to Lodge only one Appeal – The section entitles the aggrieved person to lodge only one appeal in the High Court and, therefore, when that power is once exhausted, the power of the High Court to hear and decide the appeal is exhausted and the Letters Patent Appeal against a decision of the High Court is not maintainable; *Uttam Singh* v. *National Insurance Co. Ltd.,* AIR 1988 MP 199: 1989 ACJ 38 (MP).

16. Defences Available to Insurance Company – Insurance Company in its appeal cannot raise the point that claimant is not wedded wife and legal representative of the deceased; *Oriental Fire & General Insurance Co. Ltd.* v. *Rambha Barrick,* 1989 ACJ 972 (Cal).

17. Joint Appeal by Owner and Insurer is Maintainable – When an award is made by the Tribunal, the owner of the vehicle, being a person aggrieved, can file an appeal challenging his liability on any ground, or challenge the quantum of compensation. An appeal which is "maintainable" when the owner of the vehicle files it, does not become "not maintainable" merely on account of the insurer being a co-appellant with the owner. When the insurer becomes a co-appellant, the owner of the vehicle does not cease to be a person aggrieved. So long as the owner is an appellant and he is a 'person aggrieved' in law, the question whether he is independently filing the appeal, or whether he is filing it at the instance of the insurer becomes irrelevant; *United India Insurance Co. Ltd.* v. *Shila Datta,* AIR 2012 SC 86: 2011 AIR SCW 6541: (2011) 10 SCC 509.

18. Compensation in Cases of 100% Disability – High Court without good reasons treated monthly income of appellant to be Rs. 3000 in place of Rs. 5000. No good reason assigned even for reducing the compensation of Rs. 2 lacs for pain and suffering to Rs. 1 lac and Rs. 4 lacs for permanent disability to Rs 3 lacs. Tribunal was quite justified in allowing Rs. 14.20 lacs as total compensation on the basis of monthly income of Rs. 5000. Judgement of High Court under appeal set aside and that of Tribunal restored. Interest awarded @ 9 % per annum from date of petition; *M.D. Jacob* v. *United India Insurance Ltd.,* AIR 2014 SC 988.

19. Pre-deposit of Awarded Amount – Mandatory for Maintainability of Appeal – When there is a direction given in the award to recover the amount from the owner, he is also required to pay the amount in tune with the liability already cast upon him by the award and there is no exoneration of the said appellant from the liability; *Pareeth* v. *Janaiya,* AIR 2015 Ker 1.

20. Pre-deposit of Amount – Provision Mandatory – Interpretation in Tune with Intent and Purport of Legislation to be Adopted – Only when provision is ambiguous any other mode of interpretation can be adopted; *Pareeth* v. *Janaiya,* AIR 2015 Ker 1.

21. Certified Copy of Award/Judgment – Accompanied with Memorandum of Appeal – Free copy under section 168(2) cannot be accepted in substitute of the certified copy; *Sunitha* v. *Ranju,* AIR 2015 Ker 24.

22. Violation of Statutory Provision – Plying vehicle without insurance – Liability not mulcted on financier – Appreciations by Single Judge in appeal under section 173 of Motor Vehicle Act, both on facts and law is wholly erroneous; *HDFC Bank Limited* v. *Reshma,* (2015) 3 SCC 679.

174. Recovery of money from insurer as arrear of land revenue.—Where any amount is due from any person under an award, the Claims Tribunal may, on an application made to it by the person entitled to the amount, issue a certificate for the amount to the Collector and the Collector shall proceed to recover the same in the same manner as an arrear of land revenue.

COMMENTS

Enforceability of Decision on Disputes between Insurer and Insured – The decision rendered on the claims and disputes *inter se* between the insurer and insured in the course of adjudication of claim for compensation by the claimants and the award made thereon is enforceable and executable in the same manner as provided in section 174 of the Act for enforcement and execution of the award in favour of the claimants; *National Insurance Co. Ltd.* v. *Swaran Singh,* AIR 2004 SC 1531: 2004 AIR SCW 663: JT 2004 (1) SC 109: 2004 (3) SCC 297: 2004 (1) SCALE 180: 2004 (1) Supreme 243.

175. Bar on jurisdiction of Civil Courts.—Where any Claims Tribunal has been constituted for any area, no Civil Court shall have jurisdiction to entertain any question relating to any claim for compensation which may be adjudicated upon by the Claims Tribunal for that area, and no injunction in respect of any action taken or to be taken by or before the Claims Tribunal in respect of the claim for compensation shall be granted by the Civil Court.

SYNOPSIS

1. Application of CPC in proceedings before Tribunal
2. What Claims are Excluded from Jurisdiction of Civil Court

COMMENTS

1. Application of CPC in proceedings before Tribunal – The Motor Accident Claims Tribunal constituted under the provisions of Act is a 'Court' for all intents and purposes including enforcement of its award and therefore can exercise powers under section 47 and Order XXI of Civil Procedure Code, 1908. It cannot be said that since jurisdiction of Civil Court is barred by section 175 of Act, the Tribunal would not be justified in assuming and exercising powers of the Civil Court by resorting to and applying provisions under the Code of Civil Procedure, 1908. The bar of the jurisdiction of the Civil Court is one thing and the application of the Code of Civil Procedure is entirely a different thing. Both stand on different footings. The bar of the jurisdiction of the Civil Court has been created only and simply because the Act of 1988 has created a special forum *viz.* The Motor Accident Claims Tribunal, vesting it with a special and exclusive jurisdiction to deal with the cases of motor accident claims arising out of the vehicular accidents. Obviously, no such claim proceedings for which the special motor accident claims tribunals are constituted can lie before the Civil Court. Section 175 which speaks about bar of the jurisdiction of the Civil Court has nothing to do with the application of the provisions of the Code of Civil Procedure, to the proceedings before the Claims Tribunal; *Hirabhai Nanubhai Desai* v. *State of Gujarat,* AIR 1991 Guj 1: 1991 (2) ACC 266: 1992 (2) ACJ 561.

2. What Claims are Excluded from Jurisdiction of Civil Court – Where the claim relates to damage to property exceeding Rs. 2,000 and where such a reference has been made to the Civil Court, the Tribunal ceases to have jurisdiction in respect of such a claim. It is not each and every claim which is excluded from the jurisdiction of the Civil Court but what is excluded is such which may be adjudicated upon by the Tribunal and a claim for compensation for damages to property exceeding Rs. 2,000 can be got adjudicated upon through a Civil Court at the option of the claimant; *National Insurance Co.* v. *Union of India,* AIR 1989 J&K 56: 1989 ACJ 307: 1989 Kash LJ 440.

176. Power of State Government to make rules.—A State Government may make rules for the purpose of carrying into effect the provisions of sections 165 to 174, and in particular, such rules may provide for all or any of the following matters, namely:—

(a) the form of application for claims for compensation and the particulars it may contain, and the fees, if any, to be paid in respect of such applications;

(b) the procedure to be followed by a Claims Tribunal in holding an inquiry under this Chapter;

(c) the powers vested in a Civil Court which may be exercised by a Claims Tribunal;

(d) the form and the manner in which and the fees (if any) on payment of which an appeal may by preferred against an award of a Claims Tribunal; and

(e) any other matter which is to be, or may be, prescribed.

SYNOPSIS

1. Copy of Judgment or Award – Issuance of by Court – Not for Purpose of Filing Appeal
2. Procedural Wrangles and Tangles, Hyper-technicalities

COMMENTS

1. Copy of Judgment or Award – Issuance of by Court – Not for Purpose of Filing Appeal – Such interpretation will not be in any way beneficial to the parties, as the period of limitation runs from the date of receipt of the copy; *Sunitha* v. *Ranju*, AIR 2015 Ker 24.

2. Procedural Wrangles and Tangles, Hyper-technicalities – No ground to dismiss claim petition; *United India Insurance Company Limited* v. *Brijbala*, AIR 2015 HP 34.

CHAPTER XIII

OFFENCES, PENALTIES AND PROCEDURE

177. General provision for punishment of offences.—Whoever contravenes any provision of this Act or of any rule, regulation or notification made thereunder shall, if no penalty is provided for the offence be punishable for the first offence with fine which may extend to one hundred rupees, and for any second or subsequent offence with fine which may extend to three hundred rupees.

178. Penalty for travelling without pass or ticket and for dereliction of duty on the part of conductor and refusal to ply contract carriage, etc.—(1) Whoever travels in a stage carriage without having a proper pass or ticket with him or being in or having alighted from a stage carriage fails or refuses to present for examination or to deliver up his pass or ticket immediately on a requisition being made therefor, shall be punishable with fine which may extend to five hundred rupees.

Explanation.—In this section, "pass" and "ticket" have the meanings respectively assigned to them in section 124.

(2) If the conductor of a stage carriage, or the driver of a stage carriage performing the functions of a conductor in such stage carriage, whose duty is—

(a) to supply a ticket to a person travelling in a stage carriage on payment of fare by such person, either wilfully or negligently,—

(i) fails or refuses to accept the fare when tendered, or

(ii) fails or refuses to supply a ticket, or

(iii) supplies an invalid ticket, or

(iv) supplies a ticket of a lesser value, or

(b) to check any pass or ticket, either wilfully or negligently fails or refuses to do so,

he shall be punishable with fine which may extend to five hundred rupees.

(3) If the holder of a permit or the driver of a contract carriage refuses, in contravention of the provisions of this Act or rules made thereunder, to ply the contract carriage or to carry the passengers, he shall,—

(a) in the case of two-wheeled or three-wheeled motor vehicles, be punishable with fine which may extend to fifty rupees; and

(b) in any other case, be punishable with fine which may extend to two hundred rupees.

179. Disobedience of orders, obstruction and refusal of information.—(1) Whoever wilfully disobeys any direction lawfully given by any person or authority empowered under this Act to give such direction, or obstructs any person or authority in the discharge of any functions which such person or authority is required or empowered under this Act to discharge, shall, if no other penalty is provided for the offence be punishable with fine which may extend to five hundred rupees.

(2) Whoever, being required by or under this Act to supply any information, wilfully withholds such information or gives information which he knows to be false or which he does not believe to be true, shall, if no other penalty is provided for the offence, be punishable with imprisonment for a term which may extend to one month, or with fine which may extend to five hundred rupees, or with both.

180. Allowing unauthorised persons to drive vehicles.—Whenever, being the owner or person in charge of a motor vehicle, causes or permits, any other person who does not satisfy the provisions of section 3 or section 4 to drive the vehicle shall be punishable with imprisonment for a term which may extend to three months, or with fine which may extend to one thousand rupees, or with both.

181. Driving vehicles in contravention of section 3 or section 4.—Whoever drives a motor vehicle in contravention of section 3 or section 4 shall be punishable with imprisonment for a term which may extend to three months, or with fine which may extend to five hundred rupees, or with both.

COMMENTS

Driving Vehicles in Contravention of Section 3 or Section 4 – The minor person came from behind on the motorcycle and hit the scooter of the deceased from behind. The responsibility in causing the accident was, therefore, found to be solely that of the minor. However, since he was a minor and it was the responsibility of the petitioner to ensure that his motorcycle was not misused and that too by a minor who had no licence to drive the same, the Motor Accident Claims Tribunal quite rightly saddled the liability for payment of compensation on the Petitioner and, accordingly, directed the Insurance Company to pay the awarded amount to the awardees and, thereafter, to recover the same from the Petitioner. The story that the minor came into the house of the petitioner and took the keys of the motorcycle without any intimation to the petitioner, appears to be highly improbable and far-fetched. It is difficult to accept the defence of the petitioner that the keys of the motorcycle were taken by the minor without his knowledge. Thus there is no case of contributory negligence on the part of the deceased; *Jawahar Singh* v. *Bala Jain*, AIR 2011 SC 2436: 2011 AIR SCW 3625: (2011) 6 SCC 425.

182. Offences relating to licences.—(1) Whoever, being disqualified under this Act for holding or obtaining a driving licence drives a motor vehicle in a public place or in any other place, or applies for or obtains a driving licence or, not being entitled to have a driving licence issued to him free of endorsement, applies for or obtains a driving licence without disclosing the endorsement made on a driving licence previously held by him shall be punishable with imprisonment for a term which may extend to three months, or with fine which may extend to five hundred rupees or with both, and any driving licence so obtained by him shall be of no effect.

(2) Whoever, being disqualified under this Act for holding or obtaining a conductor's licence, acts as a conductor of a stage carriage in a public place or applies for or obtains a conductor's licence or, not being entitled to have a conductor's licence issued to him free of endorsement, applies for or obtains a conductor's licence without disclosing the endorsements made on a conductor's licence previously held by him, shall be punishable with imprisonment for a term which may extend to one month, or with fine which may extend to one hundred rupees, or with both, and any conductor's licence so obtained by him shall be of no effect.

[1][**182A. Punishment for offences relating to construction and maintenance of vehicles.**—Any person who contravenes the provisions of sub-section (3) of section 109, shall be punishable with a fine of one thousand rupees for the first offence and with a fine of five thousand rupees for any subsequent offences.]

183. Driving at excessive speed, etc.—(1) Whoever drives a motor vehicle in contravention of the speed limits referred to in section 112 shall be punishable with fine which may extend to four hundred rupees, or, if having been previously convicted of an offence under this sub-section is again convicted of an offence under this sub-section, with fine which may extend to one thousand rupees.

(2) Whoever causes any person who is employed by him or is subject to his control in driving to drive a motor vehicle in contravention of the speed limits referred to in section 112 shall be punishable with fine which may extend to three hundred rupees, or, if having been previously convicted of an offence under this sub-section, is again convicted of an offence under this sub-section, with fine which may extend to five hundred rupees.

(3) No person shall be convicted of an offence punishable under sub-section (1) solely on the evidence of one witness to the effect that in the opinion of the witness such person was driving at a speed which was unlawful, unless that opinion is shown to be based on an estimate obtained by the use of some mechanical device.

(4) The publication of a time table under which or the giving of any direction that any journey or part of a journey is to be completed within a specified time shall, if in the opinion of the Court it is not practicable in the circumstances of the case for that journey or part of a journey to be completed in the specified time without contravening the speed limits referred to in section 112 be *prima facie* evidence that the person who published the time table or gave the direction has committed an offence punishable under sub-section (2).

1. Ins. by Act 54 of 1994, sec. 54 (w.e.f. 14-11-1994).

184. Driving dangerously.—Whoever drives a motor vehicle at a speed or in a manner which is dangerous to the public, having regard to all the circumstances of the case including the nature, condition and use of the place where the vehicle is driven and the amount of traffic which actually is at the time or which might reasonably be expected to be in the place, shall be punishable for the first offence with imprisonment for a term which may extend to six months or with fine which may extend to one thousand rupees, and for any second or subsequent offence if committed within three years of the commission of a previous similar offence with imprisonment for a term which may extend to two years, or with fine which may extend to two thousand rupees, or with both.

185. Driving by a drunken person or by a person under the influence of drugs.—Whoever, while driving, or attempting to drive, a motor vehicle,—

[1][(a) has, in his blood, alcohol exceeding 30 mg. per 100 ml. of blood detected in a test by a breath analyser, or]

(b) is under this influence of a drug to such an extent as to be incapable of exercising proper control over the vehicle,

shall be punishable for the first offence with imprisonment for a term which may extend to six months, or with fine which may extend to two thousand rupees, or with both; and for a second or subsequent offence, if committed within three years of the commission of the previous similar offence, with imprisonment for a term which may extend to two years, or with fine which may extend to three thousand rupees, or with both.

Explanation.—For the purposes of this section, the drug or drugs specified by the Central Government in this behalf, by notification in the Official Gazette, shall be deemed to render a person incapable of exercising proper control over a motor vehicle.

COMMENTS

Breath Analyser Test not Available to Driver who Fled from Scene – The Breath Analyzer Test has a different purpose and object. The said test is required to be carried out only when the person is driving or attempting to drive the vehicle. The expressions "while driving" and "attempting to drive" in that above sections have a meaning *"in praesenti"*. In such situations, the presence of alcohol in the blood has to be determined instantly so that the offender may be prosecuted for drunken driving. A Breath Analyzer Test is applied in such situations so that the alcohol content in the blood can be detected. The breath analyzer test could not be applied when the accused had escaped from the scene of the accident. Plea that when procedure has been laid to detect intoxication no finding that driver was drunk could be reached without subjecting driver to such test is not available to driver who had fled from the scene; *State Tr. P.S. Lodhi Colony, New Delhi* v. *Sanjeev Nanda,* AIR 2012 SC 3104: 2012 Cr LJ 4174: 2012 AIR SCW 4506.

186. Driving when mentally or physically unfit to drive.—Whoever drives a motor vehicle in any public place when he is to his knowledge suffering from any disease or disability calculated to cause his driving of the vehicle to be a source of danger to the public, shall be punishable for the first offence with fine which may extend to two hundred rupees and for a second or subsequent offence with fine which may extend to five hundred rupees.

187. Punishment for offences relating to accident.—Whoever fails to comply with the provisions of clause (c) of sub-section (1) of section 132 or of section

1. Subs. by Act 54 of 1994, sec. 55, for clause (a) (w.e.f. 14-11-1994).

133 or section 134 shall be punishable with imprisonment for a term which may extend to three months, or with fine which may extend to five hundred rupees, or with both or, if having been previously convicted of an offence under this section, he is again convicted of an offence under this section, with imprisonment for a term which may extend to six months, or with fine which may extend to one thousand rupees, or with both.

COMMENTS

Duty of Driver, Bystanders and Passenger in Motor Accident – Duty of every citizen is to help a motor accident victim, moreso when one is the cause of the accident, or is involved in that particular accident. Situations may be there, in a highly charged atmosphere or due to mob fury, the driver may flee from the place, if there is a real danger to his life, but he cannot shirk his responsibility of informing the police or other authorized persons or good samaritans forthwith, so that human lives could be saved. Failure to do so, may lead to serious consequences. Passengers who are in the vehicle which met with an accident, have also a duty to arrange proper medical attention for the victims. Further they have equal responsibility to inform the police about the factum of the accident, in case of failure to do so they are aiding the crime and screening the offender from legal punishment. No legal obligation as such is cast on a bystander either under the Motor Vehicles Act or any other legislation in India. But greater responsibility is cast on them, because they are people at the scene of the occurrence, and immediate and prompt medical attention and care may help the victims and their dear ones from unexpected catastrophe. Good samaritans who come forward to help must be treated with respect and be assured that they will have to face no hassle and will be properly rewarded. Thus the Supreme Court considering the need directed the Union of India and State Governments to frame proper rules and regulations and conduct awareness programmes so that the situation like this could to a large extent, be properly attended to and, in that process, human lives could be saved; *State Tr. P.S. Lodhi Colony, New Delhi* v. *Sanjeev Nanda,* AIR 2012 SC 3104: 2012 Cr LJ 4174: 2012 AIR SCW 4506.

188. Punishment for abetment of certain offences.—Whoever abets the commission of an offence under section 184 or section 185 or section 186 shall be punishable with the punishment provided for the offence.

189. Racing and trials of speed.—Whoever without the written consent of the State Government permits or takes part in a race or trial of speed of any kind between motor vehicles in any public place shall be punishable with imprisonment for a term which may extend to one month, or with a fine which may extend to five hundred rupees, or with both.

190. Using vehicle in unsafe condition.—(1) Any person who drives or causes or allows to be driven in any public place a motor vehicle or trailer while the vehicle or trailer has any defect, which such person knows of or could have discovered by the exercise of ordinary care and which is calculated to render the driving of the vehicle a source of danger to persons and vehicles using such place, shall be punishable with fine which may extend to two hundred and fifty rupees or, if as a result of such defect an accident is caused causing bodily injury or damage to property, with imprisonment for a term which may extend to three months, or with fine which may extend to one thousand rupees, or with both.

(2) Any person who drives or causes or allows to be driven, in any public place a motor vehicle, which violates the standards prescribed in relation to road safety, control of noise and air-pollution, shall be punishable for the first offence with a fine of one thousand rupees and for any second or subsequent

offence with a fine of two thousand rupees.

(3) Any person who drives or causes or allows to be driven, in any public place a motor vehicle which violates the provisions of this Act or the rules made thereunder relating to the carriage of goods which are of dangerous or hazardous nature to human life, shall be punishable for the first offence which may extend to three thousand rupees, or with imprisonment for a term which may extend to one year, or with both, and for any second or subsequent offence with fine which may extend to five thousand rupees, or with imprisonment for a term which may extend to three years, or with both.

191. Sale of vehicle in or alteration of vehicle to condition contravening this Act.—Whoever being an importer of or dealer in motor vehicles, sells or delivers or offers to sell or deliver a motor vehicle or trailer in such condition that the use thereof in a public place would be in contravention of Chapter VII or any rule made thereunder or alters the motor vehicle or trailer so as to render its condition such that its use in a public place would be in contravention of Chapter VII or any rule made thereunder shall be punishable with fine which may extend to five hundred rupees:

Provided that no person shall be convicted under this section if he proves that he had reasonable cause to believe that the vehicle would not be used in a public place until it had been put into a condition in which it might lawfully be so used.

[1][**192. Using vehicle without registration.**—(1) Whoever drives a motor vehicle or causes or allows a motor vehicle to be used in contravention of the provisions of section 39 shall be punishable for the first offence with a fine which may extend to five thousand rupees but shall not be less than two thousand rupees for a second or subsequent offence with imprisonment which may extend to one year or with fine which may extend to ten thousand rupees but shall not be less than five thousand rupees or with both:

Provided that the court may, for reasons to be recorded, impose a lesser punishment.

(2) Nothing in this section shall apply to the use of a motor vehicle in an emergency for the conveyance of persons suffering from sickness or injuries or for the transport of food or materials to relieve distress or of medical supplies for a like purpose:

Provided that the person using the vehicle reports about the same to the Regional Transport Authority within seven days from the date of such use.

(3) The court to which an appeal lies from any conviction in respect of an offence of the nature specified in sub-section (1), may set aside or vary any order made by the court below, notwithstanding that no appeal lies against the conviction in connection with which such order was made.]

[1][**192A. Using vehicle without permit.**—(1) Whoever drives a motor vehicle or causes or allows a motor vehicle to be used in contravention of the provisions of sub-section (1) of section 66 or in contravention of any condition of a permit relating to the route on which or the area in which or the purpose for which the vehicle may be used, shall be punishable for the first offence with a fine which may extend to five thousand rupees but shall not be less than two thousand

1. Subs. by Act 54 of 1994, sec. 56, for section 192 (w.e.f. 14-11-1994).

rupees and for any subsequent offence with imprisonment which may extend to one year but shall not be less than three months or with fine which may extend to ten thousand rupees but shall not be less than five thousand rupees or with both:

Provided that the court may for reasons to be recorded, impose a lesser punishment.

(2) Nothing in this section shall apply to the use of a motor vehicle in an emergency for the conveyance of persons suffering from sickness or injury or for the transport of materials for repair or for the transport of food or materials to relieve distress or of medical supplies for a like purpose:

Provided that the person using the vehicle reports about the same to the Regional Transport Authority within seven days from the date of such use.

(3) The court to which an appeal lies from any conviction in respect of an offence of the nature specified in sub-section (1), may set aside or vary any order made by the court below, notwithstanding that no appeal lies against the conviction in connection with which such order was made.]

193. Punishment of agents and canvassers without proper authority.—Whoever engages himself as an agent or canvasser in contravention of the provisions of section 93 or of any rules made thereunder shall be punishable for the first offence with fine which may extend to one thousand rupees and for any second or subsequent offence with imprisonment which may extend to six months, or with fine which may extend to two thousand rupees, or with both.

194. Driving vehicle exceeding permissible weight.—[1][(1) Whoever drives a motor vehicle or causes or allows a motor vehicle to be driven in contravention of the provisions of section 113 or section 114 or section 115 shall be punishable with minimum fine of two thousand rupees and an additional amount of one thousand rupees per tonne of excess load, together with the liability to pay charges for off-loading of the excess load.]

(2) Any driver of a vehicle who refuses to stop and submit his vehicle to weighing after being directed to do so by an officer authorised in this behalf under section 114 or removes or causes the removal of the load or part of it prior to weighing shall be punishable with fine which may extend to three thousand rupees.

195. Imposition of minimum fine under certain circumstances.—(1) Whoever having been convicted of an offence under this Act or the rules made thereunder commits a similar offence on a second or subsequent occasion within three years of the commission of the previous offence, no Court shall, except for reasons to be recorded by it in writing, impose on him a fine of less than one-fourth of the maximum amount of the fine imposable for such offence.

(2) Nothing in sub-section (1) shall be construed as restricting the power of the Court from awarding such imprisonment as it considers necessary in the circumstances of the case not exceeding the maximum specified in this Act in respect of that offence.

196. Driving uninsured vehicle.—Whoever drives a motor vehicle or causes or allows a motor vehicle to be driven in contravention of the provisions of

1. Subs. by Act 54 of 1994, sec. 57, for sub-section (1) (w.e.f. 14-11-1994).

section 146 shall be punishable with imprisonment which may extend to three months, or with fine which may extend to one thousand rupees, or with both.

197. Taking vehicle without authority.—(1) Whoever takes and drives away any motor vehicle without having either the consent of the owner thereof or other lawful authority shall be punishable with imprisonment which may extend to three months, or with fine which may extend to five hundred rupees, or with both:

Provided that no person shall be convicted under this section if the Court is satisfied that such person acted in the reasonable belief that he had lawful authority or in the reasonable belief that the owner would in the circumstances of the case have given his consent if he had been asked therefor.

(2) Whoever, unlawfully by force or threat of force or by any other form of intimidation, seizes or exercises control of a motor vehicle, shall be punishable with imprisonment which may extend to three months, or with fine which may extend to five hundred rupees, or with both.

(3) Whoever attempts to commit any of the acts referred to in sub-section (1) or sub-section (2) in relation to any motor vehicle, or abets the commission of any such act, shall also be deemed to have committed an offence under sub-section (1) or, as the case may be, sub-section (2).

198. Unauthorised interference with vehicle.—Whoever otherwise than with lawful authority or reasonable excuse enters or moves any stationary motor vehicle or tampers with the brake or any part of the mechanism of a motor vehicle shall be punishable with fine which may extend to one hundred rupees.

199. Offences by companies.—(1) Where an offence under this Act has been committed by a company, every person who, at the time the offence was committed, was in charge of, and was responsible to, the company for the conduct of the business of the company, as well as the company, shall be deemed to be guilty of the contravention and shall be liable to be proceeded against and punished accordingly:

Provided that nothing in this sub-section shall render any such person liable to any punishment provided in this Act, if he proves that the offence was committed without his knowledge or that he exercised all due diligence to prevent the commission of such offence.

(2) Notwithstanding anything contained in sub-section (1), where an offence under this Act has been committed by a company, and it is proved that the offence was committed with the consent or connivance of, or is attributable to any neglect on the part of any director, manager, secretary or other officer of the company, such director, manager, secretary or other officer shall also be deemed to be guilty of that offence and shall be liable to be proceeded against and punished accordingly.

Explanation.—For the purposes of this section—

(a) "company", means any body corporate and includes a firm or other association of individuals; and

(b) "director", in relation to a firm, means a partner in the firm.

200. Composition of certain offences.—(1) Any offence whether committed before or after the commencement of this Act punishable under section 177, section 178, section 179, section 180, section 181, section 182, sub-section (1) or sub-section (2) of section 183, section 184, section 186, [1][section 189, sub-section (2) of section 190], section 191, section 192, section 194, section 196, or section 198, may either before or after the institution of the prosecution, be compounded by such officers or authorities and for such amount as the State Government may, by notification in the Official Gazette, specify in this behalf.

(2) Where an offence has been compounded under sub-section (1) the offender, if in custody, shall be discharged and no further proceedings shall be taken against him in respect of such offence.

SYNOPSIS

1. Composition of Offences
2. Compounding of Offence not Mandatory

COMMENTS

1. Composition of Offences – Section 200 does not in any way authorize the State Government to permit the excess weight to be carried when on various inspection it is noticed that there is carriage of load beyond the permissible limit. It only gives an opportunity of compounding so that instead of the amounts fixed, lesser amounts can be accepted by the authorised officers. The intention of uploading the excess weight is apparent from a bare reading of the section 194(1). The liability to pay charge for uploading of the excess load is fixed on one who drives a vehicle or causes a motor vehicle to be driven in contravention of the provisions of sections 113, 114 and 115. Compounding can be done either before or after the institution of the prosecution in respect of the enumerated offences. Notifications issued by State Governments permitting carriage of excess weight after compounding runs counter to the clear import of section 194 and has no validity. After compounding the excess load, same cannot be permitted to be carried in the concerned vehicle. Such carriage would amount to infraction of section 113 of the Act. It is indisputable that the power of compounding vests with the State Government but the notification issued by various State Governments in that regard cannot authorize continuation of the offence which is permitted to be compounded by payments of the amounts fixed. If permitted to be continued, it would amount to fresh commission of the offence for which the compounding was done; *Parmajit Bhasin* v. *Union of India*, AIR 2006 SC 440: 2005 AIR SCW 6097: JT 2005 (10) SC 238: 2005 (12) SCC 642: 2005 (9) SCALE 238: 2005 (7) Supreme 518.

2. Compounding of Offence not Mandatory – For violation of section 113 to 115, section 194 accords penal sanction and on conviction for violation thereof, the section sanctions punishment with fine. Section 194 gives guidance to the State Government as a delegate under the statute to specify the amount for compounding the offences enumerated under sub-section (1) of section 200. It is not mandatory that the authorised officer would always compound the offence. It is conditional upon the willingness of the accused to have the offences compounded. It may also be done before the institution of the prosecution case. In the event of the accused persons willing to have the offence compounded, the authorised officer gets jurisdiction and authority to compound the offence and call upon the accused to pay the same. On compliance thereof, the proceedings, if already instituted, would be closed or no further proceedings shall be initiated. It is a matter of violation or willingness on the part of the accused either to accept compounding of the offence or to face the prosecution in the appropriate Court; *P. Ratnakar Rao* v. *Government of Andhra Pradesh*, AIR 1996 SC 2523: 1996 AIR SCW 3133: JT 1996 (6) SC 624: 1996 (5) SCC 359: 1998 (5) Supreme 225.

201. Penalty for causing obstruction to free flow of traffic.—(1) Whoever keeps a disabled vehicle on any public place, in such a manner, so as to cause

1. Subs. by Act 54 of 1994, sec. 58, for "section 189" (w.e.f. 14-11-1994).

impediment to the free flow of traffic, shall be liable for penalty up to fifty rupees per hour, so long as it remains in that position:

Provided that the vehicle involved in accidents shall be liable for penalty only from the time of completion of inspection formalities under the law:

[1][Provided further that where the vehicle is removed by a Government agency, towing charges shall be recovered from the vehicle owner or person in-charge of such vehicle.]

[2][(2) Penalties or towing charges under this section shall be recovered by such officer or authority as the State Government may, by notification in the Official Gazette, authorise.]

202. Power to arrest without warrant.—(1) A police officer in uniform may arrest without warrant any person who in his presence commits an offence punishable under section 184 or section 185 or section 197:

Provided that any person so arrested in connection with an offence punishable under section 185 shall, within two hours of his arrest, be subjected to a medical examination referred to in sections 203 and 204 by a registered medical practitioner failing which he shall be released from custody.

[3][(2) A police officer in uniform may arrest without warrant any person, who has committed an offence under this Act, if such person refuses to give his name and address.]

(3) A police officer arresting without warrant the driver of a motor vehicle shall if the circumstances so require take or cause to be taken any steps he may consider proper for the temporary disposal of the vehicle.

203. Breath tests.—[4][(1) A police officer in uniform or an officer of the Motor Vehicles Department, as may be authorised in this behalf by that Department, may require any person driving or attempting to drive a motor vehicle in a public place to provide one or more specimens of breath for breath test there or nearby, if such police officer or officer has any reasonable cause to suspect him of having committed an offence under section 185:

Provided that requirement for breath test shall be made (unless it is made) as soon as reasonably practicable after the commission of such offence.]

(2) If a motor vehicle is involved in an accident in a public place and a police officer in uniform has any reasonable cause to suspect that the person who was driving the motor vehicle at the time of the accident had alcohol in his blood or that he was driving under the influence of a drug referred to in section 185 he may require the person so driving the motor vehicle, to provide a specimen of his breath for a breath test—

(a) in the case of a person who is at a hospital as an indoor patient, at the hospital,

(b) in the case of any other person, either at or near the place where the requirement is made, or, if the police officer thinks fit, at a police station specified by the police officer:

---

1. Ins. by Act 54 of 1994, sec. 59 (w.e.f. 14-11-1994).
2. Subs. by Act 54 of 1994, sec. 59, for sub-section (2) (w.e.f. 14-11-1994)
3. Subs. by Act 54 of 1994, sec. 60, for sub-section (2) (w.e.f. 14-11-1994).
4. Subs. by Act 54 of 1994, sec. 61, for sub-section (1) (w.e.f. 14-11-1994).

Provided that a person shall not be required to provide such a specimen while at a hospital as an indoor patient if the registered medical practitioner in immediate charge of his çase is not first notified of the proposal to make the requirement or objects to the provision of a specimen on the ground that its provision or the requirement to provide it would be prejudicial to the proper care or treatment of the patient.

(3) If it appears to a police officer in uniform, in consequence of a breath test carried out by him on any person under sub-section (1) or sub-section (2) that the device by means of which the test has been carried out indicates the presence of alcohol in the person's blood, the police officer may arrest that person without warrant except while that person is at a hospital as an indoor patient.

(4) If a person, required by a police officer under sub-section (1) or sub-section (2) to provide a specimen of breath for a breath test, refuses or fails to do so and the police officer has reasonable cause to suspect him of having alcohol in his blood, the police officer may arrest him without warrant except while he is at a hospital as an indoor patient.

(5) A person arrested under this section shall while at a police station, be given an opportunity to provide a specimen of breath for a breath test there.

(6) The results of a breath test made in pursuance of the provisions of this section shall be admissible in evidence.

Explanation.—For the purposes of this section "breath test", means a test for the purpose of obtaining an indication of the presence of alcohol in a person's blood carried out on one or more specimens of breath provided by that person, by means of a device of a type approved by the Central Government by notification in the Official Gazette, for the purpose of such a test.

COMMENTS

Breath Analyser Test not Available to Driver who Fled from Scene – The Breath Analyzer Test has a different purpose and object. The said test is required to be carried out only when the person is driving or attempting to drive the vehicle. The expressions "while driving" and "attempting to drive" in that above sections have a meaning *"in praesenti"*. In such situations, the presence of alcohol in the blood has to be determined instantly so that the offender may be prosecuted for drunken driving. A Breath Analyzer Test is applied in such situations so that the alcohol content in the blood can be detected. The breath analyzer test could not be applied when the accused had escaped from the scene of the accident. Plea that when procedure has been laid to detect intoxication no finding that driver was drunk could be reached without subjecting driver to such test is not available to driver who had fled from the scene; *State Tr. P.S. Lodhi Colony, New Delhi* v. *Sanjeev Nanda,* AIR 2012 SC 3104: 2012 Cr LJ 4174: 2012 AIR SCW 4506.

204. Laboratory test.—(1) A person who has been arrested under section 203 may, while at a police station be required by a police officer to provide to such registered medical practitioner as may be produced by such police officer, a specimen of his blood for a laboratory test if,—

(a) it appears to the police officer that the device, by means of which breath test was taken in relation to such person, indicates the presence of alcohol in the blood of such person, or

(b) such person, when given the opportunity to submit to a breath test, has refused, omitted or failed to do so:

Provided that where the person required to provide such specimen is a female and the registered medical practitioner produced by such police officer is a male medical practitioner, the specimen shall be taken only in the presence of a female, whether a medical practitioner or not.

(2) A person while at a hospital as an indoor patient may be required by a police officer to provide at the hospital a specimen of his blood for a laboratory test—

(a) if it appears to the police officer that the device by means of which test is carried out in relation to the breath of such person indicates the presence of alcohol in the blood of such person, or

(b) if the person having been required, whether at the hospital or elsewhere, to provide a specimen of breath for a breath test, has refused, omitted or failed to do so and a police officer has reasonable cause to suspect him of having alcohol in his blood:

Provided that a person shall not be required to provide a specimen of his blood for a laboratory test under this sub-section if the registered medical practitioner in immediate charge of his case is not first notified of the proposal to make the requirement or objects to the provision of such specimen on the ground that its provision or the requirement to provide it would be prejudicial to the proper care or treatment of the patient.

(3) The results of a laboratory test made in pursuance of this section shall be admissible in evidence.

Explanation.—For the purposes of this section, "laboratory test" means the analysis of a specimen of blood made at a laboratory established, maintained or recognised by the Central Government or a State Government.

205. Presumption of unfitness to drive.—In any proceeding for an offence punishable under section 185 if it is proved that the accused when requested by a police officer at any time so to do, had refused, omitted or failed to consent to the taking of or providing a specimen of his breath for a breath test or a specimen of his blood for a laboratory test, his refusal, omission or failure may, unless reasonable cause therefor is shown, be presumed to be a circumstance supporting any evidence given on behalf of the prosecution, or rebutting any evidence given on behalf of the defence, with respect to his condition at that time.

COMMENTS

Breath Analyser Test not Available to Driver who Fled from Scene – The Breath Analyzer Test has a different purpose and object. The said test is required to be carried out only when the person is driving or attempting to drive the vehicle. The expressions "while driving" and "attempting to drive" in that above sections have a meaning *"in praesenti"*. In such situations, the presence of alcohol in the blood has to be determined instantly so that the offender may be prosecuted for drunken driving. A Breath Analyzer Test is applied in such situations so that the alcohol content in the blood can be detected. The breath analyzer test could not be applied when the accused had escaped from the scene of the accident. Plea that when procedure has been laid to detect intoxication no finding that driver was drunk could be reached without subjecting driver to such test is not available to driver who had fled from the scene; *State Tr. P.S. Lodhi Colony, New Delhi* v. *Sanjeev Nanda,* AIR 2012 SC 3104: 2012 Cr LJ 4174: 2012 AIR SCW 4506.

206. Power of police officer to impound document.—(1) Any police officer or other person authorised in this behalf by the State Government may, if he has reason to believe that any identification mark carried on a motor vehicle or any licence, permit, certificate of registration, certificate of insurance or other document produced to him by the driver or person in charge of a motor vehicle is a false document within the meaning of section 464 of the Indian Penal Code, 1860 (45 of 1860) seize the mark or document and call upon the driver or owner of the vehicle to account for his possession of or the presence in the vehicle of such mark or document.

(2) Any police officer or other person authorised in this behalf by the State Government may, if he has reason to believe that the driver of a motor vehicle who is charged with any offence under this Act may abscond or otherwise avoid the service of a summons, seize any licence held by such driver and forward it into the Court taking cognizance of the offence and the said Court shall on the first appearance of such driver before it, return the licence to him in exchange for the temporary acknowledgment given under sub-section (3).

(3) A police officer or other person seizing a licence under sub-section (2) shall give to the person surrendering the licence a temporary acknowledgment therefor and such acknowledgment shall authorise the holder to drive until the licence has been returned to him or until such date as may be specified by the police officer or other person in the acknowledgment whichever is earlier:

Provided that if any Magistrate, police officer or other person authorised by the State Government in this behalf is, on an application made to him, satisfied that the licence cannot be, or has not been, returned to the holder thereof before the date specified in the acknowledgment for any reason for which the holder is not responsible, the Magistrate, police officer or other person, as the case may be, may extend the period of authorization to drive to such date as may be specified in the acknowledgment.

COMMENTS

Power to Demand Production of Documents – The power to demand productions of and to examine the documents cannot be divorced from the purpose behind the conferment of the said power. The purpose is to enable the Police Officers concerned to check such vehicles for the commission of any violation of the provisions of the Act and to take such follow up action as may be necessary. Therefore the power to demand the production of the documents including the permit and the power to impound the same in certain situations preferred to in section 206 as also the power to seize the vehicle in the circumstances mentioned in section 207 are all exercisable by a Police Officer. The very fact that there is an amendment to section 130, sub-section (2) and (3) of the Act, by which the power to ask the conductor to produce his licence has been taken away and conferred upon an officer of the Motor Vehicles Department does not in the least affect the powers of the Police Officers under the aforesaid three provisions. The exercise of power under sections 158, 206 and 207 was in no way dependent upon the availability of the power under section 130(2) so as to make the former redundant in the absence of the later. The Amendment of section 130 sub-section (2) has a very limited effect and does not render the other provisions of the Act particularly sections 158, 206 and 207 nugatory. The power exercisable under the later provisions continues to be available to he Police Officers and could have been therefore legitimately exercised by them; *M.S. Palaksha* v. *Union of India,* AIR 1996 Kant 209: 1996 (2) Kant LJ 256: ILR 1996 Kant 1582.

207. Power to detain vehicles used without certificate of registration permit, etc.—(1) Any police officer or other person authorised in this behalf by the State Government may, if he has reason to believe that a motor vehicle has been or is being used in contravention of the provisions of section 3 or section 4 or section 39 or without the permit required by sub-section (1) of section 66 or in contravention or any condition of such permit relating to the route on which or the area in which or the purpose for which the vehicle may be used, seize and detain the vehicle, in the prescribed manner and for this purpose take or cause to be taken any steps he may consider proper for the temporary safe custody of the vehicle:

Provided that where any such officer or person has reason to believe that a motor vehicle has been or is being used in contravention of section 3 or section 4 or without the permit required by sub-section (1) of section 66 he may, instead of seizing the vehicle, seize the certificate of registration of the vehicle and shall issue an acknowledgment in respect thereof.

(2) Where a motor vehicle has been seized and detained under sub-section (1), the owner or person incharge of the motor vehicle may apply to the transport authority or any officer authorised in this behalf by the State Government together with the relevant documents for the release of the vehicle and such authority or officer may, after verification of such documents, by order release the vehicle subject to such conditions as the authority or officer may deem fit to impose.

STATE AMENDMENT

Rajasthan.—In section 207, in the proviso to sub-section (1) the expression "or without the permit required by sub-section (1) of section 66" as occurring between the expression "section 3 or section 4" and the expression "he may", shall be deleted.

[Rajasthan Act 2 of 1993, sec. 3 (w.e.f. 30-1-1993)].

SYNOPSIS

1. Power of Transport Authority is very Wide
2. Detention and Seizure of Vehicle
3. Detention of Vehicle
4. Power to Demand Production of Documents
5. Power of Seizure to be Exercised with Extraordinary Care and Caution
6. Powers to Detain and Seize Vehicle

COMMENTS

1. Power of Transport Authority is very Wide – The transport authorities of the State have a power to check a vehicle so as to ascertain whether payment of tax is being evaded. They have been conferred with the power to detain a vehicle. They can release the vehicle only when tax as demanded is paid. Even the power of the Court to release the vehicle has been taken away unless tax is paid and the Court can satisfy itself as to whether a tax is paid or not only on the receipt of the certificate issued by the transport authorities of the State. The power of the transport authorities, therefore, is very wide. Only because a wide power has been conferred the same by itself would not lead to a presumption that the same is capable of misuse or on that count alone the provisions of article 14 of the Constitution would be attracted. When a statute confers a wide power upon a statutory authority, a closer scrutiny would be required; *Hardeo Motor Transport* v. *State of Madhya Pradesh,* AIR 2007 SC 839: 2007 AIR SCW 556: 2006 (8) SCC 613: 2006 (11) SCALE 15.

2. Detention and Seizure of Vehicle – The police officer would be authorised to detain a vehicle, if he has reason to believe that the vehicle has been or is being used in contravention of any condition of such permit relating to the route on which or the area in which or the purpose for which the vehicle may be used. The condition of permit relating to the route on which or the area in which or the purpose for which the vehicle could be used if contravened, would only authorise the police officer to detain the vehicle and not each and every condition of permit on being violated or contravened, the police officer would be entitled to detain the vehicle. The expression "purpose for which the vehicle may be used" could not be construed to mean that when the vehicle is found to be carrying passengers more than the number prescribed in the permit, the purpose of user is otherwise. The purpose would only refer to a contingency. When a vehicle having a permit of stage carriage is used as a contract carriage or vice versa or where a vehicle having a permit for stage carriage or contract carriage is used as a goods vehicle and vice versa. But carrying passengers more than the number specified in the permit will not be a violation of the purpose for which the permit is granted. If the legislature really wanted to confer power of detention on the police officer for violation of any condition of the permit, then there would not have been the necessity of adding the expression "relating to the route on which or the area in which or the purpose for which the vehicle may be used. The power of seizure has been conferred upon the appropriate authority, which power is in fact a sovereign power of the State and has been delegated to the police officer in discharge of their duties of law enforcement and in the enforcement of an orderly society. The power, therefore, is required to be exercised with care and caution and the power has to be exercised only when the pre-condition for exercise of power is fully satisfied; *State of Maharashtra* v. *Nanded-Parbhani Z.I.B.M.V. Operator Sangh,* AIR 2000 SC 725: 2000 AIR SCW 261: JT 2000 (1) SC 290: 2000 (2) SCC 69: 2000 (1) SCALE 211: 2000 (1) Supreme 204.

3. Detention of Vehicle – If the holder of the vehicle obtains a contract carriage, the owner may carry a passenger or passengers for hire or reward on contract, whether expressed or implied, for the use of such vehicle as a whole for the carriage of passengers mentioned therein and entered into by a person with a holder of a permit in relation to such vehicle or any person authorised by him in this behalf on a fixed or an agreed rate or sum. In other words, the very permit for which the contract for carriage of the passengers granted should contain the names of the passengers to carry from one destination to another destination without picking up or setting down en route for hire or reward but when the holder of a permit is another and permits them to carry the passengers and make the contract *de hors* those mentioned in the list of passengers enclosed to the permit as contract carriage and take the passengers from one destination to another, even without picking up or setting down en route, the necessary consequence would be that the vehicle has been or is being used as a stage carriage but not a contract carriage. Detention of vehicle for contravention of permit is Proper; *Nirmala Jagdishchandra Kabra* v. *Transport Commissioner,* AIR 1997 SC 1405: 1997 AIR SCW 1530: JT 1997 (2) SC 743: 1997 (9) SCC 227: 1997 (2) SCALE 280: 1997 (2) Supreme 483.

4. Power to Demand Production of Documents – The power to demand productions of and to examine the documents cannot be divorced from the purpose behind the conferment of the said power. The purpose is to enable the Police Officers concerned to check such vehicles for the commission of any violation of the provisions of the Act and to take such follow up action as may be necessary. Therefore the power to demand the production of the documents including the permit and the power to impound the same in certain situations preferred to in section 206 as also the power to seize the vehicle in the circumstances mentioned in section 207 are all exercisable by a Police Officer. The very fact that there is an amendment to section 130, sub-section (2) and (3) of the Act, by which the power to ask the conductor to produce his licence has been taken away and conferred upon an officer of the Motor Vehicles Department does not in the least affect the powers of the Police Officers under the aforesaid three provisions. The exercise of power under sections 158, 206 and 207 was in no way dependent upon the availability of the power under section 130(2) so as to make the former redundant in the absence of the later. The Amendment of section 130 sub-section (2) has a very limited effect and does not render the other provisions of the Act particularly sections 158, 206 and 207 nugatory. The power exercisable under the later provisions continues to be available to he Police

Officers and could have been therefore legitimately exercised by them; *M.S. Palaksha* v. *Union of India,* AIR 1996 Kant 209: 1996 (2) Kant LJ 256: ILR 1996 Kant 1582.

5. Power of Seizure to be Exercised with Extraordinary Care and Caution – The power of seizure *is* nothing else than a sovereign power which is delegated to the police in the discharge of their duties of law enforcement and in the enforcement of an orderly society. The power of seizure, the power of arrest, are sovereign powers which have to be exercised with extraordinary care and caution: *K. Laxmi* v. *Sub-Inspector of Police (Traffic-West),* AIR 1989 Kant 311: (1988) 2 Kant LJ 292: (1988) 27 Reports 400.

6. Powers to Detain and Seize Vehicle – Though the State of West Bengal and the State of Bihar had entered into a reciprocal agreement in 1988 for issue of a certain number of permits, the State Transport Authority, Bihar exceeded the quota of permits for the inter-State route and there was no concurrence in general or for a particular occasion for issue of the temporary permit in favour of the respondent for the route from Motihari in Bihar to Siliguri in West Bengal. There was no countersignature of the State Transport Authority, West Bengal, on the temporary permit issued by the State Transport Authority (Bihar), the respondent did not have a valid permit for the part of the route inside the State of West Bengal. The plying of the vehicle of the respondent in the Siliguri region within the State of West Bengal was thus in contravention of section 66(1) of the Motor Vehicles Act which provides that no owner of a vehicle shall use or permit use of the vehicle as a transport vehicle save in accordance with the conditions of a permit granted or counter-signed by the Regional or State Transport Authority. The appellants, therefore, were well within their powers to detain and seize the vehicle of the respondent under section 207 of the Motor Vehicles Act for contravention of section 66 of the said Act; *State of West Bengal* v. *Mani Bhushan Kumar,* AIR 2012 SC 184: 2011 AIR SCW 6366: (2011) 10 SCC 147.

208. Summary disposal of cases.—(1) The Court taking cognizance of any offence (other than an offence which the Central Government may by rules specify in this behalf) under this Act,—

(i) may, if the offence is an offence punishable with imprisonment under this Act; and

(ii) shall, in any other case,

state upon the summons to be served on the accused person that he—

(a) may appear by pleader or in person; or

(b) may, by a specified date prior to the hearing of the charge, plead guilty to the charge and remit to the Court, by money order, such sum (not exceeding the maximum fine that may be imposed for the offence) as the Court may specify, and the plea of guilt indicated in the money order coupon itself:

Provided that the Court shall, in the case of any of the offences referred to in sub-section (2), state upon the summons that the accused person, if he pleads guilty, shall so plead in the manner specified in clause (b) and shall forward his driving licence to the Court with his letter containing such plea.

(2) Where the offence dealt with in accordance with sub-section (1) is an offence specified by the Central Government by rules for the purposes of this sub-section, the Court shall, if the accused person pleads guilty to the charge and forwards his driving licence to the Court with the letter containing his plea, make an endorsement of such conviction on his driving licence.

(3) Where an accused person pleads guilty and remits the sum specified and has complied with the provisions of sub-section (1), or as the case may

be, sub-sections (1) and (2), no further proceedings in respect of the offence shall be taken against him nor shall he be liable, notwithstanding anything to the contrary contained in this Act, to be disqualified for holding or obtaining a licence by reason of his having pleaded guilty.

209. Restriction on conviction.—No person prosecuted for an offence punishable under section 183 or section 184 shall be convicted unless—

(a) he was warned at the time the offence was committed that the question of prosecuting him would be taken into consideration, or

(b) within fourteen days from the commission of the offence, a notice specifying the nature of the offence and the time and place where it is alleged to have been committed was served on or sent by registered post to him or the person registered as the owner of the vehicle at the time of the commission of the offence, or

(c) within twenty-eight days of the commission of the offence, a summons for the offence was served on him:

Provided that nothing, in this section shall apply where the Court is satisfied that—

(a) the failure to serve the notice or summons referred to in this sub-section was due to the fact that neither the name and address of the accused nor the name and address of the registered owner of the vehicle could with reasonable diligence have been ascertained in time, or

(b) such failure was brought about by the conduct of the accused.

210. Courts to send intimation about conviction.—Every Court by which any person holding a driving licence is convicted of an offence under this Act or of an offence in the commission of which a motor vehicle was used, shall send intimation to—

(a) the licensing authority which issued the driving licence, and

(b) the licensing authority by whom the licence was last renewed,

and every such intimation shall state the name and address of the holder of the licence, the licence number, the date of issue and renewal of the same, the nature of the offence, the punishment awarded for the same and such other particulars as may be prescribed.

CHAPTER XIV
MISCELLANEOUS

211. Power to levy fee.—Any rule which the Central Government or the State Government is empowered to make under this Act may, notwithstanding the absence of any express provision to that effect, provide for the levy of such fees in respect of applications, amendment of documents, issue of certificates, licences, permits, tests, endorsements, badges, plates, countersignatures, authorisation, supply of statistics or copies of documents or orders and for any other purpose or matter involving the rendering of any service by the officers or authorities under this Act or any rule made thereunder as may be considered necessary:

Provided that the Government may, if it considers necessary so to do, in the public interest, by general or special order, exempt any class of persons from the payment of any such fee either in part or in full.

SYNOPSIS

1. Services of Weighbridges
2. Determination of Laden Weight and Unladen Weight
3. Implementation of Order which is not Implemented
4. Act when Repealed be Considered never Existed
5. Repealed Act Continues to be Operative Till Expiry of its Period
6. Application for Renewal is Saved
7. Claim for Condonation of Delay be Governed by Law in Force at Time of Delay
8. Old Permit will not Operative and Effective once Period Expired

COMMENTS

1. Services of Weighbridges – Services of the weighbridges are required to be obtained by the drivers/owners of the trucks for fulfilment of their statutory obligations. They cannot obtain such services free of any charges. When private parties are given the right to set up such weighbridges, indisputably they would be entitled to reasonable profit; *J.H. Truck Owners Assocn.* v. *S.A. Coal Dealer and Truck Owner Assocn.,* AIR 2009 SC 3041: 2009 AIR SCW 4881: 2009 (8) SCC 492: 2009 (9) SCALE 469.

2. Determination of Laden Weight and Unladen Weight – The provisions of the Act mandate that the unladen weight and laden weight must be determined. Indisputably, weighing devices had to be provided for the said purpose. It is true that for the said purpose Rules may have to be framed. It is, however, a well settled principle of law that even in a case where the statute provides for certain things to be done, subject to Rules, any action taken without framing the Rules would not render any action invalid. If a statute is workable even without framing of the Rules, the same has to be given effect to. The law itself except in certain situations does not envisage vacuum. Non-compliance of the provisions relating to "laden weight" and "unladen weight" being penal in nature must be held to be imperative in character; *J.H. Truck Owners Assocn.* v. *S.A. Coal Dealer and Truck Owner Assocn.,* AIR 2009 SC 3041: 2009 AIR SCW 4881: 2009 (8) SCC 492: 2009 (9) SCALE 469.

3. Implementation of Order which is not Implemented – The action which had been taken under the earlier enactment which has been validated even after the commencement of the new Act, would continue to be governed by the provisions of the new Act. The order of variation though made while the repealed enactment was in force has to be deemed to have been made under the corresponding provisions of the 1988 Act; *Anna Transport Corporation Ltd.* v. *N. Ramasamy,* AIR 1996 Mad 82: 1995 (2) Mad LW 584.

All that section 217(2)(b) of the Act says that the action which had been taken under the earlier enactment which has been validated even after commencement of the 1988 Act, used continue to be governed by the provisions of the repealed enactment, *i.e.,* Act of 1939. An order which had not been implemented and is to be implemented for the first time after the 1988 Act came into force, is not governed by section 217(2)(b); *Anna Transport Corporation Limited* v. *N. Ramaswamy,* AIR 1996 Mad 82: 1995 (2) Mad LW 584.

4. Act when Repealed be Considered never Existed – Whenever an Act is repealed it must be considered, except as to transactions past and closed as if it had never existed. The effect thereof is to obliterate the Act completely from the record of the Parliament as if it had never been passed by it, it never existed except for the purpose of those actions which were commenced, prosecuted and concluded while it was existing law. Legal fiction is one which is nor actually a reality and which the law recognises and the Court accepts as a reality, Therefore, in case of legal fiction the Court believes something to exist which in reality does not exist. It is nothing but a presumption of the existence of the state of affairs which in actuality is non-existent. The effect of such a legal fiction is that a position which otherwise would not obtain is deemed to obtain under the circumstances. Therefore, when section 217(1) of the New Act repealed 1939 Act w.e.f. July 1, 1989, the law in 1939 Act in effect came to be non-existent except as regards the transactions, past and closed or saved; *Gajraj Singh* v. *State Transport Appellate Tribunal*, AIR 1997 SC 412: 1996 All LJ 1767.

5. Repealed Act Continues to be Operative Till Expiry of its Period – The permit issued under the repealed Act will continue to be operative for the period for which it was issued as if new Act had not been passed and the repealed Act continues to be in operation. With expiry of the period of grant given in the permit under the repealed Act, by necessary implication the operator has to make fresh application in the prescribed manner to the concerned Regional Transport Authority or State Transport Authority and seek a grant under section 72. The grant of renewal is no more than a fresh permit to operate the transport service for a fresh period mentioned in the renewed permit. Therefore, the operation of the permit issued under section 58 of the repealed Act I.V of 1939 is a terminus with the expiry of the period of the grant and the operation of the Act IV of 1939 ceases to have effect from that date. The right to renewal under the Act 1939 stands repealed with the expiry of the period of grant of the permit made under the repealed Act. Where the application was not made for fresh grant under the Act, the rejection of the renewal application under Act 1939 or under the Act is perfectly legal; *Secy. Q.D.M. Transport Workers' Co-op Socy. Ltd.* v. *R.T.A.*, AIR 1995 SC 82: JT 1994 (5) SC 426: 1994 AIR SCW 4095.

Notwithstanding the repeal of the Motor Vehicles Act, 1939 the permit issued under the repealed Act continues to be operative for the period for which it was issued as if this Act had not been passed and the repealed Act continues to be in operation with the expiry of the period of grant given in the permit under the repealed Act, by necessary implication the operator has to make fresh application in the prescribed manner to the concerned Regional Transport Authority or State Transport Authority and seek a grant under section 72; *Secretary, Quilon District Motor Transport Workers' Co-operative Society Ltd.* v. *Regional Transport Authority*, AIR 1995 SC 82: JT 1994 (5) SC 426.

6. Application for Renewal is Saved – When before repeal of the old Act the holder had filed an application for renewal and his application had been notified, he can be said to have acquired the right to get his application for renewal processed and considered in accordance with 1939 Act. This right is saved by section 217(4) of the Act as there is no express provision in the new Act debarring renewal of permits applied for, under old Act. The new Act is a legislation on the same subject. Section 81 of the new Act specifically provides for renewal. The scheme of renewal having been continued even under new Act mere absence of preference clause in section 81 of the new Act could not be construed as destroying the claim for renewal set in motion under the old Act; *Gurcharan Singh Baldev Singh* v. *Yashwant Singh*, AIR 1992 SC 180: 1991 AIR SCW 2889: JT 1991 (6) SC 256: 1992 (1) SCC 428.

7. Claim for Condonation of Delay be Governed by Law in Force at Time of Delay – Where the accident took place when the old Act was in force, however, the claim petition was filed after the repeal of the old Act and the new Act came into force, the case would be covered by the new Act and delay for a longer period than six months could not be condoned. There is a vital difference between an application claiming compensation and a prayer to condone the delay in filing such an application. Liberty to apply for a right is not in itself an accrued right or privilege. Moreover, claimant's right to claim compensation was not affected at all by the substitution of one Act with another. Since the period of limitation remained the same there was no question of the claimant being taken by surprise. Further, the right or privilege to claim benefit of a provision for condonation of delay can be governed only by the law in force at the time of delay; *Vinod Gurudas Raikar* v. *National Insurance Co. Ltd.*, AIR 1991 SC 2156: 1991 AIR SCW 2503: JT 1991 (3) SC 660: 1991 (4) SCC 333.

8. Old Permit will not Operative and Effective once Period Expired – Clause (b) of sub-section (2) of section 217 provides that permit granted under the Motor Vehicles Act, 1939 (4 of 1939) shall continue to have effect even after the commencement of the

Act for a period for which it has been granted under the Act of 1939. It means that the permit will expire and its life will come to an end on the expiry of the period provided in the permit, it will live even after the repeal of the 1939 Act for the unexpired period of the permit, even after the enforcement of the Act. But once the period had expired its life span came to an end, clause (b) does not provide that old permit will continue to be operative and effective; *Fatima Begum* v. *Karnataka State Transport Authority*, AIR 1998 Kant 119: 1998 (1) ACC 506: 1997 (4) Kant LJ 57.

212. Publication, commencement and laying of rules and notifications.—(1) The power to make rules under this Act is subject to the condition of the rules being made after previous publication.

(2) All rules made under this Act shall be published in the Official Gazette, and shall unless some later date is appointed, come into force on the date of such publication.

(3) Every rule made by any State Government shall be laid, as soon as may be after it is made before the State Legislature.

(4) Every rule made by the Central Government under this Act, every scheme made by the Central Government under sub-section (1) of section 75 and sub-section (1) of section 163 and every notification issued by the Central Government under sub-section (4) of section 41, sub-section (1) of section 58, sub-section (1) of section 59, the proviso to sub-section (1) of section 112, [1][sub-section (4) of section 163A] and sub-section (4) of section 213 shall be laid, as soon as may be after it is made, before each House of Parliament while it is in session for a total period of thirty days which may be comprised in one session or in two or more successive sessions, and if, before the expiry of the session immediately following the session or the successive sessions aforesaid, both Houses agree in making any modification in the rule, scheme or notification or both Houses agree that the rule or scheme should not be made or the notification should not be issued, the rule, scheme or notification shall thereafter have effect only in such modified form or be of no effect, as the case may be; so, however, that any such modification or annulment shall be without prejudice to the validity of anything previously done under that rule, scheme or notification.

COMMENTS

State Rules of 1992 in Terms of Section 212(3) – Are in conformity with scheme envisaged in Central Act; *Shekhar Bhushan Nag* v. *State of Jharkhand*, AIR 2015 Jhar 26.

213. Appointment of motor vehicles officers.—(1) The State Government may, for the purpose of carrying into effect the provisions of the Act, establish a Motor Vehicles Department and appoint as officers thereof such persons as it thinks fit.

(2) Every such officer shall be deemed to be a public servant within the meaning of the Indian Penal Code, 1860 (45 of 1860).

(3) The State Government may make rules to regulate the discharge by officers of the Motor Vehicles Department of their functions and in particular and without prejudice to the generality of the foregoing power to prescribe the uniform to be worn by them, the authorities to which they shall be subordinate, the duties to be preformed by them, the powers (including the powers exercisable

1. Ins. by Act 54 of 1994, sec. 62 (w.e.f. 14-11-1994).

by police officers under this Act) to be exercised by them, and the conditions governing the exercise of such powers.

(4) The Central Government may, having regard to the objects of the Act, by notification in the Official Gazette prescribe the minimum qualifications which the said officers or any class thereof shall possess for being appointed as such.

(5) In addition to the powers that may be conferred on any officer of the Motor Vehicles Department under sub-section (3), such officer as may be empowered by the State Government in this behalf shall also have the power to,—

(a) make such examination and inquiry as he thinks fit in order to ascertain whether the provisions of this Act and the rules made thereunder are being observed;

(b) with such assistance, if any, as he thinks fit, enter, inspect and search any premises which is in the occupation of a person who, he has reason to believe, has committed an offence under this Act or in which a motor vehicle in respect of which such offence has been committed is kept:

Provided that,—

(i) any such search without a warrant shall be made only by an officer of the rank of a gazetted officer;

(ii) where the offence is punishable with fine only the search shall not be made after sunset and before sunrise;

(iii) where the search is made without a warrant, the gazetted officer concerned shall record in writing the grounds for not obtaining a warrant and report to his immediate superior that such search has been made;

(c) examine any person and require the production of any register or other document maintained in pursuance of this Act, and take on the spot or otherwise statements of any person which he may consider necessary for carrying out the purposes of this Act;

(d) seize or take copies of any registers or documents or portions thereof as he may consider relevant in respect of an offence under this Act which he has reason to believe has been committed;

(e) launch prosecutions in respect of any offence under this Act and to take a bond for ensuring the attendance of the offender before any Court;

(f) exercise such other powers as may be prescribed;

Provided that no person shall be compelled under this sub-section to answer any question or make any statement tending to incriminate himself.

(6) The provisions of the Code of Criminal Procedure, 1973 (2 of 1974) shall, so far as may be apply to any search or seizure under this section as they apply to any search or seizure under the authority of any warrant issued under section 94 of the Code.

214. Effect of appeal and revision on orders passed by original authority.— (1) When an appeal has been preferred or an application for revision has been made against any order passed by an original authority under this Act, the appeal or the application for revision shall not operate as a stay of the order passed by the original authority and such order shall remain in force pending the disposal of the appeal or the application for revision, as the case may be, unless the prescribed appellate authority or revisional authority otherwise directs.

(2) Notwithstanding anything contained in sub-section (1), if an application made by a person for the renewal of permit has been rejected by the original authority and such person has preferred an appeal or made an application for revision under this Act against such rejection, the appellate authority or, as the case may be, the revisional authority may by order direct that the permit shall, notwithstanding the expiration of the term specified therein, continue to be valid until the appeal or application for revision is disposed of.

(3) No order made by a competent authority under this Act shall be reversed or altered on appeal or revision on account of any error, omission or irregularity in the proceedings, unless it appears to the prescribed appellate authority or revisional authority, as the case may be, that such error, omission or irregularity has, in fact, occasioned a failure of justice.

215. Road Safety Councils and Committees.—(1) The Central Government may, by notification in the Official Gazette, constitute for the country a National Road Safety Council consisting of a Chairman and such other members as that Government considers necessary and on such terms and conditions as that Government may determine.

(2) A State Government may, by notification in the Official Gazette, constitute for the State a State Road Safety Council consisting of a Chairman and such other members as that Government considers necessary and on such terms and conditions as that Government may determine.

(3) A State Government may, by notification in the Official Gazette, constitute District Road Safety Committee for each district in the State consisting of a Chairman and such other members as that Government considers necessary and on such terms and conditions as that Government may determine.

(4) The Councils and Committees referred to in this section shall discharge such functions relating to the road safety programmes as the Central Government or the State Government, as the case may be, may, having regard to the objects of the Act, specify.

216. Power to remove difficulties.—(1) If any difficulty arises in, giving effect to the provisions of this Act, the Central Government may, by order published in the Official Gazette, make such provisions, not inconsistent with the provisions of this Act as appear to it to be necessary or expedient for removing the difficulty:

Provided that no such order shall be made after the expiry of a period of three years from the date of commencement of this Act.

(2) Every order made under this section shall, as soon as may be after it is made, be laid before each House of Parliament.

217. Repeal and savings.—(1) The Motor Vehicles Act, 1939 (4 of 1939) and any law corresponding to that Act in force in any State immediately before the commencement of this Act in that State (hereafter in this section referred to as the repealed enactments) are hereby repealed.

(2) Notwithstanding the repeal by sub-section (1) of the repealed enactments,—

(a) any notification, rule, regulation, order or notice issued, or any appointment or declaration made, or exemption granted or any confiscation made, or any penalty or fine imposed, any forfeiture, cancellation or any other thing done or any other action taken under the repealed enactments, and in force immediately before such commencement shall, so far as it is not inconsistent with the provisions of the Act, be deemed to have been issued, made, granted, done or taken under the corresponding provision of this Act;

(b) any certificate of fitness or registration or licence or permit issued or granted under the repealed enactments shall continue to have effect after such commencement under the same conditions and for the same period as if this Act had not been passed;

(c) any document referring to any of the repealed enactments or the provisions thereof, shall be construed as referring to this Act or to the corresponding provisions of this Act;

(d) the assignment of distinguishing marks by the registering authority and the manner of display on motor vehicles in accordance with the provision of the repealed enactments shall, after the commencement of this Act, continue to remain in force until a notification under sub-section (6) of section 41 of this Act is issued;

(e) any scheme made under section 68C of the Motor Vehicles Act, 1939 (4 of 1939) or under the corresponding law, if any, in force in any State and pending immediately before the commencement of this Act shall be disposed of in accordance with the provisions of section 100 of this Act;

(f) the permits issued under sub-section (1A) of section 68F of the Motor Vehicles Act, 1939 (4 of 1939) or under the corresponding provision, if any, in force in any State immediately before the commencement of this Act shall continue to remain in force until the approved scheme under Chapter VI of this Act is published.

(3) Any penalty payable under any of the repealed enactments may be recovered in the manner provided by or under this Act, but without prejudice to any action already taken for the recovery of such penalty under the repealed enactments.

(4) The mention of particular matters in this section shall not be held to prejudice or affect the general application of section 6 of the General Clauses Act, 1897 (10 of 1897) with regard to the effect of repeals.

[1][**217A. Renewal of permits, driving licences and registration granted under the Motor Vehicles Act, 1939.**—Notwithstanding the repeal by sub-section (1) of section 217 of the enactments referred to in that sub-section, any certificate of fitness or registration or licence or permit issued or granted under the said enactments may be renewed under this Act.]

1. Ins. by Act 27 of 2000, sec. 5 (w.e.f. 11-8-2000).

[1][*THE FIRST SCHEDULE*

MANDATORY SIGNS OF THE FIRST SCHEDULE OF THE MOTOR VEHICLES ACT, 1988

PART A

No. M. 1. — Stop
Normal Size 90 c.m.
Small Size 60 c.m.

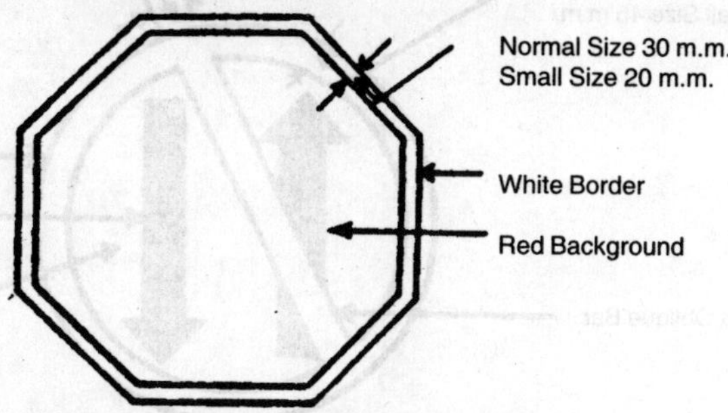

Note.—Till the road users are familiar with this sign a definition plate may be attached with the sign carrying the word 'Stop' in English and other languages as necessary.

No. M. 2 — Give Way
Normal Size 90 c.m.
Small Size 60 c.m.

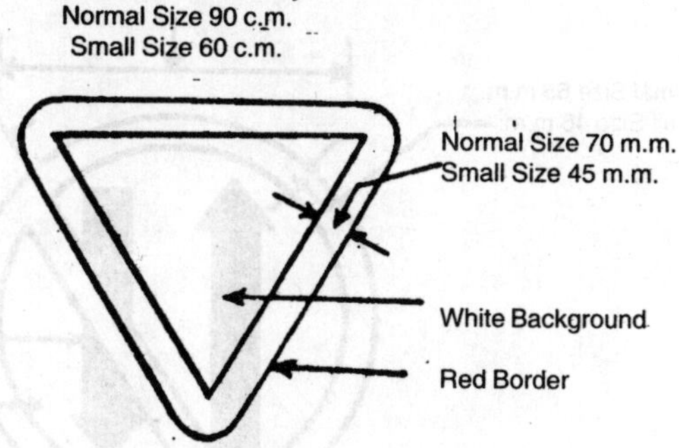

Note.—Till the road users are familiar with this sign, a definition plate may be used with the sign, carrying the message "give away" in English and other languages as necessary.

No. M 3 — Straight Prohibited or No Entry

Normal Size 60 c.m.
Small Size 40 c.m.

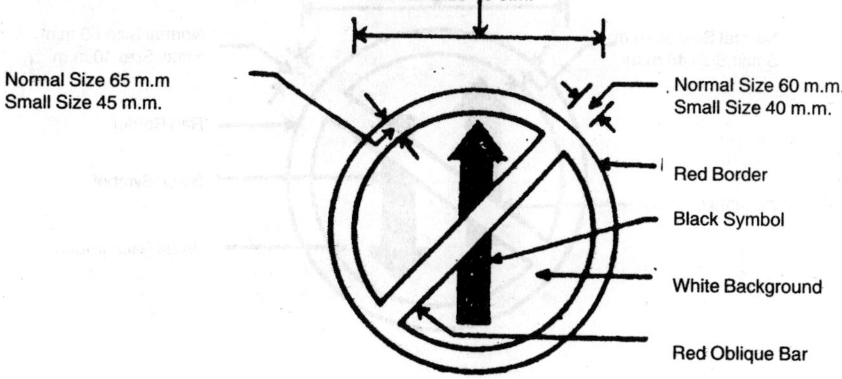

No. M 4A — One way sign—Vehicles Prohibited in one Direction

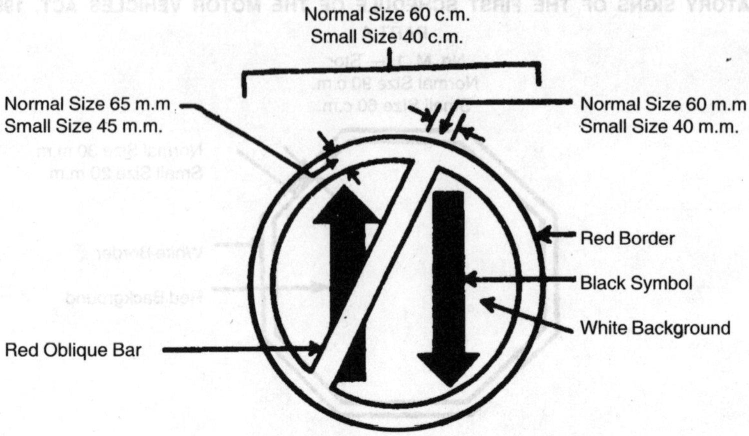

No. M 4B — One way sign—Vehicles Prohibited in one Direction

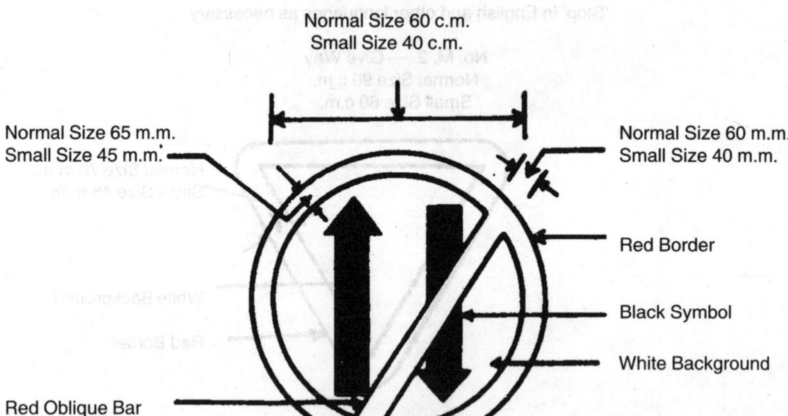

No. M 5 — Vehicles Prohibited in both Directions

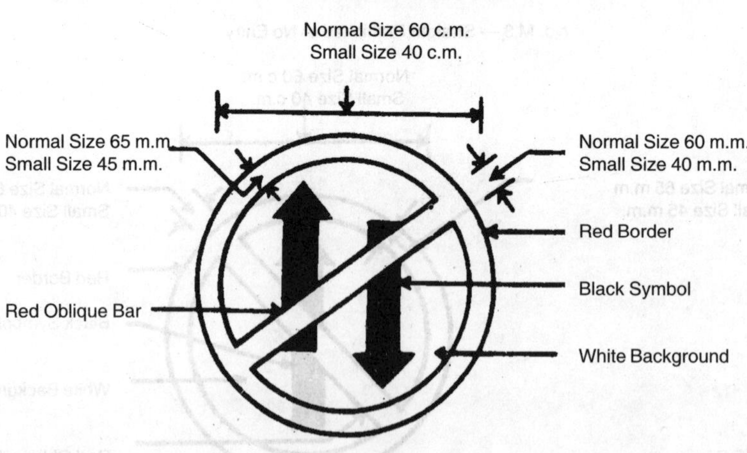

No. M 6 — All Motor Vehicles Prohibited

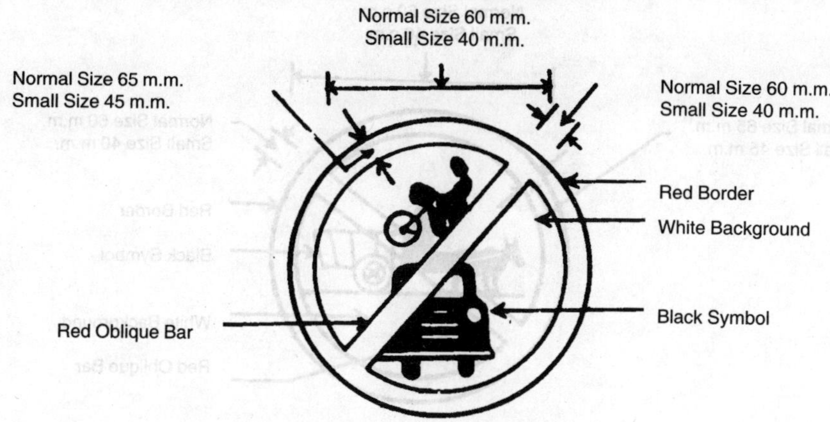

No. M 7 — Trucks Prohibited

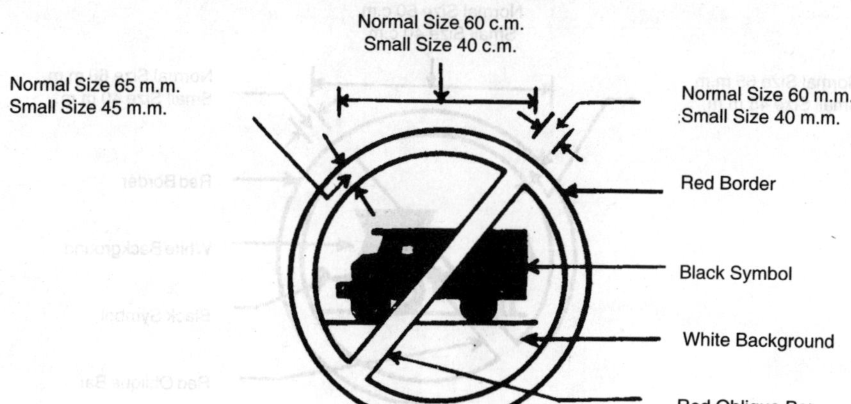

No. M 8 — Bullock Carts and Hand Carts Prohibited

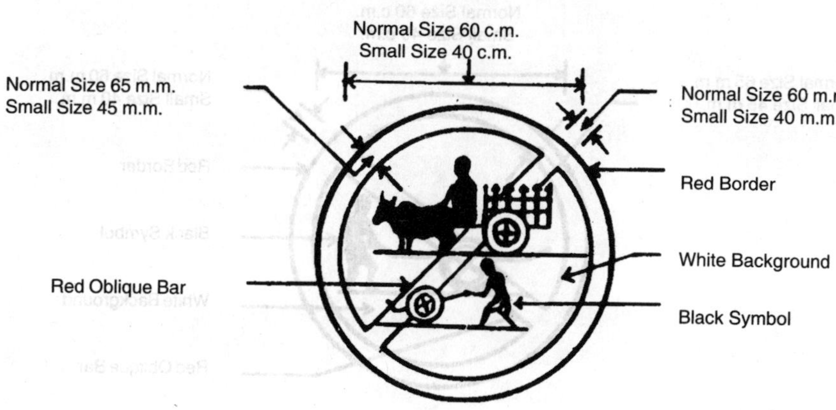

No. M 9 — Bullock Carts Prohibited

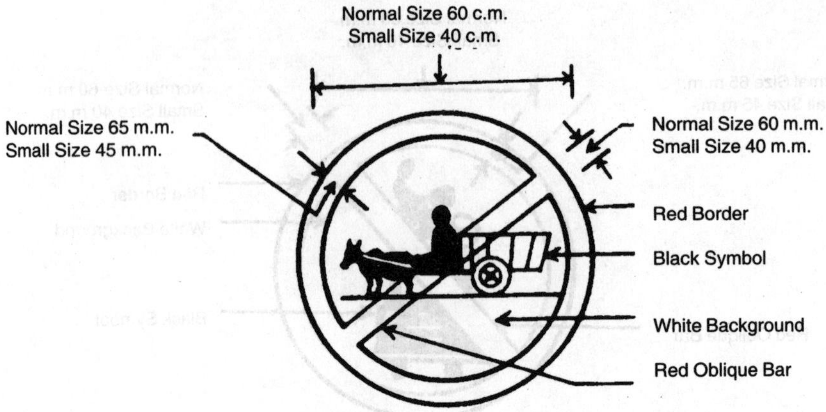

No. M 10 — Tongas Prohibited

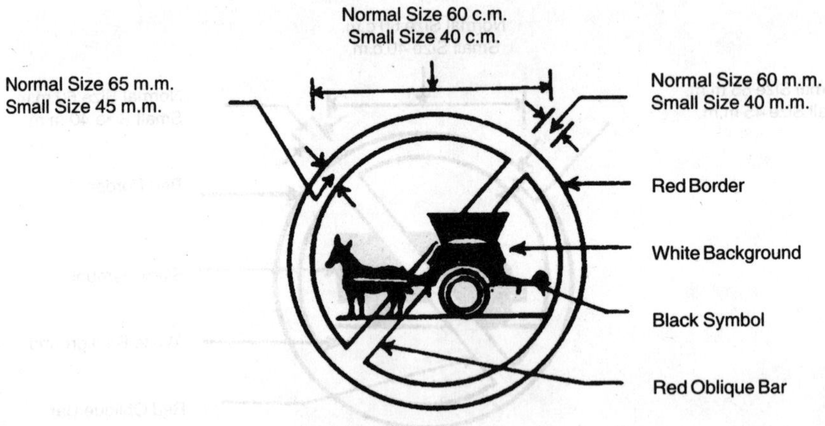

No. M 11 — Hand Carts Prohibited

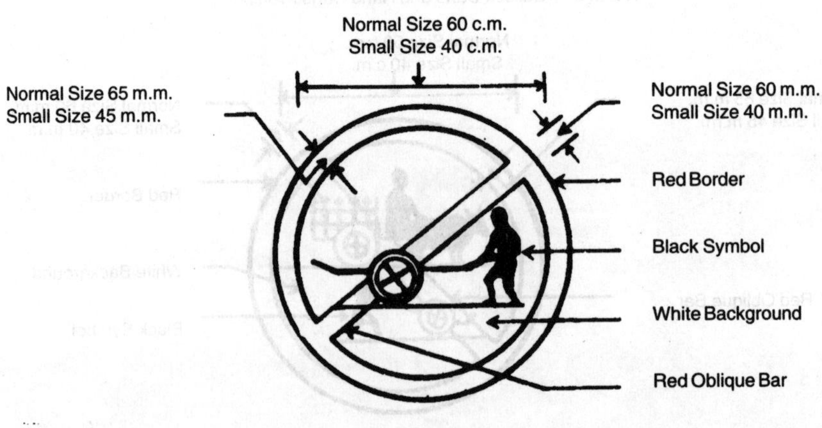

No. M 12 — Cycles Prohibited

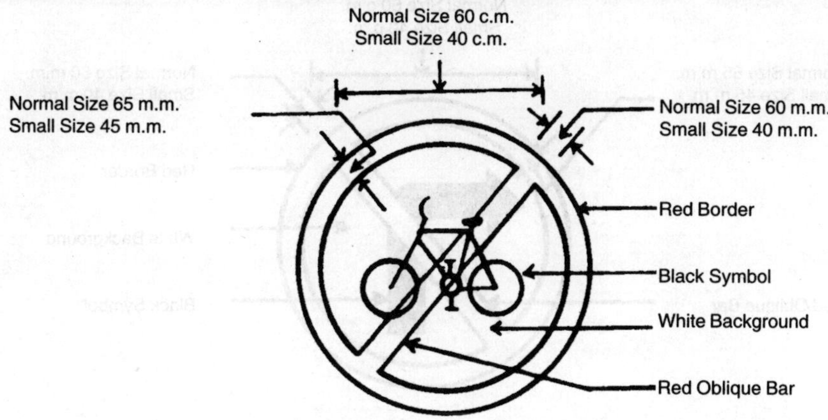

No. M 13 — Pedestrians Prohibited

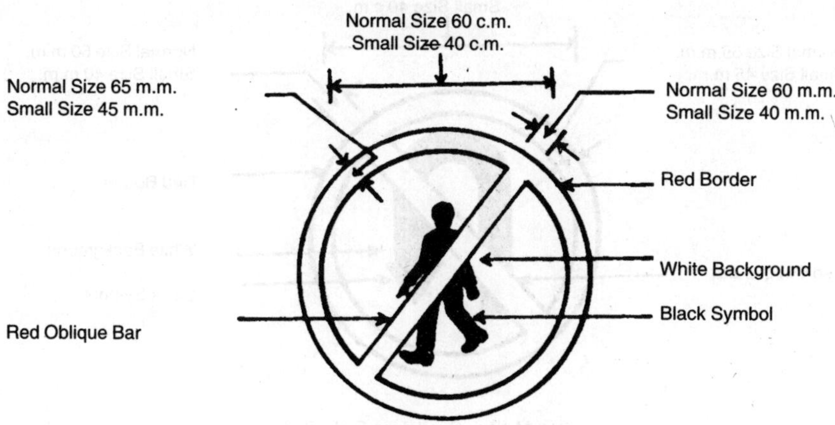

No. M 14 — Right Turn Prohibited

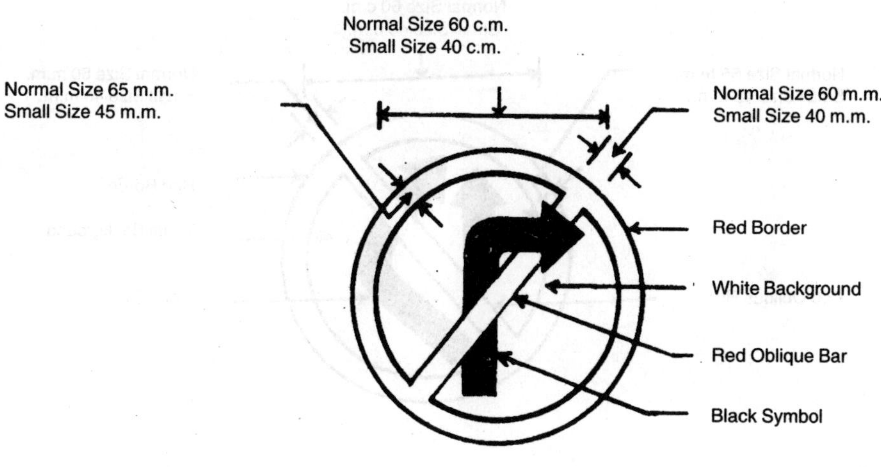

No. M 15 — Left Turn Prohibited

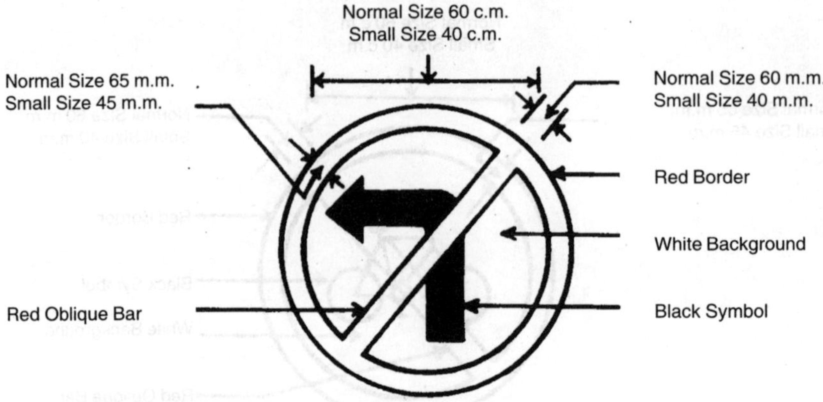

No. M 16 — U.Turn Prohibited

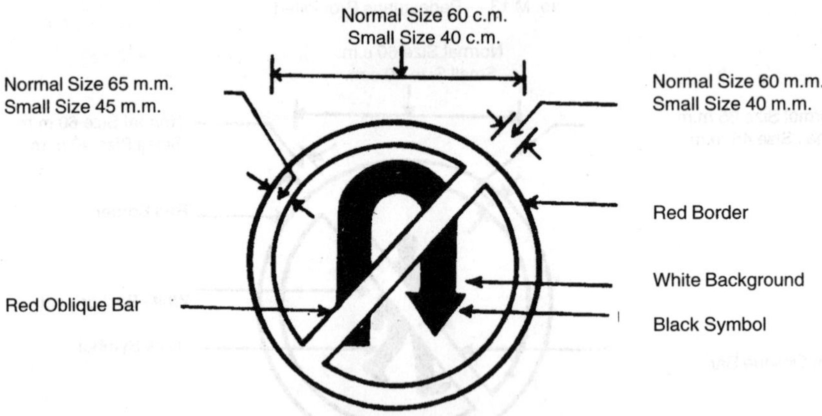

No. M 17 — Overtaking Prohibited

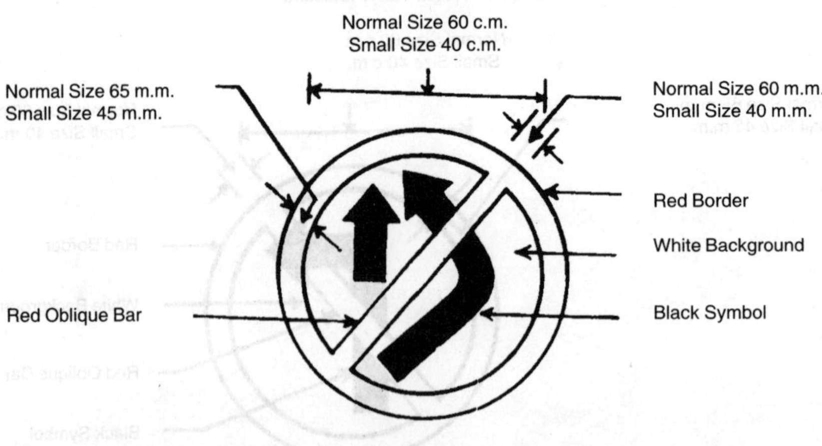

No. M 18 — Horns Prohibited

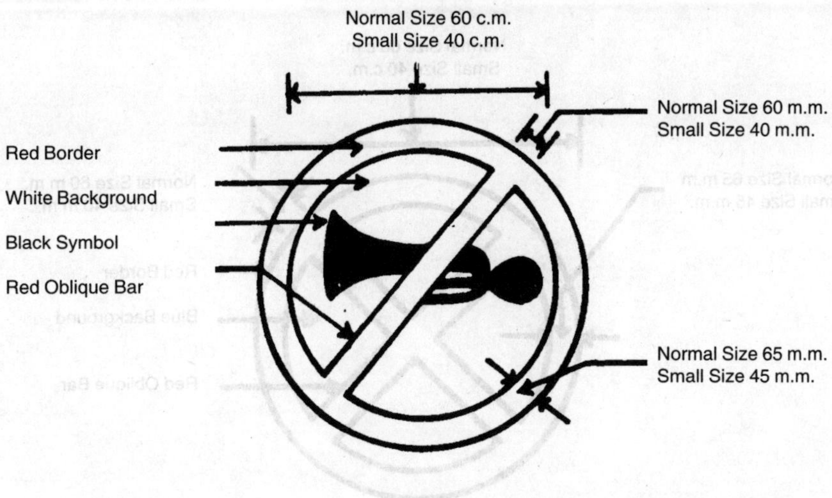

No. M 19 — No Parking

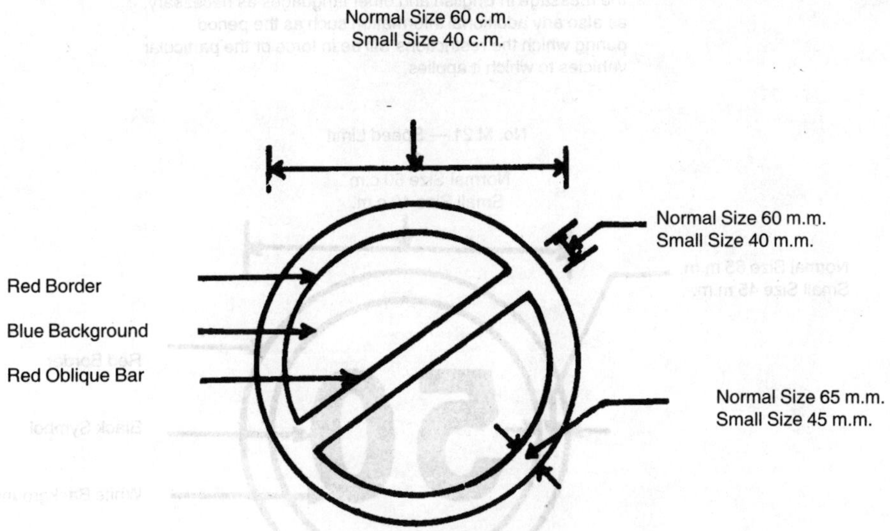

Note.—A definition plate may be attached with the sign carrying the message in English and other languages as necessary, as also any additional information such as the period during which the restrictions will be in force or the particular vehicles to which it applies.

No. M 20 — No Stopping or Standing

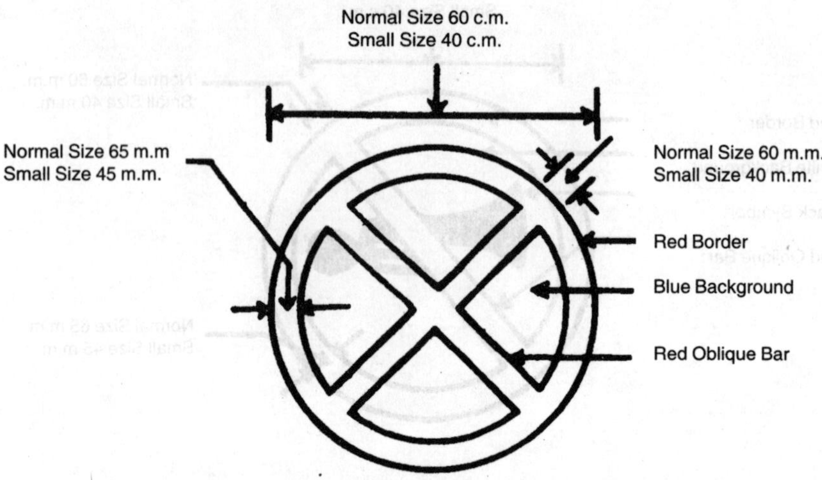

Note.—A definition plate may be attached with the sign carrying the message in English and other languages as necessary, as also any additional information such as the period during which the restrictions will be in force or the particular vehicles to which it applies.

No. M 21 — Speed Limit

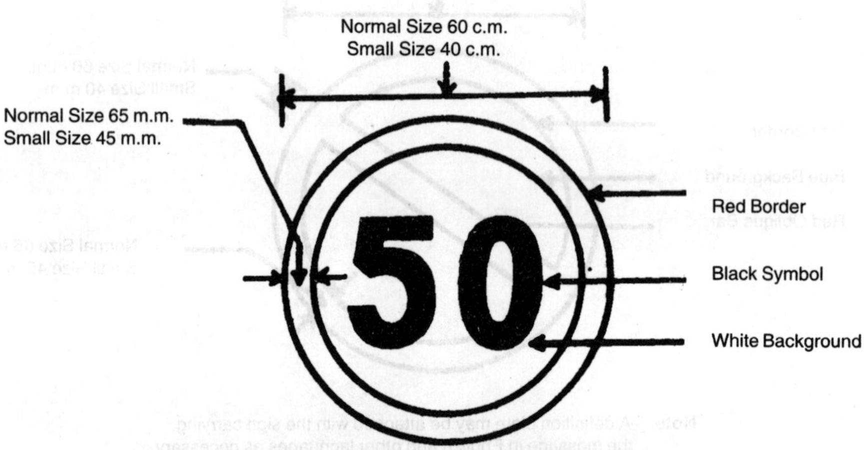

Note.—Where speed limit is imposed only on certain class or classes of motor vehicles, this may be specified on a definition plate. Where in addition to general speed limit a special speed limit is imposed on motor vehicles of certain class or classes, the latter together with the class or classes of vehicles may be specified on a definition plate.

No. M 22 — Width Limit

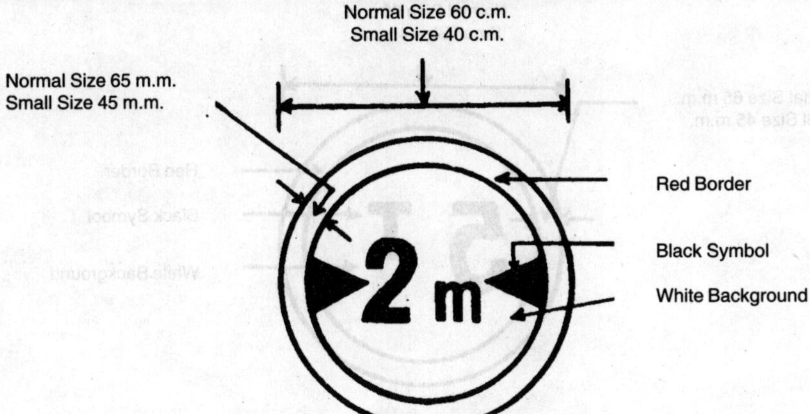

No. M 23 — Height Limit

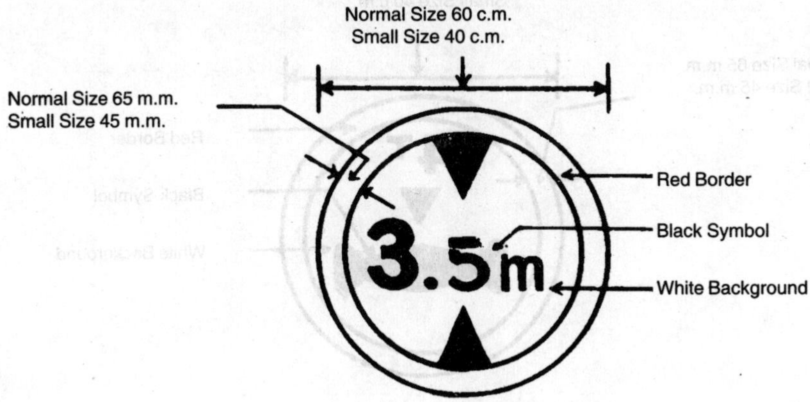

No. M 24 — Length Limit

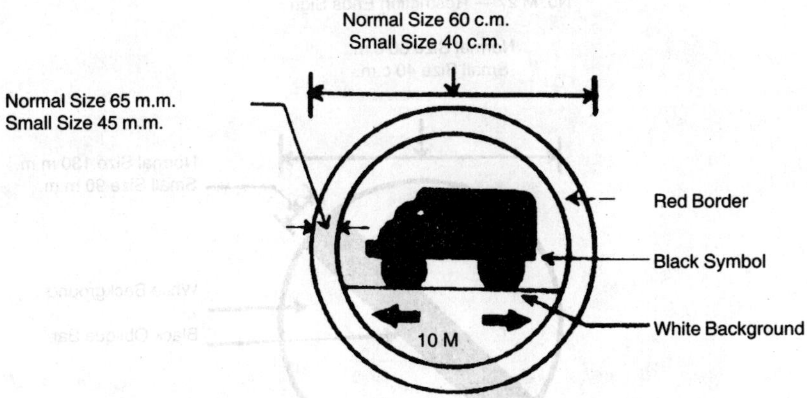

No. M 25 — Load Limit

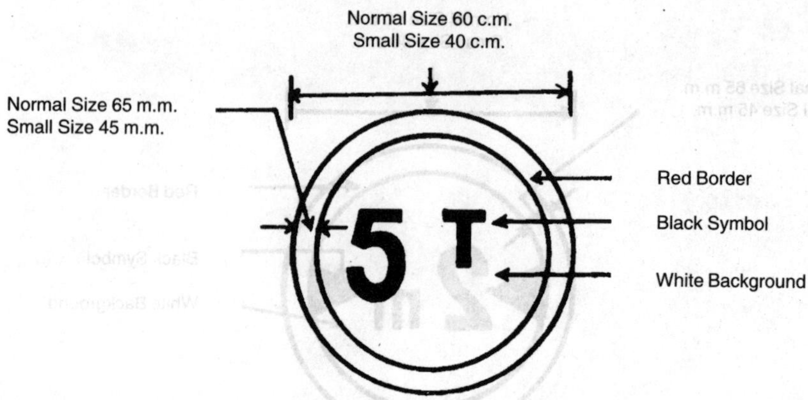

No. M 26 — Axle Load Limit

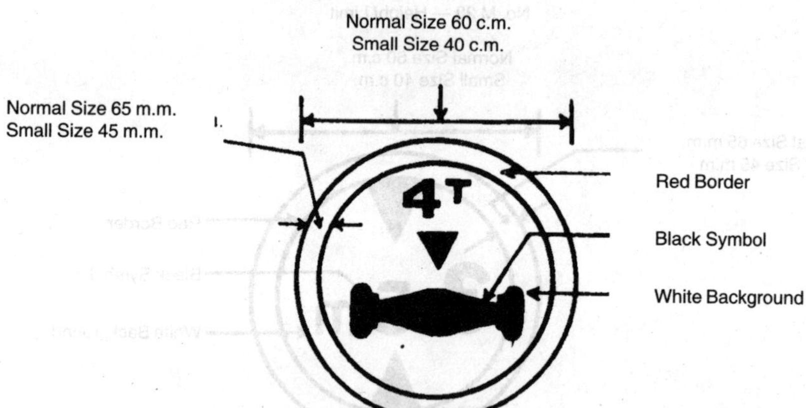

No. M 27 — Restriction Ends Sign

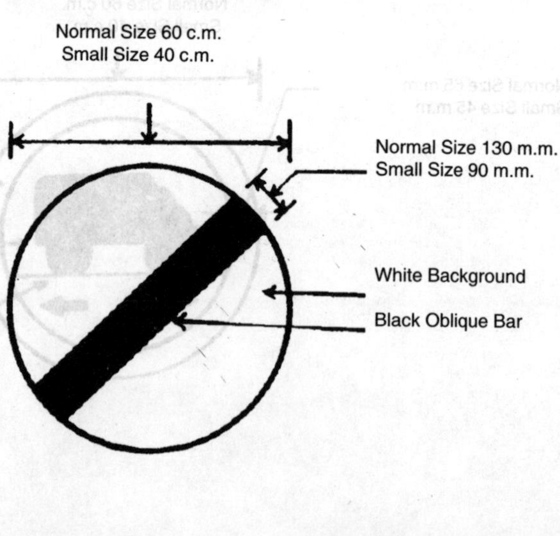

No. M 28 — Compulsory Turn Left
(Right if Symbol is Reversed)

Normal Size 60 c.m.
Small Size 40 c.m.

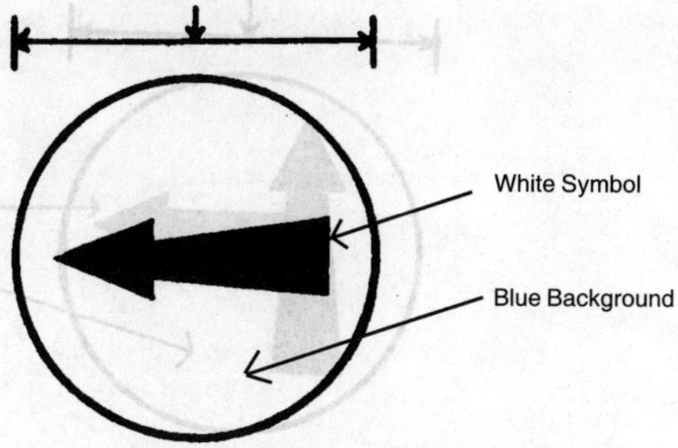

No. M 29 — Compulsory Ahead Only

Normal Size 60 c.m.
Small Size 40 c.m.

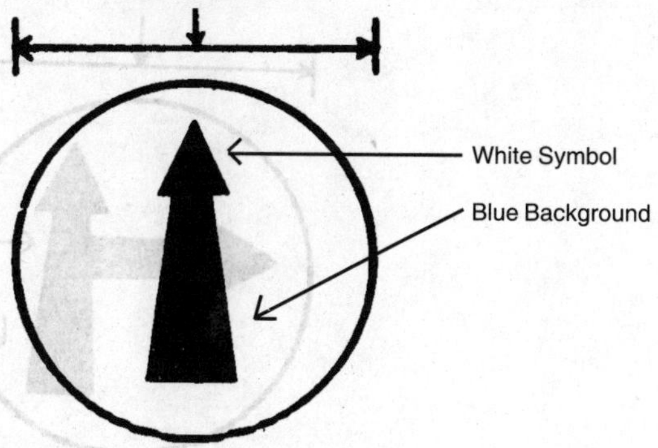

No. M 30 — Compulsory Turn Right Ahead
(Left if Symbol is Reversed)

Normal Size 60 c.m.
Small Size 40 c.m.

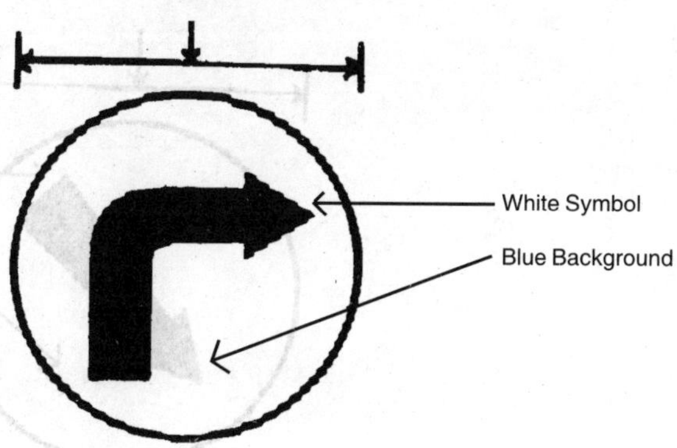

No. M 31 — Compulsory Ahead or Turn Right

Normal Size 60 c.m.
Small Size 40 c.m.

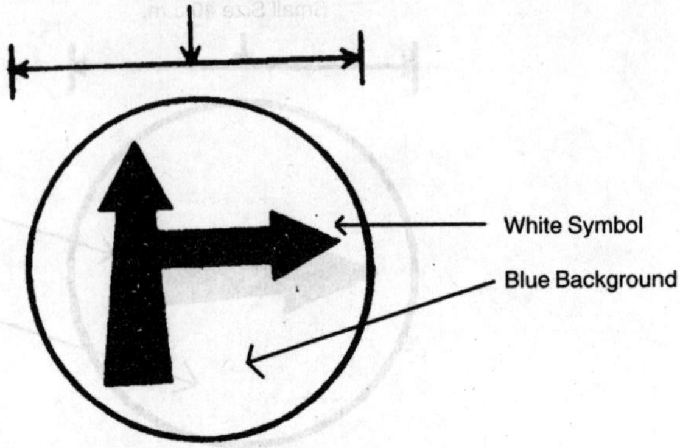

No. M 32 — Compulsory Ahead or Turn Left

Normal Size 60 c.m.
Small Size 40 c.m.

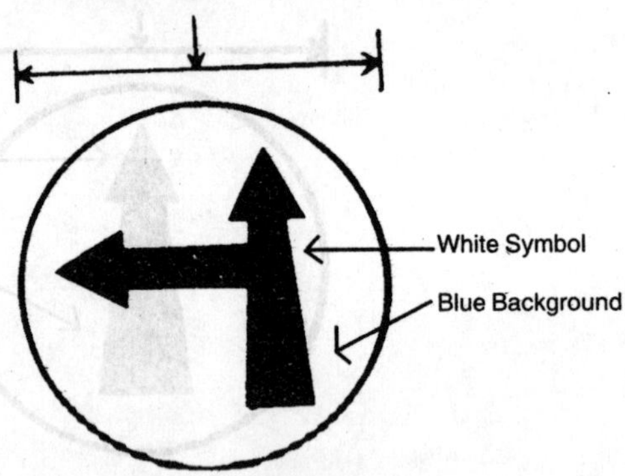

No. M 33 — Compulsory Keep Left

Normal Size 60 c.m.
Small Size 40 c.m.

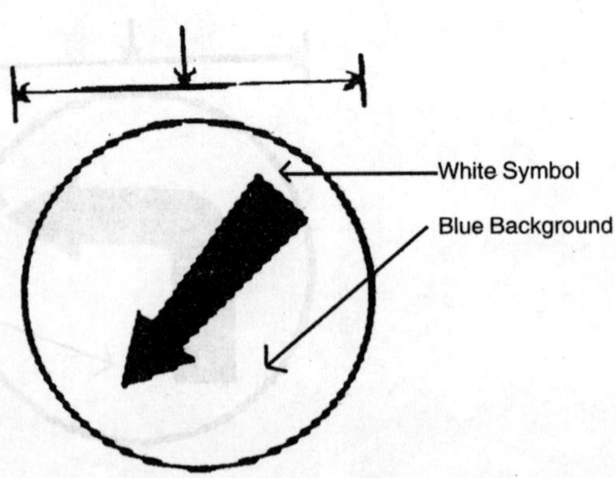

No. M 34 — Compulsory Cycle Track

Normal Size 60 c.m.
Small Size 40 c.m.

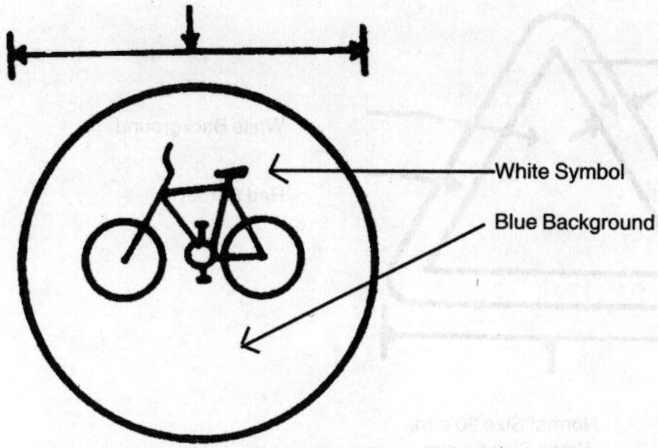

No. M 35 — Compulsory Sound Horn

Normal Size 60 c.m.
Small Size 40 c.m.

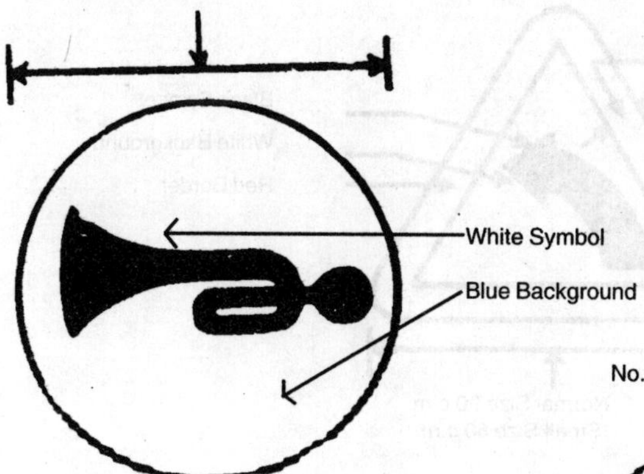

No. M 36 — Compulsory Bus Stop

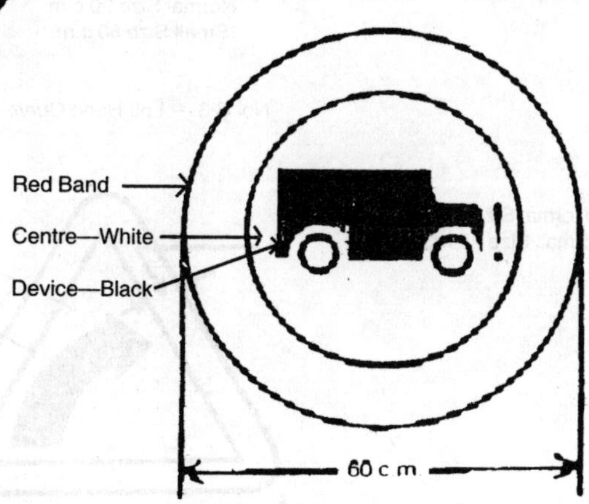

PART B

Cautionary signs of the First Schedule of The Motor Vehicles Act, 1988

No. C 1 — General Design

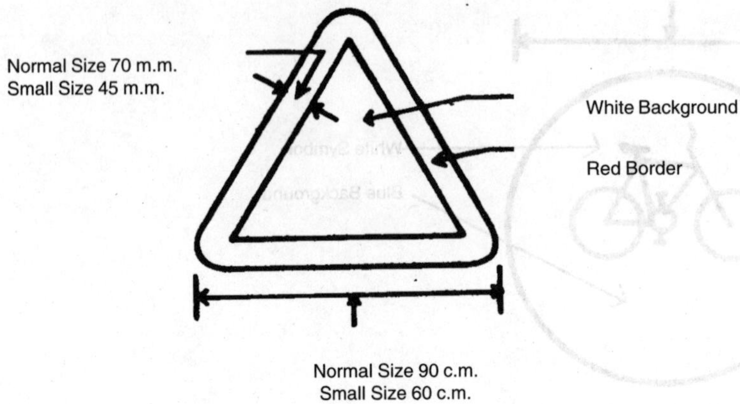

No. C 2 — Right Hand Curve

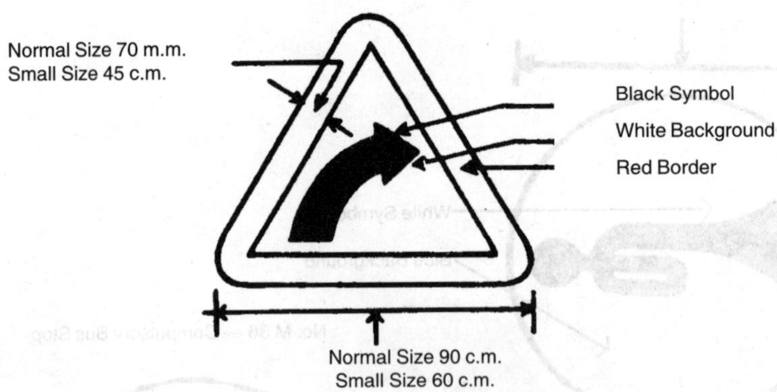

No. C 3 — Left Hand Curve

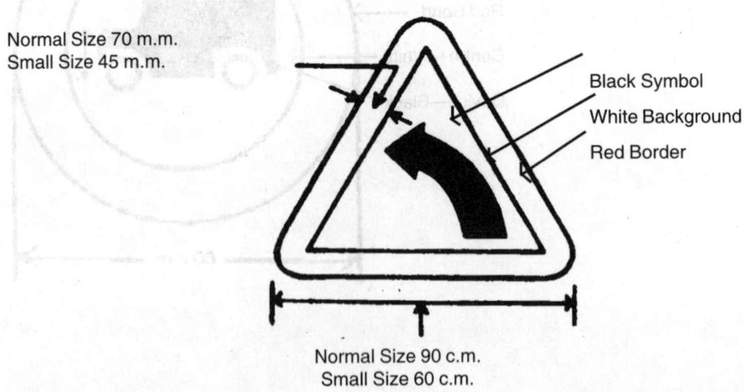

No. C 4 — Right Hair Pin Bend

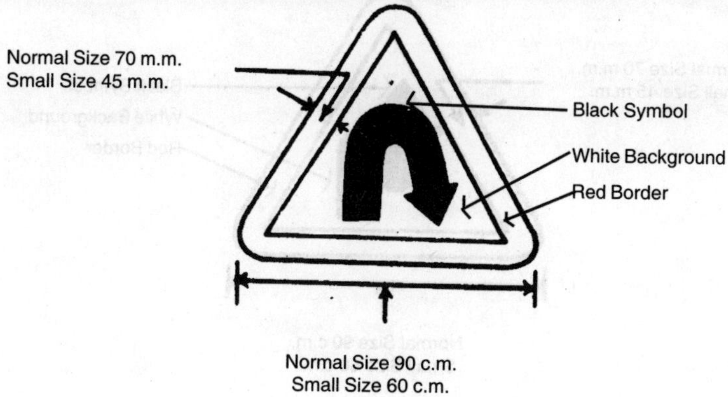

No. C 5 — Left Hair Pin Bend

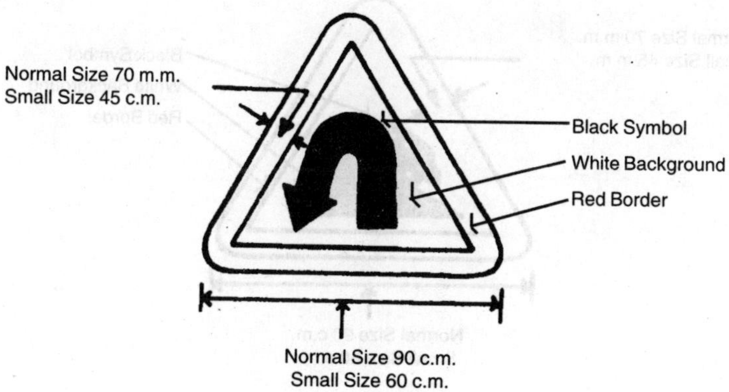

No. C 6 — Right Reverse Bend

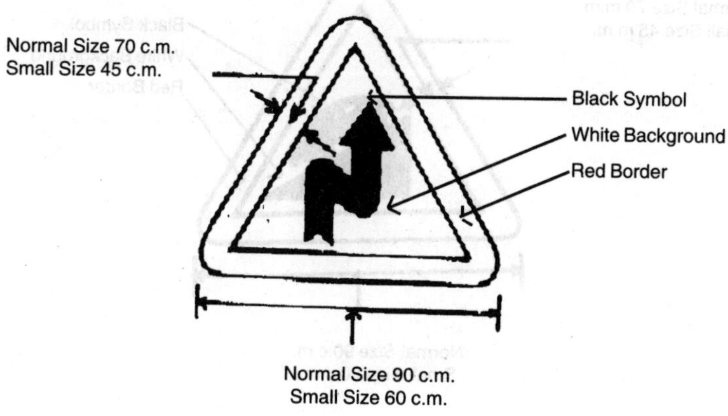

No. C 7 — Left Reverse Bend

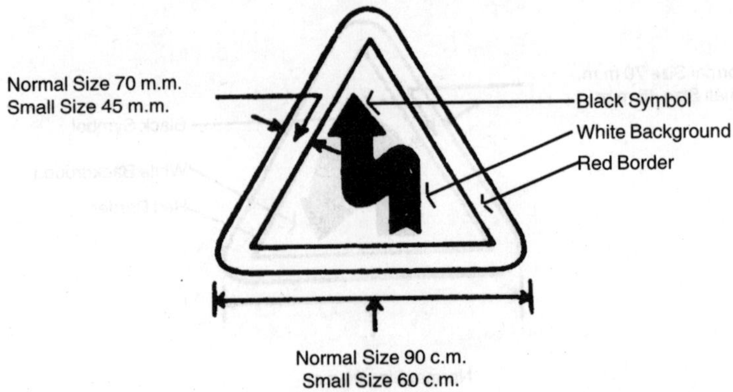

No. C 8 — Steep Ascent

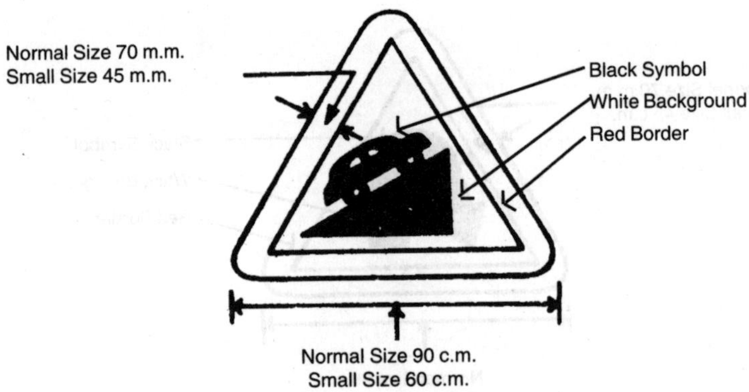

No. C 9 — Steep Descent

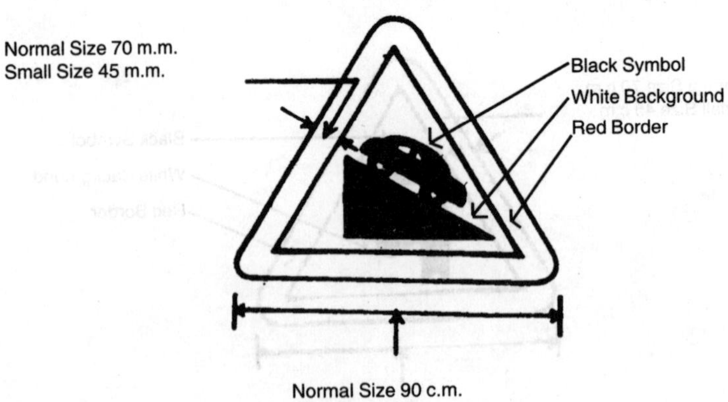

No. C 10 — Narrow Road Ahead

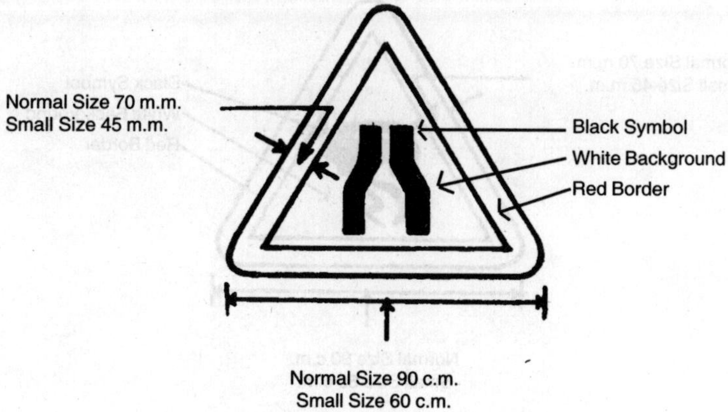

No. C 11 - Road Widens Ahead

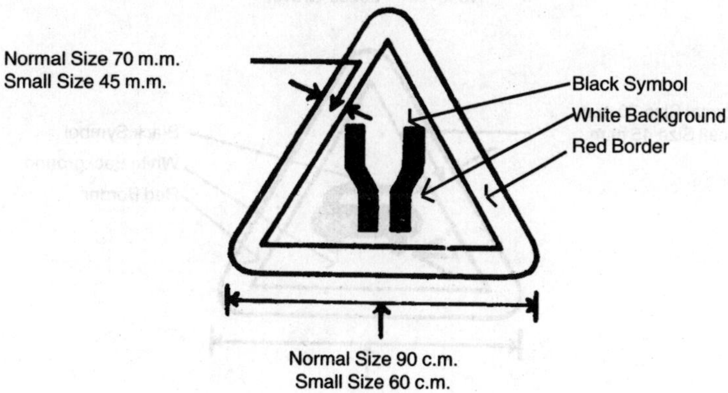

No. C 12 — Narrow Bridge

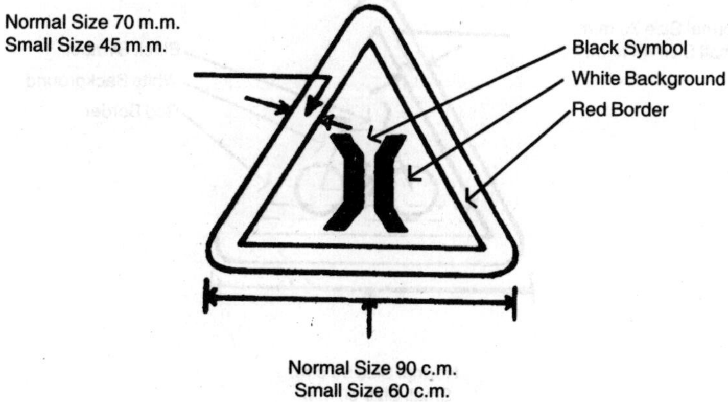

No. C 13 — Slippery Road

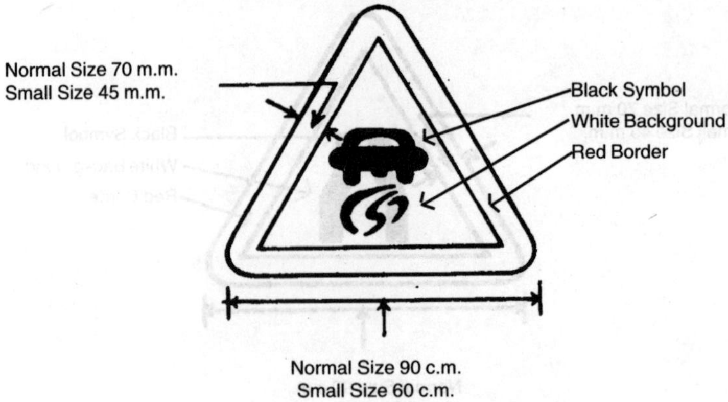

No. C 14 — Loose Gravel

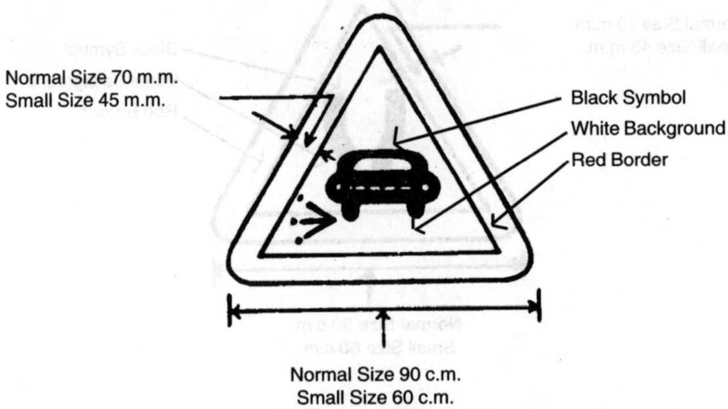

No. C 15 — Cycle Crossing

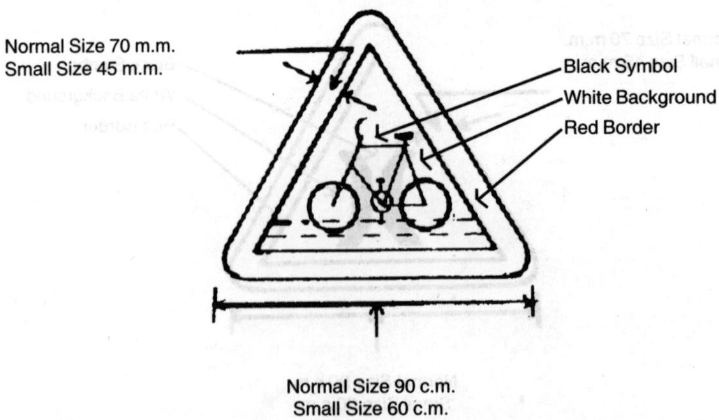

No. C 16 — Pedestrian Crossing

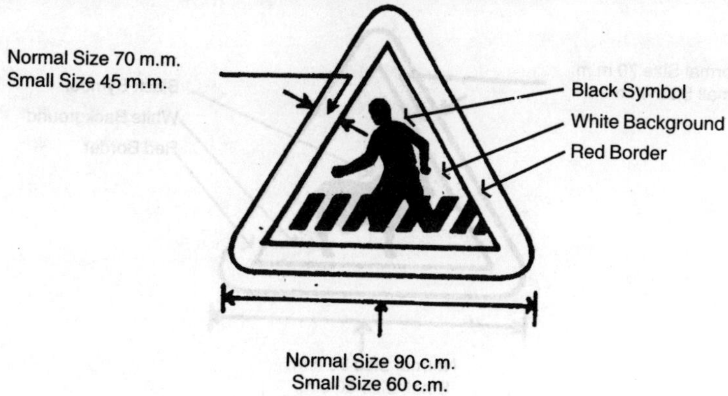

No. C 17 — School Ahead

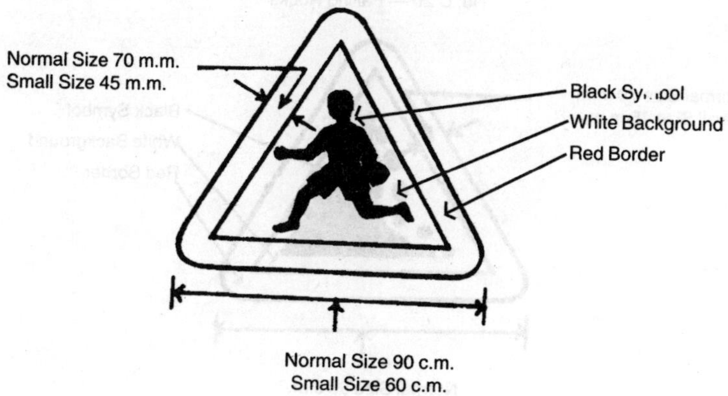

No. C 18 — Men At Work

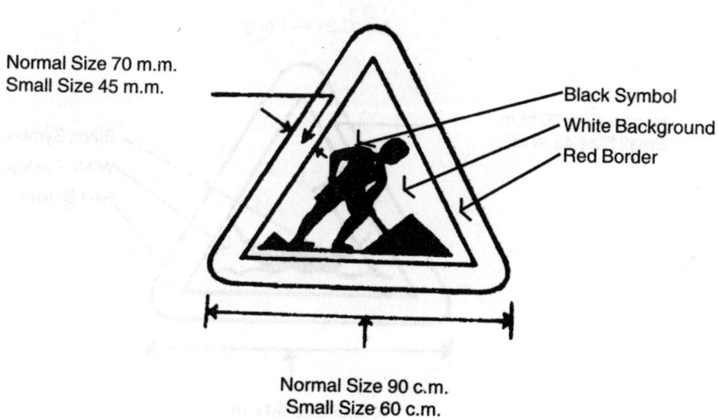

No. C 19 — Cattle

No. C 20 — Falling Rocks

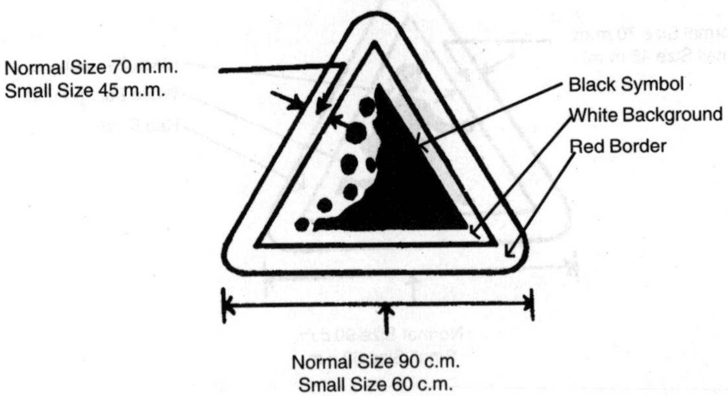

No. C 21 — Ferry

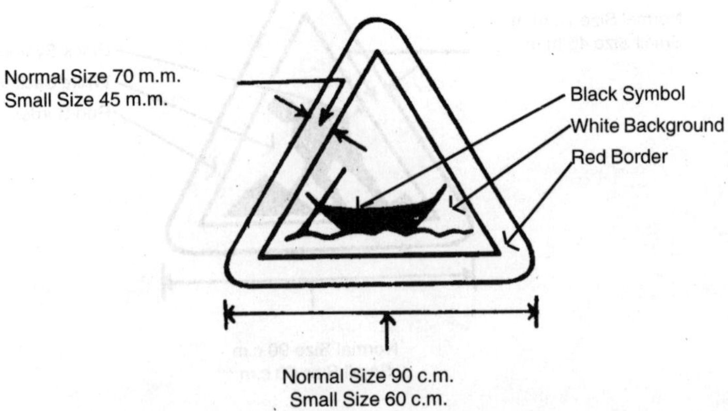

No. C 22 — Cross Road

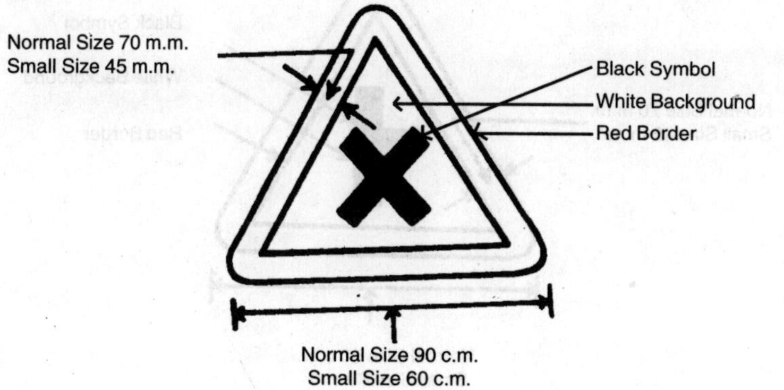

No. C 23 — Gap in Median

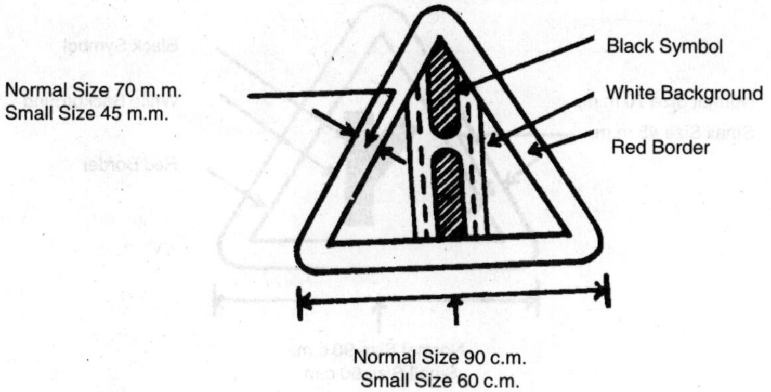

No. C 24 — Side Road Right

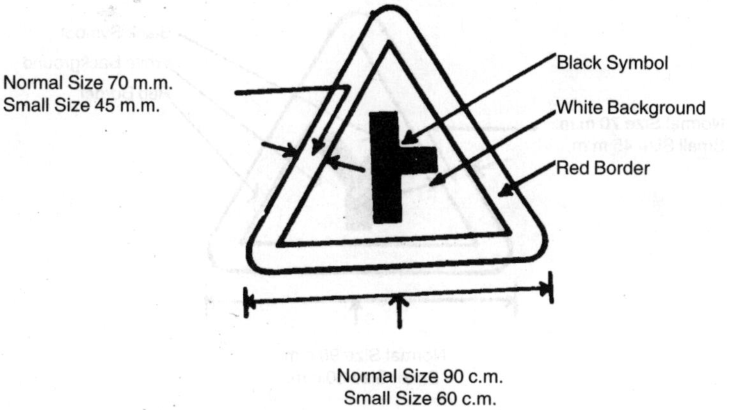

No. C 25 — Side Road Left

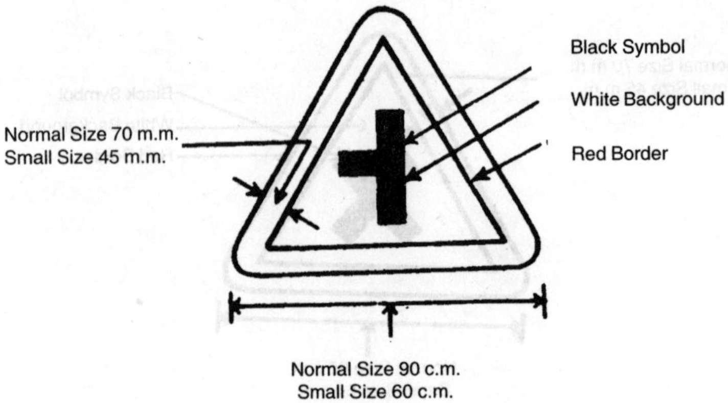

No. C 26A — Y—Intersection

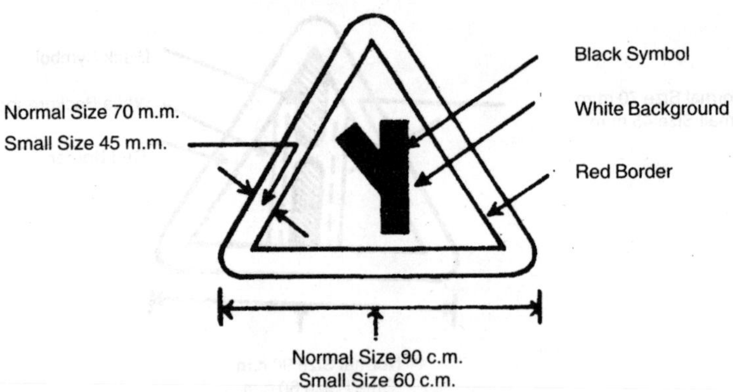

No. C 26B — Y— Intersection

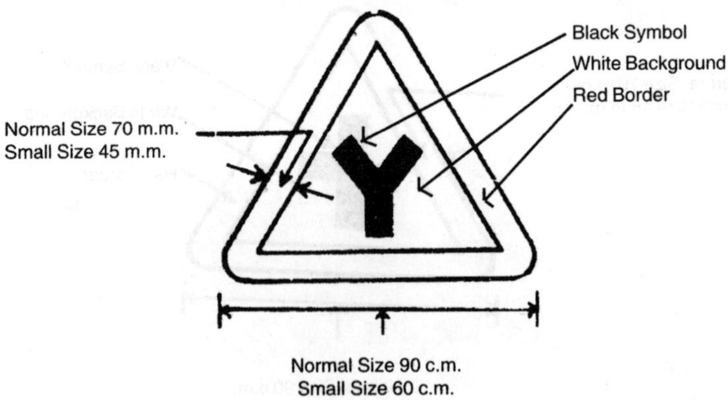

No. C 26C — Y — Intersection

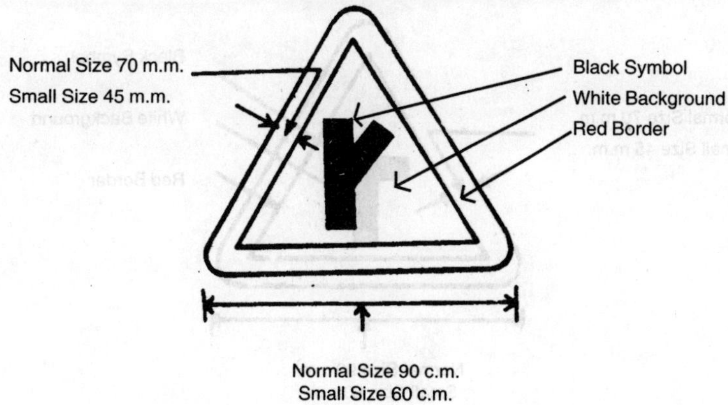

No. C 27 — T — Intersection

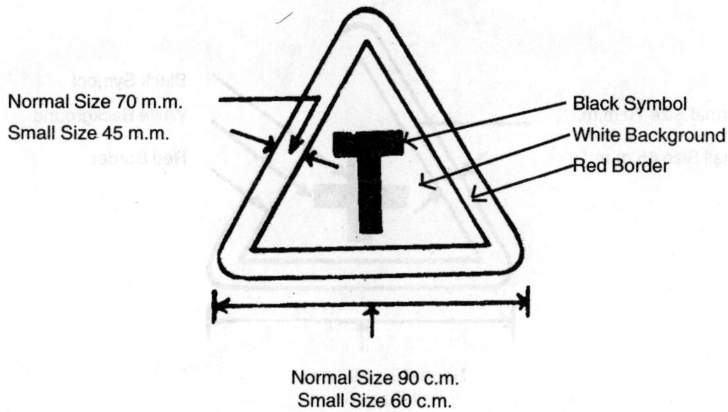

No. C 28A — Staggered Intersection

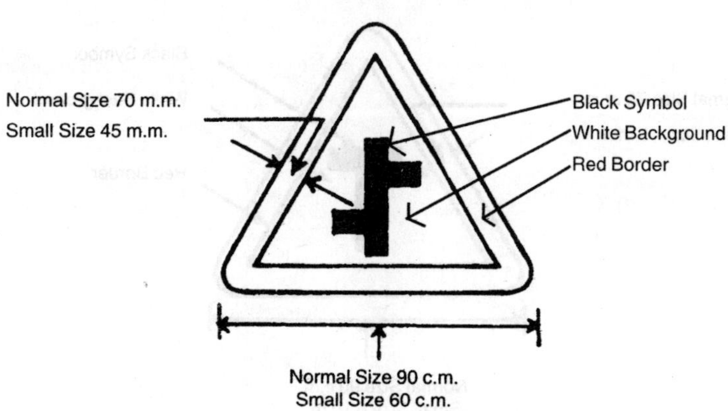

No. C 28B — Staggered intersection

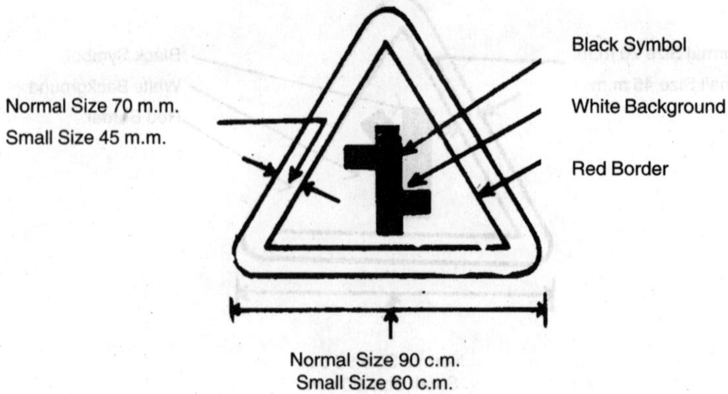

No. C 29A — Major Road Ahead

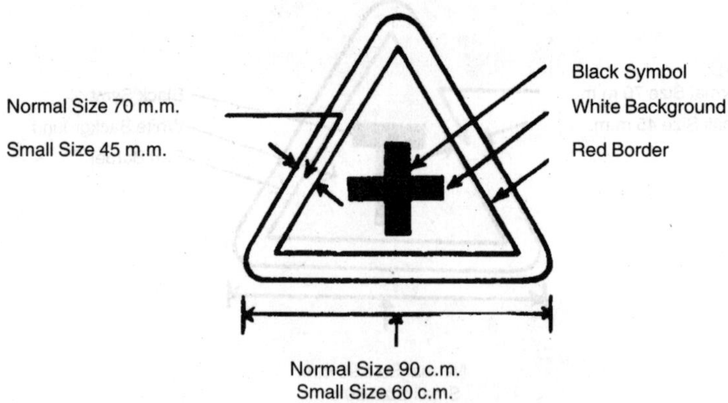

No. C 29B — Major Road Ahead

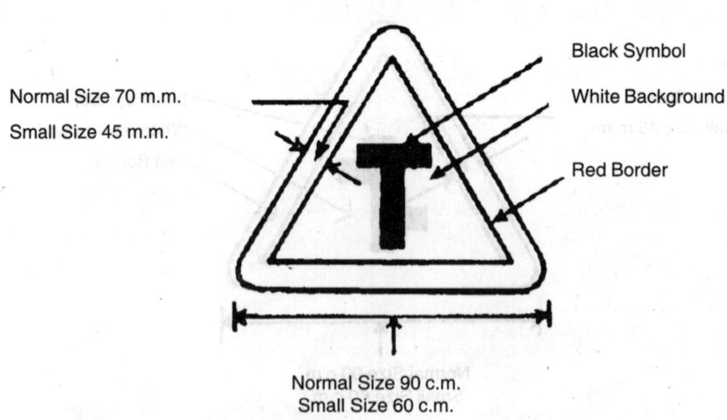

No. C 30 — Roundabout

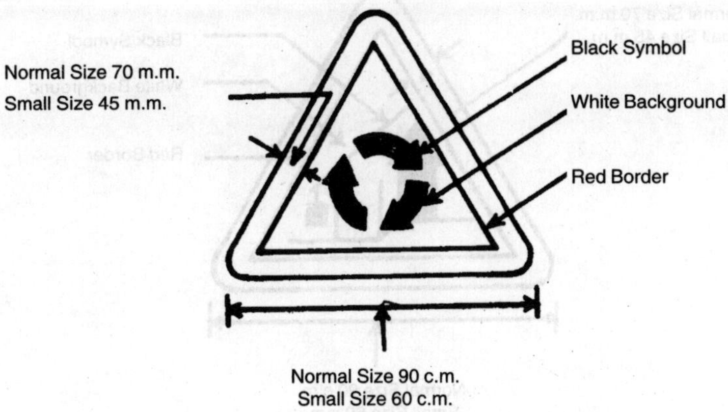

No. C 31 — Dangerous Dip

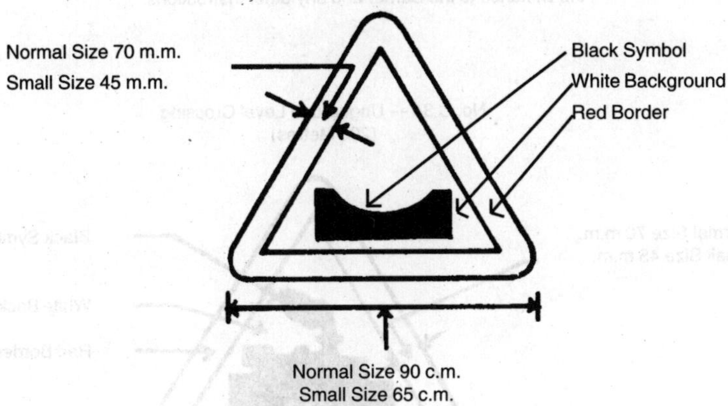

No. C 32 — Hump or Rough Road

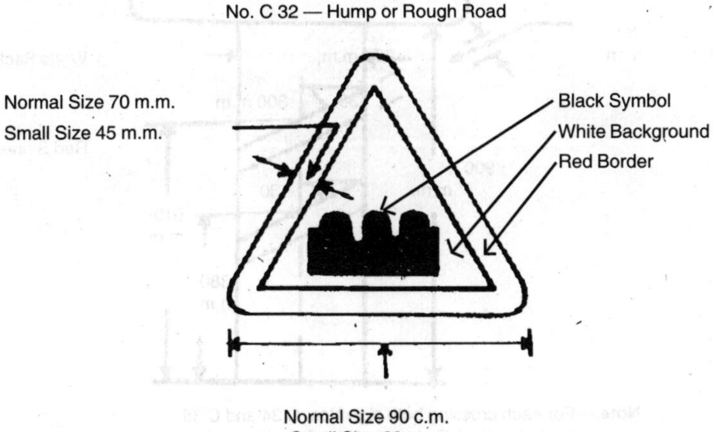

No. C 33 — Barrier Ahead

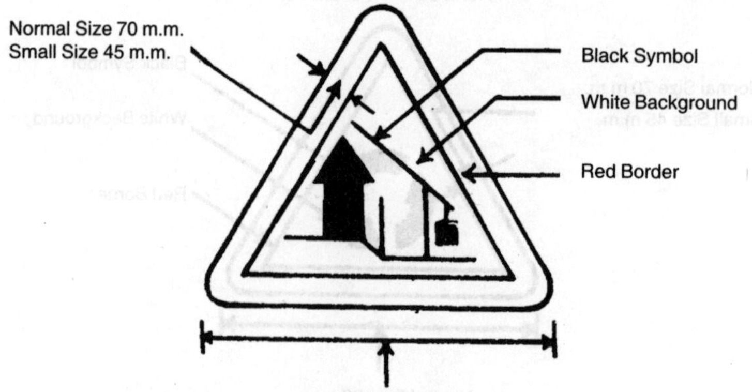

Note.—A Definition Plate may be attached with the sign indicating the Distance to the Barrier and any other instructions.

No. C 34 — Unguarded Level Crossing
(200 Metres)

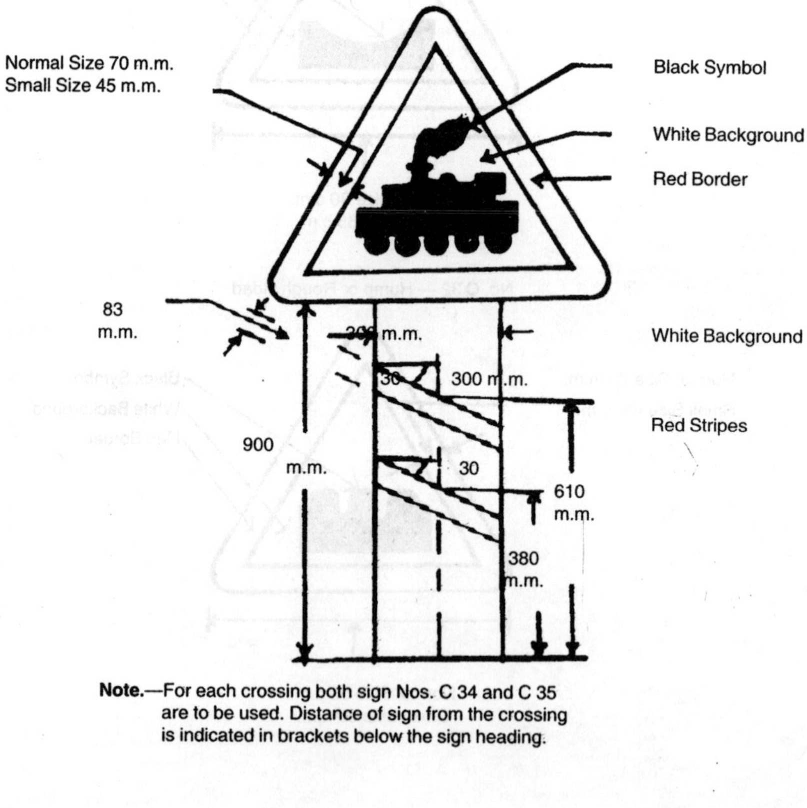

Note.—For each crossing both sign Nos. C 34 and C 35 are to be used. Distance of sign from the crossing is indicated in brackets below the sign heading.

No. C 35 — Unguarded Level Crossing
(50-100 Metres)

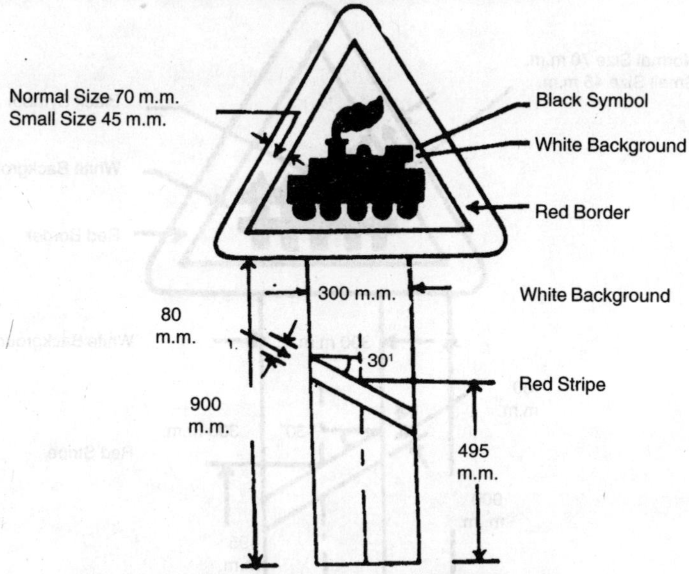

Note.—For each crossing both sign Nos. C 34 and C 35 are to be used. Distance of sign from the crossing is indicated in brackets below the sign heading. In hilly terrain distance may be reduced to 30-60 m.

No. C 36 — Guarded Level Crossing
(200 Metres)

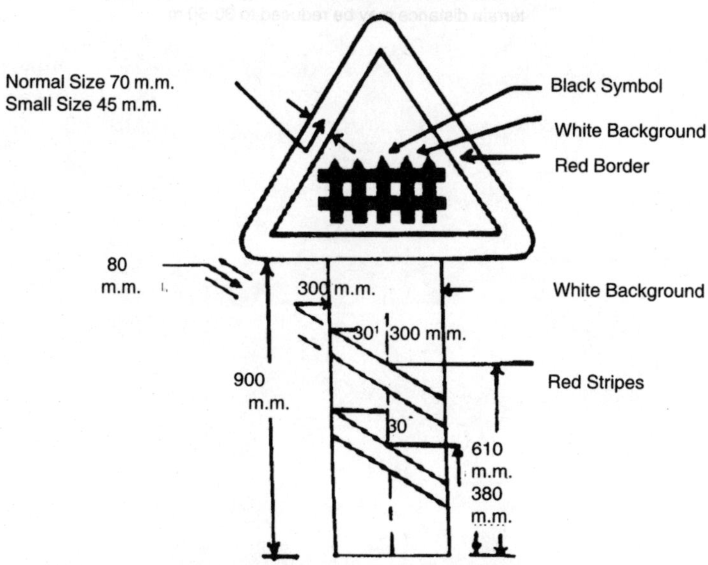

Note.—For each crossing both sign Nos. C 36 and C 37 are to be used. Distance of sign from crossing is indicated in brackets below the sign heading.

No. C 37 — Guarded Level Crossing
(50—100 Metres)

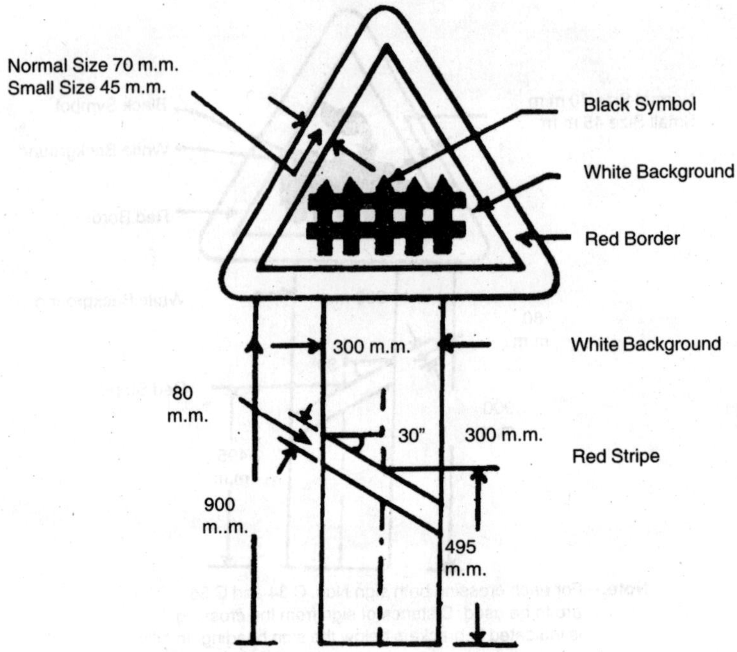

Note.—For each crossing, both sign Nos. C 36 and C 37 are to be used. Distance of sign from the crossing is indicated in brackets below the sign heading. In hilly terrain distance may be reduced to 30-60 m.

PART C

Informatory signs of the First Schedule of The Motor Vehicles Act, 1988

No. E 1 — Advance Direction sign

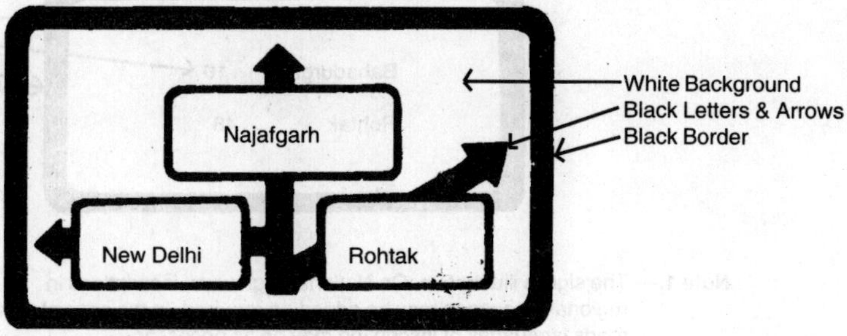

Note 1.—The sign is illustrative. On National Highways, inscriptions in regional languages may be added as required. In the case of other roads languages of inscription may be as necessary.

Note 2.—The size of the sign depends on the message and size of letters.

No. E 2 — Destination Sign

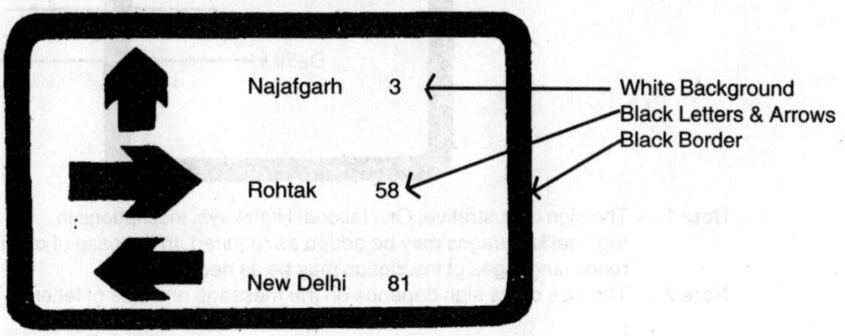

Note 1.— The sign is illustrative. On National Highways, inscriptions in regional languages may be added as required. In the case of other roads languages of inscription may be as necessary.

Note 2.— The size of the sign depends on the message and size of letters.

No. E 3 — Direction Sign

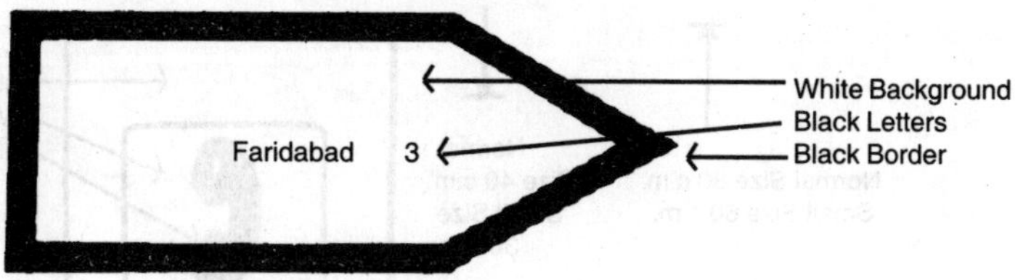

Note 1.— The sign is illustrative. On National Highways, inscriptions in regional languages may be added as required. In the case of other roads languages of inscription may be as necessary.

Note 2.— The size of the sign depends on the message and size of letters.

No. E 4 — Re-Assurance Sign

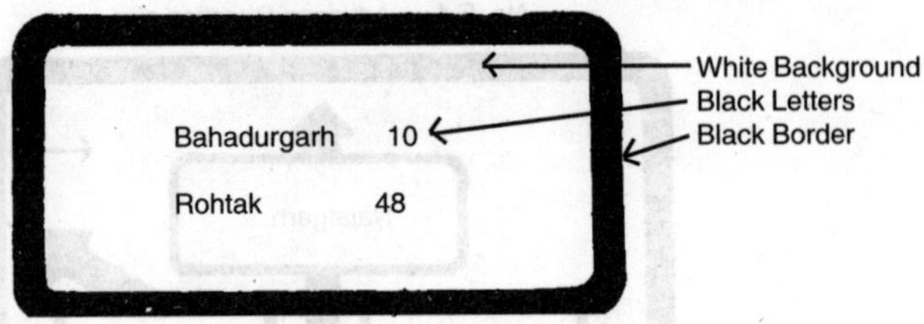

Note 1.— The sign is illustrative. On National Highways, inscriptions in regional languages may be added as required. In the case of other roads languages of inscription may be as necessary.

Note 2.— The size of the sign depends on the message and size of letters.

No. E 5 — Place Identification Sign

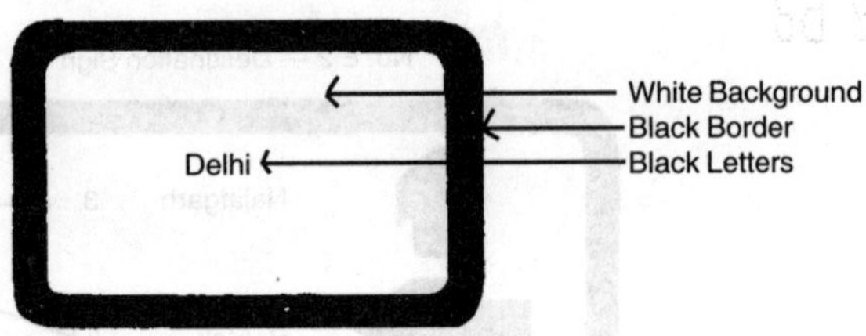

Note 1.— The sign is illustrative. On National Highways, inscriptions in regional languages may be added as required. In the case of other roads languages of inscription may be as necessary.

Note 2.— The size of the sign depends on the message and size of letters.

No, E 6 — Public Telephone

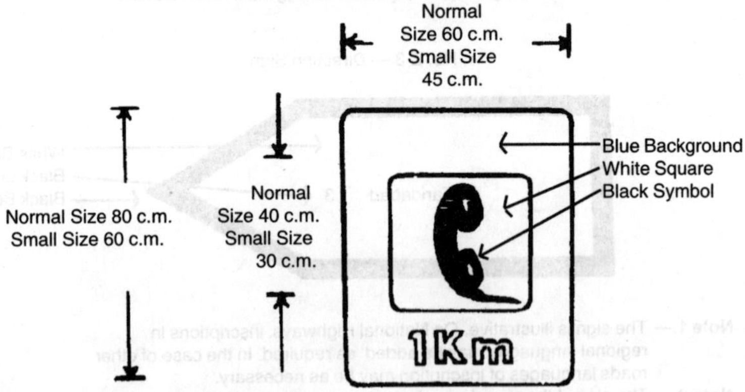

Note.— On the blue band at the bottom of the sign, the distance to the facility or the direction may be inscribed in white. Such inscription shown in the sign above is only illustrative.

No. E 7 — Petrol Pump

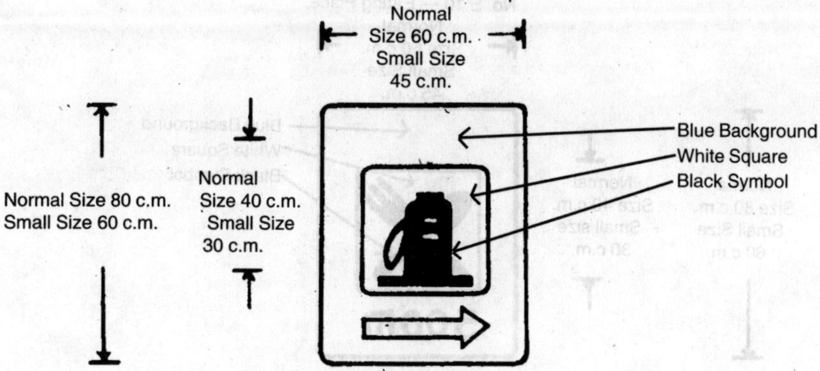

Note.—On the blue band at the bottom of the sign, the distance to the facility or the direction may be inscribed in white. Such inscription shown in the sign above is only illustrative.

No. E 8 — Hospital

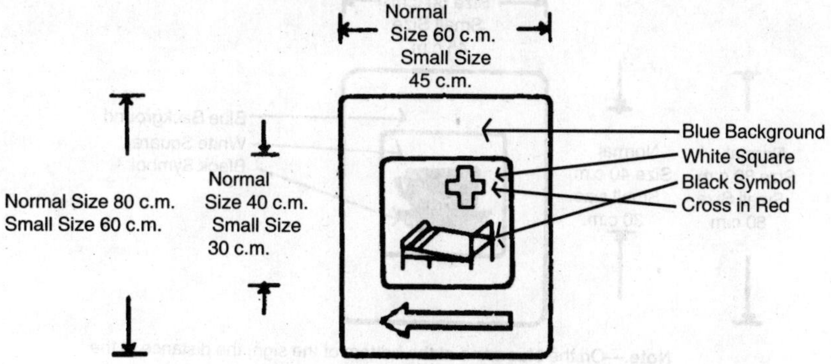

Note.—On the blue band at the bottom of the sign, the distance to the facility or the direction may be inscribed in white. Such inscription shown in the sign above is only illustrative.

No. E 9 — First-Aid Post

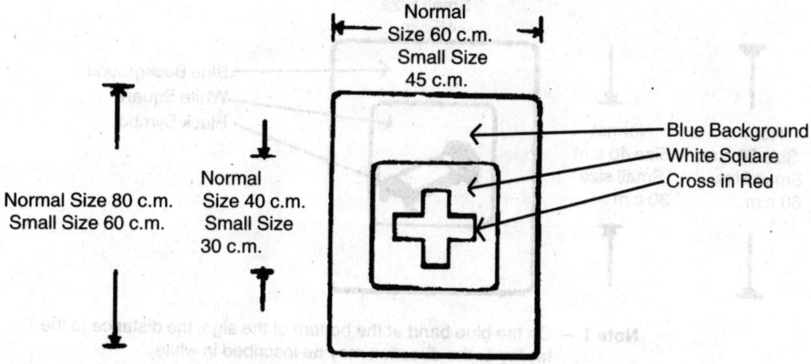

Note.—On the blue band at the bottom of the sign, the distance to the facility or the direction may be inscribed in white.

No. E 10 — Eating Place

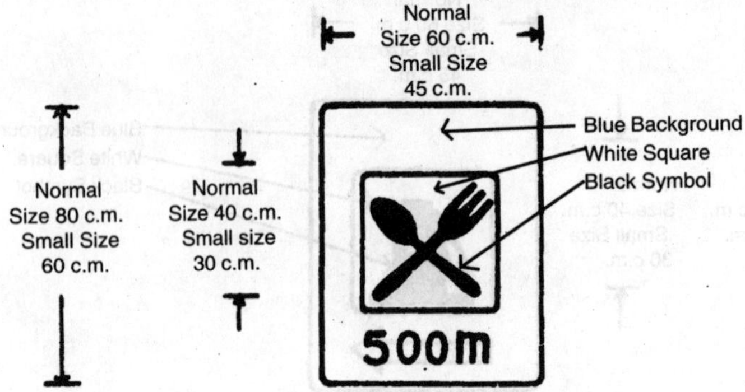

Note.—On the blue band at the bottom of the sign, the distance to the facility or the direction may be inscribed in white. Such inscription shown in the sign above is only illustrative.

No. E 11 — Light Refreshment

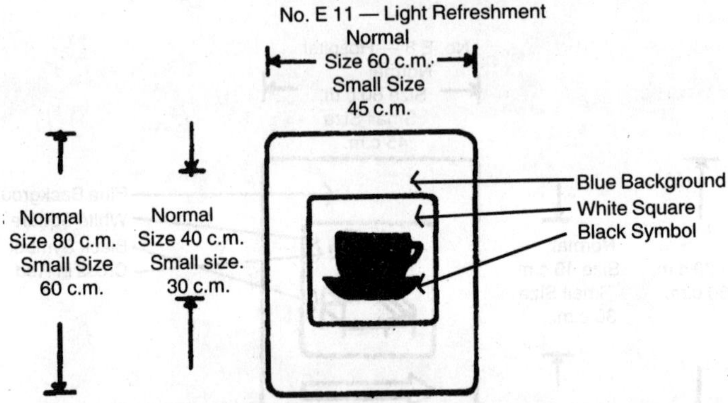

Note.—On the blue band at the bottom of the sign, the distance to the facility or the direction may be inscribed in white.

No. E 12 — Resting Place

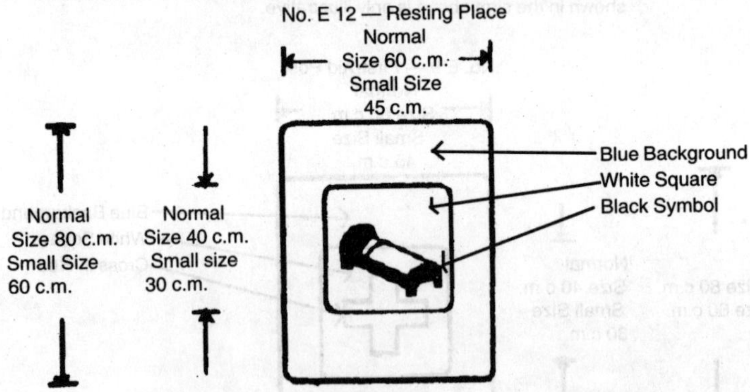

Note 1.— On the blue band at the bottom of the sign, the distance to the facility or the direction may be inscribed in white.

Note 2.—A definition plate may be attached indicating whether the place is rest house, hotel or motel.

No. E 13 — No Thorough Road

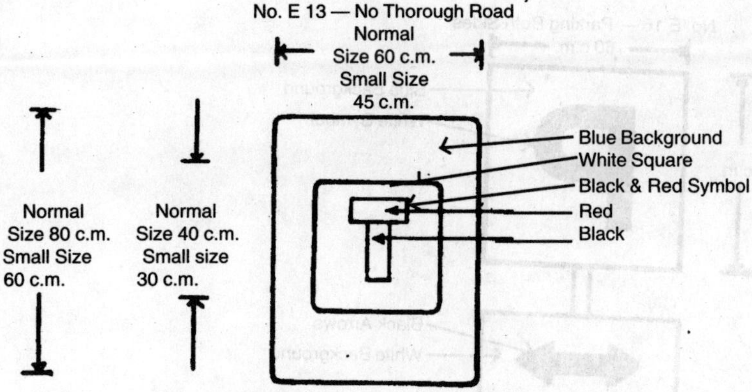

Note.—On the blue band at the bottom of the sign, the distance to the facility or the direction may be inscribed in white.

No. E 14 — No Thorough Side Road

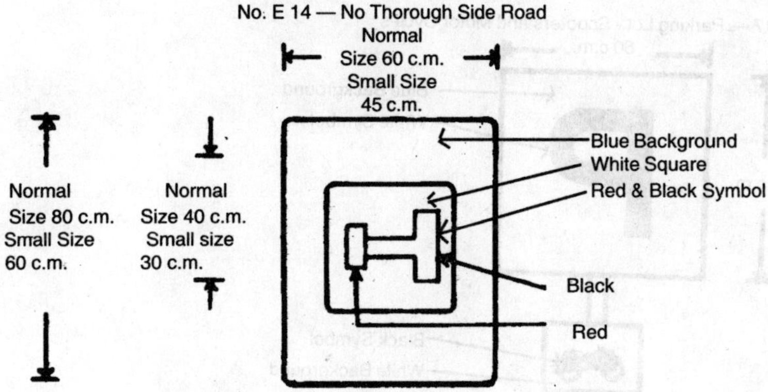

Note.—On the blue band at the bottom of the sign, the distance to the facility or the direction may be inscribed in white.

No. E 15 — Park This Side

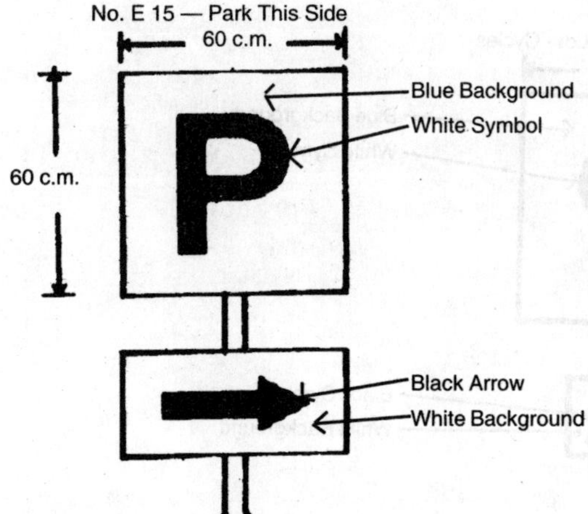

No. E 16 — Parking Both Sides

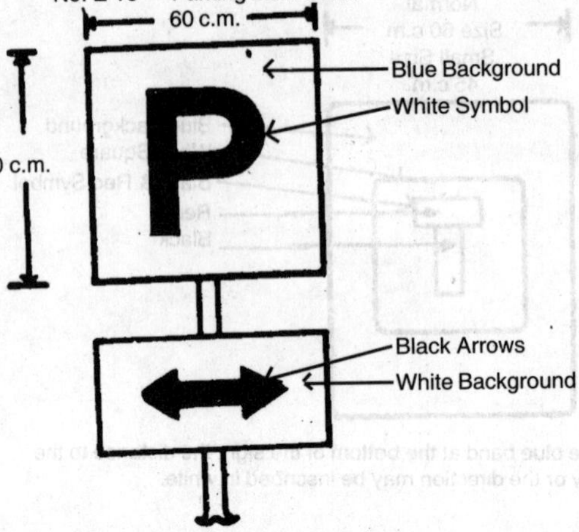

No. E 17 — Parking Lot - Scooters and Motor Cycles

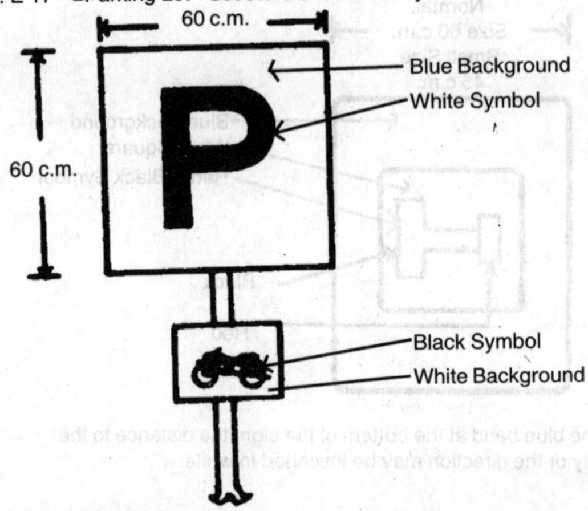

No. E 18 — Parking Lot - Cycles

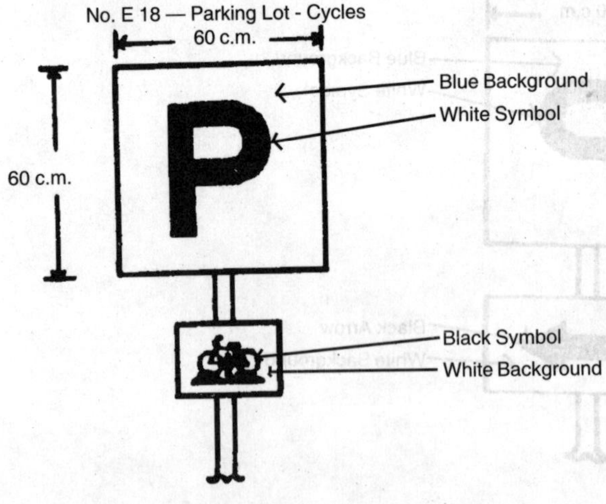

No. E 19 — Parking Lot — Taxis

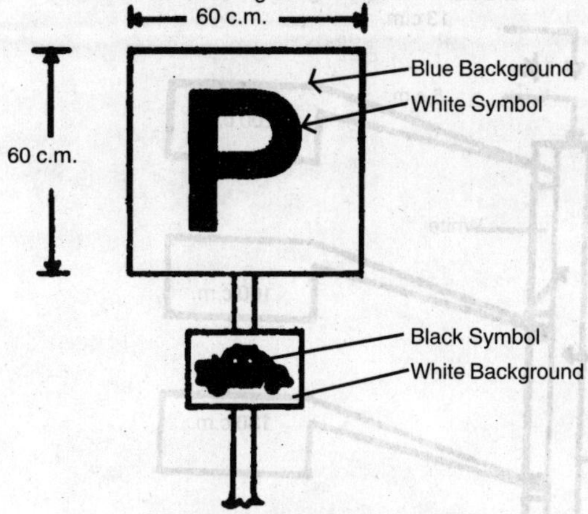

No. E 20 — Parking Lot — Auto Rickshaws

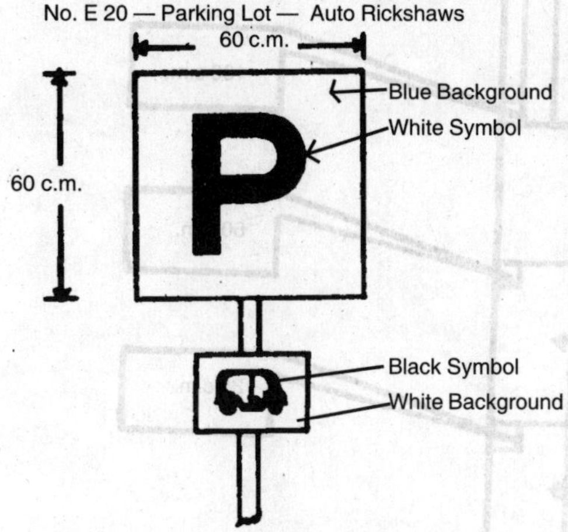

No. E 21 — Parking Lot — Cycle Rickshaws

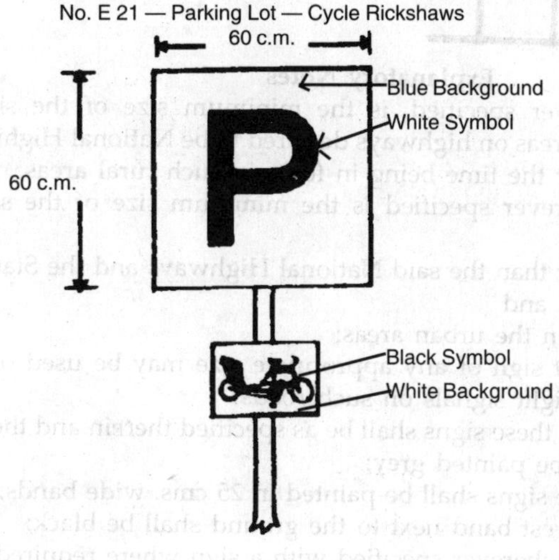

No. E 22 — Flood Gauge

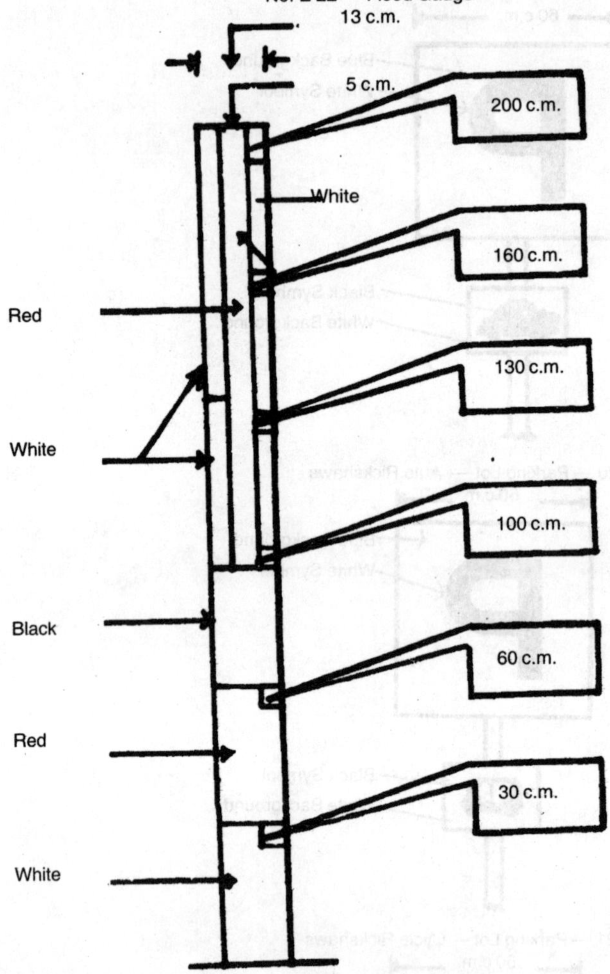

Explanatory Notes

(i) Normal Size, wherever specified, is the minimum size of the sign which is intended to be used in rural areas on highways declared to be National Highways or State Highways under any law for the time being in force in such rural areas;

(ii) the Small Size, wherever specified is the minimum size of the sign which is intended to be used,—

(a) on all roads, other than the said National Highways and the State Highways, in the rural areas, and

(b) on all roads within the urban areas:

Provided that sign of any appropriate size may be used on ballards or alongside traffic light signals on such roads;

(iii) the colour scheme of these signs shall be as specified therein and the reverse side of all such sign plates shall be painted grey;

(iv) the posts of all these signs shall be painted in 25 cms. wide bands, alternatively black and white and the lowest band next to the ground shall be black;

(v) the definition plate, wherever specified with a sign where required to make the meaning of a sign more explicit shall have white background, black letters and black border 20 mm. wide and shall be of adequate size for legibility but not too large as to be obtrusive.]

[1][*THE SECOND SCHEDULE*

(*See* section 163A)

SCHEDULE FOR COMPENSATION FOR THIRD PARTY FATAL ACCIDENTS/INJURY CASES CLAIMS

1. Fatal Accidents:

Annual Income		Rs. 3000	Rs. 4200	Rs. 5400	Rs. 6600	Rs. 7800	Rs. 9000	Rs. 10200	Rs. 11400	Rs. 12000	Rs. 18000	Rs. 24000	Rs. 36000	Rs. 40000
AGE OF VICTIM	MULTIPLIER	(RUPEES IN THOUSANDS) (compensation in case of death)												
		Rs.	Rs.	Rs.	Rs.	Rs.	Rs.	Rs.	Rs.	Rs.	Rs.	Rs.	Rs.	Rs.
Up to 15 yrs.	15	60	84	108	132	156	180	204	228	240	360	480	720	800
Above 15 yrs. but not exdg. 20 yrs.	16	57	79.8	102	125.4	148.2	171	193.8	216.6	228	342	456	684	760
Above 20 yrs. but not exdg. 25 yrs.	17	54	75.6	97.2	118.8	140.4	162	183.6	205.2	216	324	432	648	720
Above 25 yrs. but not exdg. 30 yrs.	18	51	71.4	91.8	112.2	132.6	153	173.4	193.8	204	306	408	612	680
Above 30 yrs. but not exdg. 35 yrs.	17	50	67.2	86.4	105.6	124.8	144	163.2	192.4	192	288	384	576	640
Above 35 yrs. but not exdg. 40 yrs.	16	50	63	81	99	117	135	153	171	180	270	380	540	600
Above 40 yrs. but not exdg. 45 yrs.	15	50	58.8	75.6	92.4	109.2	126	142.8	159.6	168	252	336	504	560
Above 45 yrs. but not exdg. 50 yrs.	13	50	50.4	64.8	79.2	93.6	108	122.4	136.8	144	216	286	432	480
Above 50 yrs. but not exdg. 55 yrs.	11	50	50	54	66	78	90	102	114	120	180	240	360	400
Above 55 yrs. but not exdg. 60 yrs.	 8	50	50	50	52.8	62.4	72	81.6	91.2	96	114	192	286	320
Above 60 yrs. but not exdg. 65 yrs.	 5	50	50	50	50	50	54	61.2	68.4	72	108	144	216	240
Above 65 yrs.	 5	50	50	50	50	50	50	51	57	60	90	120	180	200

Note.—The amount of compensation so arrived at in the case of fatal accident claims shall be reduced by 1/3rd in consideration of the expenses which the victim would have incurred towards maintaining himself had he been alive.

1. Ins. by Act 54 of 1994, sec. 64 (w.e.f. 14-11-1994).

2. Amount of compensation shall not be less than Rs. 50,000.

3. *General Damages (in case of death):*

The following General Damages shall be payable in addition to compensation outlined above:—

(i) Funeral expenses —Rs. 2,000/-

(ii) Loss of Consortium, if beneficiary is the spouse —Rs. 5,000/-

(iii) Loss of Estate —Rs. 2,500/-

(iv) Medical Expenses—actual expenses incurred before death supported by bills/vouchers but not exceeding —Rs. 15,000/-

4. *General Damages in case of Injuries and Disabilities:*

(i) Pain and Sufferings

(a) Grievous injuries —Rs. 5,000/-

(b) Non-grievous injuries —Rs. 1,000/-

(ii) Medical Expenses—actual expenses incurred supported by bills/vouchers but not exceeding as one time payment —Rs. 15,000/-

5. *Disability in non-fatal accidents:*

The following compensation shall be payable in case of disability to the victim arising out of non-fatal accidents:—

Loss of income, if any, for actual period of disablement not exceeding fifty two weeks.

PLUS either of the following:—

(a) In case of permanent total disablement the amount payable shall be arrived at by multiplying the annual loss of income by the Multiplier applicable to the age on the date of determining the compensation, or

(b) In case of permanent partial disablement such percentage of compensation which would have been payable in the case of permanent total disablement as specified under item (a) above.

Injuries deemed to result in Permanent Total Disablement/Permanent Partial Disablement and percentage of loss of earning capacity shall be as per Schedule I under Workmen's Compensation Act, 1923.

6. *Notional income for compensation to those who had no income prior to accident:*

Fatal and disability in non-fatal accidents:

(a) Non-earning persons —Rs. 15,000 p.a.

(b) Spouse —Rs. 1/3rd of income of the earning/surviving spouse.

In case of other injuries only "general damage" as applicable.]

•••